Date Due

THE THEOLOGY
OF ST PAUL

THE THEOLOGY
OF SAINT PAUL

BY FERNAND PRAT, S.J.

Translated from the Eleventh French Edition

BY JOHN L. STODDARD

VOLUME I

THE NEWMAN BOOKSHOP
Westminster, Md.

1956

227.12
P88tE
1956
cop.2

NIHIL OBSTAT :
G. H. JOYCE, S.J.,
Censor Deputatus.

IMPRIMATUR :
EDM. CAN. SURMONT,
Vicarius generalis.

WESTMONASTERII,
die 15ª Julii, 1926.

Reprinted, 1946
Reprinted, 1950
Reprinted, 1952
Reprinted, 1956

ALL RIGHTS RESERVED

PRINTED IN THE UNITED STATES OF AMERICA

48029

NOTE

1. The bibliography and index will be found in the second volume. There will be found here only the necessary bibliographical references relating to special questions.

2. Except when otherwise stated, the patristic references are to Migne's *Patrology,* the roman numeral indicating the volume and the arabic the column. The author's name indicates sufficiently whether the Latin or Greek Patrology is referred to. For example, Hilary, *De Trin.,* viii, 47, X, 22, means : the *De Trinitate* of St Hilary, book viii, No. 47, Migne's *Latin* Patrology, vol. X, column 22. The Greek or Latin fathers who have already appeared in the Leipzig or Vienna editions are quoted according to these editions.

3. The key-number printed after and above a title denotes the edition. Thus, Cornely, *Introd.*[2], means : second edition of the *Introductio historica et critica in S. Scripturam* of P. Cornely. When there is no possibility of confusion, the title is often given in an abridged form.

4. In the case of ancient or modern commentators, it has not seemed necessary always to mention the volume and page. If Estius or Theodoret are quoted on Rom. viii, 28, it will easily be understood that recourse must be had to the commentary on the text in question.

5. For the Greek text of St Paul, we usually follow Nestle's edition, which everyone has at hand (*Novum Testamentum Graece et Latine,*[5] Stuttgart, 1914) ; but we depart from it in regard to certain orthographical peculiarities, and sometimes also as regards punctuation. The Latin text is, of course, that of the Clementine Vulgate.

CONTENTS

INTRODUCTION

BOOK II

THE CHURCH OF CORINTH

CHAPTER I.—DISORDERS AND DANGERS

CHAPTER II.—CASES OF CONSCIENCE

CONTENTS

BOOK III

GALATIANS AND ROMANS

BOOK IV

THE CAPTIVITY

CHAPTER I.—THE EPISTLES OF THE CAPTIVITY

CHAPTER II.—THE PRE-EMINENCE OF CHRIST

CHAPTER III.—THE CHURCH, THE MYSTICAL
BODY OF CHRIST

CONTENTS

BOOK V

THE PASTORAL EPISTLES

BOOK VI

THE EPISTLE TO THE HEBREWS

DETACHED NOTES

A—THE CHRONOLOGY OF ST PAUL'S APOSTOLATE

B—PAUL AND THE OLD TESTAMENT

C—THE DECREE OF JERUSALEM

D—THE "CHARISMATA"

APPENDIX: ANALYSIS OF THE EPISTLES

INTRODUCTION

CHAPTER I

QUESTIONS OF METHOD

I—BIBLICAL THEOLOGY

1. Definition. 2. Course to be followed.

1. IN the most general meaning of the term theology is the science of revealed religion. It is called *positive* theology when it undertakes to make an inventory of dogma, the historical development of which it does not hesitate to trace.

If, after setting forth in order the elements of revelation, it enriches this material with rational conclusions, in order to make of it a vast, harmonious structure, all of whose parts unite and support one another, it is *scholastic* theology.

Biblical theology is only a section of positive theology. Of the two sources of revealed truth—Scripture and Tradition—it draws from the first only. Its duty is to collect the results of exegesis, to bring them together for comparison, to assign to them their place in the history of revelation, the upward progress of which it endeavours to follow, and finally to furnish thus to scholastic theology a sure foundation and thoroughly prepared materials. In a word, biblical theology is the fruit of exegesis and the germ of scholastic theology.

But it is not itself either scholastic theology or exegesis. Exegesis studies particular texts, but does not trouble itself overmuch about their mutual relations. Its method is that of analysis. Biblical theology adds to analysis synthesis, for it must verify the results of the exegesis which has preceded it, before employing them to reconstruct a system, or, rather, a line of thought. Its characteristic is synthesis. Scholastic theology, on the other hand, is only the putting into form, by the reason, of the facts acquired by positive theology. Without the foundation thus laid, it would have nothing to stand on. Biblical theology must precede it and enlighten it, but must also take good care not to encroach upon its aim or to borrow its method, which is usually that of deduction. We may say, therefore, that biblical theology ends where scholastic theology begins, and begins where exegesis finishes.

Biblical theology would be Protestant in character, if it claimed to constitute the whole of theology. It would be so in principle, because, by a fortunate inconsistency, neither Lutherans, Calvinists nor Anglicans have ever confined themselves exclusively to biblical theology; and it would be rationalistic in character if it put itself in contradiction to itself or to the other facts of revelation. Guided by the infallible teaching power, which expresses itself through the definitions of the Church or through legitimate tradition, it could not aim at absolute autonomy. Nevertheless, it must not expect to find in the inspired Scriptures the whole Catholic doctrine stated in its present degree of clarity and certainty. That would be to forget the fundamental principle of the life of dogma. Finally it must remember that the theology of a single author, even if that author be St Paul himself, does not constitute the whole of theology. It covers only a more or less limited portion of the vast field of written revelation. Hence one will find in it omissions, lack of continuity, and a want of harmony and proportion. All the books of the New Testament are to some extent works originating from circumstances, and this is perhaps truer of the works of Paul than of the others. His Epistles are not so much the regular extension of his preaching, as an extraordinary, almost abnormal means of guarding against unforeseen difficulties and of meeting local needs. If the Galatians had been more accessible, he would probably not have written an Epistle to them. We are doubtless indebted for the two Epistles to the Corinthians to the disorders and divisions in their city. Even the Epistle to the Romans, which is the least polemical of all, perhaps owes its existence to the judaizing peril. For Paul had received a commission, not to baptize or to write, but to preach, and when, under divine inspiration, he takes up the reed of the scribe, he is provoked to it, and, as it were, constrained to do so by a special command. The result is that the development of his written doctrine, subordinated as it was to external influences, does not always run parallel to the logical evolution of his thought. He does not write *as* he preaches, and he does not write *what* he preaches. His Epistles are often dominated by the necessities of controversy, and all controversy distorts proportions and enlarges certain features to the detriment of others. In order to regain the true perspective, we must place ourselves at a distance and at the right point of view.

2. The difficulties of our task are, therefore, apparent. If we follow the chronological order, we separate facts united by a common origin, and we disconnect doctrines, the mere juxtaposition of which would be illuminating; while if we prefer to adhere to the logical order, we inevitably mix up

teachings of all epochs, and many features, viewed outside of their historic setting, present themselves in a false light. We have thought it possible to obviate most of these difficulties by dividing this work into two parts. The first will restore the teachings of the Apostle to the place where they naturally belong, and will try, by tracing from actual life the progress of his revelations, to make evident the ever-ascending evolution of his thought. Here the reader will perhaps be inclined to find the portion given to history excessive, and he would be right, if a man's thought could be properly understood independently of the historic circumstances which give to it its motive power, or if the history of the apostles were not in itself theology. But the apostles transmit revelation to us by their deeds as well as by their words and writings; and what do we mean by theology, if we deny that name to the decrees of the assembly of Jerusalem, to the dispute at Antioch, or to the attitude of St Paul towards the Mosaic Law?

In the second part we shall endeavour to give a general view of the theology of the great Apostle, to discover its dominant idea, to note its continuity and growth, and to follow its ramifications. This synthetic view, which restores to unity the doctrinal elements dispersed by the chance of external circumstances, is especially necessary for a study of the person and work of Christ, for the doctrine of the Sacraments, for eschatology, and finally for morals, the principles and deductions of which are often very loosely connected with the developments of dogma. It is impossible to think of distributing the preaching of St Paul among the carefully prepared moulds of modern theology. These moulds are not made for it, being at once too broad and too narrow. Many classical dissertations would thus be rendered almost devoid of substance, while others would overflow into questions, no doubt vitally important in the century of the apostles, but at the present time of much less interest.

The terminology of St Paul has merited special attention. If the study of the language of the Bible is peculiarly the province of exegesis, it re-enters the domain of theology when it includes a certain number of characteristic facts, gravitating around a central teaching. Who can flatter himself that he has penetrated the thought of the Apostle if he has not weighed the value of terms which fall continually from his pen, such as "flesh and spirit," "grace and charism," "faith and law," "sin and prevarication," "justice and justification," "vocation and election," "gospel," "mystery," the "parousia," "redemption," "salvation," "glory," and many others? In order to avoid encumbering our text and rendering its exposition dull, we have explained these terms in exegetical and philological notes, according to their importance. It was necessary to guard against two dangers : one of supposing *a priori* that the vocabulary of Paul is identical with that of his apostolic colleagues; and the other, of blindly admitting that the definitions which were subsequently formulated by scholastic theology, under the influence of Aristotelian philosophy, are always applicable to it. Since no human expression of divine truth can adequately attain its object, Christian thought aspires unceasingly to a higher degree of precision and exactitude.

Perhaps we shall be able to establish the fact that in St Paul himself there was a constant effort towards improvement. We need not separate the language of the apostles from the common dialect of their day, but it is fair to recognize in their style a certain number of verbal meanings which are specifically Christian, and correspond to the characteristic ideas of the new doctrine.

Because the significance of the language of the Bible was formerly exaggerated, must we now rush to the opposite extreme and deny to the new dogmas the use of an appropriate expression?

II—THE SOURCES

1. The Authentic Epistles. 2. The Discourses in the Acts of the Apostles.

1. The exclusive sources of biblical theology are the canonical books of the Bible; it was one of the errors of the historical theology of the last century to have failed to recognize this. When one puts profane writings on the same footing with the Bible, one can indeed have the history of the philosophical and religious ideas of an epoch, but this mixture is not theology, and still less is it biblical theology. The question of *canonicity* is decided by the authoritative pronouncement of the Church; that of *authenticity* is decided generally by criticism and history. Referring the reader to dissertations on the introduction to the Scriptures for a more detailed examination of this subject, we wish here only to indicate our route by a few signposts.

It is well known that the Tübingen school, by reason of its *a priori* conception of the origin of Christianity, assigned the greater part of the Books of the New Testament to the second century. It also declared that all biblical writings are apocryphal which are characterized by a conciliatory tone or a mild sort of polemics, and which do not portray with sufficient energy the opposition which is supposed to have existed from the very first between Hellenism and Judæo-Christianity. It conceded to Paul the authorship of the four great Epistles only, in which it thought it could discern the liberal and universalist, yet at the same time extreme and uncompromising spirit of the doctor of the Gentiles. These speculations never gained much credit outside Germany, and even there they remained confined to the historians of dogma, who had been won over in advance to the Hegelian system of evolution. In general, exegetes and philologists, the most competent judges in a matter concerning authenticity, refused to adhere to them. But, while the disciples of Baur have slowly retraced their steps, a party still more radical and much more noisy has tried, on the contrary, to advance still further. This group, called by its opponents sceptical, falsely critical, hyper-critical, and anticritical, is known by the name of the Dutch School, because, with the exception of one Swiss and one American, it has not succeeded in recruiting adepts outside the Netherlands. It boldly rejects the authenticity of *all* the Pauline Epistles, and for the very reasons which were alleged at Tübingen against the lesser letters.

Is it likely, these audacious critics ask, that Paul wrote to the Christians at Rome, who were unknown to him, what the Epistle to the Romans attributes to him? Would he, who has recourse to so many subtleties and subterfuges in dealing with his spiritual children of Corinth and Galatia, take such a high hand with those of Rome? If the Epistles in question are authentic, it is impossible, they say, to give a reasonable explanation of his attitude either to the former or to the latter, and it is impossible also to understand anything about the mutual relations of the various coteries and sects. The doctrinal and religious data of these letters reveal, it is claimed, a development of Christian life and thought so broad and deep that it cannot have been attained in the space of a few years after the death of Christ. One cannot attribute to Paul, or to any other contemporary, such an extensive experience, such a great spiritual effort, and such an enlargement of the field of vision. In the great Epistles there is already visible *a system of traditional* doctrine, with which their readers are deemed familiar, and which they either follow with keen enthusiasm and the simplicity of children, or else attack with fury and obstinacy.

Many of the adversaries of Paul at Corinth have passed beyond the stage of Paulinism and might be called *hyper-pauline*. Others, like the judaizing Christians of Galatia, remain with the rearguard, and even return to Judæo-Christianity. The existence of these two clearly defined parties during the lifetime of Paul is inconceivable. To the real author of the Epistles Paul is evidently already a figure of the past. The complete transformation of primitive Christianity had already been effected. The disciples of Jesus had already abandoned their national aspirations; their old conception of Jesus as the Messiah had given place to the more spiritual conception of Jesus as the Son of God; the Law had been eclipsed by the Gospel. Now, all this, they say, must have required much time, even in those hours of high moral tension which marked the beginnings of Christianity. Can anyone imagine that the first Christian generation debated such questions as the relation of the Law to the Gospel, justification by faith or by works, election and reprobation, Christ " according to the flesh " and Christ " according to the spirit," celibacy and marriage, and the signs of a true apostolate? No, the religion which one sees dawning in the pages of the great Epistles cannot be made to harmonize with the period that preceded the death of Paul. Everything in it denotes a more recent date—the end of the first century or the commencement of the second.

Thus do the *enfants terribles* of criticism reason, and in so doing have infuriated the last defenders of Tübingen, of whom they are the living condemnation, because they are only pushing to the extreme the method and the principles of their predecessors. Let us leave them to settle their quarrels between themselves. It is not displeasing to us to see to what an excess of extravagance the abuse of the subjective method can lead them. Moreover, these revelries in hypercriticism have borne their fruits. A marked reaction has set in. Holsten, who has remained to the last faithful to the spirit of Tübingen, is obliged to acknowledge it. Harnack, after having pointed out the fact of this retreat, insists on retiring farther in the direction of tradition.

Few scholars to-day refuse to recognize Paul as the author of the Epistle to the Philippians, the letter to Philemon, and the two Epistles to the Thessalonians, at least the first. This will be the uncontested dogma of to-morrow, and it is superfluous to delay acknowledging the demonstration of a proposition which will soon have no more opponents. The authenticity of the Epistle to the Colossians is also gaining ground every day, and one could say almost as much of its twin sister, the Epistle to the Ephesians; but here we find more delay and hesitation. However, the symptoms of its acknowledgement are more and more favourable, and we think that the last clouds of opposition will soon disappear.

If we regard the Epistle to the Ephesians as being addressed exclusively to them, we encounter almost insurmountable difficulties. The Church of Ephesus was perhaps the one most dear to the heart of the Apostle. He had consecrated to it three whole years of labour. It was there that he had suffered wellnigh unto death, and had sustained against the agitators of Corinth an unequal conflict, from which he had come out victorious. There, too, he had received, by way of compensation, indescribable consolations and the most touching marks of filial attachment. Who can forget the heart-rending scene of his farewell to the elders of Ephesus? Now, the Epistle which he sends them, if the address as we have it is not erroneous, resembles not so much a letter as a dissertation, devoid of local colour, lacking in personal allusions, and without any of those delicate and amiable traits of which he is so lavish, even with the Romans and Colossians, whom he has never seen. Moreover, there is some doubt of the authenticity of the words " at Ephesus," which we read now at the head of the Epistle. Our two oldest Greek manuscripts do not have them at first hand; St Basil affirms that in his time the oldest copies did not contain them either; Ambrosiaster is ignorant of them, and very probably St Victorinus also. Origen shows clearly enough by his commentary that he knows nothing of them, and, finally, Marcion designated the Laodiceans as those to whom the Epistle was addressed, which he could not have done if he had read the suspected words in the text which he possessed, and one fails to see also what dogmatic reason he could have had for suppressing them.

All the difficulties, however, are smoothed away if we adopt the hypothesis of a circular Epistle addressed to the Churches of Asia, of which the Church of Ephesus was the mother. The impersonal tone of the letter, its expressions of doubt, and its general salutations become, then, indispensable, and the absence of the words " at Ephesus " in the oldest manuscripts is no longer surprising. The subsequent tradition in regard to the title is also easily explained, for the Ephesians were the principal persons to whom the Epistle was sent, even if they were not the only ones. This being granted, no serious opposition to its authenticity is possible; not in respect to the choice of words, for the proportion of *hapax legomena* is not here above the average, but rather less; not in respect to style, for the compacted phrases, the articled genitives, the synonyms united in couples, sentences without sequence, and long digressions often starting from a single word, are wholly characteristic of the style of Paul; nor yet in regard to doctrine, for this, too, is found in substance in the Epistle to the Colossians; and the new features in the Epistle to the Ephesians are either not sufficiently marked to indicate a different author, or else have their point of similarity and their equivalent in the Epistles whose authenticity is uncontested. We think that the recent labours of the critics have proved this superabundantly.

The authenticity of the pastoral Epistles will be studied at the beginning of the book devoted to them. As to the Epistle to the Hebrews, whatever opinion one may hold in regard to its origin and to the more or less intimate relations

which its author may have had with the Apostle Paul, it
requires a treatment by itself; it has a language and a
conception too peculiarly its own for it to be possible to
combine its study with that of the other Epistles. There
remains the " Acts," which we need to consider here only
from the point of view of its veracity.

2. It was formerly the fashion to regard the Acts of the
Apostles as a document written with a definite object to
promote, with little literary honesty or historic sense, and as
the late compilation of a narrow mind, anxious to attenuate
the violent conflicts which marked the unfolding of Christianity, and, contrary to all the evidence, to represent Peter
and Paul as two comrades in arms, always united in the most
touching brotherly affection. The new rationalist school sets
little value on these fanciful ideas. It assures us that the
book of " Acts " is legendary, that its tone is edifying, and
that it has an apologetical way of expressing itself, all of
which is sufficient for its condemnation as history; but that
nevertheless it does not offer the least trace of intentional
tendencies, and that its object is not at all to reconcile the
partisans of Peter and Paul, nor to defend the latter against
his enemies, nor to elevate him to the rank of the Prince of
the Apostles.

If the author is mistaken, he is so in good faith; he is
sincere enough, but too far removed from the events for him
to know their exact details or possess a just view of the
whole movement. Imagination and legend must, they claim,
have supplemented his lack of documentary information.

In our days, however, a great step forward has been made.
The critics are now almost unanimous in regarding the
author of the third Gospel and that of the Acts as one and
the same writer. They are willing also to concede that the
passages in which the author puts himself forward by using
the first person can be only the recital of an eyewitness
identical with the author of the entire work. How could we
indeed suppose that such a delicate artist (assuming that he
does not wish to deceive us) would have inserted so
awkwardly in his own work fragments of another document?
Finally, after having tried, without the least success, to
identify this companion of Paul with Timothy, Silas, or
Titus, the majority of independent critics return to St Luke,
who alone, even apart from tradition, satisfies all the requirements of the problem. The honour of bringing about this
change of view belongs largely to Adolf Harnack. But
then we used to think that he placed the sacred rights
of history above the petty prejudices of national infatuation. The only question still in dispute among non-
catholics is to know whether Luke published his book a little

before or a little after the year A.D. 70. Blass, Lumby, and Harnack favour the former hypothesis; Sanday, Ramsay, and Headlam the latter. But if the author of the Acts is St Luke, the friend and collaborator of Paul, what does it matter whether he wrote a few years later or a few years earlier than that date? He is in either case a contemporary of the events which he relates, has often been an actor in them and a spectator of them, and composes his narrative in the lifetime of eyewitnesses who are able to confirm or refute his assertions.

No one was better situated than he for seeing well nor better able to describe what he had seen. Endowed with a high intellectual culture, his principles regarding the method of writing history were as sound as those of Thucydides or Tacitus. He knew that it is necessary, above all, to interrogate the actual witnesses, to compare their testimony, to go back to the best sources, to use his material in an artistic manner, and to follow attentively the movement and the progress of events in order to satisfy exacting readers and to disarm severe criticism. Such is the programme which he sketches at the head of his Gospel and carried out in his two books with equal success, taking into account the difference in the subjects and situations of both.

In the Acts he relates what has passed before his own eyes, or, at least, within the limits of his horizon. Note that his entire narrative converges towards Antioch, which is precisely his birthplace and his post of observation. Even if we neglect the curious reading in the Western text, which makes him one of the first members of the community of Antioch,[1] it is certain that he lived at an early date in intimate relations with his principal hero, and that he was in continual contact with the associates of the Apostle.

He had as companions in his travels and apostolate Sopater of Berea, Aristarchus and Secundus of Thessalonica, Caius of Derbe, Tychicus and Trophimus of the province of Asia,[2] and, above all, Mark,[3] Silas,[4] and Timothy.[5] At Cæsarea he was the guest of Philip, one of the first seven deacons,[6] and the number and quality of these personages are a guarantee for sure and complete information.

---

[1] Acts xi, 28: συνεστραμμένων δὲ ἡμῶν. This takes place in A.D. 43 or 44.

[2] Acts xx, 4-5. Companions of the Apostle from Corinth to Jerusalem.

[3] Col. iv, 10-14; 2 Tim. iv, 11. Mark and Luke are together with Paul during his two captivities—at least, during the first.

[4] Acts xvi, 10. Silas was with Paul when Luke joined them.

[5] Luke met Timothy in the course of his second mission, then on the journey from Corinth to Jerusalem; and finally he lived with him at Rome beside Paul, when the latter was a prisoner.

[6] Acts xxi, 8. It is natural to think that he owes to him the details given in chaps. vi-viii.

St Luke is an exceptionally well-informed witness and attentive observer. His scrupulous exactitude includes a multitude of features, in the presentation of which the awkwardness of a forger would infallibly betray itself.

He knows, for example, that the magistrates of Thessalonica are called *politarchi* (Acts xvii, 6-8), and that the Governor of Malta bore the special title of "First" of the island (Acts xxviii, 7). We ourselves were ignorant of this until the day when a chance discovery informed us of it. He knows that the magistrates of Philippi, called *Strategoi,* had at their service *lictors* (Acts xvi, 35-39); which was, indeed, the case in certain Roman colonies anxious to imitate on a small scale the customs of the mother-country. He gives the proper name to the *proconsuls* of Cyprus and Achaia (xiii, 7, 8-12 ; xviii, 12); and this designation, correct for that epoch, would have been incorrect a few years earlier or a few years later. The attitude of the *Pharisees* and *Sadducees* (iv, 1 ; v, 17 ; xxiii, 6-8) is presented by him under an aspect which the Gospel had not exhibited, and which nevertheless alone enables us to understand the relations of the primitive Church with the Synagogue. There are a hundred chances to one that an amateur of the second century would not have succeeded in painting so vividly the riot at Ephesus ; and that he would more than once have betrayed his ignorance in speaking of the *Asiarchs* favourable to Paul, of the city as *neocoros* (guardian of the temple), of the *clerk* of the city, so different from the personages bearing elsewhere the same name, of the *theatre* also as a place of assembly on extraordinary occasions, and finally of the official title due to the goddess, the *great Artemis* of the Ephesians (xix, 31-35).

The geographical exactitude of St Luke calls forth admiration from the man (Ramsay) who, at the present time, is best acquainted with the places where the drama of the Acts of the Apostles was unfolded, and his admiration is shared by all who have studied thoroughly the episode of Paul's sojourn at Athens and the events described in the last chapters. A perfect mastery of the subject was essential to avoid anachronisms, incorrect names, confusion in regard to persons, and little errors of topography and archæology.

The test of criticism has resulted favourably for the Acts. The more its details have been scrutinized, the more truthful it has shown itself. Every time that it has been possible to verify the narrative, either by comparing it with the Epistles of St Paul, or by Jewish contemporaneous records, or by the monuments of profane history, it has emerged from the triple comparison with honour.

Do the discourses in the Acts deserve the same credence? These short speeches, the delivery of which would never require more than five or six minutes, are evidently not verbatim reports, but do they present at least a faithful résumé? We shall ask why the author, so scrupulously exact in his descriptions, should be less conscientious here. The sources of his information were neither less sure nor less numerous. The style of the discourses is his in a certain measure, but the ideas are very plainly those of the speakers put upon the stage. Paul does not speak like Stephen, nor Stephen like James, nor the latter like Peter. The speeches of Paul, in particular, are always perfectly suited to the situation. This is a presumption in his favour. It may be said that the writer was clever enough to compose them from his own invention; but instead of imagining this pretty trick, which was scarcely a characteristic of that time, is it not more natural to believe that he had in his hands records worthy of belief? Through passages in the Epistles we know what Paul preached and also a little how he preached, and we find all that again in the speeches which St Luke attributes to him, and even recognize in them also his favourite terminology. All these facts inspire confidence, and we do not hesitate to regard the speeches of Paul recorded in the Acts as a direct and sincere echo of his preaching.[1]

[1] For more details, see "St. Luke and the Acts of the Apostles " in *Études*, 1913, vol. cxxxvii, pp. 737-760, and " Les sources des Actes des Apôtres " in the *Recherches de science religieuse*, 1913, vol. iv, p. 275.

In a more recent work (" The Composition and Date of Acts," No. 1 of *Harvard Theol. Studies*, Cambridge, 1916), Prof. Torrey maintains that the first part of Acts (chap. i-xv) is simply a translation of *a single* Aramaic document; for the Greek of this part is *translated* Greek, which becomes sometimes intelligible only by returning to the original. St Luke, it is thought, annexed to this translation the second part of Acts, composed at Rome during the captivity of St Paul, before A.D. 64. We do not think that Torrey has succeeded in proving his thesis, although we willingly admit that St Luke must have had in his possession some Greek or Aramaic manuscripts. See the criticism of P. Vosté, O.P. (*Rev. biblique*, 1917, pp. 300-303). Charles Anderson Scott (*Exposit. Times*, February, 1920) gives a lucid explanation of the controversy created in America and England by Prof. Torrey's theory.

CHAPTER II

THE VESSEL OF ELECTION

I—SAUL OF TARSUS

1. The Situation and the Man. 2. The Hellenic School of Tarsus.

1. IF divine action on the human will and intelligence were merely a mechanical impulse, if the inspired man were only a stringed instrument becoming resonant under the fingers of God, or a reed merely registering the thoughts of the celestial scribe, it would be idle to try to ascertain what the physiognomy and surroundings of the sacred writer were. But the latter is neither a piece of inert matter nor an inanimate instrument. He feels, wills, and thinks, and his thoughts and sentiments cannot fail to colour the revelation which penetrates them, as a liquid tints the luminous ray which passes through it. Isaias and Ezechiel do not deliver the same divine message in the same tone. It is not a simple matter of diction. In whatever translation they may appear, the visions of Osee will never resemble those of Amos; and no one will be in danger of mistaking a chapter of St Mark for a page of St John. Hence all the exegetes rightly maintain the necessity of studying the individual character of the sacred writers, their habits of mind, the ordinary course of their thoughts, their education, their social environment, and the outward circumstances of their life and action.

One has only a very imperfect knowledge of a man, especially of a writer, so long as one is ignorant of the intellectual and moral environment in which he has grown up. From our environment we derive that marvellous instrument of mental activity, language, and with it the unconscious association and habitual turn of our thoughts, as well as a more or less rich inheritance of ideas which have been elaborated through many generations before falling to our heritage. All this combined forms the constitution of man's mind, just as blood, race, training, and style of life form the constitution of his body. Education sometimes modifies this original stock of atavism, but usually strengthens it; even divine inspiration itself does not eliminate it, for grace, far from suppressing man's nature, elevates and transforms it, while leaving its original bent and individuality perfectly distinct.

By his birth and education Saul would lead us to expect a complex nature, in which all sorts of contrasts will be united. "A Jew by race, a native of Tarsus, a Roman citizen" (Acts xxi, 29; compare Acts xxii, 3; xxii, 27), such is the civil status furnished by himself to the magistrate charged with examining his case. According to St Jerome, Giscala was the cradle of his family;[1] the thirteenth Apostle would therefore also be a Galilean. Then, as now, the Jews were the most cosmopolitan of men. Hunted down in Palestine by rival powers, driven away by invaders, tempted abroad by the allurement of gain and the instinct of trade, they had planted their colonies in all parts of the empire. Sure of meeting everywhere from their compatriots a welcome as well as aid and protection, they changed their country at the least alarm. The world was their country.

At that time Tarsus was one of the most flourishing cities of Asia. Loaded with favours by Rome, free and exempt from taxes ever since the time of Pompey the Great, and the metropolis of Cilicia since the reign of Augustus, its superb situation caused it to be a trading-place of the first rank and one of the most active markets of the empire. From the heights adjoining the city, above its groves of palm-trees, the gaze embraced simultaneously the snow-crowned mass of the Taurus Mountains, and the white sails of the Mediterranean ships, for which the River Cydnus—at that time navigable—made the approach to the city possible, and finally the Cilician plain, chequered with numberless canals and covered with crops as far as the eye could reach.

This smiling and magnificent panorama seems to have left no trace in Paul's imagination. Later, he will traverse localities made wonderful by the gifts bestowed on them by nature or by the charm of historical associations without, however, betraying the slightest thrill of admiration or enriching his style by any colour or comparison whatever. From this point of view he is the very opposite of the prophets and evangelists. Efforts have been made to explain this phenomenon, either by supposing in Paul a congenital weakness of vision or a lack of the gift of observation. In reality, lifeless nature does not appeal to this self-concentrated mind, absorbed by the spectacle of the painful struggle of which his soul is both the theatre and the prize. He sees inanimate nature only in its relations with man. His domain is psychology. It has long since been remarked that his figures of speech are almost all drawn, not from the sight of the physical world and its activities, but from the outward manifestations of human life. He observes with interest and describes with skill and delicacy the Hellenic games, Roman soldiers supple and active under the weight of their arms, markets swarming with slaves, and even grand edifices,

[1] *De Viris illust.*, 5.

temples, and palaces, in which the power and genius of man are revealed. But figures borrowed from the life of the fields do not stand forth prominently in his writings, and his technical expressions, derived from the theatre or the stadium, and, above all, his military phraseology would offer two subjects of study as curious as they would be instructive.

2. About the age of six years the Jewish child went to school. Schools in Tarsus were numerous and famous. All the sciences were taught in them, and especially philosophy. The Tarsians in this respect were the rivals of the Sophists of Alexandria and Athens, and were even considered to be superior to them. Their speciality was to furnish tutors for the masters of the world. The teacher of Augustus, Athenodorus the Stoic, came from Tarsus; so did the preceptor of Marcellus and Tiberius. Both returned to die in their native city, loaded with gold and honours. Where science is lucrative there is never a lack of experts.

Paul did not learn the elements of letters from these rhetoricians. His Greek is not the Greek of the schools; it is a language picked up through using it and through chance conversations. It is lively, full of imagery, picturesque, admirable in expression, originality, and movement, but foreign to the rules of official grammarians.

The Jews, wherever they were numerous, had their private schools, and the books of the pagans were rigidly excluded from them. The principal object of study in them, if not the only one, was the Bible; only in the Diaspora this was read in Greek. To such a school young Saul must have been sent by his father, who was a rigid Pharisee.

His three quotations from the poets are not sufficient to prove that he was very well acquainted with pagan writers. As Aratus was from Cilicia, and perhaps from Tarsus itself, it is possible that the Apostle borrows from him directly the line quoted before the Areopagus : " For we are also his offspring." But this flowing and harmonious passage was one of those which poets gladly slipped into their productions when the subject lent itself to them. In fact, we come upon it also in Cleanthes' *Hymn to Jupiter*.[1] The verse from Menander's *Thais* which, it is thought, he copied from Euripides, was only a proverbial maxim in common use; and the form which St Paul gives to it, according to the best manuscripts, proves that he was not very familiar with the system of the iambic trimeter.[2] Finally, the satirical common

[1] Acts xvii, 28: Τοῦ γὰρ καὶ γένος ἐσμέν. Aratus, *Phenomena*, ii, 429; Cleanthes, *Hymn to Jupiter*, 5.
[2] 1 Cor. xv, 33: Φθείρουσιν ἤθη χρηστὰ ὁμιλίαι κακαί (χρηστά without elision, instead of χρησθ'). Menander, *Thais* (Ed. Meinecke, frag. 75), Socrates, *Hist. eccl.*, iii, 6, affirms that the verse is from Euripides.

saying that "The Cretans are always liars, evil beasts, slothful bellies," which one reads in the *Oracles* of Epimenides and in part in the *Hymn to Jupiter* of Callimachus, must have been often thrown at the Cretans by their enemies and rivals. We see that each of these three texts is found in two different authors at least.[1]

No secular book has left in the writings of Paul a perceptible trace of its influence. The Apostle seems never to have read the theosophical speculations of his great contemporary, Philo of Alexandria; and this is not to be wondered at, since their turn of mind was so different. Sometimes the expressions "image of God," "firstborn of creation," applied to the pre-existent Christ are referred to Philo; but it is much more natural to seek the original source of them in the Book of Wisdom. Nor does Paul find inspiration in other philosophers. His code of morals, apart from several profound differences, has some traits in common with that of the Stoics, and one could perhaps discover in it, by a very strict interpretation, a souvenir of his education. The philosophers of that period, especially those of Tarsus and Cilicia, prided themselves very much on their stoicism, and it may be that the Apostle in his maturer years disputed with them. But nothing, either in his ideas or his terminology, indicates clearly that he was of their school, and it is not necessary to caution the reader that his pretended correspondence with Seneca is only a literary fraud or the futile amusement of an idle mind.

Taken all in all this first sojourn in Tarsus did not make a deep impression upon his mind. His family was quite unaffected by the surrounding atmosphere. His father, a Jew of the old school, appears to have had little taste for Hellenic culture and the social customs of the Greco-Roman world. Subsequently, Paul calls himself "a Hebrew of the Hebrews, a Pharisee of the Pharisees," so little had his Greek entourage affected him. But one day he comes back to Tarsus in his maturity, after the grace of God has changed him, and then he remarks the absurdities of these pretended philosophers who profess to sell wisdom, their secret intrigues, their mean jealousies, and the ignoble insults which they shower upon one another, their greed of gain, their scarcely veiled corruption, and their insupportable

---

[1] Titus i, 12 : *Κρῆτες ἀεὶ ψεῦσται, κακὰ θηρία, γαστέρες ἀργαί.* The *entire* verse is derived from the *Oracles* of Epimenides, as St Jerome assures us in his commentary. Callimachus (*Hymn to Jupiter*, 8) retains only the first half of it. Rendel Harris, "St Paul and Epimenides" in the *Expositor*, October, 1912, referring to an article published in the same review in October, 1906, has proved that the verse in question was taken from the poem entitled *Minos*, from which Paul also had borrowed the phrase quoted before the Areopagus—ἐν αὐτῷ γὰρ ζῶμεν καὶ κινούμεθα καὶ ἐσμέν (Acts xvii, 28).

pride, based upon an immense amount of ignorance. The portrait which he draws for us in the Epistle to the Romans of those fools, who call themselves wise, has not so much the appearance of a copy made from memory as of a picture drawn from life.

During the different sojourns which he made in his native city, he familiarized himself with the Septuagint. He knows the Bible in the two languages, but he quotes it almost always in Greek, either because the version of the Septuagint was really more familiar to him or because, when writing in Greek, the text of the Septuagint came more naturally to his memory. According to a calculation subject to revision, but the general result of which is correct, out of eighty-four quotations thirty-four agree exactly with the Septuagint, thirty-six differ from it very little, ten present notable differences, two are made from the Hebrew, but allow us to suppose that the text of the Septuagint was in the mind of the author, and, finally, two only are wholly independent translations or belong to another version. In short, the Apostle does not like to depart from the generally received version, and remains faithful to it even in cases when it seems to us that he would have gained by abandoning it.

Under the name of Septuagint we understand all the books admitted into the Alexandrian canon, which was that of the Hellenic Jews. Paul certainly had read the Book of Wisdom, and he is influenced by it when he sets forth the philosophical proof of the existence of God and describes the panoply of the Christian virtues. The comparison of the potter and other similar reminders give additional testimony to this fact. His relations with the Book of Ecclesiasticus, although less pronounced, are, in our opinion, sufficient to render a literary connection between them probable.[1]

Paul's erudition is not derived from *books;* he has learned only one science thoroughly, and that is revealed religion; he knows only one book—the Bible.

---

[1] Compare Rom. i, 20-25 with Wisdom xiii, 1-17; Rom. i, 26-29 with Wisdom xiv, 11-17. The panoply of Paul, Eph. vi, 11-17, reminds us of Isa. lix, 17, and of Wisdom v, 17-20. In the allegory of the potter, compare Rom. ix, 19-20 with Wisdom xii, 12; Rom. ix, 21 with Wisdom xv, 7; Rom. ix, 22 with Wisdom xii, 20, taking into consideration modifications caused by the remembrance, conscious or unconscious, of Jer. xiii, 3-6; Isa. xxix, 16; xlv, 9; Ecclus. xxxiii, 13-14. For details, see Grafe, *Das Verhältniss der paulin. Schriften zur Sap. Salom.*, in the *Theolog. Abhandlungen*, dedicated to Weizsäcker, Freiburg im Breisgau, 1892, pp. 251-286. Vollmer (*Die neutest. Citate bei Paulus*, Freiburg im Breisgau, 1895, pp. 67-68 and 84-85) has not succeeded in proving that Paul was acquainted with Philo.

II—At the Feet of Gamaliel

1. The Jewish School at Jerusalem.   2. Use of the Old Testament.
3. Saul the Pharisee.

1. Saul was about thirteen years of age when he went to Jerusalem to complete his education. We do not know whether his parents accompanied him thither. Forty years later the son of one of his sisters, who had established her residence in the holy city, was to save his life. We are already acquainted with the travelling customs of the Jews of that time. We must accustom ourselves more and more to these continual changes from place to place which the history of the apostolic age records on every page. The child was destined for the profession of a scribe, an ambiguous kind of occupation which prepared men for all careers and opened the door to all honours, since the scribe was, either at the same time or by turns, advocate and attorney, magistrate and jurist, counsellor and preacher, lawyer and churchman, man of letters, rhetorician, and grammarian.

The students at Jerusalem were at this time divided in two rival schools, whose founders, Hillel and Shammai, of legendary memory, respectively personify in the eyes of posterity narrow views and petty-mindedness and the broad ideas of an enlightened liberalism, but if we are to believe the Mishna, the most authoritative source of Jewish traditions, nothing justifies this contrast. Their differences extended only to trifles; for example, to the question whether an egg laid on the Sabbath might be eaten the same day or if the particoloured top-knot, called in Hebrew *zizith,* was indispensable for night attire. With the exception of these trifles, the two schools were in agreement. Both held to the strict observance of the Law, revered the ritual and historical traditions which had been added to the written Torah, and, in a word, were imbued with the purest Pharisaism. Still, if it is permissible to conjecture any difference between them, perhaps the school of Hillel inclined in general towards the less strict interpretation.

The successor of Hillel, heir to his principles if not his blood, was then Gamaliel the Elder. Although revered by the Christians for having defended the apostles, his posthumous reputation has not suffered on that account among his co-religionists. Gamaliel has remained the type of the ideal Pharisee. " Since his death," says the Mishna, " there is no more respect for the Law; the purity of Pharisaism died with him." As for the rest, his history is very obscure, and he is very often confounded with his grandson of the same name, Gamaliel II, who witnessed the ruin of the Temple and the supreme agony of the Jewish people.

It is, then, at the feet of Rabbi Gamaliel, as he was honourably called, that the young Saul came to sit. He was now laboriously to acquire a knowledge of sacred learning in the very centre of the national life, and at the moment when Jesus, older than he by a few years, was growing in grace and in wisdom in an obscure corner of Galilee. We have asked ourselves if and in what measure Paul's native soil had influenced his thought. As far as Jerusalem is concerned, there can be no doubt of it. Tarsus was his civic country, where he received, together with the envied title of Roman citizen, a knowledge of that Hellenic tongue which made him, in a way, a citizen of the world; but Jerusalem was the fatherland of his soul and his intelligence as much as, or more than, that of his heart. It is towards Jerusalem that he will always gravitate in the course of his earthly pilgrimage, and he is fully conscious of having received there the indelible imprint of his religious and moral character. It is there that, strictly speaking, he was instructed and brought up at the feet of Gamaliel. He was in a good school. In spite of their childish subtleties and practical inconsistencies, the Pharisees remained the true depositaries of sacred learning and the most authoritative interpreters of the divine Law. Jesus, their implacable enemy, was constrained to render them this testimony, that one should follow their teaching, but not imitate their conduct.

2. The Jewish school was only an annex of the Synagogue. The instruction given in it was exclusively religious. Mathematics, geography, secular history, philosophy—all these did not exist for the orthodox Jew; there were taught only morals, statutory law, and sacred history; and all this meant the Bible. He learned to read by spelling its pages; many scribes knew it by heart, as some exceptional Israelites know it still to-day. We find Paul constantly quoting it from memory, and even when he does not quote, his language is a tissue of unconscious or voluntary reminiscences. His style, like that of St Bernard or Bossuet, is wholly impregnated with biblical expressions, which spring spontaneously from his memory. This presupposes a detailed and minute acquaintance, the fruit of long years of study.

The stream of revelation, which has its source on Mount Sinai, or rather in Eden, had continued to flow, always increased by new revelations, down to the threshold of the Christian era. The Jews who were contemporaries of the apostles spoke of God, of his infinite transcendence, his creative power, and his paternal providence in terms which Christianity has not had to disavow. The doctrine of ultimate designs—the recompense of the just, the punishment reserved for the wicked, the resurrection of the dead, and a last judgement—had not far to go to find a place in the Gospel. I would say as much also of the doctrine of the original fall of man. The way of looking on Scripture as the word of God and as an expression of his intelligence and will could be accepted without any modification by the heralds of the new faith. We shall pass without delay over this heritage received from the prophets and over all the patrimony of religious truths accumulated in the course of centuries until the day when the light of the Gospel came to eclipse the torch of the Synagogue; a rich deposit surely, but one which does not belong distinctively to the teacher of the nations.

On the other hand, we cannot refrain from seeking in the writings of the Apostle the traces of his rabbinical education in the school of Jerusalem. It is to Jewish tradition that he owes his typical interpretation of Scripture, his employment of the so-called *accommodative* sense, and his frequent use of allegory.

Since the Old Testament furnished the foundations of the New, it is natural that the Holy Spirit, the author of the whole Bible, should have given to it a prophetic or figurative sense, which arises either from the narratives themselves or from the manner of relating them. This sense, superimposed upon the letter of Scripture, is called the spiritual sense; in calling it *typical,* we have the double advantage of discarding an ambiguous term and of conforming to the terminology of Paul. The Apostle declares that the first Adam was the *type* of Jesus Christ, who was the Adam to come, and he develops this typology in two famous passages.[1] Similarly, the fate of the Israelites in the desert has a *typical* character, and was committed to writing for our instruction. From this fact these *figurative* events assume a spiritual signification which the literal narration does not exhaust.[2] In the same way the Law of Moses was the *shadow* of things to come, of which the body, substance, and veritable being were identical with the Christian system.[3] Finally, the institution of marriage, re-established by Jesus Christ in its original unity and indissolubility, appears mysterious only by reason of its symbolic value.[4] But let us not think that St Paul recognizes the typical meaning only where he mentions it by name. For him the Synagogue is the figure of the Church;[5] the ancient

---

[1] Rom. v, 12-19; 1 Cor. xv, 22, 45, 49: ὅς ἐστιν τύπος τοῦ μέλλοντος (Rom. v, 14).

[2] 1 Cor. x, 6: Ταῦτα δὲ τύποι ἡμῶν ἐγενήθησαν.—x, 11: Ταῦτα δὲ τυπικῶς συνέβαινεν ἐκείνοις, ἐγράφη δὲ πρὸς νουθεσίαν ἡμῶν.

[3] Col. ii, 17: ἅ ἐστι σκιὰ τῶν μελλόντων, τὸ δὲ σῶμα (ἐστι=belongs to, is understood) Χριστοῦ .

[4] Eph. v, 32   [5] 1 Cor. iii, 16; 2 Cor. vi, 16.

sacrifices, and in particular the paschal lamb, are figures of Christ;[1] and certain of his arguments are of value only by admitting a double sense, one literal, the other typical, and both intended and confirmed by the Holy Spirit.

Nevertheless, let us avoid excess here. When the Apostle boasts of preaching only where the name of Christ has not yet been heard,[2] when he exhorts the Corinthians to give alms, in order to establish between Christians that sort of equality which reigned among the Jews when they were collecting the manna,[3] and when he relies, in both cases, on the formal quotation of a biblical text, we are not obliged to admit that he sees in these texts a typical sense, as if the Holy Spirit, as well as and beyond the literal meaning of the words, had meant to foretell the collection of alms for Jerusalem or to define the action of Paul. It is merely a case of accommodation pure and simple. It is the privilege of preachers to employ Scripture thus, and it is the right of everyone to express his thoughts in the words of the sacred books. The form of quotation makes no change in either right or privilege.

By *accommodating* is meant not precisely a scriptural sense, but the application of a biblical text to a fact or to an analogous case. The Psalmist, in speaking of the heavens, which in their own way celebrate the glory of the Creator, says :

> " Their sound hath gone forth into all the earth ;
> And their words unto the ends of the world."

St Paul applies these words, without the form of quotation yet with an evident allusion to the Psalmist's verses, to the preaching of the apostles.[4] Certain interpreters of Scripture think themselves obliged to conclude from this that, during the lifetime of St Paul, the Gospel had been preached throughout the whole world (St Chrysostom), or, at least, was known there by reputation (St Thomas). Most of them see in it merely a hyperbole; a rather strong hyperbole, if the words in question were those of the Apostle, but quite natural from the moment that it is simply an allusion. An allusion does not require to be verified literally, a relation of proportion or of analogy is enough.

The most extensive instance of *accommodation* is that which fills a chapter in the Second Epistle to the Corinthians,[5] It is founded on the narrative in Exodus, according to which Moses talked with God with uncovered face, but veiled

---

[1] 1 Cor. v, 7 ; Eph. v, 2.
[2] Rom. xv, 20, 21, quoting Isa. lii, 15.
[3] 2 Cor. viii, 14-15, quoting Ex. xvi, 18.
[4] Rom. ix, 18, quoting Ps. xviii (xix), 5.
[5] 2 Cor. iii, 7-18, based on Ex. xxxiv, 34-35.

himself to speak to the people. Paul draws from this a
double application, partly by analogy and partly by contrast.
The preachers of the Gospel—and even, to a certain degree,
all Christians—communicate with God face to face and are
transformed, little by little, into the image of God; but when
they address the people they do not cover themselves with
a veil, which is a symbol of fear and servitude. On the contrary, his Jewish contemporaries have their hearts covered
with a thick veil, like Moses on returning from his heavenly
conversations; but one day, when they shall be converted to
the Lord, they will throw aside the veil, as did Moses when
going to meet God.

The following example of *oratorical accommodation* is still
more remarkable because it seriously changes the text used
and mingles with it an appearance of argumentation. Paul
applies to the law of grace a passage in which the reference
is really to the Mosaic Law, and this in order to show that
the new order of things is superior to the old one. The
application is in Rom. x, 6-9, referring to Deut. xxx, 11-14,
as follows :

> The justice which is [born] of faith speaketh thus : *Say not* in thy heart,
> *who shall ascend into heaven?* That is, to bring Christ down; or, *who
> shall descend into the deep?* that is, to bring up Christ again from the
> dead. But what saith the Scripture ? *The word is nigh thee, even in
> thy mouth and in thy heart.* This is the word of faith, which we preach.
> For if thou confess with thy mouth the Lord Jesus, and believe in thy
> heart that God hath raised him up from the dead, thou shalt be saved.

At first sight this use of Scripture is disconcertingly
arbitrary. Not only is the text abridged and quoted
piecemeal, but its design is changed. Instead of " Who will
pass beyond the seas," Paul puts " Who shall descend into
the deep?" in order to fit his application to the resurrection
of Christ. Then he presents three interpretations of the
Midrash order, which the text did not appear to suggest.
Finally, he turns against the Law that which the Scripture
had said of the Law itself.

These difficulties are removed, or, at least, very much
attenuated, by the following observations : Paul *is not arguing;* he is merely describing, *illustrating,* the character of
the new law. *He does not even quote the Scripture;* he limits
himself to putting into the mouth of Justice personified what
Moses had said of the Law. The text of Deuteronomy had
become almost proverbial as a means of making anyone
comprehend that a thing was possible and easy. The conclusion of St Paul—that faith is easier and more within our
reach than the Law—is undeniable, and his manner of explaining it is a most legitimate instance of oratorical accommodation. It amounts to this : Moses said of the Law that,
in order to know it, it is not necessary to ascend into the

heavens or to cross the seas; and that this is even *more* true
of the Gospel. In truth, it is not necessary to ascend into
the heavens to bring Christ down from them, since Christ is
already incarnate; nor is it necessary to plunge into the deep
to bring Christ up, since Christ is already risen from the
dead. It is sufficient to believe with the heart and to
confess with the mouth that he is the Lord and that he has
risen from the dead.

We would also gladly see an example of oratorical accommodation in the passage in which Hagar and Sarah represent
the two Testaments.[1] Is that a biblical type or a symbol? In
other words, did the Holy Spirit when inspiring the sacred
writer who related the history of Abraham wish to teach us
therein the different character of the two covenants, or only
to permit us to make use of it in order to understand that
character better? That is the question. St Paul does not
speak of a type, but of an *allegory*; and if the majority of the
old exegetes decide for the spiritual sense, we know that they
give to this term a very elastic signification.

It was a custom among the rabbis to rest all obtainable
traditional opinion, whether historical or juristic, upon a
text in the Bible. That was precisely the object of their
exegesis. They distinguished six kinds of proof, which
subdivisions increased to thirteen : a *fortiori*, analogy, logical
inference, eight kinds of analysis, context, and parallel
passages. Several of these proofs lack force. In practical
matters the a *fortiori* is not decisive, analogy is only a
" reason of propriety," logical inference is not always a
scriptural sense. What is curious is that the rabbis were
not dupes of their methods, the weakness of which they
perceived perfectly. When Rabbi Simeon maintained that if
the Ammonite and Moabite women were admitted into the
Synagogue, from which the men of their country were for
ever excluded, then Egyptian women could with greater
reason be admitted, he hastened to invoke tradition (*halacha*)
in order to cut short the objection which the a *fortiori* argument suggests.[2] Since tradition had in the eyes of the rabbis
a value independent of the biblical text with which they
sought to support it, the scriptural proof became a mere
formality. One could do without it in case of need, and
content oneself with *remez* (allusion); but something was
always necessary. The abuse of *remez* was destined to
make Jewish exegesis a sort of game as arbitrary as it was
puerile.

When, therefore, we are confronted by a biblical citation

[1] Gal. iv, 21-31. See below, p. 187.
[2] *Cf.* Weber, *Jüdische Theologie*, Leipzig, 1897, ix; " Der Schriftbeweis,"
pp. 109-125.

made by St Paul, we must first ask ourselves whether we have to do with an allusion or an accommodation, a literal application or a real argument; and in the last-mentioned case, whether the argument is scriptural, or theological, or oratorical. The formula " as it is written " does not always indicate an argument in the proper meaning of the word. The case is, no doubt, different when the formula *"for* it is written " or the participle " therefore " (οὖν) is used at the beginning of a conclusion immediately following a scriptural quotation. We must, then, examine what the precise point is which St Paul wishes to establish and under what particular aspect he is considering his text. For often in a complex affirmation everything is not to be proved, and frequently in a text adduced as proof there is many a circumstance which has nothing to do with the thing which one wishes to demonstrate.

Even when the sacred writer relies on Scripture he may be arguing as an orator rather than as a theologian, and his proof may not be strictly scriptural; or, rather, it would not be so if, in distinction from the ordinary theologian or preacher, the conclusion of the inspired writer did not have an absolute value independent of his argument. Moses said : " Thou shalt not muzzle the ox that treadeth out thy corn on the floor."[1] Paul deduces from this the lesson that the apostolic worker may live from the Gospel. That is an *a fortiori* argument which was used by the rabbis. But the conclusion, strictly speaking, is not a scriptural meaning. It would be what theologians call a logical sequence. Unless we adopt the theory of " many meanings " presented by St Augustine, the fact that a thing may be *suggested* by the reading of the Bible, or that one can derive it thence by way of theological or oratorical deduction, is not enough to constitute a sense of scripture. The oratorical proof cannot always be resolved into a rigorous syllogism. Analogy, comparison, similitude, everything that causes the speaker's thought to enter more deeply into the mind of his auditor, fixes and impresses it there, and is used as a means of elucidation or illustration, can be called an oratorical proof; it is not an argument after the manner of Aristotle. But why should one refuse to the sacred writer the use of literary procedures which are universally allowed? Nobody frees himself completely from the methods of his time and of the school in which he has been trained. If it is easy to recognize by their language and their turn of thought the difference in the social rank and intellectual culture of the prophets, why should one wish Paul to be exempt from the same law? The interests of truth did not require him to unlearn all that he had been taught.

[1] I Cor. ix, 9, quoted from Deut. xxv, 4, repeated in I Tim. v, 18.

3. At that time he was noted for the strictness of his Pharisaism. " I was," he said, " full of zeal for [the Law of] God.[1] . . . I lived as a Pharisee according to the strictest sect of our religion."[2]   When his enemies subsequently boast of their scrupulous fidelity to the Law, he answers them : " I also was a Pharisee, a zealous persecutor of the Church, and blameless from the point of view of legal justice."[3]

Enveloped, as it were, in a narrow net by the six hundred and thirteen rules of the Mosaic code, which were themselves reinforced by numberless traditions, the life of the Pharisee was an intolerable servitude.   The ritual purifications, pre-scribed after defilements caused by the mere contact of im-pure objects, fill several chapters of the Talmud.   The last book of the Mishna,[4] comprising twelve dissertations or chapters, is entirely consecrated to these minute rules.   It was impossible to leave one's house, to take food, or to do any action whatever without exposing oneself to a thousand infractions of the Law.   The fear of falling into these paralyzed the mind and obliterated the higher sense of natural morality.   All religion degenerated into a petty formalism.   A man was tempted to believe himself the author of his own justice, and, no longer owing anything to anyone but himself, he became the creditor of God.   Of what use were repentance or humble, ardent prayer, or the sighs addressed to heaven by the sinner and the publican?   Was not he the just man, who fasted twice a week—on Mondays and Thursdays—after the custom of his sect, who paid exactly the tithe on mint, anise, and cummin, and who never forgot any traditional rite?   Pharisaism nourished self-love, self-conceit, and presumption.   It also fomented hypocrisy. The ideal of the Pharisee was lofty, but in order to attain it he had only his pride.   When this impulse failed, his only resource was to conceal his weaknesses or to turn them into virtues before the vulgar (*'am haarez*), whom he feared and despised.   What stratagems of cunning casuistry were employed to mitigate the severity of fasting and to relieve the inconvenience of the Sabbath !   Thus the treatise *Erubin* allows one to locate a *fictitious* domicile at the limit of sabbatical rest in order to prolong the journey by just so much, and to unite several domiciles *fictitiously,* so that one could carry food from one to the other without violating the law of rest.   The Pharisee sought to make up for his own sacrifices and miseries by a savage intolerance.   Saul, in despair at being so far from his ideal of legal perfection, made himself a persecutor through zeal and remorse.

He kept watch over the garments of Stephen, perhaps because he was not qualified to be the judge and the execu-

---

[1] Acts xxii, 3.   [2] Acts xxvi, 5.
[3] Phil. iii, 6.   [4] *Seder Teharôth.*

tioner of the martyr. But in his heart of hearts he sanctioned and approved everything. Passion agitated him too violently to let him listen to the words of the holy deacon, and if he had heard that discourse, so suddenly cut short by death, it would not have affected him. We do not find in his Epistles any allusion to that event. He remembers only that he had persecuted the Church of Christ. His four references to this deplorable past are of the highest importance in enabling us to judge his psychological condition at the moment of his conversion : " I persecuted the Church of God beyond measure and wasted it, and made progress in the Jews' religion above many of my equals in my own country."[1] " I am the least of the apostles, who am not worthy to be called an apostle, because I persecuted the Church of God."[2] " I was formerly a blasphemer, a persecutor, and contumelious ; but I obtained the mercy of God, because I did it ignorantly in unbelief.[3]—A Pharisee according to the Law, a persecutor of the Church through zeal, and blameless from the point of the justice that comes from the Law."[4] In the discourse which he addressed to the inhabitants of Jerusalem after his seizure[5] and in that which he pronounced at Cæsarea before the procurator Festus in the presence of the King Agrippa,[6] he recalls indeed the part taken by him in the martyrdom of Stephen, but without giving us to understand that he then experienced any other feeling than one of satisfaction at a desire gratified. Moreover, all the details seem to be confusedly mingled in his memory like the tormenting vision of a frightful nightmare.

III—THE ROAD TO DAMASCUS

1. Apparition of Christ. 2. Theological Beginnings.

1. The martyrdom of Stephen had only increased his thirst for Christian blood. Not content with being present at the torture of the victims, he entered into houses and dragged out the inmates, both men and women, to hale them to the dungeon. Soon, through lack of sufficient supply of such persons, the persecution died out in Jerusalem, and Saul had to carry his unappeased fury elsewhere. He begged the high priest[7] to give him an official mission to seek out the secret disciples of Jesus in the synagogues of Damascus, and to bring them, loaded with chains, before the Sanhedrim. It is there that the finger of God awaited him.

---

[1] Gal. i, 13-14. [2] 1 Cor. xv, 9.
[3] 1 Tim. i, 13. [4] Phil. iii, 6.
[5] Acts xxii, 3-5. [6] Acts xxvi, 4-11, especially xxvi, 19-20.
[7] This was perhaps still Caiaphas. In fact, Caiaphas was deposed only in A.D. 36 by Vitellius, governor of Syria, who substituted for him Jonathan, the son of the former High Priest Annas.

Since the conversion of St Paul is, next to the resurrection of the Saviour, the miracle which is best attested, the least capable of any natural explanation and consequently the most annoying to freethinkers, we cannot be surprised that rationalistic criticism has made desperate efforts to weaken its convincing force. As in the case of the resurrection of Jesus Christ, so here the attempt has been made to make the testimonies disagree. In the Book of Acts there are three narratives of the vision at Damascus : one made by St Luke on his own account,[1] the other two put into the mouth of St Paul.[2] It is conceded by everyone that the three narratives agree in all important points—viz., the occasion, the place, the time of the event, the dazzling light with which the caravan was enveloped, the dialogue between Saul, prostrate on the earth, and the mysterious voice, his temporary blindness, his baptism, his recovery, and the absolute change in his point of view, which suddenly made a persecutor an apostle. In a search for contradictions the most insignificant details are scrutinized with the closest strictness, trifles which one would blush to notice in the case of a secular historian, circumstances external to the fact itself and relating only to the impressions experienced by the companions of the principal actor, impressions necessarily subjective and perhaps diverse.[3] The most curious thing about all this is to find these objections precisely among the critics who suspect the author of having forged the discourses in the Acts in order to harmonize them with his own narrative. But it is necessary to choose between two methods of attack which exclude each other. For either St Luke himself

---

[1] Acts ix, 1-19.　　　　[2] Acts xxii, 3-21; xxvi, 12-20.

[3] The differences are not irreconcilable. Four are noted:

(a) According to one account, the companions of Saul hear the voice (Acts ix, 7); according to another they do not hear it (Acts xxii, 9). The expression used in the two cases is not the same. Ἀκούοντες τῆς φωνῆς (genitive), in Acts ix, 7, means : They perceived the sound of the voice (without understanding it); τὴν φωνὴν (accusative) οὐκ ἤκουσαν τοῦ λαλοῦντος μοί, in Acts xxii, 9, means that they " did not comprehend the voice of the one who spoke to me " (although perceiving the sound).

(b) Here they see no one, Acts ix, 7; there they see a light, Acts xxii, 9. Where is the contradiction ? Is a light a person ?

(c) In one case they remain standing (Acts ix, 7); in the other they fall to the ground (Acts xxii, 9). Εἱστήκεισαν ἐνεοί does not mean necessarily that they were standing, struck with stupefaction. It can be translated : They were, or they remained, out of themselves, as in Latin steterunt signifies in similar cases. One can convince oneself of this by consulting any Greek lexicon.

(d) Finally, it is objected that the words of Jesus are different in the different narratives. Literally, yes; but in meaning, no. The principal divergence consists in the fact that the author, according to a usage permitted at that time, unites in one single discourse (Acts xxvi, 15-18) words uttered by Jesus Christ on two distinct occasions (Acts xxii, 8 and 21): perhaps also words uttered by Ananias (Acts xxii, 14-15) in the name of Christ.

composed the discourses which he places in the mouth of his
characters, and in that case it would be unnecessary to speak
either of inconsistencies or contradictions; or else he inserted
them in his narrative, on the authority of documents, in
spite of their divergences from his story, and then we must
recognize and highly praise his conscientiousness as an
historian.

The miracle of the apparition is denied, but no trouble is
taken to explain the moral miracle, even more inexplicable
if we suppress the first, of the conversion of Paul. The
whole life of the Apostle, the serious character of his Pharisaism, and the immovable steadfastness of his Christian
faith protest against any system of thought that makes him
a visionary or a fanatic. His writings also protest against
it no less strongly.[1] There is no halting-place in his conversion, no gradual progress towards faith. Jesus Christ
arrested him suddenly in the midst of his career, and the
blow which felled him to the ground was terrible and irresistible. Nothing presaged it, nothing had prepared it; it
was simply a result of omnipotent grace. Does anyone
suggest that he had had previous relations with Christians?
But he knew them only as an executioner knows his victims.
He knew nothing of their doctrine, except the fact that it
was incompatible with the Law of Moses, irreconcilable with
Judaism, and therefore hateful and worthy of extermination.
That was enough for him, and he desired to know nothing
more about it. Does anyone charge him with hesitations,
anxieties, and remorse? He replies that he had experienced
no trouble, no uneasiness, and that he believed sincerely that
he was doing God service; that he acted in good faith, and
that it was owing to his ignorance that he had obtained mercy.
In presence of these affirmations the hypotheses so laboriously
constructed by the rationalistic critics are not tenable. In
order to do away with one miracle they invent a psychological
miracle still more marvellous. It is better to give up trying
to explain the inexplicable.

Certainly grace found in the fertile nature of Paul a
propitious soil and even precious germs. Strong convictions
in the service of passion are easier to turn to the good than
scepticism fortified by indifference. God enters more easily
into hearts and minds which have not sinned against the
light. The inborn need of justice and the profound sense of
his impotence spontaneously inclined his soul towards the
Christian doctrine, in which both those tendencies were to
find satisfaction and repose.

[1] Indeed, the declarations of the Apostle are explicit. He has *seen* the
Lord (1 Cor. ix, 1); Christ has *appeared* to him finally and after all the
others (1 Cor. xv, 8); God has *revealed* his Son in him at the moment when
he least thought of such a thing (Gal. i, 15-16).

2. The apparition at Damascus exercised on the theology of St Paul a manifold influence, some features of which it is well to note here. One of the boldest and most original theories of the Apostle is certainly that of incorporation with Christ, by virtue of which Christ is all in all, and all are one in him. But is not this idea contained in embryo in the question of Jesus: " Saul, why persecutest thou me?" Paul was not attacking directly the person of Christ, hence there is a mysterious identity between Jesus and his followers, if, in striking his disciples, one can reach the Master also.

In the conversion of Paul the work of grace is evident. The transformation is instantaneous.; it is like a blinding flash of lightning, a swift compliance with the divine call of a will which is scarcely aware of having consented. Whoever has known such a crisis has the clearest feeling and keenest intuition that all the honour of the change belongs to God, and he loves to picture to himself the work of grace as overwhelming, his faith as an act of obedience, a free act, of course, but one which, as soon as it is made, casts him immediately into a new world of rights and duties, of obligations and privileges. That is precisely the faith expressed in the Epistles to the Galatians and Romans, that active faith in which the heart has as large a share as the mind, that faith which revolutionizes the whole being, permeates all the powers of the soul, and instantaneously determines the direction of the whole life.

Finally, Christ thus seen leaves in the memory of Paul an ideal never to be forgotten. From that time on his gaze remains passionately fixed upon the incomparable model. He aspires to the measure and to the fulness of Christ, and wishes others also to do so. It will never be attained, but no matter ! It must always be our aim. Paul's moral teaching is thoroughly impregnated with this living memory, and instead of proposing to us to follow the example of Jesus in his mortal life, it invites us to imitate Christ risen from the dead and glorified.

It is, however, going too far to reduce all the theology of St Paul to the fact of his conversion, fertilized, it may be, by his religious experience. The Damascus vision is the clearest and most heartfelt of revelations, but it is only the first; and religious experience can extract from a fact only what it actually contains. Christian faith cannot be reduced to a subjective impression, and our dogmas are not the voluntary and conditional products of the individual consciousness. To attenuate the rôle of revelation to this point is no less opposed to truth than to the explicit testimony of the Apostle. The facts themselves will make this plain.

IV—PROGRESSIVE REVELATION

1. The Series of Revelations.   2. Elaboration of the Divine Element.
3. Meaning and Direction of the Progress.

1. Neither nature nor grace proceeds by leaps and bounds. The religious education of St Paul was not to be accomplished in a day any more than that of the other apostles. After a sudden crisis has indicated its commencement its further development takes a normal and progressive course. If the Damascus vision first opened the way to a theological system, the system itself was the fruit of a slow and continuous revelation.

The voice had said to him : " Arise, and go into the city, and there it shall be told thee what thou must do."[1] On this occasion Ananias was the channel of the heavenly communications. After his baptism, the neophyte retired into the desert of Arabia, either to meditate on the revelation he had received, or to prepare his soul for new light. The voice speaks to him again, three years later, in the Temple at Jerusalem.[2] Heaven always takes care to enlighten and lead him. It is by the aid of revelation that he goes to plead the cause of the Gentiles before the apostles.[3] The spirit of God hinders him from preaching in Asia,[4] closes to him the frontiers of Bithynia,[5] and urges him irresistibly towards Macedonia,[6] it encourages and consoles him at Corinth after the check experienced at Athens ;[7] it brings him back by force to Jerusalem in spite of the prospect of a long captivity.[8] Then, when all hope of seeing Rome seemed lost, it renews the assurance of it to him.[9] In short, providence leads him continually, as it were, by the hand.

It shows as much anxiety to instruct him as to guide him. But the divine illumination, wisely graduated, reveals itself

---

[1] Acts ix, 6: λαληθήσεταί σοι ὅ τι σε δεῖ ποιεῖν.

[2] Acts xxii, 18. New vision of Jesus during an ecstasy (ἐν ἐκστάσει).

[3] Gal. ii, 2: Ἀνέβην δὲ κατὰ ἀποκάλυψιν.

[4] Acts xvi, 6 : Vetati sunt a Spiritu sancto.

[5] Acts xvi, 7 : Non permisit eos Spiritus Jesu.

[6] Acts xvi, 9-10. Nocturnal apparition of the Macedonian (ὅραμα).

[7] Acts xviii, 9. Apparition of the Saviour during the night (δι' ὁράματος).

[8] Acts xx, 22-23. One may ask, it is true, if δεδεμένος τῷ πνεύματι means "bound by the Holy Spirit," irresistibly urged by him, or "bound in spirit"; that is, sure in advance of going to captivity. In any case the vision of chains and tribulations ahead of him comes to him from the Holy Spirit (τὸ Πνεῦμα τὸ ἅγιον διαμαρτύρεται, Acts xx, 23). Some days later, at Tyre, the brethren warn him by (revelation of) the Spirit not to go to Jerusalem (Acts xxi, 4, διὰ τοῦ Πνεύματος). The warning of danger comes from the Holy Spirit, but the advice is dictated by the filial affection of the Christians, and Paul does not think he ought to follow it. A little later, at Cæsarea, there is a new warning, always from the Holy Spirit (Acts xxi, 11).

[9] Acts xxiii, 11. Here it is the Lord who speaks during the night. But Paul had already, through an inspiration from the Holy Spirit (Acts xix, 21: ἐν τῷ Πνεύματι) formed the resolution to go to Rome.

only little by little : " I have appeared to thee," he is informed
the first time, "that I may make thee a minister and a
witness of those things which thou hast seen, and of those
things wherein I will appear to thee."[1] Innumerable visions,
of which Paul might justly be proud, if he did not prefer to
glory in his weakness which renders the more glory to his
Master; sublime revelations, the excess of which it pleased
the Lord to moderate and the brilliancy to soften, by giving
him a thorn in the flesh, a messenger of Satan to buffet
him.[2]

Alas! why can we not restore at a distance the whole
series of these revelations? The Apostle at one time alludes
to his being caught up into the third heaven, where he heard
ineffable words which it is neither possible nor permitted to
man to utter.[3] This great ecstasy, which made upon Paul
such a lasting impression, but the nature of which he never
succeeded in explaining, almost coincides with the beginning
of his active apostolate.[4] Was this an immediate preparation for his missions among the Gentiles, and a closer insight
into the truths which he was going to preach to them? We
cannot tell. It is, nevertheless, true that he constantly claims
for his preaching a divine authority and origin. " I give you
to understand," he writes to the Galatians, " that the Gospel
which was preached by me is not according to man. For
neither did I receive it of man, nor did I learn it, but by the
revelation of Jesus Christ."[5]

The extent of the signification of this declaration depends
a little on the meaning attached to what St Paul calls his
Gospel. When he affirms that he explained to the faithful
at Jerusalem and, in particular, to his colleagues in the
apostolate the Gospel preached by him to the Gentiles, and
that they found nothing in it either to find fault with or add
to,[6] does he mean all the Christian catechetical teaching,
including the whole body of elementary dogmas, the summary
of morals, and the symbolism of the sacraments, together
with the short story of the life and death of Jesus? This is

---

[1] Acts xxvi, 16: ὧν τε ὀφθήσομαί σοι.

[2] 2 Cor. xii, 1: ἐλεύσομαι εἰς ὀπτασίας καὶ ἀποκαλύψεις κυρίου.

[3] 2 Cor. xii, 4: ἃ οὐκ ἐξὸν ἀνθρώπῳ λαλῆσαι.

[4] It was the fourteenth year (at its beginning or end), before A.D. 56 or 57,
the date of the Second Epistle to the Corinthians—that is, between A.D. 42
and 44. Now the first great mission began in A.D. 45.

[5] Gal. i, 11-12: Οὐκ ἔστι κατὰ ἄνθρωπον—that is, "does not accommodate
itself to the desires or imaginations of men." Indeed (note the γάρ), it
is not human either in its first origin (οὐδὲ γὰρ ἐγὼ παρὰ ἀνθρώπου παρέλαβον),
nor in its transmission as far as I am concerned (οὔτε ἐδιδάχθην). It is
divine in all respects—in its first source and in its immediate source—since
I have it through a revelation from Jesus Christ, who is God.

[6] Gal. ii, 2. Paul speaks of his Gospel in the following passages:
Rom. ii, 16, xvi, 25 ; 2 Tim. ii, 8 (κατὰ τὸ εὐαγγέλιόν μου); 2 Cor. iv, 3
(ἡμῶν, cf. 1 Thess. i, 5; 2 Thess. ii, 14); 1 Cor. xv, 1 (τὸ εὐαγγ. ὃ εὐηγγελ-

hardly probable. There were too many points in common which did not come at all in question. Paul, no doubt, means by *his Gospel* the special form which the message of salvation took in passing from the Jews to the Gentiles, the quality which characterizes his preaching in pagan circles. This would be, then, first the equality of men in the scheme of redemption, the admission of the Gentiles into the Church on the same footing as the Jews, the abolition of the Mosaic Law, the liberty which results from it for all, especially for the Christians who have come out of paganism, the justification of men through faith, independently of the works of the Law, the incorporation of the faithful into Christ by baptism, the union of all in him, with the communion of saints which is its corollary; in a word, all the properties of the mystical body of Christ.

When he wishes that the Romans may be confirmed in "his Gospel," Paul identifies this Gospel with the *Mystery,* formerly hidden and now revealed,[1] a mystery of which the Epistles of the captivity give us the secret and the definition. The Apostle would, then, ascribe to the immediate revelation of Jesus Christ only the particular points of his preaching which had made the judaizing Christians accuse him of preaching a Gospel different from that of the Twelve. It is true the doctrine of the mystical body has numerous ramifications, and it may be that the institution of the Eucharist, the indissolubility of marriage, and the destiny of the righteous at the day of the *parousia,* about which subjects

---

ισάμην ὑμῖν); Gal. i, 11 (τὸ εὐαγγ. τὸ εὐαγγελισθὲν ὑπ' ἐμοῦ); Gal. ii, 2 (τὸ εὐαγγ. ὃ κηρύσσω). The opinion mentioned by St Jerome (*De Vir. ill.* 7, xxiii, 621): *Quidam suspicantur, quotiescumque in epistolis suis Paulus dicit "juxta Evangelium meum" de Lucae significare volumine,* cannot be considered.—The meaning which we adopt is that of the best exegetes, in particular that of Cornely (*Comment. in Rom.* ii, 16): *Indicari hac locutione (secundum Evangelium meum) aliquid videtur, quod ab ipso magis, quam a reliquis, doceatur ipsiusque praedicationi quasi sit proprium et essentiale.* Cf. *Ibid.,* in xvi, 25: *Confirmari ergo eos desiderat in "Evangelio suo," quo nomine illam praedicationis evangelicae formam intelligit quam ipse semper secutus est.* It is better not to compare with this the Gospel of the circumcision and the Gospel of the uncircumcision (Gal. ii, 7-8), because these two expressions can designate, not the *matter* or the *form* of the preaching, but the *special* field in which the apostolate of Paul and Peter was carried on.

[1] Rom. xvi, 25: *Juxta evangelium meum . . . secundum revelationem mysterii.* In Greek, where the same preposition κατά corresponds to *juxta* and to *secundum,* the apposition is more apparent, Eph. vi, 19: τὸ μυστήριον τοῦ; εὐαγγελίου; elsewhere (Col. i, 26-27, ii, 2, iv, 3; Eph. i, 9, iii, 3-9) it is the mystery of God or of Christ.—In Rom. ii, 16; *In die, qua judicabit Deus occulta hominum, secundum evangelium meum, per Jesum Christum,* one may ask what is specially pointed out as belonging to the Gospel of Paul. It is not the *judgement,* preached constantly by all the apostles, and moreover too far removed from the clause *secundum evangelium meum;* it is therefore either *occulta hominum* (Cornely referring to 1 Cor. iii, 13, iv, 5, xiv, 25; 2 Cor. v, 10, etc); or *per Jesum Christum* (but note John v, 22).

Paul seems to claim a special revelation, are directly connected with it. He himself clearly indicates the relation which exists between the communion of the faithful in the body of the Saviour and their union in the mystical body : " We are one bread, one body, for we all partake of one bread " (1 Cor. x, 17); a little farther on he states that he has " received from the Lord what he also has delivered "[1] to the neophytes at Corinth—namely, the fact of the Eucharist and the manner of its institution. Now, it does not seem possible to understand this reception as having been made through an intermediary, which would in no way distinguish Paul from the most insignificant of believers. Jesus Christ, therefore, must have communicated this mystery to him directly. As for the two other points mentioned above, doubt is permissible. When the Apostle says : " To them that are married, not I, but the Lord commandeth that the wife depart not from her husband, and that the husband put not away his wife " (1 Cor. vii, 10-11), it may be that he is alluding to the Saviour's precept recorded in the Gospel. However, the mystical significance of the conjugal tie, which symbolizes the union of Christ and the Church (Eph. v, 32), pleads in favour of a direct revelation. As for the declaration made to the Thessalonians " in the word of the Lord " (1 Thess. iv, 15, ἐν λόγῳ Κυρίου) referring to the fate of the righteous who will see the day of the parousia, perhaps it is a remark made by Jesus during his mortal life and transmitted by tradition, although this hypothesis is not very probable. Here also we are inclined to admit a direct revelation; and so much the more as the resurrection of the just and the glorification of the living are, for St Paul, very closely connected with the theory of the mystical body.

Is it necessary to go farther and refer to the same divine source all that the Apostle ever preached, even what he could easily have learned through an intermediary, such as the life, the miracles, and the discourses of Jesus? We do not think so. In that case Paul would have been much more favoured than his colleagues in the apostolate, who were obliged to learn from the narration of others many facts of which they had not been eyewitnesses. Providence, which does nothing uselessly, employs, even in working a miracle, a certain economy of means. No doubt, as Estius wisely remarks, it was no more difficult for the Lord to teach him in a single moment all the truths of the Christian faith than to convert him miraculously; but God wished to make use of the services of Ananias in order that, by seeing the doctor of the Gentiles instructed by a man, no one should ever disdain human agency. In this there is nothing contrary to the

---

[1] 1 Cor. xi, 23. In itself alone the preposition ἀπό would not exclude an indirect transmission.

claims of Paul. " He received the elements of faith, like the others who received instruction, at the moment of his baptism; but Christ reserves to himself the right to teach him personally the profoundest mysteries of Christianity."

2. The action of divine light on the intelligence of man is no less mysterious than that of grace upon the will. How are infused truths to be distinguished from knowledge naturally acquired? Whence comes to the prophet the certainty that he has heard God and is delivering his true message? We cannot say; scarcely can we conceive it. As St Thomas, following St Augustine, remarks : the prophets of the Old Testament were enlightened usually by emblems or symbols, the meaning of which an internal light explained to them. Their language, abounding in colours, images, allegories, and parables, retained the indelible trace of this mode of revelation. In St Paul there is nothing of the sort. His mind receives the divine ray directly and reflects it, like a mirror. He comprehends the plan of redemption intuitively, and enters into the essence and rationale of the great mystery. If his revelations sometimes seem to assume a tangible form, if he represents the Church as a perfectly organized body, or as a tree the growth of which has no limits, or as a temple which projects its harmonious lines far into the sky, we quickly perceive that these images do not stand out prominently or possess durability, but mingle and blend in one another; that the imagination does not succeed in reconstructing them; that they are reminiscences of the Old Testament; and that, far from floating in the mind of Paul like a vision, they are the attempt of an idea to become concrete. What the Apostle wishes most for his disciples is a clear knowledge (ἐπίγνωσις) of the truth; and when he claims for himself a comprehension (σύνεσις) of the mysteries, he uses the best word to express God's action upon him.

Not that a providential event did not favour the unfolding of the revelation, or that reason did not also intervene to enrich its growth. The mind of Paul was neither passive nor inert. The exaggerated spirit of concession shown by Peter made him comprehend the danger of maintaining the Law in the mixed churches; the claims of the judaizing Christians caused him to adopt, better and sooner than the others, the principle of Christian equality and its consequences; denial and doubt often gave the shock from which sprang forth supernatural light. In short, what distinguishes his revelations is their intellectual character and their relevancy to the matter in hand.

The present question is necessarily meaningless to rationalistic theologians, who suppress revelation in fact even if they retain it in name. Some, devotees of the pantheism of Hegel, make the ideas of Paul develop by continuous movements or by imperceptible changes. Since the whole being is contained in its immediate causes, progress is merely the result of the conflict between two opposing elements, which are reduced to unity by a superior principle. Whoever endeavours to reconstruct the theology of Paul on these Hegelian data, seeks it entirely in its pre-existent elements— either Greek Hellenism, or rabbinical Judaism, or a mixture of the two in more or less unequal doses, without denying, nevertheless, that this primitive stock might have been en- riched by the analysis of its contents or by a process of reasoning. Thus Paul would be merely an ideologist, an idle dreamer, passing his life in combining ideas and framing systems; in fact, the very opposite of the inspired and practical man whom we learn to know from his admirable Epistles.

Time has condemned these fanciful notions which do not stand the test of facts. Now, rationalistic theologians, imbued with Kant's philosophy, prefer to extol the psycho- logical method. The doctrine of Paul, they say, "is not a speculative theology, logically deduced from one general idea, but a really positive theology, whose point of departure is the inward reality of faith." By faith, and above all by love, Paul identifies himself with Christ. "He has become a member of Christ; he is possessed by him; he has the in- vincible assurance that Christ is not only the cause, but the ever-active author of his spiritual life and thought." What he experiences in his personal life "the Apostle finds again, and indicates as a law, in the history of humanity." To sum it all up, "the thought of Paul always followed· his religious experience, never preceded it. Born in the sphere of the individual life, it has ascended, by way of generaliza- tion, into the social and historical sphere; and as it tended by a continual effort towards unity and final principles, it succeeded at last in blossoming out into the sphere of meta- physics. . . . The historical views of the Apostle were born from his own peculiar philosophy of man; his speculative ideas came from his construction of history, and all these developments together were contained in his primitive faith, as the plant already exists in the germ that produces it."[1] Going to the bottom of these metaphors, we find this : Paul gives body to his feeling, he generalizes his experience, he objectifies his own idea of Christ. It matters little on what this idea is based, or to what this feeling responds, or what

[1] According to Sabatier, *L'Apôtre Paul* 3, 1896, pp. 295-297. We quote Sabatier, because he is the clearest—or anyway the least nebulous—of the disciples of Ritschl.

this experience is worth. Paul's theology reduces itself to a subjective impression.

All these weavers of theories plainly exceed the limit of their prerogatives. The rôle of theologians is not to substitute themselves for the Apostle, or to imagine what he ought to say, or what they would have said in his place, or to try to find out how he arrived at his conception of the supernatural world, supposing that he is moving in the domain of the unreal and chimerical. If anything is certain, it is that Paul is neither an Hegelian nor a Kantian. We must take him as he is. He would not recognize himself in the reconstructions of his thought, which are as elaborate as they are arbitrary. What anathemas would he not have fulminated against these unworthy interpreters of his work, he who wrote to the Galatians : " The Gospel which was preached by me is not according to man. For neither did I receive it of man, nor did I learn it, but by the revelation of Jesus Christ " !

3. We have a totally different conception of the progress of Paul's Gospel. It is neither a feeling objectified nor an idea developed by analysis. The impulse comes from without, from divine inspiration accommodating itself to outward events. Let us not forget that the Apostle did not draw up a systematic exposition of his doctrines, nor keep a diary of his revelations; that all his Epistles are polemical works or letters of admonition, written under the compulsion of special circumstances; that if they explain his preaching, they always take it for granted, and that consequently they reflect the difficulties which confronted the spread of the faith and the internal work which accompanied the unfolding of Christianity. The progress which they reveal runs, therefore, parallel to the progress of the life of the primitive Church, and this it is which constitutes its absorbing interest for us.

At the moment of their conversion the neophytes gave the apostolic preaching their unqualified assent. They received the words of Paul, not as those of man, but as the utterances of God, as in their origin and object they really were. It never occurred to anyone to criticize Paul's teaching. It is surprising to see with what facility the pagan populations accepted monotheism. The Christian code of morals produced a strong impression from the first by the evidence of its perfection; nor does the rôle of the Redeemer seem to have raised any serious objection. It was the dramatic account of the end of the world which sometimes disturbed their minds by exciting their imaginations and agitating their hearts. It was believed that the supreme hour was at hand, and people prepared themselves for the speedy arrival of the Judge and speculated on the relative advantages of the living and the dead; several even went so far as to neglect the cares of this world, which were insignificant in comparison with the great interests which they believed were at stake.

The Epistles to the Thessalonians testify to these lively apprehensions. As they form the only document of this epoch which remains to us, we might be tempted to believe, through a very natural mistake of perspective, that the apostolic catechesis was only one of eschatology, instead of being a succinct résumé of dogma and morals. But because the article referring to the end of the world had made such a strong impression on his hearers, the Apostle in his first writings is obliged to revert several times to the subject of the *parousia*.[1] Perhaps he subsequently took more effective measures to avoid the recurrence of such misunderstanding.

This period of simple faith and absolute confidence could not always last. The question of the observances of the Law, which had presented itself from the first moment of the preaching of Jesus and had precipitated the rupture between him and the Pharisees, was to be for a long time the vital problem of the infant Church. The compromise made at Jerusalem had not satisfied the judaizing Christians; the dispute at Antioch, settled by the triumph of the ideas of Paul, did not disconcert them. The Apostle met them everywhere on his travels—in Galatia, at Corinth, at Ephesus, as at Antioch and in Jerusalem. Scarcely had he founded a Christian community, when they hastened to follow in his steps and to organize a counter-mission; the churches of Macedonia alone seem to have escaped their unbridled propaganda. In order to contest the Gospel of Paul effectively they even dared to attack his person, to challenge his apostolate, to put him far below the Twelve, and to leave him only that secondary rôle which was not refused to apostles of the second order—to such men as Apollos and Barnabas. Paul contended for a whole year with these disloyal adversaries. We need not regret it, for his four great Epistles are the result of this struggle. If polemics occupies a large space in them, it could scarcely be otherwise. Nevertheless, the Apostle makes the controversy soar far above petty questions of persons; he goes back to the fount of grace and the origin of sin; he analyzes the nature of justification and the value of faith; he studies the impotence of the Law and the need of a redemption common to all; in a word, he keeps himself on the lofty summits of his principles with which, by means of corol-

---

[1] The word παρουσία (the Second Coming of Christ), which reappears only in 1 Cor. xv, 23, is the salient word in these Epistles—1 Thess. ii, 19, iii, 13, iv, 15, v, 23; 2 Thess ii, 1-8. No one is ignorant of the fact that eschatological ideas are the almost exclusive subject treated in them.

laries, he solves the most obscure problems.[1] But that is only
one of the aspects of his teaching during this phase of his
instruction. While the intrigues of the Judaizers forced him
to elucidate the harmony of the two Testaments and the
subordination of the old régime to the Gospel, a multitude of
theoretical and practical doubts arose in the Church about
different points of the primitive catechesis. The First Epistle
to the Corinthians gives us an idea of the numerous cases
of conscience which the Apostle had often to settle, orally or
by writing, in order to explain and complete his preaching.
And we may be certain that the treatment of Christians who
created scandals, the recourse to pagan tribunals, the
question of animals sacrificed to idols, the veiling of women,
the celebration of the *agape* and of the Eucharist, the usage
of *charismata,* the dogma of the resurrection, and the manner
of making collections, were not the only subjects of advice
addressed by him to the infant Churches.

Scarcely had the judaizing controversy begun to be settled
when a new heresy threatened the purity of the Gospel. The
Christian faith was coming into contact with profane
science; the name of philosophy had just been uttered. This
was not Greek philosophy, always more or less rational even
in its errors, but a kind of oriental theosophy, so much the
more dangerous that its outlines, being more vague, offered
less scope for refutation. Above all, the person and the
rôle of the Christ engrossed all minds. Men wanted to know
what he had been before his appearance on the earth; what
relations united him to God, to the world, to humanity; what
his rank was among those legions of supernatural beings,
intermediaries between God and man, with whom oriental
imaginations were peopling the skies. In his Epistles
of the captivity, Paul not only satisfies these desires to
know and comprehend; he elevates Christ to such a height
that nothing can any longer be compared to him. He places
him in the very bosom of God, as John places his Logos, so
as to form with God an indivisible unity. Then, taking
occasion better to explain the functions of Christ in the order
of salvation, he presents him as the universal source of grace
and the principle of union between all believers, and thus
completes the theory of the mystical body, already previously

---

[1] The course of ideas which is dominant in the great Epistles, naturally
influences their vocabulary. The word " Law " is employed here more than
110 times, and reappears elsewhere only 6 times; δικαιοσύνη, 45 times
(elsewhere 12 times) ; δικαιοῦν, 25 times (elsewhere twice, in the Pastorals) ;
δικαίωμα (5 times) and δικαίωσις are peculiar to the Epistle to the Romans.
Christian *liberty* (ἐλευθερία, 7 times; ἐλευθεροῦν, 5 times; ἐλεύθερος, 14
times) is an idea which Paul no longer makes prominent after it is no
longer contested. A statistical examination of the words *sin, death* (in
the moral sense), *life* (in the same sense), *vivify,* etc., would give similar
results.

outlined. New words, or words employed here in an entirely new sense, such as *super-knowledge* (ἐπίγνωσις), *mystery, pleroma, Head* of the Church, testify to this new current of ideas, which has its most complete expression in the formula *in Christo Jesu.*[1]

Some modern critics question the authenticity of the pastoral Epistles because they do not find the law of progress, as they conceive it, realized in them. "With the Epistle to the Philippians," they say, "*vital progress* stops; with the pastorals begins the conservative tradition." But is that not precisely what the situation calls for? Paul, who sees the end of his life approaching, feels the need of organizing the churches from which death is about to remove him, and of defending them against the invasion of strange doctrines. He thinks no more of creating, but of maintaining. His motto will henceforth be : "Keep the deposit" of faith and of tradition. He has fought the good fight; he is finishing his course; he awaits now only the never-fading crown of the apostolate and of martyrdom.

---

[1] We shall see that the formula *in Christo Jesu* is four times more frequent in the Epistles of the captivity than in the others. The words ἐπίγνωσις and μυστήριον are characteristic of this group, without being exclusively peculiar to it; but πλήρωμα ·and κεφαλή (*Head* of the Church) are not found elsewhere in the technical sense.

BOOK I
THE APOSTLE OF THE GENTILES

THE WORK OF THE MINISTRY

CHAPTER I

THE APOSTOLATE

I—Preparation and Beginnings

1. Damascus and Sinai. 2. First Mission.

1.

POPULAR imagination loves to connect the conversion of Paul with his active apostolate. In the morning he is the devouring wolf that ravages the sheepfold of Christ; in the evening he is the conqueror who brings to the foot of the cross, vanquished and captive, the enemies of the Gospel. In reality, six or seven years at least pass in the interval; a period of fruitful preparation, in which his thought matures and is perfected in solitude, silence, and prayer. It is also an obscure period, in which history often loses his traces and has for a guide only the narrative of the Acts, full of life and movement, but intermittent and fragmentary.

After his baptism and recovery from blindness, the neophyte remained in Damascus only a very few days; just enough to console and edify the faithful and to bear witness to his faith in Christ. Hastily visiting, one after the other, the synagogues of the city, he declared to his former co-religionists that Jesus was truly the Son of God. No doubt he limited himself to an account of what he had seen with his own eyes and heard with his own ears. Was this not the most decisive, as well as the most simple, of demonstrations? This Jesus, who, as everybody knows, was dead and buried, who said he was the Son of God, and gave proof of it by his resurrection, is alive, he has risen from the dead; I have seen him, he has spoken to me. The Jews, not daring to doubt his word, remained dumb with amazement.

But Saul was eager to flee from the noise of cities. After the moral shock which he had just experienced he felt the need of facing his own soul and of being alone with God. He departed for Arabia, either into the Nabathean kingdom, the capital of which was Petra, or to the sacred mountains where Jehovah had communicated the Law to Moses and conversed familiarly with Elias. It is doubtful whether he was drawn thither by any thought of the apostolate; although destined to bear the name of Jesus to the ends of the earth, he awaited without impatience or uneasiness the hour chosen by God. He wanted to probe the depths of his soul, to meditate on the Scriptures, to collect his thoughts under the eye of the Lord, and to listen to that interior voice which is heard more distinctly in proportion as the echoes of the world become distant and subdued.

He passed a year there, possibly two. Nothing helps us to penetrate the mystery of this retreat. St Luke does not say a word about it, although he seems to indicate two sojourns at Damascus, between which the journey to Arabia fits itself in quite naturally. On his return, Saul was armed for the controversy. His preaching was fortified with irresistible proofs. It was no longer, as on the first occasion, merely the testimony of an eyewitness; it was the well-considered teaching of the theologian and the inspired message of the prophet. Incapable of answering him, his adversaries resolved to close his mouth. The ethnarch of King Aretas, who had been bribed by them, undertook to satisfy their vengeance. In order to outwit the vigilance of the hired assassins, who watched day and night at the gates of Damascus, it was necessary to hide the Apostle in a basket and lower him down the wall by a postern gate. After this striking mode of escape, Paul went in haste to Jerusalem to see Peter. New perils, however, awaited him there, this time prepared by the Hellenist Jews. At the end of a fortnight, the brethren in alarm brought him to Cæsarea, and saw him safely on the road to Tarsus, which he reached by land. Then for three or four years, at least, we lose sight of him.

2. The official evangelization of the Gentiles was about to begin. Already some fugitives from the persecution let loose after the death of Stephen had come to Antioch and preached Christ Jesus there to the pagans themselves.[1] The conversions were numerous, and in order to confirm them the mother Church sent to the capital of Syria one of its best missionaries, Barnabas. This man, who had perhaps known Paul at the school of Gamaliel, and had seen him again, as a Christian, at Jerusalem, hastened to seek out in Tarsus one whom he knew to be the vessel of election, expressly chosen by God to bring the good tidings to the Gentiles. For a whole year they together cultivated the field which providence had sown for them.[2] Nevertheless, the influence of Paul increased every day. When it was necessary to carry to Jerusalem the offerings of the Church of Antioch in view of the famine predicted by Agabus, Barnabas and Paul were

---

[1] Acts xi, 20. The true reading is : Ἐλάλουν καὶ πρὸς τοὺς Ἕλληνας, and not Ἑλληνιστάς, which hardly makes sense. The evangelization of the Hellenists had begun from the first moment, but now they preached publicly even (καὶ) to the Greeks, to the pagans. The Vulgate renders it : Loquebantur et ad Graeco. The critics, except Westcott and Hort, are in favour of the reading Ἕλληνας.

[2] Acts xi, 21-26.

appointed to the task.[1] They did not find the apostles there. It was at the height of the persecution of Herod—James the Greater had just offered Jesus the testimony of his blood; Peter, miraculously set at liberty, had left the city; the others were scattered abroad. Their mission being fulfilled, the two envoys returned to Antioch about the time when, in a horrible malady followed by a frightful death, the persecuting king received the punishment of his crimes.

Henceforth the Church of Antioch was able to provide for itself. The Holy Spirit bestowed upon it many *charismata*. There were in the community prophets and doctors—Barnabas, Simon surnamed Niger, Lucius of Cyrene, Manahen, foster-brother of Herod the Tetrarch, and Saul. The construction of the Greek phrase seems to indicate that the last two held the rank of doctors and that the other three were counted among the prophets.[2] Saul still appears to occupy a subordinate position. But the spirit of God has designated him with Barnabas for the apostolate to the Gentiles on a large scale.

The two apostles began their tour at the island of Cyprus, where Barnabas was born. The proconsul Sergius Paulus embraced the faith. From that moment the rôles were reversed. Saul, suddenly become Paul,[3] assumed the leadership of the evangelical expedition, and Barnabas, with a simplicity equal to his modesty, effaced himself behind the man whose call by providence he recognizes and whose glorious destiny he foresees.

In this change of name we need not seek to find a mystery. Contemporary manuscripts inform us that a great many persons then had two names, one native, the other Roman. Saul, a Roman citizen, takes his Latin name at the moment when he is entering into relations with the masters of the world, so much the more as his Hebrew name, pronounced in Greek *Saulos,* contained a meaning somewhat ridiculous. The change of rôles is more remarkable; the apostolic company of travellers will be henceforth called "the retinue of Paul" (οἱ περὶ Παῦλον). Whereas previously Barnabas had had the supremacy, the contrary is now the case. Apparent exceptions to this are easily explained: at Lystra,[4] by the reception of the Lycaonians, struck by the imposing appearance of Barnabas; at Jerusalem,[5] by the fact that Barnabas is named first in the letter of the council, and

---

[1] Acts xi, 27-30.
[2] Acts xiii, 1. The first three names are joined by the conjunction καί, the last two by τε . . . καί. Barnabas, the first named, was the most important personage. Saul, by analogy, would be the last of the five. We think that the "laying on of hands" (Acts xiii, 3), preceded by fastings and prayers, is the episcopal consecration, needed by the two missionaries for the founding of churches.
[3] Acts xiii, 9 : Σαῦλος δὲ ὁ καὶ Παῦλος.
[4] Acts xiv, 12-14.
[5] Acts xv, 12-25.

is the first to speak. In this case Luke is only a reporter; but when he expresses his own thought he reverses the rôles and always gives Paul the place of honour.

After Cyprus, the missionaries, crossing again to the continent of Asia, preach the Gospel, one after the other, in Antioch of Pisidia, Iconium, Lystra and Derbe. Their method of preaching is always the same. They install themselves in the synagogue, so far as the Jews and the proselytes are willing to hear them. When the doors are closed to them, or when a riot drives them away, they address themselves to the Gentiles, not without making to their compatriots this solemn declaration : " To you it behoved us first to speak the word of God; but because you reject it, and judge yourselves unworthy of eternal life, behold we turn to the Gentiles.''[1] The intrigues and plots of the Jews drive them from Antioch and Iconium; at Lystra Paul is stoned by them and left for dead; and at Derbe they no doubt bar their way, for, instead of re-entering Syria by the direct route through Cilicia, they make the same journey back again, preaching in Perga, which on the first trip they had merely passed through, and embark at Attalia for Antioch.

Thus in a period of time which cannot have exceeded four or five years, they founded at least seven Christian communities : two in Cyprus (Salamina and Paphos), two in Lycaonia (Lystra and Derbe), one in Pamphilia (Perga). Having returned to Antioch, " whence they had been delivered to the grace of God,''[2] they related to the brethren, called together in a full assembly, what God had done with them and by them, and how they had opened the door of faith to the Gentiles. This was an event, the import of which it is impossible to exaggerate. The expansive force of the Church had just broken through the narrow framework of Judaism, and the prophecies which promised it the conquest of the world were beginning to be realized.

II—PAUL AND THE TWELVE

1. The Assembly at Jerusalem. 2. The Incident at Antioch.

1. The return of the missionaries was the signal for a tempest, in which infant Christianity might have perished if the ideas of Paul had not triumphed. It was a question of

---

[1] Acts xiii, 46. This declaration was first made in Antioch of Pisidia. However, we find the missionaries again in the synagogue of Iconium (Acts xiv, 1). Paul begins his preaching in the Jewish oratory at Philippi (xvi, 13), at the synagogue in Thessalonica (xvii, 1), in that of Berea (xvii, 10) ; he is driven from the synagogue at Corinth, where he renews his declaration (xviii, 4-6). Even during his third mission, he succeeds in preaching for three months in the synagogue at Ephesus (xix, 8).

[2] Acts xiv, 26 : παραδεδομένοι τῇ χάριτι τοῦ Θεοῦ. Cf. xv, 10.

knowing on what conditions the Gentiles should be admitted into the Church, and what position they should occupy in it. The mother Church of Jerusalem still adhered so closely to the Synagogue that it might have passed for a Jewish sect. Distinctions between foods that were clean and foods that were unclean, visits to the Temple, sacrifices, legal purifications—all these almost identified, outwardly at least, the new disciples of Christ with devout Israelites. Their assiduous attendance at the Temple was exemplary;[1] Peter and John went there to pray at the ninth hour, according to the custom;[2] several years later, Peter had not yet touched any food forbidden by the Law.[3] Even in 57 or 58 A.D. the brethren were still zealous observers of the Mosaic code, and it was in order not to scandalize them that Paul submitted to a ritual ceremony.[4] On the other hand, the liturgical meetings for the ministry of the word, the *agape* and the Eucharist, escaped the notice of the uninitiated. The Christians of Jerusalem evidently tried to treat their compatriots and former co-religionists with consideration. A violent rupture, cutting short all hope of proselytism, would have caused the infant Church to waste away in its cradle.

Confined at first to Jewish circles, the Gospel freed itself from them only gradually. An express command from heaven had been necessary to decide Peter to baptize the centurion Cornelius, and notwithstanding the striking miracle which sanctioned it, this exception did not pass without exciting some astonishment among the faithful.[5] The admission of the Samaritans, who were circumcised and half Jews in spite of their heresy and hereditary hatreds, raised no serious difficulty; at the first announcement of their conversion, Peter and John were sent to them.[6] The first mixed church was at Antioch. Christians from Cyprus and Cyrene, scattered broadcast by the storm which followed the death of Stephen, had preached Christ there even to the Greeks.[7] This was an unprecedented fact, but one which the apostles hastened to ratify, sending Barnabas as a delegate to Antioch.[8] There Jews and converted Greeks, designated now by the name of Christians, which distinguished them as a special religious association,[9] seem to have agreed very well together. Perhaps the Jews of Antioch were less irreconcilable than their brethren of Palestine, or the Christians who had come from paganism were more accommodating; perhaps also they made mutual concessions. But the question arose,

---

[1] Acts ii, 46. *Quotidie perdurantes unanimiter in templo.*
[2] Acts iii, 1. [3] Acts x, 14.
[4] Acts xxi, 20-26. [5] Acts xi, 1-18.
[6] Acts viii, 5-14. [7] Acts xi, 20.
[8] Acts xi, 22.
[9] Acts xi, 26. This name quickly became general (Acts xxvi, 28).

imperious and menacing, when Paul and his companion announced that they had opened wide the doors of faith, that the pagans were rushing in *en masse,* and that Christian communities were being formed from which the Jewish element was almost excluded, and which claimed to live on an equal footing with the others.

Meanwhile, there came from Jerusalem to Antioch some folk who must have enjoyed a certain amount of credit, and who, in any case, gave themselves an air of great importance. They preached openly that circumcision was an essential condition for admission into the Church and for hope of salvation. The excitement was great. Paul and Barnabas violently opposed these new pretensions. The moment was a fateful one. The world was about to see whether the Christian society would claim the universality which its Founder had promised it; or whether, persisting in remaining a Jewish sect, it would disappear in oblivion after a few years of sterile agitation. To retain circumcision, with the whole observance of the Law which it implies, meant abandoning the hope of conquering the world. The world would never become Jewish. The question of principle was still more serious. To make a Mosaic practice the essential condition of salvation was virtually to deny the transitory character of the old order, the sufficiency of redemption, and the efficacy of the blood and merits of Christ; it was to overturn the fundamental dogma of Christianity.

It was decided to submit the question to the mother Church of Jerusalem. Paul and Barnabas were chosen to represent the Church of Antioch. No doubt Paul, admirably suited for this task by his dominant position and by the leading part which he had just played in the evangelization of the Gentiles, offered himself for it voluntarily, for a revelation had bidden him to go and plead his cause in person. Let us hear his own account of it :

Then, after fourteen years, I went up again to Jerusalem with Barnabas, taking Titus also with me. And I went up according to revelation, and communicated to them the Gospel which I preach among the Gentiles, but severally to them who were of high reputation; lest perhaps I should run, or had run in vain. But neither, Titus, who was with me, being a Greek, was compelled to be circumcised: and that because of false brethren, unawares brought in, who came in privately to spy our liberty which we have in Christ Jesus, that they might bring us into servitude. To whom we yielded not by subjection, no, not for an hour, that the truth of the Gospel might continue with you. But of them who were of high reputation (what they were sometime, it is nothing to me; God accepteth not the person of man), for to me they who were of high reputation added nothing to me. But contrariwise, when they had seen that to me was committed the Gospel of the uncircumcision, as to Peter was that of the circumcision (for he who wrought in Peter to the apostleship of the circumcision, wrought in me also among the Gentiles); and when they had known the grace that was given to me, James and Cephas and John, who seemed to be pillars, gave to me and Barnabas the right hands of fellowship, that we should go unto the Gentiles, and they unto the circumcision. Only [they urged] that we should be mindful of the poor ; which same thing also I was careful to do.[1]

With almost all the critics and exegetes, we are of opinion that this narrative and that of St Luke in Acts xv refer to the same event. In fact, *the actors are the same:* Paul and Barnabas on one side, Peter and James on the other. The Epistle to the Galatians mentions in addition Titus, included in the " some others " referred to in the Acts, and Paul mentions John, whom Luke passes over in silence, because he did not take an active part in the proceedings. *The scene is the same:* Antioch and Jerusalem. Paul goes from Antioch to Jerusalem, charged (according to St Luke) with an official mission and also impelled to do so by a revelation, as he himself declares. Now it is evident that the two motives complete and do not exclude each other. *The discussion is the same:* one party wishes to oblige the Gentiles to be circumcised, in spite of the protestations of Paul and Barnabas. Luke designates the authors of these manœuvres : they are former Pharisees. Paul is content to stigmatize them with the name of intruders and false

---

[1] Gal. ii, 1-10. Their relations with the Twelve may be summed up as follows :

A. *Paul explained to them his Gospel in private :*

'Ανεθέμην αὐτοῖς τὸ εὐαγγέλιον ὃ κηρύσσω ἐν τοῖς ἔθνεσιν, κατ' ἰδίαν δὲ τοῖς δοκοῦσιν, μήπως εἰς κενὸν τρέχω ἢ ἔδραμον (ii, 1).—(*a*) As αὐτοῖς can refer only to the whole church of Jerusalem, the οἱ δοκοῦντες are the heads of the church, and probably only those who are subsequently named (ii, 9 : οἱ δοκοῦντες στῦλοι εἶναι), James, Peter and John. The Vulgate translation *qui videbautur esse aliquid* (ii, 2, 6) is capable of giving the false impression that Paul contests their real superiority, but the Greek expression suggests nothing of the kind, and the Greek Fathers have not even suspected it. For them, as for the classical writers, οἱ δοκοῦντες or οἱ δοκοῦντες εἶναί τι meant simply " the principals, the chiefs, the conspicuous personages." At the very most, one might see in this phrase, four times repeated, a slight irony intended for those who thought they could lower Paul's prestige by reserving that title for the Twelve.—(*b*) The sense of μήπως is interrogative : " *si* (*si forte*) I run or have run in vain," with a negative reply understood. One could also take μήπως in a *final* sense (*ne forte*) ; but as the context plainly excludes all doubt on Paul's part, it would then be necessary to supply something :—" *For fear* of running or having run in vain " (if my position is not accepted). This second explanation appears less natural.

B. *Titus was dispensed from circumcision :*

ἀλλ' οὐδὲ Τίτος ὁ σὺν ἐμοί, ῞Ελλην ὤν, ἠναγκάσθη περιτμηθῆναι· διὰ δὲ τοὺς παρεισάκτους ψευδαδέλφους. . . . οἷς οὐδὲ πρὸς ὥραν εἴξαμεν τῇ ὑποταγῇ, ἵνα ἡ ἀλήθεια τοῦ εὐαγγελίου διαμείνῃ πρὸς ὑμᾶς (ii, 2-5).—(*a*) Paul expressly states that Titus was not circumcised.—(*b*) He gives the last reason for his refusal: to maintain among the Gentiles and in their favour " the truth of the Gospel," the right which the Gospel grants to them.—(*c*) And he explains the determining motive for this : to resist the unjust demands of " spies and false brethren " who might have been able to take advantage of his concessions, and to whom he could not properly " yield, even for one moment." To interpret this, with Pelagius, Primasius and some modern Protestants, as " I was not forced to circumcise Titus, but

brethren. If he alone relates the pressure brought to bear on Titus, it is because it is characteristic and touches him more closely. *The date is the same.* All the attempts which have been made to disconnect the two recitals have been in vain. Finally, *the result is the same:* Paul's ideas triumph. Nothing is found to object to in his preaching, and the pillars of the Church sanction his Gospel fully. St Luke is no less explicit. According to him, the abettors of discord are disavowed, and the apostles, acknowledging the liberty of the Gentiles, declare them exempt from the law.

This first victory of Paul was a brilliant one. The strict adherents of the Law demanded the circumcision of Titus, whom he had taken as his companion, perhaps not unintentionally. He decidedly refused. In a somewhat complicated phrase he gives us to understand that he might have been able to show more compliance under other circumstances; but that it was then necessary to reject any concession which might have been used subsequently as a precedent, and to baffle the machinations of the false brethren, to safeguard Christian liberty, and to maintain intact the rights of the Gentiles, which one moment of weakness would have compromised. Therefore, " Titus, Greek though he was, was not compelled to undergo circumcision " precisely because the adversaries claimed to impose it; and the Apostle " did not yield to their demands even for a moment "; although he would consent

---

I did so voluntarily, on account of false brethren who had intruded into the meeting," is to do violence to terms and to impute to Paul a contradiction. To make this interpretation acceptable, it would be necessary, like Tertullian, Victorinus and Ambrosiaster, not to read the words *quibus nec* (οἷς οὐδέ), which are certainly authentic.

C. *The leaders of the Twelve were of no use to Paul:*

ἐμοὶ γὰρ οἱ δοκοῦντες οὐδὲν προσανέθεντο (ii, 6). Whatever their authority might be elsewhere (ὁποῖοί ποτε ἦσαν, *qualescumque essent*, rather than *quales aliquando fuerint*) concerns me little (οὐδέν μοι διαφέρει), or that has nothing to do with the question. As far as I am concerned, they added nothing to me, they gave me nothing *of their own* (the proper meaning of the middle voice) that I did not possess already: *nihil mihi contulerunt.* That is perfectly clear; and it is useless to understand as implied either " They added nothing *to my Gospel* " or " They imposed upon me *no new obligation.*" There is nothing to be supplied.

D. *On the contrary, the leaders among the Twelve were fully in accord with him* (ii, 7-10).

James (first named because he was considered to be the most hostile to the Pauline Gospel), as well as Peter and John, recognizing the divine mission of Paul (γνόντες τὴν χάριν τὴν δοθεῖσάν μοι), concluded an agreement of unity with him (δεξιὰς ἔδωκαν ἐμοὶ κοινωνίας), by virtue of which they divided the fields of the apostolate between him and Peter; giving to Peter the Gospel of the circumcision; to Paul and his companions that of the uncircumcision. But this division was not exclusive, and neither Paul nor Peter ever understood it so. See Belser, " Die Selbstverteidigung des hl Paulus im Galaterbriefe," Freiburg im Breisgau, 1896 (*Biblische Studien,* vol. i, fasc. 3).

willingly to the circumcision of Timothy when that act of opportunism could not be misrepresented.

After this manifestation of authority, it was easy for Paul to make his view prevail. He demanded for ·the Gentiles the privilege of being freed from the Mosaic legal observances, and this opinion Peter amplified greatly, reminding all Christians that the liberty of the Gentiles had been proclaimed with equal power by the Holy Spirit himself. But it was James who had the honour of proposing a really practical solution, which everyone finally adopted. He advised declaring the Gentiles exempt from the whole Mosaic Law, with the exception of four restrictions, intended to facilitate their relations with the Jewish Christians. They were to refrain from meats offered up to idols, from fornication (that is, according to all probability, from marriage with blood-relatives, which was forbidden by the Law), from meat of animals which had been strangled, and from blood. These four points had been formerly prescribed under penalty of death to all foreigners resident in Israel; and although they do not agree precisely with the Noachian precepts imposed—according to the artificial legislation of the Talmud—on proselytes of the second rank, they were no doubt observed then by all pious men who frequented the synagogue. Some circumstances deserve consideration.

The recruits from the ranks of the Gentiles *are formally discharged from the burden of the Law;* and nothing suggests the fact that they find themselves thereby in a condition of inferiority in comparison with the recruits from Judaism. The four prohibitions—sacrifices to idols, fornication, blood, and bloody meat—are imposed upon them, not by the Law of Moses, but *in virtue of the authority of the apostles.* They chose *observances which were to render possible table and social relations* between the two sections of the Christian community; for they could not hope to see the Jews put aside so soon their instinctive horror of animals sacrificed to idols and of meats which had not been drained of blood. Finally, *the decree concerned only the mixed Church of Antioch,* in which the controversy had arisen, and the Churches of Syria and Cilicia, which were in a similar condition.

In fact, it was a complete triumph for the ideas of Paul. The freedom of the Gentiles having been recognized in principle, their evangelization having been explicitly approved, and the Pauline churches having been maintained *in statu quo,* Paul is able to say with strict truth that the chief apostles had changed nothing in his Gospel nor added anything to it. He recalls with confidence this solemn act of adhesion and brotherhood which sanctioned his work and consecrated his mission. If he does not mention the apostolic decree, it is because he does not feel himself aimed at in it; but he will-

ingly assumes the spirit of it, and he causes it to be
observed to the letter in other mixed communities, where, as
in Antioch, the Jewish element formed a large part. For, if
no one is more unyielding than he in questions of principle,
yet no one is more accommodating when it is a matter of
avoiding controversies and of quieting the scruples of the
timorous.

2. The decree of Jerusalem did not remove all doubts.
Although the Gentiles were officially dispensed from the Law,
did they not remain free to observe it, if they liked, to its full
extent? Was there not for them merit and perfection in
doing so? The four restrictions which were imposed upon
them *by necessity* (ἐπαναγκές), without specifying the nature
of this necessity, seemed to liken them to the Jewish proselytes of the second rank. Were they not placed thus, in
regard to the racial Jews, in a condition of humiliating
inferiority, which they could do away with by assuming
the entire observance of the Law? On the other hand,
if the measure adopted by the apostles gave satisfaction
to the moderate Jewish Christians, it did not suppress the
objections of the Judaizers. We must not imagine that the
strict Pharisees believed they had a right to deal freely with
proselytes who were restricted only to the Noachian precepts,
or that they regarded as their equals even the proselytes
of justice. In the eyes of the extremists nothing filled
up the abyss which yawned between the impure offspring
of the Gentiles and the child of Abraham. Were these
uncompromising specimens of Judaism, imbued with such
pharisaical maxims, going to treat Gentile converts as equals,
as brothers? It was soon evident that they had no such intention. Hence the painful incident which we let the principal
actor in it relate :

> But when Cephas was come to Antioch, I withstood him to the face,
> because he was to be blamed. For before that some came from James,
> he did eat with the Gentiles; but when they were come, he withdrew
> and separated himself, fearing them who were of the circumcision.
> And to his dissimulation the rest of the Jews consented, so that Barnabas
> also was led by them into that dissimulation. But when I saw that
> they walked not uprightly unto the truth of the Gospel, I said to Cephas
> before them all :—If thou, being a Jew, livest after the manner of the
> Gentiles, and not as the Jews do, how dost thou compel the Gentiles
> to live as do the Jews ?[1]

---

[1] Gal. ii, 11-14. Note (*a*) that in ἐλθεῖν τινας ἀπὸ Ἰακώβου, the preposition
ἀπό refers more naturally to the neighbouring word τινας than to the verb
ἐλθεῖν, and it is better, therefore, to interpret " from " as " associated with,"
not as " sent by " James.—(*b*) Remark the imperfect tenses indicating habit
(συνήσθιεν) on the one hand, and on the other ὑπέστελλεν καὶ ἀφώριζεν ἑαυτόν,
characterizing the double attitude of Peter *before* and *after* the arrival of the
Jews from Jerusalem.—(*c*) In changing his conduct Peter "was to be

Three points are to be regarded as gained. The Cephas reproved by Paul is indeed Peter; history knows no other person of that name capable of counterbalancing the authority of the doctor of the Gentiles and sufficiently influential to make Barnabas himself waver. Hence the supposition of *two* Peters, proposed in ancient times by Clement of Alexandria and by some obscure anonymous writers, whose opinion is cursorily mentioned by St Jerome, St John Chrysostom, and St Gregory the Great, is only a poor subterfuge, which ought not to have tempted certain mediocre modern exegetes, anxious to preserve the prestige of the Prince of the Apostles. Secondly, the difference between them was serious and not simulated; it was not a mere spectacle, arranged beforehand between the two great apostles, in order to instruct the faithful by a dramatic contradictory debate. On that point the good sense of Augustine easily triumphed over the cavils of Jerome, which were inspired by Origen. Finally, the discussion took place *after and not before* the meeting at Jerusalem; for there is no reason for imagining a chronological inversion in the recital given in the Epistle to the Galatians. Nor can we either place the incident after the second mission, since Barnabas was at that time no longer with Paul. It is necessary, therefore, to place it as occurring during the apparently short sojourn which the latter made at Antioch immediately after the apostolic meeting.

What was the precise object of the conflict? On the question of principle the two apostles were fully agreed. Indeed in the Church of Antioch, where the Jews were only a minority, Peter was wont to eat with the Gentiles (συνήσθιεν, imperfect tense, denoting habit), breaking thus abruptly with the claims of the extremely strict Pharisees. 'And Paul reminds him of this in those words which, on any other hypothesis, would have no sense: "You, who are a Jew, live like the Gentiles and not as do the Jews." The change of attitude was occasioned by the arrival of the judaizing party from Jerusalem. It is said that they came *from* James, or even, perhaps, were sent *by* James—for the Greek preposition (ἀπό) can convey both meanings—but it is nowhere said or insinuated that they were sent in order to thwart the influence of Paul, or to bring about a schism in the two divisions of the Church, or to curb the liberty

blamed." The word is not κατέγνωστο, which would suppose an *act* of condemnation, but κατεγνωσμένος ἦν—that is, he was in a *state* of condemnation, consequently "blameworthy." It is necessary to take this participle as an adjective, like κεκορεσμένοι (1 Cor. iv, 8), and κεκαλυμμένον (2 Cor. iv, 3), etc.—(*d*) Paul warns him before them all (ἔμπροσθεν πάντων), not secretly, surreptitiously, but *before all*. The Greek κατὰ πρόσωπον means merely in his presence or face to face, with no hostile intention, and without the defiant air suggested by the Latin *in faciem*.

so solemnly granted to the Gentiles in the assembly of the apostles. Whether these intriguers claimed St James, the brother of the Lord, as their patron or not, they pretended that the tolerance of the council applied to the Gentiles only, and that the whole burden of the Law continued to rest on the racial Jews. But the complete observance of the Law, understood in the sense of the Pharisees, involved no longer taking meals with those who did not observe it. Peter was afraid of these schemers and thought it well to handle them cautiously, either because he feared to make apostates of them (as Chrysostom thought), or because he dreaded their threats and manœuvres (as Irenæus believed), or for some other unknown motive. So, from that day forth, he was accustomed to decline the invitations of the faithful of Gentile origin and to avoid their company. The spirit of conciliation led him too far. His conduct was really dissimulation, as St Paul was soon to tell him reproachfully, since he was acting contrary to his closest convictions, and appeared to accept an obligation the need of which he did not admit in conscience. This had, however, two disastrous results which he had not foreseen. The other Jews of Antioch and Barnabas himself, who previously had had no scruples about not fulfilling the requirements of the Law, thought it necessary to imitate him, because his example had such weight. On the other hand, the converted pagans, whose freedom from the Law had been recognized, saw themselves threatened with isolation if they did not live after the manner of the Jews. Placed in the alternative of renouncing their privileges, or of no longer sharing meals with the apostles and their Hebrew brethren, they were morally compelled to follow Jewish customs.

Paul saw at a glance the more or less remote, yet fatal, consequences of this false situation. He understood that Peter and his imitators were not "walking uprightly unto the truth of the Gospel." Their "dissimulation," although prompted by avowable motives, injured the rights of a portion of the Church, under the colour of charity, and might bring about a division in the Christian community. Paul knew the loyalty, humility and grandeur of soul which characterized the chief of the apostles. He did not, therefore, fear to reproach him publicly, not with a fault, but with a dangerous example; not with an error, but with an inconsistency. Peter certainly yielded to the arguments of Paul. If he had persisted obstinately in his mode of action, this whole affair, far from being an argument in favour of the Gospel of Paul, would have been a formidable objection, the remembrance of which the latter would not have been able to evoke, without utterly ruining the principle which was so dear to him.

III—Missionary and Preacher

1. Sermons to the pagans. 2. Discourse at Antioch in Pisidia.
3. Discourse at Lystra. 4. Speech at Athens.

1. The first sermons of the apostles must have been cast in a uniform mould. The rough draft, shaped in advance by the necessities of the moment, comprised two points—sincere conversion and faith in Jesus Christ the Saviour. Conversion also presupposed an act of the mind and a movement of the heart; the exclusive worship of the true God and repentance for the past, inspired by the prospect of divine judgement. Before a Jewish audience, already imbued with monotheism, the preaching was, therefore, summed up in the two words repentance and faith. But faith in Christ had assumed at that time a special character; it was no longer merely faith in Jesus, who had died for our sins and whose redeeming mission God had sanctioned by the miracle of the resurrection, it was faith in the Messiah predicted by the prophets, the hope of Israel, the crowning of the promises.

The Epistles have preserved for us some rare echoes of St Paul's preaching. Recalling to the Thessalonians the very recent hour of their conversion, the Apostle says to them : " You turned to God from idols, to serve the living and true God, and to wait for his Son from heaven, whom he raised up from the dead, Jesus, who hath delivered us from the wrath to come."[1] A complete break with the past, profession of monotheism, expectation of salvation through the mediation of the Son ; such were the acts of the will and the intelligence which the herald of the Gospel had preached to them and which had made them Christians. In the beginning the article concerning the judgement of God readily took the dramatic form of the *parousia,* a consolation to believers, a terror to unbelievers.

---

[1] I Thess. i, 9, 10 : ᾿Επεστρέψατε πρὸς τὸν Θεὸν ἀπὸ τῶν εἰδώλων, δουλεύειν Θεῷ ζῶντι καὶ ἀληθινῷ, καὶ ἀναμένειν τὸν υἱὸν αὐτοῦ ἐκ τῶν οὐρανῶν, ὃν ἤγειρεν ἐκ τῶν νεκρῶν, ᾿Ιησοῦν τὸν ῥυόμενον ἡμᾶς ἐκ τῆς ὀργῆς τῆς ἐρχομένης. The two infinitives δουλεύειν and ἀναμένειν depend on ἐπεστρέψατε. " You were converted *in order to* serve the true God *and* to await his Son." It is pressing the meaning of ἐπεστρέψατε too far to seek in it the idea of *a return* to a primitive state from which the pagans had fallen ; this word is often used to express the conversion of the Gentiles (Acts ix, 35 ; xi, 21, etc.), without any idea of *a return* to God, but with that of separation (ἀπό) from idols. The biblical appellation of God as the " living and true " (2 Kings xix, 4-16 ; 2 Par. xv, 3) must have been suggested by the mention of vain and lifeless idols. Two things are comprised in conversion : (*a*) the resolve to serve God by carrying out all his will, (*b*) an act of faith and hope in regard to the Son, who is to come in the heavens, whom the Father has raised from the dead, and who even now saves us (ῥυόμενον in the present) from the wrath ready to fall upon us. It is remarkable that Jesus Christ does not appear here as a judge, but as an advocate and defender before his angry Father.

When a hearer, touched by the grace of God, had once said " I believe," there began for him the teaching of Christian doctrine in the true sense of the word. The initial dogma was that of the resurrection of Christ, which belongs rather to the preliminaries of faith, because it contains the most solid as well as the most accessible proof of the divinity of Christianity. Paul insisted on this particularly, for it was for him the key to the sacramental value of baptism and one of the foundations of his system of morals. " For I delivered unto you, first of all, that Christ died for our sins, according to the Scriptures, and that he was buried and that he rose again the third day, according to the Scriptures, and that he was seen by Cephas and after that by the Twelve " (1 Cor. xv). There followed a long list of eyewitnesses who rendered the fact of the resurrection indubitable for any unprejudiced mind. Although the Corinthians came for the most part from the Gentiles, the first religious instruction had been given to them in the synagogue at the outset, and afterwards in an adjoining house. This explains why the fundamental Christian dogma was presented to them as the realization of the prophecies : the New Testament forming a sequel to the Old without any break in continuity. The author of the Epistle to the Hebrews numbers among the elementary truths, of which no Christian is supposed to be ignorant, and which were, therefore, to form the first subjects of catechetical teaching, the following items : repentance from dead works, faith in God, the doctrine of baptisms, the laying-on of hands, the resurrection of the dead, and eternal judgement. In reality, the first two subjects and the last two always formed part of the sermons addressed to unbelievers in order to induce them to believe; only the explanation regarding baptism and the laying on of hands could be reserved for the converts under instruction.

2. The Acts of the Apostles gives us an interesting specimen of St Paul's preaching before an audience in which the Jewish element predominated.[1] On the first Sabbath after their arrival at Antioch in Pisidia, the missionaries went and seated themselves in the midst of the Jews and proselytes who were filling the synagogue. After the reading of the Law and the Prophets they were invited to speak. This was an act of politeness which they did not fail to show to strangers of distinction. Paul reckoned on it. So, when the *chazzan* advanced towards him on the part of

---

[1] Acts xiii, 15-41. The three parts of the discourse are clearly indicated by the apostrophe three times repeated ἄνδρες ἀδελφοί (verses 15, 26 and 38). The first part, under colour of showing God's providence towards Israel, leads to Jesus ; the second shows that Jesus, although denied and crucified by his people, is nevertheless the Messiah ; the third concludes by stating the necessity of believing and hoping in him.

the chiefs of the synagogue, he rose at once and with a gesture claimed the silence and attention of the congregation. Whether his exordium had been suggested to him by the *haphtara* or the *parascha* of the day or not, he began to develop one of the favourite ideas of the Scriptures—the divine vocation of Israel and the special providence of which Israel was the object in the time of the Patriarchs, in Egypt, in the desert, under the judges, during the institution of royalty. Up to this point nothing would excite any distrust in his hearers, and the most unorthodox Pharisee would not have spoken otherwise. But having come to David, the orator imperceptibly gives his discourse another direction, without, however, leaving the prophetic groundwork. It is from the race of David that, according to the promise, the Saviour of Israel is to be born ; and this Saviour has appeared, he is called Jesus, and he has had for a forerunner and guarantee a man whose testimony they cannot deny, since he belongs to them and they have revered him as a worker of miracles and a prophet, St John the Baptist.

Here properly begins the substance of the sermon, of which, doubtless, Luke gives us only a very brief résumé. Paul follows exactly the course which he tells us he had adopted in the evangelization of Corinth, a method, moreover, so natural and conformable to his doctrine that it might have been anticipated. He proves by Scripture that the death, the burial, and the resurrection of Christ had been foretold for a long time, that the executioners of Jesus had contributed, without knowing it and without wishing it, to the fulfilment of the prophecies, and that God has put his seal upon it by raising his Son from the dead. The actual fact of the resurrection is proved, as always, by the testimony of eyewitnesses who are still alive and whose testimony everyone can verify. In view of the conciseness of the text the scriptural evidence is more difficult to apprehend, and we are ignorant, in particular, of the rôle which the *argumentum ad hominem* may play in it ; but it is clear that the words, " Thou wilt not suffer thy Holy One to see corruption," pronounced by David, less as a prayer than as a prophecy, did not have in him (David) their fulfilment. They can, therefore, refer only to him, of whom David was the symbol, to the Holy One *par excellence,* who has known death indeed, but not the corruption of the tomb.

The demonstration finished, the Apostle concludes in these terms : " Know therefore, my brethren, that the remission of sins through him is proclaimed to you. The justification which you have not been able to obtain by the Law of Moses every believer finds in him." It is impossible not to feel here the touch of Paul. There is not one idea, hardly one word, which is not characteristic of his style and language. Everything in it is typical : the opposition between faith and the Law, the impotence of the latter, the remission of sins by the mediation of Christ, and justification by faith in the person of the Redeemer. But it is not only the conclusion that is in the spirit and method of Paul. A multitude of other features and expressions remind us of the Epistles : the harmony of the two Testaments, one of which is the continuation of the other; the seed of David which realizes the promises; the death of Jesus verifying the prophecies, with the special mention of the burial, passed over in silence by the other apostles but always displayed conspicuously by St Paul by reason of the mystical and sacramental burial in baptism, which symbolizes it.[1] In truth, if St Luke, as is claimed, composed on his own initiative the discourses of the Acts, it must be confessed that he is profoundly imbued with Paul's doctrines and that he knows how to express them with a skill capable of putting us on the wrong scent.

Attention has been called to a certain similarity between this discourse and the speech of St Stephen to his executioners; but the resemblance, in any case limited to the exordium, is a superficial one. It is wholly in the style of the *midrash,* which was adopted by both speakers : Paul for his entry into the main subject; Stephen for the whole of his discourse, which treats only of this truth, of which Scripture is the perpetual confirmation : " You and your fathers have always resisted the Holy Spirit." The Apostle, on the contrary, never loses sight of this thesis, towards which every one of his sentences converges : " Jesus is the Messiah promised to the Jews, the only one whose mission it is to save them and who can justify them." His opening is no mere *hors d'œuvre;* aside from the fact that it is imposed

---

[1] It is enough to indicate the following comparisons : (A) ver. 23 : τούτου (Δαυείδ) ἀπὸ σπέρματος, Jesus of the race of David, a Pauline expression (Rom. i, 3 ; 2 Tim. ii, 8).—(B) ver. 23 : κατ' ἐπαγγελίαν; and ver. 32 : ὑμᾶς εὐαγγελιζόμεθα τὴν πρὸς τοὺς πατέρας ἐπαγγελίαν γενομένην. The word ἐπαγγελία is very Pauline and still more so is the idea which it expresses. Outside the writings of Paul, who uses it twenty-seven times, and outside the Epistle to the Hebrews ἐπαγγελία is found almost exclusively in St Luke who, curiously enough, puts it four times in the mouth of Paul (Acts xiii, 23, 32; xxiii, 21 ; xxvi, 6).—(C) ver. 38 : διὰ τούτου ὑμῖν ἄφεσις ἁμαρτιῶν καταγγέλλεται, ἀπὸ πάντων ὧν οὐκ ἠδυνήθητε ἐν νόμῳ Μωϋσέως δικαιωθῆναι, ἐν τούτῳ πᾶς ὁ πιστεύων δικαιοῦται. In this singular phrase in which everything reminds us of Paul, it is necessary especially to note : (a) that the remission of sins is attributed, not to baptism, but directly to the mediation of Christ, as in Eph. i, 7 and Col. i, 14 ; (b) the impotence of the Mosaic Law to produce justification (Rom. viii, 3, τὸ ἀδύνατον τοῦ νόμου), cf. Gal. iii, 21 ; (c) the characteristic expression πᾶς ὁ πιστεύων, Rom. i, 16, 22 ; iv, 11 ; x, 4, 11, etc.; (d) the no less characteristic expression δικαιοῦσθαι ἐν Χρίστῳ, Gal. ii, 17 ; (e) the rare construction of δικαιοῦσθαι with ἀπό, Rom. vi, 7 ; (f) the technical term δικαιοῦσθαι itself.—(D) ver. 46: ὑμῖν ἦν ἀναγκαῖον πρῶτον λαληθῆναι τὸν λόγον τοῦ Θεοῦ. The πρῶτον is justified by all Paul's teaching (Rom. i, 16 ; ii, 9-10 ; iii, 2).—(E) ver. 29 : The mention of Christ's burial between his death and resurrection would seem utterly idle, apart from the doctrine of Paul (1 Cor. xv, 4 ; Rom. vi, 4).

upon him by the circumstances, it has the merit of conducting his hearers of the synagogue without any shock to the threshold of the Church, by showing them the connection between the two covenants, through which the providence of God works uninterruptedly on his people.

The eloquence and logic of Paul did not have the desired effect. The Jews of Antioch, startled for a moment, were not long in recovering their self-possession, and on the following Sabbath the missionaries, in taking their departure, cast in their faces that warning which they were subsequently so often to repeat : " Since you judge yourselves unworthy of eternal life, lo, we turn to the Gentiles." It is, indeed, to the Gentiles that Paul received a special mission to preach. His Hellenic education and his lively sympathy for the Greeks fitted him for it better than the others. He knew that conscience is always alert in the human heart, and he perceived at the bottom of even the most degraded religious sentiment a sort of latent monotheism which it was necessary to redeem. God is the God of the Gentiles as well as of the Jews, and it is only needful to point that fact out to a well-disposed mind to make it recognized.

3. To the inhabitants of Lystra, who raise altars to them because they take them for gods, Paul and Barnabas are content to say : " Brethren, what do ye? We too are mortals, men like unto you, preaching to you to be converted from these vain things to turn to the living God, who made the heaven and the earth and the sea and all things that are in them ; who, in times past, suffered all nations to walk in their own ways. Nevertheless, he left not himself without testimony, doing good from heaven, giving rains and fruitful seasons, and filling our hearts with food and gladness."[1] These sentences, unfortunately too short, contain an exhortation, an apology, and a condensed justification of God's providence. The exhortation is couched in the same terms which the Apostle subsequently repeats to the Thessalonians : to turn from idols and to be converted to the living God. The apology has for its aim to prevent the scandal caused by the apparent forgetfulness of God, which seems contrary to his providence. God has allowed man to make a bad use of his free will, as if he had abandoned him to his errors ;[2]

---

[1] Acts xiv, 15-17. The following comparison is instructive :

ACTS xiv, 15 :	I THESS. i, 9 :
ἐπιστρέφειν.	ἐπεστρέψατε.
ἀπὸ τῶν ματαίων.	ἀπὸ τῶν εἰδώλων.
ἐπὶ Θεὸν ζῶντα.	δουλεύειν Θεῷ ζῶντι.

[2] Acts xiv, 16. The same idea is in the Athenian discourse (Acts xvii, 30), τοὺς χρόνους τῆς ἀγνοίας ὑπεριδὼν ὁ Θεός, and in Rom. iii, 25. Those

but this abandonment, replies the Apostle, was only temporary, and was to end with the centuries of ignorance when the fulness of time had come; and it was only partial, because God had continued always to furnish testimony to himself. In any case, those times are past, and the preaching of the Gospel inaugurates a new era. Of the two principal proofs of the existence of God, the cosmological argument is only outlined; the physical argument, on the contrary, which is more accessible to the common mind, because the idea of causality is in it more concrete and more personal, is skilfully portrayed.[1] The beautiful order which reigns in the universe already speaks loudly to our intelligence, but the providential considerations which manifest themselves therein appeal both to heart and mind. From high heaven God pours out his blessings upon the world, and each of us has his share in them. Of all these benefits the most keenly felt is the fertility of the earth, enriched by periodic rains and by the regular return of the ripening seasons. At sight of this spectacle, which touches him so intimately, the heart of man expands with joy. It is also a divine benefit which awakens the religious sentiment instinctively and irresistibly. This is God's testimony to his own existence. The error of polytheism was to stop halfway, and to worship the forces of nature, instead of adoring their Author. The three attributes of God made especially prominent—his impassibility, his creative power, and his beneficent providence—are also those most accessible to human reason.[2]

4. The discourse of Paul at Athens brings us into a thoroughly pagan society. The sight of this polite, mocking, superstitious yet sceptical, curious and frivolous city seems

---

past times, in which God seemed to sleep, are always placed in contrast to the present, the fullness of time (Gal. iv, 4; Eph. i, 10). We see in this a divine plan which unrolls itself, and the objection against providence is turned into an argument for it.

[1] Acts xiv, 17 : οὐκ ἀμάρτυρον αὐτὸν ἀφῆκεν ἀγαθουργῶν οὐρανόθεν, ὑμῖν ὑετοὺς διδοὺς καὶ καιροὺς καρποφόρους, ἐμπιπλῶν τροφῆς καὶ εὐφροσύνης τὰς καρδίας ὑμῶν. The three participles depend on οὐκ ἀμάρτυρον αὐτὸν ἀφῆκεν, but they are not co-ordinate, but subordinate. God has not left himself without testimony, *seeing* that he showers his benefits from heaven (referring οὐρανόθεν to what follows is too awkward); for these benefits *consist* especially in the rains and the rotation of seasons, and these sources of fruitfulness *in their turn* fill us with joy and incline the heart of man to gratitude.

[2] The Apostles protest at first that their bodies have *feelings* like all other men's (ἡμεῖς ὁμοιοπαθεῖς ἐσμεν ὑμῖν ἄνθρωποι; *cf.* James v, 17), and that they are therefore not immortal gods, *impassibility* (ἀπάθεια) being the recognized privilege of divinity.—The living God is defined as the *universal Creator* by the usual biblical formula (Ex. xx, 11 ; Ps. cxlvi, 6 ; Isa. xxxvii, 36 ; Jer. xxxii, 17 ; Acts iv, 24).—On the other hand, the dogma of *providence* takes the apologetic turn peculiar to Paul. He has to explain why God has permitted the errors of men and delayed his supernatural intervention so long.

to have disconcerted him. He chafed inwardly at the spectacle of the innumerable idols with which the temples, streets, and squares swarmed. Everywhere could be seen ex-votos, altars, and pedestals surmounted by busts. Some of these were dedicated to anonymous deities, and Paul perceived a monument with the inscription : " To the unknown God." The idea did not occur to him—it could not occur to a Jew—that it was consecrated to the true God; but his pity redoubled for these poor blind Athenians who, not finding in their pantheon the wherewithal to satisfy their thirst for the divine, went so far as to invoke a nameless God, unconscious adorers of invisible perfection and a mysterious Beyond. This circumstance was soon to furnish him with an appropriate exordium.

One day when he was walking in the market-place, which was filled with idlers, sophists, and curiosity-mongers, some disciples of Epicurus and Zeno, desirous of hearing him, conducted him to the Areopagus, apparently to hear him more at their ease without being disturbed by the cries of the shopkeepers and the tumult of the passers-by.[1] The attitude of his hearers was not very encouraging; the curiosity and spirit of criticism, so natural to the Athenians, were dominant, irony was visible under a show of affected politeness. The beginning of Paul's speech was remarkably pertinent and full of local colour and Attic style : "Athenians, I perceive that you are in all respects the most religious of men. For passing by and seeing your temples, I found an altar on which was written *To the unknown God.* What therefore you worship without knowing it, that I preach to you."[2] In order not to offend their jealous susceptibilities, yet without betraying the rights of truth, he uses a word which was admirably chosen. He designates their love of the marvellous and their passion for the divine by a term which signifies either piety or superstition, according as it is the expression of the normal religious sentiment or of one that has been led astray. His hearers could take it as a eulogy, and in their disposition of mind they were led to adopt the more favourable meaning. By promising to solve the enigma of the unknown God, Paul piqued their curiosity. This anonymous God, to whom they erected altars without know-

---

[1] In reference to the *local colour* of the narrative given in the Acts, E. Curtius may be read with interest (" Paulus in Athen " in *Sitzungsberichte der Akademie der Wissenschaften zu Berlin*, Nov. 9, 1893, vol. xliii, pp. 925-938). Curtius believes that the Areopagus, of which St Luke speaks, is the Archon's office of the magistracy in the Agora or near it (the royal Portico), where Socrates and Euthyphro were judged.

[2] Acts xvii, 22, 23 : κατὰ πάντα ὡς δεισιδαιμονεστέρους ὑμᾶς θεωρῶ. Formerly the word δεισιδαίμων had not an unfavourable sense. In Xenophon and Aristotle it is synonymous with θεοσεβής, "pious." However, in the time of Paul it was taken often in the sense of "superstitious." The religiosity of the Athenians was proverbial. *Cf.* Josephus, *Contra Apion.*, ii, 11 : Pausanias, *Attic.*, 24.

ing him, and the true God had this in common—that they were both unknown and mysterious. But "the God who created the world and all that it contains, the Lord of the heaven and the earth" ought not to be "unknown," for the testimony which he furnishes of his existence in his works speaks clearly to all minds.

It will be noted that the Apostle does not dwell upon the proof of the existence of God. Platonism exercised at that time sufficient influence on the different philosophical schools for them not to deny, at least in theory, the existence of a supreme God, far superior to the poor divinities of vulgar polytheism. Remembering that the greater part of his hearers were Stoics and Epicureans, Paul insists upon the dogma of providence, disfigured by both, and on the nature of God, of which both Stoics and Epicureans held such an erroneous idea. "God hath made of one all mankind to dwell upon the whole face of the earth, determining appointed times and the limits of their habitation; that they should seek God, if happily they may feel after him or find him, although he be not far from everyone of us. For in him we live and move and are; as some also of your own poets said, *For we are also his offspring.*"

The truths clearly announced in this passage are the following : the unity of the human race as opposed to the fables of pagan cosmogonies (ἐξ ἑνὸς πᾶν ἔθνος ἀνθρώπων); the divine providence which distributes humanity over the surface of the earth (ἐποίησε . . . κατοικεῖν), separates the different nations by natural boundaries, seas, rivers, or mountains (ὁροθεσίας), determines for all specific times (ὁρίσας προστεταγμένους καίρους), either the allotted centuries in which their history unrolls itself or the periodic return of the seasons on which to a great degree the salubrity of climates and the fertility of the soil depend; the obligation imposed upon man to seek out God (ζητεῖν τὸν θεόν), an obligation founded on a positive wish of God, which forms one of the motives of his providential conduct; and the possibility of finding him, correlative to the duty of seeking him. This last point requires some explanation.

God is not far from us; he is within us and we are in him; that is a truth which the pagans themselves had perceived, and which the Stoics were no doubt less disposed than anyone to dispute. And we are not in him as in a strange element—like the bird in the air or the fish in the water; we are not only lost in his immensity, but contained in him as in our own efficient cause, which at every moment gives us fresh life, movement, and being by preserving them for us. It is for this that he is so near to us, to our intelligence; and it is for this that it is so easy to feel his presence (ψηλαφήσειαν) and to find him (εὕροιεν). That this is really the idea of Paul is proved by the reason that he gives for this nearness : "For we are of his offspring." God is more than our efficient cause, he is our exemplary cause. We are made in his image, and although the poets quoted by the Apostle did not understand it in the biblical sense, their formula, taken in itself, was the expression of a profound truth.

St Paul in passing draws some conclusions from his principles, and weaves them with much skill into the tissue of his teaching. He has deduced the immensity of God from his sovereign dominion over earth and heaven, and his independence from his creative omnipotence; now he deduces his spirituality from the fact that man is made in his image. Certainly the supreme intelligence, of which we are a spark, cannot resemble the works of an artisan or the products of his imagination. To designate God, the Apostle here very skilfully employs the word which the philosophers and poets were wont to use to express the superior and transcendent nature, which in their eyes comprised all the divine ($\tau\grave{o}$ $\theta\epsilon\hat{\iota}o\nu$) and had nothing in common with the deities of the popular pantheon.

So long as the missionary remained in the domain of philosophy all listened to him in silence and with attention. They remembered having read something similar in the classic authors. Moreover, these high ideas about the nature of God were not of a character to displease the Stoics, for in spite of their tendency to pass into pantheism they themselves used a scarcely different language. Many Epicureans, too, ashamed of what was gross and low in their system, had in the course of time become imbued with Platonism. But all this was only an exordium, and passing on to the real subject of his speech he broke the charm. Paul could deliver only one still unfinished phrase of it. But he took care to put into it the quintessence of his preaching to the Gentiles : " God indeed having winked at the times of this ignorance, now declareth unto men that all should everywhere repent. Because he hath appointed a day wherein he will judge the world in equity by the man whom he hath appointed, giving faith to all by raising him from the dead. . . ." At this word resurrection some began to mock, while others, concealing their disappointment under a politely indefinite phrase, said to him, not without a touch of irony : " We will hear thee again concerning this matter." And there Paul had to stop, without having been able even to utter the name of Jesus. If he consoled himself for his partial success with a few conversions, he concluded, nevertheless, that Athens was not yet ripe for the Gospel, and he departed for Corinth.

CHAPTER II

CORRESPONDENCE WITH THESSALONICA

I—Paul's Letters

1. General traits.   2. Letters or Epistles?   3. The Style of the Letters.

1.   THE two Epistles to the Thessalonians, written about the year 51 A.D. in the midst of the second apostolic journey, clearly mark the transition between Paul's oral, simple, and familiar teaching and the dogmatic controversies of the great letters.

Affectionate, courteous, delicate, and full of vivacity, earnestness, and fine irony, with that instinctive power of putting himself into the state of mind of others and of comprehending and sharing their joys and sorrows, which has been so well called the gift of sympathy, Paul was pre-eminently endowed for the epistolary style. Without study or research, he had created for himself a mode of writing in which spontaneity and naturalness ally themselves charmingly with profundity of thought and force of argument. What one admires most in it is the blending on the same page, or even in the same sentence, of the highest lessons of theology and the most familiar practical applications of them in daily life.

There is nothing like it in classic literature, as can be seen by comparing Paul's note to Philemon with the letter written by Pliny the Younger on an almost identical subject in similar circumstances.[1] The comparison is entirely favourable to the Apostle. How dry and stiff seem the forms of greeting in use among the Græco-Romans compared with the corresponding formulas in the letters of Paul, so free, so varied, and so unconventional! To find anything even distantly reminiscent of the latter's style rather would the papyri recently exhumed from the Egyptian sands repay examination.[2]

All his letters have a very marked family air. The order in them is almost always the same : first, a formal and very characteristic superscription; then a eulogy of those to whom the letter is addressed in the form of a thanksgiving; then an announcement of the subject with proofs and confirmations;

---

[1] Plinius Sabiniano, *Epist.* ix, 21.
[2] Numerous examples in Deissmann's *Licht vom Osten*[2], Tübingen, 1909, pp. 104-163.

then moral recommendations; and, finally, a wish and benediction in the autograph of the Apostle.

The *superscription* is not to be confounded with the address. The latter was written on the back of the letter in such a manner as to remain visible when it was closed and sealed. As it offered no special interest, further developed as it was in the superscription inside, no copy of it was made. The present titles, though very ancient, do not go back to the time of St Paul. The superscription comprises three elements, which follow one another in this order: the name and quality of the writers; name, titles and merits of those to whom the letter is addressed; wishes for the welfare of these last. Paul gives himself usually the title of apostle,[1] and almost always joins some companions with him: Timothy, Silvanus or Silas, Sosthenes, all the brethren who are with him.[2] When they are not wholly personal, like the Epistles to Titus and Timothy, they are addressed to a particular church, or to the members of a church, or to a church and its members, or to the faithful and the clergy, or to a local church and to all the Christians of the province and even of the entire world, or to some individuals as well as to the local church.[3] Even in the personal letters there is a greeting to the church. If we except the Epistle to the Galatians, the mention of the addressees, collective or individual, is always followed by a word of praise or by honorary titles. Paul wishes to all grace and peace; the two letters to Timothy add mercy.[4]

The *introduction to the subject* is an act of thanksgiving or a sort of doxology.[5] The absence of this formula in the Epistle to the Galatians is explained by the Apostle's indignation. The familiar tone of the Pastoral Epistles may account for the abrupt exordium in the letter to Titus and the first to Timothy. To the thanksgiving are attached some eulogistic words for the addressees, some souvenirs of the past, and some details about present circumstances, whether happy

[1] Except in 1 and 2 Thess., Phil. and Philemon.

[2] Timothy with the title of brother (2 Cor., Col., Philemon); with that of servant of Jesus Christ (Phil.); with no title (1 and 2 Thess.); Sosthenes with the title of brother (1 Cor.); Silvanus or Silas without any title, but before Timothy (1 and 2 Thess.); all the faithful present (Gal.).

[3] Special church (1 and 2 Thess.); members of a church (Rom., Eph. and Col.); faithful and clergy (Phil.); churches of a region (Gal.); special church and Christians of the province (2 Cor.); of the whole world (1 Cor.); individuals and local church (Philemon).

[4] These blessings are described as coming *from God our Father* (Col.), or *from God our Father and from the Lord Jesus Christ* (2 Thess., 1 and 2 Cor., Rom., Phil., Eph., Philemon); or *from God the Father and from our Lord Jesus Christ* (Gal., i, 1 and 2 Tim., and Titus). 1 Thess. does not indicate the source.

[5] Εὐχαριστῶ τῷ Θεῷ (Rom., 1 Cor., Phil. and Philemon); Εὐχαριστοῦμεν (1 Thess., Col.); εὐχαριστεῖν ὀφείλομεν (2 Thess.); Χάριν ἔχω τῷ Θεῷ (2 Tim.); εὐλογητὸς ὁ Θεός (2 Cor., Eph.).

or sad; for he finds in everything a reason for giving thanks. Sometimes the thanksgiving is prolonged to the point of intruding upon the substance of the letter and of becoming the framework of it;[1] at other times it is clearly separated from it;[2] most frequently it loses itself at last in the principal subject, which it introduces imperceptibly.[3]

The body of the letter naturally varies according to the difference in the subjects treated. When it is a thesis it is announced at the beginning, after the exordium,[4] and the development of the subject follows, regular and methodical in the Epistles to the Romans and Galatians, freer and more oratorical in the Epistles to the Ephesians and Colossians. The letters devoted to a thesis present this peculiarity, that the moral teaching is separate from the dogma, so that the division is in two parts;[5] while the letters treating of various subjects cannot be divided according to this principle, the moral teaching in them being as many-sided as the dogmatic teaching. Let us add that in several Epistles the division is not clearly marked or is even non-existent, which is not surprising, since a letter is, after all, only a written conversation.

The *conclusion* begins generally with personal communications, news of an intimate character, followed by a recommendation of the messenger. Then comes usually a more or less lengthy list of greetings. At this moment Paul himself seizes the pen and adds a few words or phrases in his own handwriting, as a sort of signature. We may take the Epistle to the Colossians as a typical instance, but each one has its interesting peculiarities.

2. Does St Paul write letters or epistles? The question may seem a strange one; but it is not without interest or importance both for the exegete and the theologian. A letter is a conversation carried on at a distance. A letter-writer of antiquity well defines it thus: " A writing telling someone who is absent what we wanted to say to him in speech if he were present." If the separation did not exist, there would be no necessity for the letter; a visit would be a substitute for it. What distinguishes it from an epistle is not its length, for there are conversations which are very lengthy; nor is it the subject, for a conversation can treat of the most serious questions; nor the style, for certain persons naturally assume an oratorical tone and polished language; nor is it the fact that it is not published, for there

---

[1] 1 Thess. [2] 1 and 2 Cor. and Phil.
[3] Rom., Eph., Col., 2 Thess., 2 Tim., Philemon.
[4] Rom. i, 17 ; Gal. ii, 16 ; Eph. i, 22, 23 ; Col. i, 15-18.
[5] Rom. i-xi and xii-xvi; Gal. i-iv and v-vi ; Eph. i-iii and iv-vi ; Col. i-ii and iii-iv.

are epistles, intended by their authors for publication, which have never seen the light; and such a letter, exhumed from an old Egyptian city, has recently received the honour of a publicity which its composer hardly expected. What distinguishes an epistle from a letter is the fact that one is a composition intended for the public, while the other is a composition that is intimate and private.

We must not imagine that the ancients were less anxious than we to assure the secrecy of their letters. The Romans sealed with lead, pitch, or wax the extremities of the cord which fastened their tablets, in order to guard their contents from indiscreet eyes; the Greeks often pushed their precaution so far as to introduce this bond through the coils of the roll of papyrus, which could not be violated without tearing it; finally, the Chaldeans and Assyrians covered their letters with an envelope of fire-hardened clay, which yielded only to the hammer. Every real letter is by its very nature secret. Although it is the property of the addressee, the latter has never had the right to publish it during the lifetime and without the consent of his correspondent. Fictitious letters are not real letters, neither are public letters; and *open* letters are so little real letters that the writer does not always take the trouble to send them to the person to whom they are addressed. But, between these extreme types, there are infinite varieties. There is the circular letter, sometimes so nearly an epistle as to be hardly distinguishable from it. There is the collective letter, which so easily turns into the epistle. There is the letter, in which its author, not intending to limit the benefit of his composition to one reader only, aims at a much more extended public, above and beyond the actual addressee. Finally, there is the letter, the divulging of which is foreseen : it loses so much the more of its intimate private character, as the writer has an indefinite public more in view. Cicero has very well noted this psychological phenomenon. Who can doubt that the thought of outside readers has sometimes caused aberrations to the pens of our most celebrated letter-writers? Their letters are epistles in proportion as the image of a possible public floats before their mind.

It is to one of these intermediary types that all the letters of Paul belong. What is lacking in that charming page which constitutes the little note to Philemon to prevent its being a letter in the full sense of the word? What could be more familiar, more personal, more full of life? In it Paul appears as a friend and father, rather than as an apostle. However, on studying it closely, he associates with Philemon, in addition to Appia and Archippus, who may be of the family, the whole Christian community.[1] It is, therefore, a collective letter. Moreover, the Apostle passes in it naturally

---

[1] Philemon 2.

and unconsciously from the singular to the plural : " Prepare *thou* for me a lodging, for I hope that I shall soon be given unto *you.*"[1] He did not think it necessary to close it, and he must have handed it open to Onesimus, who could not have been ignorant of the contents.

The Pastorals are administrative letters. Paul writes them by virtue of his apostolic authority,[2] and he speaks in them to his delegates, as a superior to his subordinates. Perhaps they contained details too intimate to be read, as a whole, before the Church, in the presence of those principally interested, but it is certain that Paul, in his thought, always associates with Titus and Timothy the Christian communities of which they temporarily have the oversight. Sometimes, forgetting that he is addressing one correspondent only, he makes his counsels and commands general; he greets the Churches of Ephesus and Crete directly, he passes from the singular to the plural with extreme facility, as in " Grace be with you,"[3] or " with you all."[4] If this is not sufficient to take from the Pastorals the character of real letters, it shows at least that the Apostle, whether he preaches or writes, hopes that his words may be heard as far as possible, that his communications are not of an entirely private nature, and that, far from avoiding publicity, he greatly desires it.

The letters to the Thessalonians, Galatians, and Philippians have this in common with the note to Philemon and the Pastorals, that they owe their existence to a passing need of the addressees, and that they would not have been written if Paul had been able to go to his neophytes in person. From this point of view they are also true letters. But if they had a personal character in their origin, they have nothing secret in them. The Apostle foresees that they will have a large circulation, and he is far from wishing to prevent it. Knowing that his letters pass from hand to hand,[5] he is careful to forewarn the faithful against forgers, and he does away with the possibility of frauds by sending them a specimen of his handwriting ;[6] but the idea does not occur to him of checking the circulation of the letters, which, on the contrary, is exactly what he wants.

By the nature of their contents, those which he addressed to the Corinthians and Colossians seemed unsuited for circulation outside of these Churches. In them he reproves the guilty severely ; he corrects the disorders at Corinth with a harshness of which he was tempted to repent; and he condemns unreservedly the errors of the Colossians. Nevertheless, he demands that the letter sent to the faithful at Colosse be communicated to the Christians of Laodicea,

---

1 *Ibid.,* 22.
2 Παῦλος ἀπόστολος stands at the head of the three.
3 2 Tim. iv, 22.
4 Titus iii, 15.
5 2 Thess. ii, 2.
6 2 Thess. iii, 18.

who also are to send the one which is in their possession.[1]
The letters of Paul circulate during his lifetime, and by his
orders, in the other Churches. Could the Corinthians keep,
as their exclusive deposit, the letters addressed " to the
saints that are in all Achaia,"[2] or even, beyond the narrow
horizon of Greece, " to all those who invoke the name of our
Lord and Saviour Jesus Christ, in every place of theirs and
ours?"[3]

If the letter is less truly a letter in proportion as the
addressee is more indefinite and the object of the correspondence less personal, that which Paul writes to the
Romans ought rather to be called an epistle. Paul is writing
to a Church which as yet he knows only by reputation, and
except for the sake of preparing the ground for an approaching apostolate, it is not clear why he explains to the Romans,
in preference to others, his thesis on justification and on the
relations between the Law and the Gospel. In its quality of a
circular letter, the Epistle to the Ephesians is still more impersonal and its addressees are more indeterminate. In order
to feel the difference existing between these two kinds of
writings, one has only to compare the Epistles to the Romans
and Galatians on the one hand and the Epistles to the
Ephesians and Colossians on the other.

Paul is accustomed to inscribe at the head of his letters the
names of his companions in the apostolate. This fact is not
without importance in the question before us. It takes something from the personal and private character of his correspondence and transforms his letters into semi-official
documents, susceptible of an ever-increasing publicity. Not
that it is necessary to attach too much importance to the use
of the plural instead of the singular. If the theory, according to which Paul, when he speaks of himself in the plural,
always mentally associates with himself Christians in
general or his companions in the apostolate, is untenable,
prodigies of subtlety, and of a subtlety of poor quality, are
necessary to discover in this " we " a trace of modesty or
authority, or any other special intention. This figure of
rhetoric was so common among the literate and illiterate
contemporaries of the great Apostle that it had lost all
particular signification.[4]

At the end of our inquiry we have the right to conclude
that all the writings of Paul are true letters, really sent to
their addressees in order to supplement the Apostle's absence

---

[1] Col. iv, 16.   [2] 2 Cor. i, 1.   [3] 1 Cor. i, 2.
[4] The continual interchange of singular and plural in one chapter (2 Cor. x),
where Paul is certainly speaking of his own person and where he distinguishes
himself formally from all his companions (2 Cor. x, 1 : Αὐτὸς δὲ ἐγὼ Παῦλος)
defies any preconceived theory and is only to be explained by the usage
of that time.

and to provide for necessities more or less urgent. But, neither in the opinion of the author nor in that of his correspondents were they written in order to remain the exclusive property of one family or of one church; they were to carry on Paul's preaching both in time and space; they were epistles which the Christian communities were eager to collect, and which they soon acquired the habit of reading aloud in the Church's liturgical meetings.

3. And these Epistles, so marked in character, are written in a still more personal style. In general the Fathers of the Church agree with the Apostle when he refuses to use fine language : *imperitus sermone.* St Irenæus reproaches him for his inversion of the natural order of words; Origen, for his obscure phrases; St Epiphanius, for his involved sentences; St Gregory of Nyssa, for using words which are obsolete or distorted from their usual meaning; St Chrysostom, for carelessness in style; St Jerome, for unsuitable words, idioms peculiar to Cilicia, and even for grammatical errors. Bossuet sums them up well when he writes in his celebrated *Panégyrique:* " This man, ignorant of the art of fine writing, with his rude forms of speech, with a phraseology which betrays the foreigner, will go to polished Greece, the mother of philosophers and orators, and, in spite of the opposition of the world, will there found more churches than Plato ever gained disciples by that eloquence of his which was thought divine. He will preach Jesus in Athens, and the most learned of its senators will pass from the Areopagus into the school of this barbarian.'' But here is the other side of the picture. St Jerome praises Paul's force, energy, and overwhelming power; St Augustine, his passionate eloquence; St Chrysostom, his charm and powers of persuasion; even the pagan Longinus, his oratorical fire and the vigour of his reasoning.

Into style, broadly speaking, there enter three elements : vocabulary, grammar, and composition. It is recognized that Paul's vocabulary is, above all, biblical. The words foreign to the language of the Septuagint are most often of popular origin. St Jerome called them *Cilicisms,* because, not having met them in the authors with whom he was familiar, he erroneously thought them peculiar to the soil of Cilicia. A certain number of these have been recently found in the papyri or inscriptions of that epoch; and the further this kind of research is pursued, the more will be shortened the list of terms, the peculiar form of which had previously been attributed to the sacred writers. These writers did not endeavour to create new words which no one would have understood; they turned to all possible advantage the words in common use by giving to them, in case of need, new shades of meaning. When addressing the people, they used the popular language, which was rich, picturesque, and pleasing.

Paul has been reproached with "a singular poverty of expression," which is too summary a judgement and one contradicted by the facts. No other writer of the New Testament has at his command so extensive a vocabulary. We know that he is fond of heaping up words which are almost synonymous, the various shades of which he wishes to expose. He likes also to use words similar in sound, as well as puns and antitheses, all of which presupposes an author's complete mastery of his language. The frequent repetitions of words are not a proof of linguistic indigence; it is rather a dialectical or oratorical procedure, intended and well considered, in order to fix the attention of the reader and better to imprint the thought upon his mind.

His syntax is certainly not classical syntax. If the solecisms, which can be rightly called so, are wholly exceptional,[1] Hebrew expressions, although less numerous than has been claimed, are not rare. But his letters swarm with anacoluthons—*i.e.*, unfinished sentences or such as end in a changed construction.[2] Two curious peculiarities are to be noted : the series of incidents which overload the phrase, breaking continually the thread of the discourse; and, especially, constructions with the genitive and article, in which the exact relation of each genitive with the preceding word remains rather indefinite. Many of these cases of carelessness can be explained by improvisation. Paul did not write his letters himself. The habit of dictation was then so common that to "dictate" meant in general to "compose." Certain allusions of the ancients would lead us to believe that the manual labour of the scribe was considered incompatible with the work of thought. The Apostle conformed to this usage, which the weakness of his eyes rendered more imperative for him. Hence his uncompleted phrases, changes of construction, incidents, parentheses, sudden passages from one thought to another, and frequent recurrences of the same idea. But while the stylists kept on carefully revising their first sketch, in order to cut down the faults in it and to efface its harshness, Paul packed it off just as it was, or with additions and new digressions. If he wishes—and perhaps without trying—he writes pages of flawless Greek; he handles in a masterly way the most delicate part of an idiom—the particles; and he clearly speaks Greek as his mother tongue and not as a foreign language, learned late in life and imperfectly acquired.

[1] *Cf.* 2 Cor. viii, 23 and Phil. ii, 1 ; but this last text must be corrupted, for Paul was not ignorant of the gender of σπλάγχνα, of which he makes use quite frequently.

[2] Rom. ii, 17-21 ; v, 12-14 ; ix, 22 ; xvi, 25-27 ; 1 Cor. xiv, 1 ; Gal. ii, 6, etc.

More intimate and more personal than anything pertaining to vocabulary and syntax is the order, the mode of expression, and the arrangement of the ideas in his letters. In a very true sense it has been said that the style is the man himself : " The language of Paul is his living image. As the body of the Apostle, a vessel of clay, bends under the weight of his ministry, so the words and forms of his language bend and break under the burden of his thought. But from this contrast spring forth the most wonderful effects. What power is in this weakness ! What riches in this poverty ! In this infirm body what a soul of fire ! All the force, all the movement, all the beauty here come from his thought; it is not the style which carries the thought, it is the thought that carries the style. His thought rushes on, almost over-weighted, breathless, swept along, dragging the words after it. . . . Words and their ordinary signification are not sufficient to carry this overflowing plenitude of ideas and feelings. Each one of them has been obliged, so to speak, to carry a double or triple load. In a preposition or in the juxtaposition of two words Paul has placed an entire world of ideas. It is this which makes the exegesis of his Epistles so difficult, and their translation absolutely impossible."[1]

The best way to understand them is to read them again and again. We must get used to this strange way of speaking, which at first repels and disconcerts us by its singularity. We meet with sentences whose sections somehow slide into one another, like the draws of a telescope; clauses running on and on without end and broken up into digressions and parentheses, the whole of which the eye seeks vainly to combine. The Greek period, very elastic though it is, does not run to such lengths; and the phrases of St Paul are not periods. One can simplify them, free them from the details which encumber them, and liberate them from the weight of their subordinate clauses without altering their aspect or disturbing their method of procedure. The principal idea forms a sufficiently apparent framework, in which are arranged, after the manner of separate enclosures, definitions and explanations. With practice and a little reflection it can be disentangled without too much trouble. The general object in view serves as a guiding-mark, and it is by keeping this always in sight that the reader succeeds in finding his way.

Paul is a vigorous reasoner, who moves at ease through the labyrinths of a long and abstruse argument. He never recoils before a useful digression, even though his work must thereby suffer from a literary point of view. Certain chapters of his present the appearance of geological conglomerates

[1] A. Sabatier, *L'apôtre Paul*[2], 1896, pp. 150-151.

formed from sedimentary deposits and solidified lava; but the thought proceeds always, like an uninterrupted metallic vein, through these apparently heterogeneous masses. The incidental question having been settled, he returns to his subject by boldly emphasizing a word rather than by a definite transition. If he is not tormented by words, as he is accused of being, he is drawn on beyond all measure by the idea which is pursuing, and it is true that his thought sometimes revolves about a word. He is fond of running through the whole gamut of the various meanings of a word in order to display his idea under all its aspects. Every occurrence of the slightest difference puts him on new ground, and he glides from one meaning to another with such ease that the transition is not always perceptible.

Moreover, he has a supreme indifference for his fame as an author. He laughs at the rules of rhetoric and sometimes also at the rules of grammar. If he frequently attains to the highest eloquence it is, St Augustine says, without aiming at it. In him everything flows from the source, and from a mind overflowing with ideas and a heart able to impart emotion almost involuntarily. When Tertius or some other of his secretaries reads a letter of Paul's dictation over to him, do not think that the Apostle stops to polish an involved sentence or to correct a solecism, an inversion of the natural order of words, or a lack of sequence. On the contrary, he adds to them those exuberances with which his style is bristling, as if he feared by too much study and refinement to take away something from the virtue of the Gospel and by a display of human wisdom to cast a shadow on the brilliant triumph of the cross.

II—THE FIRST EPISTLE TO THE THESSALONIANS

1. The Converts' Fear. 2. Near Prospect of the *Parousia*.
3. The Fate of the Living.

1. It was an immense joy to the heart of the Apostle, hunted from city to city by the hatred of the Jews, while still under the painful impression of his lack of success at Athens, and feeling keenly his isolation in Corinth, to learn that the neophytes in Thessalonica, whom he had left exposed to persecution, were unflinchingly holding out against the assaults of a furious storm.[1] Their faith, their steadfastness in trial, their admirable piety, their brotherly charity were everywhere extolled.[2] There was, however, a shadow on the picture. They pitied excessively the fate of their brethren, prevented

[1] Acts xvii, 14-16; xviii, 5, compare with I Thess. iii, 1-6.
[2] I Thess. i, 3-6.

by death from witnessing the triumphal return of Christ, which they evidently regarded as near at hand. Paul's real object in writing to them is to correct the erroneous idea which they cherished in regard to the inferior state of the deceased Christians as compared with the living, but before coming to the principal point he opens his heart and seems to wish to exhaust his vocabulary of affection. With what charming, graceful, and picturesque words does love inspire him! By turns he is the father who exhorts, encourages, and animates each of his children, and the mother who warms her darling nursling with ardent caresses. Full of love for them, he would like to give them not only truth and happiness, but his life and his soul.[1] The loftiest teachings of dogma and morals which reveal these amiable traits appear to be lost in this effusion of paternal tenderness. All the first part of the letter is song of gratitude and a hymn of thanksgiving. It is this which makes its unity and constitutes its plan; thanksgiving for the way in which the Thessalonians have welcomed the Gospel and caused it to bring forth fruit, thanksgiving for the success of his preaching, thanksgiving for the safe return of Timothy and the good news of which he is the bearer.[2] A very simple framework this, which lends itself wonderfully to the calling up of memories and makes of this letter, in which the words "you remember," "you know" are repeated lavishly, a real conversation at a distance.[3]

A faithful echo of the preaching of Paul, the First Epistle to the Thessalonians is full of allusions to the Judge who is to come, to the kingdom of heaven, the object of our hopes, to the wrath of God ready to be poured out on the unbelieving Jews,[4] and to the severity of the divine judgements. The *parousia* of the Lord[5] is mentioned four times, and this it is, in the opinion of all, that forms the principal subject of the letter. It is very likely that the Apostle is replying to a formal question addressed to him by the Thessalonians which may have been conveyed by Timothy. The sudden transition and the rigid formula twice repeated, "Concerning them that are asleep" and "But of the times and moments," recalls exactly his replies to the doubts of the Corinthians. Between the two portions of this theological advice there is this difference, that the latter is content to appeal to the memories of the neophytes and does not lead us to hope for new teachings, while the former promises a revelation "in the name of the Lord."

[1] I Thess. ii, 7-11.
[2] Εὐχαριστοῦμεν (i, 2 ; ii, 13) ; Τίνα γὰρ εὐχαριστίαν (iii, 9).
[3] i, 3·5 ; ii, 1, 2, 5, 9, 11 ; iii, 3, 4 ; iv, 2 ; v. 2.
[4] i, 10; ii, 12; ii, 16, etc.
[5] ii, 19; iii, 13; iv, 15; v, 23.

And we will not have you ignorant, brethren, concerning them that are asleep, that you be not sorrowful, even as others who have no hope. For if we believe that Jesus died and rose again, even so them who have slept through Jesus will God bring with him. For this we say unto you in the word of the Lord, that we who are alive, who remain unto the coming of the Lord, shall not prevent them who have slept. For the Lord himself shall come down from heaven with commandment and with the voice of an Archangel and with the trumpet of God, and the dead who are in Christ shall rise first. Then we who are alive, who are left, shall be taken up together with them in the clouds to meet Christ into the air, and so shall we be always with the Lord. Wherefore comfort ye one another with these words. . . .

But of the times and moments, brethren, you need not that we should write to you ; for yourselves know perfectly that the day of the Lord shall so come, as a thief in the night. For when they shall say " peace and security," then shall sudden destruction come upon them as the pains upon her that is with child, and they shall not escape. But you, brethren, are not in darkness, that that day should overtake you as a thief. For all of you are the children of light and children of the day. We are not of the night nor of darkness. Therefore, let us not sleep as others do ; but let us watch and be sober. For they that sleep, sleep in the night ; and they that are drunk, are drunk in the night. But let us, who are of the day, be sober, having on the breastplate of faith and charity, and for a helmet the hope of salvation. For God hath not appointed us unto wrath, but unto the purchasing of salvation by our Lord Jesus Christ, who died for us, that, whether we watch or sleep, we may live together with him. For which cause comfort one another and edify one another, as you also do.[1]

The last paragraph does not announce any new revelation. " Concerning the times and moments " the faithful *know* all that they are to know and can know, that " the day of the Lord shall so come as a thief in the night." All curiosity in this respect is vain and out of place. The day of the Lord is known to no one, say the Synoptics—not even to the Son, adds St Mark[2]—but it will come suddenly when men are least expecting it. The comparison to a thief in the night was classical; it is employed by St Matthew, St Luke, St John, St Peter, and St Paul, and it was to enter into all the sermons on the *parousia*.[3] The metaphor of a woman in travail is borrowed from the prophets; in the dramatic description of the Day of the Lord it formed a necessary part of the representation; it then passed into the apocalyptic style, and pictures marvellously the suddenness of the

---

[1] iv, 12–v, 11. Note the symmetry of the two paragraphs at the beginning and the end.

[2] Mark xiii, 32. See Matt. xxiv, 36 ; compare Acts i, 7 (οὐχ ὑμῶν ἐστι γνῶναι χρόνους ἢ καιροὺς οὓς ὁ Πατὴρ ἔθετο ἐν τῇ ἰδίᾳ ἐξουσίᾳ) with 1 Thess. v, 1 (περὶ τῶν χρόνων καὶ τῶν καιρῶν οὐ χρείαν ἔχετε ὑμῖν γράφεσθαι), and note the parallelism of ideas and words.

[3] 1 Thess. v, 4 (ὡς κλέπτης), v, 2 (ὡς κλέπτης ἐν νυκτί). The comparison to a thief is in Matt. xxiv, 43 ; 1 Peter iv, 15 ; 2 Peter iii, 10 ; Apoc. iii, 3 ; xvi, 15. See Luke xii, 39. It is the phrase of St Matthew in another context.

surprise, the anguish, and the despair.[1] From a practical point of view, the Thessalonians have no need of counsels; in obedience to the Gospel rule they are vigilant, they are armed—vigilant against nocturnal attacks, armed against malefactors.[2] The three theological virtues serve for their armour—hope as a helmet, faith and charity as a breast-plate. Watching constantly, there is for them no night; they are "children of the day and of the light." The thief can come; he will not take them unawares.

While this second part does not depart from the usual category of eschatological predictions, the first presents to us a revelation which the Apostle had not previously received, or which he had not deemed it proper to communicate till now. Paul refers it expressly to a "word of the Lord,"[3] either to a word uttered by Jesus in the course of his mortal life and not recorded by the Evangelists, or to a word whispered within and attributed to the Master with the certainty of inspiration. "On the day of the *parousia*, the living will not take precedence of the dead," such is the message which he is commissioned to transmit. The neophytes imagined that at the coming of the supreme Judge the living would have some advantage over the dead. He destroys this illusion. At the last day the dead will not envy the living, nor will the living pity the dead. Both the dead and the living will then go to meet the Lord, the latter with their actual bodies transfigured and transformed, the former with their previous bodies reconstituted and glorified; together they will be carried into space and together they will rejoin their Master and will begin with him a reign that shall have no end. If there does exist any difference between them it is rather in favour of the dead; for the dead shall rise *first* (πρῶτον) before the presence of the glorified Christ transforms the living.

The trembling of nature, the cloud which serves the Judge

---

[1] Matt. xxiv, 8 ; Mark xiii, 8 : ἀρχὴ ὠδίνων, like our ὥσπερ ἡ ὠδίν, recalls the numerous texts of the prophets relating to the Day of the Lord, Isa. xiii, 6-8 , xxxvii, 3 ; Jer. xiii, 21 ; xxii, 23 ; xxvii, 43 ; Hos. xiii, 13 ; Mich. iv, 9.   This figure of the pains of childbirth carries with it, moreover, several shades of meaning; it expresses sometimes the *pain*, sometimes the *certainty*, sometimes the *proximity* of the event which it presages, sometimes, as in 1 Thess. v, 3, the *suddenness* (ἀιφνίδιος αὐτοῖς ἐπίσταται ὄλεθρος ὥσπερ ἡ ὠδὶν τῇ ἐν γαστρὶ ἐχούσῃ). St Luke xxi, 34 uses also, to depict the suddenness and surprise of the last day, the word ἀιφνίδιος, but with the comparison of a *snare* falling suddenly.

[2] The apocalyptical counsels relative to the expectation of the great Day emphasize especially vigilance, sobriety, and the need of being armed.   Matt. xxiv, 36-51 ; Mark xiii, 37 (γρηγορεῖτε) ; Luke xxi, 34-36 (ἀγρυπνεῖτε); see xii, 45 ; Apoc. xvi, 5 ; 1 Peter i, 13.   The idea of armour is borrowed from the Old Testament (Isa. lix, 17 ;   Sap. v, 19), and is treated with much liberty by St Paul (Eph. vi, 14-17 ; 1 Thess. v, 8).

[3] 1 Thess. iv, 15 : τοῦτο ὑμῖν λέγομεν ἐν λόγῳ Κυρίου.

for a chariot or throne, the attendant multitude of angels, the shouts of the spectators, and the blare of the trumpet are features common to all the apocalyptical writings.[1] They are borrowed from the terrifying apparition of Jehovah on Mount Sinai, which had made an ineffaceable impression on the national imagination. To what degree will these allusions to the past be verified in the future, and how much of them may be due to imagery and symbolism? That is God's secret.

2. It is an undeniable fact that the Christians of the apostolic age believed that they were approaching the end of the world, and St Peter saw himself obliged to justify the long delay of Christ.[2] Their error, due in part to desire and hope, was also connected with the universal conviction of the Jews of that time, with a pessimistic notion of contemporaneous events, and perhaps with a false interpretation of the remark of the Saviour : " This generation shall not pass till all these things be done."[3] It was persistently believed that some privileged persons, like the beloved disciple, would live till that time. There was nothing—even to the very name *parousia,* which we translate " second coming," but which literally means " presence," and by which the triumphal return of Christ was usually designated—which did not arouse the idea of a speedy arrival; and it is well known that the prophets, accustomed as they were to project all future events in the same perspective, seem to make the beginning of the messianic era coincide with the consummation of the world. Did Paul share the common illusion? In principle there is nothing to prevent his having done so, for inspiration does not impart universal knowledge and could not in any case give him the knowledge of the last day, which the heavenly Father has reserved to himself. Apart from the truth of which he is the depositary, the sacred writer can be ignorant, hesitate, base an opinion on probabilities or likelihoods, and set out in search of the truth by using the means which all men have at their disposition. The essential thing is that he should not teach error. Paul, knowing better than anyone that the date of the last day by no means forms the object of the revelation, does not teach that the world is about to end; he even declares solemnly that the consummation of things is not imminent; but for want of special light on the subject, he abides by the statement of the Gospel. Nevertheless, he does not seem to look forward to a long series of centuries. Doubtless those words, " We

---

[1] Trumpet and angels (Matt. xxiv, 31 ; Mark xiii, 27) ; clouds (Matt. xxiv, 30 ; xxvi, 64 ; Mark xiii, 26 ; Luke xxi, 27 ; Dan. vii, 13, etc.).
[2] 2 Peter iii, 9.
[3] Matt. xxiv, 34 ; Mark xiii, 30 ; Luke xxi, 32.

who are alive and remain shall go to meet the Lord "[1] exclude any premature judgement of the matter, for the Church will not perish, and all Christians can identify themselves with it as if they were to witness its triumphs and its trials personally in a distant future. Nevertheless, would the Apostle have spoken thus if he had had a clear knowledge of the fact that thousands of years separated him from the end? Subsequently the prospect will become more distant. The longer the world lasts, the more will men become accustomed to its duration. The idea of a *parousia* will become rarer; the word itself will finally be lost. What we cannot admit, with certain modern exegetes, is that the mind of Paul changed its attitude in the short space of time which elapsed between the two Epistles to the Corinthians. To these he uses to the last the same language that he uses to the Thessalonians.

3. Nor did he vary in his teaching that the last generation of the just will be clothed upon with immortality without experiencing death : " The dead who are in Christ will rise first; then we who are alive and who remain shall be taken up with them in the clouds into the air to meet Christ, and so shall we be always with the Lord." St Augustine confessed that he had never been able to read these words attentively without finding in them the meaning that the last generation of the just will be exempt from death. And what embarrassed him at times was precisely the text which ought to have anchored him most firmly in this opinion, which was the common opinion of the Church Fathers, if, in place of the incorrect Latin translation " We shall all rise," he had understood the true lesson of St Paul, " We shall not all die, but we shall all be transformed. . . . The trumpet will sound, and the dead shall rise again incorruptible, and we, we shall be changed."[2] It is impossible to understand these words otherwise than the Corinthians themselves understood them, who earnestly desired the privilege of being the last survivors of the world. Death is horrible to us both because it is a punishment and because it violently breaks the natural ties of the human body. Like the Corinthians, we would like to be clothed upon with immortality without having to undergo death. This desire is legitimate, replies the Apostle, if it has in it nothing contrary to the established order; it is supernatural, provided that it takes

---

[1] I Thess. iv, 17 : Ἡμεῖς οἱ ζῶντες οἱ παραλειπόμενοι ἅμα σὺν αὐτοῖς ἁρπαγησόμεθα is not exactly translated by " we who are alive, who remain," etc.   There is needed, as in the Greek, a present participle (*nos viventes*) or else an adjective (*nos superstites*), which, being in correlation with a verb in the future tense, would itself take the sense of the future, as " we who shall be alive, who will survive," etc.

[2] I Cor. xv, 51.   For the true lesson of this text see the subsequent chapter on the Resurrection of the Dead.

nothing from our confidence and our resignation; and it is
realizable, provided the second Advent of Christ finds us still
alive : *Si tamen vestiti non nudi inveniamur.* This will be
the lot of a small number. After all, what does it matter?
Whether we live or whether we die, we are the Lord's.[1]

How can affirmations, so clear and thrice repeated, have
given room for doubt? The reason lies, as we have said, in
the old Latin version, which read either *" Omnes resurgemus,"*
or *" Omnes moriemur,"* supposing in both cases universal
death. Ambrosiaster, wishing to smooth away all difficulties,
conceived the idea of making the just who were to be witnesses
of the *parousia* die and revive again during their rapid passage
through the air.[2] Augustine, who knew of this hypothesis,
was tempted to adopt it, but did not dare to embrace it
heartily, and in his " Retractations " he records his confession
of an unconquerable hesitation to do so : " Either they will
not die, or else they will pass from life to death and from
death to life so quickly that they will not be conscious of
death."[3] The " Master of the Sentences," citing St Jerome
and Ambrosiaster, whom he takes for St Ambrose, also
refuses to pronounce his opinion, as if the two authorities
neutralized each other. St Thomas, while maintaining the
probability of the two opinions, already finds Ambrosiaster's
more certain and more generally held. From the thirteenth
century on, the opinion of the Fathers on this point fell
behind so much that Soto and Catharinus call it rash. They
themselves are sharply rebuked by Suarez for their temerity
in adopting such an extreme opinion. But the reading in
the Vulgate has always occasioned difficulty, and it was only
in our time that, together with the sound exegesis of
St Paul, a return has been made to the patristic tradition
of Tertullian, of St. Jerome, of St Epiphanius, of St Gregory
of Nyssa, of St Chrysostom, of Theodoret, of Primasius, and
many others.[4] Few theological theses have experienced
more singular vicissitudes.

---

[1] 2 Cor. v, 1-9. This passage will be commented on elsewhere.

[2] Commentary on 1 Thess. iv, 14 (XVII, 450) : *In ipso raptu mors
proveniet et quasi per soporem, ut egressa anima in momento reddatur.
Cum enim tollentur morientur.*

[3] The history of his hesitations is curious. In 418, *Epist. ad Mercator.*,
193 (XXXIII, 872), he is very firm in the usual opinion. *Ad Dulcit.*, qu. 3a
(XL, 159), he has not yet changed his mind. In the *Civitas Dei*, xx, 20
(XLI, 688), the opinion of Ambrosiaster, met with in the interval, perplexes
him. In his *Retractations*, ii, 33, his doubt is complete.

[4] Chrysostom and Theodoret, *Comment. on* 1 Cor. xv, 51 : *Omnes im-
mutabimur etiam qui non moriemur ;* Primasius (LXVIII, 644) ; Tertull.,
De resurr. carnis, 41-42 (II, 853) ; Epiph., *Haeres.*, lxiv, 70 (XLI, 1193) ;
Hieron., *Ep.* 59 *ad Marcell.* (XXII, 587) ; Greg. Nyss., *De opif. hom.*, 22
(XLIV, 208). For Origen compare *Contra Cels.*, ii, 65 (XI, 900) with
St Jerome, *Ep.* 119 *ad Minerv.*, 9 (XXII, 974, 975). The text of Rufinus,
Expositio Symboli, 33 (XXI, 369), probably corrupt, is in any case so
obscure that one can get nothing out of it.

This return to the past has its reaction on the manner of explaining the seventh article of the Creed.[1] Instead of seeing in the "dead and the living" the sinners and the righteous (as St Augustine supposes), or the dead and the living at some moment or other in the duration of the world (St Thomas), or the dead and the living with relation to the one who is reciting the Creed (as Suarez thinks), by the dead and the living are understood simply the dead and living whom the coming of the Supreme Judge will find on the earth.

III—The Second Epistle to the Thessalonians

1. New Terrors.   2. The Obstacle to the Appearance of Antichrist.

1. Only a few months had passed after the first message to the Thessalonians when a new misunderstanding arose. Although reassured now in regard to their dead, the neophytes were more than ever convinced of the nearness of the *parousia*, and this conviction, far from urging them to good, troubled and paralyzed them. Some even, neglecting their duties, wandered from door to door, in idleness and unemployment, like people whose days are numbered. Whence came their foolish fears? St Paul insinuates it quite clearly in the advice which he gives them :

> We beseech you, brethren, concerning the *parousia* of our Lord Jesus Christ and of our gathering together unto him that you be not easily moved from your mind, nor be frighted, neither by spirit, nor by word, nor by epistle, as sent from us, as if the day of the Lord were at hand.[2]

Three causes of error could have been operative here : a supposed or misunderstood revelation, an expression attributed rightly or wrongly to St Paul or to some other person of distinction, an apocryphal letter of the Apostle or even an authentic letter wrongly interpreted. It was not the First Epistle to the Thessalonians which could have borne any such ambiguous meaning, and the words "as from us" really seem to indicate a forgery. To prevent frauds, Paul will henceforth add the final salutation in his own handwriting, and this will serve as his signature.

---

[1] This article, borrowed textually from 2 Tim. iv, 1 (*qui judicaturus est vivos et mortuos*), or from 1 Peter iv, 5 (*qui paratus est judicare vivos et mortuos*), was one of the fundamental points of the apostolic preaching, Acts x, 42 : *Praecepit nobis praedicare populo et testificari, quia ipse est qui constitutus est a Deo judex vivorum et mortuorum.* All the forms of the Symbol, both Greek and Latin, contain this article, which subsequently passed into the Symbol of Nicaea. See Denzinger, *Enchiridion*, 10, pp. 1-9. It was understood by all in this sense, that Jesus Christ will judge *all* men, although there was a difference about the precise meaning of the *dead* and the *living*. Cf. Rufinus, *Expos. Symboli*, 33 (XXI, 369); St Cyril of Jerusalem, *Catech.*, xv, 26 (XXXIII, 909).

[2] 2 Thess. ii, 1-2. The Vulgate translates *per adventum ;* but ὑπέρ has not this sense, at least in the New Testament.

The custom of dictating letters, at that time common, rendered this precaution necessary. We think that the " spirit," to which he makes allusion, is a manifestation of the kind known as *charismata*. In their ecstatic prayers those who had the gift of tongues often used to say *Maranatha*. Ναί, ἔρχομαι ταχύ ! (*Ecce, veniam cito !*) Being unskilled in the discernment of spirits, the hearers of these words may have taken them, not for pious desires, but for prophecies destined to be fulfilled in a short time. But the origin of the misunderstanding is of little importance. The Apostle defends himself from having given rise to it either by his discourse or by his writings. No, the end is not so near.

> Let no man deceive you by any means, for unless there come a revolt first, and the man of sin be revealed, the son of perdition, who opposeth and is lifted up above all that is called God, or that is worshipped, so that he sitteth in the temple of God, showing himself as if he were God. Remember you not that, when I was yet with you, I told you these things ? And now you know what withholdeth, that he may be revealed in his time. For the mystery of iniquity already worketh ; only that he who now holdeth do hold, until he be taken out of the way. And when that wicked one shall be revealed, whom the Lord Jesus shall kill with the spirit of his mouth, and shall destroy with the brightness of his coming, him, whose coming is according to the working of Satan, in all power and signs and lying wonders.[1]

Paul merely recalls here, with a few allusions, some features of his oral preaching. He takes it for granted that the Thessalonians are familiar with these ideas, for the instructions given to the neophytes always included a chapter on the last things associated with the *parousia*. The Apostle contents himself with refreshing their memory of them. He formerly taught orally, and now he repeats in writing—but in terms the conciseness of which makes them enigmatical for us—that the last day is to be preceded by two great crises—the apostasy and the appearance of Antichrist. He speaks of

---

[1] 2 Thess. ii, 3-12. It is necessary to mention the numerous cases of an association of ideas and expression between this passage and the apocalypse of the Synoptists.—(*a*) παρουσία (ii, 1) ; Matt. xxiv, 3, 27, 37, 39.—(*b*) Ἐπισυναγωγή (ii, 1) ; Matt. xxiv, 31 ; Mark xiii, 27, ἐπισυνάξει τοὺς ἐκλεκτοὺς αὐτοῦ.—(*c*) Ἡ ἀνομία (ii, 3, 7) ; Matt. xxiv, 12.—(*d*) Ἡ ἐπιφάνεια τῆς παρουσίας αὐτοῦ (ii, 8) ; Matt. xxiv, 27 : ὥσπερ ἡ ἀστραπὴ φαίνεται . . . οὕτως ἔσται ἡ παρουσία.—(*e*) Ἐνέργεια πλάνης (ii, 11) ; Matt. xxiv, 24 : ὥστε πλανῆσαι καὶ τοὺς ἐκλεκτούς ; Mark xiii, 22 : πρὸς τὸ ἀποπλανᾶν. It is also necessary to compare the allusions to the Old Testament.—(*a*) The name of Antichrist (ὁ ἄνομος, ii, 8 ; ὁ ἄνθρωπος τῆς ἀνομίας, ii, 3 ; *another reading*, τῆς ἁμαρτίας) may have been suggested by Ps. lxxxviii, 23 : υἱὸς ἀνομίας, or Ps. xciii, 20 : Θρόνος ἀνομίας.— (*b*) The description of Antichrist (ii, 3-4) contains reminiscences of Ezechiel, xxviii, 2 : Θεός εἰμι ἐγώ, κατοικίαν Θεοῦ κατοίκηκα ἐν καρδίᾳ θαλάσσης ; and especially of Daniel : ὑψωθήσεται ἐπὶ πάντα θεὸν καὶ ἐπὶ τὸν Θεὸν τῶν θεῶν ἔξαλλα λαλήσει. *Cf.* vii, 25 ; ix, 27 ; also for the idea, Isa. xiv, 13-14.—(*c*) And the defeat of the Antichrist (ii, 8) recalls Isa. xi, 4 : καὶ πατάξει γῆν τῷ λόγῳ τοῦ στόματος αὐτοῦ, καὶ ἐν πνεύματι διὰ χείλεων ἀνελεῖ ἀσεβῆ.

both as of things well known which do not need explanation. The apostasy indicates certainly a religious defection, a revolt against God or his representatives. It appears to be closely connected with the acts and wonders wrought by the great adversary. The latter, formally distinguished from Satan, who lends him his aid and uses him as an agent, is described with the traits and characteristics of the persons of whom he is the antitype. He will lift himself up above all that is God or is called God, like Antiochus Epiphanes; he will give himself out for God and will wish to be treated as God, like the Prince of Tyre in Ezechiel and the King of Babylon in Isaias; he will sit in the very Temple of God, like the abomination of desolation predicted by Daniel. These reminders are not so much new prophecies as allusions to old texts; it is not necessary to expect the literal verification of them, they are symbols realizable according to a law of proportion unknown to us. When we read that the Lord Jesus " will destroy the wicked one with the spirit (breath) of his mouth," these words recall to us the way in which the Son of David, according to Isaias, is to destroy impiety; but what can we conclude from them as to the real way in which those things will take place? What is said, aside from figures of speech, is that Antichrist will work false miracles, signs, and wonders, will seduce a great many souls, and also cause a schism in the Church, but that he will finally be conquered, and that his fall will be the signal for the *parousia*.

2. In one point only does Paul go beyond his predecessors. He speaks of an obstacle which hinders the immediate coming of Antichrist, and gives us the following description of it: It is a person or something personified (ὁ κατέχων, masculine), and at the same time a physical or moral force (τὸ κατέχον, neuter). The obstacle is already active (ἄρτι) and it checks the mystery of iniquity (τὸ μυστήριον τῆς ἀνομίας); it prevents the advance of the wicked one (ὁ ἄνομος). As soon as this obstacle disappears the field will be open to Antichrist, whose appearance (παρουσία) seems likely to precede but shortly the appearance (παρουσία) of the Son of God. What is this obstacle? The Thessalonians had learned what it is from the mouth of the Apostle, but we are ignorant of it now, and everything leads us to suppose that we shall always be ignorant of it. The proverbial obscurity of this passage has given rise to innumerable solutions.

With brotherly unanimity, Albigenses, Waldenses, Hussites, the disciples of Wyclif, of Luther and Calvin, and ancient and modern Anglicans, down to the nineteenth century, have seen in Antichrist the Pope and in the obstacle which opposes the triumph of the former, first the Roman Emperor and later the German Emperor. In 1518, when the first ideas of revolt were fermenting in him, Luther had a slight suspicion that the Pope might indeed be Antichrist; in 1519, he whispered it to a confidant; from the beginning of 1520 he was almost sure of it, and at the end of that year, when the rupture with Rome was complete, he had become entirely certain of it. Ten years later, he was indignant that the Augsburg confession had made no mention of such a fundamental article of faith. The mistake was remedied at Smalkalde, where it was declared that "the Pope is the true Antichrist who has elevated himself against Christ and above him." The only divergence among the Protestants is that some have admitted two Antichrists—one for the East, namely Mohammed and Islam; the other for the West, the Pope and the Papacy. One bolder commentator has even discovered that if the Pope is always Antichrist, of course the mystery of iniquity is Jesuitism, while the temple of God is the pure Lutheran doctrine, and the obstacle which resists the advent, not of Antichrist, as the text of St Paul requires, but of Jesus, is still the Pope. It is not long since the Lutherans, Calvinists and Anglicans gave up this exegesis, which was for them more sacred than the most solemn definition of faith is for us. So difficult to uproot are the prejudices of sect and caste, strengthened by habit and education!

As for the rationalists, they all declare that the prophecy of St Paul has not been fulfilled and never will be. It is only a dream of the Apostle. But when they try to say precisely what the object of this dream is, they are so divided that it is impossible to find two of them with the same opinion. Some, adopting the idea of Grotius, seek the fulfilment of the apocalyptic announcement in events occurring in the life of the author. The prophecy would then be only a prediction *ex eventu,* or a case of foresight at short range. Antichrist might then be Caligula, and the wicked one Simon Magus, and the obstacle Vitellius (Grotius); or the wicked one would be Titus, and the Antichrist Nero, while the obstacle would be the civil war of the year A.D. 70 (Wetstein); or Antichrist might be Simon Magus, the defection the Gnostic heresy, the obstacle the temporary union of Judaism and Christianity (Hammond). For others the obstacle is either St Paul himself (Koppe, Schott, and Grimm), or all the apostles and especially St James (Böhme), or the prophet Elias (Ewald), or the philosopher Seneca (Kreyher). It is useless to go further.[1]

---

[1] Whoever is curious to run through this medley of contradictory systems has only to read the two long historical dissertations of Bornemann, *Die Thessalonicherbriefe* (Meyer's *Commentary*), Göttingen, 1894, pp. 400-459 and 538-708 ; or the notes of G. Wohlenberg, *Der 1 und 2 Thessalonicherbriefe*, Leipzig, 1903, pp. 170-209.

Nor can we say that Catholic commentators are any more agreed. However, in spite of infinite divergences of detail, they almost all regard the *parousia* as the personal return of Jesus Christ coming to judge the living and the dead; they see in Antichrist an individual, although St Augustine thinks rather of a tendency; in the *apostasy* they see a defection and a revolt, either religious or political, or both at the same time; in the *mystery of iniquity,* either Nero and the persecutors, or heretics and schismatics; in the *temple of God,* either the Temple of Jerusalem rebuilt or the Christian Church; finally, in the *obstacle,* they see either the Roman Empire or its heir, the Christian State. But what State to-day constructs a dyke against the invasion of evil? In despair of finding any other solution, some are forced to hold that it is the faith still living in many hearts or the divine command to preach the Gospel throughout the world.

Not only is the " obstacle " not yet found, but we doubt whether it has ever been looked for in the right direction. Paul keeps to the ideas of Jewish and Christian eschatology. Like Daniel and St John, he describes a conflict between good and evil, which has its echo on the earth, but the scene and principal seat of which are elsewhere. It is, in fact, Satan who begins it and maintains it, helping his tool with all his might (κατ' ἐνέργειαν τοῦ Σατανᾶ). The antagonist must be a power of the same order. In the prophecy of Daniel it is the commander of the heavenly hosts, the chief of the people of God, Michael, who takes up the cause of the holy nation, especially at the time of the great tribulation and on the eve of the resurrection of the dead.[1] In St John it is still Michael at the head of his angels who fights against the Dragon, the old Serpent, Lucifer, the Devil, Satan, and who finally wins the victory for Christ.[2]

The struggle between Michael and Satan goes on through the centuries. There is no need of interrogating the Apocrypha—the Book of Enoch, the Testament of the Twelve Patriarchs, or the Apocalypse of Moses[3]—to know what a leading rôle the Archangel Michael is to play at the last day. It is he, according to St Paul—the thing is scarcely doubtful—who will give the signal for the resurrection and the judgement. Will it not be also he—the protector first of the Synagogue and then of the Church—who with his legions will bar the passage of the powers of hell until the fulness of time? All the features of Paul's description are applicable to him; a personal being (ὁ κατέχων), he

---

[1] Dan. x, 13, 21 ; xii, 1. *Cf.* 1 Thess. iv, 16.
[2] Apoc. xii, 7-9.
[3] References in Hastings' *Dictionary of the Bible,* art. " Michael," and his *Dictionary of the Apostolic Church,* 1918. See also Székely, *Bibliotheca apocrypha,* vol. i, Freiburg im Breisgau, 1913.

commands an army and represents a force (τὸ κατέχον); he is immortal, and his fight against Satan, begun in the apostolic epoch (ἄρτι), runs on through history to its final climax. If his momentary disappearance (ἕως ἐκ μέσου γένηται) signified a defeat or a destruction this character would not be applicable to him, but the Apostle's words do not mean this, and need not be thus understood. Until the baffled exegetes have found a better solution it is here that we shall seek for the mysterious " obstacle " that retards the appearance of Antichrist.

Everything leads us to believe that all the anxieties about the imminence of the *parousia* were quickly allayed. We do not see that they manifested themselves elsewhere; perhaps because they arose from local circumstances in Thessalonica, or because the Apostle, taught by experience, took care thereafter to prevent all misunderstanding.[1]

[1] The Biblical Commission, under date June 18, 1915, promulgated the following three decisions :
1. It is not permitted to a Catholic exegete " to affirm that the apostles, although teaching nothing erroneous under the inspiration of the Holy Spirit, do nevertheless express their own human ideas, subject to error or illusion " (*asserere, Apostolos, licet sub inspiratione Spiritus Sancti nullum doceant errorem, proprios nihilominus humanos sensus exprimere, quibus error vel deceptio subesse possit*). This division between inspired statements and uninspired statements would be both arbitrary and dangerous. All the assertions of the sacred writers, even when they affirm their ignorance or doubt (see 1 Cor. i, 16), are inspired, and are therefore veracious, to the degree in which they formulate them.
2. The Catholic exegete must maintain that " the Apostle Paul in his writings has said nothing at all which is not in perfect accordance with that ignorance of the time of the *parousia* which Christ proclaims to be common to all men " (*Apostolum Paulum in scriptis suis nihil omnino dixisse quod non perfecte concordet cum illa temporis Parousiae ignorantia, quam ipse Christus hominum esse proclamavit*).
In fact, even independently of inspiration, it is not likely that St Paul could have been ignorant of the solemn declaration of the Saviour recorded by the three Synoptists.
3. Finally, one may not claim that the traditional interpretation (given above, p. 76) of 1 Thess. iv, 15-17 " is too far-fetched and devoid of any solid foundation."

BOOK II
THE CHURCH OF CORINTH

CHAPTER I

DISORDERS AND DANGERS

I—The Parties at Corinth

1. The State of the Church of Corinth. 2. Coteries and Factions.
3. Human Wisdom and True Wisdom. 4. The Apostle a Collaborator
of God. 5. The Apostle a Servant of Christ.

1. FOUR or five years have passed away since the
correspondence with the Thessalonians. The
narrative of St Luke, in spite of its conciseness,
allows us to follow the movements of the Apostle
step by step. We left him at Corinth, teaching in
the house of Titius Justus near the synagogue.[1]

Exposed to the attacks of the Jews, who were furious at
seeing some of their leaders[2] go over to the new faith, ill-
protected by the platonic goodwill of the proconsul Gallio,[3] he
decides at last to leave Corinth after a stay of more than
eighteen months.[4] His hosts, Priscilla and Aquila, accompany him. He leaves them at Ephesus, whither he has
resolved to return to settle down for a short time, continues
his pilgrimage to Palestine, and goes to take breath, as is
his custom between two missions, in his resting-place at
Antioch. This is not for long. His zeal gets the better of
him again; he crosses Galatia and Phrygia, multiplying his
halts in order to complete the instruction of the converts.
At last, in accordance with his plan, he arrives in Ephesus.

An event of the greatest interest had meanwhile taken
place there. An Alexandrian Jew, named Apollos, calling
himself a disciple of the Lord and, in fact, a catechumen,[5]
perhaps before leaving his country, was preaching in the
synagogue all that he knew of Jesus and was beginning to
make disciples. Unfortunately, he had remained in the preliminary stages of the faith and did not yet know anything
of Christian baptism.[6] Aquila and Priscilla completed his
instruction and, as he desired to go to Achaia, recommended

[1] Acts xviii, 7. [2] Acts xviii, 8-11.
[3] Acts xviii, 12-17.
[4] Acts xviii, 11. Eighteen months, without counting the considerable
time (ἡμέρας ἱκανάς, Acts xviii, 18) passed at Corinth after the affair with
Gallio.
[5] Acts xviii, 25. οὗτος ἦν κατηχημένος τὴν ὁδὸν τοῦ Κυρίου, a very
remarkable expression.
[6] Ibid. Ἐδίδασκεν ἀκριβῶς τὰ περὶ τοῦ Ἰησοῦ ἐπιστάμενος μόνον τὸ βάπτισμα
Ἰωάννου. The life of Jesus was, therefore, related to the catechumens,
the explanation of Christian baptism being deferred till the moment of
receiving it.

him to the brethren; but their proselytism does not seem to have gone further. Arriving at Ephesus, Paul found there a dozen disciples—probably the conquests of Apollos[1]—who knew no other baptism than that of John and who had never heard of the Holy Ghost. He baptized them and conferred the Spirit upon them by the laying on of hands.[2] The Church of Ephesus, therefore, truly owes its origin to him; there he built upon no other man's foundations.

Natural eloquence, religious enthusiasm, pure, noble diction, and the art of adapting the lofty speculations of Greek philosophy to the narratives of the Bible and of giving to the facts of Scripture an allegorical interpretation, after the manner of Philo;[3] in a word, all that charms and leads captive crowds of listeners, above all in a versatile and fickle populace like that of Corinth—all these Apollos possessed. There, in spite of himself, he had acquired some fanatical admirers resolved to belittle everyone else so as to exalt him. What a contrast between this and the simple familiar manner of the Pauline style, rough and irregular to the point of incorrectness, full of substance, yet so devoid of oratorical embellishments! The authority of the Apostle would suffer by comparison in the minds of the superficial.

Other causes of dissension had arisen. Some scandals had occurred among the neophytes. Paul had been obliged to inflict punishment. In a letter which we no longer possess he commanded that these impure persons should be kept apart from the others. Either by mistake or by malice some had pretended to see in this command an express order to avoid having anything to do with all pagans who were leading an immoral life, and this had been regarded, and with reason, as an excessive measure. But, as he will subsequently explain (1 Cor. v, 9-12), he merely wished to forbid relations with Christians guilty of scandal. Nevertheless, this misunderstanding itself proves how inclined certain disciples were to censure his acts and to emancipate themselves from his rule. This was because the Church of Corinth, founded by him at the price of so many efforts, was becoming day by day less compact and homogeneous.

---

[1] This is not said in so many words, but comes from the whole substance of the narrative. Paul's converts know only the baptism of John (Acts xix, 3-4), the only one that Apollos could have taught them.

[2] Acts xix, 5-6. Baptism and confirmation were conferred together, and the instruction concerning those two sacraments immediately preceded their reception. The Ephesian converts, not having been prepared for the baptism of Christ, naturally did not know either the nature or the effects of confirmation. They were even ignorant that there was a Holy Ghost (xix, 2).

[3] His qualifications are: Ἀνὴρ λόγιος . . . δυνατὸς ὢν ἐν ταῖς γραφαῖς (Acts xviii, 24); ζέων τῷ πνεύματι (xviii, 25); ἤρξατο παρρησιάζεσθαι (xviii, 25); συνεβάλετο πολὺ διὰ τῆς χάριτος (xviii, 27); εὐτόνως διακατηλέγχετο (xviii, 28).

A ferment of discord was becoming evident within its ranks. Members of the house of Chloe had just brought alarming news (1 Cor. i, 11). The first fervour was cooling down; coteries were being formed which threatened to degenerate into schisms; scandals were occurring publicly without provoking a sufficiently energetic repression; there were also some strange peculiarities, exaggerations of doctrine, and together with them grievous palliations of wrongdoing. The future of this Christian community was big with dangers.

A little later, Stephanas, Fortunatus, and Achaicus disembarked at Ephesus, bringing a letter in which the Corinthians asked Paul for a solution of several embarrassing cases of conscience.[1] The three messengers were to return to their country by sea. The Apostle charges them with a second letter, which is now our First Epistle to the Corinthians. In this he treats of the most varied subjects, without any other order or connection than the doubts or the needs of his correspondents. At the first glance, however, are distinguished two very clearly defined parts—the correction of abuses (i-vi) and the reply to the cases of conscience (vii-xvi).

2. The most pressing danger comes from party spirit. To this the Apostle devotes the first quarter of his letter :

> I beseech you, brethren, by the name of our Lord Jesus Christ, that you all speak the same thing, and that there be no schisms among you, but that you be perfect in the same mind and in the same judgement. For it hath been signified unto me, my brethren, by them that are of the house of Chloe, that there are contentions among you. Now this I say, that everyone of you saith : I indeed am of Paul ; and I am of Apollos ; and I of Cephas ; and I of Christ. Is Christ divided ? Was Paul then crucified for you ? Or were you baptized in the name of Paul ? I give God thanks that I baptized none of you, but Crispus and Caius, lest any should say that you were baptized in my name. And I baptized also the household of Stephanas ; besides I know not whether I baptized any other. For Christ sent me not to baptize, but to preach the Gospel, not in wisdom of speech, lest the cross of Christ should be made void.[2]

As the history of the parties at Corinth is limited almost entirely to this information, we must not be surprised if the critics have expended many hypotheses upon them. Almost all possible combinations have been exhausted. But, first of all, what were these parties? They were not schisms; the word σχίσμα had not yet the theological meaning which it

---

[1] vii, 1. περὶ ὧν ἐγράψατε. It seems almost certain that these three persons (xvi, 17) were the bearers of the letter. Out of delicacy, Paul makes no allusion to the information which they gave him orally, but it is probable that they told him of the abuses concerning the celebration of the *agape* (xi, 8 : Ἀκούω σχίσματα ἐν ὑμῖν ὑπάρχειν).

[2] 1 Cor. i, 10-17. See Rohr's monograph, " Paulus und die Gemeinde von Korinth," Freiburg i. Br., 1899 (*Bibl. Studien*, iv, 4).

has since received. They were not sects; all professed the same faith, frequented the same meetings, took part in the same eucharistic feast. Nor were they well-defined groups; they all recognize the authority of Paul, who by turns encourages, exhorts, reproves, and threatens them as his children in Christ. Thus the deposit of faith remained intact and the bond of charity was not broken; it all consisted in intrigues and personal rivalries, of which the ancient factions of Byzantium and the Lower Empire, or the coteries which still group themselves in our days around a renowned orator or lecturer, can give a fairly good idea.

At Corinth some claimed Paul as their leader, because he was their apostle, their master, and their father; others adhered to Apollos, whose talents charmed them; others exalted above all the name of Peter, the chief of the apostolic college and the pillar of the Church; and some, who thought themselves wiser and better inspired, and apparently disdained to pledge their fealty to a mere man, wished to be subordinate only to Christ. But this very claim to appropriate to themselves the whole of Christ, while despising his human ministers, revealed secret pride and overweening arrogance. Some have doubted the existence in Corinth of a party of Christ. Clement of Rome, writing to the Corinthians about forty years later, makes no allusion to it, although he does mention the three other groups.[1] Certain exegetes think that the rallying cry, " I am of Christ !" far from being the motto of one of the parties, was the watchword of Paul himself. But in that sentence—" Now this I say that everyone of you saith : ' I am of Paul, and I of Apollos, and I of Cephas, and I of Christ.' Is Christ then divided?"—it seems to us arbitrary and unnatural to detach the last one of the series in order to see in it the special formula of Paul, which formula he himself condemns as nonsense, asking if Christ be divided and if it be permissible for each one to appropriate him to himself. This appears still more clear from another passage in the Second Epistle to the Corinthians : " If any man trust to himself that he is Christ's, let him think this again with himself, that, as he is Christ's, so are we also,"[2] and with a better right than the authors of this exclusive claim.

One incontestable fact is that the persons whose names offered to the partisans a rallying cry had nothing to do with these petty rivalries. For his part, Paul laments them and is indignant over them. Very far from ascribing to Peter a doubtful rôle, he always speaks of him with deference. Apollos was so little suspected of intrigues that he was

---

[1] xlvii, 3. Funk, Patres apost.,[2] 1901, vol. i, p.160. St Clement calls the factions of Corinth by their true name (προσκλίσεις).

[2] 2 Cor. x, 7.

urgently begged to return to Corinth; but he refused to do so, fearing, perhaps, to augment the evil by his presence and displeased at the uproar made in connection with his name.[1] Moreover, the tone of the letter shows clearly enough that the most perfect harmony exists between the two apostolic labourers. Paul is no more jealous than Apollos is ambitious, but he does not wish to be underrated to the detriment of his ministry and his legitimate authority.

3. It was said at Corinth that he lacked something which his fellow-worker possessed to an eminent degree; this was *wisdom*. Wisdom suggested the idea of profound speculations or of consummate art. Aristotle had defined it as the knowledge of principles and first causes. For the Stoics it was the science of things human and divine, the queen of virtues, and the aim of life. But art in its most different forms was also called wisdom. Homer and Sophocles, Phidias and Polycletus were sages, as well as Socrates and Plato.[2] In the opinion of the Corinthians Paul had no right to this title, either as a philosopher, or an artist, or a fine speaker. After his experience at Athens he had understood that neither philosophy, nor eloquence, nor subtleties of language would convert the world. It was necessary to preach simply the *verbum crucis* and to let the word germinate and fructify of itself. Paul wished to know nothing else than Christ and Christ crucified. He purposely avoided " persuasive words of human wisdom,"[3] " in order not to render of no avail the cross of Christ." He does not affirm absolutely that his method is the only good one, but it was the only one suitable to Corinth, in this society of

---

[1] I Cor. xvi, 12.

[2] The definition of Aristotle (*Metaph.*, i, 1 : τὴν ὀνομαζομένην σοφίαν περὶ τὰ πρῶτα αἴτια καὶ τὰς ἀρχὰς ὑπολαμβάνουσι πάντες) is applied to philosophy rather than to wisdom. Cicero (*De Offic.*, ii, 43 : *rerum divinarum atque humanarum scientia*) and the 4th book of Machabees (i, 14 : σοφία ἐστὶ γνῶσις θείων καὶ ἀνθρωπίνων πραγμάτων καὶ τούτων αἰτίων) speak the language of the Stoics. But the philosophical meaning was the least common. Paul puts himself at the point of view of the Old Testament when he treats of true wisdom ; and he understands wisdom in the ordinary sense of art, skill (of a good or bad sort), when he wishes to indicate human wisdom. In qualifying himself as a σοφὸς ἀρχιτέκτων (I Cor. iii, 10), he speaks exactly like Homer (*Iliad*, xv, 412 : σοφία τέκτονος), and Pindar (*Nemes.*, vii, 25 : σοφὸς κυβερνήτης). Aristotle himself defines elsewhere σοφία (*Eth. Nicom.*, VI, vii, 1) as ἀρετὴ τέχνης, and, according to this definition, calls Phidias and Polycletus *sages*. However, wisdom is more applicable to philosophers and artists than to artisans. Cf. the verses quoted by a commentator of Aristophanes (on the *Clouds*, 144, Ed. Didot, p. 88), which are believed to be a parody of the oracle of Delphi :

Σοφὸς Σοφοκλῆς, σοφώτερος δ' Εὐριπίδης,
'Ανδρῶν δὲ πάντων Σωκράτης σοφώτατος.

[3] I Cor. ii, 1-5.

disputatious minds, prejudiced by a false wisdom, against which the best arguments would have broken down. In fact, the Church of Corinth gained as recruits "not many wise according to the flesh, not many mighty, not many noble."[1] God, according to his usual method, chose for it the foolish things of the world, the weak things, and the base things, and the things that are contemptible, and things that are not, to confound the wise and the strong, so that no flesh should glory in his sight.[2]

If secular writers understand by wisdom the lofty conceptions of philosophy, or the skill of the artist, the authors of the Old Testament saw in Wisdom the daughter of the Most High and the most precious of his gifts. To these two meanings the New Testament adds a less favourable one, originating perhaps from the abuse of this word by the Greek sophists and the rabbinical theologians. There was, therefore, room for a distinction between human wisdom, worldly wisdom, and carnal wisdom,[3] which the Corinthians vainly looked for in St Paul, and the name of which he repeats to them to satiety with an avenging irony,[4] and the true, the divine wisdom, which he everywhere loads with eulogies and which he wishes ardently that all the converts should possess.[5] Thus there is no contradiction in his assertions and opinions; he *would* not make use of human wisdom, as being unworthy of his ministry and injurious to Christ; he also *could* not teach divine wisdom to hearers who were carnal and psychical—in a word, to men.[6]

True wisdom is "hidden in mystery, ordained of God before the world unto our glory, unknown by all the princes of this world, for, if they had known it, they would not have crucified the Lord of glory."[7] From this description it appears that divine wisdom has to do with the plan of redemption, and seems to be identical with what St Paul sub-

---

[1] 1 Cor. i, 26.

[2] 1 Cor. i, 26-31. The principal idea in Paul's soteriology.

[3] Σοφία λόγου (i, 17), ἀνθρώπων (ii, 5), ἀνθρωπίνη (ii, 13), Ἡ σοφία τοῦ κόσμου (i, 20), τοῦ κόσμου τούτου (iii, 19), τοῦ αἰῶνος τούτου (ii, 6), τῶν σοφῶν (i, 19, taken from Is. xxix, 13). Σοφία σαρκική (2 Cor. i, 12), σοφοὶ κατὰ σάρκα, ἐν αἰῶνι τούτῳ (1 Cor. i, 26).—Sometimes, owing to the context, σοφία alone is to be understood as worldly or carnal wisdom (1 Cor. i, 21, 22; ii, 1-4), and σοφός receives the same unfavourable sense (1 Cor. i, 12, 20, 27; iii, 19, 20).

[4] Sixteen times in this context (1 Cor. i, 17—iii, 20), and the word "wise" ten times.

[5] Ἡ σοφία τοῦ Θεοῦ (1 Cor. i, 21; ii, 7. See Rom. xi, 33).

[6] Σαρκικοί (1 Cor. iii, 3) and σάρκινοι (iii, 1) carnal, as opposed to spiritual; ψυχικὸς ἄνθρωπος (ii, 14), *animalis homo*, the same opposition, the natural man having only his ψυχή, his reasonable soul, without the πνεῦμα of God. Man left to his own powers alone and consulting only his own intelligence is a carnal man (iii, 3): κατὰ ἄνθρωπον περιπατεῖτε, and (iii, 4): οὐκ ἄνθρωποί ἐστε; *nonne homines estis?*
1 Cor. ii, 7, 8. See Cornely's explanation of this text.

sequently calls "the Mystery"—that is to say, the great
secret of God in reference to the incorporation of men with
Christ in the unity of the mystical body. Like the Mystery,
it is hidden in the depths of the divine will; like the Mystery,
it has for its object our eternal blessedness; like the
Mystery, there was only a glimpse of it in the past, and even
the angels knew it only through the medium of the Church,
when they contemplated it in its concrete reality;[1] like the
Mystery, it can be revealed only by God or by the Spirit
which scrutinizes all the secrets of God;[2] and, finally, like the
Mystery, it is in Jesus Christ that it has its ideal realization.[3]
The divine wisdom is, therefore, something outside of man;
it is the wonderful means of our salvation. Whosoever succeeds in comprehending it—and that is the peculiar business
of the apostles and prophets—is truly wise, for he is initiated
into the wisdom of God. If he possesses at the same time,
to a high degree, the faculty of explaining it to others he
has the special *charisma* called the "word of wisdom,"
(λόγος σοφίας), very different from "wisdom of speech"
(σοφία τοῦ λόγου).[4] From this double point of view Paul
flatters himself that he yields the palm to no one.

4. Having silenced his detractors, he now comes to the
matter of the parties. The Corinthians compare and criticize
the preachers of the Gospel; they assign to them different
ranks, preferring one, disdaining another. Now, nothing is
more unreasonable than this for one who comprehends the
character, rôle, and mission of the apostolic labourers.
Indeed, since the apostles are collaborators with God the
contrast it is attempted to make between them is injurious
to Him who delegates and employs them. As "servants of
Christ and dispensers of the divine mysteries," they are not
amenable to their subordinates and have to give an account
only to their Master.[5] With each of these two ideas is
associated a celebrated passage, the context of which will
make them better understood.

If the Church is a field, the apostles are its cultivators; if
the Church is a building, they are its builders. But, by
themselves, they are nothing, absolutely nothing. Paul
plants, Apollos waters, but God alone gives the increase;
Paul, as an able architect, lays the indispensable foundation,
which is Jesus Christ; others build on this foundation, but it

---

[1] Eph. iii, 10. [2] 1 Cor. ii, 10.
[3] 1 Cor. i, 24: Χριστὸν . . . Θεοῦ σοφίαν; i, 30: ἐγενήθη σοφία ἡμῖν ἀπὸ
Θεοῦ. Cf. Col. ii, 2; i, 27.
[4] 1 Cor. i, 17: σοφία τοῦ λόγου is the art of the rhetorician; 1 Cor. xii, 8:
λόγος σοφίας is the gift of explaining the divine wisdom.
[5] 1 Cor. iii, 5-23 and iv, 1-15.

is God alone who gives solidity and cohesion to the whole. Strictly speaking, God is the only cultivator and the only builder; the faithful are the "increase of God, the building of God." The apostolic workmen are only assistants, all of whose labour would be vain without God. Since they form only one body with their Master, so they form only one body among themselves; and the preferences shown them are as injurious as they are unjust. Paul puts himself forward with Apollos, feeling sure that no one will misunderstand their mutual sentiments; but beyond this one particular[1] case, he aims at and condemns all coteries.

From the fact that the preachers of the Gospel work under orders, it does not follow that they have neither merit nor responsibility. On the contrary, they are entitled to a re-compense, a salary ($\mu\iota\sigma\theta\delta$s) in proportion to their work.[2] This salary is independent of the kind of employment exercised the talents used, and the fruits garnered; it is estimated solely by the amount of work done ($\kappa\delta\pi\circ$s); it is personal ($\iota\delta\iota\circ$s) and not to be shared with others any more than the work which it remunerates. And since it is a question of *salary,* it is idle to pretend that it is given *according* to the nature of the work and not *in view* of the work in order to recognize it and to reward it.

The metaphor of agriculture is followed without any transi-tion by that of a building. Although, strictly speaking, God is the only builder, as he is the only cultivator, the apostolic labourers themselves also build, under orders, some more or less well, others more or less badly, while a third group, which we have not to consider here, labours only to destroy.

We are God's coadjutors; you are God's husbandry; you are God's building. According to the grace of God that is given to me, as a wise architect, I have laid the foundation; and another buildeth thereon. But let every man take heed how he buildeth thereupon. For other foundation can no man lay, but that which is laid, which is Christ Jesus. Now if any man build upon this foundation, gold, silver, precious stones, wood, hay, stubble, every man's work shall be manifest; for the day of the Lord shall declare it, because it shall be revealed in fire; and the fire shall try every man's work, of what sort it is. If any man's work abide, which he hath built thereupon, he shall receive a reward. If any man's work burn, he shall suffer loss; but he himself shall be saved, yet so as by fire (1 Cor. iii, 10-17).

---

[1] iv, 6: Ταῦτα δὲ μετεσχημάτισα εἰς ἐμαυτὸν καὶ ᾿Απολλὼν δι᾿ ὑμᾶς. "It is on account of you (δι᾿ ὑμᾶς, for your profit, to teach you), that I have made of these things a figurative application to myself and to Apollos." The figure (σχῆμα) consists in solving a general question by treating a par-ticular case: *Id genus in quo per quamdam suspicionem quod non dicimus accipi volumus* (Quintilian, *Instit.,* ix, 2).

[2] iii, 8: ὁ φυτεύων δὲ καὶ ὁ ποτίζων ἔν εἰσιν, ἕκαστος δὲ τὸν ἴδιον μισθὸν λήψεται κατὰ τὸν ἴδιον κόπον. The contrast is between the *identity* of the Gospel labourers so far as they are labourers together with God and their *individuality* in relation to the work and to the corresponding reward.

In this allegory there are three points to be considered: the nature of the building, the day of the Lord, and the fire which tries the work of the labourers.

What is this *building* which the apostolic labourers are commissioned to finish? It certainly is not the inner temple which every Christian erects in his soul from the beginning of faith, which is its foundation, to the perfection of charity, which is its summit; for this temple, of which every Christian is his own architect, is multiplied according to the number of individual Christians, whereas the Apostle speaks continually of one *single* building, constructed by the preachers of the Gospel. Nor is it the Church, that temple of the Holy Spirit, constructed out of living stones placed upon the corner-stone of Christ; for then the perishable materials, which do not withstand the test of fire, would be the sinners and the rejected; and how could those, who made them enter into the substructure of the Church, be themselves saved? It refers, therefore, clearly to the Gospel, of which Paul laid the first foundation in Corinth by preaching Jesus Christ who died for our justification and rose again for our glory. No man has the right to remove this foundation, or to substitute another for it; but every preacher of the Gospel has the right and duty to continue the building. Now, as the building is of the same order and of the same nature as the foundation, the portions superadded to the edifice founded by Paul will necessarily be the doctrines of Christianity, not dead, purely speculative doctrines, without any influence on the growth of the mystical body, but active, living doctrines, capable of transforming the minds and hearts of those who make of them their rule of life. The gold, silver, and precious stones are, in various degrees, useful and fruitful doctrines; the wood, hay, and stubble, fragile and ephemeral substances, symbolize, not errors and heresies, but frivolous teachings, useless stories, good only to feed the curiosity of hearers, but without any serious influence on their moral life. The sovereign Judge will appear suddenly. A devouring fire will precede him. The gold, silver, and precious stones will resist the test; the wood, hay, and stubble will be consumed; and the imprudent workmen who employed them, seeing their work perishing, will escape through the flames.

The Apostle, as usual, suppressing all that intervenes, foreshadows on the last day, which he calls by antonomasia the *Day*,[1] the separation of the good from the evil and the

---

[1] The Vulgate has *dies Domini*, but the Greek text has only ἡ ἡμέρα, "the Day" *par excellence*. This Day is oftener called "the Day of the Lord" or "the Day of Christ" (1 Cor. i, 8; v, 5; 2 Cor. i, 14; Phil. i, 6, 10; ii, 16; 1 Thess. v, 2; 2 Thess. ii, 2; 1 Peter iii, 10, 12; Apoc. xvi, 14); but it is also designated by ἐκείνη ἡ ἡμέρα (2 Thess. i, 10; 2 Tim. i, 12, 18; iv, 8), and by ἡ ἡμέρα alone (Heb. x, 25; *cf*. Rom. xiii, 12). It is the day of judgement. There is no reason to think of the day of tribulation (Augustine), or of the day of death (Cajetan), or of an indeterminate day (Grotius).

distribution of rewards and punishments. He represents to us the Gospel labourers in the act of rearing the building of faith. They are divided into three classes. Some are demolishing or, at least, shaking the edifice, instead of building it; their punishment will be terrible; God will destroy them as they strive to destroy the temple of God. Others are constructing a solid monument and are employing only the best materials; they will receive the special recompense due to wise and faithful workmen. Finally, the remainder are using perishable material; they will suffer harm ($\zeta\eta\mu\iota\omega\theta\acute{\eta}\sigma\epsilon\tau\alpha\iota$); St. Paul does not say precisely how, but at least they will not receive the honourable distinctions accorded to the apostles, and will suffer the mortification of having laboured all in vain. Nor is this all : " They will be saved as by fire," like the workman who, using combustible materials instead of those which are fireproof, sees the conflagration burst forth in the building in process of construction, and flees from it through the flames, not without burns, as well as fear and horror. There are, therefore, some faults which are not sufficiently serious to shut them out of heaven and send them to hell, but which are punished, nevertheless, with a chastisement proportionate to their sin. The Catholic dogmas of venial sin and of purgatory thus find a very solid support in this text.

The fire which the Apostle speaks of here is not the *fire of purgatory,* for this purifies but does not try, and has nothing to do with the excellent work done, represented by the gold, silver, and precious stones. Still less is it the *fire of hell,* as has been supposed by St Chrysostom and some of his disciples; for the fire of hell punishes but does not try; and can we say, without doing violence to the text, that the damned will be " saved " ($\sigma\omega\theta\acute{\eta}\sigma\epsilon\tau\alpha\iota$), that is, kept alive, to suffer eternally? It is necessary, therefore, to choose between the *fire of the judgement* and the *fire of the final conflagration.* But the fire of the judgement is so often mentioned in Scripture, and the fire of the conflagration so rarely, that it is hardly probable that St Paul wished to indicate the latter.[1] The Apostle is speaking of a fire that tries the doctrines and actions of men, of a fire that accompanies and reveals the day of the Lord. Now this fire can be only the fire of the judgement. This fire, which forms a necessary part of the divine appearances, accompanies the chariot of the Lord coming to judge the world. It is an intelligent fire, which will make clear the contrast between good doctrines, durable like gold,

---

[1] The fire of the final conflagration is foreign to Paul's teaching. It is not to be found in 2 Thess. i, 8 ($\dot{\epsilon}\nu$ $\pi\upsilon\rho\grave{\iota}$ $\phi\lambda o\gamma\grave{o}\varsigma$ $\delta\iota\delta\acute{o}\nu\tau o\varsigma$ $\dot{\epsilon}\kappa\delta\acute{\iota}\kappa\eta\sigma\iota\nu$), for these words are a quotation from Is. lxvi, 15 (*quia igne Dominus judicabit et gladio suo ad omnem carnem*), where it is a question of the fire of the judgement.

silver, and marble; and worthless doctrines, which are as destructible as wood, hay, and straw. This same fire will try the consciences of the imprudent architects, and inflict upon them their merited punishment. " They shall be saved as by fire." Here the word "fire" has its ordinary sense; only there is also a comparison which may be developed thus : They shall be saved, but not without pain and distress, like people surprised by a sudden conflagration, and saved by rushing through the flames.

5. The apostles are still " the servants of Christ and the dispensers of the mysteries of God;[1] not the preachers only, but the dispensers; for the mysteries comprise, together with truths to be believed, saving institutions to be administered. As servants, they are dependent only on their master; as dispensers, they act only in the name and by the orders of Him who sends them. In any event, they are responsible only to the judgement of God. The judgements pronounced upon them by others are valueless, and without reliability or justice. Paul calls them disdainfully " the day of man " in contrast to the " Day of the Lord." He regards them as of no account. What is much more, he abstains from judging himself. Although not conscious of any fault in the fulfilment of his apostolic duties at Corinth, he is not sure of being justified before God.[2] A great lesson of humility this, and a precept never to be forgotten. Even if a man were another Paul, he would have to work out his own salvation with fear and trembling.

Not only did the Corinthians judge the ministers of the Gospel and assign to them different ranks according to their preferences and caprices, but they were vain of their relations to them, and boasted of belonging to one rather than to

---

[1] I Cor. iv, I : ἡμᾶς λογιζέσθω ἄνθρωπος ὡς ὑπηρέτας Χριστοῦ καὶ οἰκονόμους μυστηρίων Θεοῦ.—(a) The pronoun ἡμᾶς includes Paul and the other preachers, such as Apollos.—(b) The word ὑπηρέτης (which Suidas explains by δοῦλος) seems to indicate a subordinate position, inferior to that of the διάκονος.—(c) Although the μυστήρια in the language of Paul are the secret arrangements of the plan of redemption, the Apostle considers them here rather as institutions than as teachings, as appears from the word οἰκονόμοι (stewards or administrators). With much reserve the Council of Trent (Sess. xxi, cap. 2) says that in this text the Apostle seems clearly to insinuate (non obscure visus est innuisse) the power which the Church has always had of making, in the dispensation of the Sacraments, various incidental changes, according to the different circumstances of time, place and person.

[2] I Cor. iv, 4 : Οὐδὲν ἐμαυτῷ σύνοιδα, ἀλλ' οὐκ ἐν τούτῳ (non in hoc, non propter hoc) δεδικαίωμαι. This denies that the testimony of the conscience is a sufficient reason for believing oneself justified (δεδικαίωμαι, in the perfect tense, indicates a state which has begun in the past and which still continues). The case is individual, but the reasoning is general. The Council of Trent (Sess. vi, cap. 16) paraphrases this text, which is illumined by the contiguity of other passages, I Cor. ix, 27 ; Phil. ii, 13, etc.

another. Paul lets fly one last satirical arrow at this ridiculous fancy of theirs :[1] " For who distinguisheth thee?" Who, besides thyself, dreams of recognizing in thee any sort of superiority? But suppose that these advantages of which thou art so proud are not imaginary, " what hast thou that thou hast not received? And if thou hast received it, why dost thou glory " as if it were a personal distinction? That thou receivest it from Peter, or Apollos or Paul, after all, what does that amount to? In the last resort, to God we must always go as the original Giver. Thus is the precept verified : " He that glorieth, let him glory in the Lord," and not in men.

Nothing authorises the opinion of certain exegetes who suppose that the chiefs of the factions are alone referred to in this outburst. Those chiefs are neither named nor designated in any way. Paul addresses all the Corinthians, and warns them not to be " puffed up for anyone against another "; not more in favour of Peter or of Paul than in favour of Apollos or of any other unknown preacher. " For," he adds, " who, then, distinguisheth thee?" Who recognizes in thee these fanciful advantages with which thou dost honour to this or that apostolic labourer? Immediately after, the Corinthians are always the persons in question. There is no trace of the instigators.

It is known that, towards the end of his life, St Augustine, contrary to the usual opinion, interpreted *Quis te discernit,* as referring to the divine discernment which predestination establishes between men. Since then, our text has become classic in treating the subject of grace. Nevertheless, the councils' documents do not deduce the necessity of grace from the phrase *Quis te discernit* itself, but from the whole context, or more precisely from the words : *Quid habes quod*

---

[1] iv, 7 : Τίς γάρ σε διακρίνει; the verb διακρίνειν means to "distinguish " among several, and then to " prefer." It does not mean to give superiority or advantage. The Fathers are not agreed about the extent of the signification of σέ, in which some see only the heads of the factions, while others, whose view appears to us better founded, see in it all the faithful who take sides for this or that master. But they seem indeed to suppose that the reply to the Apostle's question is to be a negative one—viz., No one distinguishes thee. Chrysostom is very clear. Origen, whose commentary Theodoret copies word for word, is no less so (Cramer, *Catena in* 1 Cor., Oxford, 1841, p. 78). Severianus of Gabala (*Ibid.*) has a remarkable explanation : Σὲ τὸν βουλόμενον ἀπὸ τοῦδε καλεῖσθαι ἢ τόνδε καταλιμπάνειν τίς διακρίνει; οὐχὶ ἀναμένεις τὸν κριτήν; St Ephrem (*Comment. in Epist. Pauli,* Venice, 1893 : *Quis enim est qui discernat istud quod tu habes ?*) also supposes the answer : *Nemo.* The explanation of St Augustine—*Quis te discernit a massa perditorum?* which supposes the answer: *Deus*—may be irreproachable as a theological formula, but not as an interpretation of the text.

The second Council of Orange (*Araus.* ii, *can.* 6 and *conclus.*) relies only on the words *Quid habes quod non accepisti,* to prove the necessity of grace.

non accepisti? from which it can, in fact, be deduced. It is true that this requires a far from involved twofold reasoning. First an *argument of parity* is needed in order to extend to all men the words which the Apostle addresses to the Corinthians only, or even, according to certain exegetes, to the fomentors of the disorders only. Moreover, it is in virtue of an *argument a fortiori* that what Paul says of external advantages is applied to the gifts of grace. But the fact of our elevation to the supernatural state being once admitted, it is evident that everything in the order of grace, still more than in the order of nature, from the first ray of faith up to the beatific vision, is a gift of divine liberality, and that man cannot boast of it without failing to recognize his own dependence and the sovereign dominion of God.

II—CORINTHIAN SCANDALS

1. The Case of the Incestuous Man. 2. Lawsuits before Pagans.

1. Two scandalous affairs had taken place in Corinth, to which the whole community had rendered itself accessory by its tolerant indulgence.

Venus, patroness of Corinth, was honoured there by a kind of worship in which the wantonness of the Greek Aphrodite was united to the shameless deeds characteristic of the Eastern Astarte. In her temple a thousand female hierodules openly prostituted their bodies for her profit and in her honour; and sacred prostitution was raised to a sacerdotal rank. Public morals were correspondingly and lamentably lax. To live like the Corinthians was regarded, even among pagans, as a disgrace. In this pestiferous atmosphere some Christians had caught the contagion of vice. One of them was living in concubinage with his stepmother, no doubt a widow or divorced.

> It is absolutely heard that there is fornication among you, and such fornication as the like is not among the heathens ; that one should have his father's wife. And you are puffed up ! and have not rather mourned, that he might be taken away from among you, that hath done this deed.[1]

---

[1] 1 Cor. v, 1-2 : *Ὅλως ἀκούεται ἐν ὑμῖν πορνεία, καὶ τοιαύτη πορνεία ἥτις οὐδὲ ἐν τοῖς ἔθνεσιν, ὥστε γυναῖκά τινα τοῦ πατρὸς ἔχειν, κτλ.*—(a) This is no question of ordinary fornication, but of incest. The wife of the father is not the mother of the guilty man, but his stepmother (μητρυιά). St Paul gives to her the biblical name of " the father's wife," because he is alluding to the Mosaic law (Lev. xviii, 7-8 and Deut. xxii, 30) which forbids such kinds of union.—(b) The expression γυναῖκα ἔχειν designates a permanent union, either concubinage or marriage (Mark vi, 18 and Matt. xiv, 4 use for this the same expression).—(c) These unions were regarded as abominable by the Greeks and Romans (the ἔθνη, pagans of St Paul), although they were customary among the Egyptians and other peoples : *Nubit genero socrus ; o mulieris scelus incredibile et praeter hanc unam in omni vita inauditum*

It was not a case of a passing sexual relation, but of a permanent union, like that of Herod Antipas with Herodias, the wife of his brother Philip. The Roman law, so easy-going in regard to marriages, prohibited these unions, and the instances of them which profane history could offer were condemned by public opinion, which in this respect was in harmony with natural instinct. Now the Christians of Corinth did not appear to be much affected by this conduct. They continued to associate with the guilty man, and admitted him to their meetings. Perhaps they allowed themselves to be deceived by that false maxim that baptism makes of the Christian a new creature, freed from all his former ties and exempt from all legal prohibitions. It is thus that, in the eyes of the rabbis, a conversion to Judaism sundered all relations of kindred; and Maimonides expressly teaches that it is permissible for a proselyte to marry his stepmother.

Paul's indignation was great. His invariable custom was to submit all those guilty of creating scandals to a sort of excommunication, which involved a cessation of all relations with other Christians, even those of convenience and civility. He had threatened with this punishment the mischief-makers and the idle of Thessalonica if they refused to obey his òrders. Later, he will tell Titus it is his duty to avoid the obstinate heretic, meaning by that the instigator of divisions and troubles. In the letter to the Corinthians which is lost, he bade them formally to break off all connection with the unchaste.[1] What, then, is his grief now to see them tolerate this infamy! Let them at once expel the incestuous man in order not to be contaminated by him. Easter, it seems, was at hand, and this symbolical exhortation was very appropriate : " Know you not that a little leaven corrupteth the whole lump? Purge out the old leaven, that you may be a new paste, as you are unleavened. For Christ, our Pasch, is sacrificed. Therefore let us feast, not with the old leaven, nor with the leaven of malice and wickedness, but with the unleavened bread of sincerity and truth. . . . Put away the evil one from among yourselves."[2] These last words, which contain the definite sentence of Paul, are an allusion to the law in Deuteronomy,[3] prescribing the penalty of death for certain crimes. Excommunication, a kind of symbolical

---

(Cicero, *Pro Cluent.*, v, 6).—(*d*) They were also forbidden by the Roman law, but Cicero has just shown us that this prohibition was not always respected ; and perhaps the Romans let the Jews—and Christians could then pass for Jews—marry as they liked. However, the thing will be less credible, if we suppose the father to be alive. This question depends on the sense which is given to the word ἀδικηθείς (2 Cor. vii, 12).

[1] 2 Thess. iii, 14: (μὴ συναναμίγνυσθαι αὐτῷ); Tit. iii, 10 (αἱρετικὸν ἄνθρωπον . . . παραιτοῦ); 1 Cor. v, 9 (μὴ συναναμίγνυσθαι πόρνοις).

[2] 1 Cor. v, 6-8, 13.   [3] Deut. xvii, 7 ; xix, 19 ; xxii, 24, etc.

death, replaces in the Gospel the actual death of the old Law. He had at first thought of a much severer punishment, and one more in proportion to the enormity of the crime.

> I indeed, absent in the body, but present in spirit, have already judged, as though I were present, him that hath so done, in the name of our Lord Jesus Christ, you being gathered together and my spirit, with the power of our Lord Jesus, to deliver such a one to Satan for the destruction of the flesh, that the spirit may be saved in the day of our Lord Jesus Christ.[1]

Canonists, desirous of finding here an example of the greater excommunication according to the forms at present used in the Church, ask how Paul could issue it, or command the Corinthians to issue it in his name, without first instituting inquiry, the summoning of witnesses and an interrogatory. All very superfluous questions. Paul does not pronounce the sentence and he does not urge the Corinthians to pronounce it. He only expresses his opinion about the penalty due to the man notoriously guilty of incest; perhaps he hints of the rigorous measure which he is resolved to take in case the Christians should themselves do nothing. As far as he is concerned, he thinks it just and expedient to deliver the guilty man over to Satan, but he does not say what formalities would have to be observed if it came to that.

This terrible punishment evidently presupposed excommunication—that is to say, exclusion from the Church together with the deprivation of the graces and aids of which the communion of saints is the channel. But it included something still more formidable. The apostles who had received from the Lord the power of restraining devils had also the power of loosing them. The criminal who fell under this sentence, which was more serious than excommunication, was abandoned to the vengeance of the eternal enemy of men and became the prey and the plaything of Satan. But, as all the punishments inflicted by the Church

---

[1] 1 Cor. v, 3-5: Ἐγὼ μὲν γὰρ ἀπὼν τῷ σώματι, παρὼν δὲ τῷ πνεύματι, ἤδη κέκρικα ὡς παρὼν τὸν οὕτως τοῦτο κατεργασάμενον. . . . παραδοῦναι τὸν τοιοῦτον τῷ Σατανᾷ, κτλ. The verb κέκρικα does not signify here "I have judged"—that is, sentenced a guilty person—but "I have judged it best, or I have resolved (cf. ii, 2) to take severe measures in order to make up for your inaction." Note the ἤδη—i.e., "while you shuffle." The measures to be taken naturally have to do with the future and are only conditional. In the parenthesis formed by verse 4, we think that in nomine Domini nostri Jesu Christi refers to tradere hujusmodi (the man who has acted thus) Satanae, and that cum virtute Domini nostri Jesu Christi is a completion of congregatis vobis et meo spiritu. But this point is secondary; what is not secondary is to distinguish well between the punishment projected by the Apostle and that which he commands the Christians to inflict themselves. He orders them to remove the guilty man; and if this not done, he threatens to proceed himself to punish him in their name.

are curative, the final aim was always the conversion and salvation of the sinner. Once at least in his life, Paul made use of this formidable power. He delivered over to Satan Hymeneus and Alexander to teach them not to blaspheme,[1] or, rather, that they might learn that lesson at their own expense when exposed without refuge or protection to the tyranny of the devil. In regard to the Corinthian guilty of incest he is less severe; he contents himself with his exclusion, and if for a moment he thought of a severer punishment, it was always with a view to saving the soul of the criminal by afflicting his body.

Three corollaries are to be drawn from this doctrine; the Church, on account of the injunction of the Saviour and the example of the Apostle (Matt. xviii, 17, etc.), always claims the right to exclude from its fold Christians guilty of causing scandals. But this penalty, which has for its direct object the immunity of the good, aims also at the amendment of the guilty party.[2] Neither the Apostle nor the Church arrogates to itself any power over unbelievers.[3] It is for God to judge them. Far from abolishing the prohibition of marriage between relatives in the cases foreseen by the Mosaic Law[4] the infant Church hastened to sanction it and to extend it even farther.[5] We find it everywhere prevailing from the very first. The profound horror which sensual vices awakened in the preachers of the Gospel was due, in part, to a reaction against the looseness of pagan morals, and partly to a moral sensitiveness inherited from the Jews, among whom fornication and idolatry were called by the same name—πορνεία.[6] Paul feels the need of inculcating in the neophytes a well-grounded aversion to these shameful acts of lewdness, which they had perhaps accustomed themselves to look on with indifference. The three reasons which he

---

[1] 1 Tim. i, 20: Ὑμέναιος καὶ Ἀλέξανδρος, οὓς παρέδωκα τῷ Σατανᾷ, ἵνα παιδευθῶσιν μὴ βλασφημεῖν.

[2] There is no instance of a punishment inflicted by the Church where benefit of the guilty is entirely excluded.

[3] 1 Cor. v, 12-13: τί γάρ μοι τοὺς ἔξω κρίνειν; οὐχὶ τοὺς ἔσω ὑμεῖς κρίνετε; τοὺς δὲ ἔξω ὁ Θεὸς κρίνει (or κρινεῖ).—Οἱ ἔξω certainly means the unbelievers (Col. iv, 5; 1 Thess. iv, 12; 1 Tim. iii, 7), Jews or Gentiles. The Church exercises jurisdiction only over the baptized (Council of Trent, Sess. xiv, De Poenit, cap. 2).

[4] 1 Cor. v, 1, alluding to Lev. xviii, 8, Deut. xxii, 30.

[5] It is not necessary to assume a formal decree. The N.T., which came to complete the Old and make it perfect rather than abolish it, kept not only what are rightly called nature's laws but also nature's desires, and it is certain that the prohibition of marriages between near relatives by blood or alliance was included in them.

[6] Πορνεία, fornication and idolatry. So also πορνεύω (to adore idols, Jer. iii, 6; Ezech. xxiii, 19; Hos. ix, 1, etc.). The Apocalypse, which loves to use the language of the O.T., often employs these words as well as πόρνη metaphorically.

gives to them to turn them from impurity come from the depths of his mystical theology.

Fornication is an injustice, a sacrilege, and a profanation : an *injustice* towards him to whom we belong body and soul; a *sacrilege* against Jesus Christ, of whom we are members; a *profanation* of the temple of the Holy Ghost.

An *Injustice.*—We call indifferent those actions which conform to natural instinct, which wound the rights of no one, and have no direct relation with the moral life—such are eating and drinking. The stomach is made for food, and food for the stomach. But the relation of the body to fornication is entirely different. " The body belongs to the Lord, not to fornication, and the Lord belongs to the body." The body belongs to the Lord as the limb belongs to the head, and *vice versa.* And the proof of this mutual dependence is that God raises the one on account of the other. Fornication, violating the rights of Christ over us, is, therefore, an injustice.

A *Sacrilege.*—Whoever has in his mind these two elementary truths of Paul's doctrine, that the body of the Christian is a member of Christ and that, in sexual union, a man and woman become one body and one flesh, must logically conclude thence that fornication prostitutes a member of Christ to an impure woman so as to identify him with her. To name such an act is to show the sacrilegious abomination of it.

A *Profanation.*—Our body, sanctified through grace, becomes, as well as the soul, a temple consecrated by the presence of the three divine persons and by the special indwelling of the Holy Ghost. Fornication soils and violates this temple. Everywhere else the sinner abuses a creature outside himself and sins against it by turning it from its purpose. Here he himself abuses his own body and sins against it. The accomplices form only one flesh; nothing external intervenes. The body is not only the instrument of the sin, as in other faults, but is itself the subject of it.

2. Under our present conditions, the second abuse condemned by the Apostle would seem a very light one. A Christian had sued another. He had " demanded justice of the unjust;"[1] that was the current name for the pagans. Hence a twofold scandal—the quarrel itself and the wide publicity of the trial. Better suffer injustice than give the

[1] 1 Cor. vi, 1 : Κρίνεσθαι ἐπὶ τῶν ἀδίκων, καὶ οὐχὶ ἐπὶ τῶν ἁγίων. Here ἄδικοι is used rather than ἁμαρτωλοί (Matt. ix, 10; Gal. ii, 15) to designate the heathen, because it is a question of *justice* to be rendered and because the expression " to have themselves judged by the unjust " is sufficient to show the absurdity of the act charged. Paul does not deny the right to demand justice, but he does not wish that it should be made use of in these conditions at the cost of such a scandal.

heathen such a bad example and put this weapon into their hands against believers.

We know that the Jews wherever they were numerous had special courts, before which their suits were settled. The Roman authority generally tolerated and sometimes recognized this exceptional jurisdiction, which, Origen tells us, occasionally pronounced capital sentences;[1] these, however, had to be approved by the supreme power or else carried out secretly, like the sentences of the German *Vehmgericht* in the Middle Ages. There is reason to believe that the Jews voluntarily granted their magistrates the most extensive jurisdiction, and St Paul himself appears more than once to have submitted to their verdict when his position as a Roman citizen might have exempted him from it. Thus can be explained the five beatings with thirty-nine strokes, which seem to have been inflicted according to Jewish custom and as the result of a regular procedure. However this may be, he desires a similar institution for Christians. " If you have judgements," he says, " set them to judge who are the most despised in the Church." Then, catching himself up at once for fear of the Corinthians taking his biting irony seriously, he exclaimed : " Why, is there not among you one wise man that is able to judge between his brethren? But brother goeth to law with brother, and that before unbelievers !"[2] The saints—and all Christians bear this name— can certainly settle a matter of very little importance if they are one day to judge the world and even the angels themselves.[3] Some theologians, embarrassed by this judgement, have vainly imagined five or six different kinds of judgement—a judgement of comparison, a judgement of approbation, etc. The Apostle's thought is more simple. The saints will judge together with Jesus Christ, just as they will rise from the dead with him, be glorified with him, and reign with him. Forming only one being with him in the unity of the mystical body they share in all his prerogatives, and consequently in that of universal Judge. The angels, who will be submitted to the test as well as men, will be judged as men are judged, and it will be the elect together with Jesus Christ, with whom they are indissolubly united, who will judge them. It is, therefore, superfluous to suppose that " the angels " here signify priests or possibly demons; an untenable hypothesis, because it is wholly contrary to custom.

[1] *Epist. ad Afric.*, 14 (XI, 84). The *Clementine Homilies (Epist. Clem. ad Jac.*, 10) prescribe a similar tribunal, and Theodoret (*Comment. in* I *Cor.* vi, 7) calls attention to the fact that this practice is not contrary to the deference and submission due to the civil power.

[2] I Cor. vi, 4-5. It is clear that the order given in v. 4 is ironical.

[3] I Cor. vi, 3: οὐκ οἴδατε ὅτι ἀγγέλους κρινοῦμεν. This expression of astonishment shows that it is a teaching familiar to Paul's readers.

We know how zealous was Paul for the edification of the heathen. He saw in this a way of forwarding mission work which was sometimes as efficacious as direct preaching. This is the principal reason for the measure which he recommends at this time and which, from its very nature, was to be transient. It remained in force, however, through three centuries. Until the official conversion of the empire to Jesus Christ, when it lost its reason for existing and fell into desuetude, perhaps not a single lawsuit by one Christian against another can be traced.

CHAPTER II

CASES OF CONSCIENCE

I—MARRIAGE AND CELIBACY

1. Paul's Ideal. 2. Full Lawfulness of Marriage and the Conjugal Act.
3. Virginity Better. 4. Marriage Indissoluble and the Pauline Privilege.

1. THE greatest part of the First Epistle to the Corinthians is devoted to the solution of doubts proposed by the neophytes. Paul refers frequently to the questions of his correspondents,[1] but he probably inserts into his replies points of doctrine about which they had neglected to consult him. There are six principal questions: marriage and celibacy (vii); the question of things sacrificed to idols (viii-x); the *agape* and the Eucharist (xi); the use and the value of *charismata* (xii-xiv); the resurrection of the dead (xv); the great collection (xvi).

The last point will be treated in connection with the following Epistle, where it fills two entire chapters. With the celebration of the *agape* and the Eucharist is connected women's dress in church. Perhaps in the mind of the Apostle the *charismata* belong to the same subject; but it is better not to pre-judge anything and to leave the texts in their independence.

" It is good for a man not to touch a woman."[2] This sentence looks as if it were a well-known maxim, perhaps

---

[1] I Cor. vii, I : Περὶ δὲ ὧν ἐγράψατε. viii, I : Περὶ δὲ τῶν εἰδωλοθύτων. xii, I : Περὶ δὲ τῶν πνευματικῶν. xvi, I : Περὶ δὲ Ἀπολλὼ τοῦ ἀδελφοῦ. It is quite natural to think that by these identical forms of speech, forming an abrupt transition, Paul refers to the written questions (ἐγράψατε) of the Corinthians. The formula is wanting in the question about the veiling of women (xi, 2-16), the *agape* and the Eucharist (xi, 17-34) and the resurrection (xv, 1-58). On all these points the Apostle shows himself extremely well informed, and the instructions which he gives are as precise as they are practical. But it is doubtful whether the Corinthians themselves had thought of pointing out these grave abuses.

[2] vii, I : Καλὸν ἀνθρώπῳ γυναικὸς μὴ ἅπτεσθαι. This sentence is so closely connected with ἐγράψατε, that it may be asked if it did not form part of the letter of the Corinthians, or if it simply contains Paul's answer. However that may be, it is conceived in the most general terms ; man is there designated by his nature (ἄνθρωπος) and not by his quality of husband (ἀνήρ). The word καλός (beautiful, suitable, good) means often, especially in the Bible, where it corresponds to the Hebrew טוב—moral goodness. That it is necessary to understand it thus here appears from the reasons for this advice, v, 5-7, 32-38. But from the fact that an act is good, it does not follow that the contrary act is bad, as Tertullian says (*De monog.*, 3) and also St Jerome (*Contra Jovinian.*, i, 7 : *Si bonum est mulierem non tangere, malum est ergo tangere*). The Apostle, who expressly distinguishes later

adduced by the Corinthians to raise the question of the lawfulness of marriage. Paul repeats it, making it his own, and he applies it successively to abstention from conjugal relations, to celibacy, and to widowhood. In itself it is good to renounce the rights of marriage, to preserve virginity, and not to contract another marital union when death has broken the first. But, although all this is good, the contrary is also good, only *less* good. It is not a matter of precept, it is a matter of divine vocation, perfection, and counsel.

It may seem strange that such scruples should have originated in Corinth, but extreme laxity of morals sometimes provokes these exaggerated reactions. When men despair of reforming nature, they come to dream of annihilating it, and beside the Epicurean, who allows the most shameless libertinage, rises the Stoic, who is very near condemning even marriage. The Gnostics always oscillated between these two excesses. Paul comes straight to the point, and his doctrine may be summed up in three phrases : the use of conjugal rights is permissible, but continence is more perfect; marriage is good, but virginity is better; second marriages are allowed, but widowhood is preferable.

If there is one thing certain, it is that the Apostle lived in celibacy, for the discordant voice of Clement of Alexandria only accentuates the harmony of Catholic tradition in this respect. That he considered virginity as more excellent than marriage it is impossible to doubt, and the efforts of some heterodox writers to escape this annoying testimony have ended in putting it in the clearest light. " I would," says Paul, while granting husband and wife conjugal intimacy but not imposing it, " I would that all men were even as myself "—given to continence—" but everyone hath his proper gift from God, one after this manner and another after that." And that his mind may not be misunderstood, he adds immediately : " I say to the unmarried and to the widows, it is good for them if they so continue, even as I "— that is to say, evidently, free from the ties of matrimony— " but if they do not contain themselves, let them marry. For it is better to marry than to be consumed " by impure fires.

2. According to these principles, the case of the married is very simple. To them, as to everyone, is applicable the general maxim : " It is good for a man not to touch a

---

between the good (καλόν) and the better (κρεῖσσον), must have warned them against this error. Moreover, St Jerome seems to retract his words implicitly a little [f]urther on when he compares marriage to barley and virginity to pure wheat; but the expression, for all that, is no less inaccurate, and it shows too much of Tertullian's influence.

woman;" and consequently it is the same for the woman in
regard to the man, for the conditions are the same, as we
shall see later.   But to them is also applicable this other
sentence : " But for fear of fornication " (διὰ τὰς πορνείας—
i.e., acts of incontinence, the danger of which may occur)
" let every man have his own wife and let every woman have
her own husband." We think that the Apostle purposely
employs the most comprehensive formula in order to include
all legitimate sexual relations at once.   He does not speak
clearly and minutely either of making a marriage or of
exercising conjugal rights, because he is referring to both
and because he applies to both the same rule.   In itself
abstinence is better, but the use of marriage is good and in
certain circumstances may be recommended.   He supposes,
of course, that no previous engagement binds the decision.
His severe condemnation of widows who violate their faith—
a vow properly so called, or a simple promise—is well
known, and he reminds the married that they are no longer
entirely free to satisfy their desire for perfection.   For the
conjugal act is for them a real *debt,* so far as one of them
wishes to make use of his right ; and the refusal to fulfil this
duty is like a denial of justice, which deprives the other party
of a good of which he cannot be dispossessed.   In fact, since
marriage makes of them both one flesh, the body of the wife
belongs to the husband, and the body of the husband belongs
to the wife.   No doubt it is permissible for them simultaneously to give up their right, but for this Paul lays down
three conditions : mutual agreement ; a motive of a spiritual
nature, such as a desire to give oneself more freely to prayer ;
and a time limit, beyond which the ordinary relations are to
be resumed to obviate the danger of incontinence and to
prevent the temptations of Satan.   Scarcely has he given this
last counsel, however, when he hastens to add : " I speak
this by indulgence, not by commandment."[1]   He would like

---

[1] 1 Cor. vii, 6 : Τοῦτο δὲ λέγω κατὰ συγγνώμην, οὐ κατ' ἐπιταγήν.   The
word τοῦτο cannot refer to verse 2, which is too far off, nor to verses 3 and 4,
which deal with a *duty* and a *debt ;* it refers therefore to verse 5, and more
particularly to the last clause which seemed to contain a command
(καὶ πάλιν ἐπὶ τὸ αὐτὸ ἦτε).   The Vulgate translates quite accurately :
Hoc autem dico secundum indulgentiam, non secundum imperium.   But
St Augustine read in his version *veniam* instead of *indulgentiam,* and he
interpreted it in the sense of *pardon* (*De pecc. origin.,* 38 : *Evidenter dum
tribuit* veniam *denotat* culpam ; so also *De bono conj.,* 10 ; *Enchir,* 78),
thinking that the conjugal act was a *venial* sin—even when it had for its
object the avoidance of incontinence—and was excused only by the intention
of having children.   His authority also won over a number of scholastic
theologians and even some good exegetes like Estius, although they read
indulgentiam.   But clearly this view has no foundation in the original text.
It is, moreover, incredible that St Paul would advise one evil to avoid a greater
evil, and that he gives in advance absolution for all the venial sins which his
advice would cause.   Here again the influence of Tertullian (*De exhort.
castit.,* 3, Migne, II, 917) has been fatal.

to have everyone continent, like himself, but he does not wish to impose continence on anyone, and he even cannot do so, since that requires a *special gift* from God. His *permission* proves clearly that conjugal intimacy is perfectly lawful, even solely in order to avoid the temptations of the devil and the flesh, but does not therefore make it obligatory. This teaching is so clear and precise as to seem incapable of ever leaving any room for discussion or doubt.

The case of celibates and widowers differs from that of the married in this—that the former are free from any obligation; the celibates by having contracted none, the widowers by having been released through the death of their consort. It is, however, settled in accordance with the same principles. The celibate can form a marriage without committing any fault: " If thou take a wife, thou hast not sinned. And if a virgin marry, she hath not sinned."[1] Similarly, " A woman is bound by the law as long as her husband liveth; but if her husband die, she is at liberty; let her marry to whom she will, only in the Lord "[2] —that is to say, marry a Christian. The same rule applies to the father or guardian who has the guardianship of a young girl and is responsible for her conduct.[3] If by keeping her unmarried too long after the marriageable age he fears for himself or for her some unpleasant consequence—while unable to specify exactly what he fears—he will do well to follow the counsels of prudence and marry her to someone. " In acting thus, he sinneth not;" let the virgin and her betrothed be married.[4] But if, on the one hand, he has no

---

[1] 1 Cor. vii, 28.   [2] *Idem*, vii, 39. See Rom. vii, 2, 3.

[3] In an interesting study, whose data require verification, Achelis (*Virgines subintroductae, ein Beitrag zu* 1 *Cor.* vii, Leipzig, 1902) seeks to show that it is not a question of the virgin's father or guardian, but of the man, clerical or layman, who had her in his service. If the man sees that there is danger for him in this situation—Achelis makes ὑπέρακμος refer to the man and translates it by *überreizt*—he will do well, not to marry the virgin himself, but to give her in marriage to another. J. Sickenberger (in *Biblische Zeitschrift*, 1905, pp. 44-69) appears to us to have proved absolutely that it is really a question of the father and not of the companion of a *virgo subintroducta*. *Cf.* Hugo Koch (*Ibid.*, 1905, pp. 401-407).

[4] 1 Cor. vii, 36 : Εἰ δέ τις ἀσχημονεῖν ἐπὶ τὴν παρθένον αὐτοῦ νομίζει, ἐὰν ᾖ ὑπέρακμος, καὶ οὕτως ὀφείλει γίνεσθαι, ὃ θέλει ποιείτω· οὐχ ἁμαρτάνει· γαμείτωσαν. The differences between the original and the Vulgate are numerous and not without importance.—(*a*) According to the Greek there are two conditions dependent on εἰ, first the fear of the father or guardian, and then the moral necessity of proceeding to the marriage. The father thinks that he is exposing his virgin daughter to dishonour (active sense of ἀσχημονεῖν) or that he exposes himself to dishonour (passive sense), if (ἐὰν) the virgin is ὑπέρακμος, that is, if she has passed the ἀκμή, which women reach, according to Plato, at the age of twenty. This fear of the father comes evidently from the peril of her seduction ; from which there results also the second condition: οὕτως ὀφείλει γίνεσθαι. Marriage seems to be necessary.—(*b*) In this case it is expedient for the father to carry out his plan of giving his daughter in marriage. The Vulgate *quod vult faciat*

such fears, and if, on the other, he is perfectly free to do as he likes, he does well and even better, in itself considered, not to give his virgin daughter in marriage.

Certain exegetes find it singular that the father disposes of his daughter's destiny without consulting her, and that he should decide for her, as he prefers, virginity or marriage. We will not say that this is to look at the question too much from our modern point of view of extreme individualism, nor even that, when in doubt, a virtuous young girl generally follows the advice of her natural director; we confine ourselves to remarking that the consent of the daughter is implicitly shown in the clause, " Let them marry," and, if not there, it is shown in the absence of all obligation on the part of the father. Moreover, there is no reason to suppose any tyrannical intention or arbitrary despotism in the father or the guardian, and Paul has a perfect right to rule out any such exceptional case.[1]

3. The complete and entire lawfulness of marriage and of second nuptials is, therefore, indisputable. But what is no less certain is that the state of virginity or of widowhood is in itself better. No ambiguity on this point is possible : "I say to the unmarried and to the widows, it is good for them if they so continue, even as I "[2]—that is, unmarried. And it is not only a question of something *good,* but of something *better;* for it is a good which the Apostle wishes for everyone and which he would like to see realized in all, but which depends on a free gift (χάρισμα) of God. —After a vigorous eulogy of virginity, Paul adds : " And this I speak for your profit; not to cast a snare upon you, but for that which is decent and which may give you power to attend upon the Lord without impediments."[3] The object of the Apostle's recommendations, the ideal that he proposes, the means of becoming more closely united to the Lord, is evidently something better from a spiritual point of view. The father who, having reflected well and duly weighed all

---

gives us to understand that he can do either one or the other, as he likes ; but the original is to be explained differently : " let him do what he thinks he ought to do."—(c) " He sinneth not ; let them marry." The Vulgate *non peccat, si nubat* may revert to the Greek meaning by changing the subject: *Non peccat pater, si nubat virgo.* Clearly the marriage must not be repugnant to the daughter, and her father, in giving her in marriage, far from forcing her to it, anticipates her desires.

[1] vii, 37-38. Note well the four conditions :—(a) The father has no fear (ἐν τῇ καρδίᾳ αὐτοῦ ἑδραῖος).—(b) He has no reason which forces him one way or the other (μὴ ἔχων ἀνάγκην).—(c) He is free to act as he chooses (ἐξουσίαν ἔχει περὶ τοῦ ἰδίου θελήματος).—(d) Finally, all things considered, he thinks it well to keep his daughter unmarried (τοῦτο κέκρικεν ἐν τῇ ἰδίᾳ καρδίᾳ).

[2] I Cor. vii, 8.   [3] I Cor. vii, 35.

the circumstances of time and person, keeps his daughter a virgin, " doth better "[1] than if he gave her in marriage. He procures for her, therefore, a superior good. For both sexes there is perfect equality. Paul speaks in general of unmarried people (ἄγαμος). If he specially mentions virgins and widows, it is because the masculine form of these words is rarely used in Greek, and perhaps also because the lawfulness of marriage and second nuptials for men was not in question. But on several occasions he lets us see that he makes no difference between the sexes either in respect of commands or counsels.

For it is undeniable that he does give counsels : " Now concerning virgins, I have no commandment of the Lord; but I give counsel, as having obtained mercy of the Lord, to be faithful."[2] Whether " faithful " signifies " worthy of faith," or a " faithful preacher of the Gospel," matters little; in any case, the Apostle puts forward the authority given him by God to support his teaching. On a point relating to the Christian life he gives reasoned advice; he expresses an opinion supported by supernatural reasons, and which in the circumstances can be only a counsel, whatever name may be given it. When he urges widows not to marry again, assuring them that in his opinion (κατὰ τὴν ἐμὴν γνώμην) they will thus be happier, and when he appeals to the Spirit of God which he flatters himself that he possesses, he likewise gives a counsel. By the mere fact of presenting virginity and widowhood as a state more perfect, more advantageous, and more agreeable to God, and yet not commanded, he teaches that there are such things as evangelical counsels.

Was his preference for celibacy dictated by selfish considerations, utilitarian views, and a desire to escape from the annoyances of the world, in order to lead a life free from cares and troubles? Whoever imagines that he knows Paul will never be persuaded that the Apostle is subject to such worldly and base considerations; but he has himself taken care to confound such unworthy interpreters of his mind. He wishes the temporary cessation of conjugal relations to spring from the desire for more leisure for prayer. He knows that the unmarried man, if he is truly a Christian, is careful to please the Lord; and that the married man, even if a Christian, is engrossed with worldly things, and must think " how he may please his wife." He knows likewise that the virgin or the widow can have for her only care to be " holy in body and in spirit," while the married woman is distracted by her obligation to " think on the things of the world," and by her anxiety to " please her husband."

[1] 1 Cor. vii, 38.
[2] 1 Cor. vii, 25. The conclusion is independent of the meaning of γνώμη

From a spiritual point of view, the situation of the celibate is better; he can consecrate himself entirely to the service of God. Now, concludes the Apostle, I desire to " give you power to attend upon the Lord without impediment."[1]

The instability of human affairs preaches the same lesson : " I think, therefore, that this is good for the present necessity. . . . This I say, brethren, that the time is short; it remaineth that they also who have wives, be as if they had none; and they that weep, as though they wept not; and they that rejoice, as if they rejoiced not; and they that buy as though they possessed not; and they that use this world, as if they used it not; for the fashion of this world passeth away."[2] Is it possible that Paul was haunted by the near prospect of the *parousia?* We must not deny this *à priori.* As we have already said, he teaches nothing about this subject, and is aware that he knows nothing about it. But lacking certain knowledge, he might have formed an opinion based upon probabilities or conjectures, and, as soon as he tells us of his ignorance and refrains from teaching anything on the subject, it is at least possible that he guided his conduct and his counsels by such probabilities.

4. St Paul proclaims with as much force as the Synoptists the indissolubility of Christian marriage, for the law that he promulgates on this subject has the same origin : " To them that are married, not I but the Lord commandeth that the wife depart not from her husband; and if she depart, that she remain unmarried, or be reconciled to her husband. And let not the husband put away his wife."[3] By oral tradition Paul must have known the Lord's precept recorded by the three Synoptists; he here presents it in a form which resembles the text of Mark, yet with remarkable differences. By virtue of this divine command the wife is forbidden to *depart from* her husband ($\chi\omega\rho\iota\sigma\theta\hat{\eta}\nu\alpha\iota$), and the husband is forbidden to *put away* his wife ($\dot{\alpha}\phi\iota\acute{\epsilon}\nu\alpha\iota$); this gives a very delicate shade of expression to designate marital authority both from the Jewish and the Roman point of view. The Apostle foresees, however, cases of bodily separation actually taking place, and lets us understand that this may be legitimate; but under no hypothesis is the marriage tie broken. In fact, the wife separated from her husband has only two alternatives, either to be reconciled with him, which shows that the bond still exists, or to abstain from marrying another, which also proves the continuance of the first union. The putting away of the wife by the husband is prohibited without any restriction or exception, because this *putting away* ($\dot{\alpha}\phi\iota\acute{\epsilon}\nu\alpha\iota$) meant, for Jews as well as for

---

[1] 1 Cor. vii, 32, 34.   [2] 1 Cor. vii, 26-31.
[3] 1 Cor. vii, 10, 11.   *Cf.* Matt. v, 32 ; xix, 9 ; Mark x, 11-12 ; Luke xvi, 18.

Gentiles, an act which would have for its effect the legal
annulment of the conjugal contract. Since this case must
never arise, there is no need of building other hypotheses
upon it. The indissolubility of Christian marriage has, therefore, no limits put upon it by St Paul. As he loves to repeat,
marriage is broken only by death.[1] A woman will always be
called an adulteress if she contracts a new marriage during
the lifetime of her husband, and it would be the same with
the man who remarried during the lifetime of his wife; for
these two terms are correlative, and the Apostle establishes
between husband and wife, from a conjugal point of view,
perfect equality of rights and duties.

The mixed marriage-tie is weaker. Paul does not even call
it a marriage, reserving this name for the sacrament which
unites two Christians : " For to the rest I speak, not the
Lord. If any brother hath a wife that believeth not, and she
consent to live with him, let him not put her away. And if
any woman hath a husband that believeth not, and he consent
to live with her, let her not put away her husband."[2] Here
also the finer shades of thought and expression are admirably
observed. It is no longer the Lord who is speaking, it is the
Apostle, no doubt with the spirit of the Lord. He addresses
himself to the *others* (τοῖς λοίποις), to that category of
Christians whom he cannot class either among the *married,*
since he reserves this word for the Christian marriage, or
among the *unmarried,* since they are really living in the state
of matrimony. But he takes into account only the Christian
party, for the Church has not to regulate the lives of those
who do not belong to her. He forbids, therefore—and the
absolutely prohibitive form of the phrase (μὴ ἀφιέτω) makes
us think of a true prohibition rather than of a counsel—he
forbids the Christian partner to put away the unbelieving one
in the case where either party consents to live with the other.
A mistaken instinctive repugnance or baseless scruples are not
a sufficient cause for separation. "For the unbelieving husband
is sanctified by the believing wife, and the unbelieving wife
is sanctified by the believing husband."[3] The husband and
wife being of one flesh, and the Christian party being sanctified by baptism, the Christian's sanctity is communicated to
the unbelieving consort. This is not a question of internal
sanctity, for that is incommunicable, but of an extrinsic
sanctity, proceeding from association with sacred things,

---

[1] Rom. vii, 2-3.

[2] 1 Cor. vii, 12, 13. Note the absolute *equality* of rights and duties.

[3] 1 Cor. vii, 14. The meaning of ἁγιάζεσθαι and of ἅγιος in this passage
is unparalleled in the New Testament. One can compare it with 1 Tim. iv, 5 :
every creature of God is good, if one receives it with thanksgiving : "for
it is *sanctified* by the word of God and by prayer." In both cases it is a
question of an *external* sanctification ; but nowhere else is this sanctification
applied to persons.

from non-intercourse with ungodly persons, and from an introduction into the worship of God. The Corinthians admitted this for their children, most of whom had been born before their parents' conversion only three or four years before. St Paul calls their attention to the fact that the same reason militates in favour of the sanctification of married pagans by their Christian consorts.

However, "if the unbeliever depart, let the Christian depart [also]. The brother or the sister is not bound in such cases. But God hath called you (to live) in peace. For how knowest thou, O wife, whether thou shalt save thy husband? Or how knowest thou, O man, whether thou shalt save thy wife?"[1] The permission is clear; the condition not less so. The Christian *may* depart. He is no longer bound in such a case; the Apostle, in virtue of his inspiration, declares him free. Nevertheless, unless he runs the risk of a moral danger, it is allowable for him to renounce this privilege. Paul permits; at most he counsels; he does not command. But, if the case occurs, he takes from the Christian party all occasion for regret and every scruple, by reminding him that God calls us to live in peace, and that the distant and possible hope of some day converting the consort, who remains unbelieving, cannot impose upon him the sacrifice of peace, joy, and liberty. It is necessary only that the non-Christian party be the first one to depart, either by refusing to live together or by rendering their union dangerous or morally impossible by blasphemies, ill-usage, or threats, which would bring scandal or open warfare into the conjugal home. Moreover, this privilege, accorded in favour of the faith, is only an exception to the general maxim : " Let every man persevere in the condition which the Lord hath distributed to him, and let him abide in the same calling, in which he was called."

Objection has been unjustly made to an application of the Pauline privilege in the constitution of Pius V (*Romani Pontificis,* 2 August, 1571) which orders converted Indians to keep the wife who will receive baptism with them, and dismiss the others; and in the decree of Gregory XIII (*Populis ac nationibus,* 25 January, 1585), which dispenses the neophytes of Angola, Ethiopia, Brazil, and other *Indian* countries from questioning their pagan consorts in order to know whether they wish to cohabit, in case of such questioning being impossible, declaring the marriages, contracted by virtue of this dispensation, valid, *whatever may happen.* In the Pauline

---

[1] 1 Cor. vii, 15: Εἰ δὲ ὁ ἄπιστος χωρίζεται, χωριζέσθω. It is clear that the mere fact of remaining an unbeliever does not make good χωρίζεται; a positive refusal to live together is necessary. This is the opinion of St Basil (XXXIII, 673), St Chrysostom (LXI, 155), Ambrosiaster (XVII, 219), St Ambrose (XV, 1767), St Augustine (XL, 216) and others. St Chrysostom notes justly that an attempt at perversion on the part of the unbeliever would be equivalent to a refusal.

privilege the questioning is essential, if there is no other means of knowing the will of the consort. The *moral* estrangement of the latter is sufficient, but it is necessary; the accidental *physical* estrangement would not suffice. The cases of Pius V and Gregory XIII are wholly different. From sheer necessity these two Pontiffs make use of their power of dissolving a non-consummated Christian marriage, and *a fortiori* one contracted in a state of unbelief. Between the facts aimed at in the pontifical documents and the Pauline privilege there exist three great points of difference : as to the *cause,* on the one hand, there is a divine dispensation promulgated by St Paul; on the other, a papal dispensation of an ecclesiastical order; as to *time,* the dispensation of the Pope breaks the old marriage-bond from the moment it is applied or announced, while the Pauline privilege allows it to continue until the contract of a new marriage; as to the *conditions,* the Pope determines them according to his wisdom, while Paul lays down only one condition, the definite refusal, or its equivalent, to cohabit.

II—Victims Sacrificed to Idols

1. The Three Cases. 2. Solution.

1. The Græco-Roman religion consisted entirely of rites and practices. Almost anything could be said or thought about the immortal gods, provided the religious usages of the nation or the city were observed. But these usages entered into almost the entire life of the people. Family joys and mourninig, vows and thanksgivings, ritual solemnities, the games in the circus, anniversaries and a thousand other circumstances gave rise to sacrifices. When the victims were not consumed on the spot in the outer buildings of the temple or in the sacred grove they served for a family banquet or were distributed to near relatives or even sold at a very low price to retailers. This was a constant source of difficulties, scruples, and dangers for the little nucleus of neophytes, lost in the great mass of idolaters. It is probable that they had submitted to Paul three cases of conscience which presented themselves frequently : Ought they to withdraw their patronage from idolatrous butchers, suspected of selling meats offered in the temples, or of having made superstitious invocations over the animals they slaughtered? Could they sit at table with their pagan relatives or friends in spite of the well-founded fear of finding there meats consecrated to idols? Was it even permissible for them, for official reasons or for the sake of propriety, to take part in the sacred banquet which usually accompanied the sacrifice? Before approaching the question directly, the Apostle lays

down two principles : he first shows that the animal which is sacrificed to idols contracts no intrinsic impurity; and secondly, he proves that an indifferent action may become unlawful according to circumstances.

What, then, is an *" idolothyton "?* A victim sacrificed to idols. But what is an idol? A chimera, a being of the imagination, a nonentity. The idol passes for a divinity; but " there is only one God," and it is not he whom the idol represents; hence it follows that the idol is an image without an original, a representation without reality, an idea without an object. In a word, " the idol is nothing in the world." The fact that it has been sacrificed to idols cannot render a creature impure, nor withdraw it from the domain of God. " The earth is the Lord's and the fulness thereof," and it belongs to him by an inalienable right. Of course, whoever eats sacrificial meat " as sacrificed to idols "—that is to say, with the conviction that the offering of it to false gods has defiled it—would contract therefrom the impurity of an ill-trained conscience; but this would be through a lack of knowledge.

Well, an enlightened Christian, endowed with *knowledge,* must consider these weak brethren, for " Through thy *knowledge* shall the weak brother perish, for whom Christ hath died? Now when you sin thus against the brethren and wound their weak conscience, you sin against Christ. Wherefore, if meat scandalize my brother, I will never eat flesh, lest I should scandalize my brother."[1] There we have the heart and mind of Paul. In the long digression which follows he seems to lose sight of the affair of sacrifices offered to idols. In reality, he is preparing its solution. He shows by his own example the application of the maxim : ." All things are lawful for me, but all things are not expedient. All things are lawful for me, but all things do not edify. Let no man seek his own, but that which is another's."[2] Does he, Paul, make use of his rights? He is an apostle, with as good a right to the title as the Twelve; in any case, he is the undisputed apostle of the Corinthians. He could, therefore, live at the expense of the faithful; he could, like the other apostles, like Peter, like the brothers of the Lord, let himself be accompanied by a Christian woman, whose duty it should be to serve him. Every labourer is fed by his employer; Moses even forbids men to muzzle the ox that treadeth out the corn. Under the ancient Law, as under the new, the priest lives of the altar. Why, then, has he, Paul, renounced this right? Because he does not wish that his conduct should place any obstacle in the way of the diffusion of the Gospel; because he is jealous

---

[1] I Cor. viii, 13.   [2] x, 23. *Cf.* vi, 12.

of his good name and of his independence; because he aspires to the glory of an absolutely gratuitous and disinterested apostolate; because he wishes to be a model to the neophytes of detachment from worldly things and a living example of self-abnegation; because, by making himself all things to all men, a Jew with the Jews, a Gentile with the Gentiles, he hopes to save at least some of them; and finally, because he wishes to be able to say to the neophytes : Imitate me, as I imitate Christ.

2. In the light of these principles, the first two cases of conscience are already solved. Like everybody else, the Christian may buy in the market the meats to be found there without troubling himself about their origin. If they have been offered to idols, this offering does not alter anything. He can also accept invitations and eat without scruple all that is offered him. But if anyone there points out the presence of something offered to idols, then he must abstain from it. That remark would show that someone is or may be scandalized, and charity lays upon us the duty of avoiding scandal. One might think the third case similar to the preceding one; but a gulf separates them. To take part in a sacred banquet with the adorers of false gods rightly causes scandal. What would be said of a Christian seated at the table of idols? There is, moreover, imminent danger of idolatry; witness the Israelites who, after having crossed the Red Sea and passed under the luminous cloud, a twofold figure of baptism, and after having eaten the manna and drunk the miraculous water of Horeb, a type of the Eucharist under its two forms, were invited to the feast of Beelphegor and worshipped the god. But independently of the imminent danger of scandal, the participation at the sacred banquet is in itself an idolatrous act. St Paul proves this by two analogies. The Jews, who eat victims offered in the Temple, put themselves, as all allow, in communion with the altar. No Christian is ignorant of the fact that to drink of the chalice and to break the consecrated bread is to partake of the blood and the body of Christ; "I would not that you should be made partakers with devils. You cannot drink the chalice of the Lord and the chalice of devils; you cannot be partakers of the table of the Lord and of the table of devils."[1]

Among all peoples the table forms between the guests assembled round it a sort of sacred bond, which becomes

[1] 1 Cor. x, 20, 21. The three following invitations to dinner, the original text of which we possess, will make us understand, better than any dissertations, the cases of conscience of the Corinthians and Paul's solutions of them. We borrow them from Grenfell and Hunt, *The Oxyrhynchus Papyri*, London, 1898-1904.

more intimate and more sacred when the banquet is the consummation of a sacrifice. For there is in a religious feast the usual union between hosts and guests; the union with the sacrificing priest, for the consumption of the victim is the complement of the sacrifice; the real or supposed unión with the god, thought to be present in the midst of his worshippers; and the union with the victim itself, the vehicle of blessings. It is evident that these unions—at least, the last three—constitute a religious bond. Here, therefore, charity and edification are not at stake, but religion itself. An act of worship done in honour of a false divinity, whether one intends it or not, is an act of idolatry. Not that idols have a real existence, or that the offering to idols defiles a creature. St Paul has just affirmed that it does nothing of the sort, and he does not contradict himself. Only the sacrifices which are not offered to the true God are thought to be offered to devils; and it is indeed the devil who profits by them.

It has been asked how Paul's words can be made to agree with the apostolic decree at Jerusalem which had expressly,

---

(A) No. CX (vol. i, p. 177), second century.

> Ἐρωτᾷ σε Χαιρήμων δειπνῆ-
> σαι εἰς κλείνην τοῦ κυρίου Σαρά-
> πιδος ἐν τῷ Σαραπείῳ αὔριον,
> ἥτις ἐστιν ιε, ἀπὸ ὥρας θ.

(B) No. DXXIII (vol. iii, p. 260), second century.

> Ἐρωτᾷ σε Ἀντώνιο(ς) Πτολεμ(αίου) δειπνῆσ(αι)
> παρ' αὐτῷ εἰς κλείνην τοῦ κυρίου
> Σαράπιδος ἐν τοῖς Κλαυδ(ίου) Σαραπίω(νος).
> τῇ ι ἀπὸ ὥρας θ.

(C) No. CXI (vol. i, p. 177), third century.

> Ἐρωτᾷ σε Ἡραῒς δειπνῆσαι
> εἰς γάμους τέκνων αὐτῆς
> ἐν τῇ οἰκίᾳ αὔριον, ἥτις ἐστιν
> πέμπτη, ἀπὸ ὥρας θ.

(A) The invitation given by Cheremon " to dine at the table of the Lord Serapis and at the Serapeum " could not be accepted by a Christian, according to Paul's principles, for this is a question of a sacred banquet in a sacred place, that is, of an act of idolatry (cf. I Cor. viii, 10 : ἐάν τις ἴδῃ σὲ . . . ἐν εἰδωλίῳ κατακείμενον . . .).—(B) A Christian would be likewise obliged to decline the second invitation ; for although the sacred banquet was to take place at the house of Claudius, son of Serapion, it was nevertheless a sacred feast, given in honour of the Lord Serapis, and the table, at which the guests were to sit, was the table (κλείνη, the usual spelling of the papyri for κλίνη) of the god (I Cor. x, 21 : οὐ δύνασθε τραπέζης Κυρίου μετέχειν καὶ τραπέζης δαιμονίων).—(C) But he could accept the third, in spite of the fear that the wedding feast might include some sacrifice offered to idols, if, as the name would lead us to suppose, Eraïs was a pagan (cf. I Cor. x, 27). He would have then been obliged merely to abstain, in order to avoid scandal, from every dish shown to proceed from a sacrifice.

prohibited the use of things sacrificed to idols. The decree of Jerusalem was temporary and local; a simple measure of discipline, in its very nature liable to be changed, and proposed by St James to conciliate and to soften the clashings between Jewish and Gentile converts in the mixed churches; it was only directly imposed upon the faithful in Antioch, Syria, and Cilicia. St Paul thought he was bound to proclaim it also in Galatia and probably in Asia, where the composition of the Christian communities was the same; but he had no reason for extending it to Corinth, where the Jewish-Christian element must have been very small. On the other hand, the liberal solution of the question given to Corinth did not bind the future. It was natural that, after the triumph of Christianity, a stricter interpretation should be adopted. There was then no further moral necessity or reason for giving to pagan sacrifices that sort of material co-operation which seemed like an encouragement of them. Things offered to idols were, therefore, forbidden, like the games in the circus, either because of the scandal which thenceforth was inevitable, or on account of the imminent danger. We must not be astonished either if some of the Church Fathers, losing sight of the teaching of St Paul, came to regard the things offered to idols as being themselves polluted by the mere fact of being so offered and *ipso facto* forbidden.

III—THE AGAPE AND THE EUCHARIST

1. The Veiling of Women. 2. The Four Abuses of the *Agape*.
3. The Profanation of the Eucharist.

1. Wherever a body of Christians was found public meetings were provided for them. The first day of the week was chosen for these by preference, and was called, from the time of St John, the Lord's Day.[1] Were there at first, as was the case under Trajan, two distinct assemblies, one for instruction, the other for the breaking of bread? The first Epistle to the Corinthians leads us to suppose so. In fact, catechumens and pagans also were present at the meetings, where prophets and those who "spoke various tongues" displayed their divine gifts,[2] and they were probably not admitted to the celebration of the sacred mysteries.

Paul does not try to describe these meetings, but merely

---

[1] Apoc. i, 10: Ἐν τῇ κυριακῇ ἡμέρᾳ. κυριακή is not here used alone, as in S. Ignatius (*Magnes.*, ix, 1), nor have we κυριακὴ Κυρίου, as in the *Didachè*, xiv, 1. The religious meeting took place on the *first* day of the week or Sunday (1 Cor. xvi, 2, κατὰ μίαν σαββάτου), and the Eucharist was then celebrated (Acts xx, 7: ἐν τῇ μιᾷ τῶν σαββάτων). Barnabas, *Epist.* xv, 9, calls it the eighth day.

[2] 1 Cor. xiv, 23, 24 (ἄπιστος ἢ ἰδιώτης, the latter was neither a believer nor an unbeliever, and must therefore have been a catechumen).

means to correct the abuses which had crept into them since his departure. The most intimate details are not given. When they are touched upon in passing, it is hardly more than by way of allusion. Thanks to the difficulties of the Corinthians, a corner of the veil is lifted, too little to satisfy our curiosity, yet enough to allow a wary glance at the working of the churches in their earliest beginnings.

In the Greek cities in general, women enjoyed very great liberty, and Corinth was not a good school for teaching them reserve and modesty. It appears that many of them were present at the religious gatherings without veils, and even ventured to speak there. Paul condemns this practice as improper, contrary to the custom of other churches, and opposed to his own teachings.[1] In those days it was evidently the custom to go with uncovered head as a sign of authority and autonomy, while a veil symbolized fear, mourning, and subjection. Now Christianity came to emancipate woman, to raise her social condition, and restore her position of honour in the home, and did not assign her any place in the sacred functions of the ecclesiastical hierarchy. By the law of God and in the order of nature woman is made subject to her husband, and her external deportment should express this dependence. The Apostle reminds her of this, and binds her to remember it herself in church : " The head of the woman is the man, the head of the man is Christ, and the head of Christ is God."[2] This is the rightful hierarchy. Christ, the supreme head of the Church, under the high suzerainty of God, has reserved for man alone the power of rule, and it is by man that he exercises his jurisdiction; woman is in the last rank, without authority of her own. " Man " and " woman," it is seen, are taken in the collective sense, and consequently there is nothing to prevent their individual inequality nor their mutual relations, as superior and inferior. But St Paul wishes that the hierarchy of the sexes should be perceptibly expressed in the liturgical functions of the Church. A man, praying or prophesying in church with his head covered, dishonours his head, because he voluntarily abdicates the hierarchical dignity with which Christ has honoured him. A woman, praying or prophesying with uncovered head, would dishonour her head, because she would show by that act an arrogance and an effrontery unsuitable to her sex and to her lower rank.[3] It would be equivalent to having her head shaved, says the Apostle. In the heathen world only vile, disreputable people were shaved thus : in Greece the slaves, in

---

[1] 1 Cor. xi, 3-16.   [2] 1 Cor. xi, 3.   Consult Eph. v, 23
[3] This does not mean that it is permissible for her to *prophesy* in public even with her head covered. The Apostle forbids her to do so (xiv, 34), but if she did so with uncovered head, it would be an added indecorum.

Rome the female dancers and courtesans, as a distinctive mark of their ignominious calling.

The history of creation gives woman the same lesson of modesty. Man is in some sort the direct reflection of the divine majesty, while woman is like the image of an image. God said, when he made her : " Let us make man a help like unto himself." Man is taken for the model. Moreover, woman is taken bodily from him, as he himself had been taken from dead matter. Finally, woman was made with regard to man, because " it is not good for man to be alone." Here are three reasons for subordination which the Holy Spirit gives her to meditate upon.[1] Moreover, nature is in accord with revelation to teach woman modesty and decency. It has given her hair as a veil, an honour and an ornament of which it is an insult to deprive her. On the contrary, it is a shame for a man to let his hair grow like the effeminate fops who have lost all sense of decency, and who think nothing of nature's promptings.

The Apostle sums up his thought in this somewhat enigmatical phrase : " Therefore ought the woman to have on her head a [sign of man's] authority, because of the angels,"[2] who were witnesses of the original subordination of the sexes on the day of the creation, and are the invisible but severe guardians of the Christian in places consecrated to prayer and solemn rites.

These considerations are profound, and the Corinthians were likely to find them subtle. Paul foresees this objection and replies to it in advance by opposing to such reasoners the practice of the other churches and his own formal teaching.[3] From its first beginning the Church, therefore,

---

[1] Paul tempers all this, however, by setting forth woman's advantages (verses 11-12) : the woman is necessary to the man, for it is not good for him to be alone. If the woman is taken from the man, man also is born of the woman : Ὥσπερ ἡ γυνὴ ἐκ τοῦ ἀνδρός, οὕτως καὶ ὁ ἀνὴρ διὰ τῆς γυναικός. This restores the balance a little.

[2] 1 Cor. xi, 10 : Διὰ τοῦτο ὀφείλει ἡ γυνὴ ἐξουσίαν ἔχειν ἐπὶ τῆς κεφαλῆς διὰ τοὺς ἀγγέλους. The therefore refers to the subordinate rank of woman in creation (vv. 7-9) : γυνὴ διὰ τὸν ἄνδρα. Ἐξουσία (Vulgate: potestas) must be the sign or the symbol of the power of the husband, and consequently of the dependence of the woman, that is to say, the head-dress or the veil. Diodorus Siculus, Histor., i, 47, says the same : ἔχουσαν τρεῖς βασιλείας ἐπὶ τῆς κεφαλῆς, and by these three "kingdoms" he understands three diadems. It is necessary to leave the word "angels" its usual meaning, much to be preferred to all the fantastical hypotheses that people have tried to substitute for it. Probably it is a question not of angels in general, but of guardian angels. It is so understood by Theodoret, St Jerome, St Augustine, De Trinit., xii, 7, etc. At that time this was a familiar idea, Acts xii, 15 ; Matt. xviii, 10 (cf. Luke xv, 10 ; 1 Tim. v, 21). Respect for guardian angels is a powerful motive for good behaviour.

[3] 1 Cor. xi, 16. Si quis autem videtur contentiosus esse (rather, εἰ δέ τις δοκεῖ φιλόνεικος εἶναι: if anyone finds it good, or deems it proper to dispute) nos talem consuetudinem non habemus, neque ecclesia Dei. (Better ecclesiae, αἱ ἐκκλησίαι). The custom of which the Apostle speaks is not

already had its fixed customs which the believer was obliged
to follow, even when he may not have understood or appre-
ciated the reasons for them. The apostles, too, had the recognized right to issue laws and to cause them to be observed.
Their authority decided everything.

2. Paul had been informed of other abuses by witnesses
whom he had the delicacy not to name :

> Now this I ordain [as to the veiling of women] : I praise you not, that
> you come together not for the better, but for the worse. For, first of all,
> I hear that, when you come together in the church, there are divisions
> among you ; and in part I believe it. For there must be even sects
> among you ; that they also, who are approved, may be made manifest
> among you. When you come therefore together into one place, it is not
> now to eat the Lord's Supper. For every one taketh before his own
> supper to eat ; and one indeed is hungry, and another is drunk. What,
> have you not houses to eat and to drink in ? Or despise ye the Church
> of God, and put them to shame that have not ? What shall I say to
> you ? Do I praise you ? In this I praise you not.[1]

One of the most touching institutions of the apostolic age
was the *agape*. A triumph of Christian equality and
fraternity, a vivid representation of Christ's last supper
on earth, and a symbol of the feast which is to reunite
the elect around the throne of God, the *agape* was also,
as St Chrysostom eloquently says : " An occasion for
charity, a means of alleviating poverty and of making
wealth wiser, a grand spectacle of edification and a school
of humility." United with the Eucharist, which it preceded
sometimes, as a sign of fraternal union between the com-
municants and as a memorial of the Last Supper, which
it usually followed, as a sign of spiritual joy and thanksgiving, the *agape* was only an adjunct to and a complement
of the Lord's Supper. But it was very liable to lose its
liturgical character and to degenerate into a profane repast,

---

the habit of disputing, which he would call *custom* (συνήθεια) by a very
unsuitable name ; it is the custom blamed among the Corinthians, by virtue
of which women appeared at church unveiled. This abusive custom did not
exist in the other churches.

[1] i Cor. xi, 17-22. (*a*) Paul argues first from the greater to the less :
" I believe in part that there are divisions (σχίσματα) among you, for
there must be in the Church even sects (καὶ αἱρέσεις)." This last word
says more than the other, although neither σχίσμα nor αἵρεσις had then
the meaning which they acquired later. One of the reasons for the
existence of sects is that the sincere Christians (δόκιμοι) may be put to
the test and then esteemed.—(*b*) The phrase *jam non est dominicam coenam
manducare* (οὐκ ἔστιν κυριακὸν δεῖπνον φαγεῖν) is variously explained.
Many translate it, " *It is impossible* to eat the Lord's Supper (on account
of your divisions)," understanding by the Lord's Supper the Eucharist alone.
But as οὐκ ἔστιν (for οὐκ ἔξεστιν) is very rare in this sense, it is better to
adhere to the natural meaning, " *It is not* to eat the Lord's Supper (but to
make a profane feast, where selfishness reigns)," understanding by the Lord's
Supper the *whole* liturgical festival, including the *agape* and the Eucharist.

similar to that of the associations or confraternities of paganism. From the time of the apostles crying abuses had occurred; St Paul, St Peter, and St Jude were obliged to repress them. Soon the Eucharist was separated from the *agape.* Then, imperceptibly, the latter was limited to some commemorative solemnities, or transformed into a charitable repast offered to the poor by the rich. The difficulty which the Church had to extirpate these old customs proves how deeply rooted and tenacious of life they were. The liturgy has preserved feeble vestiges of them in the ceremony of the offertory, the distribution of the blessed bread, the meal given on Holy Thursday to twelve poor men, and perhaps also in the kiss of peace.

Four abuses were pointed out in the Corinthian *agape.* The Corinthians divided themselves into distinct groups, relatives with relatives, friends with friends, which destroyed the symbolical beauty of the fraternal banquet. Instead of spreading out all the food in common, each group consumed its own provisions with a selfishness at once offensive and shocking. Those who arrived first sat down at the table without consideration for late comers. Finally, a thing which brought the scandal to a climax, some guests, entirely forgetting the respect due to the assembly and the sacred character of the ceremony, drank to excess. To act in this way was evidently no longer to celebrate the Lord's Supper; it was to make a vulgar picnic, as little religious as were heathen revels.

Paul does not question the rightness of the *agape.* How highly would he who fulminates with so much force against women bold enough to appear in the assembly without a veil or to speak in public, contrary to the custom of the other Christian communities, have denounced the *agape,* already subject to so many abuses, had it been merely local and peculiar to this church. We must conclude from this fact that it was in force in the churches founded by him, as well as at Jerusalem; therefore, instead of suppressing it, he limits himself to setting it in order. He orders the Christians to wait for one another, to fraternize with all, and to remember that this liturgical banquet is not meant to satisfy hunger and thirst—people do not assemble in sacred places for that—but to commemorate in its entirety the Lord's Last Supper, to symbolize the charity and the unity of the faithful, and to make it thus a prelude to the Eucharist.[1]

3. It is, indeed, this last consideration that predominates,

[1] The only stipulation that he makes concerning the *agape* and the Eucharist is the following (xi, 33, 34): Συνερχόμενοι εἰς τὸ φαγεῖν ἀλλήλους ἐκδέχεσθε. Εἴ τις πεινᾷ, ἐν οἴκῳ ἐσθιέτω, ἵνα μὴ εἰς κρίμα συνέρχησθε. He adds that on his arrival he will settle points of less importance.

and we need not seek any other link between the two passages referring to the Eucharist and the *agape*. In reality it does not appear that abuses had crept into the celebration of the Eucharist itself. At least, St Paul says nothing about them. But, on account of their intimate connection, the disorders in the *agapes* reacted on the sacred mysteries, to which they were less a prelude than a prospective profanation.

> In this I praise you not. For I have received of the Lord that which also I delivered unto you, that the Lord Jesus, the same night in which he was betrayed, took bread, and giving thanks, broke and said: Take ye and eat; this is my body, which shall be delivered for you; this do for the commemoration of me. In like manner also the chalice, after he had supped, saying: This chalice is the new covenant in my blood; this do ye, as often as you shall drink, for the commemoration of me. For as often as you shall eat this bread and drink the chalice, you shall show the death of the Lord until he come. Therefore whosoever shall eat this bread or drink the chalice of the Lord unworthily, shall be guilty of the body and of the blood of the Lord. But let a man prove himself; and so let him eat of that bread and drink of the chalice; for he that eateth and drinketh unworthily, eateth and drinketh judgement to himself, not discerning the body of the Lord. Therefore are there many infirm and weak among you, and many sleep. But if we would judge ourselves, we should not be judged, but whilst we are judged, we are chastised by the Lord, that we be not condemned with this world (1 Cor. xi, 22-32).

Those who wish to see in Christian dogmas only the completion of a slow evolution and the result of long-continued struggles that end by combining together after long ages of antagonism must experience great embarrassment in reading this passage, which was written less than thirty years after the institution of the Eucharist, and is also of an unassailable authenticity. Does the theological language of to-day describe in any more precise and explicit terms the most consoling and ineffable of our mysteries? Paul declares expressly that he received this doctrine from the Lord himself, for his words cannot be understood as referring to a revelation through an intermediary, which would not distinguish him at all from the least favoured of the faithful.[1]

---

[1] 1 Cor. xi, 23: Ἐγὼ γὰρ παρέλαβον ἀπὸ τοῦ Κυρίου ὃ καὶ παρέδωκα ὑμῖν. The γάρ (*enim*) justifies what Paul has just said: *In hoc non laudo*. Between the conduct of the Corinthians in the celebration of the *agape* and the institution of the Eucharist which they had to commemorate, the contrast is too great: " it is not to eat the Lord's Supper," οὐκ ἔστι κυριακὸν δεῖπνον φαγεῖν.—The tradition, received directly from *the Lord*, was transmitted by the Apostle himself to the Corinthians. If Paul had not received it directly from the Lord, he would have no cause for adding ἀπὸ τοῦ Κυρίου. It is true, the direct reception would be better expressed by παρά, but ἀπό also is used to express a direct transmission (Gal. iii, 2; Col. i, 7; iii, 24; Acts ix, 13, etc.), and here the meaning was clear in itself. To say without restriction that we receive *a fact* from someone, means that we have learned it from his mouth, especially when a distinction is thus made between ourselves and those who have learned it in another way.

It has long been observed that in the account of the Eucharist Luke depends upon Paul, as Matthew and Mark seem to depend on each other, without it being possible to say with certainty which side had the priority.[1] Between Paul and Luke there are only three differences of very little importance, none of which alters the meaning. In the consecration of the bread the Evangelist expresses the verb which St Paul leaves understood. He says, "This is my body, which is given for you," while the Apostle, according to the most authorized critical reading, says simply, "This is my body which (is) for you" (τὸ ὑπὲρ ὑμῶν); but it is evident that this elliptical way of speaking requires a complement, and we can hesitate only between "given" or "sacrificed," according as we do or do not see in it an allusion to the sacrifice of Calvary. In the consecration of the chalice the correspondence of the two writers is quite as close. The words of institution are thus recorded : "This chalice is the new covenant in my blood;"[2] only St Luke adds "which is shed for you." This addition was already virtually contained in the "blood of the covenant"; for the formal allusion to the conclusion of the old covenant being given, this blood can be only the blood of the sacrifice shed for those whose pact of reconciliation it seals. The last divergence is still less important. To each of the two formulas Paul adds the precept : "Do this in remembrance of me." Luke omits this the second time as superfluous, the two parts of the sacramental rite being inseparable.

It is indisputable that in both cases the consecration of the chalice offers a certain difficulty. In the formula, "This chalice is the new covenant in my blood," with or without the addition of the words, "which is shed for you," the obscurity does not consist in the oft-found metonymy of making the chalice represent its content; it comes from a less usual figure of speech which consists in taking the cause for the effect, or *vice versa,* the covenant concluded in the blood being taken for the blood which seals the covenant. However, if we take into account the parallelism with the first consecration, "This is my body," which seems to demand, as a pendant, "This is my blood"; if we refer to

---

[1] Matt. xxvi, 26 and Mark xiv, 22 : Τοῦτό ἐστι τὸ σῶμά μου.—I Cor. xi, 14 : Τοῦτό μού ἐστι τὸ σῶμα τὸ ὑπὲρ ὑμῶν (variation, κλώμενον or θρυπτόμενον).— Luke xxii, 19 : Τοῦτό ἐστι τὸ σῶμά μου τὸ ὑπὲρ ὑμῶν διδόμενον.—All have the five essential words : Τοῦτό ἐστι τὸ σῶμά μου.

[2] Matt. xxvi, 28 ; Mark xiv, 24 : Τοῦτο γάρ ἐστι τὸ αἷμά μου τῆς διαθήκης τὸ περὶ πολλῶν ἐγχυννόμενον. (Mark omits γάρ and replaces περί by ὑπέρ; Matthew adds at the end: εἰς ἄφεσιν ἁμαρτιῶν; many manuscripts of both add καινῆς before διαθήκης).—I Cor. xi, 25, Luke xxii, 20: Τοῦτο τὸ ποτήριον ἡ καινὴ διαθήκη ἐστὶν ἐν τῷ ἐμῷ αἵματι. (Luke omits the verb and adds at the end: Τὸ ὑπὲρ ὑμῶν ἐγχυννόμενον). The two formulas evidently allude to Exod. xxiv, 8 : Ἰδοὺ τὸ αἷμα τῆς διαθήκης, ἧς διέθετο ὁ Κύριος πρὸς ὑμᾶς.

the words in Exodus, recalled in the formula; and, finally, if we reflect that in all this context St Paul employs the words "drink the chalice" and "drink the blood of the Lord" as being absolutely synonymous, we shall not hesitate to conclude that the new covenant in the blood is equivalent to the blood of the new covenant. In this complex expression Paul and Luke make prominent the effect—the covenant, whereas Mark and Matthew lay stress upon the cause—the blood. We could not, therefore, understand why St Thomas should consider the formula of Paul insufficient if, strangely enough, he did not maintain that the formula of the first two Synoptists is equally so,[1] from which it would follow that none of the four sacred writers had transmitted to us, even in substance, the true formula of the consecration, and that the Eastern Churches had never had a true sacrifice.

Do the allusions to the sacrifice in the different formulas of consecration refer to the sacrifice of the cross or to the sacrifice of the altar? No doubt it would be necessary to accept the former alternative if the future tense of the verb *tradetur* of the Vulgate exactly translated the text. But this word corresponds to a present participle ($\kappa\lambda\dot{\omega}\mu\epsilon\nu\sigma\nu$, $\theta\rho\upsilon\pi\tau\dot{o}\mu\epsilon\nu\sigma\nu$) or more probably does not correspond to anything at all, since the best reading appears to be : "This is my body which [is] for you." This impression is confirmed when we compare Paul's formula with Luke's, "This is my body which is given for you," with a present participle which indicates the simultaneousness of the gift. There is the same phenomenon in connection with the consecration of the chalice. St Paul adds nothing to the mention of the blood of the new covenant, but the addition of the three Synoptists has the verb in the present and not in the future : "Which is shed for you, which is shed for many for the remission of sins." It may be said, it is true, that the sacrifice of Calvary being so near can be treated as being present. Nevertheless, this exegesis has something forced and obscure about it. If it is rejected it will be necessary to admit that the allusions to the sacrifice refer directly to the sacrifice of the altar and not to that of the cross.

This is not the place to point out how this passage proves irrefutably the real presence of Jesus Christ in the Eucharist, or to examine whether the words of Paul authorize the use of Holy Communion under one species. One point only merits consideration. The Apostle states that "whosoever eats this bread and drinks the chalice of the Lord *unworthily,* is guilty of the body and the blood of the Lord;" that "whosoever eats and drinks *unworthily,* drinks and eats his own

---

[1] *Summa Theol.*, pars iii, qu. lxxviii, art. 3.

condemnation, *not discerning* the Lord's body." But the unworthy reception of it has infinite degrees of guilt, from irreverence to sacrilege; and it is the same with the want of discernment, more or less conscious, and more or less guilty. Paul adds that on account of this unworthy treatment and this want of discernment many of the Corinthians are " infirm and weak, and many sleep," and that these are fatherly warnings which they could avoid if they would judge themselves with greater severity. Now, hitherto he has blamed only three or four abuses connected with the celebration of the *agape,* and he gives no other command than that of celebrating this liturgical repast together and with decency. It is, therefore, very probable that by the word " unworthily " he means not only bad dispositions, but also irreverence and a lack of suitable preparation. The severe chastisements inflicted on the Corinthians could lead us to suppose more guilty dispositions, but it will be observed that St Paul does not call them punishments, but simply lessons, having for their object the correction and the salvation of the faithful. But if thoughtless conduct and a lack of respect for the Lord's Supper are punished in this way, what penalties would not a really sacrilegious partaking of Holy Communion deserve?

IV—CHARISMATA

1. Different Kinds of *Charismata.* 2. Prophecy and the Gift of Tongues.

1. When Jesus Christ ascended to heaven he promised to give those who believed in him the power to cast out devils, to heal the sick, to speak in previously unknown tongues, and to render the poison of serpents harmless.[1] His promise had been soon fulfilled. When the Holy Ghost descended on the apostles in Jerusalem,[2] on simple believers in Samaria,[3] on the first Gentile converts at Cæsarea,[4] and on the former disciples of John the Baptist at Ephesus,[5] phenomena of a most wonderful character appeared. The converts of Corinth had been so abundantly blessed with them that they consulted Paul[6] about the value of these extraordinary gifts and the use that should be made of them.

The most imperative thing was to ascertain their source. " No man, speaking by the spirit of God saith Anathema to Jesus, and no man can say that Jesus (is) Lord but by the

---

[1] Mark xvi, 17-18. [2] Acts ii, 4.
[3] Acts viii, 8. [4] Acts x, 46.
[5] Acts xix, 6.
[6] 1 Cor. xii, 1. This formula (*cf.* vii, 1 ; viii, 1 ; xvi, 1-12) shows that the Corinthians had raised the question. It is evident that τῶν πνευματικῶν is neuter, and signifies spiritual things, spiritual gifts, and not spiritual men, the possessors of *charismata.*

Holy Ghost."[1] We notice that St Paul does not pretend to offer a test applicable equally to all periods and places. In times troubled with religious discussions there is always some formula which becomes the password of the orthodox : *Homoousios* in the days of Arius, the merit of works in Luther's, sufficient grace in Jansen's. For St John faith in the Word made man is the criterion of orthodoxy, for all the heretics of that time either denied the humanity of Christ or rejected his divinity, or recognized only an accidental union between the two. For St Paul it is the supremacy of Jesus Christ. To confess that Jesus is Lord is a condensed profession of faith and an epitome of the creed; for that is equivalent to confessing that he is the Messiah, that he is the Son of God, that he is God. Jesus said of the false prophets, "You will know them by their works ;" St Paul and St John say, "You will know them by their doctrine." Hypocrisy may mislead; God alone can see through the mask; but the set rule is enough in practice, and if there is always a possibility of error, it is in such a case harmless. Besides, among the *charismata* there was one, the discernment of spirits, specially meant to ascertain the supernatural origin of these spiritual gifts.

We understand here by *charismata*[2] what the theologians call gratuitous graces (*gratis datae*) as opposed to sanctifying graces (*gratum facientes*). They are not distinguished from the others by the fact that they are gratuitous—for whoever speaks of a grace speaks of a free gift—but because, in themselves, they are not sanctifying; they contain only the notion of genus without a specific difference. The *charisma* can be defined as a gratuitous, supernatural, and transitory gift, conferred for the sake of the general good and for the edification of the mystical body of Christ. It is *gratuitous* in the sense that it has no necessary connection with sanctifying grace, and that, not being requisite for salvation, the

---

[1] 1 Cor. xii, 3 : Γνωρίζω ὑμῖν ὅτι οὐδεὶς ἐν Πνεύματι Θεοῦ λαλῶν λέγει Ἀνάθεμα Ἰησοῦς, καὶ οὐδεὶς δύναται εἰπεῖν; Κύριος Ἰησοῦς, εἰ μὴ ἐν Πνεύματι ἁγίῳ. *Cf.* John's formula : 1 John iii, 2-3.

[2] Apart from St Paul and the first Epistle of St Peter (iv, 10) the word χάρισμα is found only in Philo (*De leg. alleg.*, iii, 30), where it seems to be synonymous with χάρις. The Apostolic Fathers and more recent ecclesiastical writers borrow the word from St Paul and, using it in a very general sense, are of no assistance to us (Clement, *Ad Corinth.*, xxviii, 1 : Ignatius, *Ephes.*, xvii, 2 ; *Smyrn. initio ; Polyc.*, ii, 2). It is neither found in the *Didache* nor in *Barnabas*. St Paul has it sixteen times in all, certainly in seven cases with the technical meaning which is in question here (Rom. xii, 6 ; 1 Cor. i, 7 ; xii, 4, 9, 28, 30, 31). Elsewhere it is almost synonymous with *grace ;* the grace of redemption (Rom. v, 15, 16 ; vi, 23), the sacramental grace of Orders or rather the grace of state which is the fruit of this sacrament (1 Tim. iv, 14 ; 2 Tim, i, 6) ; finally it sometimes denotes a spiritual gift different from the *charisma* properly so called (1 Cor. vii, 7 ; 2 Cor. i, 11 ; Rom. i, 11 ; xi, 29).

Holy Spirit gives it to whom he will and when he will,[1] although there is a hope of obtaining it by asking for it.[2] It is *supernatural,* for it is a special work of the Holy Spirit within us,[3] being able, however, to graft itself on a natural aptitude in the individual, as grace in general is superimposed upon nature which it transforms and exalts. It is also *transitory,* for the Holy Spirit gives it and withdraws it at his will; it is transitory in comparison with the theological virtues which are lasting, above all with charity which never falls away; yet it possesses, none the less, a certain stability, in virtue of which a man, habitually endowed with the gift of prophecy, is called a prophet. Finally, the *charisma* is *conferred for the sake of the general good,* as Paul expressly and aptly affirms.[4] The comparison of the *charismata* to the members of the human body, whose function is to contribute to the common bodily activity and well-being, really proves the same thing. Moreover, the gifts are valued in proportion to their utility. The more profitable they are to the Christian community the more perfect they are. Bestowed for the public good rather than for individuals, they might some day disappear without depriving the Church of an indispensable organ.

2. Of all the *charismata* the most extraordinary was the gift of tongues, or *glossolalia.* We cannot say exactly what this was, but Scripture tells us at least what it was not. It was certainly not intended for the preaching of the Gospel. When the apostles on the day of Pentecost " began to speak with divers tongues, according as the Holy Ghost gave them to speak," they did not address the people; they magnified " the wonderful works of God "[5] in the various languages of those present with such animation in voice and gesture that they were accused of being intoxicated. When he has to address the multitude, Peter speaks in the name of all and, being able to speak only one language at a time, naturally speaks his own. But if there was a miracle, it was in his hearers that it was wrought, not in him. As soon as preaching began the gift of tongues ceased. After their baptism, the centurion Cornelius and his family " spoke with

---

[1] I Cor. xii, 11.   [2] I Cor. xiv, 27.
[3] I Cor. xiv, 12, 32 (πνεύματα, by metonomy); xii, 1; xiv, 1 (πνευματικά).
[4] I Cor. xii, 7; Eph. iv, 12 (εἰς οἰκοδομὴν τοῦ σώματος τοῦ Χριστοῦ). However, it does not follow that the *charismata* are unprofitable to those who possess them (*cf.* I Cor. xiv, 4).
[5] Acts ii, 4. At the moment when the *tongues of fire* (γλῶσσαι ὡσεὶ πυρός) appeared and rested on them, the apostles were filled with the Holy Ghost: καὶ ἤρξαντο λαλεῖν ἑτέραις γλώσσαις καθὼς τὸ Πνεῦμα ἐδίδου ἀποφθέγγεσθαι αὐτοῖς.—Acts ii, 11. The hearers heard them, each in his own language, celebrate τὰ μεγαλεῖα τοῦ Θεοῦ.—The preaching begins only afterwards (Acts ii, 14). Then the admiration of some and the insulting suspicions

tongues and magnified God."[1] It was the same with the twelve disciples of Ephesus who, " filled with the Holy Ghost, spoke with tongues and prophesied."[2] None of these people had to preach. Finally, and this is decisive, the man who spoke with tongues was not understood by those present unless there was an interpreter among them.[3]

Summing up all the characteristics of this *glossolalia,* we see that it was the supernatural ability to pray to or praise God in a strange language with an enthusiasm bordering on exaltation. In fact, the apostles chant " the wonderful works of God," the household of Cornelius " glorifies God," the converts of Ephesus " prophesy " in the biblical sense, those of Corinth " speak not to men but to God, and no one understands them when, under the impulse of the Spirit, they utter mysteries," the significance of which escapes their hearers. On the other hand, the excitement of the apostles is attributed to strong wine, and St Paul fears his Corinthians may be accused of madness if they make use of their gift before unbelievers or catechumens.[4]

These wonderful manifestations verified the prophecies, proved visibly the continued presence of the Holy Ghost in the bosom of the Church and symbolized the great catholic unity and universality of the Gospel, which was destined to speak all languages and to gather together all men in the profession of the same faith. But the wonderful character of the *glossolalia,* striking as it did the imagination of all beholders, was bound to make it ardently desired by the converts still imperfect and inexperienced. Paul protests vigorously against this excessive valuation of it, and recommends, on the contrary, the gift of prophecy, which seemed to be less highly esteemed.

In the Old as well as in the New Testament the prophet is one who speaks in the name of God.[5] But while the

---

of others cease. But what appears from the story of St Luke is, that under the impulse of the Holy Ghost the Apostles spoke a *real* language which could be understood by those who knew it (Acts ii, 11).

[1] Acts x, 46: Ἤκουον γὰρ αὐτῶν λαλούντων γλώσσαις καὶ μεγαλυνόντων τὸν Θεόν.

[2] Acts xix, 6: ἐλάλουν τε γλώσσαις καὶ ἐπροφήτευον.

[3] 1 Cor. xiv, 2: Οὐδεὶς γὰρ ἀκούει· Πνεύματι δὲ λαλεῖ μυστήρια. *Cf.* xiii, 2; xiv, 27.

[4] 1 Cor. xiv, 23: ἰδιῶται ἢ ἄπιστοι.

[5] This is the etymological sense (πρὸ φάναι, not *prae fari* but *pro fari,* " to speak *before* someone, in his place "), which is always maintained in profane usage, as well as in the Bible. The prophet, in pagan sanctuaries, was properly one who explained the oracles, or who served as the mouthpiece of the god: προφήτης Διός, προφῆτις Φοίβου, κτλ. It also signified, by extension, "interpreter," as in Pindar (fragment 118):

Μαντεύεο Μοῖσα, προφατεύσω δ' ἐγώ.

Philo (*Quis rerum div. heres,* 51. Mangey, vol. i, p. 510) defines the prophet very well : Προφήτης ἴδιον μὲν οὐδὲν ἀποφθέγγεται, ἀλλότρια δὲ πάντα

prophets of the Old Testament exercised a public function and a permanent ministry, those of the New are prophets in a more private and transitory capacity. These are inspired preachers; but it is not essential that they should be bearers of a revelation in the proper sense of that word. Their specific rôle is to " edify, exhort, and console."[1] If they read the depths of the heart and raise the veil of the future, it is by virtue of a prerogative superadded to their official mission. In the hierarchy of *charismata,* the prophets always come immediately after the apostles, and their spiritual gift clearly fitted them to direct the new-born communities and designated them for the functions of the regular ministry.

This is why Paul advises them to desire prophecy more than the other gifts, especially more than that of tongues.[2] It has over the latter the double advantage of being understood by the hearers and of being profitable even to the unbelievers. Everybody understands the prophet and can acquire benefit from his instructions; God alone understands the speaker with tongues, unless an interpreter comes to his assistance.[3] While the prophet edifies the Church, the speaker with tongues edifies only himself. When he feels himself acted upon by God, he himself is conscious of praising him, but what do those present gain?[4] For what is the use of a language that is not understood?[5] In former times God had threatened to make his unbelieving people hear a strange tongue which they would not understand. Should men boast so much of a privilege promised to unbelief?[6] And if only *glossolalia* would convert unbelievers! But they treat it with mockery, as they did on the day of Pentecost.

> If therefore the whole church come together into one place, and all speak with tongues, and there come in catechumens or infidels, will they not say that you are mad? But if all prophesy, and there come in one that believeth not, or a catechumen, he is convinced of all, he is judged of all. The secrets of his heart are made manifest ; and so, falling down on his face, he will adore God, affirming that God is among you indeed.[7]

ὑπηχοῦντος ἑτέρου. This use of the word is very striking in the passage of Exodus (vii, 1), where Moses objects that he does not know how to speak in public. God replies to him : " I have appointed thee the God of Pharaoh, and Aaron thy brother shall be thy prophet;" that is to say : Thou shalt treat with Pharaoh through an intermediary, as God treats with men, and Aaron shall serve you as interpreter.—But in order to be the mouthpiece of God, it is necessary that the prophet should be initiated into the secrets of God, that he should be inspired ; so he is also a " seer," and is believed to know mysteries and even the future.

[1] xiv, 3.   [2] xiv, 1.   [5] xiv, 5.
[4] xiv, 3, 4.   [5] xiv, 19.   [6] xiv, 21-22.
[7] xiv, 23-25. We can hardly give to ἰδιώτης any other sense than " catechumen," since he is neither a believer yet nor an unbeliever. Note that *prophets* are thought to be able to read the heart.

As the use of the gift of prophecy can be itself subject to abuses, St Paul regulates that gift as well as the gift of tongues. Three counsels are addressed to speakers with tongues, and two to the prophets : if the former are numerous, let two only, or at most three, speak at each meeting. Let them not all speak at once, but one after another; and let an assistant, endowed with the *charisma* of interpretation, or acquainted with the language spoken, explain what they say. If there is no interpreter present, let the *glossolalos* keep silent in public and talk with God in a low voice.[1] The following arrangements regulate the use of prophecy : two or three prophets at each meeting shall exhort the people in turn; the others, or those of the faithful who are endowed with the *charisma* of discerning spirits, will judge of their inspiration and their doctrine. If, while one is speaking, another feels himself inspired, the first, through deference and modesty, will yield the floor to him.[2] The Apostle sums up his advice in one word : " Let everything be done decently and in order."[3]

In their desire to parade their spiritual gifts, the Corinthians were too apt to lose sight of the fact that the *charismata* do not add or attribute an atom of merit to the man who possesses them, and that they are conferred upon him less for his particular benefit than for the general good of the Church. To exhibit them with complacency, therefore, is childish. The gift of tongues, especially, is one of the least, for it must be completed by the gift of interpretation. The speaker with tongues is not understood by others, and, as a rule, does not understand himself; his spirit ($\pi\nu\epsilon\hat{v}\mu\alpha$) is edified, but his understanding ($\nu o\hat{v}s$) is without nourishment. It is not without irony that Paul compares him to a musical instrument, playing an unknown air which is meaningless to everyone; both beat the air and make it vibrate in vain. Not that it is necessary to despise the gift of God or hinder its development; but it is proper to value these gifts according to their utility. Applying this standard to them, prophecy holds the highest rank after the gift of apostleship, which is not intended for communities already established. However, there is something far superior to the *charismata,* which are, after all, gratuitous favours that God distributes at will, and the lack of which takes nothing from us in his eyes; this consists in the supernatural virtues, because they remain in the soul as long as sanctifying grace abides there, and above all others stands that trio of the theological virtues—faith, hope, and charity. Such is the supreme aim which Paul offers to the ambition of the perfect, and this word charity inspires him to write a page of soul-stirring and almost lyrical beauty.

[1] xiv, 27, 28: ἀνὰ μέρος, " one after the other."   [2] xiv, 29-32.
[3] xiv, 40: πάντα εὐσχημόνως καὶ κατὰ τάξιν.

The special object of the various *charismata* is not clear, but one essential characteristic common to them all is their instability and their absolute dependence on the will of God. This does not allow their being confounded either with the other " fruits of the Spirit " or with the ordinary functions of the sacred hierarchy. No doubt, in the beginning, ecclesiastical dignitaries were often chosen from among the possessors of *charismata*. The *charisma*, indeed, prepared a man for the function, but it was not necessary for it, since sanctifying grace, which is sometimes named *charisma*, is able to make up for it. Finally, if all the gifts were supernatural, as fruits of the Spirit, it does not seem necessary that they should all be miraculous, and apparently the Apostle might have called a supernaturalized natural aptitude a *charisma*.

V—THE RESURRECTION OF THE DEAD

1. Certainty of the Resurrection. 2. Resurrection in Christ and through Christ. 3. Baptism for the Dead and the Firm Belief of the Apostles. 4. Glorification of the Dead and the Living.

1. The dogma of the resurrection of Christ and consequently of our own resurrection is, as everyone knows, one of the pivots of the theology of St Paul. It was also the most difficult to instil into the minds of the pagans. The Apostle learned this to his cost when, from the heart of the Areopagus, he heard loud laughter[1] at the mere mention of a resurrection, and when, preaching the same truth before Festus, the procurator told him bluntly: " Paul, thou art beside thyself; much learning doth make thee mad."[2] Hence, it is not extraordinary that occasional doubts about this matter should have arisen here and there in the Church of Corinth, recruited as it was almost wholly from the ranks of the Gentiles. Some said: " There is no resurrection of the dead."[3] They did not go so far, of course, as to contest its absolute possibility; they limited themselves to denying the fact. If they deigned to make an exception in favour of Jesus Christ, a unique exception justified by the pre-eminent dignity of the Son of God, they thought themselves perhaps in accord with the teaching of the Apostle by understanding, as the resurrection preached by him, baptismal regeneration— a sort of spiritual resurrection.

In the eyes of Paul, to deny our own resurrection is to deny that of Christ, for one is the corollary of the other, or,

Acts xvii, 18: Ἐχλεύαζον.   [2] Acts xxvi, 24.
[3] I Cor. xv, 12: Εἰ δὲ Χριστὸς κηρύσσεται ὅτι ἐκ νεκρῶν ἐγήγερται, πῶς λέγουσιν ἐν ὑμῖν τινες ὅτι ἀνάστασις νεκρῶν οὐκ ἔστιν; note the τινές, they are Christians (ἐν ὑμῖν), and not infidels. We must give οὐκ ἔστιν its usual meaning, " there is no."

rather, one is impossible without the other. To be logical it is necessary either to admit both or to reject them together. But if Christ is not risen from the dead, Christianity is only a lie. Vain is the preaching of the apostles who base their whole Gospel on this fragile support; vain is the faith of the believers, since it rests upon this worthless foundation; the bearers of the good tidings are only false witnesses, calumniously imputing to God a miracle which he never performed. And what would be the consequences for the Christians? If living, they remain deeply rooted in their sins; if dead, they are hopelessly lost; living and dead, their wretchedness is unequalled. Indeed, if Jesus Christ is not risen from the dead, he is neither the Son nor the envoy of God; if he is not the Messiah, he is not the Saviour; if he is not the Saviour, then faith in him and baptism in his name are without efficacy. The result is that the Gospel is nothing but an imposture, justification merely a snare, hope only a chimera, life simply a pitiable dream with annihilation or further misfortune as its goal, nothing beyond the tomb, and in this world suffering and persecutions, aggravated by voluntary privations and fanatical self-renunciations. Such, then, were there no resurrection, would be the destiny of the Christian.[1]

But, again, it is not the resurrection of Jesus Christ that is at stake. It is our own, and Paul is bent upon proving that they are united by an indissoluble bond. We are to rise from the dead *in* Christ (ἐν Χριστῷ), and we are to rise also *through* Christ (διὰ Χριστοῦ). In other words, Christ is the exemplary cause of our resurrection and he is also its meritorious cause.

Daniel tells us that the just and sinners alike shall one day rise from the dust to renew an endless life—for the latter, one of shame; for the former, one of glory. St John tells us that there are two resurrections—the one unto life, the other unto judgement. Paul also proclaimed before the procurator Festus the resurrection of the wicked as well as the resurrection of the just.[2] But in his Epistles he speaks

---

[1] I Cor. xv, 14-19. All these deductions are evident. If Christ is not risen, then faith is, on the one hand, empty and aimless (κενή) and on the other hand null and fruitless (ματαία); the disciples are false witnesses *in respect to* God (ψευδομάρτυρες τοῦ Θεοῦ, objective genitive; *falsi testes* de *Deo*), because they have brought false witness *against* God (κατὰ τοῦ Θεοῦ). It is more offensive to God, according to St Augustine and St Thomas, to impute to him what he has not done, than to deny what he has done. But if faith is vain, chimerical and deceptive, the hopes that it gives and the blessings that it promises are also vain, and we can justly conclude: Ἔτι ἐστὲ ἐν ταῖς ἁμαρτίαις ὑμῶν· ἄρα καὶ οἱ κοιμηθέντες ἐν Χριστῷ ἀπώλοντο. In the latter phrase the Apostle does not say that the soul would be annihilated, if the body did not rise again, but that eternal salvation (ἀπώλοντο) would be lost if their faith were vain and objectless.

[2] Dan. xii, 2; John v, 29; Acts xxiv, 15: ἀνάστασιν μέλλειν ἔσεσθαι δικαίων τε καὶ ἀδίκων.

only of the latter. Applied to the other, his arguments would have no point. How, indeed, could Christ be an exemplary cause for those who have neither received nor preserved his image, or a meritorious cause for those who have trampled his merits under foot?

2. The reasoning based on the *exemplary cause* is presented under two aspects : if the just rise not, Christ is not risen; if Christ has risen, the just will rise also.[1] A bond of dependence unites the two members of these conditional propositions, which must be affirmed or denied together. Now, it is certain that Christ has risen from the dead; the sceptics of Corinth do not doubt that, and, if necessary, Paul's testimony would close their mouths. The inevitable consequence is that the just will also rise. Why so? Because Jesus Christ " is risen from the dead, as the firstfruits of them that sleep."[2] The firstfruits are the promise and the pledge of the harvest; they would be no more " firstfruits " without the harvest which they announce. Even if the harvest is less esteemed and less precious than the firstfruits, it is not of a different nature; it is the fruit of one and the same seed, the product of the same field, the result of the same cultivation. Thus Christ would not have a right to the titles which belong to him, he would not be " the first-born among the dead," and " the firstfruits of them that sleep," if he alone, to the exclusion of his brethren, were raised from the grave. We see easily that the final reason of all this lies in the solidarity of the elect with their Redeemer. " As in Adam all die, so in Christ shall all be made alive."[3] To contract the debt of death in body and soul it is enough to belong to the lineage of Adam and to be one with him by means of natural generation; to receive the credit of life in soul and body it is enough to be incorporated into the second Adam and to form only one with him by means of supernatural regeneration. All those who are dead in Adam in consequence of the common nature received from him will be made alive in Christ on the condition of sharing his grace. We can see how defective this reasoning would be if Paul were speaking of the general resurrection of the dead; limited to the just it is impregnable; it has its roots in the theory of the mystical body so dear to the Apostle. As soon as we are grafted into Christ by baptism

---

[1] 1 Cor. xv, 16: *Εἰ νεκροὶ οὐκ ἐγείρονται, οὐδὲ Χριστὸς ἐγήγερται.* For the positive form of this proposition, see 2 Cor. iv, 14 (*ὁ ἐγείρας τὸν Κύριον Ἰησοῦν καὶ ἡμᾶς σὺν Ἰησοῦ ἐγερεῖ*); 1 Cor. vi, 14; Rom. viii, 11, etc.

[2] 1 Cor. xv, 20: *Νυνὶ δὲ Χριστὸς ἐγήγερται ἐκ νεκρῶν, ἀπαρχὴ τῶν κεκοιμημένων;* xv, 23: *Ἀπαρχὴ Χριστὸς ἔπειτα οἱ τοῦ Χριστοῦ.* The argument based upon *πρωτότοκος ἐκ τῶν νεκρῶν* (Col. i, 18; Apoc. i, 5) amounts to about the same thing. On the contrary, the proof drawn from the " firstfruits of the Spirit " (Rom. viii, 23) is entirely different. It will be explained with the others not touched on here, in the second part of this work

[3] 1 Cor. xv, 22: *οὕτως καὶ ἐν τῷ Χριστῷ πάντες ζωοποιηθήσονται.*

we begin to live of his life, to participate in his privileges and in his destinies, as a branch, when grafted on to the trunk, draws from it nutrition and sap. From that time on we acquire a right to a glorious resurrection. God owes it to himself to raise us from the dead as members and an integral part of Christ. It is not merely a seemly act, it is a necessity in the existing providence of God, and in the present order of things an evident corollary of God's plan of redemption.

The second demonstration, starting from the idea of a *meritorious cause,* is still more clear. No Christian can be ignorant of the fact—for this truth forms a part of elementary Christian instruction—that Jesus Christ was sent to rebuild the ruins made by the first Adam. These ruins consist principally in the forfeiture of original justice and the loss of immortality. If Christ were not the conqueror of death, as he is of sin, he would have accomplished only half his work; " By a man came death, and by a man the resurrection of the dead."[1] Among the number of enemies to be destroyed is death. It will be conquered last of all, but it must be conquered; yet it would not be conquered if Jesus Christ were unable to snatch its prey from death. Only when all that is mortal in us shall have put on immortality shall we be able to sing in an ecstasy of triumph " O death, where is thy victory? O death, where is thy sting?" Jesus would have decisively failed in his conflict with the great enemy if, content to brave it for himself, he had been unable to liberate its victims.

3. To these two arguments, founded on the essential character of the redemption, Paul adds a twofold proof, which he draws both from the personal conviction of the faithful and from the conduct of the apostles. He wishes to show in that way that the resurrection is conformable to the intentions of nature. Moreover, the conviction of the apostles is itself a form of teaching.[2]

A curious usage existed in Corinth and probably also in other Christian communities. When a catechumen died before being so far advanced as to be baptized, one of his relatives or friends received for him the ceremonies of the sacrament.[3] What precise signification was attached to this

---

[1] 1 Cor. xv, 21: δι' ἀνθρώπου θάνατος, καὶ δι' ἀνθρώπου ἀνάστασις.

[2] 1 Cor. xv, 31, 32. *Cf.* 2 Cor. iv, 11-12.

[3] 1 Cor. xv, 29: Ἐπεὶ τί ποιήσουσιν οἱ βαπτιζόμενοι ὑπὲρ τῶν νεκρῶν; εἰ ὅλως νεκροὶ οὐκ ἐγείρονται, τί καὶ βαπτίζονται ὑπὲρ αὐτῶν; whether we put the interrogation point after ἐγείρονται, as the Vulgate does, or after νεκρῶν, as the best Greek authorities do, matters little for the sense. The text in itself is quite clear, and is well explained by Ambrosiaster: *Tam securi erant de futura resurrectione, ut etiam pro mortuis baptizarentur, si quem mors praevenisset. . . . Non factum illorum probat, sed fidem fixam*

act? It is difficult to say. St Paul neither approves nor blames it; he sees in it only a profession of faith in the resurrection of the dead. In fact, baptism, symbolized by the tree of life, deposits in the body a germ of immortality; it completes, by the external rite of incorporation into Christ, the regeneration produced inwardly in the soul by invisible grace; it imprints upon the Christian an indelible seal which will cause him to be recognized at the last day as a member of Christ. That is the distinctive sign which the Corinthians wanted to supply as far as possible in the catechumens who had died without baptism. Their practice was not, in itself, superstitious; it was a solemn protestation that the deceased belonged to Jesus Christ and that he had lacked the requisite time, but not the desire, to become an effective member of the visible Church. Nor were they mistaken in thinking that through the communion of saints an act of faith and piety on their part could be profitable to the deceased. But there was danger of believing that in having themselves baptized for the dead (ὑπὲρ τῶν νεκρῶν)—that is to say, for their advantage—they had had themselves baptized in the place of the dead (ἀντὶ τῶν νεκρῶν), so as to procure for them the effects of baptism; as if death were not the terminus of the test, and as if the dead could be aided otherwise than by means of prayers. Some heretics, the Cerinthians, Montanists, and Marcionites, fell subsequently into this error and thereby came even to the point of baptizing corpses, though not without incurring the general condemnation of the Church.

Paul and his colleagues in the apostolate pay a more glorious testimony to the resurrection. They die every day through their voluntary renunciations; their life, exposed to so many dangers and privations, is only one slow and continuous sacrifice. All could say with St Paul: "I mortify my body and reduce it to subjection." But if the body has no part in the recompense, why treat it so? Will not the

---

in resurrectione ostendit. *Cf.* Tertullian, *Ad Marc.*, v, 10, *De resurrect.*, 48. When heretics of different sects had adopted this usage and attached their errors to it (*Cf.* Epiph., *Haeres.*, xxviii, 7; Philastr., *Haeres.*, 49 : Chrysost., *Comment.*), the interpreters tried to explain the text differently. They then understood by "dead," either *dead works* (Sedulius, etc.); or our body, which can be compared to a *corpse* (Chrysostom and, in another sense, Theodoret); or the *bodies* of the martyrs (Luther, giving to ὑπὲρ the sense of "on" and supposing that the baptism was given *on* the tomb of the saints); or *Christ* (Lightfoot, etc., taking the plural for a singular); or the *dying*, who are called dead by anticipation (Epiph., Estius, etc., who see in this an allusion to the *clinici*, the catechumens whose baptism was hastened through the danger of death). Others gave to the word βαπτίζεσθαι the sense of "mortifying themselves" in order to aid the dead. Our explanation, which is evidently the most natural, and the only one which does not appear forced, is also the one usually adopted.

maxim of the Epicureans then be right? And will it not be necessary to conclude either that the actions of the body are matters of indifference, or that the hope of a better life is only an illusion? One may object that the soul's survival is enough. But, besides the fact that in the existing providence of God the eternal happiness of the soul and that of the body are indissolubly united, an incomplete state of blessedness of only a part of man's composite nature does not satisfy our aspirations. Moreover, those who reject the resurrection of the body come very near denying the immortality of the soul. St Paul, as well as the Saviour himself, refutes this twofold error by the same arguments.

4. Although the fact of the resurrection corresponds to our innermost aspirations, the way in which it will be effected is somewhat disconcerting to our imagination. We have no idea of an organic body which is eternally incorruptible, nor can we conceive of a sense-life which is unchangeable or of change without alteration. When death has scattered to the four winds of heaven this handful of dust which was once our body, where can we find these atoms dispersed into a thousand new combinations, and how can they be prevented from being disbanded again? This is the objection which Paul foresees and answers in advance. "How do the dead arise, and with what body do they come?"[1] It is evident that our body must undergo a profound transformation; it must be clothed with the form of Christ, which will "glorify the body of our humiliation," our body now in a condition of misery and trial, to make it "like to the body of his glory"[2]—that is to say, to his glorified body. It must undergo transfiguration, if we consider that the personality will be exalted and ennobled without being destroyed; and transformation also, in respect to the new, supernatural form of the resurrected body. The Apostle explains this transformation or transfiguration by the metaphor of the seed. The seed is endowed with a latent life which manifests itself only through previous death and corruption; it is transfigured by perishing, and its life is transformed into a nobler life in accordance with a law of proportion established by God. "So also is the resurrection of the dead."[3] The body of the just man, in which the Holy Spirit dwells, contains a germ of supernatural life; and the transformation common to all the saints does not in any way exclude degrees of individual glory proportioned to the nature and energy of the vital principle. Plants differ in perfection

---

[1] I Cor. xv, 35: πῶς ἐγείρονται οἱ νεκροί; ποίῳ δὲ σώματι ἔρχονται ; We think that πῶς contains the general question as to the *manner* of the resurrection, and ποίῳ σώματι the special question of the *quality* of the risen bodies.

[2] Phil. iii, 21.   [3] I Cor. xv, 42.

and stars in brilliancy. What is there, then, surprising in the same thing holding true of the elect?

St Paul expressly teaches that our body, both in its humble condition and also in its glorified state, remains identical; he affirms that " this corruptible body must put on incorruption, and this mortal body must put on immortality."[1] We must not push too far the comparison of the seed, so as to maintain that there is a change in substance, for this would be equivalent to the production of another individual. The Apostle does not decide whether the grain and the plant have, or do not have, the same vital principle; for him these biological questions have little interest. His comparison refers only to the continuation of life beyond death, and he knows that the force which will transfigure and transform our body to the point of making it like the glorified body of Jesus Christ is always the same, notwithstanding the diversity of its effects and manifestations. It is the divine Πνεῦμα.

However profoundly mysterious it may be, the renewal of our being does not go so far as the creation of a new personality. The body " is sown in corruption, it is raised in incorruption; it is sown in dishonour, it is raised in glory; it is sown in weakness, it is raised in power; it is sown a natural body, it is raised a spiritual body."[2] From corruptible it becomes incorruptible and consequently immortal; from abject, vile, and subject to the most humiliating necessities, it becomes worthy of honour and respect, clothed with a beauty which reflects the restored image of God and the brilliancy of a glorified soul; from powerless, infirm, and subject to all the limitations of its nature and to all the lapses of sin it becomes superior to the elements, a victor over time, and a master of space; from carnal and terrestrial it becomes " spiritual," not aerial or ethereal, in the etymological sense of spirit, nor even like celestial spirits in its manner of being and acting, however alluring this explanation may appear, but dominated by the Spirit of God which animates it in its supernatural life, just as the soul moves it and penetrates it in its sensible life. The spiritual body is a body resembling the glorified body of Jesus. By virtue of natural generation, we inherit from the first Adam a terrestrial body (χοϊκόν) and a natural body (ψυχικόν) which weighs down the soul and fetters it in its operations; but by virtue of our supernatural descent we shall receive from the second Adam a celestial (ἐπουράνιον) body, a spiritual (πνευματικόν) body, like unto his own.[3] The characteristics of the body of Jesus Christ—immunity from suffering, brightness, and perfect liberty of action and movement—will be

[1] I Cor. xv, 53. [2] I Cor. xv, 42-44.
[3] I Cor. xv, 45-49.

ours also. That is all that revelation teaches us in regard
to it.

But Paul reminds the Corinthians that their curiosity is
mistaken in its object. They wish to know how risen bodies
will be formed; now the transformation of the living is
neither less marvellous nor less difficult to comprehend; for
" flesh and blood shall not inherit the kingdom of God."[1]
A change, equivalent to a complete transformation, is
necessary :

> Behold I tell you a mystery. We shall not all die (sleep), but
> we shall all be changed, in a moment, in the twinkling of an eye,
> at the last trumpet ; for the trumpet shall sound, and the dead shall
> rise again incorruptible ; and we shall be changed. For this corruptible
> must put on incorruption and this mortal must put on immortality.[2]

Admirable and truly mysterious is this secret which Paul
is charged to transmit to the faithful, and which he indeed
does communicate to them in three of his Epistles : " We
shall not all die, but we shall all be changed." The just
of those last days will not know death; incorruptibility will
envelop them like a mantle of glory without extinguishing
in them the spark of life. All the mortal in them will be
swallowed up in immortality at that one instant ($\dot{\epsilon}\nu$ $\dot{a}\tau\acute{o}\mu\phi$)
which the lightning-like coming of Christ shall reveal in a
flash.

Jesus Christ, the exemplary and meritorious cause of the
resurrection of the just, together with the invincible conviction of the faithful and the infallible certainty of the apostles,
these are not the only proofs of our resurrection which Paul
urges. Elsewhere he speaks of Jesus Christ, the first-born
among the dead, of the earnest of the Holy Spirit and the
supernatural desire with which He inspires us, of His indwelling in the soul and body of every Christian as in a

---

[1] 1 Cor. xv, 50.

[2] 1 Cor. xv, 51-53 : Ἰδοὺ μυστήριον ὑμῖν λέγω· πάντες (μεν) οὐ
κοιμηθησόμεθα, πάντες δὲ ἀλλαγησόμεθα. One cannot reasonably doubt that
such is the true reading. It is that of all the minuscule manuscripts
except one, and of the uncial MSS., BKLP (and D by the third hand), and
the great mass of the Greek and Syrian Fathers and of almost all the versions.
It is also the only one that suits the context and agrees with the words οἱ
νεκροὶ ἐγερθήσονται ἄφθαρτοι καὶ ἡμεῖς ἀλλαγησόμεθα. St Jerome preferred
it (Epist., cxix, 5-7, vol. XXII, 968-973) although in the Vulgate he
kept the ancient Latin version which takes for granted the reading: πάντες
μὲν ἀναστησόμεθα, οὐ πάντες δὲ ἀλλαγησόμεθα, the only authority for which
is the Greco-Latin Codex D (Claromontanus) of the sixth century. As
for the reading, πάντες μὲν κοιμηθησόμεθα, οὐ πάντες δὲ ἀλλαγησόμεθα,
adopted by one minuscule MS. (No. 17), three uncial MSS. (Ν, C, F) and the
Armenian version, all the convergent indications show it to be a dogmatic
correction. The negation was changed in place through failure to remember
that Paul is not speaking here of sinners, but of two categories of the just,
all of whom, living and dead, are to undergo a transformation in order to
reign with Jesus Christ

temple, and of grace, the seed of glory. These connected arguments, the many aspects of which we shall still have to examine, cannot but meet at some points, and must sometimes interpenetrate one another; however, they show at least the richness of the Apostle's perceptions and the vast sweep of his horizons.

CHAPTER III

THE SECOND EPISTLE TO THE CORINTHIANS

I—Misunderstandings

1. Historical Sketch. 2. Complaints against Paul. 3. Vindication.

1.   PAUL has written nothing more eloquent, more heartfelt, or more passionate than this Epistle. Sadness and joy, fear and hope, tenderness and indignation vibrate through its pages with equal intensity. The art of exalting the most ordinary incidents by applying to them the loftiest principles of faith makes of it an inexhaustible mine for the lovers of asceticism and mysticism.

In more than three years since his departure from Corinth the Apostle had seen his converts only once. This visit, which is not mentioned in the Acts, appears to us absolutely certain; for even if the words : " For the third time I am ready to come to you " may be understood as referring to a mere plan for a journey thrice renewed, we cannot so understand the words " I am coming to you for the third time " and still less " I repeat, now that I am absent, as I did when I was present the second time, that if I come again I will not pardon." To explain such words by an imaginary presence and by plans never carried into effect seems to us contrary to sound exegesis.[1]

---

[1] 2 Cor. xii, 14 : τρίτον τοῦτο ἑτοίμως ἔχω ἐλθεῖν πρὸς ὑμᾶς. We must take into account the whole context, which seems to require more than a series of mere projects. 2 Cor. xiii, 1-2 : τρίτον τοῦτο ἔρχομαι πρὸς ὑμᾶς. . . . προείρηκα καὶ προλέγω, ὡς παρὼν τὸ δεύτερον καὶ ἀπὼν νῦν. These texts seem sufficiently clear to need no commentary. The character of the second visit to Corinth is impossible to determine. If, in the phrase (2 Cor. ii, 1) Ἔκρινα δὲ ἐμαυτῷ τοῦτο, τὸ μὴ πάλιν ἐν λύπῃ πρὸς ὑμᾶς ἐλθεῖν, the word πάλιν refers to ἐν λύπῃ, it would have been accompanied by sadness ; but πάλιν may refer to ἐλθεῖν, or the Apostle may allude to his *first* arrival when he had left Athens. To conclude from 2 Cor. xii, 21, μὴ πάλιν ἐλθόντος μου ταπεινώσῃ με ὁ Θεός μου, that Paul had then to endure a humiliation, is to read too much between the lines, for πάλιν is too far from ταπεινώσῃ to qualify this verb. With much more reason may we infer from 2 Cor. xiii, 2, Ἐὰν ἔλθω εἰς τὸ πάλιν οὐ φείσομαι, that he had then to use indulgence, for πάλιν may refer to οὐ φείσομαι as well as to ἐλθεῖν On the other hand, the Apostle wishes by his visit to bring a second cause for joy (2 Cor. i, 15): ἵνα δευτέραν χαρὰν σχῆτε. The preceding visit had, therefore, been considered as a favour.—A text not much noticed (1 Cor. xvi, 7), οὐ θέλω γὰρ ὑμᾶς ἄρτι ἐν παρόδῳ ἰδεῖν, proves (a) that this second visit was short; (b) that it preceded the first Epistle to the Corinthians.— Paul, in announcing for *this time* (ἄρτι) a longer visit, evidently does not allude to his first sojourn at Corinth, which lasted eighteen months.

Upon this journey to Corinth a little romance has been built, the details of which vary according to the taste and imagination of the critics, but the usual version of it is as follows. Timothy, who had been sent to Corinth to silence objectors there, had pitiably failed. Paul then goes thither himself in the hope of restoring order, but even he also " experienced a reverse; his words are powerless; his enemies triumph. He is publicly insulted and has to retire to Ephesus, his soul overwhelmed with apostolic sadness in which anger mingles with regrets. From Ephesus he resumes the conflict; he writes to the Corinthians a terrible letter (now lost), the excessive terms of which he, for a moment, regretted, and he now sends Titus, whose conciliatory spirit and great personal authority may perhaps bring about a change. Paul's letter, supported by the words of Titus, caused a touching revival of affection and gratitude among the Corinthians. The majority of the Church, in a solemn assembly, condemned the man who had insulted the Apostle, and decided to send Paul, in writing and through the medium of Titus, unequivocal apologies and proofs of regret for the past, fervid affection for the present, and of confidence for the future."[1]

These ingenious fancies would not be worth mentioning were it not for the notoriety of the names identified with them. As one conjecture suggests another, when the hypotheses have all been exhausted, the tangle of more and more complicated and improbable theories increases. Instead of one lost letter, certain critics claim two. They insist that two journeys must have been made by Titus. But by dint of mixing up the correspondence and multiplying the various comings and goings, they are forced to lengthen the interval between our two Epistles by a whole year, and this gives a death-blow to the whole theory.[2] A *recent* visit of Paul is inadmissible. On the contrary, one of the principal complaints of the malcontents was his prolonged absence. They say he promises to come and does not keep his word; that he seems afraid to show himself; and that he prefers to settle differences from a distance. These reproaches would have no sense if the Corinthians had received a visit from him in the interval between our two Epistles. He replies that he has deferred it out of pity for the guilty ones, and that he wished to keep away as long as the misunderstandings lasted; but that he will not wait much longer, and will treat

[1] Sabatier, *L'Apôtre Paul*[3], 1896, pp. 172-173. The author declares (p. 163, note) that he has been led to modify his ideas completely through the study of Weizsäcker, who indeed (*Das apostolische Zeitalter*[3]) *reconstructs* this romantic drama almost in the same way.

[2] For an exposé and criticism of the different systems, see Heinrici, *Der zweite Brief an die Korinther*[8], 1900 (Meyer's *Kommentar*), pp. 9-32.

the proud and rebellious according to their deserts. In the hypothesis of a recent reverse and a personal insult followed by a humiliating retreat, this vindication would be nonsense, and these threats, far from inspiring salutary fear, would have excited only contempt.

The hypothesis of an intervening letter, to-day lost, raises fewer difficulties, but it is of less moment than the question whether our second Epistle forms a sequel to the first, and whether in particular the guilty person, condemned by the Church of Corinth by a majority of its members, is the man guilty of incest, whose punishment the Apostle had demanded. For our part, we see nothing in the second Epistle which obliges us to suppose a lost letter, and we think that this hypothesis gives rise to many more difficulties than it solves. The scandalous connivance of the Corinthians had pained Paul enough, and their subterfuges had injured his rightful position as an apostle and father sufficiently to make it unnecessary for us to suppose a personal insult as well. His first Epistle contained reproaches sharp enough, orders sufficiently severe, and expressions of enough harshness to make Paul, who knew by experience their sensitiveness, their tendency to be suspicious, and their spirit of insubordination, fear its bad results, and for an instant regret having written it. In a previous instance much less had been necessary on his part to alienate their hearts, and he had just learned that a new outbreak had made its appearance in Corinth among those foreign intriguers, those false apostles, those fomenters of misfortune, and those agents of Satan, who were determined to destroy his work. To suppose that his first Epistle must not have cost Paul many tears is not to understand his heart.

In spite of its undeniable unity, concerning which the best judges are now agreed, our Epistle offers this curious peculiarity, that each of its three parts forms a complete whole by itself, without any apparent connecting bond. The following headings sum up the subject sufficiently well : The Misunderstandings (i-vii); The Collection (viii-ix); The Adversaries (x-xiii).

2. The malcontents of Corinth took up arms against the Apostle for a very frivolous grievance. They accused him of fickleness and inconstancy in his plans for travelling. Before the difficulties, of which the two Epistles give us the echo, Paul had intended to go by sea to Corinth and, after a tour among the churches of Macedonia, to return thither to wait for a ship which was to convey him to Palestine.[1]

---

[1] 2 Cor. i, 15-16: Ἐβουλόμην πρότερον πρὸς ὑμᾶς ἐλθεῖν . . . καὶ δι ὑμῶν διελθεῖν εἰς Μακεδονίαν, καὶ πάλιν, κτλ. The πρότερον refers to the period before the dissensions, when their mutual confidence had not

His plans, for reasons unknown to us, were completely changed in the spring of the year 56 A.D., just when he was writing our first Epistle. He then proposed to celebrate Pentecost at Ephesus, then to go by land and, crossing Asia in short stages with a rather more prolonged stay in Macedonia, to arrive in Corinth towards the end of the summer.[1] The unforeseen uprising of the silversmiths and sculptors at Ephesus must have necessitated his speedy departure from that city. The result of this was that Titus, sent by him to Corinth and whom he hoped to find again in Troas, was not yet there. Paul, therefore, went to wait for him in Macedonia, probably at Philippi; and, as he did not wish to appear again in person at Corinth before all the difficulties there had been settled, he consigned to him our second Epistle.[2] Now the new itinerary which he announced to the Corinthians in his first Epistle had been a surprise and a disappointment to them. They had counted on seeing him sooner. In vain did he hold out to them the prospect of a longer sojourn as a brilliant compensation : " And with you perhaps I shall abide or even spend the winter; . . . for I will not see you now by the way, for I trust that I shall abide with you some time, if the Lord permit."[3] In vain did he insist on the necessity of again first seeing the Macedonians, a visit to whom, in the first plan, had been placed after that to Corinth. Already tampered with, doubtless, by the ringleaders of the plot, the converts did not accept these explanations. " What do these delays mean?" they ask. " Why should he promise something if he is not sure of keeping his promise?" " Did I use lightness," asks Paul, " when I was thus minded? Or the things that I purpose, do I purpose according to the flesh, that there should be with me ' yea ' and ' nay '? But God is faithful, for our preaching which was to you was not ' yea ' and ' nay.' "[4] If he has deferred his visit it was out of compassion for them. He would have had to be severe, and he does not wish that his return to them should be clouded by sadness. He has, therefore, given the clouds time to disperse.

To this ridiculous grievance were added reproaches much

---

been troubled by any discord and when he could truthfully say: καύχημα ὑμῶν ἐσμεν καθάπερ καὶ ὑμεῖς ἡμῶν (2 Cor. i, 14). Note the transition between this phrase and the following : καὶ ταύτῃ τῇ πεποιθήσει ἐβουλόμην, and observe the reasons for deferring the journey, which will be subsequently mentioned.

[1] I Cor. xvi, 5-9. Here the Apostle tacitly retracts a plan previously formed, which was known by the Corinthians : " Now I will come to you, when I have passed through Macedonia ; *for I am passing through Macedonia.*" This remark would be singular, if the passing through Macedonia had not something unexpected in it and contrary to the hope of the faithful.

[2] 2 Cor. ii, 12-13 ; vii, 6 ; xiii, 10.

[3] I Cor. xvi, 6-7.   [4] 2 Cor. i, 17-18.

more serious. Paul was accused of duplicity in his preaching, of arrogance in his language, and of tyranny in his
administration. The imputations of the evil-disposed persons,
recalled here and there by Paul ironically, serve us as land-
marks in our pursuit of a thought, the thread of which
slackens at times, but never breaks. Paul's defence, which
never descends to petty questions of persons and maintains
itself at a serene height, can be summed up thus : The Apostle
proceeds with head erect and without dissimulation or ·con-
cealment, because he has the honour of being the messenger
of the Gospel. What is called arrogance is only the legitimate consciousness of his dignity, and of the fact that his
real strength lies in his weakness. He speaks and acts
boldly, but his quality as ambassador of Christ authorises
this apostolic liberty.

3. Disloyalty, knavery, policy, offensive names, and absurd
suspicions directed against this man—such, indeed, were the
precise terms in which he was accused. They found insinua-
tions, intentional ambiguities, and the finesse of a trickster
in his letters; and he replies : " We do not write to you any
other things than you are able to read and understand. I
hope that you will understand at last. . . . We are not as
many, adulterating the word of God, but with sincerity, as
from God, before God and in Christ we speak."[1] The contrast is between the sincerity of the Apostle, who preaches
the word of God as it really is without any mingling of what
is foreign to it or falsification of any sort, and the dishonest
tricks of those intruders who accommodate it to the taste of
their hearers, as innkeepers adulterate their wine ($\kappa\alpha\pi\eta\lambda\epsilon\acute{u}o\nu\tau\epsilon\varsigma$)
by means of skilful dilutions or suspicious mixtures in order
to get more money out of it. We see that sincerity is the
word needed here. How could an apostle of Jesus Christ be
wanting in integrity? Ought he to blush for his mandate or
to falsify his message? The ministry of the old covenant
flooded the face of Moses with such a dazzling light that the
children of Israel could not bear its splendour; but that was
only the ministry of the letter, while the Gospel is the ministry
of the spirit; that was the ministry of condemnation, while
the Gospel is the ministry of justification; that was the
ministry of servitude, while the Gospel is that of freedom; that
was the ministry of fear, but the Gospel is that of filial confidence; that was a ministry destined to end, while the Gospel
is to endure for ever.[2] Let Moses cover his face with a veil

---

[1] 2 Cor. ii, 17 : $O\dot{u}$ $\gamma\acute{a}\rho$ $\dot{\epsilon}\sigma\mu\epsilon\nu$ $\dot{\omega}s$ $o\acute{\iota}$ $\pi o\lambda\lambda o\grave{\iota}$ $\kappa\alpha\pi\eta\lambda\epsilon\acute{u}o\nu\tau\epsilon\varsigma$ $\tau\grave{o}\nu$ $\lambda\acute{o}\gamma o\nu$ $\tauo\hat{u}$ $\Theta\epsilon o\hat{u}$,
$\dot{a}\lambda\lambda$' $\dot{\omega}s$ $\dot{\epsilon}\xi$ $\epsilon\grave{\iota}\lambda\iota\kappa\rho\iota\nu\acute{\iota}as$ . . . $\lambda\alpha\lambda o\hat{u}\mu\epsilon\nu$. Note the great number of synonyms
expressing these connected ideas: sincerity ($\epsilon\grave{\iota}\lambda\iota\kappa\rho\iota\nu\acute{\iota}a$, i, 12; ii, 17);
confidence ($\pi\epsilon\pi o\acute{\iota}\theta\eta\sigma\iota s$, i, 15; iii, 4; x, 2); frankness ($\pi\alpha\rho\rho\eta\sigma\acute{\iota}a$, iii, 12;
vii, 4); courage ($\theta\alpha\rho\rho\hat{\omega}$, v, 6-8; vii, 16; x, 1-2); liberty ($\dot{\epsilon}\lambda\epsilon\upsilon\theta\epsilon\rho\acute{\iota}a$, iii, 7).
[2] 2 Cor. iii, 6-16.

when speaking to the people—well and good ! Let this veil
of Moses pass over the eyes and hearts of all who read him ;
so be it ! But Moses himself, when he turned towards the
Lord, threw his veil far from him ; and his blind disciples at
the consummation of time will tear off theirs also when they
shall be converted to Jesus Christ. For us, the preachers of
the law of grace, every sort of veil would be unseemly :

> But we all, beholding the glory of the Lord with open face, are
> transformed into the same image from glory to glory, as by the spirit
> of the Lord. Therefore, seeing we have this ministration, according
> as we have obtained mercy, we faint not ; but we renounce the hidden
> things of dishonesty, not walking in craftiness, nor adulterating the
> word of God ; but by manifestation of the truth commending ourselves
> to every man's conscience in the sight of God. And if our Gospel be
> also hid, it is hid to them that are lost, in whom the God of this world
> hath blinded the minds of unbelievers, that the light of the Gospel
> of the glory of Christ, who is the image of God, should not shine unto
> them.[1]

The other two complaints are so intimately connected and
touch each other at so many points that we can hardly
separate them. Hence the Apostle refutes them together
without dividing them. What his enemies treat as arrogance
and vainglory is only a just appreciation of his sacred
character ; and what they call tyranny and excess of power
is merely the obligatory exercise of his apostolic mandate :

> And such confidence we have through Christ in God. Not that
> we are *sufficient* to think anything of ourselves, as of ourselves ; but
> our *sufficiency* is from God, who hath also *made us sufficient* ministers
> of the new covenant.[2]

He has just spoken of himself in terms that might cause
him to be accused of conceit and presumption.[3] He excuses

---

[1] 2 Cor. iii, 18–iv, 4.

[2] 2 Cor. iii, 4-6 : Πεποίθησιν δὲ τοιαύτην ἔχομεν διὰ τοῦ Χριστοῦ πρὸς τὸν
Θεόν · οὐχ ὅτι ἀφ' ἑαυτῶν ἱ κ α ν ο ί ἐσμεν λογίσασθαί τι ὡς ἀφ' ἑαυτῶν, ἀλλ' ἡ
ἱ κ α ν ό τ η ς ἡμῶν ἐκ τοῦ Θεοῦ, ὃς καὶ ἱ κ ά ν ω σ ε ν ἡμᾶς διακόνους καινῆς
διαθήκης.
The Latin translation, *non quod sufficientes simus cogitare aliquid a nobis,
quasi ex nobis,* might give the impression that *a nobis quasi ex nobis* depends
on *cogitare ;* but in the Greek the position of the words shows us that *a nobis*
(ἀφ' ἑαυτῶν) modifies *sufficientes simus* (ἱκανοί ἐσμεν, or rather the complex
expression *sufficientes simus cogitare aliquid*). It is evident that *quasi ex
nobis* explains and determines *a nobis* which is less precise, ἀπό (*a*) designating the origin of any title, ἐκ (*ex*) marking more distinctly the immediate
source. The verb λογίζεσθαι, translated *reputare* by St Jerome and
aestimare by Ambrosiaster, does not mean simply " to think, to conceive,"
but really " to esteem, to appreciate "; it indicates a practical judgement
directing the action. Note the play upon words (ἱκανός, ἱκανότης, ἱκάνωσεν)
brought about by the question in ii, 16 : καὶ πρὸς ταῦτα τίς ἱκανός ; Paul
uses the turn of phrase which he employs ordinarily to avoid possible misunderstandings : " I do not say that we are of ourselves capable of conceiving anything " (οὐχ ὅτι, *cf.* i, 24 ; not to be confounded with ὅτι οὐ).

[3] 2 Cor. ii, 14-17.

himself with equal tact and wit[1] by saying : No, our assurance (mine and that of my companions in the apostolate) is not excessive. It is supernatural in its source and in its object; it comes *from* Christ, our universal Mediator in the order of salvation; and it tends *towards* God, as to its goal and support. It is, therefore, legitimate, for it is not based upon our own resources, but upon the overflow of divine grace. By ourselves we can do nothing; we are incapable and *insufficient* even to conceive and appreciate the means of fulfilling our sacred ministry. All our *sufficiency* comes from God alone, who has *rendered us sufficient* for our sublime functions. Far from attributing to himself the success of his apostolate, the Apostle asserts that he has need of divine aid even to decide what he is to do, and all the more to carry it into execution.

When theologians deduce from this passage the necessity of grace for every salutary act in the supernatural order, we may well ask if their proof comes from the analysis of the text itself, or if it is a conclusion reached by a more or less intricate course of reasoning. It is well known that St Augustine in his later works understood *sufficientia nostra* of *all* Christians, and *cogitare aliquid* of *every* thought having reference to salvation.[2] In this way the necessity of grace would be deduced formally from our text for our initial faith and all the more for other saving acts. But if, with all the commentators, St Thomas included, we understand *non quod sufficientes simus* and *sufficientia nostra* of Paul and his fellow-workers, and if, moreover, with the best interpreters, we understand by *cogitare aliquid* thoughts which have relation to the apostolic ministry, we arrive at that conclusion only by a twofold parity of reasoning, or, if you will, by a double *a fortiori* argument, legitimate and founded on the literal meaning, but going beyond it. Canon 7 of the second Council of Orange does not settle the question.

From the standpoint which Paul has taken, he has a good chance against his adversaries. The apostles are the depositaries of the Gospel truth. What matters it whether they are or appear to be insufficient from a human point of view? " We have this treasure in earthen vessels, that the excellency (of the results obtained) may be of the power of God, and not of us."[3] Although human nature, destined to become the receptacle of the divine gifts, is in itself sufficiently base to

---

[1] iii, 1-3.

[2] *De praedest. sanctor.*, 2 ; *Contra duas epist Pelag.*, ii, 8; *De dono persever.*, 8 and 13, etc.

[3] 2 Cor. iv, 7 : Ἔχομεν δὲ τὸν θησαυρὸν τοῦτον ἐν ὀστρακίνοις σκεύεσιν, ἵνα ἡ ὑπερβολὴ τῆς δυνάμεως ᾖ τοῦ Θεοῦ καὶ μὴ ἐξ ἡμῶν. The Latin *ut sublimitas sit virtutis Dei* is obscure on account of the position of the word *sit ;* it must be understood as if it were *ut sublimitas virtutis sit Dei.*

justify the metaphor of " earthen vessels," it is probable that St Paul alludes here to the lack of external qualities which would seem to disqualify him for the apostolate : his incorrect style, his insignificant personality, and his infirm body.   Well, the poorer the instrument, the diviner will be the effect which it produces.   Under the all-powerful hand of God weakness brings forth strength, death creates life, and even nonentity becomes fertile.   Paul seems to take delight in this contrast, which has in it nothing paradoxical except the form.   Undismayed, therefore, does he behold his body falling into decay : he is even proud to perceive in it the state of death assumed by Jesus Christ.   This thought lifts him with a stroke of the wing into the loftiest regions of Christian hope.   Death reminds him of the resurrection.   The gradual falling into ruin of this earthly tabernacle recalls heaven's imperishable mansion.   He dreams, therefore, of emigrating from this world to live with Christ.   While waiting for the final triumph, the feeling that dominates him is expressed in the words : confidence, boldness, holy audacity, and apostolic liberty.

II—THE GREAT COLLECTION

1. Gifts for the Church in Jerusalem.   2. Three Reasons for Almsgiving.

1. At the time of the apostolic council, in A.D. 49 or 50, Paul had promised not to forget the brethren in Jerusalem during his missionary work among the Gentiles.[1]   These brethren had lived for a long time on alms, and the sort of communism which they had tried at first[2] could not have increased their wealth.   The Apostle never lost sight of his promise.   He saw in it a proof of gratitude, deference, and veneration towards the church in which the Gospel had been born.   These voluntary gifts tightened the bonds between the two sections of the Christian community, which were too much inclined to keep apart; they revived the brotherly feeling, of which they were the tangible expression; they taught to all generosity and unselfishness; and, finally, they symbolized that great principle of Catholic solidarity, the communion of saints.   The Hellenist Jews assessed themselves every year on behalf of the needs of the Temple : was it fitting for Christians to do less for the centre of their unity?

Paul had already preached to the Churches of Galatia the necessity of a collection.[3]   Those of Macedonia, divining his wishes, had anticipated them.[4]   It was now the turn of Corinth and Achaia.   In his first Epistle, replying doubtless to the inquiries of the Corinthians, he had given definite

[1] Gal. ii, 10.   [2] Acts iv, 32.
[3] 1 Cor. xvi, 1.   [4] 2 Cor. viii, 3, 4.

instructions on this point.[1]   Every Sunday he wanted each
one to put aside his offering, so that all should be ready on
his arrival.   Evidently the rôle of collector annoyed him and
questions of money were repugnant to him.   His precautions
to safeguard his own reputation for integrity and disinterestedness appear to us to-day almost excessive.   He
would do nothing without witnesses, and was not even
willing, alone, to carry the amounts collected to those for
whom they were destined.[2]   At Corinth, Titus had prepared
the way for him by organizing the collection.   The Apostle,
on giving this Epistle to him, charged him to terminate the
affair as soon as possible.   Chapters viii and ix are really
what to-day would be called a charity sermon.   What a
delicate touch he uses in order to suggest his idea without
becoming importunate!   What care and skill are used to
stimulate generosity while avoiding insisting on it!   What
flights into the realm of the supernatural in order to correct
the fatal and inevitable element of the commonplace!   The
word "collection" is not once used, nor the expression
"almsgiving"; it is always an act of beneficence and pity,
a sacred ministration, a means of uniting themselves with
the brethren and of sharing in their prayers; it is assistance
destined for the saints; finally, it is a grace, more blessed for
him who gives than for him who receives.[3]

2. Paul appeals to three motives which rarely miss the
mark: emulation, *amour propre,* and self-interest.[4]   These
feelings are all powerful for good as well as for evil.   They
have only to be rightly directed and introduced into the
sphere of the supernatural.   This the Apostle knows how
to do wonderfully well, and he gives us in these two pages an
exquisite model of this kind of preaching.

He first puts forward the motive of *emulation.*   The
Christians in Macedonia, at the height of their persecution
and in spite of their great poverty, have urgently asked
permission to contribute to the collection: "I bear them
witness that they, according to their power and beyond their

---

[1] 1 Cor. xvi, 1-4.   [2] 2 Cor. viii, 6-16; ix, 2.   *Cf.* Acts xx, 4.
[3] The word λογία (collection) is found in the first letter (1 Cor. xvi, 1-2),
but not in the second.   Here it is εὐλογία (ix, 5), διακονία (ix, 13), or
διακονία εἰς τοὺς ἁγίους (viii, 4; ix, 1), λειτουργία (ix, 12), chiefly χάρις
(viii, 1, 4, 7, 19), but it is a question of a grace which falls upon the bene-
factors.   The most complete expression is the phrase (viii, 4): τὴν χάριν
καὶ τὴν κοινωνίαν τῆς διακονίας τῆς εἰς τοὺς ἁγίους.   Still more to extol
almsgiving and to show its supernatural character, Paul calls it also a
grace of God (viii, 1) and compares it to the *grace* which Jesus Christ has
given us by making himself poor for us (ix, 8).
[4] Emulation (viii, 1-11), *amour-propre* (ix, 1-5), one's own good (ix, 6-15).
The conclusion of chap. viii explains the proper measure that should be
kept in almsgiving (viii, 12-15), and contains praise for Titus and the two
other messengers (viii, 16-24).

power, were willing. They have not only fulfilled our hope; they have given their own selves, first to the Lord, then to us by the will of God." The good example of others is a lesson easy to understand. " O Corinthians, as you abound in all things, in faith, in word, in knowledge, and in all carefulness, moreover in your charity towards us, so in this grace also may you abound. I speak not as commanding, but by the carefulness of others, approving also the good disposition of your charity. For you know the grace of our Lord Jesus Christ, that, being rich, he became poor for your sakes, that through his poverty you might be rich."[1] It is no longer a question of the Christians of Philippi or of Thessalonica. Paul looks up far into the heavens; he opens them and shows us the Son of God divesting himself of his divine attributes and clothing himself with our poverty in order to associate us with his glories and riches. Who could resist such an example and remain deaf to such an invitation?

Self-respect is a more difficult theme to handle, and praise is a dangerous specific for one who does not know in what doses to administer it. Paul reminds the Corinthians that for a year they have been making a collection, and this of their own initiative without any external pressure. "I know," he says, " your forward mind, for which I boast of you to the Macedonians, and I repeat to them that Achaia also has been ready for a year, and your emulation hath incited very many."[2] If, then, the Macedonians, when they accompany the Apostle to Corinth, should find the collection not yet

---

[1] viii, 9: Γινώσκετε γὰρ τὴν χάριν τοῦ Κυρίου ἡμῶν Ἰησοῦ Χριστοῦ, ὅτι δι' ἡμᾶς ἐπτώχευσεν πλούσιος ὤν, ἵνα ὑμεῖς τῇ ἐκείνου πτωχείᾳ πλουτήσητε. It is difficult to read this text without at once thinking of Phil. ii, 6-8 and of Matt. viii, 20 and Luke ix, 58. Poverty is the characteristic note of Christ's life, and his incarnation inaugurates his self-denudation. It is very true that πτωχεύειν signifies " to be poor," not to " become poor"; but just as the aorist ἐβασίλευσεν means " he inaugurated his reign and continues to reign," so the aorist ἐπτώχευσεν may very well mean " he entered into his condition of self-denudation, to continue in it." It is, there-fore, probable that St Paul is thinking at the same time of the denudation involved in the incarnation and of the voluntary poverty which was the consequence of it. No doubt the first act belongs to the divine will and the other to the human will, but this is not a decisive objection, so keen in Paul is the thought of the personal union in Christ. The dominant idea would then be the exchange of heaven for earth (as in Phil. ii, 6), but with an allusion to the life of poverty which followed (Matt. viii, 20). In any case, πλούσιος ὤν refers to the divine nature, and, as it is in correlation with ἐπτώχευσεν, if we understand by this word the incarnation alone, the sense will be : " He exchanged the riches of heaven for the poverty of humanity"; if we understand by it the mortal life only, then the meaning will be : " Being rich, as God, he accepted poverty as man " ; if we understand by it both the incarnation and the mortal life, the sense will be : " Being and remaining rich, as God, he embraced voluntarily the condition of destitution, character-istic of the incarnation, and also the state of poverty characteristic of a life of indigence.   [2] 2 Cor. ix, 2.

ready, Paul would have to blush before them, or, rather, the Corinthians themselves would be covered with shame. It would then be seen how little deserved were the praises which had been given them so freely. Certainly it is not a question of making themselves poor in order to aid others; let everyone consider his own means and give accordingly; what is important is that the offering should be the spontaneous gift of a generous heart and not the obligatory contribution of a miser. The object of the almsgiving is the establishment of a certain equality between Christians;[1] the rich surrender to the poor the superfluity of their temporal goods, while the poor make them the return of spiritual aid by their prayers and benedictions. We see that the tone grows constantly more lofty and brings us anew every moment into the domain of the supernatural.

This last thought prepares us for the third motive drawn from the *advantages* of almsgiving. Almsgiving is the seed of spiritual and even of temporal blessings, and there exists between the seed and the harvest a strict law of proportion. Whoever sows with parsimony must expect to reap sparingly; whoever sows abundantly prepares for himself a rich harvest.[2] Only when it is a question of alms the amount is a secondary matter; what is most important is the charitable intention, the promptitude of the act, and the expansion of the heart. *Hilarem datorem diligit Deus.*[3] The miser may give against his will, by constraint, or out of consideration for others, but he is not thus sowing for heaven. Whoever gives to the poor lends to God. God undertakes to make this loan of value, and he owes it to himself not to let it lie unproductive. " God is able to make all grace abound in you; that you always, having all sufficiency in all things, may abound to every good work. . . . He that ministereth seed to the sower will both give you bread to eat and will multiply your seed and increase the growth of the fruits of your justice; that, being enriched in all things, you may abound unto all simplicity which worketh through us thanksgiving to God."[4] To spiritual benefits and to temporal profits is added also another advantage of a higher and more general character : God is glorified and Christ is blessed.[5] And these prayers and thanksgivings, called forth by almsgiving, return in benedictions on the author of the benefaction. That is why almsgiving is a sacred ministration, an act of worship, a kind of " liturgy,"[6] according to the beautiful expression of St Paul.

Charity, actuated by such motives, is neither burdensome to the giver nor humiliating to the receiver.

---

[1] viii, 13-15.   [2] ix, 6.   [3] ix, 7 ; Prov. xxii, 8 (Septuagint).
[4] ix, 8-11.   [5] ix, 12, 14.
[6] ix, 12 : ἡ διακονία τῆς λειτουργίας ταύτης.

III—Paul's Adversaries

1. Strangers and Intruders.   2. Their Doctrines and Aims.   3. Paul's
Works and Heavenly Favours.   4. The Thorn in the Flesh.

1. Certain critics, struck by the difference of tone which
prevails between the two parts of our Epistle, have deduced
from this a difference of place. They have supposed that the
four last chapters formed originally a distinct letter. No
external proof corroborates this hypothesis, and it has
but few supporters. It is, indeed, very improbable that anyone would have had the idea of mutilating two of Paul's
authentic letters to make them one, the parts of which do
not fit in well. Hence the majority of contemporaneous
critics, maintaining the indisputable unity of the Epistle,
look for some other explanation of the change of tone
and manner. Full of joy over the good news which
Titus has just brought him, the Apostle at first pours out
his heart; he thanks, he praises, he exhorts, he advises, he
again treats paternally his dear Corinthians, who have come
back to a better course of life. The words "console" and
"consolation," which he repeats a dozen times in the first
two chapters, well express the sentiment with which his
heart overflows. Then, finding himself thoroughly master of
the situation, and sure of the sympathy, docility, submission,
and obedience of his spiritual children, he turns against the
agitators and, writing thenceforth in his own name,[1] overwhelms them with sarcasms, threatens them with reprisals,
and hurls his lightnings upon them. A similar course has
been remarked in Demosthenes' *De corona;* but what in the
Greek orator was a subtle refinement of art is in St Paul the
spontaneous inspiration of an eloquent nature.

Who, then, were these intriguers who were following on
the heels of St Paul in an attempt to rob him of the fruit
of his apostolate? They were, in the first place, strangers,
since they needed letters of introduction in order to gain
admission.[2] The Apostle always takes great care to distinguish between these intruders and the community of
Corinth. Although their intrigues suffice to trouble the
entire Church, they form only a very small minority in the
great body of Christians; they are only "some;"[3] the vague
and collective term "one who comes"[4] accentuates still
more their alien origin. They usurp "the work of others,"
and boast of it as if it were their own; they install themselves

---

[1] The letter is written (i, 1) in the names of Paul and Timothy. But
from 2 Cor. x, 1 on, Paul remains alone in evidence: Αὐτὸς δὲ ἐγὼ Παῦλος.
[2] 2 Cor. iii, 1.   [3] x, 2, 7, 12; xi, 20, 21 (τίς or τίνες).
[4] xi, 14: ὁ ἐρχόμενος. In the Vulgate the expression *is qui venit* marks
less clearly the character of the stranger, the intruder.

in the churches already founded, and invade the "domain occupied by others."[1] They are "false apostles, perfidious workmen, who deck themselves out as apostles of Christ; ministers of Satan who transfigure themselves into ministers of justice, as Satan, their chief, transforms himself into an angel of light."[2] Their special characteristic seems to be the love of money. They exploit the Gospel. They adulterate the word of God, less no doubt for the pleasure of corrupting it than through a desire to make more money out of it.[3] They pillage, devastate, shear, and devour the flock of which they take charge.[4] Their covetousness devises a singular complaint against Paul. They blame the delicacy which makes him sacrifice his rights and decline gifts. They attribute it to suspicious motives, to ambition, to distrust, and calculations unworthy of a man of honour. In reality, they want Paul to imitate them in order to be able to justify themselves by his example or at any rate to escape the odium of contrast.[5]

2. It would be very interesting to know what they preached and whence they came. One lately common hypothesis attributes to them a Gospel opposed to that of Paul and makes them emissaries of the Church of Jerusalem. In spite of the natural attraction of novelty and the disfavour associated with old opinions, we are obliged to reject this twofold hypothesis as totally devoid of proofs.

The conjecture of an anti-pauline Gospel is founded solely on the most obscure text of the Epistle. Paul writes to the Corinthians : "If he that cometh preacheth another Christ, whom we have not preached, or if you receive another Spirit, whom you have not received, or another Gospel which you have not had, you might well bear with him."[6] The last clause might be rendered "You would bear" or "You bear well with him." Everything here depends on a variant of one letter, more or less.

---

¹ x, 15, 16.   ² xi, 13-15.
³ ii, 17. The Vulgate translates καπηλεύοοντες by *adulterantes*, but the Greek has an additional idea of illicit gain. καπηλεύειν is literally to sell again, especially as an innkeeper (κάπηλος). Plato in his *Protagoras* amusingly represents the sophists as peddling their erudition from city to city, to sell it and to give it out piecemeal (πωλοῦντες καὶ καπηλεύοντες). Lucian (*Hermot.*, 59) says the same thing of the philosophers, and adds that they cheat, adulterate and give bad measure, ὥσπερ οἱ κάπηλοι. That is probably the idea expressed by St Paul. The tavern-keepers put water in their wine in order to gain more profit, and mix with it other substances in order to make it appear of a better quality or to recommend it to the perverted taste of their customers, but they do not put poison in it. Such were the intruders at Corinth who adulterated and falsified the word of God (iv, 2 : δολοῦντες τὸν λόγον τοῦ Θεοῦ) in order to make money out of the Gospel.
⁴ xi, 20.   ⁵ xi, 7-12 ; xii, 13-17.
⁶ xi, 4 : Εἰ γὰρ ὁ ἐρχόμενος ἄλλον Ἰησοῦν κηρύσσει ὃν οὐκ ἐκηρύξαμεν, ἢ πνεῦμα ἕτερον λαμβάνετε ὃ οὐκ ἐλάβετε ἢ εὐαγγέλιον ἕτερον ὃ οὐκ ἐδέξασθε,

Whatever be the reading adopted, the meaning remains ambiguous and is to be determined by the context. Now, if Paul's enemies had preached another Jesus, another Holy Spirit, and another Gospel, if they had succeeded in seducing the Corinthians from the faith, and if they were still carrying on their underhand intrigues, and were working to ruin the teaching of the Apostle, is it credible that Paul would content himself with replying to them with an irony so veiled that the majority of interpreters do not perceive it? And if there is no irony expressed, is it conceivable that he would limit himself to this cold statement of facts, he who in the Epistle to the Galatians hurls anathemas against whoever would preach a Gospel contrary to his own? Would he make not a single allusion to those wicked doctrines, and no effort to warn the neophytes against error? Would he riddle with railleries the morals of the false apostles, their lust for gain, their childish vanities and unseemly intrigues, and yet not have a word of indignation or blame for their heresies, heresies so fundamental, too, as were theirs? It is claimed that the enemies of Paul were Judaizers, like those who threw the Churches of Galatia into commotion. But the Epistle makes not the slightest reference to judaizing practices. It contains nothing about justification by faith, nothing about the impotence and uselessness of the Mosaic Law, and circumcision is not even named.

The Apostle, therefore, must here be facing an absurd hypothesis, which its very absurdity dispenses him from refuting. If the intruders were really bringing another Gospel, another Holy Spirit, and another Christ, if they were adding something to the spiritual blessings already possessed by the Corinthians, the latter would be right in listening to them. But no; there are not two Christs, two Holy Spirits, two Gospels. The agitators of Corinth are endeavouring to supplant Paul without, however, directly finding fault with his preaching; if they adulterate the Gospel it is less with the design of changing it than of gaining more money from it by means of suspicious additions and clever omissions.

Some exegetes think they have discovered the description of these intriguers. They are Hebrews; they have allowed

---

καλῶς ἀνείχεσθε. The hypothesis is evidently absurd and obliges us to supply mentally: " But, it is not so." Paul gives the reason for this " For " (note this *for*, which refers to the understood negation) " I think that I have done nothing less than the great apostles," and consequently my Gospel is not different from theirs. The translation of the Vulgate *recte pateremini* supposes the reading which we have adopted, ἀνείχεσθε (understanding ἄν, as often happens, as in Rom. vii, 7 : τὴν ἐπιθυμίαν οὐκ ᾔδειν εἰ μὴ ὁ νόμος ἔλεγεν. The reading ἀνέχεσθε, given only by the *Vaticanus* and the *Codex Bezae*, can hardly be adopted. It could, moreover, yield the same meaning.

themselves to be called " superior apostles "; they are at the
head of " the party of Christ "; therefore, they belong to the
mother-church of Jerusalem and are perhaps sent by the
directors of this church in order to counterbalance the influence of Paul. Unfortunately, these honourable titles refer
to the true apostles, not to those agents of the devil. Who
will be made to believe that, in saying : " Are they Hebrews?
So am I. Are they Israelites? So am I. Are they the seed
of Abraham? So am I. Are they the ministers of Christ?
(I speak as one less wise) I am more,"[1] St Paul wishes to
compare himself with those whom he has just called false
apostles, impostors, and ministers of Satan? It may be
replied that he is treating them ironically as " ministers of
Christ." But the phrase has nothing ironical in it. He does
not dispute any of these titles as not being rightly possessed
by them; he simply claims them also for himself. At the
same time he takes a thousand oratorical precautions to have
his boastfulness, and, as he says more than once, his folly,
pardoned. Would he treat with so much honour those whom
he has just crushed with his contempt? And would he give
himself so much trouble to raise himself to their level? Of
course not. In these superior apostles (οἱ ὑπερλίαν ἀπόστολοι)
to whom he is not inferior in spite of his nothingness, Paul
sees the true apostles, the true ministers of Christ. He has
laboured more than they have, he has suffered more than
they have. He is confronted with the great name of the
Twelve. Well, whatever it costs his humility to do it, and
whatever may be the appearance of vainglory and folly that
this pretension may furnish, he is ready to maintain a comparison with them. As a representative of Christ he is
inferior to no one, not even to these apostles *par excellence,*
who are set so high in order to humiliate him.

3. We are tempted to rejoice that calumny compelled the
Apostle to speak to us of himself and to tell us, together

---

[1] xi, 22 : Ἑβραῖοί εἰσιν; κἀγώ. Ἰσραηλῖταί εἰσιν; κἀγώ. Σπέρμα Ἀβραάμ
εἰσιν; κἀγώ. Διάκονοι Χριστοῦ εἰσιν; παραφρονῶν λαλῶ, ὑπὲρ ἐγώ.
To find irony in these phrases, one must put it there oneself. The
Apostle apologizes twenty times for making his own panegyric ; and he
repeats several times that he is speaking as a fool (ἐν ἀφροσύνῃ, xi, 17-21 ;
παραφρονῶν, xi, 23, etc.). The only irony discoverable in these two affirmations : (xi, 5) λογίζομαι γὰρ μηδὲν ὑστερηκέναι τῶν ὑπερλίαν ἀποστόλων,
and (xii, 11) οὐδὲν γὰρ ὑστέρησα τῶν ὑπερλίαν ἀποστόλων, εἰ καὶ οὐδέν
εἰμι, would be addressed to the agitators. Paul does not deny to the
Twelve or to the leaders among the Twelve the quality of ὑπερλίαν ἀπόστολοι,
but he takes satisfaction in putting his *nothingness* on the same sublime
height ; and he repeats, perhaps purposely, the honourable title, which his
adversaries exploit in their effort to lower him. We shall see in the Epistle
to the Galatians a similar polemical procedure : Peter, James and John are
expressly called the *pillars* or the *eminent personages* of the Church (οἱ
δοκοῦντες, ii, 2, 6, 9), titles which the Judaizers bestowed upon them so
emphatically in a sense hostile to Paul.

with the great things which he has done for God, a part of the favours which God has heaped upon him in return.

In truth, the purposely sober and circumscribed narrative of the Acts lets us divine the perils of every sort through which St Paul had to pass, at the hands of robbers, false brethren, Jews, and Gentiles. His apostolic wanderings in almost unexplored regions, situated on the confines of the Empire, among hostile or prejudiced populations, without any display of authority and power, brought with them almost inevitably superhuman fatigue, prolonged fasting, hunger and thirst, cold and privations. We have heard already of the stoning of Paul at Lystra, the imprisonment and beating at Philippi, the hazardous escape from Damascus, the dramatic riot at Ephesus, the precipitate flights from Jerusalem, Antioch in Pisidia, Iconium, Thessalonica, Berea, and Corinth. But nothing made us suspect the three shipwrecks which preceded the one the exciting episodes of which St Luke describes to us, nor the day and night passed in the sea, no doubt on a floating plank, nor the thirty-nine lashes inflicted on him by the Jews on five different occasions, nor the two other beatings given him by the order of governors in spite of his title of Roman citizen, which ought to have protected Paul from such an infamous punishment.[1] All these details, elsewhere omitted and mentioned here only as if by chance, must take from us the hope of reconstructing the entire course of his life with the help of incomplete documents.

But if Paul laboured more than the others, if he braved more prisons, more tortures, more threatened deaths, he was also favoured with more distinguished graces.

> If I must glory (it is not expedient indeed) ; but I will come to visions and revelations of the Lord. I know a man in Christ, above fourteen years ago (whether in the body, I know not, or out of the body, I know not ; God knoweth), such a one rapt even to the third heaven. And I know such a one (whether in the body or out of the body, I cannot tell ; God knoweth) : that he was caught up into paradise, and heard secret words, which it is not granted to man to utter. For such a one I will glory ; but for myself I will glory nothing but in my infirmities.[2]

In this curious duplication of his being, Paul distinguishes the part of God in it, in which he can glory, since it glorifies God himself. He retains for himself only his infirmity, and he glories in that just because it reveals by contrast the wonderful work of God in him.

There is not a perfect agreement about the exact meaning of *visions* and *revelations* here. It is probable that " revelations " is the generic term, including " visions." The Apostle relates only one of them, which he is careful to date exactly, either the more to emphasize its reality and certainty or to

---

[1] 2 Cor. xi, 23-33.
[2] 2 Cor. xii, 1-5. On this difficult text, see Cornely.

suggest that it formed an epoch in his life. It happened, in fact, towards the beginning of his active ministry, at the end of his long retirement in Cilicia, when Barnabas came to take him at Tarsus to make him a co-worker in the flourishing Christian community at Antioch.[1] Unfortunately for our curiosity, if Paul is certain of the fact, he is entirely ignorant of how it occurred. He knows that he was caught up to the third heaven and that he heard there ineffable words, but he does not know whether his body shared this favour with his soul or not.[2] However, even this doubt is instructive. for it permits us to conclude that the vision or the revelation was purely intellectual. If the senses had had any part in it, Paul's doubt could not be explained. The rapture was, therefore, accompanied by ecstasy and a complete alienation of the faculties of the senses. In regard to the rapture itself, commentators are much divided. Some suppose that the Apostle does not know whether he was transported to heaven in body and in soul. In case the soul only had been transported, the body would have remained on earth in the condition of a corpse. But other exegetes, who are supported by the authority of St Augustine and of the Angelic Doctor, find with reason that this change of place is neither necessary nor probable when the soul is alone in question. The soul is ravished unto heaven, when the mysteries of heaven are unveiled before it, and when God reveals to it his intimate secrets. The faithful angels carry heaven with them everywhere, and the paradise of the elect is the happiness of possessing God. But whether the soul of Paul was actually transported through space to the abode of the blessed, or whether heaven was transported ideally into Paul's soul, it is useless to go back to rabbinical fantasies concerning the *seven* heavens superimposed upon the earth. According to a customary form of speech, which would be distorted if analyzed, Paul really said that he had been caught up *as far as* the third heaven—that is, to the loftiest height of divine contemplation.

4. To keep him in a state of humility by reminding him constantly of his weakness, God implanted in his flesh a

---

[1] The second Epistle to the Corinthians was written during the autumn of A.D. 56 or 57, and his being "caught up" would take place in A.D. 43 It is possible to make it coincide with the second visit to Jerusalem, made with Barnabas on the occasion of the famine (Acts xi, 30), but not with the vision which Paul had in the Temple (Acts xxii, 17) at the time of his first visit several years before.

[2] It is to be remarked that the twice repeated phrase εἴτε ἐκτὸς τοῦ σώματος οὐκ οἶδα, ὁ Θεὸς οἶδεν is always taken absolutely, and refers to the subject and not to the verb (ἁρπαγέντα, ἡρπάγη) which it precedes. The ignorance of Paul would relate, therefore, not to the participation of his body in the transportation, but to the *relation of the body to the soul*, at the moment when the latter was favoured with its celestial vision.

thorn or a goad.[1] The Latin *stimulus carnis,* which is obscure and not very accurate, has finally sanctioned an opinion of no great intrinsic probability, which was unknown to the whole ancient world and is hardly reconcilable with the original text. The σκόλοψ τῇ σαρκί—" the thorn in the flesh," or " the goad to the flesh "—it is said, designates an inclination to carnal pleasures, a source of painful and humiliating conflicts. Neither old age, which he was approaching, nor the gift of continence, which he says he had received, put him at all beyond the reach of temptation, and it is impossible to prove that he was exempt from this trial. But without fear of contradiction we may affirm that nothing in his words authorizes such an explanation. Even if it be supposed that σκόλοψ τῇ σαρκί could have this meaning, would not Paul be playing the game of his enemies by revealing to them the existence of such a conflict known to himself and God alone? How could he delight in it and number it among the infirmities in which he glories?

Putting aside carnal temptations, we are confronted by two interpretations which divide the ancient commentators : (1) persecutions and (2) sickness. But it is difficult to understand how external persecutions can be called a thorn in the flesh, and why the Apostle should be humiliated by them is still less clear. These persecutions are so much the lot of the Christian and are so clearly announced as coming to everyone who wishes to live piously in Christ Jesus, that we do not see how he could regard them as a personal preservative, especially against temptations to pride. And how can we believe that Paul prayed three times to be delivered from them?

There remains sickness : " It is said that physical pain made him suffer cruelly ; bodily pains are very often due to the messengers of Satan, but not without divine permission." Thus speaks St Augustine, and almost all modern exegetes are of his opinion. What malady are we to suppose? They have surmised neuralgia, gout in the feet, ophthalmia, epilepsy, and various kinds of fever. This difference of opinions proves that a sure diagnosis is impossible. If it be supposed that in the Epistle to the Galatians[2] Paul alludes to

---

[1] 2 Cor. xii, 7 : ἐδόθη μοι σκόλοψ τῇ σαρκί, ἄγγελος Σατανᾶ, ἵνα με κολαφίζῃ.

[2] Gal. iv, 13. Paul calls the malady which obliges him to remain among the Galatians against his purpose ἀσθένεια τῆς σαρκός, πειρασμὸς ἐν τῇ σαρκί. He congratulates the Galatians on not having repulsed him (*non sprevistis, neque respuistis,* οὐδὲ ἐξεπτύσατε) ; from this certain critics have concluded that he was attacked by epilepsy, the custom being to *spit* on the epileptics through disgust or superstition. He thanks them for having interested themselves in his recovery to the point of being ready to give him their own *eyes.* Whence the conclusion has been drawn by other still more ingenious critics that he suffered from ophthalmia.

Cf. Menzies Alexander, " St Paul's Infirmity," in the *Expository Times,* July and September, 1904. After having criticized the hypotheses of his

the same infirmity, we obtain the following symptoms : the malady from which the Apostle suffered must have been acute and violent, for he designates it metaphorically as a thorn or sting embedded in his flesh. It must also have had about it something repellent, for he thanks the Galatians for not having turned away from him with horror. It must have been humiliating, for he considers it as an antidote to pride and a buffet from Satan. Finally, this infirmity must have seemed to form an obstacle to his apostolate, since he prayed to God three times to be delivered from it, and ceased only on receiving this assurance : " My grace is sufficient for thee."

Whether ulcers of the eyes, malaria, or nervous attacks were the malady, the pathological term is of very little importance to us.

---

predecessors : (1) *Acute Ophthalmia* (Howson, Lewin, Farrar, Plumptre, etc.) ; (2) *Epilepsy* (Holsten, Ewald, Klöpper, Lightfoot, Schmiedel, etc.) ; (3) *Malaria* (Ramsay), the author brings forward his own theory. He thinks it was a question of the Maltese fever, known at Gibraltar, Naples, Constantinople, and elsewhere on the shores of the Mediterranean. The proofs are not very strong, but the criticism of the different opinions is interesting.

More recently a well-known specialist, Seeligmüller (*War Paulus Epileptiker ? Erwägungen eines Nervenarztes*, Leipzig, 1910), has examined Paul's case from a pathological point of view. He concludes, above all against Krenkel, that the malady of the Apostle does not present any of the characteristics of epilepsy. He himself inclines to neuralgia or malaria. Fischer (*Die Krankheit des Apostels Paulus*, Gr.-Lichterfelde, 1911) has tried to answer him. While recognizing that Paul's intellectual faculties were not affected, he makes the symptoms of epilepsy consist in an increasing nervousness and a certain tendency to moral depression. It must be confessed that this diagnostic is very doubtful.

BOOK III
GALATIANS AND ROMANS

CHAPTER I

THE JUDAIZING CRISIS IN GALATIA

I—THE PREACHING OF A NEW GOSPEL

1. The Epistle to the Galatians.   2. Agitators' Attacks upon the Apostle.

1. A CRISIS much more terrible than that of Corinth had just broken out at another point of the vast empire conquered by St Paul for Jesus Christ. We are indebted to it for the Epistle to the Galatians and, also, by its reactive force, for the Epistle to the Romans. At Corinth the infatuation for new ideas was still far from heresy; party spirit did not go so far as to produce schism; the abuses, crying though they were, did not affect the very essence of Christianity; if doubts began to assert themselves in opposition to its fundamental teachings, they were small and circumscribed; it is true, the authority of Paul was threatened, his mission disputed, and his acts and intentions misrepresented, but his adversaries had not yet become so bold as to throw off the mask and preach a Gospel openly contrary to his. The Judaizers of Galatia, further away from the Apostle and seeing him contending with difficulties which he seemed incapable of settling, had this audacity. Our Epistle is the reply to their defiance.

Concerning the date of this letter there is the greatest difference of views among the critics. While some give it the first rank in the chronological order, others assign it the last; the majority place it immediately after the correspondence with Thessalonica; finally, other authors, whose reasons seem to us preponderant, make it go lower in the order of time and follow the Epistles to the Corinthians. We cannot persuade ourselves that a long interval separates it from the Epistle to the Romans. In both the mind of Paul is evidently moving in the same circle of thoughts; there are the same reasonings, the same quotations, and the same theological formulas; only, what is merely outlined in the first is expressed with more precision, fulness, cohesion, and breadth in the second.

The letters written at about the same date—the two Epistles to the Thessalonians, the two Epistles to the Corinthians, the two Epistles to the Colossians and Ephesians, the Pastoral Epistles—have between them close relations of ideas and style. Our two Epistles, Galatians and Romans, compared with each other, present relations still more striking. We remark especially : the identical thesis, expressed in almost the same terms ;[1] the story of Abraham, mentioned twice with quite similar applications ;[2] the theological use of the same three texts of Scripture, serving to support the same doctrinal conclusions ;[3] and finally, a conjuncture of phrases far too frequent not to show a state of mind preyed upon by the same anxieties.[4] These subtle conjunctures, continual and, for the most part, characteristic, appear to settle the question of *simultaneousness*. As to the relative *precedence* of the Epistle to the Galatians, we think it has no need to be discussed. That Epistle is not the resumé of the Epistle to the Romans; it is rather the sketch and first draft of it.

Up to the end of his sojourn in Ephesus, the Apostle seems to have had perfect confidence in his beloved Galatians. It is on his arrival in Macedonia that the ordeal comes upon him from all sides; fears within, combats without, one source of uneasiness after another, afflictions after afflictions. The situation is, indeed, just suited to our Epistle, and, for want of more explicit indications, we believe it to have been written in Macedonia during the period of anxious waiting which followed the second Epistle to the Corinthians. Who were these Galatians, whose sudden danger brings to the heart of Paul so severe a blow? Were they the descendants of those adventurers who came forth from the depths of Gaul in 280 B.C. and swept like a torrent into Illyria, Greece, and Thrace, and, crossing the Hellespont, carved out for themselves an empire in the heart of Asia

---

[1] Rom. iii, 28 ; Gal. ii, 16.
[2] Rom. iv, 1-25 ; Gal. iii, 6-18, and again Rom. ix. 7-9 ; Gal. iv, 21-24.
[3] Gen. xv, 6 (Rom. iv, 3-9; Gal. iii, 6); Lev. xviii, 5 (Rom. x, 5 ; Gal. iii, 12); Hab. ii, 4 (Rom. i, 17 ; Gal. iii, 11).
[4] Among others, compare the following passages :

Galatians.	Romans.
ii, 9 : τὴν χάριν τὴν δοθεῖσάν μοι.	xv, 15 : τὴν χάριν τὴν δοθεῖσάν μοι.
iii, 22 : συνέκλεισεν ἡ Γραφὴ τὰ πάντα ὑπὸ ἁμαρτίαν.	xi, 32 : συνέκλεισεν, ὁ Θεὸς τοὺς πάντας εἰς ἀπείθειαν.
iii, 23 : εἰς τὴν μέλλουσαν πίστιν ἀποκαλυφθῆναι.	viii, 18 : πρὸς τὴν μέλλουσαν δόξαν ἀποκαλυφθῆναι.
iii, 27 : ὅσοι εἰς Χριστὸν ἐβαπτίσθητε.	vi, 3 : ὅσοι ἐβαπτίσθημεν εἰς Χριστόν.
iv, 6 : τὸ Πνεῦμα τοῦ Υἱοῦ αὐτοῦ . . . κρᾶζον · Ἀββᾶ ὁ πατήρ.	viii, 15 : Πνεῦμα υἱοθεσίας ἐν ᾧ κράζομεν · Ἀββᾶ ὁ πατήρ.
iv, 30 : ἀλλὰ τί λέγει ἡ Γραφή;	iv, 3 : τί γὰρ ἡ Γραφὴ λέγει;
v, 7 : ἀληθείᾳ μὴ πείθεσθαι.	ii, 8 : ἀπειθοῦσι τῇ ἀληθείᾳ.
v, 18 : εἰ δὲ Πνεύματι ἄγεσθε.	viii, 14 : ὅσοι Πνεύματι Θεοῦ ἄγονται.
v, 18 : οὐκ ἐστὲ ὑπὸ νόμον.	vi, 14 : οὐ γάρ ἐστε ὑπὸ νόμον.

Compare Gal. i, 15, 16 with Rom. i, 1; Gal. ii, 20 with Rom. viii, 37 ; Gal. iv, 4 with Rom. viii, 3 ; Gal. iv, 13 with Rom. vi, 19 ; Gal. iv, 28 with Rom. ix, 7 ; Gal. v, 8 with Rom. ix, 12 ; Gal. v, 10 with Rom. xiv, 14 ; Gal. v, 16 with Rom. viii, 1-4, etc.

Minor at the expense of Phrygia, Cappodocia, and Paphlagonia? Or must we see in them the inhabitants of Isauria, Pisidia, and Lycaonia—that is to say, of the southern regions of that immense province of Galatia, which in 25 B.C. had succeeded to the heterogeneous kingdom of Amyntas? Very plausible reasons are alleged in support of both hypotheses; but as we decline to determine by the national character of the Galatians the nature of their errors, this question, so vehemently debated in our day, is for us a side issue. Whether Greeks, Celts, or aborigines, matters little to us; it is sufficient for us to know that they were not Jews racially. And it is certain that they came from the Gentiles. Paul speaks always of the Judaism of the Galatians as of something imported from without; he expressly distinguishes his ancestors from theirs;[1] he reminds them of the time when they were free from the Jewish observances with which they wish to burden themselves to-day; when he dissuades them from subjecting themselves "again to the rudiments of the world,"[2] he does not mean that they were formerly subjected to the Mosaic Law; but he lowers the latter to the level of practices dictated by religious instinct; to embrace the Law of Moses is to return to something analogous to their ancient religion. The allusions to a Jewish element among the Christians of Galatia are vague and indistinct. If it exists, this element can include only a very small minority.

So much the more strange is the presence in Galatia of the Judaizers. Whence came these intruders? Whose names did they make use of? What mission did they pretend to have? Were their undertakings sporadic and pushed forward haphazard, or did they form part of a vast plot, a formidable revolt against the Apostle? All that we know is that the emissaries of Judaism preached "a different Gospel."[3] The

---

[1] Gal. i, 13, 14; iii, 23-29; iv, 3-7.

[2] iv, 9. *Cf.* iv, 3 and iii, 23.

[3] Gal. i, 6-7: Θαυμάζω ὅτι οὕτως ταχέως μετατίθεσθε ἀπὸ τοῦ καλέσαντος ὑμᾶς ἐν χάριτι Χριστοῦ εἰς ἕτερον εὐαγγέλιον, ὃ οὐκ ἔστιν ἄλλο, εἰ μὴ τινές εἰσιν οἱ ταράσσοντες ὑμᾶς καὶ θέλοντες μεταστρέψαι τὸ εὐαγγέλιον τοῦ Χριστοῦ. (A) The expression οὕτως ταχέως is not relative, but absolute; it does not mean " so soon " but " so quickly "; it does not allude to the last journey of St Paul to Galatia or to the recent conversion of the Galatians (for this circumstance, as Chrysostom remarks, would attenuate their faul:, instead of aggravating it), but it indicates the *rapid* change which is going on among them (μετατίθεσθε, present tense).—(B) The Galatians are being removed from " him who called them " (ἀπὸ τοῦ καλέσαντος ὑμᾶς). These words do not designate St Paul, for a man is never presented as the author of the vocation; or Jesus Christ (a meaning obtainable by bringing Χριστοῖ nearer to τοῦ καλέσαντος), but God the Father, to whom the efficacious call to the faith is always referred by appropriation.—(C) Although in the New Testament ἕτερος and ἄλλος can be employed as synonyms, ἕτερον εὐαγγέλιον must be given its proper value—viz., " a different Gospel." There is only one Gospel, that of Christ, and the Judaizers do not claim to preach *another*, but they preach it *differently*.

Gospel of St Paul was a charter of liberty in regard to the Mosaic regulations, while that of the Judaizers was a code of subjugation to the Law; the Gospel of Paul was the Gospel of grace independent of works, while that of the Judaizers was the Gospel of meritorious works, independently of grace; finally, the Gospel of Paul was the true Gospel of Jesus Christ, which that of the Judaizers would destroy.

The first tenet of this new " Gospel " was the necessity of circumcision for converted pagans, either as an essential condition of salvation, according to the extreme doctrine of the Judaizers at Antioch and Jerusalem, or, more likely, as a last perfection and indispensable complement of Christianity.[1] They showed forth complacently the spiritual and temporal advantages of it : the participation in the prerogatives and blessings of Israel, the quieting of the refractory Jews, the harmonizing of the two factions of the Church, and the facilities for proselytism under the cover of a lawful religion. Without laying stress on the burdensome obligations of circumcision, they extolled the splendour of the Jewish solemnities, which were all the more welcome to converts, since they made up for the poverty of the Christian form of worship, which was scarcely outlined as yet. However, the majority of the faithful, although disturbed, still resisted the new doctrines. " Stand fast," St Paul wrote to them, " and be not held again under the yoke of bondage. . . . If you be circumcised, Christ shall profit you nothing. . . . They will have you to be circumcised, only that they may glory in your flesh."[2] When he addresses the whole Church, he has always hope and confidence, he hastens to soften the gloomy words that grief draws from him, and he ascribes the attempts at perversion to a small number of mischief-makers. If the Judaizers have already some victims, they have not yet succeeded in making themselves masters of the situation.

The sense therefore is : " I am astonished that you go over *so quickly* . . . to a *different* Gospel, which (in reality) is not anything else than that some people are spreading trouble among you and wish to overthrow the Gospel of Christ." In other words, " This pretended Gospel *consists only in this,* that certain people are seeking to destroy the true Gospel." All other explanations either neglect the delicate difference which exists between ἕτερον and ἄλλο, or do not take into account the meaning of εἰ μή, which forms with ἄλλο one expression, and ought to be separated from it, at most, only by a comma.

[1] Gal. iii, 3 : *Sic stulti estis ut cum spiritu coeperitis, nunc carne consummemini.* " Whether one takes the verb ἐπιτελεῖσθε in the passive, "you are led to perfection," as do the Vulgate and the Greek Fathers, or in the middle voice, " you finish, you crown the work," as most modern exegetes do, circumcision is opposed to baptism as the end is opposed to the beginning, and the completed work to the sketch. This ironical touch lets us understand that the Judaizers of Galatia presented circumcision as the perfection of Christianity for Christians who had come from the Gentiles.

[2] Gal. v, 1-2; vi, 13. See also iii, 5; iv, 11-17; v, 10.

2. Their only chance of success was to ruin Paul in the estimation of the neophytes. They brought three complaints against him.

First, they reproached him with arguing for or against, according to the occasion and the interest at stake. Launching an anathema against his detractors, Paul thus ironically addresses them : " For do I now persuade men, or God? Or do I seek to please men?"[1] As they wished to make him contradict himself by recalling the history of Timothy, he replies with indignation mingled with sarcasm : " If I yet preach circumcision, why do I yet suffer persecution? Then is the scandal of the Cross made void. I would they were even cut off, who trouble you."[2]

Secondly, they reproached him with being only the disciple of the disciples of Christ, and of teaching what he had never himself properly learned. Here is his reply : " I give you to understand, brethren, that the Gospel which was preached by me is not according to man. For neither did I receive it of man, nor did I learn it, but by the revelation of Jesus Christ."[3] They all know, at least by hearsay, the former ardour of his pharisaism and his fury as a persecutor. Not then, indeed, could he have conversed with Christians and gone to school to them. One day he was stopped short in his career and turned about instantly. It had pleased God to reveal his Son within him. Satisfied with this inner light, he hid himself in the desert ; after three years he goes to see Peter, but remains with him only fifteen days ; it is only after fourteen years that he finds himself at last in contact with his colleagues in the apostolate. He is not indebted to them for his Gospel. Jesus Christ has been his only master.

Finally, they accuse him of being in opposition to the Twelve, the pillars of the Church, the principal apostles, as they were called to humiliate him. Well, James, John, and Peter, to whom he set forth his Gospel, found nothing to object to, nothing to change, and nothing to complete in it. They formally recognized his right to the apostolate ; they gave him the right hand in token of fraternity ; they concluded an alliance with him. In refusing to yield to the demands of the Judaizers, who loudly insisted upon the circumcision of Titus, they sanctioned the liberty of the Gentiles. In another case the Prince of the Apostles listened to the counsel of Paul, and did not hesitate to say that he was right. All this proves that there is a unity of principles and doctrines between the preachers of the faith, and that the imputation of the Judaizers, who wish to make out that Paul is a dissenter and a schismatic, is pure calumny.

[1] Gal. i, 10.   [2] Gal. v, 11, 12.   [3] Gal. i, 11, 12.

Thus ends the historical and apologetic part of the Epistle; the central portion of it is that which treats of dogma.

II—JUSTIFICATION BY FAITH WITHOUT THE WORKS OF THE LAW

1. Thesis of the Epistle. 2. Justifying Faith. 3. Justified by Faith. 4. The Three Proofs of Justification by Faith. 5. Paul and James.

1. Paul formulates his principal thesis in the same terms which the Prince of the Apostles had accepted at the assembly of Antioch six or seven years before :

> We by nature are Jews, and not sinners of the Gentiles. But, know-ing that no man is justified by the works of the Law, but by the faith of Jesus Christ, we also believe in Christ Jesus, that we may be justified by the faith of Christ, and not by the works of the Law, because by the works of the Law no flesh shall be justified. But if, while we seek to be justified in Christ, we ourselves also are found sinners, is Christ then the minister of sin ? God forbid. For if I build up again the things which I have destroyed, I make myself a prevaricator. For I, through the Law, am dead to the Law, that I may live to God; with Christ I am nailed to the Cross. And I live now not I, but Christ liveth in me. And that I live now in the flesh, I live in the faith of the Son of God, who loved me and delivered himself for me. I cast not away the grace of God. For if justice be by the Law, then Christ died in vain.[1]

In these incorrect, breathless phrases, bending under their weight of ideas, as difficult to understand as they are im-possible to translate, Paul accumulates all the reasons which militate in favour of Gospel liberty and against the persistent bondage of the Law. He sketches, cursorily, five or six different proofs. Here is the outline of his reasoning :

Argumentum ad Hominem.—Peter and Paul, although racially Jews, have recognized that man does not attain justification by the works of the Law, and, thus persuaded, they have believed in Jesus Christ and given up legal ob-servances.[2] To go back, and to wish to lead others back to it, would constitute an anomaly and a contradiction.

Scriptural Argument.—No flesh, according to the Psalmist,

[1] Gal. ii, 15-21. We suppose, like all the ancient and a large number of modern scholars, that this whole passage forms part of the discourse addressed by St Paul to St Peter before the faithful of Antioch. The beginning (*Nos natura Judaei*, etc.) is certainly addressed to Peter, and not to the Galatians ; and no reason or indication allows us to assert that the interlocutors changed subsequently.

[2] ii, 15, 16 : *Nos in Christo Jesu credimus, ut justificemur ex fide Christi et non ex operibus legis.* Instead of *credimus*, we should read or understand *credidimus* (ἐπιστεύσαμεν), as ancient manuscripts of the Vulgate have it. Peter's conviction that, by embracing the faith, he shook off the yoke of the Law, appears from ii, 14 : Σὺ Ἰουδαῖος ὑπάρχων ἐθνικῶς καὶ οὐκ Ἰουδαϊκῶς ζῆς. It appears also from the fact that he accepts the general principle laid down by Paul (ii, 15).

is justified before God by its own efforts;[1] hence, since the
terms used are general, it is no more justified by observance
of the Law than by any other method.

Reductio ad Absurdum.—It is through having relied upon
the sufficiency of grace and the superabundant redemption
of Christ that the Jewish Christians (and among them Peter
and Paul) have believed themselves dispensed from the Law,
and have acted accordingly. If this fact made them sinners,
their sin would reflect on Christ, the author and the object
of their faith.

Theologico-scriptural Argument.—Through the Law the
Jews are dead to the Law, in order to live to Jesus Christ.
Hence, to regard the Law as still capable of imposing duties,
is to go against its purpose; it is to violate it. This subtle
reason requires explanations, for which this is not the place.

Theological Argument.—The death of Christ, source of all
graces, has an infinite value. To establish any other means
of reaching justice or the perfection of justice is to do injury
to grace and equivalently to deny the redemptive virtue of
the cross.

2. Before treating Paul's thesis, it is well to analyze the
two terms : justice and faith.

Whatever may be the etymology of the word "just," it is
certain that justice is conformity to the supreme rule of our
conduct. Expressing the normal relation between the human
and the divine will, it identifies itself, for the Jew, with the
complete observance of the Law, which is regarded as the
adequate enunciation of the will of God. It includes, therefore, the entire moral life of man. "Just" is synonymous
with "right, good, perfect, innocent"; and its antitheses are
"wicked, impious, sinful." Everyone is agreed on this point,
and the controversy between Protestants and Catholics turns
on the meaning of "justifying," not on that of "just."
Protestants maintain that to justify (δικαιοῦν), in spite of
its causative form, means to *declare* just, but not to *make*
just. They say that this is the usual meaning of the word
among secular writers, and that the verbs of this form are
not causative when they are derived from an adjective that
expresses a moral quality.

To this reasoning there would be much to say. We know
that the idea of a God sanctifying man was completely unknown to the pagans. This is why, in secular authors, "to

---

[1] ii, 16: Ὅτι ἐξ ἔργων νόμου οὐ δικαιωθήσεται πᾶσα σάρξ. It is a slightly
changed citation from Ps. cxlii, 2: Ὅτι οὐ δικαιωθήσεται ἐνώπιόν σου πᾶς
ζῶν. The Apostle here and in Rom. iii, 20 replaces ἐνώπιόν σου by ἐξ ἔργων
νόμου. But he has a right to do so, since the Psalmist, affirming that no
man will be justified before God (by his own efforts), Paul only applies the
universal proposition to a particular case. Note that in the Vulgate *propter
quod* ought to be understood as *propterea quod* (ὅτι).

justify " signifies always " to declare just, to regard or treat as just, to judge," and by extension " to approve " and by a euphemism " to condemn or punish." It will be the same in the Bible whenever this verb has a finite being as subject; for it belongs to God alone to confer justice. But when the subject is God, or man himself aided by God, the verb " to justify " may quite well retain its causative value. Most often, it is true, the part of God in the justification of the sinner is expressed by grace and mercy, and when the just man, whether innocent or repentant, is brought before the tribunal of the sovereign Judge, the justification is only a favourable sentence or a verdict of " no case." But it is sometimes otherwise.[1]

Moreover, it is evident that the judgement of God is necessarily conformable to truth, and that no one can be declared just by the infallible Judge if he be not actually so. When God " justifies the wicked " it must be that he finds him or makes him just, otherwise we should be brought into the following dilemma : either God declares someone to be just who is not so, and himself sins against truth, or else the sinner who is declared just has become so by his own efforts, which is the reverse of Paul's doctrine; in any case, to justify the wicked, while leaving him so, is an impossibility and nonsense. " Paul," writes Sabatier, " would not have had words severe enough to brand such a gross misinterpretation of his thought." Very well; but we are disconcerted to see the same writer attributing " to the scholasticism of the Middle Ages this forensic justification, which only makes God's sentence alike insufficient and arbitrary,"[2] as if all Catholics, scholastic and others, had not always rejected this with horror. Luther, who invented it, did not succeed in persuading Melanchthon, and, in spite of the profession of faith of Smalkalde, the Lutherans have never been able to come to an understanding on so fundamental a doctrine. In order to give some support to such strange theories, they would have to produce a scriptural text, in which the sinner justified by God is still called a sinner. Such a text does not exist. The faithful are called " saints " for the one

---

[1] The Psalmist (lxxii, 13) *justified* his heart (ἐδικαίωσα τὴν καρδίαν μου), which means, by virtue of parallelism, that he purified himself of his faults (*et lavi inter innocentes manus meas*).—The Servant of Jehovah, the Messiah, *will justify* many (Isa. liii, 11) ; which is explained by *et iniquitates eorum ipse portabit.* Ecclesiasticus (xviii, 22) exhorts the reader not to cease to *justify himself* until death. See also Dan. xii, 3. Only an obstinate prejudice can refuse to see in these examples the meaning of "making just." We are forced to omit all the texts which have God for their subject, because our adversaries object to them. But, when the Almighty enters upon the scene, why could not δικαιοῦν from δίκαιος mean " to make just," as λευκοῦν from λευκός means " to make white," or as τυφλοῦν from τυφλός means " to make blind "?

[2] *L'Apôtre Paul*[3], p. 321.

reason that they are Christians and deemed worthy of that title. In them justice is not simply a fiction; it is as real and as personal to them as the sin which it replaces. It is not either merely the prelude of a new life, and as it were the negative side of a divine operation, of which sanctification is the positive complement. It is the new life itself, and is indeed the same thing as sanctification. It is sufficient, in order to be convinced of this, to meditate of these three series of testimonies :

Justification is a " justification of life "[1]—that is, an act which confers the supernatural life. It alternates with regeneration and renewal by the Holy Spirit, which are the fruit of baptism.[2] The Holy Spirit is a " Spirit of life,"[3] because he brings the life of grace wherever he dwells, and he does dwell in all the just; or, as St Paul says again : " He liveth because of justification."[4]

If we turn to the justification that comes from faith, the result will be the same; for " the just man liveth by faith."[5] We cannot imagine a just man who does not live by the life of grace, and consequently we can very well establish a difference in definition and concept between justification and sanctification, but we cannot separate them, nor consider as separated these two inseparable things.

The first effect of baptism is to graft us upon Christ and to make us participate in his life.[6] It is impossible that we should die to the old man without beginning to live to the new. Now this new man is " created according to God in justice and sanctification."[7] Justice and sanctity, therefore, are two equivalent notions; so much so, that St Paul does not fear to reverse the order, and to say that Christ has become for us " sanctification, justice, and redemption."[8] Moreover, reminding the converts of the first moment of their regeneration, he tells them, without any beating about the bush, as if he wished to refute in advance the cavillings of the heterodox : " And such some of you were " (idolaters, adulterers, thieves, etc.), " but you are washed, you are sanctified, you are justified in the name of our Lord Jesus Christ and the Spirit of our God."[9] The unique moment of baptismal regeneration brings at the same time purification,

---

[1] Rom. v, 8.
[2] Titus iii, 5-7.
[3] Rom. viii, 2.
[4] Rom. viii, 10.
[5] Rom. i, 17 ; Gal. iii, 11.
[6] Rom. vi, 3-5.
[7] Eph. iv, 24.
[8] 1 Cor. i, 30. See Eph. ii, 9-10.
[9] 1 Cor. vi, 11 : καὶ ταῦτά τινες ἦτε· ἀλλὰ ἀπελούσασθε, ἀλλὰ ἡγιάσθητε, ἀλλὰ ἐδικαιώθητε. In regard to this text, Liddon, with the approval of Sanday (The Epistle to the Romans³, 1898, p. 38), writes that justification and sanctification can be distinguished by the scholar, as the arterial and the nervous systems are distinguished in the human body, but that in the living soul these are coincident and inseparable things. This is not the former orthodox Protestant standpoint

sanctification, and justification, and this concluding gift is mentioned last to show that it is not merely a means of access to and, as it were, the vestibule of, the other two.

It was fitting that the moral renovation of man should begin with a human act, the product of the two intellectual faculties, reason and will; this act is faith.

Faith is understood by the Apostle in very different ways. It is not proved that it ever signifies "confidence"; all the passages quoted in support of this can be interpreted as referring to a faith in the strict sense of the word, accompanied, it is true, by confidence, a sentiment which faith engenders spontaneously, when it has promises for its object. All the more, then, it is not that blind and unreasonable confidence which would make us regard our sins as being veiled, without being forgiven, and ourselves as being treated by God as just although we are not so. But leaving aside the rarer meanings, good faith, fidelity, the faith to perform miracles,[1] we distinguish in faith, properly so called, the act, the object, and the supernatural habit—that is, we believe in God by faith, we submit our minds to faith, and we have faith.[2]   Paul knows the last sense and still more the second; but when it is a question of justification by faith, it is almost always actual faith, the act of believing, that he has in view.   It must not be imagined, however, that he proceeds here with the strict analysis of a metaphysician, who makes subtle distinctions about the entities of reason.   The psychologist does not consider man under the two forms of a reasoning animal only : he studies him as he is in his concrete reality.   Thus does Paul in regard to the act of faith; he surveys it in its normal conditions of existence and with some properties which its strict definition does not contain.

Faith is a complex act.   It is the amen of the intelligence and the will to divine revelation, presented with the degree of moral certainty suited to historic facts.   Paul speaks from

---

[1] Rom. xiv, 23 (cf. xiv, 1-22) : *practical certainty* being liable to error and having nothing in common with theological faith.—The *faithfulness* of God (Rom. iii, 3), of servants (Titus ii, 10), of widows (1 Tim. v, 12). In this last case the meaning is " sworn faith."—*Faith to perform miracles* (1 Cor. xiii, 2) which presupposes theological faith and superadds to it only a new element.

[2] The first sense—the *act* of faith—is so common, that it is superfluous to give examples of it. The second sense—the *object* of faith—is found whenever faith is opposed to the Law as a providential institution (Rom. iv, 14): *Si enim qui ex Lege, heredes sunt : exaninita est* fides, *abolita est* promissio ; (Gal. i, 23): *nunc evangelizat* fidem, *quam aliquando expugnabat;* (Gal. iii, 24, 25) : *Itaque Lex paedagogus noster fuit in Christo. . . . At ubi venit* fides, *jam non sumus sub paedagogo.* The third sense—*habitual* faith—suits such expressions as " to persevere, to remain, to be confirmed, to live in and to be in faith," Rom. x, 20 ; 1 Cor. xvi, 13 ; 2 Cor. i, 24 ; xiii, 5 ; Gal. ii, 20 ; Col. i, 23 ; ii, 7 ; 1 Tim. ii, 15, etc.

experience. He describes what he has experienced in the crisis from which he emerged a Christian, and what most of his readers very recently had experienced, like himself. One day a herald of the Gospel, with an accent of irresistible conviction, spoke to them of Jesus, of his death, his resurrection, his divine mission, and of every man's duty to believe in him and to practise his doctrine in order to be saved. Illumined and supported by grace, they said : " We believe !" They did not forget that decisive moment in which they had given themselves over, bound hand and foot, to the Gospel and to Jesus Christ.

The faith which justifies contains, therefore, the following elements :

An *act of the intelligence* holding unreservedly to the word of God, because he is as incapable of deceiving as of being deceived.[1] The intellectual element, which is always at the basis of the act of faith, can become predominant to the point of obscuring all the others. This happens especially when the object to be believed is a fact of the past which is not within the range of confidence, or a truth without any direct relation to salvation. Such is the Christian's faith in the mysteries and miracles of the Gospel. Such was the faith of Abraham, although the object of it was still to come ; on the word of God, he believed the improbable, the impossible, without allowing himself to be overcome by hesitation or doubt.

When, from its nature, the object comes into the sphere of hope, it is difficult for faith, if it is sincere, not to be *confident*.[2] Faith and hope are two sisters, almost in-

---

[1] 1 Thess. ii, 13: παραλαβόντες λόγον ἀκοῆς παρ' ἡμῶν τοῦ Θεοῦ (which may be translated, " Having received the word of God preached by us," or, " Having received from us the announcement of God's word," no matter which) ἐδέξασθε οὐ λόγον ἀνθρώπων, ἀλλὰ κάθὼς ἀληθῶς ἐστιν, λόγον Θεοῦ.— iv, 13: *Si enim credimus quod Jesus mortuus est, et resurrexit.*—Rom. x, 9 : *Quia si confitearis in ore tuo Dominum Jesum, et* in corde tuo credideris *quod Deus illum suscitavit a mortuis, salvus eris.* In this last instance there is nothing to object to in the word " heart," for we know very well that, in Biblical psychology, the heart is the seat of thoughts as well as of feelings.— The intellectual character of the act of faith appears again from the fact that it is contrasted, not with a lack of confidence, but with unbelief (Rom. iv, 20, οὐ διεκρίθη τῇ ἀπιστίᾳ), and that it has often for its object an inanimate thing which cannot evoke confidence (ii, 12, 13, πιστεύειν τῇ ἀληθέια, πίστις ἀληθείας), Col. ii, 12 (faith in the power of God who raises Christ from the dead) ; *cf.* 1 Cor. xv, 2 ; Rom. x, 16, etc.

[2] It is possible to discover, at the bottom of every act of faith, a feeling of confidence, but this is not the Protestant's confidence. πίστις comes from πείθειν, " to persuade, to try to convince," and corresponds to the middle voice of the verb πείθεσθαι, " to allow oneself to be convinced or persuaded." This arrangement necessarily requires that the believer *should have confidence* in him who speaks, and that he listen to him *with confidence.* Some Protestants in our day thus explain the confidence inherent in the act of faith ; but this is no longer the pure doctrine of Luther. *Confidence*, understood in this way, is not faith ; it merely serves as a preliminary to the act of faith ; **any** more than *hope* is faith, even when it accompanies faith.

separable; when one stumbles, the other totters also, and it is difficult to imagine a case where hope alone fails. Faith is involuntarily trustful, as hope is faithful. But if confidence naturally is added to faith in the promises, it is rather a mode of it than an intrinsic element. What proves this is the fact that hope is so often mentioned side by side with faith, and that they together with charity form the trio of the virtues which abide, in contrast to the gifts (*charismata*) which pass.

There is furthermore in faith a *twofold act of obedience*: an obedience of the will inclining the intelligence to accept the testimony of God, and an obedience of the whole man to the divine will known through revelation. This is why in St Paul "to believe" and "to obey the faith" are synonymous expressions; unbelief is described as a want of submission, a revolt.[1] Obedience is such an essential element that, without it, faith, whose object always has a certain obscurity and does not force the understanding, could not show itself. With still greater reason must active, normal faith, which expresses itself in the inquiry: *Domine quid me vis facere?* or by that other: *Quid faciemus viri fratres?* contain an act of obedience, since it includes the implicit desire to do all that God commands: it is the faith, the form of which is charity, the faith which works under the impulse of charity, the faith which justifies.

Paul affirms, therefore, that man is justified *by* faith (διὰ πίστεως or πίστει), *in virtue* of faith (ἐκ πίστεως), *on* faith (ἐπὶ πίστει): the first expression points out the means or instrument; the second, the principle; the third, the foundation of justification. Once justified, man continues to live *in* faith (ἐν πίστει), as in a supernatural atmosphere of which his life has henceforth need, and *from* faith (ἐκ πίστεως), as from a force the energy of which is lasting and always active.[2] All these expressions already designate an instrumental causality of the moral order. The texts which follow will enable us to be more specific.

3. Man's justification by faith is expressed in two ways, which differ slightly: *Man is not justified by the works of the Law, but by the faith of Jesus Christ.*[3] *Man is justified by faith without the works of the Law.*[4]

---

[1] Acts vi, 7 says "to obey the faith": ὑπακόνειν τῇ πίστει. Paul speaks of "obedience to the faith": εἰς ὑπακοὴν πίστεως (Rom. i, 5; xvi, 26; *cf*. xv, 18; vi, 17). The crime of the Jews is not to have submitted (οὐχ ὑπετάγησαν, Rom. x, 3); and not to have obeyed (Rom. x, 16) the faith. *Cf*. Rom. ii, 8; xi, 30, 31.

[2] ἐκ πίστεως (Rom. i, 17; iii, 26, 30; iv, 16; v, 1; ix, 30, 32; Gal. ii, 16; iii, 8, 11, 22, 24; v, 5; *cf*. Gal. iii, 25); διὰ πίστεως (Rom. iii, 22, 25, 30; Gal. ii, 16; iii, 14, 26; Eph. ii, 8; iii, 12, 17; Phil. iii, 9; 2 Tim. iii, 15; Rom. iii, 25; xi, 20; 1 Cor. i, 24); ἐπὶ τῇ πίστει (Phil. iii, 9); ἐν πίστει (1 Cor. xvi, 13; 2 Cor. xiii, 5; Gal. ii, 20; 1 Tim. i, 4; ii, 15, etc.).

[3] Gal. ii, 16.　　　　　[4] Rom. iii, 28.

That it is a question here of the first justification, of the passage from the state of sin to that of justice, is proved clearly by the context in both cases. In the Epistle to the Romans the Apostle devotes three chapters to proving that all men, reduced to their own strength or to the resources of the Law only, are sinners; now he examines whence comes the justice which excludes sin, consequently the first justice. In the Epistle to the Galatians Paul reminds Peter of the reason which impelled them formerly to embrace the faith; this reason is that justice comes from faith only—that is to say, looking at the situation, the *first* justice. Let us note, in passing, that the Protestant interpretation " to be declared just " does not suit the verb δικαιοῦσθαι, either in the one case or in the other. In fact, Paul does not say that man is justified by God *in view of faith* (διὰ πίστιν), for then we might strictly understand it as a declaration of justice; he says that man is justified *by faith* (διὰ πίστεως or πίστει, instrumental dative). Now in what language would the phrase " Man is declared just by faith " have a rational meaning?

The Law here in question is the Mosaic Law; no one can doubt it. But a great number of Catholic commentators, ancient and modern, think that the Apostle is speaking only of the ritual Law concerning circumcision, the Sabbath and the sacrifices, on which the controversy with the Judaizers turned. It seems to us much more probable that Paul, as is usual with him, designates the Law in general, since he opposes it to faith. Could he without self-contradiction let it be understood that the moral Law, without faith, is able to justify?

Finally, even if the Apostle here refers directly to the act of faith which produces justification, we think that he has also in view the Gospel, from which the act of faith derives its efficacy. He designates both dispensations by their characteristic qualities, but he no more denies that works are necessary in the new dispensation than he excludes faith from the old. It is in vain, therefore, for certain Protestant theologians to try to prove that faith is not a *work* (ἔργον), and that in consequence it is not an *act*—for the Mosaic Law also prescribed internal acts—but something purely passive. They arrive thus at the beautiful result of depriving faith of all ethical value; and we ask ourselves then what part it can have in the renewal of man and how it is capable of glorifying God.

Let us now return to Paul's own declarations. That of the Epistle to the Romans is the simplest : " Man is justified by faith without the works of the Law." The requirement of the argument as well as the order of the sentence makes the emphasis fall on the last words of this statement which resolves itself into two propositions : " Man is justified without the works of the Law, independently of them "—the principal proposition ; " Man is justified by faith "—an incidental proposition. It will be remarked that the Apostle here is not concerned with the part which works play *after* justification. That they are then necessary appears from his system of morals, and that they increase the justice already acquired follows from his principles ; but in the controversy with the Judaizers the debate turns chiefly on first justification— namely, on the passage from the state of sin to that of grace. The works of the Law are neither the cause nor the essential condition, nor even, in themselves, the occasion of it; and according to the most elementary principles of the Pauline theology one could say as much of natural works done before justification, and with more reason. But note well the fact that St Paul does not say that faith is the only disposition required, and we know by other passages that it must be accompanied by two complementary sentiments : repentance for the past and acceptance of the divine will for the future.

The second text is : " Man is not justified by the works of the Law, but by the faith of Jesus Christ." By making St Paul say that man is not justified by works alone, but by works joined to faith, we get a meaning diametrically opposed to his doctrine and exactly what he fought against in the case of the Judaizers. The essentially complex phrase must be resolved thus : " Man is not justified by the works of the Law; he is justified only by the faith of Jesus Christ." Whether the faith of Jesus Christ is the faith of which he is the author, or the faith of which he is the object—faith in himself, his person and his preaching—matters little ; in either case it is the sum total of the Christian revelation, the Gospel as opposed to the Mosaic Law. We remark as before, that it is a question of works anterior to justification, and that the absolute necessity of faith does not exclude the other dispositions required.

4. The proofs of justification by faith independently of works are three in number : the proof of fact or experience, the theological proof, and the proof from Scripture.

The proof of fact is fairly clear. The Galatians, being Gentile converts, had never observed the Law of Moses. It is, therefore, impossible that the observance of this Law (ἔργα νόμου) had influenced their justification in any way whatever, either as cause, essential condition, or previous disposition. However, it is not at all doubtful that they had been really justified at baptism; they had, as a pledge of it, the gift of the Holy Spirit, whose presence then manifested itself by extraordinary signs, such as the *charismata,* and continued to assert itself by visible wonders. Let no one object, as the Judaizers of Galatia probably did, that the justice acquired by faith perfects and completes itself through the Law; for the author of justification is able to preserve it and to perfect it without any external aid; and it is folly, when one has begun by the Spirit, to wish to finish by the flesh. Not to have perceived a consequence so clear, shows that the Galatians must have lost sight of the redemptive value of the death of Christ. Paul can only attribute their error to some fascination.[1] He had depicted to them in flaming words the image of the Crucified. A look at Jesus Christ, who died to obtain for us the justice which the Law had not been able to give, ought to break the spell. To maintain the necessity of the Law in the face of Calvary is to deny the value of the divine blood and the sufficiency of redemption.

This last consideration, merely hinted at here, leads us to the *theological proof.* To apprehend its force it must be remembered that the Apostle relies upon two postulates, which he thought quite conclusive, and the statement of them reappears frequently in his Epistles under different forms: Justification is a free gift, which man does not deserve and cannot deserve; man never has a right to boast before God, or, if he boasts, it can be only of divine benefits received.[2]

Given this, the Apostle reasons thus: Justification by faith is gratuitous, and does not warrant any man's boasting; it fulfils, therefore, the two conditions required. Justification by works would not be gratuitous, and it would warrant man's boasting; it is, then, chimerical.[3]

Justification by faith is gratuitous because, faith being a gift of God, the whole edifice which it supports is the work

---

[1] Gal. iii, 1-5: τίς ὑμᾶς ἐβάσκανεν;

[2] The two postulates of St Paul, which have become for us articles of faith. since they form part of his teaching, are united in the short phrase in Eph. ii, 8-9: *Gratia enim salvati estis per fidem et hoc non ex vobis, Dei enim donum est ; non ex operibus ut ne quis glorietur.* The twofold subordinate clause, *et hoc non ex vobis, Dei enim donum est,* must be considered as a parenthesis, at the two extremities of which *per fidem* and *non ex operibus* are set in contrast, as usual. Then the *hoc* refers not precisely to *fides* but to the adverbial expression *per fidem.* This way of salvation *per fidem* is not of yourselves, it comes from God ; hence it follows clearly that faith is a gift of God and a grace. To make the *hoc* refer to *salvati estis,* as some commentators do, would be to attribute to St Paul a tautology : *Gratia salvati estis . . . et hoc non ex vobis.* In *Ut ne quis glorietur* the *ut* (ἵνα) may be consecutive, " in such a way that no one should glory," or final, " in order that no one may glory." In the latter case, it is not Paul's intention that is indicated (" I say this, in order that . . .") but that intention or one of those intentions which God had in view in establishing the present order of salvation. This intention is well known to us through other texts, 1 Cor. i, 29-31 ; Rom. iii, 27, etc.

[3] This proof, the details of which are scattered, is unfolded quite clearly in Rom. iv, 1-9.

of God. The act of faith presupposes essentially the divine call made at the propitious moment. Now, since these two things (the divine call and the appropriateness of it) depend exclusively on the pleasure of God, the priority of grace, from an ontological point of view, is undeniable, and God always commences the work of man's salvation before man himself does. On the contrary, the justification which the works of the Law would produce, or, in a more general way, the works done before faith (admitting that to be possible), would be the fruit of the labour of man; it would be due to him, as a salary is due to the workman; and he could boast of it as being his rightful property. If the feignedly just, the Pharisees, regard their justice as due to their natural activity, and flatter themselves that they can obtain it *ex opere operato* by the material observance of the Law—the really just, Abraham and David, think very differently. " Abraham believed God, and it was imputed to him for justice." Not that faith is justice or its equivalent, but it is a disposition that God wishes to find in the heart of man in order to confer upon him a more excellent good—justice. For his part, David cries : " Blessed are those whose iniquities are covered. . . . Blessed is the man to whom God imputeth not sin." Of works and merits, not a word. David attributes everything to mercy. That is what differentiates the two tendencies. The Pharisee, who wishes to conquer justice by a hard conflict, claims it like a debt. The believer, on the contrary, claims nothing; he surrenders at discretion; he confesses by his very act both his unworthiness and his impotence; he stands before God like a mendicant before his benefactor; he gives to God the glory which he refuses to himself.

To sum up the case : he who obtains justice by his own works is not justified by grace ($\kappa\alpha\tau\grave{\alpha}\ \chi\acute{\alpha}\rho\iota\nu$), but by right ($\kappa\alpha\tau'\ \acute{o}\phi\acute{\epsilon}\iota\lambda\eta\mu\alpha$); he would not, therefore, have true justice, the justice of God ($\delta\iota\kappa\alpha\iota\sigma\acute{\nu}\nu\eta\ \Theta\epsilon\sigma\tilde{\nu}$), the most essential element of which is its gratuitousness.

Whoever is justified by faith independently of works is justified gratuitously, because faith has no proportion with justice, and because the act of faith, being only the assent of the reason and of the will to the divine call made at an opportune moment, is by that very fact a grace.

The necessity of faith and of the other dispositions required does not injure the gratuitousness of justice any more than the suppliant gesture of the beggar destroys the liberality of the alms given, even if it were a necessary condition for it. And there is this difference, that the gesture of the mendicant is his own, while the act of faith is a gift of God.

Finally, the believer, by the avowal of his impotence and

the implicit recognition of divine mercy, relinquishes all right to vainglory and so much the more glorifies the Author of all good : *Dans gloriam Deo.*

The theological proof prepares the way for the *scriptural proof,* drawn from the history of Abraham.[1] Abraham was justified and proclaimed father of the faithful *before* his circumcision. It follows, first, that there is no necessary bond between circumcision and justice, and that one can be just without being circumcised; secondly, that the paternity of Abraham, a reward for his faith, is equally independent of circumcision and can be extended to the Gentiles who imitate the faith of Abraham. Being derived not from the Law but from the promise, not from the flesh but from the spirit, it is not the appanage of a race; it is the privilege of all believers.

That Abraham was justified *before* his circumcision is a fact which appears clearly from the comparison of dates. In chapter xv of Genesis, it is said of him : " Abraham believed God and this was imputed to him unto justice." In chapter xvii only is the divine precept of the circumcision for all the family of Abraham reported. Justice comes first. Why, then, the circumcision? It is the visible sign of the alliance previously concluded and the material seal of the justice vouchsafed to faith, in a state of uncircumcision.

For his spiritual paternity the reasoning is almost the same. It was said to the patriarch : " In thee shall all nations be blest." This is not " all Jews " or " the Jews only," but all the nations of the earth. The blessings promised to the father of the faithful, passing beyond the particularism of the Synagogue, are as extended and as universal as the Church itself was to be. And these blessings are bestowed without any restriction or condition long before the covenant of Sinai. Now common sense says that a wholly gracious concession, received from God by Abraham as a testament, and bequeathed by him to his spiritual lineage in the form of an inheritance, could not be revoked without injustice or without arbitrary action in consequence of a later act.

A man's testament, if it be confirmed, no man despiseth, nor addeth to it. To Abraham were the promises made and to his seed. He saith not : And to his seeds, as of many, but as of one, And to thy seed, which is Christ. Now this I say, that the testament, which was confirmed by God, the law, which was made after 430 years, doth not disannul, to make the promise of no effect. For if the inheritance be of the law, it is no more of promise. But God gave it to Abraham by promise.[2]

---

[1] Proof developed in Rom. iv, 10-25 and Gal. iii, 7-14.

[2] Gal. iii, 15-18. For the details of the text see Lagrange, *Galatians,* Paris, 1918, pp. 71-81, noting that the author uses constantly *lignage* for *lignée.*

5. Such is the doctrine of St Paul concerning justification by faith. At first sight, that of St James seems at the very antipodes. The teacher of the Gentiles says : " Man is justified by faith without the works of the Law,"[1] or still more forcibly : " Man is not justified by the works of the Law, but by the faith of Jesus Christ."[2] The Lord's brother says : " Man is justified by works and not by faith only."[3] Moreover, each bases his thesis upon the same biblical example and on the same text of Scripture : " Abraham believed God and it was reputed to him unto justice."[4] Now, while Paul draws this conclusion : " If Abraham were justified by works, he hath whereof to glory; but not before God,"[5] James forms the contrary conclusion : " Was not Abraham our father justified by works, offering up Isaac, his son, upon the altar? Seest thou that faith did co-operate with his works, and by works faith was made perfect?"[6] Is there not here an irreconcilable opposition, if not a flagrant contradiction?[7] It is said that Luther, in a fit of joviality and buffoonery, promised his Doctor's cap to anyone who would remove the contradiction. If at times he called St James " an excellent man, although a little narrow in his views," he usually designated his Epistle as an epistle of straw, which did not contain a syllable worthy of Christ.

The two apostles, although using the same words, are not speaking of the same things. The faith of St Paul is a concrete, active faith, which receives from charity its impulse and its form; the faith of St James is a simple assent of the mind comparable to that which the devils themselves give to evident truths.[8] It is clear that this act, which is necessary and purely intellectual, cannot influence the justification of man at all. The works of which St Paul speaks are the works which *precede* faith and justice, chiefly the works of the Law, which is the object of discussion in the controversy with the Judaizers; the works of St James are the works which

---

[1] Rom. iii, 28. [2] Gal. ii, 16.
[3] James ii, 24. [4] Gen. xv, 6.
[5] Rom. iv, 2. [6] James ii, 21, 22.
[7] See B. Bartmann, " St Paulus und St Jacobus über die Rechtfertigung," Freiburg i. B. 1897 (in *Biblische Studien*, vol. iii, part 1). Not very different are the conclusions of Ménégoz, " Étude comparative de l'enseignement de S Paul et de S Jacques sur la justification par la foi " (in *Études de théol. et d'hist.*, etc., Paris, 1901, pp. 121-150).
[8] James ii, 19: Σὺ πιστεύεις ὅτι εἷς Θεός ἐστιν; καλῶς ποιεῖς· καὶ τὰ δαιμόνια πιστεύουσιν. For the argument to be effective, something must be supplied. " You do well to believe in God," (but that is not sufficient, for) " the devils themselves believe." Estius thus explains the comparison : *Quemadmodum daemonibus ad salutem nihil prodest omnis illa notitia quam de rebus divinis habent, quia non adest bona voluntas; ita christiano quamdiu non studet bonis operibus, fides ad salutem prodesse non poterit.* It does not follow that the *faith* of the demons is of the same nature as the imperfect faith of sinners.

follow faith and justice, since he addresses himself to Christians already in possession of the supernatural life. The justice of which St Paul speaks is *first* justice—that is, the passage from a state of sin to a state of holiness, as the very object of the polemics and the reiterated explanations of the Apostle abundantly prove; the justice of St James is *second* justice, otherwise called the increase of justice, the regular development of the Christian life. In a word St Paul places himself *before* the justification of man, St James *after* it; the former speaks of *living* faith, the second of a faith which may be *dead,* and which is in any case inactive; one declares to the *unbeliever* that without faith he cannot obtain justification; the other teaches the *Christian* to see to it that his conduct shall harmonize with his faith, for faith alone is not sufficient for him.

The doctrine of Paul, drawn from the depths of his theology, went beyond ordinary minds. It was easy to give to it a paradoxical turn, or to make a bad use of it in order to lead an evil life. We know that the Apostle himself had sometimes to protest against false interpretations of his theories. Was the Lord's brother also proposing thus to obviate the injurious conclusions which ignorance or bad faith might deduce from the principle : Man is justified by faith without works? In other words, was he referring to St Paul, and did he wish, not to rectify his teaching, but to explain it by presenting it in a new light? Many exegetes have thought so. The example of Abraham and the text from Genesis, common to both apostles, would not be sufficient to prove it. This example and this text almost inevitably suggested themselves to a Jewish writer when he was treating the subject of faith and justice. Thus Philo, in the long treatise entitled *The Life of the Just,* which he devotes to the father of the faithful, quotes this same text more than ten times, while the Talmud also expounds it with its usual prolixity. What would show an intentional allusion and not an accidental coincidence would be the contrast maintained between faith and works, the similar terminology applied to different ideas, and the way in which St James formulates his thesis by taking the opposite side to the thesis of St Paul. However that may be, the polemic of James, if polemic there be, is directed against short-sighted or ill-disposed readers of Paul and not at all against Paul himself, whose Gospel James, at the council of Jerusalem, had solemnly approved, without finding in it anything to correct or to complete.

III—THE PART PLAYED BY THE LAW

1. The Reason for the Law. 2. The Childhood of Humanity
under the Régime of the Law.

1. The opinions of St Paul concerning the Mosaic Law
are, at first sight, contradictory. Sometimes he extols it to
the skies, at other times he seems to bring it down below
the natural law. The Law is holy and spiritual;[1] its aim is
to give life;[2] at the last day those who observe it will be
declared just.[3] It was established by the angels, with Moses
as mediator;[4] it is one, and not the least of the nine prerogatives of the children of Israel;[5] it leads men to Christ,[6] whom
it had the honour to prophesy;[7] in Christ it has its end and
its accomplishment,[8] and finally, to sum up all his praises
of it, it is not the Law of Moses, it is the Law of God.[9]
But here is the reverse side. The Law has brought
nothing to perfection;[10] it is rather the artisan of divine
wrath;[11] it has slipped in surreptitiously behind sin in order
to aggravate its transgression.[12] It gives the knowledge of
sin[13] without the strength to avoid it. All those who are
dependent on its works and put their confidence in it fall
under a curse.[14]
Thus the Law is at the same time a pledge of the goodness
of God and a precursor of his wrath. To-day it is the
messenger of heaven and the way which leads to life; to-
morrow it will become the weapon of sin[15] and an instrument
of death. It is powerless to justify, and yet those who
observe it will be declared just. What, then, is the solution
of this enigma?

[1] Rom. vii, 12-14: ὁ νόμος ἅγιος, πνευματικός ἐστιν.
[2] Rom. vii, 10: Εἰς ζωήν naturally in the sight of God, for the effect has
been a contrary one. Cf. Rom. x, 5.
[3] Rom. ii, 13: Factores legis justificabuntur. Cf. Rom. x, 5; Gal. iii, 12.
[4] Gal. iii, 19: Ordinata (διαταγείς) per angelos in manu mediatoris.
However, this mode of transmission has something imperfect in it.
[5] Rom. ix, 4: Νομοθεσία. Cf. Rom. ii, 13: Quid ergo amplius Judaeo
est? . . . Primum quidem quia credita sunt illis eloquia Dei.
[6] Gal. iii, 24: παιδαγωγὸς ἡμῶν γέγονεν εἰς Χριστόν.
[7] Col. ii, 16. It is the shadow (σκία), of which Christ is the body.
[8] Rom. x, 4: τέλος means only "end," "term," but the meaning
"accomplishment" comes from the preceding text. Cf. Matt. v, 17,
[9] Rom. vii, 22-25; viii, 7.   [10] Heb. vii, 19.
[11] Rom. iv, 15: Lex enim iram operatur.
[12] Gal. iii, 19: Propter transgressiones posita est (προσετέθη, apposita
est, addita est). Rom. v, 20: Lex subintravit (παρεισῆλθεν, it entered
secretly [παρά] behind sin), ut abundaret delictum.
[13] Rom. iii, 20: Per legem cognitio peccati. Cf. Rom. vii, 7, 8.
[14] Gal. iii, 10: Quicumque enim ex operibus legis sunt, sub maledicto sunt.
Note in St Paul and in St John the force of the expression εἶναι ἐκ, " to be
dependent on a thing, to be fastened to it."
[15] I Cor. xv, 56. Virtus peccati lex (its mode of action, the instrument
of its power).

We shall endeavour to give it in connection with the Epistle to the Romans. It is a question here only of the *raison d'être* of the Law. The Apostle has just proved that it contributes in no way to man's justification; he has shown that, if the inheritance of the Messianic blessings is derived from the Law, it cannot be derived from the wholly gratuitous promise made to the father of the faithful, as Scripture teaches. He continues thus: "Why, then, was the Law? It was added because of transgressions, until the seed should come to whom He made the promise."[1] From the first, Paul's doctrine has always seemed hard to the exegetes, and they have tried to soften it by understanding it as " in order to diminish, repress, and punish transgressions." But they have not reflected that transgression is the violation of a positive law, and that consequently, if no positive law had been given, there could have been no transgression: *Ubi non est lex nec praevarieatio* (παράβασις).[2] The Law could not, therefore, have the effect of diminishing or repressing transgressions, which, but for it, would have no existence. On the contrary, it engenders them; it is at least the occasional cause of them, in view of the present corruption of man and his inclination to sin. This is the constant teaching of the Apostle, who elsewhere calls the Law an active force (δύναμις)[3] of sin, and who says in so many words: *Lex autem subintravit ut abundaret delictum.* Far from diminishing the falls (παράπτωμα) from rectitude it could only aggravate and multiply them. The reason which Paul furnishes for this is clear; it is that the Law instructs man in regard to his duties without remedying his weakness: *Per legem cognitio peccati.*[4] By promulgating the code of Sinai, God foresaw the acts of disobedience of which it would be the occasion, but he at the same time foresaw the way in which he would turn to account these very faults; by awakening the conscience, by humbling the sinner, by convincing him of his impotence, and by making him desire divine aid. Thus good triumphs over evil, and God who cannot himself love

---

[1] Gal. iii, 19: Τί οὖν ὁ νόμος· τῶν παραβάσεων χάριν προσετέθη ἄχρις οὗ ἔλθῃ τὸ σπέρμα ᾧ ἐπήγγελται. In St Paul and in general in the New Testament τί is often equivalent to διὰ τί, "why"; it is in this sense that we take it here, for the phrase that follows expresses less the *essence* than the *object* of the Law. The other possible translation, "What is the Law?" harmonizes, therefore, less with the context.

[2] Rom. iv, 15. [3] 1 Cor. xv, 56.

[4] Rom. iii, 20: Διὰ γὰρ νόμου ἐπίγνωσις ἁμαρτίας. St Paul does not say γνῶσις but ἐπίγνωσις, " clear knowledge," because there may be a certain knowledge of sin even without the Law. Although designating the Law of Moses, νόμου is without the article, as often happens in these prepositional expressions. The absence of the article before ἁμαρτίας may be due to attraction (the other words of the sentence being without an article), or to indeterminateness. In the latter case it would be a question, not of original sin only, but of all that is sin,

evil, is pleased to repair it and to bring it back to good.
But, when he permits it in view of the good which results
from it, the Scripture usually says that he wishes and orders
it. St Paul well expresses these two occasions of the will of
God, overlooking the evil of which he is not the author, as
being a means of attaining the end which he proposes to
himself : " The Law entered in, *in order* that sin might
abound; . . . *so that* grace might reign by justice unto life
eternal.[1]

The Law, being what it was, could not last for ever. It
was only an intermediary in the great drama of humanity.
On the day when the promises shall be realized, it will lose
all its reason for existing. The manner in which it was
given already presaged this. Moses was its mediator. But
the presence of a mediator presupposes two contracting
parties; and the act which results therefrom is a bilateral
contract, producing on both sides rights and duties, the
stability of which is conditional, since it can be cancelled by
common consent, or annulled through the violation of it by
one of the contracting parties.[2] Very different will be the
promise. Here God alone is concerned, and there is in
him no fear of inconstancy, forgetfulness, or unfaithfulness.
He binds himself by an oath in order to inspire man with
more confidence. His promise is not dependent on the
consent or the merit of anyone; and, as it is absolute and
free of all conditions, it will not be repented of.

2. But these explanations themselves appear contradictory.
If the promise is absolute and wholly gratuitous, why was
this burdensome condition added later? Why this insupportable load which has crushed the Hebrews by its weight?
" Is the Law opposed to the promises of God?" " No," the
Apostle answers : it would be contrary to the promises of
God only if it gave the advantages which are the object of
the promises,[3] or if it were still to endure when the moment
for the fulfilment of the promises should have come. But it

[1] Rom. v, 20 : Νόμος δὲ παρεισῆλθεν ἵνα πλεονάσῃ τὸ παράπτωμα.
If the ἵνα is consecutive, it marks only the effect produced by the intervention of the Law; if it is final, it expresses an intention of God, who wishes
the increase of falls, as a means of obtaining an end worthy of him. But he
wishes such falls only by a *consequent* volition, when once he sees them take
place through the fault of man.

[2] Gal. iii, 19, 20. That is the sense of the enigmatic διαταγεὶς δι' ἀγγέλων,
ἐν χειρὶ μεσίτου · ὁ δὲ μεσίτης ἑνὸς οὐκ ἔστιν, ὁ δὲ Θεὸς εἷς ἐστιν.

[3] Gal. iii, 21. Lex (ὁ νόμος = the Mosaic Law) *ergo adversus promissa
Dei ? Absit !* (an energetic denial which Paul uses in order to repel impossible hypotheses or absurd propositions). *Si enim data esset lex, quae
posset vivificare, vere ex lege esset justitia.* The thought remains in suspense,
but it is completed easily by adding mentally : " And then the Law would be
really contrary to the promises, which announced to us justice as a gratuitous
gift."

is not so. The Law is not capable of giving life, it does not confer supernatural justice. On the other hand, it is only a state of transition, a halting-place before the terminus, an episode before the ending. It has not driven back the empire of evil; it has rather strengthened it, but with a wholly providential end in view : " Scripture hath included all things under sin, that the promise which is by the faith of Jesus Christ may be given to them that believe."[1] While waiting for this term, it was important that man should not be able to escape, and that, whether he wished it or not, he should be brought to the gates of faith. The hard régime of the Law rendered this service to the Jews : " Before the coming of faith we were kept under the Law as prisoners, closely confined in order to be handed over to the faith, which was, one day, to be revealed."[2] Faith was to be revealed in the fulness of time. It represents the mature age of humanity, and the régime of the Law is consequently its infancy. This idea suggests to Paul a twofold comparison, which puts the final touch to the revelation of his thought. Before the coming of Christ man was a minor, a pupil; the Law was his pedagogue and tutor.

The pedagogue of ancient times had little resemblance to the modern teacher. A reliable and faithful slave, often very ignorant, he accompanied his pupil everywhere. He took him also to school—carrying his books, if one accepts as accurate that detail, given by St Augustine—and was present at the master's lessons, sometimes comprehending nothing of them. His unwavering integrity, which might help to form the lad's character, contributed above all to make adolescence a thing to be desired. For the young Roman it was a happy day when, laying aside the golden *bulla* with the *toga praetexta,* he assumed the *toga virilis.* The farewell words to the *paedagogium,* scrawled in such numbers at the foot of the Palatine, do not contain regrets. Through the strictness of its precepts the Law caused the liberator to be longed for; by its prophecies, which became more and more clear, it allowed him to be recognized in advance; it prepared the hearts of mankind for this event by maintaining them, almost in spite of themselves, in monotheism : and thus it led them to Christ, who is its object and its end.[3]

> Now I say, as long as the heir is a child, he differeth nothing from a servant, though he be lord of all ; but is under tutors and governors until the time appointed by the father ; so we also, when we were children,

---

[1] Gal. iii, 22. *Sed* [it is not so, for] *conclusit Scriptura omnia sub peccato* (it has shown *all* men, Jews and Gentiles, as being subject to sin), *ut promissio ex fide Jesu Christi daretur credentibus.*

[2] Gal. iii, 23. Faith means here the Gospel, as a new system, opposed to the régime of the Law.

[3] Rom. x, 4 : τέλος γὰρ νόμου Χριστὸς εἰς δικαιοσύνην.

were serving under the elements of the world. But when the fulness of the time was come, God sent his Son, that he might redeem them who were under the law, that we might receive the adoption of sons.[1]

The centuries which preceded the coming of Christ were for the human race the age of minority. Men were heirs by virtue of the Messianic promises, for these promises were a testament concerning the Gentiles as well as the Jews, and the Gospel is their common heritage. But, in order to enter into possession of their patrimony, both Jews and Gentiles were obliged to wait until the world had attained its majority. Until then they were subject to rudimentary institutions, which, however, prepared them for a more perfect state, and led them to it by degrees. Did the Apostle conceive of the testator as living or dead? The second hypothesis is the more likely. During the lifetime of his father the pupil would be neither heir nor proprietor, nor under a state of dependency on lawyers and guardians. It is objected that the Roman law did not allow the testator to fix the age of his son's emancipation; but Paul is not considering Roman law, but is adhering to the natural law, which, binding the will of the testator less strictly, seems more suitable to represent the divine decree. Moreover, it is not certain that the Roman law, above all in the provinces, definitely fixed the legal age of majority. However that may be, the father's free choice must be taken into account, because the fulness of time, which puts an end to the childhood of humanity, depends on the pleasure of God.

There is also not a perfect agreement in regard to the meaning of the *elementa mundi* (τὰ στοιχεῖα τοῦ κόσμου), to which men were subject before the coming of Christ. By comparing different passages of St Paul with one another, we shall elsewhere show that he means by this the rudimentary institutions, the products of a still imperfect revelation or of the religious instinct, which governed Jews and Gentiles before the régime of the Gospel. The appearance of Christ delivers them both, but in a different way : it takes from the Jews the yoke of the Law, and it confers on all the adoptive sonship which had been promised to all the spiritual children of Abraham without distinction of race, but of which the Jews were *de facto* the depositaries. Now there is no more difference; Jews and Gentiles simultaneously attain to the "fulness of time," and are together emancipated and called to claim their rights as heirs.

[1] Gal. iv, 1-5. The parallel proceeds with much symmetry :

Quanto tempore heres parvulus,	*Nos cum essemus* parvuli,
Nihil differt a servo,	*Eramus* servientes,
Sed sub tutoribus et actoribus *est*,	Sub elementis *mundi ;*
Usque ad praefinitum tempus,	*At ubi venit* plenitudo temporis,
Cum sit dominus *omnium,*	*Ut* adoptionem filiorum *reciperemus.*

A scriptural allegory finally explains Paul's mind. He sees in the two wives of Abraham the symbol of the two testaments. Hagar, the bondwoman, represents the Synagogue; Sarah, the free woman, is the symbol of the Church. Hagar gives birth *according to the flesh,* and conformably to the laws of nature, to a son, who is a slave like herself; Sarah gives birth, *according to the spirit* and by virtue of a miraculous promise, to a son who, like her, is to be free. It is a universal principle of law that sons partake of the condition of their mothers. Consequently, Sinai, of which Hagar was the symbol, will give birth only to slaves; but the heavenly Jerusalem, the Church represented by Sarah, will give to the world only free men. The allegory is clear.[1] The Jews, like Ishmael, are indeed children of Abraham according to the flesh, but they are not the true heirs of Abraham any more than Ishmael is. Christians, like Isaac, are the descendants of Abraham according to the spirit, and, like Isaac, they inherit promises and spiritual blessings. It results from this that the Judaizers of Galatia, who wish to be under the Law, in spite of the indications of the Law itself, are retrograding and renouncing their privileges, and are making themselves liable to be excluded from the patrimony of their father, like their prototype Ishmael.

The Apostle calls this exegetical application an *allegory.* He is certainly not speaking of an allegory in the strict sense of the term which would suppress the reality of the story of Genesis, to give it only a figurative meaning. Does he wish to designate a biblical *type,* which the Holy Spirit had had in view when inspiring that recital? This would have to be admitted if its development were regarded as a scriptural argument meant to prove that the Christian is no longer under the Law; and then we should have to ask how much is type and how much is accommodation, for it is difficult to believe that the Holy Spirit meant to include all

---

[1] Gal. iv, 21-31. Allegorical analogies (ἅτινά ἐστιν ἀλληγορούμενα):

The *two wives* of Abraham.	The *two Testaments.*
Hagar, the *bondwoman.*	The Synagogue, *a slave.*
Birth *in Arabia.*	Birth *at Sinai.*
A slave *according to the flesh.*	Slaves *according to the Law.*
Sarah, the *free* woman.	The *free* Church.
Birth *for Zion.*	Birth *for heaven.*
A *free* man.	*Free* men.
By virtue of the *promise.*	By means of *faith.*

The vertical columns contain respectively ideas of the same order ; on one side the type, on the other the antitype, if we admit the strictly spiritual sense; or, on one side the biblical fact, on the other the oratorical (allegorical) application, if we take the accommodative sense. The horizontal lines present the different elements of the typical sense or the accommodative sense ; the ideas placed in relation have a harmony of affinity (συστοιχεῖ, Vulgate, *conjunctus est*) between them.

the details of the antitype. But is not Paul also an orator? Have not comparisons, analogies, and contrasts often more power to set forth a truth in its true light than the driest and most concise theological argument? If so, why should we refuse him the right, which we concede to every orator, of drawing accommodated applications from a biblical text?

With this allegory the dogmatic development ends. The Epistle to the Galatians has this peculiarity, that the ethical element is embodied in the dogma; it is its immediate corollary. Paul, therefore, concludes with an ardent appeal to the liberty of Christ.[1] Yet this Gospel liberty must not degenerate into licence, and the yoke of the Law must not be shaken off to fall under that of the flesh.[2] Such is the Apostle's last word, and the end of the Epistle.

[1] Gal. v, 1. The numerous readings of this text do not substantially alter the meaning. We can read: *Qua libertate Christus nos liberavit, state et nolite iterum jugo servitutis contineri*, or, by punctuating otherwise: *Non sumus ancillae filii sed liberae: qua libertate Christus nos liberavit. State*, etc. The most authorized reading is τῇ ἐλευθερίᾳ ἡμᾶς Χριστὸς ἠλευθέρωσεν, στήκετε οὖν καὶ μὴ πάλιν ζυγῷ δουλείας ἐνέχεσθε, instead of τῇ ἐλευθερίᾳ οὖν ᾗ Χριστός, κτλ, in the received text.

[2] Gal. v, 13: *Vos enim in libertatem* (ἐπ᾽ ἐλευθερίᾳ = *in order to* enjoy liberty) *vocati estis fratres: tantum ne libertatem in occasionem detis carnis* (better *carni*, τῇ σαρκί), *sed per charitatem Spiritus servite invicem.* There follows the enumeration of the works of the flesh (*opera carnis*) and of th fruits of the spirit (*fructus Spiritus*), Gal. v, 19-24.

CHAPTER II

THE EPISTLE TO THE ROMANS

FIRST SECTION

THE JUSTICE OF GOD THE ONLY WAY OF SALVATION

I—IMPOTENCE OF NATURE AND THE LAW

1. General Idea of the Epistle to the Romans. 2. Nature Powerless among the Gentiles. 3. The Law Powerless among the Jews.

1. FOR a long time the gaze of the Apostle had been fixed on Rome. A vehement desire to visit the little growing church there harrowed his mind. He kept saying to himself : " I must see Rome."[1] It was not the sort of fascination that the capital of the world exercised upon provincials and foreigners. A voice within him urged him thither irresistibly.[2] His tactics had ever been to make his assault upon great cities, thus to strike Paganism at its heart, convinced that through the power of attraction which always draws country districts towards a metropolis, they would follow sooner or later. Perhaps, too, he had a supernatural presentiment that the centre of the world was predestined to be also the centre of the Church. Moreover, it seemed to him that his work in the East was finished — having firmly planted the Gospel at Antioch, Corinth, and Ephesus, and in the principal cities of Galatia and Macedonia, the rest was only an affair of time. The seed had been sown; it would spring up of itself under the breath of divine grace. Others could garner the harvest. He had preached the glad tidings from Jerusalem to the confines of Illyria; there was no longer a place for him in those vast regions. The intrigues of the Judaizers, the danger threatening the Galatians, the disorders at Corinth, and the care of so many churches exposed to temptation, had thus far detained him. Now he is free, and his plan is made. After having carried to the saints at Jerusalem the result of the collections, he will see Rome. And, beyond Rome, Spain, with the mysterious boundary of the West, invites his zeal—an entire unknown world to conquer for Christ !

Paul turned these thoughts over in his mind during the winter that he passed at Corinth in the midst of that turbulent Christian community which had come back to a more orderly

---

[1] Acts xix, 21 ; Rom. i, 11-15 ; xv, 23.   [2] Acts xxiii, 11.

life. He only awaited the opening of navigation early in March for his departure.[1] A woman of Cenchrea, a neighbouring port of Corinth, was going directly to Rome. To her he gave a letter in which he expounded his doctrine concerning the relations between faith and the Law, nature and grace, more fully than he had done in the Epistle to the Galatians. The latter letter, in which feeling overflows and passion boils, has not the methodical advance and the calm serenity which are suited to his present design. He uses it as his groundwork; but here he intends to go further and mount higher, beyond a transient episode, and above a local controversy.

The humble beginnings of the Church of Rome are very obscure. The faith, brought thither by emigrants from the provinces or by pilgrims from Jerusalem, spread gradually from one to another, secretly and noiselessly, for the soil was eminently favourable to exotic cults and to all sorts of proselytism. Had the Church its origin there, as almost everywhere else, in the Synagogue? It is possible, even probable. In the troubles which gave rise to the expulsion of the Jews about the year 49 A.D., some have seen signs of a violent rupture between the Synagogue and the Church, and the words of Suetonius seem to furnish some basis for this hypothesis.[2] Anyhow, it is certain that at the moment when Paul was writing his Epistle, the Christian community at Rome was mixed, but with a non-Jewish element in the majority.[3] When the Apostle addresses them in general, he calls them *Gentiles*;[4] and he bases his right to address them on the fact of his being the teacher of the Gentiles.[5] No doubt, before their conversion, a certain number of neophytes had experienced in different degrees Jewish influence which rendered them more exposed to the judaizing peril. Those scrupulous individuals who distinguish between one kind of food and another and between " days," may be Jews or former proselytes, but they form only a small fraction of the Church. These the others have to endure patiently; they do not give the community its tone. Instead of launching an anathema against them, the Apostle assures to these " weak in the faith " the widest tolerance.[6] How far we are here from the Judaizers of Galatia! Here we find no proof of Paul's adversaries having already woven their net of intrigues. Nothing savours of direct polemics; nothing pro-

---

[1] His intention was to go to Syria by sea (Acts xx, 3) in order to reach Jerusalem for the Passover. But the lying in wait (ἐπιβουλή) of the Jews obliged him to take the land route, and he arrived there only at Pentecost.

[2] *Claudius, 3: Claudius Judaeos impulsore Chresto assidue tumultuantes expulit.*

[3] Rom. i, 5-6; xi, 13; xv, 15-16, etc.

[4] Rom. i, 13; xi, 13.

[5] Rom. i, 5-14; xv, 16.

[6] xiv, 1; v, 1.

claims the presence of active enemies. If dangers there are, they are for the future to take care of; and the solemn warning against fomenters of troubles,[1] or rather the whole Epistle, is meant to conjure them away.[2]

Impersonal, like the Epistle to the Ephesians, although somewhat less so, it has almost the character of a treatise on theology. But it would be a great mistake to look for an entire résumé of Paul's teaching in it. St Paul always assumes that the foundations of Christianity are known to his correspondents; he does not revert to the creed, or does so only by way of allusion. The Epistle to the Romans, therefore, is not a catechism, as the Protestants formerly affected to believe; it is only a fundamental thesis which may be called in a limited sense the Gospel of Paul, but is really only the first half of it.

Granted that it is a thesis, it is very important to find out what it enunciates, and happily, for once, the exegetes are agreed on this point. Its central idea resides in the following words, placed immediately after the Apostle has entered upon his subject-matter :

> I am not ashamed of the Gospel. For it is the power of God unto salvation for every one that believeth, to the Jew first, and to the Greek. For the justice of God is revealed therein from faith unto faith, as it is written : The just man liveth by faith.[3]

From this complex statement several truths of the greatest importance can be derived : (1) The universality of God's salvation, for he means the Gospel for all men and, through the Gospel, invites all to faith—that is, to salvation; (2) the equality of all, Jews and Gentiles, as to the conditions of salvation, with a certain priority *de facto* and *de jure* in favour of the Jews; (3) a natural and, in respect to God, necessary bond between justification and glorification, between the starting-point and the goal; (4) the justice of God communicated to men by the faith of Jesus Christ, to the exclusion of nature, left to itself, and of the Mosaic Law. On the whole, the first four chapters are a commentary on

---

[1] xvi, 17-18.

[2] Against our opinion is given Rom. iv, 1 (Abraham *our* father according to the flesh). But this text is explained naturally like 1 Cor. x, 1, where Paul, addressing the Corinthians, who were certainly Greeks, calls the ancient Hebrews " *our fathers* " (οἱ πατέρες ἡμῶν). The passage Rom. vii, 1-6 also offers some difficulty. Paul says to his readers that they are dead to the Law (vii, 4: ὑμεῖς), which seems to presuppose a former state of subjection. But, besides the fact that he sometimes addresses minorities, as if they were all, the pre-Christian Mosaic Law had claims even on the Gentiles, since it was then the only religious institution sanctioned by God. In chaps. ix-xi, dealing directly with the Jews, Paul speaks of them always in the third person.

[3] Rom. i, 16, 17. See H. Denifle, O.P., *Die abendländischen Schrift ausleger bis Luther über Justitia Dei* (Rom. i, 17) *und Justificatio*, Mayence, 1905.

this last proposition; the next four develop the last proposition but one; while chapters ix-xi reply to the objection drawn from the unbelief of the Jews, and to the apparent violation of their prerogative. Finally, the universality of salvation in the plans of God is everywhere presupposed and affirmed several times without being the subject of a special exposition. The conclusion is devoted, as usual, to moral applications of his thesis and to greetings.

It is evident that the interest and also the difficulty centre in this statement : *The justice of God is by the faith of Jesus Christ*. We have spoken in the Epistle to the Galatians of justification by faith; we now have to examine the particular characteristic which the Apostle imprints upon his thesis in replacing justification by the justice of God. It cannot be denied that the justice of God designates usually a divine attribute, and some few exegetes understand it so here. The justice of God would then be his holiness, or his fidelity, or his resolve to pardon man only after a satisfaction in proportion to his offence. This, it is said, is the ordinary meaning in the Old Testament; it is also sometimes the meaning in St Paul.[1] Moreover, the contrast between the wrath of God which reveals itself from heaven and the justice of God which reveals itself in the Gospel, invites us to conceive of a justice which forms a pendant to his wrath, and consequently of the immanent justice of God.

These arguments have some force, but they are counter-balanced by more convincing reasons; for no one can fail to recognize the parallelism in thought and expression between our text and the following passage from the Epistle to the Philippians : " Not having my justice which is of the Law, but that which is of the faith of Christ Jesus, God's justice stayed on faith."[2]   Justice coming from the Law without the complement of grace, if that were possible, would be the absolute property of man, and he could therefore, strictly speaking, call it *his* justice; but this justice could not please God, who loves nothing in us that he has not implanted in us; on the contrary, the justice which comes from God, even while being the property of the man to whom it is given and who really possesses it, belongs also to God, from whom it is derived.   Even without departing from our text, the quota-

---

[1] Rom. iii, 5 (εἰ ἡ ἀδικία ἡμῶν Θεοῦ δικαιοσύνην συνίστησιν) ; iii, 25-26 (εἰς ἔνδειξιν τῆς δικαιοσύνης αὐτοῦ).   In all other cases, it is a question of the divine justice which is in man; or at least the meaning is open to discussion.

[2] Phil. iii, 9 : μὴ ἔχων ἐμὴν δικαιοσύνην τὴν ἐκ νόμου, ἀλλὰ τὴν διὰ πίστεως Χριστοῦ, τὴν ἐκ Θεοῦ δικαιοσύνην ἐπὶ τῇ πίστει.   Here *God's justice* is described by its five characteristics : (1) It is not the exclusive property of man (μὴ ἔχων ἐμὴν δικ.).—(2) It does not come *from* the Law (ἐκ νόμου).—(3) It is produced *by* the faith of Jesus Christ (διὰ πίστεως).—(4) It originates *from* God (ἐκ Θεοῦ).—(5) It continues to depend *on* faith (ἐπὶ τῇ πίστει).

tion from Habacuc can evidently apply only to a justice inherent in man, although it has its source in God : " The justice of God is revealed therein from faith unto faith, as it is written : *The just man liveth by faith.*"[1] Moreover, the justice of God is defined later on, and the definition leaves no doubt of its true nature. It is " the justice of God by the faith of Jesus Christ unto all and upon all them that believe in him."[2] Such a justice does not remain confined in God; it spreads, propagates, and communicates itself, and becomes personal to man by means of faith.

Thus " God's justice " is sometimes the attribute which pertains to him as judge; but here it is the regeneration of man by faith and charity, a real creation with God alone for its author. The originality in Paul's doctrine lies in his making our justification originate in God's intrinsic justice and not in his power. God exercises and manifests his justice in justifying us by his grace. Such is the apparent paradox which we must examine after having proved that true justice, that which God wishes to find and which he crowns in us, is placed outside of the sphere of our efforts, and that consequently " we are justified *freely* " by the faith of Jesus Christ.[3]

This justice, which is at the same time God's and man's, " has been revealed in the Gospel." The revelation of a thing is not always its first manifestation. A truth is said to be revealed when it is illumined by a new light. Such is the mystery of redemption; and such is justification by faith, dimly foretold by the life of Abraham and by the signs of the prophets, and especially by Habacuc. This doctrine was almost uncomprehended, because no one could reconcile it with the declarations of Moses, which seemed to make all real justice depend upon the Law. Now, thanks to the Gospel, the question is cleared up. It is proved that, without faith, the Law can do nothing, and that faith can do everything even without the Law. It is a revelation : *Justitia Dei in eo revelatur.*

The words *ex fide in fidem* could be ignored without doing much harm to the meaning. They take the place of an adverbial phrase, qualifying either God's justice or the re-

---

[1] Rom. i, 17: Δικαιοσύνη γὰρ Θεοῦ ἐν αὐτῷ ἀποκαλύπτεται ἐκ πίστεως εἰς πίστιν καθὼς γέγραπται· ὁ δὲ δίκαιος ἐκ πίστεως ζήσεται. The sentence, united to the preceding one by the particle γάρ, explains why the Gospel is a " power of God unto salvation for every one that believeth."

[2] Rom. iii, 21, 22: Νυνὶ δὲ χωρὶς νόμου δικαιοσύνη Θεοῦ πεφανέρωται . . . δικαιοσύνη δὲ Θεοῦ διὰ πίστεως, κτλ. Compare Phil. iii, 9. This is evidently not the immanent justice of God: (a) which is revealed independently of the Law ; (b) which was predicted by the Law and the Prophets ; (c) which is produced by faith ; (d) which causes man to be justified freely. It is, therefore, a question of man's personal justice.

[3] Rom. iii, 24: δικαιούμενοι δωρεάν.

velation of it which is made in the Gospel. The simplest
exegesis consists in regarding them as expressing a gradation, a progress : from faith beginning to faith increasing,
from imperfect faith to full faith. Scripture is full of such
texts : " They shall go from virtue to virtue; they shall be
changed from glory into glory; from death unto death; from
life to life."

2. The powerlessness of the Law and of nature to justify
man can be proved by their very definition, by the notion of
supernatural justice, and by the present conflict between the
flesh and the spirit. The Apostle does not object to this kind
of demonstration; but in the first three chapters of the
Epistle to the Romans his mode of reasoning assumes a
simpler and more popular form. He seems to say : Run
through the history of humanity; do you find there the ideal
of justice which we all bear imprinted in our souls? No;
among both Jews and Gentiles sin has reigned without
hindrance. Reason could not resist the inclination to evil,
and the Law was too weak a barrier to it. Hence, unless we
are to despair of salvation, the goal of our aspirations, it is
necessary to ask this justice from the Gospel which promises
it and gives it.

The case against the Gentiles is argued with a vigour and
conciseness worthy of Paul. What is needed to deprive them
of all excuse? The knowledge of God and of the natural
Law, combined with a course of life diametrically opposed to
these lights :

> For the wrath of God is revealed from heaven against all ungodliness
> and injustice of those men that detain the truth of God in injustice.
> Because that which is known of God is manifest in them. For God
> hath manifested it unto them. For the invisible things of him from the
> creation of the world are clearly seen, being understood by the things
> that are made; his eternal power also and divinity, so that they are
> inexcusable. Because that, when they knew God, they have not glorified
> him as God, or given thanks; but became vain in their thoughts and
> their foolish heart was darkened. For professing themselves to be
> wise, they became fools. And they changed the glory of the incorrup-
> tible God into the likeness of the image of a corruptible man; and of birds
> and of four-footed beasts and of creeping things. Wherefore God gave
> them up to the desires of their heart.[1]

The wrath of God *is revealed,* not in the private tribunal
of the conscience, nor in the threatening warnings of Holy

---

[1] The whole passage (Rom. i, 18-32) is merely an immense period, of which
verses 18-23 form the protasis and verses 24-32 the apodosis. The idea is
condensed in verse 18 and developed in the rest, but in an inverse order:
(a) verses 19-20, knowledge of God (development of τὴν ἀλήθειαν κατεχόντων);
(b) 21-23, conduct opposed to this knowledge (ἐπὶ πᾶσαν ἀσέβειαν καὶ
ἀδικίαν ἀνθρώπων); (c) 24-32, the vengeance of an angered God
(ἀποκαλύπτεται ὀργὴ Θεοῦ ἀπ' οὐρανοῦ). It seems certain that ἀπ' οὐρανοῦ
refers to ἀποκαλύπτεται, and not to ὀργή or to Θεοῦ.

Scripture, nor in the dread scene of the *parousia,* as many exegetes think, but in this world—note the present tense ἀποκαλύπτεται—in the punishment inflicted by God upon ungodliness, and in a terrible blindness, the consequences of which are idolatry and shameful conduct. The heathen have both known God and disregarded him; that is their sin and the cause of God's wrath. The distinction, imagined by some exegetes, between philosophers and the vulgar masses is without foundation. Paul is speaking of the heathen in general; he proves that all have sinned, that they are all inexcusable, and that their sin consists precisely in having refused God, whom they knew, the honour which they owed him. Philosophers may be more guilty for having sinned more against the light, but they are not the only guilty ones. To limit the argument of the Apostle to them alone is to lose sight of his thesis and to weaken his reasoning.

The heathen knew God: this Paul affirms several times with remarkable clearness. He does not say that they *could* have known him; he says they knew him.

"They keep the truth captive in injustice."[1] Although the Gentiles are not named, there can be no doubt that they are intended. The whole context refers to them, and they are sufficiently indicated by their ungodliness (ἀσέβεια). The truth which they keep captive and oppress by hindering it from producing its natural fruits is the knowledge of God; and the Vulgate is right to add the word *Dei,* which is wanting in the original. They must, therefore, possess to some degree this truth, which they keep unjustly.

"That they know God is manifest in them; for God hath manifested it unto them."[2] This is not simply a potential

---

[1] i, 18: ἐπὶ πᾶσαν ἀσέβειαν καὶ ἀδικίαν ἀνθρώπων τῶν τὴν ἀλήθειαν ἐν ἀδικίᾳ κατεχόντων. The word κατέχειν signifies to "possess" and "keep." It can be well translated by "arrest" in the sense of "keeping hold of what one has in one's hand, to hinder it from acting or escaping," but not in the sense of "keeping off from oneself what one does not yet hold, in order to prevent it from approaching." The two texts quoted against this (Luke iv, 42 and 2 Thess. ii, 6-7) do not prove the contrary. Thus, in all probability "to hold fast (κατέχειν) the truth in injustice" is either to possess it, or to hinder it from acting, which presupposes possession. Bengel in his *Gnomon N.T.* gives the idea well: *Veritas in mente nititur et urget, sed homo eam impedit.* It is of little importance to our present purpose, whether the words ἐν ἀδικίᾳ mean "unjustly" or "through injustice," or "unjust as they are."

[2] i, 19: διότι τὸ γνωστὸν τοῦ Θεοῦ φανερόν ἐστιν ἐν αὐτοῖς · ὁ Θεὸς γὰρ αὐτοῖς ἐφανέρωσεν. The reason why (διότι) God's wrath is revealed is that they know God, yet do not honour him. The verbal adjective γνωστός, which in Plato means "knowable," in the Bible has only the meaning of "known." However, as Paul does not employ it elsewhere, we are free to choose. The Vulgate's translation, *quod notum est Dei,* has the appearance of tautology, which is avoided by taking, with Chrysostom, τὸ γνωστὸν τοῦ Θεοῦ in the sense of ἡ γνῶσις τοῦ Θεοῦ, the knowledge which one has of God, as in τὸ δυνατόν (Rom. ix, 22), τὸ χρηστόν (Rom. ii, 4), τὸ ἀσθενὲς τοῦ Θεοῦ

knowledge, but an actual knowledge, which has God for its author, and which appears plainly in the mind of the Gentiles (ἐν αὐτοῖς).

" Knowing God, they have not glorified him as God."[1] St Paul does not say *being able to know,* but *knowing* or *having known.* The heathen are inexcusable *because* they have known God without honouring him. And it is a question of the great mass of Gentiles, not of some rare, privileged individuals. Their crime is that of not having honoured God according to their lights, not possible but real. Could actual knowledge be expressed more clearly?

" Who having known the justice of God—that is to say, that they who do such things are worthy of death; not only do them, but also approve of them that do them."[2] According to the Latin, the heathen would know God *theoretically* (*cum cognovissent*), but would be ignorant of him *practically* (*non intellexerunt*). According to the original, they know him unreservedly, but act in a way contrary to their knowledge, either by doing evil or else by approving it in others; which denotes a greater degree of malice, as the Fathers justly remark. Paul does not relegate the knowledge which the heathen had of God to a distant past; he speaks of it as something notorious at the present time. Whoever knows the law of God and the penalties inflicted by him upon sin, knows divine justice; but whoever knows a divine attribute knows God himself.

Finally, the Apostle describes with admirable precision the twofold way which leads every rational man to a knowledge of God, as obscure and imperfect as you will, but, neverthe-

---

(1 Cor. i, 25). Only in our text τοῦ Θεοῦ is an objective genitive. Let us add that ἐν αὐτοῖς is not equivalent to αὐτοῖς and does not signify " among them " but " *in* them," in their reason and conscience. Similarly, ἐφανέρωσεν can be understood only as a "manifestation" of the truth perceived, and not as a presentation of the truth, to which they had closed their eyes.

[1] i, 21 : διότι γνόντες τὸν Θεὸν οὐχ ὡς Θεὸν ἐδόξασαν.

[2] Rom. i, 32 : οἵτινες τὸ δικαίωμα τοῦ Θεοῦ ἐπιγνόντες, ὅτι οἱ τὰ τοιαῦτα πράσσοντες ἄξιοι θανάτου εἰσίν. The relative οἵτινες "seeing that" (*quippe qui*) suggests the cause of the punishment inflicted by God. The heathen knew perfectly (ἐπιγνόντες, stronger than γνόντες) the δικαίωμα of God. Δικαίωμα=the sentence, what God declares just (δίκαιον); according to the context, it is a question here of a sentence of condemnation, for the purport of it is expressed immediately; it is that the authors of these crimes are " worthy of death " everlasting. In order to make the Vulgate conform to the Greek text, we must omit the words : (1) *non intellexerunt ;* (2) *et* (before *non solum*) ; (3) and the word *qui* twice ; and note further that *justitia Dei* is not the immanent justice of God, but his judgement (τὸ δικαίωμα). The literal translation would be : *Qui cognoscentes judicium Dei (quod qui talia agunt digni sunt morte) non solum ea faciunt, sed etiam applaudunt facientibus.* The critical edition of the Vulgate by Wordsworth and White omits the *et* before *non solum,* and the following word *qui* twice.

less, a real knowledge; the spectacle of the created universe and the moral law engraved upon our hearts.

The cosmological proof of the existence of God, reminding us of the Book of Wisdom, makes us think also of Aristotle and Philo. The latter compares created beings to a series of steps, which raise us to the conception of God; but, too much of a Platonist, he seems to admit only a probable argument and only a conjectural knowledge. According to Aristotle : " God, all invisible as he is, makes himself visible by his very works." The Book of Wisdom goes a step further by suggesting the mode of proof : " Through the grandeur and beauty of created objects, he who orders them is perceived by analogy." Paul emphasizes this still more : " The invisible things of God, his eternal power and divinity, intellectually perceived in his works, are clearly seen in the creation of the world."[1] All four well show the origin of our knowledge; but Paul is the only one to specify that aspect of the divine being (God's eternal power and divinity), which is the conclusion of the mental operation. For him God's creatures are a means of proof, as well as a kind of mirror wherein God reflects his principal attributes. In fact, the spectacle of the finite, the incidental, and the relative leads by the triple way of negation, causality, and analogy to a knowledge of the infinite, the necessary, and the absolute. The bond of union between God and man is intelligence (νοῦς) ; the animals, like ourselves, behold the world, but, through lack of thinking, do not see God in it.

The three divine attributes reflected in the world are, according to St Paul, his power, eternity, and divinity. God is in the world as the cause is in the effect, but he is not generally perceived there under the abstract notion of cause. The spectacle of the universe suggests to the mind rather the idea of an *omnipotent* creator. This power, as the simplest reasoning shows, must have always existed,

---

[1] Philo, *De praem. et poen.*, 7 (Mangey, vol. ii, p. 415): Οἷα διά τινος οὐρανίου κλίμακος ἀπὸ τῶν ἔργων εἰκότι λογισμῷ στοχασάμενοι τὸν δημιουργόν. Aristotle, *De mundo*, 6: Ἀθεώρητος ἀπ' αὐτῶν τῶν ἔργων θεωρεῖται. Wisdom xiii, 5: Ἐκ μεγέθους, καλλονῆς καὶ κτισμάτων ἀναλόγως ὁ γενεσιουργὸς αὐτῶν θεωρεῖται (another reading, καὶ καλλονῆς κτισμάτων). Rom. i, 20: τὰ γὰρ ἀόρατα αὐτοῦ ἀπὸ κτίσεως κόσμου τοῖς ποιήμασι νοούμενα καθορᾶται, ἥ τε ἀΐδιος αὐτοῦ δύναμις καὶ θειότης. As the mode of demonstration appears to be expressed here by two equivalents (τοῖς ποιήμασιν and ἀπὸ κτίσεως κόσμου), certain exegetes, on the pretext of avoiding tautology, translate these last words by "since the creation of the world," a meaning that ἀπό has in Matt. xxiv, 21, Luke xi, 50 and Mark x, 6. But the phrase "since the creation of the world" seems quite useless, and a comparison of the four formulas hardly permits us to suppose that the word ἀπό, which is deductive in the others, is not so in St Paul's sentence. We may avoid the pretended tautology very easily by taking *per modum unius* the expression τοῖς ποιήμασι νοούμενα (perceived intellectually *in* the works or *by* the works), and joining ἀπὸ κτίσεως κόσμου to καθορᾶται.

since it cannot produce itself, and since, if we suppose it
to be produced by another, this other would be God : it is,
therefore, *eternal*. To these two attributes of power and
eternity (ἡ ἀίδιος δύναμις) Paul adds *divinity* (θειότης). The
word is admirably chosen. Above the gods of Olympus, who
were gods only through an abuse of language, the heathen
placed a *supremum summumque numen,* called by the Greeks
τὸ θεῖον, or ὁ θεός, whose character was incomparable highness
and unapproachable majesty, in a word, transcendence.
This, we think, is what Paul desires to express by this third
attribute. He speaks here neither of wisdom, although it is
so apparent in the order of the universe; nor of goodness,
although it shines forth so radiantly in the special providence
of which man is the object; but his enumeration of attributes
is not intended to be a complete one, and he nowhere affirms
that the mirror of this world, known to our senses, reflects
no other divine attribute.

Without having to go outside of themselves, the pagans
found God in the depths of their hearts. The natural law is
engraved there in indelible characters. We have seen that
the pagans "know the judgement of God, and are aware
that sinners merit death;" but the knowledge of the sanction
implies the knowledge of a supreme Lawgiver, who is none
other than God. It is true that in the classic passage in
which the Apostle teaches the existence of the natural law,
he does not put it explicitly in relation with God. This is
because he speaks of it incidentally and, as it were,
parenthetically, in connection with the principles of justice
which direct the divine verdicts.

> There is no respect of persons with God. For whosoever have sinned
> without the law, shall perish without the law ; and whosoever have
> sinned in the law, shall be judged by the law. For not the hearers of
> the law are just before God, but the doers of the law shall be justified.
> (For when the Gentiles, who have not the law, do by nature those things
> that are of the law, these, having not the law, are a law unto themselves.
> Who show the work of the law written in their hearts, their conscience
> bearing witness to them, and their thoughts between themselves accusing,
> or also defending one another.)
> [So shall it be] in the day when God shall judge the secrets of men
> by Jesus Christ, according to my Gospel.[1]

---

[1] Rom. ii, 11-16. We think that the principal thought is continuous
at the two ends of the parenthesis : " The doers of the law shall be justified
. . . in the day when God," etc. But it is only the parenthesis (ii, 14, 15)
which must occupy us here.

(*a-d*) Ὅταν γὰρ ἔθνη τὰ μὴ νόμον ἔχοντα φύσει τὰ τοῦ νόμου ποιῶσιν,

(*e*) οὗτοι νόμον μὴ ἔχοντες ἑαυτοῖς εἰσι νόμος·

(*f*) οἵτινες ἐνδείκνυνται τὸ ἔργον τοῦ νόμου γραπτὸν ἐν ταῖς καρδίαις αὐτῶν.

(*g*) συμμαρτυρούσης αὐτῶν τῆς συνειδήσεως,

(*h*) καὶ μεταξὺ ἀλλήλων τῶν λογισμῶν κατηγορούντων ἢ καὶ ἀπολογουμένων.

(*a*) *When* (ὅταν) indicates, not a hypothesis, but a fact, *quotiescumque.—*
(*b*) *The Gentiles* (ἔθνη, indeterminate), any pagan. The abstract is for the

It is a fact that the Gentiles sometimes conform to the requirements of the Mosaic Law, so far as it is moral law. The case is not chimerical, and the Apostle does not give it as such. That he is speaking of the heathen and not of Christians who have come from the Gentiles is indubitable, and had it not been for the controversies connected with Pelagianism, St Augustine would never have imagined the contrary. The heathen, therefore, sometimes conform to the Law of Moses, with which they are not acquainted. It is not a question of an involuntary, accidental concurrence, which would prove nothing, but of a free and deliberate act. By the very fact they show the existence of an inward light, which leads them and takes the place of a law for them, they are a law unto themselves, not their ultimate law, which supposes the power to lay upon them an obligation with a proportionate sanction, but their immediate law, which is the promulgation of

---

concrete, as appears from the masculine pronouns (οὗτοι, οἵτινες) which refer to it.—(c) *By nature* (φύσει) can signify only "by their natural light"; for the law in all this context is considered only as a supernatural light. —(d) *Do those things that are of the Law* (what the Law prescribes, τὰ τοῦ νόμου ποιῶσιν—i.e., ἔργα or δικαιώματα being understood) without any indication of few or many. Paul says τὰ τοῦ νόμου and not τὸν νόμον, because the heathen do not observe the Law, even when doing what the Law commands.—(e) *They are a law unto themselves.* They find in themselves the equivalent of the Law, in so far as it is a guide. The reason for this is given immediately (οἵτινες, *quippe qui*).—(f) In τὸ ἔργον τοῦ νόμου the word ἔργον may be active or passive. If it is passive, as the majority of exegetes think, the meaning will be "the work done conformably to the Law" (a synonym for τὰ τοῦ νόμου); but then how can this work be written in the heart? If it is active, the sense will be "what the Law does"; the Law having for its aim to enlighten and to guide man, the heathen finds in his heart, in his conscience, this guidance and this light.—(g) *Their conscience bearing witness* (συμμαρτυρούσης) to the existence of this inward law. If translated "their conscience bearing witness *to them*," the οὖν of the composite verb would remain unexplained. The Latin *illis* corresponds to nothing in the Greek and is probably not authentic.—(h) The most important and most difficult incidental phrase is the last. The present Vulgate is not very clear: *et inter se invicem cogitationibus accusantibus aut etiam defendentibus.* Some exegetes see in this only a paraphrase of the testimony of the conscience, but most try to find in it the verdict of reason as far as it is distinct from conscience. But here they divide. Most of them believe that it is a question of the same individual who voluntarily judges himself. Only the μεταξὺ ἀλλήλων, if referred to the judgements of an individual passed upon himself, is then very difficult to explain. Indeed, either it is a question of the *same act* about which the individual judgements are in conflict, though this struggle and uncertainty are rather opposed to the existence of a conscience; or else it is a question of different acts, some of which are condemned and others absolved by the interior verdict; but then the μεταξὺ ἀλλήλων has no longer any *raison d'être.* It is better, therefore, to understand these words as of *different individuals*, who condemn or absolve one another (μεταξὺ ἀλλήλων). In this way the natural law is proved by the conscience *and* by reason, which makes us approve or blame our fellow-creatures. See Quirmbach (Catholic), *Die Lehre des heil. Paulus von der natürlichen Gotteserkenntnis und dem natürlichen Sittengesetz,* Freiburg i. B., 1906, pp. 60-85.

a superior law; they let others see the work of the Law written in their hearts. Nature does for them what the Mosaic revelation did for Israel; it instructs them and guides them authoritatively. The words *by nature* (φύσει), which the Pelagians made a bad use of, can signify only "guided, enlightened, impelled by nature." It is useless, therefore, to ask whether the Gentiles, without the aid of grace, have observed few or many of the precepts of the natural law; for this is not a matter of a little more or a little less, and the rôle of grace is not the question with which we are concerned. If they had observed only one of its precepts, with or without the aid of grace, they would have shown that they knew it. They show it, according to St Paul, in three ways: by the fact that they follow an inward standard of moral goodness; by the testimony which their conscience adds to this when, after the action, it approves or condemns them; finally, by the amount of blame or praise which they are wont to bestow on one another.

The heathen, therefore, knew God as First Cause and Supreme Lawgiver. The Fathers of the Church remarked— and the comparative history of religions confirms their view —that the religious ideas of peoples are often independent of their degree of civilization, and are in any case much superior to their mythology. Only read St Justin, St Irenæus, Theophilus of Antioch, Arnobius, St Jerome, and especially St Augustine, Tertullian, Clement of Alexandria on this subject. Tertullian distinguishes himself above all by the virile vigour of his logical eloquence, and his *De testimonio animae* is the best indirect commentary on this chapter of St Paul.

The Vatican Council, relying on our text, has defined that God *can* be known by man: (*a*) with certainty; (*b*) by the light of reason alone; (*c*) by means of his creation; (*d*) as Creator and Lord, as the only and true God. But St Paul goes further; he speaks of the *fact,* not merely of the *possibility* of this. St Thomas perfectly apprehended his thought when he summed it up in his commentary thus: *Fuit in eis quantum ad aliquid vera cognitio Dei.* Those who have wished to understand by this a potential knowledge seem to us to have been influenced by considerations foreign to the exegesis. It is scarcely necessary to observe how far the doctrine of the first reformers differed on this point from the Apostle's teaching. Extreme traditionalism finds in this also its condemnation. The same is true of ontologism. As for moderate traditionalism, the most favourable thing one can say of it is that it harmonizes very badly with the theology of Paul.

Having disregarded the God whom their reason had made them know, the heathen underwent the most terrible of punishments : they were delivered over to themselves—that is to say, to their passions, to the spirit of error and falsehood, and to sensual depravity. To deliver someone over to his mortal enemies is not only to allow him to fall under their blows. The attitude of the general who exposes his army to rout by ceasing to lead it, or that of the physician who dooms his patient to death by suspending his remedies, is not purely a passive one. In this complex act of divine justice three elements can be distinguished : permission, without which no evil is possible; partial abandonment—that is to say, a withdrawal of chosen graces which leaves intact the free will with moral responsibility, but increases the probability of falling into sin by reason of diminished aid; finally, a judgement, by which God withdraws his graces, as a punishment for men's malice, ingratitude, and obstinacy. Thus the first sin becomes the cause (not necessary but incidental) of the second; and the second is the real, though indirect punishment of the first.

In this way the origin and progress of idolatry in the world are explained. Before being the mother of so many disorders, it was itself the daughter of sin. There were two phases in the process of degeneracy : first, the gradual clouding of the mind, and then the perversion of the heart and the obliteration of the moral sense. For having found delight in their sophistries, the pagans are left to their own lights, which are only darkness, and to their own wisdom, which is merely folly. For having dishonoured God by prostituting the worship of him to that of his creatures, they are delivered over to the shame which they mutually bring on one another. Victims of divine justice, they are also its executioners upon one another. It is the punishment of the *lex talionis* applied in all its strictness. However, the Apostle does not wish it to be supposed that there is enough conscience among the heathen to excuse them. Hence, after his historical review of the origin, progress, and consequences of idolatry, he comes back to his point of departure and shows, in concluding, the Gentiles still in possession of the idea of God and of the natural law : " Who, knowing the justice of God, who declares that they who do such things are worthy of death, not only do them, but also praise them that do them."

Such is the dark picture of heathenism which Paul draws for us. He does not contradict himself in his other Epistles, and the testimony of profane writers proves that he does not exaggerate. All the Jews, with the Mosaic code in their hands, judged the Gentiles very severely; heathen and sinner, idolater and fornicator were for them synonymous terms. They were especially disgusted by the unnatural vices of which the Greco-Roman world presented a hideous spectacle.

What distinguishes Paul from his compatriots is his sympathetic attitude towards the heathen; he pities them without despising them, and accuses them without condemning them beyond the hope of pardon. He puts them on the same footing as the Jews, and if he includes them all in one and the same act of accusation, he leaves to both the hope of the Gospel.

3. As long as the Apostle was conducting his case against the Gentiles, he heard the approving murmur of the Jews applauding all his words. It is now against them that he is about to direct his denunciation. This was in appearance an easy task, yet in reality a very delicate one; easy, for it was sufficient for him to appeal to facts and to the testimony of Scripture; delicate, for he had to safeguard the privileges which raised the monotheistic Jews above the idolatrous Greeks. He shows that these prerogatives either do not belong to them exclusively, or, in the sense in which they are really theirs, aggravate their guilt instead of lessening it.

The testimony of fact is crushing; it fills the whole of chapter ii: "Thou art inexcusable, O man, whosoever thou art that judgest. For wherein thou judgest another thou dost condemn thyself, for thou dost the same things which thou judgest."[1] It is impossible to plead ignorance or good faith. "Thou that teachest another teachest not thyself; thou that preachest that men should not steal, stealest; thou that sayest men should not commit adultery, committest adultery; thou that abhorrest idols, committest sacrilege; thou that makest thy boast of the Law by transgression of the Law dishonourest God."[2]

The testimony of Scripture is still more decisive:

> There is none that doeth good, no, not one; there is none that understands and seeks God; they are all gone aside, they are become unprofitable altogether; there is none that doeth good, no, not one.[3] Their throat is an open sepulchre; with their tongues they acted deceitfully;[4] the poison of asps is under their lips;[5] their mouth is full of cursing and bitterness;[6] their feet are swift to shed blood. Destruction and unhappiness are in their ways; the way of peace have they not known;[7] there is no fear of God before their eyes.[8]

In this collection of biblical texts all the parts have not the same convincing force. The first passage only is wholly

---

[1] Rom. ii, 1. Paul's skill lies in compelling the Jews, without directly accusing them, to pronounce their own condemnation.

[2] Rom. ii, 21-23. The words which follow (ii, 24) are less a quotation in the true sense of the word, than an accommodation of Isa. lii, 5 in the free LXX version which adds ἐν τοῖς ἔθνεσι.

[3] Ps. xiii, 1-3. That which proves that the Apostle has this passage in view and not Ps. lii, 2-4, which is almost identical, is the word χρηστότης.

[4] Ps. v, 10.   [5] Ps. cxxxix, 3.   [6] Ps. ix, 28.

[7] Isa. lix, 7-8.   [8] Ps. xxxv, 2.

general : the Psalmist complains of the malice of men, among whom he does not find one that doeth good; Isaias addresses the Jews of his time; the third and fourth texts apply to the enemies of David; the other two concern sinners and the ungodly, without any hint of their number. But the argument formed by this series of texts, which recalls the rabbinical method of the *haraz*, is sufficient for the Apostle's present design. Wishing to close the mouth of the Jews, who were so proud of their origin and prerogatives, among a thousand texts which accuse them, he takes at random five or six well-known passages, enough to remind them of the constant reproofs heaped upon them by the prophets. He does not pretend that there has never been, in the mass of the Hebrew people, a little group of just men faithful to Jehovah, but he maintains that the vast majority was unfaithful.

In spite of these partial exceptions, the thesis which he defends is a most delicate one, for he has to beat down the pride of the Jews without touching their privileges, and to establish the equality of all in regard to sin and in the presence of grace without contesting the pre-eminence of the chosen people. From this come his apparent hesitations and sudden reversions. These may be judged by the following curious dialogue which we present in the form of a slightly paraphrased translation :[1]

Objector: "What advantage, then, have the Jews, and what is the profit of circumcision?"

Paul: " [Their advantage is] much every way. First, because the words of God were committed to them."

Objector: "But what if some of them have not believed [or even a great number of them]?"

Paul: " [What matters that?] Shall their unbelief make the fidelity of God without effect? God forbid. God is necessarily true, and every man a liar, as it is written : That thou mayest be justified in thy words, and mayest overcome when thou art judged."[2]

Objector: "But if our injustice make the justice of God prevail, what shall we say? Is not God unjust when he executeth wrath? I speak according to man."

Paul: "Certainly not. For how could God judge this world [if he were not an upright judge]?"

Objector: "Yet if the truth of God hath more abounded unto his glory through my lie, why am I still judged as a sinner [since my lie hath served the cause of God]? Would it not rather be right to say : Let us do evil, that good may come?"

Paul: "Certain people slander us by saying that we teach that; but they shall be punished as they deserve."

---

[1] Rom. iii, 1-9.　　　　　　　　[2] Ps. li, 6.

Objector: "Well, do we [Jews] have an advantage [over the others? Yes or no.]"

Paul: "Not entirely. For we have just shown that all Jews and Gentiles are under the [yoke of] sin."

Paul here confronts an objector, whose five objections he demolishes one by one; or rather he talks to himself and replies to himself in order to instruct the reader. His last word brings him back to his thesis, and he sums up in this concise form the first three chapters: *Omnes sub peccato esse.* All men are equal in having sinned, and in the light of God's grace. Now, side by side with the evil, he is going to place the remedy. He does so briefly and without commentary, because this is a question of ideas which were the subject of the apostolic catechesis, and must have been well known to all his readers.

II—SALVATION THROUGH THE GOSPEL

1. The Respective Share in this of the Father, Christ and Man.
2. Harmonies in the Plan of Redemption.

1. The history of mankind before Christ, then, may be concisely stated as follows: "All men, Jews and Greeks, are under the dominion of sin." But Paul, who believes in a supernatural providence, does not leave us under the weight of this painful statement. He shows us God, meditating plans of mercy, and entering upon the scene at the moment when the impotence of nature and of the Law is clearly evident.

> But now without the law the justice of God is made manifest, being witnessed by the law and the prophets, even the justice of God by faith of Jesus Christ unto all and upon all them that believe in him. For there is no distinction; for all have sinned and do need the glory of God, being justified freely by his grace, through the redemption that is in Christ Jesus. Whom God hath proposed to be a propitiation through faith in his blood, to the showing of his justice for the remission of former sins, through the forbearance of God for the showing of his justice in this time; that he himself may be just and the justifier of him, who is of the faith of Jesus Christ.[1]

---

[1] Rom. iii, 21-26:

A. (21) Νυνὶ δὲ χωρὶς νόμου δικαιοσύνη Θεοῦ πεφανέρωται, μαρτυρουμένη ὑπὸ τοῦ νόμου καὶ τῶν προφητῶν, (22) δικαιοσύνη δὲ Θεοῦ διὰ πίστεως Ἰησοῦ Χριστοῦ, εἰς πάντας [καὶ ἐπὶ πάντας] τοὺς πιστεύοντας.

B. οὐ γάρ ἐστιν διαστολή· (23) πάντες γὰρ ἥμαρτον καὶ ὑστεροῦνται τῆς δόξης τοῦ Θεοῦ, (24) δικαιούμενοι δωρεὰν τῇ αὐτοῦ χάριτι διὰ τῆς ἀπολυτρώσεως τῆς ἐν Χριστῷ Ἰησοῦ,

C. (25) ὃν προέθετο ὁ Θεὸς ἱλαστήριον διὰ πίστεως, ἐν τῷ αὐτοῦ αἵματι, εἰς ἔνδειξιν τῆς δικαιοσύνης αὐτοῦ διὰ τὴν πάρεσιν τῶν προγεγονότων ἁμαρτημάτων (26) ἐν τῇ ἀνοχῇ τοῦ Θεοῦ, πρὸς τὴν ἔνδειξιν τῆς δικαιοσύνης αὐτοῦ, ἐν τῷ νῦν καιρῷ, εἰς τὸ εἶναι αὐτὸν δίκαιον καὶ δικαιοῦντα τὸν ἐκ πίστεως Ἰησοῦ.

Let us put aside, for the moment, the idea of *justice of God*, which will be studied in the second volume, and the two words *propitiation* and *redemption*, which form the subject of Note E.

This passage has appeared to some authors the epitome and mother-idea of St Paul's theology. There are few passages certainly which go more deeply into the very heart of his doctrine, and which are richer in their instruction. But an understanding of it is dependent on four or five questions, which it is impossible to treat here, because they touch upon the Apostle's general soteriology : What is God's anger? Does it imply his active enmity? How can we reconcile that with his ever-active mercy? What is reconciliation? Is it one-sided or reciprocal? In other words, is God content to reconcile us to himself, or does he also reconcile

---

Section A.—It is expedient to examine the time, manner, instrument and subject of this justice.—(*a*) *The time* is the present, the régime of the Gospel (νυνί), in contrast to the past and to the régime of the Law. The νυνί cannot indicate a logical consequence, for what follows is not the result of what precedes, but *vice versa*. Moreover, Paul is accustomed to indicate a contrast between the past and present by means of the conjunction νῦν (or νυνί), often joined to the verb φανεροῦσθαι, Rom. xvi, 26 ; Col. i, 26 ; 2 Tim. i, 10, etc. The particle δὲ in δικαιοσύνη δὲ Θεοῦ is not adversative it only causes the resumption of the subject of the sentence, according to a usage familiar to Paul, and might be translated by "I say."—(*b*) *The manner.* The justice of God *is manifested* permanently in the Gospel (Rom. i, 17 : ἀποκαλύπτεται) ; but it *was manifested* at the death of Christ with a brilliancy which still endures (hence the perfect πεφανέρωται). It was manifested without the Law, *independently of it* (χωρὶς νόμου) ; seeing that the Law revealed sin, not justice (iii, 20). It was nevertheless manifested *conformably to the Law and the prophets* and with their *testimony*, for the Law (Gen. xv, 6) relates that Abraham was justified by faith, and Habacuc (ii, 9) asserts that the just shall live by faith.—(*c*) *The instrument.* Faith is not justice, but justice is *by* faith (διὰ πίστεως) ; for faith is the first step towards justice, the condition to which justice is attached, and the means which God uses to produce justice in us. And this is not any kind of faith, as for example the faith of which Christ is the author (as Berlage claims), nor that of which he is the subject (as Haussleiter and Kittel suppose), but that of which he is the object : faith *in* Jesus Christ.—(*d*) *The subject.* This is *all* believers and believers *only*. The extension of supernatural justice is determined in two ways : it exists only where faith is found, for, independently of faith, there is no distinction between men (iii, 23) ; it is found everywhere where true faith exists, for it is produced by faith (iii, 22, 24, 26). This is what Paul expresses when he says that it is directed by a spontaneous movement *unto* (εἰς) all who believe, to whom it is equally destined, and that it rests *upon* (ἐπί) all who believe. If the words καὶ ἐπὶ πάντας are authentic, as is probable, they cannot be explained otherwise, for it is entirely arbitrary to say that εἰς refers to the Jews and ἐπί to the Gentiles, or that the two propositions are absolutely synonymous.

Section B.—This section, forming a parenthesis, offers a certain number of difficulties of detail, which fortunately have no serious influence on the sense of the whole passage.—(*a*) The punctuation of the Clementine Vulgate leaves something to be desired. *Non enim est distinctio* ought not to be separated by a period from what follows, nor should *justificati* be separated from what precedes ; it is the same sentence which continues : "There is no distinction, [*for* all have sinned and are deprived of the glory of God, *in view of the fact that they* are and should be] justified," etc. *Non enim est distinctio, omnes enim peccaverunt* repeats the thought expressed previously (iii, 9) : *Causati sumus Judaeos et Graecos omnes sub peccato esse.*—(*b*) *Justificati* ought to be understood as if there were a present participle (δικαιού-

himself to us? Is redemption, through the death of Christ, on the part of the Father an act of justice or a pure act of goodness? Is Christ's death itself a true sacrifice of expiation, or a simple manifestation of love? For want of a previous reply to all these questions, more than one point is left unexplained; yet our text may contribute valuable help towards their solution.

A striking feature of it, which is entirely in the spirit of Paul's theology, is the Father's initiative. Man's reconciliation is absolutely impossible, unless God takes the first steps. The Son accepts the rôle of Saviour and even desires it, but

---

μενοι); otherwise there would be an evident contradiction with what has just been said : *egent gloria Dei*.—(*c*) Does the *glory of God* refer to celestial glory, or to grace, the seed of glory ? or to the commendation and approbation of God ? or to the reason for glorying before God ? or to a sort of supernatural brilliancy, divine light, comparable to the *Shekinah* of the Hebrews (in the Septuagint δόξα, *gloria*) or to the *hvarenah* of the Persians ? The last idea is too far-fetched, and the reason for glorying is called by St Paul καύχημα (*gloriatio*) and not δόξα (*gloria*). As ὑστεροῦνται has lost its etymological meaning (*to be left behind* in a race, or *to miss the prize* in a contest), and hardly means anything more than *to miss* or *be deprived* of a thing which one ought to have or could have, it is better to understand δόξα τοῦ Θεοῦ as the *grace of God*, of which the sinner is really deprived, either sanctifying grace (the formal cause) or divine favour (the efficient cause), of justification.—(*d*) The words *justificati gratis per gratiam ipsius* do not comprise a tautology : " Justified *freely* (δωρεάν) by the *merciful goodness* of God " (τῇ αὐτοῦ χάριτι). It is useless to seek in these last words the formal cause of justification.

Section C.—(*a*) We might be tempted to compare προέθετο with πρόθεσις (the eternal decree of God), and we should then paraphrase it thus : " God had formerly, from all eternity, *decided* that Christ should one day be a *propitiation.*" But there are three objections to this : (1) *the context*, all the characteristics of which indicate a brilliant manifestation of divine justice (πεφανέρωται, εἰς ἔνδειξιν, πρὸς τὴν ἔνδειξιν); (2) the *parallelism* with Gal. iii, 1 (κατ' ὀφθαλμοὺς προεγράφη); (3) the *ordinary meaning* of the verb, especially in the middle voice. The use of the middle voice is explained by God's *intention* to manifest *his* justice. The preposition in προέθετο does not, therefore, denote time, but *place*, as in the Latin *proponere*, to *put before* the sight or the mind of someone.—(*b*) What God exposes thus publicly, in order that all may see it and appropriate it to themselves, is a *means of propitiation* (see Note E) *by faith* (which assures the application and individual efficaciousness of it) *in his blood* (in the blood of the Son, who confers upon it its intrinsic virtue). The two phrases διὰ πίστεως and ἐν τῷ αὐτοῦ αἵματι are independent of each other and refer directly to ἱλαστήριον.—(*c*) God wishes in this way to repair the negligence which he seems to have shown formerly in regard to sin (διὰ τὴν πάρεσιν, διά final with the accusative). The word πάρεσις indicates " the action of allowing to take place, to overlook " the sins of men without appearing to take notice of them. This attitude is explained by ἐν τῇ ἀνοχῇ τοῦ Θεοῦ, " while God suffered them."—(*d*) And this extraordinary long-suffering, this apparent indifference in regard to sin, is justified by God's *design* of making the manifestation of his justice still more glorious, when the moment came (πρὸς τὴν ἔνδειξιν τῆς δικαιοσύνης αὐτοῦ· πρὸς final, *in order* to prove).—(*e*) The definitive result of all this divine plan is " to be [and to be recognized as] just " by acting thus, and " to justify the believer " (εἰς τὸ εἶναι αὐτὸν δίκαιον καὶ δικαιοῦντα). It might almost be translated : " to be just *in* justifying those who believe."

it is his Father who acts first : " He was in Christ reconciling the world to himself."[1] The initiative always belongs to him. On Calvary " he shows forth his Son openly as a victim of propitiation." He wishes to display before the eyes of the whole human race his justice, too long concealed by his forbearance. For centuries he tolerated men's crimes, or inflicted upon them only punishments disproportionate to their number and wickedness. Men might have wondered whether sin was really hateful to him. Now he shows, or rather *demonstrates* (εἰς ἔνδειξιν) his justice in the sight of heaven and earth by attaching the sinner's justification to an act and to a fact which place in bold relief his own justice. In this way the justice of man will be able to be called the justice of God, not only because God takes the initiative in it, and is its first cause, but because he makes it originate in his immanent justice.

The rôle of the Son is summed up thus : He is made a propitiation (ἱλαστήριον); he effects redemption (ἀπολύτρωσις); and this in his blood (ἐν τῷ αὐτοῦ αἵματι) or by his blood.

We shall prove elsewhere that the death of Jesus has the character of a sacrifice, and of a propitiatory sacrifice. Christ dying is compared to all the victims of the ancient Law, to the paschal lamb, to the blood of the covenant and of expiation, to the offering for sin ; almost all the terms of the ritual of sacrifices are applicable to him; and the way in which he himself speaks of his own death hardly permits us to doubt that the teaching of the apostles goes back to him. On the other hand, the remission of sins is constantly associated with the death of Jesus Christ; it is the sprinkling of his blood that purifies souls, appeases the wrath of God, renders him propitious and annuls the effect of sin. This is how Jesus on the Cross is propitiatory, or to come more closely to the meaning of St Paul—a " means of propitiation " in the hands of the Father; and this is how he is a redeemer, paying for our deliverance with his divine blood.

Nevertheless, man does not play a purely passive rôle. Jesus Christ wins for him supernatural justice; the Father offers it to him; but he must himself take it. He is an actor, not a mere spectator, in this drama; and his salvation is not effected without him. His contribution is faith. For " the justice of God is *by* the faith of Jesus Christ,"[2] by the faith of which he is the meritorious cause and the first object. Jesus Christ is a " propitiation *by* faith."[3] A pleasing and holy victim, independently of faith, he contains an infinite power of satisfaction and propitiation for sin ; but the pro-

[1] 2 Cor. v, 18-19. He is in Christ (ἐν Χριστῷ) when he effects the reconciliation of the world, and he uses Christ as an instrument of reconciliation (διὰ Χριστοῦ).

[2] Rom. iii, 22 : δικαιοσύνη δὲ Θεοῦ διὰ πίστεως Ἰησοῦ Χριστοῦ.

[3] iii, 25 : ἱλαστήριον διὰ πίστεως ἐν τῷ αὐτοῦ αἵματι. It is beyond doubt that we must connect ἐν τῷ αὐτοῦ αἵματι not with διὰ πίστεως, but with ἱλαστήριον,

pitiation becomes efficacious only by means of faith. Without faith, the satisfaction, all sufficient and superabundant as it is, remains inactive. God " justifies *him who is of the faith of Jesus Christ,*"[1] but he does not justify otherwise. Justification " comes to *all who believe*[2] and rests upon them all," but it comes to them only.

2. The plan of salvation, in the mind of the Apostle, must fulfil three conditions :

It must be universal, like grace and mercy. This is a consequence of monotheism. Since there is only one God, he is necessarily the God of the Gentiles as well as of the Jews. On the other hand, he sees in man no reason for preference, for " all have sinned and feel themselves deprived of the glory of God." Consequently, the time for privileges is past ; the era of equality in the Gospel has begun.

It must confound the pride of man. There is, in the eyes of Paul, no sentiment more unreasonable, more impious, and more insulting to God than man's vainglory in regard to salvation. God, wishing that no flesh should be able to boast in his sight, chose faith as an instrument of salvation in order to compel him to give thanks to him.

Finally, it must conform to the old revelation, or, at least, not be contrary to it. The Old Testament is the type, the prophecy, and the preparation for the New ; moreover, it is evident that God, the Author of the Law as well as of the Gospel, cannot contradict himself.

Now the method adopted by God, when he makes salvation depend on faith, satisfies the three conditions required. It is *universal,* for there is no feeling more general, more simple and spontaneous than faith ; and since it was necessary to require something from man in order not to save him in spite of himself and with no action on his part, he could be asked for nothing more suitable. It is *the thing best adapted to mortify pride,* for faith is the humble gesture of the poor man imploring charity, and receiving it in the very instant that he asks for it.[3] It *agrees with the Scripture records,* and is " attested by the Law and the Prophets " ; far from contradicting the Law, it " confirms " it.[4] Witness David,

---

or, if preferred, to προέθετο ἱλαστήριον. The διὰ πίστεως is then the instrument which applies to the believer the propitiation of Christ or the virtue of his redeeming blood.

[1] iii, 26 : τόν ἐκ πίστεως, " he who takes faith for a guide or for a lever." Cf. οἱ ἐξ ἐριθείας (ii, 8) and ὅσοι ἐξ ἔργων νόμου (Gal. iii, 10).

[2] Note the insistence with which Paul extends justice to *all* who believe (Rom. i, 16 ; iii, 22 ; iv, 11 ; x, 4-11, etc.), and makes of all men potential believers. [3] Eph. ii, 8. For this text see p. 275.

[4] Rom. iii, 21 : μαρτυρουμένη ὑπὸ τοῦ νόμου καὶ τῶν προφητῶν. Here the Law evidently means the Torah, the Pentateuch—iii, 31 : νόμον οὖν καταργοῦμεν διὰ τῆς πίστεως ; μὴ γένοιτο, ἀλλὰ νόμον ἱστάνομεν.

who speaks in the name of the prophets, and Abraham, who personifies the Law.

The Psalmist, conscious of his sins and desirous of recovering his lost justice, does not seek to conquer the friendship of God by force. He does not put his confidence in sacrifices or observances of the Law. He raises his eyes to heaven and cries : " Blessed are they whose iniquities are forgiven and whose sins are covered. Blessed is the man to whom the Lord hath not imputed sin,"[1] and he confesses by his humble prayer the free gift of grace, counting only on faith.

The justification of the Father of the faithful is marked by three characteristics which make it the striking type of Christian justification. First, it is anterior to the Law of Moses, and even to the circumcision; consequently, it is independent of them : Scripture affirms that faith was imputed to him unto justice even before circumcision was mentioned; circumcision was only the seal of justice received, the sacred sign that rendered him fit to become the father of the Jews, as he was already by faith the father of them that believe. Furthermore, it is free, for it is given in return for a thing which is not equivalent to justice, and which is itself a gift of God. Finally, it glorifies God so much the more as it takes from man all occasion for vainglory.

The faith of Abraham was four times put to the proof; when he left his native country ; when he believed, against all hope, in the birth of Isaac; when he restored to him (Isaac) the right of primogeniture; and when he set about immolating him. But it was after the second trial, when God asked him only to believe, that Scripture gives him this testimony : " Abraham believed God, and it was imputed to him unto justice."[2] This reflection is general and qualifies, on one

---

[1] Rom. iv, 7-8. Quotation from Ps. xxxi, 1, 2.

[2] Rom. iv, 3 (*cf.* Gal. iii, 6 ; James ii, 23) quoting Gen. xv, 6 according to the Septuagint. Instead of the passive, the Hebrew has the active : " Abraham believed God and God imputed it to him unto justice "; but clearly the sense is not changed. Λογίζεσθαι τινί τι is a business expression which really means " to put a thing to the credit of someone "—for example, " to credit someone with a sum which he has paid." With εἰς, followed by an accusative, the meaning is " to reckon to someone something for so much." Now God, who is just, cannot reckon a thing for less than it is worth; but because he is merciful, he can accept a thing at a price higher than its actual value. It is thus that he imputes faith unto justice, although faith is not justice and is not equivalent to justice. Indeed, Paul distinguishes in God two sorts of imputations : one which is in the nature of commutative justice (κατὰ ὀφείλημα, Rom. iv, 4), the other which is in the nature of grace (κατὰ χάριν), and it is the second which God employs when he confers justice in return for faith. In respect to the context, St Thomas is right when he says : *Dictum est* reputatum est illi ad justitiam. *quod consuevit dici, quando id, quod minus est ex parte alicujus, reputatur ei gratis ac si totum fuisset.* All the Catholic commentators express themselves in the same way, and Estius, who appears to have another opinion,

side, the attitude of Abraham towards God, and on the other, the conduct of God towards Abraham. It matters little at what precise moment Abraham became just. All that it is necessary to remember is that justice was conferred upon him in return for faith; but not at the price of faith, for faith is not justice, and, if the reasoning of St Paul proves anything, it is not equivalent to justice.

SECOND SECTION

CERTAINTY OF OUR HOPE

I—CHRIST TRIUMPHS OVER SIN FOR US

1. General View.   2. Adam and Sin.   3. Christ and Sin.

1. Paul has proved that the justice of God comes to man through Jesus Christ, and only through him. His programme is, however, not yet finished, for he undertook to show that the Gospel is not only the source of justification, but an instrument of salvation in the hand of God. It is a long way from justification to salvation; there is the duration of this life of trial; there is the distance from earth to heaven.

Chapters v-viii are meant to prove that these two things, initial justice and final salvation, although separated by time and space, are united by a bond of causality. They are the extreme links of a chain indissoluble in the thought and plans of God, although it is the sad privilege of our free will to be able to break it. Grace is the germ of glory, faith is the pledge of the vision, the gifts of the Holy Spirit are the pledge of blessedness, and the happy state of the elect is only the tardy but spontaneous florescence of charity, which is itself a particular aspect of justice. "We are saved by hope" and "hope confoundeth not," there is the key of the situation. Final salvation is only a matter of patience and of time. Evidently the certainty of this hope is not in us, it is in God; but it is precisely the excessive love of God for us, even to the point of pouring into our hearts the most consoling and most precious of his gifts, the Holy Spirit, that fully guarantees us the future. Indeed, it needs more power to justify the sinner than to maintain justice in him, and more goodness to withdraw him from the abyss than to prevent him from falling into it again.

---

corrects his view enough for him to adopt the usual explanation : *Fides . . . reputari dicitur ad justitiam . . . quia fides vera justitia est*, saltem quoad inchoationem.

God commendeth his charity toward us, because, when as yet we were sinners, Christ died for us; much more, therefore, being now justified by his blood, shall we be saved from wrath through him. For if, when we were enemies, we were reconciled to God by the death of his Son, much more, being reconciled, shall we be saved by his life.[1]

However, three formidable obstacles rise before us : sin, death, and the flesh. In this section the Apostle affirms that we shall triumph over them with Jesus Christ, or rather that Jesus Christ triumphs over them for us. At last all our motives for hope are united, as in a bundle, and the three Persons of the Trinity, together with the whole creation, confirm our hope.[2]

2. The first obstacle with which our hope collides is sin. St Paul loves to personify it; he imagines it as the union of the moral forces which are hostile to God. Sin reigns,[3] it has a body,[4] servants,[5] an army to which it pays wages;[6] after having killed us,[7] it kills Christ himself.[8] Death is its constant companion, a queen but a suzerain.[9] The Mosaic

[1] Rom. v, 8-9. The whole passage v, 1-11 connects this second section with the preceding one. The first five verses state the subject and indicate the proof ; the following six verses establish it by a series of arguments *à fortiori*. Here are their essential phrases : (*a*) *Justificati ergo ex fide pacem habeamus ad Deum* . . . (*b*) *et gloriamur in spe gloriae filiorum Dei* . . . (*c*) *spes autem non confundit quia charitas Dei diffusa est in cordibus nostris* . . . (*d*) *Si enim cum inimici essemus, reconciliati sumus Deo per mortem Filii ejus : multo magis reconciliati salvi erimus in vita ipsius.*— (*a*) Δικαιωθέντες ἐκ πίστεως, résumé of the first four chapters; εἰρήνην ἔχωμεν πρὸς τὸν Θεόν, subject of the four following chapters. One would expect rather ἔχομεν (the reading of many manuscripts and Fathers), which gives a more natural conclusion, peace being the immediate fruit of justification. If we keep the subjunctive ἔχωμεν of the critical editions, we must translate : Let us preserve peace with God (Chrysostom) ; or, Let us enjoy peace (Sanday). In any case, peace designates the cessation of hostilities between man and God, with appeasement on the part of God and security on the part of man.—(*b*) καὶ καυχώμεθα " and we exult " (meaning peculiar to the Septuagint) ; ἐπ' ἐλπίδι, based *upon* the hope, as on an unshakable foundation; τῆς δόξης τοῦ Θεοῦ ; the Latin *filiorum* is a gloss which does not alter the meaning. Here the glory of God is eternal blessedness, since it is presented as an object of hope.—(*c*) Ἡ δὲ ἐλπὶς οὐ καταισχύνει [allusion to Ps. xxi, 6 ; xxiv, 20] ὅτι ἡ ἀγάπη τοῦ Θεοῦ ἐκκέχυται ἐν ταῖς καρδίαις ἡμῶν. In spite of the authority of St Augustine, who has drawn a certain number of scholastics after him, it is a question here and in viii, 39 of the love of God for us, and not of our love for God. In fact, it is not precisely our actual love for God which reassures us and is the foundation of our hope, but the love which God has for us.—(*d*) The verses 8-9 contain our four principal reasons for hope: the love of God for us, the death of Christ for us, the actual state of justification (δικαιωθέντες νῦν), and an *a fortiori* argument drawn from the contrast between the past and the present (πολλῷ μᾶλλον).

[2] Victory over sin (chap. v) ; over death (chap. vi) ; over the flesh and the Law (vii, 1 ; viii, 11) ; motives for hope and a hymn of thanksgiving (viii, 12-39).

[3] Rom. v, 21.   [4] Rom. vi, 6.   [5] Rom. vi, 17-20.
[6] Rom. vi, 23.   [7] Rom. vii, 11-13.   [8] Rom. vi, 10.
[9] Rom. v, 14.

Law—who would believe it?—is in its train; it is the effective tool of sin; *Virtus peccati lex*.[1] Sin personified is, therefore, not only original sin; it is that indeed, but accompanied by all its escort. This is why in the same context, frequently in the same sentence, we glide so easily from one meaning to another, sin designating sometimes the deprivation of original justice, sometimes the lust which results from it, and at other times the actual sin which is the effect of it.

When personified, as it almost always is in this section, *sin* takes in Greek the definite article; without the article it would be the generic notion of sin.[2] But we must be on our guard against estimating the biblical value of this word by its secular signification. Among classical authors sin (ἁμαρτία, *peccatum*) is most often merely an error of judgement or appreciation, a failure to observe the usages or proprieties of society; if it ever is a moral fault it is generally one that is quite venial.[3] The Hebrew *chattath*, on the contrary, although corresponding etymologically with the Greek ἁμαρτία and with the Latin *peccatum*, indicates a perversion of will, which, in alienating us from God, our supreme end draws upon us his wrath and makes us his enemies. Whether it be considered as an act or as a state, sin is, therefore, the sovereign evil of man; and this explains why Paul so often contrasts it with justice in its most comprehensive sense. We must distinguish from sin two words which are only in a limited sense synonymous with it. A *fault* (παράπτωμα, *delictum*), a moral slip or *faux pas*, expresses actual sin, whether of Adam or of his descendants. A *prevarication* (παράβασις, *praevaricatio*) is the transgression of a positive law, and is used especially to designate the violation of the precept imposed upon our first father. Every transgression is a sin, but every sin is not a transgression. *Ubi non est lex, nec praevaricatio*.[4]

The end of the incarnation is the destruction of sin. By Jesus Christ, the Apostle has just said, we have peace with

---

[1] 1 Cor. xv, 56: ἡ δὲ δύναμις τῆς ἁμαρτίας ὁ νόμος.

[2] In this section (chaps. v-vii) ἁμαρτία occurs thirty-one times with the article and eleven times without the article. The distinction appears very clearly in this phrase: "But (the) *sin*, that it may appear *sin*," etc. (the former with the article, the latter without it); vii, 13: ἡ ἁμαρτία ἵνα φανῇ ἁμαρτία; and in this: "Is the Law then *sin*? No; but I have known (the) sin only by the Law" (vii, 7: ὁ νόμος ἁμαρτία; μὴ γένοιτο· ἀλλὰ τὴν ἁμαρτίαν οὐκ ἔγνων εἰ μὴ διὰ νόμου). But the distinction is not always so clear, and the gnomic expression of a thought, the presence of a negation and certain prepositional forms in common use, may justify the omission of the article, even when the word is determinate.

[3] The notion of sin will be studied more thoroughly in the second part of this work.

[4] Rom. iv, 15: παράβασις (from παρά and βαίνω) to "go to one side" of the rule, of the Law (v, 14), παράπτωμα (from παρά and πίπτω) to "fall short" of the aim (v, 15, 16, 17, 18, 20).

God; by him access to heaven; by him reconciliation; by him the assurance and the anticipated joy of salvation.

> Wherefore as by one man sin entered into this world, and by sin death ; and so death passed upon all men, because all have sinned. For until the Law sin was in the world ; but sin was not imputed, when the Law was not. But death reigned from Adam unto Moses, even over them also who have not sinned after the similitude of the transgression of Adam, who is a figure of him who was to come.[1]

The construction is irregular, and the first phrase, which remains suspended, is not finished; but the general meaning is perfectly clear, for the mind has no difficulty in supplying the term of comparison, indicated without being uttered. The thought passes to and fro between the two extremes of this antithesis : One man has been able to ruin us ; one man, who is more than a man, will be able to save us. As the reign of sin has been the act of one man only, so the reign of justice will be derived also from one man alone. Adam, the first head of the human race, has dragged us down in his fall ; Jesus Christ, the second Adam and the Head of renewed humanity, will bear us upward with him in his ascent to God. Such is the meaning of the enigmatical word " wherefore," which begins the sentence; of the comparative particle " as," to which nothing seems to correspond; and finally, of the words " who is the figure of him who was to come," which concludes the digression, and at the same time completes the suspended comparison under a grammatically incorrect form. Paul needs for his thesis only an argument of parity, but it is impossible for him to confine himself to it. To the sin that abounds he cannot keep from opposing the grace that superabounds. A simple parallel between the two Adams seems to him disrespectful to Christ, and at every moment he unintentionally transforms it into a contrast.

---

[1] Rom. v, 12-14. On the irregular construction of the passage and on the bond which links it with what precedes it, see Note G.

The *world* is here not the universe, but the human race. This sense is frequent in St Paul (Rom. iii, 6, 19 ; xi, 12, 15 ; 1 Cor. iv, 9, 13 ; vi, 2 ; 2 Cor. v, 19, etc.), but is by no means peculiar to him. (*Cf.* John iii, 16, 17 ; xii, 19, 47, etc.). The Vulgate (*in hunc mundum*) by adding the word *hunc*, which is wanting in the Greek, might give the false impression that *this* world, into which sin enters through the act of Adam, is opposed to *another* world, into which sin had already entered in a different way. But this text makes no allusion to the previous sin of the angels.

Death is chiefly (*in recto*) physical death, the separation of the soul from the body. This meaning is absolutely required by verse 14, which explains and justifies verse 12, also by the evident allusion to the story of Genesis (ii, 17 ; iii, 19), and finally by the necessity of avoiding the tautology, which the interpretation of " spiritual death " or of " sin " attributed to θάνατος would offer. I say *chiefly,* for physical death, in St Paul, is very often put in connection with the death of the soul and with eternal death, which permits the Apostle to pass so easily from one meaning to the other (*cf.* Rom. v, 17-21).

Towards the end, however, remembering that this heaping-up of proof is unnecessary, he takes up again the argument of parity, although abandoning it once more in order to conclude with the words : *Ubi abundavit delictum superabundavit gratia.*

Let us not forget that the Apostle has in mind the story in Genesis, the authority of which his readers do not dispute. A single man, bearing mankind potentially in his loins, introduced into the world sin and death. He saw himself and his descendants deprived of the supernatural privileges of which he was the depositary. He caused himself and all his posterity to be cursed. For the contemporaries of St Paul it was almost a commonplace that Adam is the author of death and of man's inclination to evil, and that his fall is ours. The apocryphal Fourth Book of Esdras and the Apocalypse of Baruch (composed, the latter shortly before the catastrophe of 70 A.D., the former some twenty years later, but certainly in the course of the first century) are from this point of view very explicit. The Talmudic theology inherited these ideas and mingled with them also many fables. In any case, it was admitted that the human race, by the fact of Adam's transgression, is liable to death, dominated by bad desires, and doomed to the curse of the fall. If this is not in all respects original sin, as we understand it, it is something very like it; for the penalty presupposes the fault and the curse implies the offence.

Paul does not, then, propose to prove the existence of original sin. He merely makes use of the universality of the fall, known and accepted on the faith of the Scriptures, to explain and render probable the universality of redemption. All his reasoning could be very well summed up in the following complex proposition : If it is certain, as you do not doubt, that all men are made sinners by the disobedience of Adam, you should believe, with greater reason, that they will be made just by the obedience of Christ. He assumes the conditional proposition rather than proves it; but he affirms it four or five times very explicitly, and his affirmation takes for us the place of proof : " By one man sin entered into the world and death by sin."—" Death hath passed upon all men, because all have sinned."—" By one sin (there has fallen) on all men a sentence of condemnation."—" By the disobedience of one man, all, whatever their number, were made sinners."—Finally, Adam, the author of sin, is the "figure" of Christ, the author of reparation. This last truth, once proclaimed directly, is the basis of all this parallel and dominates the entire passage.

To sum up the argument, St Paul attributes to the first Adam : the reign of sin in the world, the universality of death, and a condemnation which extends to all men, and has as its antithesis the justice conferred by the second Adam.

The entry of sin into the world is not for the Apostle the mere appearance of a passing phenomenon, but the solemn inauguration of a reign : " By one man sin entered into the world and death by sin, and thus death passed upon all men because all have sinned.[1] This is not the personal sin of

[1] Rom. v, 12: δι' ἑνὸς ἀνθρώπου ἡ ἁμαρτία εἰς τὸν κόσμον εἰσῆλθεν,
καὶ διὰ τῆς ἁμαρτίας ὁ θάνατος,
καὶ οὕτως εἰς πάντας ἀνθρώπους ὁ θάνατος διῆλθεν
ἐφ' ᾧ πάντες ἥμαρτον.

Besides the points considered in Note G, let us note (A) the sense of εἰσῆλθεν and of διῆλθεν, (B) the sense of ἐφ' ᾧ, (C) the sense of ἥμαρτον.

(A) Εἰσῆλθεν cannot designate either the first or the simple appearance of sin in humanity. In fact : (a) the personal sin of Adam is not called ἡ ἁμαρτία, but παράπτωμα, παράβασις, παρακοή.—(b) Adam's sin was not the first ; according to the story of Genesis, which is evidently alluded to here, Eve sinned first. Therefore it is written: 'Απὸ γυναικὸς ἀρχὴ ἁμαρτίας (Ecclus. xxv, 24).—(c) Paul himself mentions expressly the priority of Eve's sin (2 Cor. xi, 3 ; 1 Tim. ii, 14). The entry of sin by the act of a single man is, therefore, the invasion of sin, the inauguration of a reign of sin (v, 21 ; ἐβασίλευσεν ἡ ἁμαρτία). The word διῆλθεν, employed for death, is not entirely synonymous with εἰσῆλθεν, employed for sin ; it better expresses the passage of death into each individual : καθάπερ τις κλῆρος πατρὸς διαβὰς ἐπὶ τοὺς ἐγγόνους (Euthymius).

(B) That the expression ἐφ' ᾧ signifies " because " and cannot signify anything else in this context, is now beyond question. 'Εφ' ᾧ, applied to a man, would not give a satisfactory meaning ; and it must not be wondered at that no writer of the Greek language before Theophylact ever thought of it. See Patrizi, Delle parole di San Paolo, in quo omnes peccaverunt (Rome, 1876). The meaning of the Latin in quo is less certain. There is, however, every reason to believe that the words in the Vulgate in quo omnes peccaverunt mean because all have sinned. Indeed, the expression ἐφ' ᾧ, employed three times by St Paul, is translated once in the Vulgate by eo quod (2 Cor. v, 4), another time by in quo in the sense of "because" (Phil. iii, 12). Cf. Rom. viii, 3, where in quo (because) corresponds to ἐν ᾧ (same meaning). Moreover, the words per unum hominem are much too remote for the relative pronoun of in quo to be able to refer to it, passing over the nearest substantives mundus and peccatum. The theological formula " to sin in Adam " is met with already in St Ambrose (Apol. pro Davide, ii. 71; XIV, 915): Omnes in primo homine peccavimus. It is copied from the phrase of St Paul : Sicut in Adam omnes moriuntur (1 Cor. xv, 22). The first one to find this formally in St Paul is Ambrosiaster : In quo, id est in Adam, omnes peccaverunt. St Augustine, who in A.D. 412 referred the words in quo either to Adam or to sin (De peccatorum meritis et remiss., i, 10 (11), XLIV, 115), chose finally the first explanation in A.D. 420 (Contra duas epist. Pelagianor., iv, 4 (7), XLIV, 614), when he perceived that the Greek word corresponding to peccatum was feminine. He cites as authority Ambrosiaster, whom he calls sanctus Hilarius. The Latins generally follow one of the two explanations of St Augustine : Sive in Adamo, sive in peccato (Peter Chrysol., Primasius, Bede, Peter Lombard, St Thomas, Dionysius the Carthusian, etc.) ; in quo, id est in Adamo (Sedulius, Fulgentius of Ruspe, Walafrid Strabo, Alex. of Hales, Hugh of Saint-Cher, S. Bonaventure, etc.). Among the Greeks, Theophylact also refers ἐφ' ᾧ to Adam.

(C) In the last phrase (death has passed upon all men, because all have sinned) we may ask whether it is a question of actual sin or original sin. Everything argues in favour of the second alternative, provided nevertheless that we do not consider original sin in its isolated state, but with

Adam, which is expressed in other terms—fault, transgression, disobedience—and, moreover, it is not the first sin in point of time, preceded as it was by the sin of Eve; nor is it, by metonymy, the punishment of sin, for this does not bring with it another punishment; it is, therefore, a sin common to all, multiple, and unique, in virtue of which death passed upon all men, which constitutes all men sinners and draws upon all a sentence of condemnation, to which only the justice of Christ can bring a remedy. It is, if you will, original sin, not isolated, but such as the Apostle usually presents it, followed by its train of curses.

Let us not make him say that all men have sinned *in* Adam. The formula may be very theological, and somewhere he gives the model for it by saying that "all die *in* Adam"; but after all, this formula is not his, and we must not think of translating the Greek text (ἐφ' ᾧ πάντες ἥμαρτον) or even the Latin (*in quo omnes peccaverunt*) by "*in* whom all have sinned." The Greek expression signifies undoubtedly *because;* and such is also, in the Vulgate, the sense of the corresponding phrase *in quo*. Let us hasten to add, in order to reassure the theologians, that, in translating: "Because all have sinned," as lexicon, grammar, and context demand, not only all parts of the sentence follow one another and link themselves together better, but the argument for original sin gains in clearness and convincing force. In fact, Paul affirms two things positively: (1) that all men have sinned, even those who have not imitated the prevarication of Adam: (2) that a sin, which is not actual sin, is for all a deadly debt.

Sin and death have the same universality because one is the effect and the consequence of the other. The causal bond which unites death with sin is expressed in two ways. First: "By sin death entered into the world, *and so* death passed upon all men." Secondly: "Death passed upon all men *because* all have sinned." The death of each individual cannot be attributed to his actual sins; hence it must be that there

---

its attendant evils, among which is found also actual sin: (*a*) It is untrue that all men die because they have committed actual sins, for all men are not capable of committing them through want of reason or of knowledge.—(*b*) No less is this contrary to the express affirmation of St Paul. In the following phrase he says that death has struck down even those who have not sinned after the similitude of Adam's *transgression*—that is to say, who have not imitated the actual sin of our first father; how can we think that he says here the exact opposite?—(*c*) The parallelism requires all to die by Adam, as all are made alive by Christ. Bengel says very justly (*Gnomon N.T.*): *Omnes peccarunt Adamo peccante; sicut omnes mortui sunt, salutariter, moriente Christo.* St John Chrysostom thinks the same. It must be confessed, however, that some Fathers seem to attribute death to individual sins, as St Cyril of Alexandria does in the scholia published under his name (LXXIV, 784 and 789, with the note of Mai). But they derive the actual sins from Adam's sin, which finally caused the death of all men.

is, outside of actual sins, one sin of a nature for which each man is sufficiently responsible to be required to endure its penalty. This is how the Apostle proves the premiss of this argument : In the period which elapsed between Adam and Moses, sins were committed in the world, but there was not yet any positive law which punished sinners with death. Now, a particular penalty, such as the penalty of death would be, is applied only as far as it is promulgated. Nevertheless, it is an evident fact that death was universal during that period of which we speak; it is not, therefore, explained by the personal sins of men. And it is explained still less by the fact that all " had not sinned after the similitude of the transgression of Adam "[1]—that is to say, had not imitated his disobedience. Who were these sons of Adam who had not sinned after the similitude of their father? St Paul does not say. We can think of those who have not the use of their reason, such as children in infancy, whom death spares no more than it does the others : a manifest sign that it is not the punishment of individual faults. In order to give to this argument an irresistible force, it is necessary, no doubt, to suppose, with the story of Genesis, that in the sight of God man was originally destined to immortality and could be deprived of this privilege only by disobeying the divine command, either personally or in the person of him who, as the representative of the whole human race, acted as its universal proxy in the name of all his descendants.

Therefore, as by the offence of one, unto all men to condemnation; so also, by the justice of one, unto all men to justification of life. For, as by the disobedience of one man, many were made sinners ; so also, by the obedience of one, many shall be made just.[2]

---

[1] Rom. v, 13: ἄχρι γὰρ νόμου ἁμαρτία ἦν ἐν κόσμῳ, ἁμαρτία δὲ οὐκ ἐλλογεῖται μὴ ὄντος νόμου· (14) ἀλλὰ ἐβασίλευσεν ὁ θάνατος ἀπὸ Ἀδὰμ μέχρι Μωϋσέως καὶ ἐπὶ τοὺς μὴ ἁμαρτήσαντας ἐπὶ τῷ ὁμοιώματι τῆς παραβάσεως Ἀδάμ.
There are here two distinct arguments for concluding that all men do not die on account of actual sins, but on account of original sin : (a) Before Moses there existed no divine law punishing actual sin by death ; hence death was not the penalty for actual sin.—(b) Moreover, all men have not committed actual sins, " have not sinned after the similitude of the transgression of Adam "; therefore, they die for another reason.

[2] Let us set out the text in parallel :

Verse 18:

Ἄρα οὖν ὡς δι᾽ ἑνὸς παραπτώματος   οὕτως καὶ δι᾽ ἑνὸς δικαιώματος
εἰς πάντας ἀνθρώπους   εἰς πάντας ἀνθρώπους
εἰς κατάκριμα,   εἰς δικαίωσιν ζωῆς.

Verse 19:

Ὥσπερ γὰρ διὰ τῆς παρακοῆς   οὕτως καὶ διὰ τῆς ὑπαχοῆς
τοῦ ἑνὸς ἀνθρώπου   τοῦ ἑνὸς
ἁμαρτωλοὶ κατεστάθησαν οἱ πόλλοι, δίκαιοι κατασταθήσονται οἱ πολλοί.

Whether the first member δι᾽ ἑνὸς παραπτώματος and δι᾽ ἑνὸς δικαιώματος mean " the fault of one only, the merit of one only "—(which corresponds

These two phrases, which explain each other, should not be separated. The second interprets and justifies (γάρ) the former, and determines every word of it. The one fault (παράπτωμα) which resolves itself into a sentence of condemnation for all men is the disobedience of Adam; the one meritorious act (δικαίωμα) which resolves itself for all men into a verdict of justification is the obedience of Christ. This sentence of condemnation makes of all men sinners. St Paul expressly asserts it. We may wrestle with his text as much as we like, we shall never obtain from it anything but what he proclaims with the greatest plainness—namely, that all men have been actually constituted, made, or rendered sinners; and not merely regarded or treated as sinners. This last interpretation would come into conflict with the two-fold impossibility of conceiving that God regards and treats as sinners those who are really not so, and of finding a reasonable meaning for the phrase : " All have been treated as sinners by the disobedience of Adam."

---

better to the parallelism)—or " a single fault, a single meritorious act," has almost no importance from a theological point of view. What is important is the synonymy suggested by the corresponding parts of the two phrases : παράπτωμα is explained by παρακοή, as is δικαίωμα by ὑπαχοή, as εἰς κατά- κριμα is explained by ἁμαρτωλοὶ κατεστάθησαν, and as εἰς δικαίωσιν ζωῆς is explained by δίκαιοι κατασταθήσονται, and finally as εἰς πάντας ἀνθρώπους explains οἱ πολλοί and vice versa. This last example shows that οἱ πολλοί does not exclude universality, but on the contrary includes it ; only οἱ πολλοί (those who are numerous=all, in spite of their number) is chosen by preference instead of πάντες in order to contrast directly the one sinful or meritorious act with the one author of sin or of justice.

Finally, the comparison of verse 19 contains in its two members three identical terms : (a) to be constituted (καθίστασθαι) ; (b) all, in spite of their number (οἱ πολλοί) ; (c) one man only; no more couples of antithetical terms ; (d) obedience, opposed to disobedience (ὑπακοή and παρακοή) ; (e) just as opposed to sinners (δίκαιοι and ἁμαρτωλοί).

The meaning of καθίστημι is not doubtful. Construed with εἰς it sig- nifies " to establish, to put into a position, into a condition "; for example εἰς ἀρχήν, εἰς ἀπορίαν, "to make a head, to put into embarrassment." Construed with two accusatives (of which, in the passive, one becomes the subject and the other the predicate), it signifies " to establish, to institute, to constitute, to render someone this or that"; πολλάκις με ἔρημον καὶ ἄπορον κατέστησεν (Plato, Phil., 16 B). The other two examples in the New Testament are very clear. James iv, 4 : Quicumque voluerit amicus esse saeculi hujus, inimicus Dei constituitur (καθίσταται=is really rendered such) ; 2 Peter i, 8 : Haec si vobiscum adsint, et superent, non vacuos nec sine fructu vos constituent (καθίστησιν=render you, make you).

Catholic commentators, therefore, are right in affirming that the dogma of original sin and that of real justice are deducible from our text with equal evidence. Many Protestant exegetes agree to this to-day, at least for what relates to original sin. If others hold a contrary opinion, it is in order to find in original sin an imputation, which corresponds to their so-called imputative justice. This prepossession shows itself in Godet (2nd edition, p. 527), still more in Zahn (pp. 284-5), and especially in Weiss (Meyer's Kom- mentar, p. 257).

THE EPISTLE TO THE ROMANS 219

3. The justice conferred by Christ being " a justification of life," the sin bequeathed by the first Adam cannot be either less true or less real. It is objected that in fact all men are not justified in Christ. St Thomas replies thus : "*All* men born of Adam, according to the flesh, sin and die in him and by him; so *all* men who are born spiritually in Christ are justified and vivified in him and by him." A simple reflection will dispel the obscurity which this reply still leaves. By the merits of Christ all men are potentially justified, and would be in fact, if they fulfilled the requisite conditions. The universality of sin is absolute, because it comes from a condition inherent in our existence; the fact which constitutes us men and children of Adam constitutes us sinners. On the contrary, we do not become members of Christ as we become members of the human family, without our own participation. The faith, which makes us children of grace, and the baptism which regenerates us, are something superadded to our nature. With this reservation the universality of sin and that of justice are in the same relation.

Let us briefly finish the parallel, or rather the contrast, between the first and the second Adam. As Adam is the type of Christ, and as the type is, by its nature, less perfect than the antitype, besides these relations, there will be also differences :

> But not as the offence, so also the gift. For if by the offence of one, many died ; much more the grace of God and the gift by the grace of one man, Jesus Christ, hath abounded unto many. And not as it was by one sin, so also is the gift. For judgement indeed was by one unto condemnation ; but grace is of many offences unto justification. For if by one man's offence death reigned through one, much more they who receive abundance of grace and of the gift and of justice, shall reign in life through one, Jesus Christ.[1]

---

[1] The contrast can be shown by an arrangement of the text, which reveals at the same time the value of the contrasted terms.

Verse 15 : Ἀλλ' οὐχ ὡς τὸ παράπτωμα, οὕτως καὶ τὸ χάρισμα·

Εἰ γὰρ	πολλῷ μᾶλλον
τῷ τοῦ ἑνὸς παραπτώματι	ἡ χάρις τοῦ Θεοῦ καὶ ἡ δωρεὰ ἐν χάριτι τῇ τοῦ ἑνὸς ἀνθρώπου ᾽Ι. Χ.
οἱ πολλοὶ ἀπέθανον,	εἰς τοὺς πολλοὺς ἐπερίσσευσεν.

Verse 16 : καὶ οὐχ ὡς δι᾽ ἑνὸς ἁμαρτήσαντος τὸ δώρημα·

τὸ μὲν γὰρ κρίμα	τὸ δὲ χάρισμα
ἐξ ἑνὸς	ἐκ πολλῶν παραπτωμάτων
εἰς κατάκριμα,	εἰς δικαίωμα.

Verse 17 :

Εἰ γὰρ	πολλῷ μᾶλλον
τῷ τοῦ ἑνὸς παραπτώματι	οἱ τὴν περισσείαν τῆς χάριτος καὶ τῆς δωρεᾶς τῆς δικαιοσύνης λαμβάνοντες
ὁ θάνατος ἐβασίλευσεν	ἐν ζωῇ βασιλεύσουσιν
διὰ τοῦ ἑνός.	διὰ τοῦ ἑνὸς ᾽Ιησοῦ Χριστοῦ.

Thus there are two great differences : a difference in the causes and a difference in the effects. On one side, a man, Adam; on the other, a God-man, Jesus Christ; such is the moral cause. On one side, sin; on the other, justice; such is the formal cause. But it is evident that Jesus Christ better represents humanity than does Adam, and reason teaches that good surpasses evil in power. It follows that the reparation will be more efficacious than the destructive act. The causes being unequal, the effects must be so likewise. Also we see that the point of departure of the ruin is a unique sin transmitted from one to another; but the point of departure of the restoration is an infinite number of sins to be expiated. The superabundance of grace is rendered still more striking by the very abundance of sin : *Ubi abundavit delictum superabundavit gratia*.

From the preceding data three corollaries may be deduced :

The reign of sin in humanity goes back to a single cause; it comes originally and definitely from a single act, the disobedience of our first father. Therefore, the rehabilitation (or to maintain the antithesis, the reign of justice) can be referred to one and the same cause, the person of Christ, and comes originally from one meritorious act, the obedience of Christ even to the death of the cross. For this it is sufficient that the author of the reparation should have the same relation with the human race as the author of the fall; in other terms, that Christ should be the Head of humanity and the antitype of Adam.

From this unique source flow respectively, on the one hand, universal death, the tyranny of the flesh, and the ever-increasing flood of actual sins; on the other hand, regeneration, the pouring out of grace, and the fruits of the Holy Spirit.

The sin, which invades the human race by the fault of one man, is not a mere external name; it renders all men sinners, even those who have not imitated the transgression of Adam; it brings upon all a sentence of condemnation; it becomes the peculiar property of each one, like the grace, the justice, and the life which Christ brings to them.

In what precisely consists this original sin? How is it communicated? Why is it imputed to us? In what sense does it become ours? That it consists in the deprivation of the original justice of which Adam was the depositary, and which he could not retain; that it is imputed to us by virtue of the solidarity which makes of Adam's will the will of his whole race; and that it is transmitted by the natural way of

---

The parallel still continues, but on one point only—the unique cause (διὰ τοῦ ἑνός) and the multiple effect (οἱ πολλοί). All the rest is contrast (οὐχ ὡς) and difference by excess (πολλῷ μᾶλλον) on the part of Jesus Christ.

generation as its contrary is transmitted by the fact of supernatural regeneration; this is what the words and reasoning of
St Paul permit us to infer. But these deductions and speculations exceed the object of biblical theology, and it is fitting
that we leave them to another branch of science.

II—Christ makes us Triumph over Death

1. Baptism, Mystical Death.   2. Mystical Death, Principle of Life.

1. Life and death being two correlative notions, it is impossible that a modification of the meaning undergone by one
should not react on the signification of the other. For St
Paul, as for St John, life in all its fulness is at the same time
the life of grace and the life of glory, participation in the
justice of Christ, the celestial blessedness which is the spontaneous florescence of charity and the glorious existence of
the resuscitated body, which is the complement of blessedness. In the same way death signifies sometimes the physical
separation of the soul from the body, sometimes the deprivation of sanctifying grace, sometimes the eternal perdition
called by St John a second death, sometimes all these things
together, united as they are to one another by a bond of
intimate dependency. All the effects of sin are comprised
under the name of death; all the effects of grace are comprised under the name of life : " The wages of sin is death;
the gift of God is life everlasting."[1]

It would be limiting the wages of sin too much to confine
it to physical death, for it has its counterpart in eternal life,
which is not only the restoration of man's composite nature,
but the participation in the life of Christ, on earth by grace,
in heaven by glory. We live in proportion as we are
associated with the life of Christ. Now it is in his death that

---

[1] Rom. vi, 23: Τὰ γὰρ ὀψώνια τῆς ἁμαρτίας θάνατος, τὸ δὲ χάρισμα τοῦ
Θεοῦ ζωὴ αἰώνιος. In order properly to understand this text it is necessary
to compare it with vi, 16, where the Apostle says that man puts himself
voluntarily into the service "either of sin unto death, or of obedience
unto justice" (ἤτοι ἁμαρτίας εἰς θάνατον ἢ ὑπακοῆς εἰς δικαιοσύνην).
Sin is, therefore, conceived as an emperor or general who enrolls soldiers, and
owes them pay. On the contrary, God gives to those who serve him a
grace (χάρισμα). Tertullian translates it as *donativum*, the largess granted
by the emperors to their army in certain circumstances, but this is perhaps
pushing too far the harmony of the metaphors. However this may be, all
the effect of sin is called *death* (cf. vi, 21). Doubtless the direct effect of
sin is the death of the soul (Rom. vii, 10: εὑρέθη μοι ἡ ἐντολὴ ἡ εἰς
ζωήν, αὕτη εἰς θάνατον. viii, 6: τὸ φρόνημα τῆς σαρκὸς θάνατος, τὸ
δὲ φρόνημα τοῦ πνεύματος ζωὴ καὶ εἰρήνη), as the direct effect of justice or of
grace is the life of the soul, but there is almost always joined to it by associa
tion an allusion to further consequences. It may be interesting to note
that Philo frequently sets the death of the soul in opposition to the life of sin
(κακίας, *Alleg. leg.*, i, 33 ; *De profug.*, 21, etc.), and that he knows also of
death eternal (ἀΐδιος, *De poster. Cain*, 11).

Jesus Christ makes us participate in his life; we live in him only so far as we die in him. This takes place *de jure* on Calvary, *de facto* at baptism. For one who has once become thoroughly imbued with the Apostle's thought, his mode of reasoning is very simple. Baptism applies to us the fruit of Calvary. In it Jesus Christ associates us, in a mystical yet very real way, with his death and his life. By associating us with his death, he neutralizes the active principle which sin had implanted in us, and which constituted the old man; by associating us with his life, he destroys all the germs of death and confers upon us the privilege of an endless life: life of the soul and life of the body, life of grace and life of glory. No doubt we possess in hope only a portion of these favours, but " hope confoundeth not." God wishes to perfect his work in us, and he binds himself to do so by granting us a certain pledge of his fidelity; we have only to let ourselves live.

> Know you not that all we, who are baptized in Christ Jesus, are baptized in his death? For we are buried together with him by baptism into death, that as Christ is risen from the dead by the glory of the Father, so we also may walk in newness of life. For if we have been planted together in the likeness of his death, we shall be also in the likeness of his resurrection.[1]

Plainly, the Apostle has in mind both the primitive rite of baptism and the etymology of the Greek word " to baptize." To " baptize " means to " immerse," and the primitive rite brought both to the imagination and to the eyes this etymological meaning. Immersion, symbol of burial, and consequently of death—for only the dead are buried—was immediately followed by *emersion*, emblem of resurrection and of life. To be baptized into Christ (ϵὶς Χριστόν) is not simply to be made subject to him, like a slave to his master, or like a liegeman to his lord, nor is it merely to be bound to him by an oath like a soldier to his general, nor even to be consecrated to him as a temple to a divinity; it is still more and above all to be incorporated with him, to be immersed in him, as if in a new element, to become a part of him as another self. Not content with affirming that at baptism we are immersed in Christ, St Paul says that " we are immersed in the death of Christ"—in other words, in the dying Christ. In fact, we are associated with Christ and become members of him just when he himself becomes the Saviour. Now this moment, in the case of Jesus, coincides with that of his death, symbolized and mystically realized for us at baptism. From that time on, we have everything in common with Jesus Christ; we are crucified, buried, and raised from the dead with him; we share his death and his new life, his glory, his reign, and his

---

[1] Rom. vi, 3-5: Ἡ ἀγνοεῖτε ὅτι ὅσοι ἐβαπτίσθημεν εἰς Χριστὸν Ἰησοῦν, εἰς τὸν θάνατον αὐτοῦ ἐβαπτίσθημεν; all the aorists show that it is a question of an act definitely fixed in time.

heritage. Ineffable union, compared by Paul to the grafting, which intimately mingles two lives even to the point of blending them, and absorbs into the life of the trunk the life of the grafted branch; a marvellous operation, which makes both Christ and ourselves σύμφυτοι (animated by the same vital principle), σύμμορφοι (subject to the same active principle), or, as Paul says elsewhere, clothes us with Christ and makes us live of his life.[1]

2. It is evident that for St Paul baptism is not a purely figurative imitation of the death of Christ, nor a simple act of the neophyte who seeks to appropriate to himself the Saviour's death by considering it as his own, for this fiction would not at all change the reality of things; baptism truly deadens the old man in us, truly infuses into our veins the divine sap and truly creates in us a new being. As a sacramental rite and independently of faith, which is not even named here, it works these wonderful effects. It is not to misrepresent the thought of the Apostle to translate it thus in modern theological style : The sacraments are efficacious signs which produce ex opere operato what they signify. Now baptism represents sacramentally the death and the life of Christ. It must, therefore, produce in us a death, mystical in its essence but real in its effects, death to sin, to the flesh, to the old man, as well as a life in conformity with the life of Jesus Christ risen from the dead. The major in this argument belonged to the Church's elementary teaching; the minor was so well known to Paul's hearers that he merely reminds them of it; the conclusion is one of the most solid foundations of his system of morals.

But the efficacy of baptism is not his principal objective; he takes it for granted rather than proves it. His design is to show that baptism is the entering into an immortal and never-failing life. All the neophytes know that baptism destroys sin and puts us, as regards sin, into a condition of death which, according to the intention of God, is to be lasting and definite. This same baptismal rite, the Apostle concludes, will have no less efficacy in so far as it symbolizes and reproduces the resurrection and the glorified life of Christ. " If we have been planted together in the likeness of his death, we shall be also in the likeness of his resurrection."[2]

---

[1] In the allegory of the graft, Rom. xi, 17-24, the trunk symbolizes the chosen people, on which the Gentiles are grafted (ἐγκεντρίζειν) ; but the wild olive tree in its entirety represents the Church—that is, the mystical body of Christ—and takes the place of the true vine of St John xv, 1.

[2] Rom. vi, 5 : Εἰ γὰρ σύμφυτοι γεγόναμεν τῷ ὁμοιώματι τοῦ θανάτου αὐτοῦ, ἀλλὰ καὶ τῆς ἀναστάσεως ἐσόμεθα. We may ask whether σύμφυτοι τῷ ὁμοιώματι is well translated in the Vulgate by complantati similitudini, and if it would not be better translated by complantati (Christo) similitudine mortis ejus, regarding the Greek dative as instrumental. We prefer the

But this new life being destined to last for ever, God, in giving it, binds himself to preserve it : " If we be dead with Christ, we believe that we shall live also together with Christ; for in that he died to sin, he died once; but in that he liveth, he liveth unto God. So do you also reckon that you are dead to sin, but alive unto God in Christ Jesus."[1] The new life received at baptism is in our own hands; it depends on us to preserve it or lose it. As far as God is concerned, he wishes that it may be immortal, and that grace may be changed to glory at the end of our probation.

We end, therefore, always at the same starting-point : " Hope confoundeth not."

III—VICTORY OF THE SPIRIT OVER THE FLESH

1. The Law at the Service of the Flesh. 2. The Flesh subdued by the Spirit.

1. The third obstacle to salvation is the flesh, of which the Mosaic Law was the unconscious auxiliary. Origen had already remarked that one of the principal difficulties in the seventh chapter of the Epistle to the Romans is the continual change of meaning which the word *law* undergoes there.[2] When he designates by antonomasia the Mosaic Law, he usually takes the Greek definite article; but he can also do without it, either in certain often used genitive or prepositional expressions, or because it is then considered as a sort of proper name. Moreover, the Law may signify the Mosaic code itself or the book which contains it, or the whole of the Old Testament as contrasted with the Gospel. But the ambiguity does not stop there.

---

second meaning, as more conformable to the context, but the former is grammatically more simple. The future ἐσόμεθα does not indicate something to come, but expresses a logical consequence : " *If we are* united to Christ in his death, *we shall be* united also to him (we are necessarily united to him) in his resurrection."

[1] Rom. vi, 8-11 : Εἰ δὲ ἀπεθάνομεν σὺν Χριστῷ, πιστεύομεν ὅτι καὶ συνζήσομεν αὐτῷ . . . ὃ γὰρ ἀπέθανε, τῇ ἁμαρτίᾳ, ἀπέθανεν ἐφάπαξ · ὃ δὲ ζῇ, ζῇ τῷ Θεῷ, κτλ. The words ὃ γὰρ ἀπέθανε form a nominative or rather an accusative absolute : *As to his death, or as far as his death is concerned.* . . . It will be noticed that the parallel between Christ and ourselves is not finished. Christ has died once only *for* sin (τῇ ἁμαρτίᾳ) in order to live to God eternally ; so we should die once only *to* sin (τῇ ἁμαρτίᾳ) in order to live to God for ever. The emphasis of the discourse rests upon " once only "; and the identity of the Greek expression is sufficient to justify the other comparison, although the relation of death to sin is entirely different in us and in Christ. Christ dies *for* sin, with relation to sin, in so far as he has done with the sin which God had laid upon him (2 Cor. x, 21), and which he had laid upon himself ; we die *for* sin in so far as we shake off its yoke and repudiate our allegiance to it.

[2] *In Rom.*, vii, 7 (Greek in *Philocalia*, chap. ix).

I find in myself this *law*, that when I have a will to do good, evil is present with me. For I am delighted with the *law* of God, according to the inward man; but I see another *law* in my members fighting against the *law* of my mind and captivating me in the *law* of sin, that is in my members.[1]

In this brief text the word *law* is taken in five different meanings, which we shall now enumerate, in the order in which they are presented : the *law of experience,* defined by the fact that when man wishes to do good he perceives in himself the presence of evil; the *law of God*—that is, the Mosaic Law, for although St Paul recognizes the existence of the natural law, he does not give it the name of law, above all, that of the law of God; *the law of the members,* or more exactly, the law which is in the members—concupiscence and perverse instincts; *the law of reason,* which is the dictate of conscience, or the law of God so far as it is promulgated in the understanding; the *law of sin,* in other words the power of evil which weighs on fallen humanity. This preliminary observation will find its application in the reasoning of the Apostle :

> Know you not, brethren (for I speak to them who know what a law is), that the law hath dominion over a man, as long as it liveth ? For the married woman is bound by a law to her husband [as long as he] liveth. But if her husband be dead, she is loosed from the law of her husband. Therefore, whilst her husband liveth she shall be called an adulteress, if she be with another man ; but if her husband be dead, she is delivered from the law; so that she is not an adulteress, if she be with another man. Therefore, my brethren, you also are become dead to the law by the body of Christ, that you may belong to another who is risen again from the dead, to bring forth fruit to God.[2]

---

[1] Rom. vii, 21-23.

[2] Rom. vii, 1-4. The word " law " recurs six times in this short passage : four times with the definite article and twice without any article. The last time (ὑμεῖς ἐθανατώθητε τῷ νόμῳ) it undoubtedly refers to the Mosaic Law ; the first time (γινώσκουσιν γὰρ νόμον λαλῶ) it refers to the law in general, although this fact is contested. The other cases are doubtful. In the aphorism : ὁ νόμος κυριεύει τοῦ ἀνθρώπου, κτλ, the law means the Law of Moses, or more probably " all law," all that enters into the *genus* law (thus the definite article is explained). The married woman is bound to her husband by *a* law (νόμῳ), either by *an* order of the Mosaic Law, or more likely by a moral bond, called " law " metaphorically. When her husband is dead, she is free from *the* law of the husband (ἀπὸ τοῦ νόμου τοῦ ἀνδρός) : either *from* the point of the Mosaic Law which concerns the husband, or rather from that moral bond determined by the context and by the added genitive.

To give to the allegory a sort of balance, the equations may be put thus :

> The woman = the *ego*, changeless in its different states.
> The husband = the old man who is subject to the *ego*.
> The law of the husband = sin inherent in the old man.
> The death of the husband = baptism, death of the old man.
> The new marriage = union with Christ.

The great difficulty of this passage no doubt consists in the different meanings of the word *law,* the precise sense of which remains sometimes dubious; but it arises especia'', from a very striking lack of harmony between the terms of the comparison, so that the conclusion does not seem to correspond to the premisses. How is this lack of harmony to be explained? In the fact that the Apostle is at the same time aiming at two theses of unequal importance : the principal one, which he has just brought out at the end of chapter vi; and the other, which he is going to develop at length in the sequel of chapter vii. The first can be formulated thus : "The Christian, dead in baptism, is freed from sin and becomes capable, united to Christ, of bearing the fruits of justice." The second could be expressed as follows : "The Mosaic Law was the unconscious auxiliary of sin; but hereafter it is no further hindrance to the fruits of salvation."

Paul appeals first to a fact of experience and common sense : a law, or in a more general sense any moral bond whatever, binds a man only till death. Rome, the motherland of the most famous lawyers, must have known so clear a legal principle as this better than any other place. For example, a married woman becomes free at the death of her husband, and it is permissible for her to contract a second marriage without being accused of adultery. We should expect this inference : "In the same way the Law is dead for you, and you are delivered from its yoke." But if the Apostle lets us divine it, he does not dwell upon it because it is only an accessory. He remembers that baptism is a mystical death to all the past and the point of departure of a new life, a life of justice and holiness. He, therefore, gives his thought a different turn : "So, my brethren, are you dead to the Law by the body of Christ, that you may belong to another who is risen from the dead, to bring forth fruit to God." Formerly, subject to the flesh, they brought forth only fruits of death. "But now we are loosed from the Law, being dead to this Law which detained us" under its empire, and nothing any longer hinders our supernatural fruitfulness. It is probable that the idea of marriage floats continually before the mind of Paul; for, like the prophets, he likes to present the union of the soul with God under this symbol. In fact, he uses here, to designate our attachment to Christ, the very word which expresses the relation of a woman to her second husband.

In baptism, the death of the Christian to sin (the law of the husband) being *ipso facto* the death of sin to the Christian, the Apostle may infer as he pleases, either that we are dead to the law or that the law is dead to us. Only this law is not directly the Mosaic Law ; but there is between them a necessary connection : for to die to sin is to die to the Law.

One thing is certain; it is that the Law is dead for the Christian, and that the Christian is dead for the Law. In other words, there is nothing in common between the Law and the Christian; and this is justice, for it was the auxiliary of sin and the flesh. This last consideration will be expounded by the Apostle in one of the boldest pages of his work :

What shall we say, then? Is the Law sin? God forbid. But I do not know sin but by the law ; for I had not known concupiscence, if the Law did not say : Thou shall not covet. But sin, taking occasion by the commandment, wrought in me all manner of concupiscence. For without law sin was dead. And I lived some time without the law. But when the commandment came, sin revived, and I died. And the commandment that was ordained to life, the same was found to be unto death to me. For sin, taking occasion·by the commandment, seduced me and by it killed me. Wherefore the Law indeed is holy, and the commandment holy and just and good. Was that then which is good made death unto me? God forbid. But sin, that it may appear sin, by that which is good, wrought death in me; that sin, by·the commandment, might become sinful above measure. For we know that the Law is spiritual; but I am carnal, sold under sin. For that which I work, I understand not. For I do not that good which I will; but the evil which I hate, that I do. If then I do that which I will not, I bear witness to the Law, that it is good. Now then it is no more I that do it, but sin that dwelleth in me. For I know that there dwelleth not in me, that is to say, in my flesh, that which is good. For to will is present with me; but to accomplish that which is good, I find not. For the good which I will, I do not; but the evil which I will not, that I do. Now if I do that which I will not, it is no more I that do it, but sin that dwelleth in me. I find then a law, that when I have a will to do good, evil is present with me. . . . Unhappy man that I am, who shall deliver me from this body of death? Thanks be to God through our Lord Jesus Christ !¹

Who is the hero of all this lugubrious drama, and how comes it that the Law, designed to give life, has ended by giving death? Such are the two preliminary questions suggested by the reading of this passage.

The opinion formerly maintained by St Methodius in a long explanation of this text² must be formally rejected. According to that, the " I " of this chapter would indicate humanity included in the first man ; the *law* would be the prohibition to

---

¹ Rom. vii, 7-25. This passage may be summed up thus : The Law is good, since it is from God ; but I am carnal, that is to say, subject to sin. The Law, by teaching me my duty, awakens in me the natural concupiscence which revolts at every law. So that the Law becomes for me an occasion for sin ; and that is how it is an agent, an instrument of sin.

According to the best authorities, the Apostle wrote (Rom. vii, 14) : ἐγὼ δὲ σάρκινός εἰμι (not σάρκικός). Theoretically, σάρκινος would mean *carneus*, " of the flesh "; and σαρκικός would mean *carnalis*, " having relation to the flesh." But this distinction practically amounts to nothing, and the exchange of the two adjective-forms in 1 Cor. iii, 1-3 shows that Paul regards them as wholly synonymous.

² *De resurrect.*, ii, 1-8 (edit. Bonwetsch, 1891, pp. 189-204). The opinion of St Methodius and Cajetan has been taken up again in our days by a small number of Protestant exegetes, followed by Father Lagrange (*Ep. aux Romains*, 1916, p. 168).

touch the forbidden fruit; *sin* would be the devil. Man, in the earthly paradise, lived at first *without law;* but when the divine *commandment* came, the *devil* began his work; and man *died*—that is to say, was smitten with a sentence of death. Can we be surprised that such a strange exegesis secured only one adherent, Cajetan?

That Paul is speaking from experience, and that he is evoking the painful remembrance of unavailing struggles and humiliating defeats, is possible, even probable, so poignant with emotion is his accent here. But he does not make himself the solitary actor in the scene, and everyone agrees that the " I " which he uses is to some degree fictitious. Is he assuming the rôle of the Jew tormented by the Law and conscious of his weakness, or the rôle of the Christian regenerated by grace, but still tempted by nature? Starting out from the Pelagian disputes, Augustine made himself the champion of the second hypothesis, which, thanks to him, found numerous adherents among the scholastics, who were subsequently joined by the leaders of Protestantism. In changing his opinion, he yielded, he says, to the authority of interpreters of Scripture, among whom he numbers (certainly erroneously) St Ambrose. Some expressions of St Paul would seem at first to favour this exegesis. " I am delighted with the Law of God "; is that the remark of a sinner? " It is not I that do evil," can anyone but the just man speak thus? If he is called " carnal, sold like a slave to sin," it is because his deliverance is still incomplete. He does not *do* the good that he would like to, because he wishes to *do it perfectly.*

Such are the reasons given by Augustine. It will be noted, first, that his distinction between doing and doing perfectly is illusory, for it rests on an incorrect translation of the text; the contrast indicated by St Paul is not between doing and doing perfectly, but between doing and willing.[1] The argument which seemed conclusive to the Bishop of Hippo—namely, that only the just man can say : " I am delighted with the Law of God according to the inward man," has no longer much force. We find among the heathen—and *a fortiori* among the unbelieving Jews—a great number of similar avowals : they love and approve what is good, but they embrace and do what is evil.[2] Moreover, in adopting his new opinion, the eminent Doctor did not condemn the old

---

[1] Rom. vii, 18 : *Velle adjacet mihi*, perficere *autem bonum non invenio.* It is by mere chance that the Vulgate translates here κατεργάζεσθαι by *perficere.* Everywhere else (five times in this context) it translates it by *facere* (vii, 20) or *operari*, without any idea of perfection.

[2] The thought is frequent, especially among the writers of tragedy. The words of Ovid are often quoted (*Metam.*, vii, 19):

Video meliora proboque, deteriora sequor.

one : " I formerly explained," he says, " the words of the
Apostle, in which is exposed the conflict between the spirit
and the flesh, as referring to man subject to the Law before
the reign of grace. Only much later did I understand that
they *could also be understood*—and that with more probability
—of the spiritual man."[1]

That the words of the Apostle *can* be applied to the just
man himself, we grant to St Augustine, who asks nothing
more. Mystical writers, like Cassian and St Hilary, have
always turned to account this accommodative meaning. But
that is not the question. We seek for the true thought of
Paul, and the whole context from the first line to the last
tells us clearly that the *"I"* represents man struggling with
concupiscence under the *régime* of the Law, and too weak
not to fall in that unequal conflict. Such was the universal
opinion of the Fathers before St Augustine, and such is once
more the common opinion of the exegetes. It alone accounts
for expressions which would be more than strange in the
mouth of a just man under the law of grace. Phrases like :
Ego autem carnalis sum, venumdatus sub peccato, or *Perficere
bonum non invenio,* or *Sentio legem captivantem me in lege
peccati,* if understood as referring to a man transformed
by baptism, are diametrically opposed to the letter and
spirit of all the Epistles. But, above all, let us remember
the subject treated here. The Apostle wishes to prove
that the Mosaic Law had to perish because it was the

Cf. rather Epictetus: "Every sin presupposes a combat, a struggle" (πᾶν
ἁμάρτημα μάχην περιέχει). Certain phrases remind one greatly of St Paul.
For example (*Dissert.*, ii, 26) : " The sinner does not do what he wants to do ;
he does what he does not want to do " (ὃ θέλει οὐ ποιεῖ, καὶ ὃ μὴ θέλει
ποιεῖ).

[1] *Retract.*, i, 23, 24, 26; ii, 1.—In four of his works Augustine still maintains the common opinion, *Expositio quarumd. propos. ex. epist. ad Rom.*,
prop. xxxviii-xlvi (XXV, 2070-2); *Comm. in Gal.*, 47 (XXXV, 2139); *De* 83
diversis quaestion., qu. lxvi (XL, 60-66); *Ad Simplician.*, i, 1, Nos. 7 and 9
(XL, 115-117).—His new exegesis of this chapter must be sought in *Contra
duas epist. Pelagian.*, i, 16-23 (XLIV, 559-562), for in the *Contra Julian.*, vi, 11
(XLIV, 1520) and *De Praedest sanctor.*, 8 (XLIV, 966), he contents himself
with referring the reader to the *Retractations.*
The Greek and Latin commentators understand the *ego* in chap. vii
as we do; for example, St Irenæus (*Contra haeres.*, iii, 20); Tertullian
(*De Pudicitia*, 17) ; St Basil (*Reg. brev. tract.*, 16) ; St Ambrose (*De Abraham*,
ii, 6 ; *De Jacob*, i, 4 ; *De Isaac*, 2, etc.) ; St Jerome, *In Daniel*, iii, 29 ; *Ad
Algas. epist.* cxxi, 8), etc. Pelagius, however, exaggerates when he reproaches
Augustine with being the only one of that opinion and with having against
him *all* the ecclesiastical authors (in Aug., *De Gratia Christi*, XLIV, 379).
Augustine could cite in his favour St Hilarius, *In Psalm*, 118, *litt. ghimel*, 3
(edit. Zingerle, Vienna, 1891, p. 379), which cursorily applies to the just
man Rom. vii, 24. Later (between A.D. 428 and 431) Cassian, *Coll.*, xxiii,
10-17 (edit. Petschenig, Vienna, 1886, pp. 654-667), puts into the mouth
of Abbot Theonas, a long similar explanation. But neither of them pretends to give the literal meaning.

auxiliary of sin, and because it provoked the divine wrath
by multiplying transgressions. He must, therefore, put
himself in imagination once more under the Law before
the régime of grace; and this is what he really does. The
final exclamation : " Thanks be to God by Jesus Christ our
Lord," is the cry of relief uttered by a man who wakes,
as from a dream, happy to see that this was nothing but a
frightful nightmare.

But how has the Law, which is good, spiritual, and holy,
augmented sin, nourished concupiscence, and contributed to
produce death? It is sufficient to remember what a law is,
the Mosaic Law as well as the others. Law is a light, but in
itself it is not a force. Without it prevarication, the transgression of a positive desire of God, would be impossible :
Ubi non est lex, nec praevaricatio. It has, therefore, for its
first result to increase the number of sins and to aggravate
their malice : *Lex autem subintravit ut abundaret delictum.*
Law makes us learn by painful experience the disorder of our
nature : *Per legem cognitio peccati.* It is the means by which
sin acts, and its instrument of governing : *Virtus peccati lex.*
Sin utilizes it for its own ends in order to attack our wavering will; without it sin would not have all the force it now
possesses, it would be half dead or would possess only a
latent life : *Sine lege enim peccatum mortuum est.* If this
be so, who can be surprised that it provokes the divine anger?
Lex enim iram operatur.[1] But this is not all. Law is a moral
barrier which irritates man without restraining him; a goal
placed beforehand for his free activity, humiliating him without attracting him. For a weak and variable will so many
new precepts are only so many occasions of sin. For the
prohibition stimulates desire, the commandment kindles
pride, the forbidden fruit appears more delicious. Temptation, long repressed, longs for revenge; it suddenly bursts
through; it obsesses the will, which becomes as dazed as a
traveller on the edge of an abyss. The part of law is to say :

---

[1] Let us consider the six texts which condemn the Law.—(a) Rom. iv, 15 :
οὗ δὲ οὐκ ἔστιν νόμος οὐδὲ παράβασις. The word νόμος has no definite
article ; it is therefore better to understand by it "any law whatever";
although, if it were a question of the Law of Moses, the negation might
explain the absence of the article.—(b) Rom. v, 20: νόμος δὲ παρεισῆλθεν
ἵνα πλεονάσῃ τὸ παράπτωμα. Although the word νόμος is without an article.
it certainly refers to the Mosaic Law; but it designates it under its general
concept, which could apply to every law.—(c) Rom. iii, 20: διὰ γὰρ νόμου
ἐπίγνωσις ἁμαρτίας. The phrase is gnomic and all the articles are omitted,
but the context shows that the Apostle has in view the Mosaic Law; ἁμαρτία
may be original sin or actual sin, for the Law gives us a clearer knowledge
(ἐπίγνωσις) of both.—(d) I Cor. xv, 56 : ἡ δὲ δύναμις τῆς ἁμαρτίας ὁ νόμος.
Here there is no doubt ; it is the Mosaic Law and original sin.—(e) Rom.
vii, 8 : χωρὶς γὰρ νόμου ἁμαρτία νεκρά. A gnomic turn as above; but the
context shows that it is a question here especially of the Mosaic Law and
original sin.—(f) Rom. iv, 15: ὁ γὰρ νόμος ὀργὴν κατεργάζεται. Here
again it is clearly a question of the Mosaic Law.

Do this; avoid that. Proposed to beings of perfect rectitude, to whom it would be sufficient to point out the good to make them love it, it would have only advantages. But the present condition of humanity is entirely different. Law has slipped in noiselessly behind original sin to assist it, and the result of this is this strange paradox that the "commandment that was ordained to life ends in death."[1]

This brings us back to the psychological problem studied by St Paul, from which, to tell the truth, we have never gone far away. Do you wish to know, he asks, how sin kills us by means of the Law? "I lived some time without Law,"[2] and you, O Jews, to whom I am speaking, and whose rôle I am now representing, lived so also. This time can be only that of infancy, before the first awakening of reason; for from that moment to the hour of baptism the Law has not ceased to claim its rights on those whom blood subjected to it. From the day when the Decalogue, promulgated by the Law, revealed to my conscience its imperative character, sin, which appeared to be, and really was, dead, soon came to life again.[3] It manifested its presence at once by revealing another law, the law of the flesh, contrary to the Law of God. The result of the conflict was the death of the soul: *Ego autem mortuus sum*. True, it is not the Law which directly caused my spiritual death; it is sin which is responsible for that; it has seized upon the occasion of the Law and has abused a thing good in itself in order to cause my death. But it is none the less certain that, without the Law, sin would have remained in a state of inertia, languor, and impotence.

To this reasoning two objections can be urged: the first, that without the Mosaic Law the natural law would have produced the same result; the second, that one could argue in the same way against the law of grace. Both objections are due to a misunderstanding.

For the Jew the natural law is blended with the positive law. Paul knew sin only by the Law, and he means the

---

[1] Rom. vii, 10: Εὑρέθη μοι ἡ ἐντολὴ ἡ εἰς ζωήν, αὕτη εἰς θάνατον. The word εὑρέθη seems to express an unexpected discovery, the following antithesis of which accentuates its paradoxical character. It matters little whether the μοι signifies "by me" or "for me."

[2] vii, 9: Ἐγὼ δὲ ἔζων χωρὶς νόμου ποτέ. If the emphasis is put on ἔζων, the Apostle means that he *was living*, before the age of reason, the life of grace; and this is the most natural sense. But it is possible to join it to χωρὶς νόμου and to interpret it simply as: I was living without Law—that is, I was not subject to (or dependent on) the Law.

[3] vii, 9: ἐλθούσης δὲ τῆς ἐντολῆς ἡ ἁμαρτία ἀνέζησεν, ἐγὼ δὲ ἀπέθανον. Here again we are tempted to give to the verb ἀνέζησεν all its force: "lived again, resumed life"; so much the more as, thanks to circumcision or to the providential remedy which formed the prelude to baptism, original sin was *dead* in the Jewish child. However, the preposition ἀνά in compounds sometimes only strengthens the sense of the simple word.

Mosaic code, for he adds immediately : " I had not known concupiscence, if the Law did not say : Thou shalt not covet."[1] He chose purposely the commandment of the Decalogue where reason most needs to be enlightened by revelation; but he could say the same thing of the others. The Jewish child knew the Law by heart before understanding it, and the Law laid hold of him as soon as his conscience awoke. In fact, he knew the disorder of his nature only by the Law. If someone had objected to Paul that reason, left to itself, would have been able to render the same service, he would not have denied it; but he would have remarked that this was shifting the question, and that he was not considering this new hypothesis.

What he would not have agreed to is that his reasoning could be applied to the law of grace. This, as its name indicates, bears in itself its antidote, for grace is inherent in that law. On the contrary, grace was added as an external element to the Mosaic Law. Not that God commands the impossible, and refuses to proportion his aid to the obligations which he imposes; but under the old dispensation grace was derived from a foreign principle, and in discussing the worth of the Law, we must take account of that only which belongs to it intrinsically.

The Mosaic Law, therefore, had to disappear, and to disappear *entirely,* for Paul did not make the distinction, so familiar to us to-day, between the ceremonial law and the moral law. For him the Law forms one whole; it stands or falls together. It can be affirmed that he never appeals to the Law of Moses in his ethical exhortations. He asks of it scarcely more than a simple *confirmatur;*[2] he may sometimes quote it as a revelation, but not as an imperative rule.[3] He does not even depend upon the written Decalogue, if he mentions it in passing, it is only to say that all its precepts are comprised in the law of love.[4] The Law is, therefore, abolished for ever. Christians are dead to the Law, and the Law is dead to them.[5] Christ was its end ($\tau \acute{\epsilon} \lambda o \varsigma$), the goal whither it tended and the terminus where it must cease.[6] It has been torn to pieces, nailed to the cross.[7] And let it not be said that the thought of Paul developed, and with time became either more hostile or more favourable to the Mosaic Law. Before he had written a single line of his Epistles, from the time of the assembly at Jerusalem, his ideas were fully formed on this point, and the contradictions among

---

[1] Rom. vii, 7 : alluding to Exod. xx, 14-17 ; Deut v, 18-21.
[2] 1 Cor. xiv, 34. Cf. 1 Cor. ix, 8 ; 1 Tim. v, 18.
[3] Rom. xii, 19.
[4] Rom. xiii, 8 ; Gal. v, 14. *Cf.* 1 Tim. i, 5.
[5] Rom. vii, 4 ; Gal. ii, 19; iv, 31
[6] Rom. x, 4.   [7] Col. ii, 14 ; Eph. ii, 15

the critics show that a change of attitude on his part is imaginary.[1]

The Law perishes because it was an instrument of sin and increased transgressions and kindled the divine anger. It gives place to a more perfect institution because it was only a transient phase in the scheme of redemption, and because, having been made impotent by the flesh,[2] it thwarted the designs of God. This last consideration brings us back to our subject. We must now examine how the vanquished flesh is no longer a hindrance to our hope.

2. A new antagonist now enters on the scene—the spirit, which will engage successfully against the flesh in the struggle in which the Law has succumbed through weakness.

The flesh and the spirit are almost always acting through one another, and therefore the one can hardly be defined otherwise than by the other. They are opposed to each other in three principal ways : as integral parts of the human being (a physical opposition); as complete substances, having a common characteristic in life, and being differentiated by materiality (ontological opposition); as antagonistic principles of good and evil in the supernatural order (moral and religious opposition).

It is the third opposition alone which interests us at this moment. It is evident that from this point of view the flesh is in relation with sin, and the question is to determine the nature and origin of this relation.

Quite a large group of radical theologians and exegetes have had the idea of attributing to St Paul the dualism of the Greeks. The flesh, they say, being essentially evil, is in itself and fatally sinful. But they have not reflected that the antithesis of matter and spirit is not biblical; and they have,

---

[1] Clemen (*Die Chronol. der paulin. Briefe*, 1893) pretends that Paul, at first favourable to the Law, subsequently became hostile to it, and that the Epistles to the Romans and Galatians mark the turning-point. Sieffert, on the contrary, tries to prove (in the *Theolog. Studien* in honour of Weiss, 1897) that the opposition of Paul to the Law increased steadily. Clemen has since then retracted (in the *Theol. Lit. Zeitung*, 1902, part viii), but several critics maintain his first point of view ; among these are Hausrath, Halmel, Franke, etc. They base their conclusions chiefly on Gal. v, 11 : Ἐγὼ δὲ, ἀδελφοί, εἰ περιτομὴν ἔτι κηρύσσω τί ἔτι διώκομαι; but this text is easily explained by Paul's acts of condescension (Acts xvi, 3 ; *cf.* Gal. i, 10 ; ii, 3-5) which caused him to be accused by his enemies of having been formerly a partisan of the circumcision. Sounder are the views of Zahn (*Das Gesetz Gottes nach der Lehre und der Erfahrung des Paulus*,[2] 1892) on the attitude of Paul towards the Law.

[2] Rom. viii, 3 : τὸ γὰρ ἀδύνατον τοῦ νόμου, ἐν ᾧ ἠσθένει διὰ τῆς σαρκός, κτλ. Concerning the nominative or accusative absolute and the (active or passive) value of ἀδύνατον, see Sanday, *Commentary*, pp. 191-192. The meaning adopted is independent of these controversies.

above all, failed to perceive how much Greek dualism was always antipathetic to Hebrew monotheism. To every Jew, instructed by the reading of the Bible, God is the Creator of all things, and all that he has made is good; for him there is no uncreated and autonomous matter, no demiurge independent of God. Hebrew logic never escaped from this dilemma : If matter is evil in itself, either God is the author of evil, or evil ceases to be evil. If it be supposed that the flesh is evil in itself, far from thinking of making it holy, it would be necessary to try to annihilate it; the Christian ideal would then be Hindu asceticism, a prelude to the Buddhist Nirvana. But such is not the ideal of Paul. For him the body is accessible to the influences of the Holy Spirit, of which it is the temple here on earth. The Apostle urges Christians to purify themselves " from all uncleanness of the flesh and of the spirit;" he hopes for himself that the life of Jesus may manifest itself in his mortal flesh, while he awaits the moment of being clothed with a spiritual body. We are here a world away from Platonic dualism, which longs to get rid of the body in order to restore to the soul its native liberty. How could Christ restore human nature if it were essentially sinful? How could he be sinless if sin is inherent in the flesh? And how will he condemn sin in the flesh if he himself is a sinner?

The relation of sin to the flesh is not, therefore, essential but accidental; it does not have its foundation in the nature of things, but in an historic fact. We have already seen that the sin of one man has constituted all men sinners. Human nature is no more what it was intended to be in the sight of God. It is carnal, and sold, like a slave, to sin. St Paul reproaches the Corinthians with being men and walking after the manner of man; he means after the manner of man as sin has made him and not as grace can remake him. But if this disorder includes the whole of man, if the entire man is constituted a sinner; if the understanding can become carnal when it is disordered; if Paul reproves the vices which depend upon the intellect, such as pride, enmity, dissensions, envy, and idolatry, as energetically as he does those which originate in the sphere of the senses, whence comes it that sin is usually so closely associated with the material part of the human entity? For, if we eliminate all the difficult texts,[1] we cannot deny that, according to Paul, the flesh is a flesh of sin, in which sin resides, and in which there dwells nothing good.[2] And to show that it is indeed a question of the

---

[1] Col. iii, 5: νεκρώσατε τὰ μέλη τὰ ἐπὶ τῆς γῆς, πορνείαν, ἀκαθαρσίαν, κτλ. Are these "members which are upon the earth" those of the old man, or those of sin personified, or are they to be understood as members of the body, considered as organs of the passions?

[2] Rom. vii, 18-20.

material organism, the Apostle substitutes sometimes for the flesh, the body or the members of the body.[1] He longs to shake off his body of death, which he subdues and chastises in order not to be its victim;[2] he regards it, therefore, as the special breeding-place of sin.

It is because, if the disorder is general, it is more apparent and even more real in the sensual appetites. In spite of the fall, our reason always keeps some affinity with God and the things of God; it is the seat of conscience; it approves the divine law and imposes its yoke upon us. On the contrary, the sensual instincts are deaf and blind; instead of obeying, as order requires, they aspire only to command; their violence and brutality unseat the reason; they overthrow completely the harmony of our nature; they almost always have their part in the derangement of our higher faculties, and this part is preponderant.

But if we stop here the explanation is incomplete. We must go back further. The origin and invasion of sin are very plainly referred by St Paul to the transgression and disobedience of Adam. The flesh plays no part therein. But the sin of Adam is common to us all because we are one and the same *flesh* with him. At a given moment *all flesh* was concentrated in Adam. It is because we descend from him *according to the flesh* that we have this solidarity with him, by virtue of which his sin is ours. The river of human life has been defiled at its source, and it is by the propagation of the flesh that the defilement is transmitted from one to another.

It is as an antidote to the actual power of the flesh that God confers upon us the Holy Spirit. We shall prove elsewhere, in studying the psychology of St Paul, that he calls " spirit," not only the third person of the Trinity, but the whole combination of gifts, properties, and graces—in a word, the new nature which the presence of the Holy Spirit produces in us. Between this new principle and the flesh the incompatibility is absolute. " They that are according to the flesh, mind the things that are of the flesh; but they that are according to the Spirit, mind the things that are of the Spirit. For the thought of the flesh is death, but the thought of the Spirit is life and peace. Because the thought of the flesh is an enemy to God. . . . And they who are in the flesh cannot please God. But you are not in the flesh but

---

[1] Rom. vi, 12 (sin reigning in the *body ;* vii, 23, the law of sin in the *members*) ; viii, 13, etc., the *body of sin* (Rom. vi, 6: τὸ σῶμα τῆς ἁμαρτίας) compared to the *body of death* (Rom. vii, 24: τοῦ σώματος τοῦ θανάτου τούτου) and to the *carnal body* (Col. ii, 11 : τοῦ σώματος τῆς σαρκός), must also designate the body as the principal breeding-place of concupiscence.

[2] 1 Cor. ix, 27 ; Rom. vii, 25

in the Spirit, since the Spirit of God dwelleth in you."[1] The spirit is extinguished in proportion as the flesh progresses; while the flesh retires in proportion as the spirit triumphs; and this antagonism goes on without intermission until the final victory of the spirit.

For this victory is certain from the moment that the Spirit of God dwells in us. We have not received the spirit of bondage, but the spirit of sonship; and what proves this is the name of "Father" which falls from our lips with confidence and love; it is the testimony that the Holy Spirit imparts to our own spirit, and the aspirations and holy desires which he suggests to us.[2] For this divine guest to produce in us the results which his presence promises, and finally to effect the total destruction of the body of death and sin, it is sufficient not to quench the spirit, and to give ourselves up to its leadership. Here again our hope is made sure.

It will be perhaps objected that the Apostle is marking time without advancing; that he is always bringing up for conflict, under different names, the same antagonists; that, with the exception of the Law, which has slipped in behind sin in order to come to the aid of the flesh, the struggle between good and evil in chapters v-viii of the Epistle to the Romans resolves itself into these three antitheses, the terms of which appear respectively identical :

> Sin and justice (v).
> Death and life (vi).
> The flesh and the spirit (vii and viii).

The objection is only partially justified. Sin, death, and the flesh on the one hand, and justice, life, and the spirit on the other, are notions which are closely related yet distinct. They could be translated into terms of modern theology by these equivalents :

> Original sin and the grace of Christ.
> Habitual sin and sanctifying grace.
> Concupiscence[3] and actual grace.

---

[1] Rom. viii, 4-9. It is necessary to observe the entirely new meaning which the nearness and the contrast of the Holy Spirit or his action in us give to the expressions ἐν σαρκί and κατὰ σάρκα. In other places (Gal. ii, 20; Phil. i, 22-24; 2 Cor. x, 3) ζῆν, περιπατεῖν, ἐπιμένειν ἐν σαρκί mean simply to "live this mortal life." *Cf.* 1 Tim. iii, 16; Col. ii, 1; Eph. ii, 11. In the same way κατὰ σάρκα does not always have (for example, Rom. i, 3; iv, 1; ix, 3, 5; 1 Cor. i, 26) the derogatory meaning which we see in it here.

[2] viii, 9, 15, 16, 23.

[3] St Augustine has taken pains to define concupiscence, *Enarr. in Psalm,* cxviii (XXXVII, 1522): *Non omnis concupiscentia desiderium est. Concupiscuntur enim et quae habentur et quae non habentur; nam concupiscendo fruitur homo rebus quas habet, desiderando autem absentia concupiscit.* A little before this he explains *concupiscentia carnis* by *mala dilectio,* and *concupiscentia spiritus* by *bona dilectio.* We willingly accept this

These are, of course, only approximations. Original sin and the grace of Christ are generally considered by Paul in their causes, the revolt of Adam in the one case, the voluntary death of Christ in the other, but including all their possible consequences. Habitual sin and sanctifying grace are rarely considered apart from eternal death and a blessed resurrection, which are respectively their natural endings. Finally, the Apostle almost always connects actual grace with the source from which it springs, the Spirit of holiness, and includes what theologians call concupiscence under the generic name of flesh. If we have ourselves avoided the word concupiscence, it is because it is now ambiguous and often signifies bad desire, or even sensual desire, instead of designating in general the corruption of our nature, intellectual and sensible, the inclination to evil, the *yetser hara* of Talmudic theology.

IV—Sure Reasons for our Hope

1. Testimony of Creation and of the Holy Spirit.   2. Testimony of the Father and the Son.   3. St Augustine's Different View.

1. The second part of the Epistle to the Romans closes with a song of triumph. Paul has written nothing more stirring or more lyrical. Emotion bears us aloft with him, while he unrolls before us vistas of Christian hope, beautiful as dreams.

Let us cast a glance backward. Our three great enemies (four, counting the Law) lie powerless before the cross of Christ. Sin is destroyed : " There is now, therefore, no condemnation to them that are in Christ Jesus."[1] Death is vanquished in advance by the seeds of immortality planted within us. The Law, which was in connivance with sin, is abolished. The flesh alone still struggles against the spirit ; but with the aid of grace victory is assured. The present guarantees to us the future, and our fate is in our own hands : " We are saved by hope," but our hope is certain. In order to certify this close, intimate, and necessary connec-

---

definition, but we fear that it may not be sufficiently apprehended by all readers.—St Thomas, at least in the *Summa*, looks at concupiscence from the philosophical point of view and defines it thus (Ia, IIae, qu. xxx, a. 1) : *Concupiscentia, proprie loquendo, est in appetitu sensitivo, et in vi concupiscibili, quae ab ea denominatur.* It is not, therefore, the appetite in general, as Sylvius justly remarks, nor even the sensible appetite in its full extent, and still less is it the corruption of nature, which theologians call *fomes peccati.*—Although the *flesh* is not *concupiscence* thus extended, Paul is accustomed to establish between the flesh and the sensible appetite a relation which we shall have to examine in studying the psychology of the Apostle.

[1] Rom. viii, 1.—Victory over sin, chap. v ; over death, vi ; over the Law, vii ; over the flesh, viii, 1-18.

tion between grace and glory, Paul appeals to four witnesses; the whole creation, the Holy Spirit, God the Father, and Jesus Christ. In the testimony of these four witnesses there is a crescendo of movement, light, and certainty.[1] *The material creation,* associated formerly, in spite of itself, with our fall and forfeiture, has the presentiment and promise that it shall one day be associated with our glorification. *The Holy Spirit* gives us here below so many pledges of blessedness that he guarantees to us in advance its possession. *God the Father* has established a natural bond between the results of his mercy which mutually invoke one another, from the first spark of faith to the clear vision of heaven. Finally, *the love of Jesus Christ* for us speaks a language still more eloquent, and we know that nothing will ever be able to separate us from it, except ourselves. Let us listen, first, to the voice of creation :

> For the expectation of the creature waiteth for the revelation of the sons of God. For the creature was made subject to vanity, not willingly, but by reason of him that made it subject in hope ; because the creature also itself shall be delivered from the servitude of corruption into the liberty of the glory of the children of God. For we know that every creature groaneth and travaileth in pain even till now.[2]

" Made subject to vanity not willingly," material nature is now subjected to a master who profanes and prostitutes it. St Paul lends to it life and feeling; he makes us hear its lamentations; he describes it as trembling under an abhorred yoke and sighing for deliverance. For it knows that its servitude will finally end, and that its glorification is linked with ours. God promised this solemnly to it when he made it serve rebels for a time. An untranslatable word (ἀποκαραδοκία) represents it with head raised, forehead stretched forward, and eyes ardently fixed on the goal of its hope, which is still distant. Let us, however, seek in this imagery only what the Apostle wished to express in it. He nowhere speaks of a physical renovation of nature. The new heavens and the

---

[1] The hearing of the witnesses (Rom. viii, 19-39) takes place in the following order : nature (viii, 19-25) ; the Holy Spirit (viii, 26-27); the Father (viii, 28-33) ; the Son (viii, 34-39).

[2] Rom. viii, 19-22 : Ἡ γὰρ ἀποκαραδοκία τῆς κτίσεως τὴν ἀποκάλυψιν τῶν υἱῶν τοῦ Θεοῦ ἀπεκδέχεται, κτλ.—(a) The creature or creation (κτίσις, four times in this context) is the material creation, with the exception of rational beings.—(b) Life and feeling are given to it by personification. It expects (ἀπεκδέχεται), it hopes (ἐπ᾽ ἐλπίδι), it is impatient (ἀποκαραδοκία), it feels repugnance (οὐχ ἑκοῦσα), it groans and experiences the pangs of childbirth (συνστενάζει καὶ συνωδίνει, the σύν expressing a *collective* sentiment rather than a sentiment *shared* with us).—(c) Nature was wronged in some way when, after the advent of sin, it was subjected to profitless and profane usages (τῇ ματαιότητι); it submits, however, to the command of God (διὰ τὸν ὑποτάξαντα), but on this twofold assurance, that it shall one day be delivered and glorified together with man.

new earth, however they may be understood, are not found in his eschatology. He makes himself only the interpreter of the wishes of creation, certain that the state of violence into which sin has brought it will cease at the moment appointed for our glorious transformation.

The testimony of the Holy Spirit is more distinct than that of nature; above all, it is more intimate. By the desires which he suggests to us, by the prayers which he brings to our lips, and by his very presence, he attests our future glory. With sanctifying grace, the gifts inherent in the sacraments, not to speak of the *charismata* which are the lot of the privileged, we possess even here below all the firstfruits of the Spirit. Now the firstfruits are the announcement of the harvest. But while between the firstfruits and the vintage a thousand accidents can happen, there is between glory and grace, which is its germ, no other peril to be feared save that of our own inconstancy. Meanwhile, the guest of our souls does not remain inactive. The desires with which he inspires us express themselves in sighs which cannot be voiced in words, because they have for their object that which the eye of man hath not seen, nor his ear heard, nor his heart felt. Neither these desires nor these groanings can be disappointed, for they have for their author the Spirit of truth himself. It is likewise so with the prayers which he forms within us without our aid, knowing better than we what it is fitting that we should ask. When he causes the name of the Father, *Abba, Pater,* to rise to our lips, he testifies to us of our adopted sonship. "But if we are sons, then heirs, heirs indeed of God, and joint-heirs with Christ; yet so, if we suffer with him, that we may be also glorified with him." A part of our heritage, and the principal one, is celestial glory. We do not possess it yet, being saved only by hope; but we have a right to it, and no one can disinherit us without our consent. Such is—as far as it is expressed in this passage—the triple testimony of the Holy Spirit.[1]

---

[1] The testimony of the Holy Spirit (viii, 15-17 and viii, 23-27) is cut in two by that of creation. In the first part the Holy Spirit, who is a spirit of adoption (πνεῦμα υἱοθεσίας) and not a spirit of servile fear (πνεῦμα δουλείας), bears witness to our quality as sons and therefore to our title of heirs of God (κληρονόμοι Θεοῦ) and joint-heirs of Christ (συνκληρονόμοι Χριστοῦ). In the second part the Holy Spirit, by implanting within us the desire for eternal happiness, which is the spontaneous florescence of the state of grace (viii, 23 : ἀλλὰ καὶ αὐτοὶ, τὴν ἀπαρχὴν τοῦ Πνεύματος ἔχοντες, ἡμεῖς καὶ αὐτοὶ ἐν ἑαυτοῖς στενάζομεν υἱοθεσίαν ἀπεκδεχόμενοι, τὴν ἀπολύτρωσιν τοῦ σώματος ἡμῶν), bears testimony to our glorious destiny. He gives an analogous testimony — and a still clearer one — by causing us to ask for our future glorification. For it is the spirit rather than ourselves who is the author of that prayer and of those sighs (viii, 26 : αὐτὸ τὸ Πνεῦμα ὑπερεντυγχάνει στεναγμοῖς ἀλαλήτοις, viii, 27 : κατὰ Θεὸν ἐντυγχάνει ὑπὲρ ἁγίων).

2. If the whole creation longs for our future glorification, and if the Holy Spirit suggests to us the wish and the request for it, it is the Father who gives to us the explicit assurance of it.

> We know that he maketh all things work together unto good to them that love God, to such as are called according to his purpose.
>
> For whom he foreknew he also predestinated to be made conformable to the image of his Son, that he might be the first-born amongst many brethren. And whom he predestinated, them he also called, and whom he called, them he also justified. And whom he justified, them he also glorified. What shall we then say to these things? If God be for us, who is against us? He that spared not even his own Son, but delivered him up for us all, how hath he not also, with him, given us all things? Who shall accuse against the elect of God? God that justifieth. Who is he that shall condemn?[1]

The beginning of this passage is also the key to it. But it raises two controversies: one accessory, although not deprived of importance; the other capital and decisive for the understanding of the whole.

What is the subject of the sentence? Is it the word "all" (πάντα), and must we translate it: "All things work together for the good of them that love God"? Or is it "God" who has just been named and whom it is, moreover, so easy to understand in a proposition of this kind? The meaning would then be: "Those who love God he comes to help in every way for good," or giving to the Greek verb the transitive signification, which it allows: "God makes everything work to the good of those who love him."[2] Three principal reasons make me prefer the last translation: first, the authority of the Greek Fathers, more sensitive to the fine distinctions of their language; then the word used (συνεργεῖν), which is said of persons rather than of things, and in which the prefix συν seems to indicate a concurrence of causalities, a common action; and finally, the context, which requires one and the same subject for this phrase and the following one, the subject of which is certainly God, although God is not directly named in it. But, I repeat, this question of philology is secondary.

---

[1] Rom. viii, 28-30. See Note H on the exegesis of the Fathers.

[2] Rom. viii, 28: Οἴδαμεν δὲ ὅτι τοῖς ἀγαπῶσι τὸν Θεὸν πάντα συνεργεῖ εἰς ἀγαθόν, τοῖς κατὰ πρόθεσιν κλητοῖς οὖσιν. The Vulgate adds after *vocati sunt* the word *sancti*, which is not in the Greek, but which changes nothing in the meaning, for according to St Paul all the *vocati* are Christians, and all Christians are *sancti*. A more serious alteration lies in the fact that it translates the passage as if πάντα were the subject of συνεργεῖ, while "God" is more probably the subject of that verb. The reading συνεργεῖ ὁ Θεός is supported by an important group of authorities (see the commentaries of Sanday and Meyer-Weiss). Many of the Greek Fathers, without reading ὁ Θεός, derive this subject from the accusative τὸν Θεόν which immediately precedes. Augustine also reads *cooperatur* as his text shows, although editors often make him say *cooperantur*. Estius rejects this reading under the curious pretext that, in speaking of God, it is necessary to say *operatur* rather than *co-operatur*.

The other problem is not secondary. It is a question of knowing whether the words "called according to his purpose" explain the words "those who love God," with which they are found in apposition, or whether, on the contrary, they limit them; in other words, whether all those who love God are called according to his purpose, or whether the latter form a privileged class among the friends of God. In the second hypothesis, the helpful concurrence of God, of which St Paul speaks, would be promised only to one class of Christians, those whom God called according to his purpose; in the first, it is promised to all the just.

We unhesitatingly choose the first hypothesis, basing our conviction on the constant language of St Paul, on his actual reasoning, and on patristic tradition. We know that for the Apostle vocation (κλῆσις) is always the efficient call to faith. The *called* (κλητοί) are those who have really responded to the call of God. It is, therefore, almost a synonym for Christians, but with an allusion to divine favour. The distinction between two classes of the called, some of whom come while others do not come—a distinction justified by the parable of the invited guests in St Matthew—is absolutely foreign to Paul's usage. For him all the called are necessarily called according to the divine purpose—that is to say, according to the benevolent design of God, because the purpose (πρόθεσις), as he understands it, has for its object the bestowal of sanctifying grace and not, at least directly, that of celestial glory. It follows that in adding: "Those who are called according to his purpose," he does not intend either to limit or restrict his preceding assertion, but he is expressing only the motive of divine benevolence towards all those who love God: this motive is the call to faith with which they have been favoured.

If there remained the shadow of a doubt, the reasoning of the Apostle would dissipate it. In the second part of the Epistle to the Romans, and especially in chapter viii, he enumerates our many reasons for hoping. He speaks to *all* Christians, for *all* are bound to hope. His reasoning amounts to saying that God will finish his work, that grace is a germ of glory, that the three divine Persons are favourable to us, and that any obstacle to our salvation can henceforth come only from ourselves. God the Father "makes all things work together unto good to those who love him, those whom he has called according to his [benevolent] purpose"; for, in calling them, he gives them a precious pledge and sure earnest of his future benefits. If the words "called according to his purpose" restricted the meaning of "friends of God" instead of explaining it, the Apostle would reason thus: *All* must hope, because *some* are protected by God against every eventuality; the hope of *all Christians* is certain, because *the* predestined obtain infallibly what they hope for. It is impossible to argue with less logic. Is it surprising that the Fathers did not understand the Doctor of the Gentiles thus?

When certain exegetes give a limited sense to the call according to God's purpose, on the ground that, as a matter of fact, all things do not work together for the good of God's friends, since many, ceasing to love him, fall under his disfavour, they do not reflect that Paul is speaking of God's arrangements for the just. These benevolent arrangements are universal, although they may be thwarted by man's free will. All must say with the Apostle : *Si Deus pro nobis, quis contra nos?* The condition of our co-operation is understood; the danger of our weak will also. Therefore, in spite of all assurances, fear, so often inculcated by St Paul and his colleagues in the apostolate, remains always useful and necessary. But this is not the question. As we have said already, and as cannot be too often repeated, the immovable steadfastness of our hope comes from God and not from ourselves. Now, divine aid is assured to us, for the long series of God's benefits is to us an authentic proof of his enduring love.

But, it will perhaps be said, why is the call to faith a sure guarantee of the Father's benevolent arrangements in regard to us? It is so because it has not its end in itself, but goes back to the profound mysteries of the divine counsels; it is a " call according to the purpose." This purpose is the purpose of God, not of man : the exaggerated care of some Greek Fathers to safeguard free will and their excessive fear of Gnostic fatalism formerly made them prefer the second interpretation; but there is no longer any reason for modifying Paul's thought, which would become an insoluble enigma, if he based our hope on the wavering support of human dispositions.

God's acts in reference to our salvation are linked together and succeed one another in the following order :

> Prescience ($\pi\rho o\acute{\epsilon}\gamma\nu\omega$).
> Predestination or purpose ($\pi\rho o\acute{\omega}\rho\iota\sigma\epsilon\nu$).
> Vocation or election ($\acute{\epsilon}\kappa\acute{a}\lambda\epsilon\sigma\epsilon\nu$)
> Justification ($\acute{\epsilon}\delta\iota\kappa a\acute{\iota}\omega\sigma\epsilon\nu$).
> Glorification ($\acute{\epsilon}\delta\acute{o}\xi a\sigma\epsilon\nu$).

The vocation or efficient call to faith is an intermediary act which, preceding justification and glorification, succeeds prescience and predestination. Predestination is not prescience. Practically to confound these two things, as did Calvin and the usually better-informed Estius,[1] is

---

[1] Thus Calvin : *Dei praecognitio, cujus hic Paulus meminit, non nuda est praescientia, sed adoptio qua filios suos a reprobis semper discrevit.* So also Estius : *Praescientia est praedilectio ac praeordinatio in bonum . . quos*

gratuitously to impute to Paul an insufferable tautology. How much wiser is the distinction of St Thomas, who sees in prescience an act of intelligence, and in predestination an act of will.[1] If *to know beforehand* is the same thing as *to love beforehand,* would this be true of a love unenlightened by foreknowledge? But how is it possible to suppose that such a blind love exists in God? The will follows the intelligence; it does not precede it. Assuredly God beholding what is good cannot help loving it, just as when beholding evil he cannot help hating it; but it does not follow that even for God to foresee or to know in advance signifies to approve and to love in advance. Search as one may in Scripture or elsewhere, no instance of this strange interpretation will be found.

Since prescience, therefore, is an act of the understanding, and since the divine gaze fixed upon the future has a limitless range, it is necessary to draw the limitation from the context itself; for it is evident that in this phrase : " For whom he foreknew, he also predestinated to be made conformable to the image of his Son,"[2] the two verbs have the same extension of meaning, which cannot be universal, since, as a matter of fact, all men do not receive filial adoption. The limitation of the relative pronoun (οὕς) can be found in what precedes : " those who love God, those who are called according to the purpose " ; or else in what follows : "predestinated to be made conformable to the image of his Son." The first construction is more natural and much simpler, in that the causative particle (ὅτι, more expressive than *nam*) closely unites the two members, and invites us, unless we wish to impute a sophism to Paul, to seek in the second construction the

---

praescivit, id est ab aeterno praedilexit et amicos habere voluit. Estius adds that Rickelius, Sasboldus, Pererius and other moderns and even Origen are of his opinion. As to Origen, Estius is certainly mistaken ; and the authority of the other three mentioned, even added to that of Estius and Cajetan, is not sufficient to establish a signification so unusual and so contrary to the opinion of the Fathers.

[1] *Praescientia importat solam notitiam futurorum, sed praedestinatio importat causalitatem quamdam respectu eorum.*

[2] Rom. viii, 29 : *Ὅτι οὕς προέγνω, καὶ προώρισεν συμμόρφους τῆς εἰκόνος τοῦ υἱοῦ αὐτοῦ, εἰς τὸ εἶναι αὐτὸν πρωτότοκον ἐν πολλοῖς ἀδελφοῖς.* It is not necessary to take into account the opinion of some exegetes (Corn. a Lapide and others), who see in the phrase an anacoluthon and who translate it : " For those whom he foresaw and predestined to be made conformable to the image of his Son," etc. Not only do they gain nothing by attributing to Paul a grammatical inaccuracy, but the ὅτι (because) then remains unexplained, since it is not followed by any verb, the relative clause not belonging to it ; or else it is necessary to consider the relative οὕς as a demonstrative pronoun, which is absolutely impossible. The period is, therefore, complete, οὕς προέγνω forming the protasis, and καὶ προώρισεν the apodosis. Consequently καί signifies " also " and the members have the same extension.

exposition of God's benefits towards those who love him and whom he has favoured with the initial gift of faith. But, on the whole, the sense does not change; and it remains always true that the expressions "those who love God," "those whom he has called according to the purpose," "those whom he foreknew," "those whom he predestinated," have the same extension of meaning and apply to the same persons.

I am well aware that commentators are not agreed about the meaning of the phrase "to be made conformable to the image of his Son."[1] While the majority and the most distinguished of the commentators understand by this conformity the *resemblance,* still imperfect but very real, which sanctifying grace confers, some see in it the completed assimilation which celestial glory gives. From the theological point of view this diversity of opinions is unimportant, for the efficient call to faith and final perseverance are determined by the same principles. But if we hold to the texts of St Paul, the first are right. In fact, in his language "to predestine" never has for its end—at least, for its exclusive end—the glory of heaven. God *predestines* man to grace or grace to man. He has predestined us to filial adoption, and this sonship is fully ours already here below. So that, for St Paul, all the just are predestined in the sense that they are all called and all chosen; for calling and election are with him two synonymous words, with an idea of preference or choice which election implies and which, in itself, the calling does not include. If we reflect on the way in which the Apostle is wont to describe our conformity with Jesus Christ, which he supposes to be accomplished now; on the universality of his expressions, which include all who love God—that is to say, all the just; on the bond which he always establishes between the absolute call to the grace

---

[1] Some commentators, like Cornely, understand by the *image of the Son* the glorified body of Christ. They base their opinion on Phil. iii, 21 (ὃς μετασχηματίσει τὸ σῶμα τῆς ταπεινώσεως ἡμῶν σύμμορφον τῷ σώματι τῆς δόξης αὐτοῦ), where συμμόρφος is applied to the glorified body, and on I Cor. xv, 49 (τὴν εἰκόνα τοῦ ἐπουρανίου), where Paul teaches that at the resurrection we shall bear the image of the heavenly Adam. Others, like Estius, understand by it the glory of heaven in its entirety for both body and soul; they quote, to support their theory, the same texts as above. The most authorized interpreters of Paul's thought (see Note H) understand by conformity *to the image of the Son of God,* the *conformity* which sanctifying grace bestows, filial adoption, the presence and intimate action of the Holy Spirit. It is indeed in that way that we participate in the *form* of the Son (Gal. iv, 19 : μέχρις οὗ μορφωθῇ Χριστὸς ἐν ὑμῖν) ; it is thus that Christ becomes the first-born among many brethren (Rom. viii, 29: εἰς τὸ εἶναι αὐτὸν πρωτότοκον ἐν πολλοῖς ἀδελφοῖς, which explains this *conformity* exactly). St Paul invites us to *transform* ourselves thus (Rom. xii, 2: μεταμορφοῦσθε) and indicates to us the means of reproducing within us, already here below, this *image* of Christ (2 Cor. iii, 18 : τὴν αὐτὴν εἰκόνα μεταμορφούμεθα).

of faith and the conditional election to celestial glory; on his manifest design of establishing our hope upon a sure foundation; on the care he takes to present our glorification as realised already in this life, by right and by power if not in fact and in deed, the common opinion will be found much more plausible. It is by sanctifying grace that we participate gradually in the *form* of Son; it is by this grace that Christ becomes the firstborn among many brethren; St Paul invites us to *transform* ourselves in this way and shows us the means of obtaining, already in this world, this transformation. Let us add only that *conformity to the image of the Son,* effected by grace and filial adoption, is not to be considered as a thing that *differs* from the complete resemblance conferred at the termination of our probation.

This being settled, the remainder of the text is without difficulty : " Those whom he predestined, them he also called. And whom he called, them he also justified. And whom he justified, them he also glorified."[1] The *efficient call* to faith—it is always this which St Paul means—infallibly follows predestination to this same call, just as justification is connected with the calling and glorification with the granting of justice. Is the glorious state, of which the Apostle speaks, that of the just on earth or that of the elect in heaven? St Thomas asks the question, and leaves it undecided. On the contrary, St John Chrysostom and the other Greek Fathers resolutely adopt the first interpretation. They are naturally led to do so by the past tense of the verb ($\dot{\epsilon}\delta\acute{o}\xi\alpha\sigma\epsilon\nu$, *glorificavit*), which otherwise must be taken either as a proleptical past tense, or as an aorist either gnomic or habitual, uses very rarely found in the New Testament. It is certain that the glory granted by God to men must sometimes, when the context requires it, refer to celestial blessedness; but it signifies no less frequently the glorious condition inherent in sanctifying grace. We think that St Paul designates both *per modum unius.* We thus

---

[1] Rom. viii, 30 : οὓς δὲ ἐδικαίωσεν, τούτους καὶ ἐδόξασεν. In what sense has God glorified those whom he has justified ? St Thomas asks himself the question without solving it. Hos et magnificavit (this was the reading in many manuscripts instead of the present text *glorificavit*); *et hoc dupliciter, scilicet uno quidem modo per profectum virtutis et gratiae; alio autem modo per exaltationem gloriae.* . . . *Ponit autem praeteritum pro futuro,* si intelligatur de magnificatione gloriae, *vel propter certitudinem futuri, vel quia quod in quibusdam est futurum, in aliis est completum.* It is certain that the glory granted by God to man must be understood sometimes as the glory of heaven, Rom. v, 2 (ἐπ' ἐλπίδι τῆς δόξης τοῦ Θεοῦ); viii, 18 (πρὸς τὴν μέλλουσαν δόξαν); 1 Cor. xv, 43; Phil. iii, 21; Col. i, 27; 1 Tim. iii, 16; 2 Tim. ii, 10; but it is said also of the glorious state which sanctifying grace confers, Rom. ii, 10; iii, 23; 1 Cor. ii, 7 ; 2 Cor. iii, 18 (ἡμεῖς δὲ πάντες ἀνακεκαλυμμένῳ προσώπῳ τὴν δόξαν κυρίου κατοπτριζόμενοι τὴν αὐτὴν εἰκόνα μεταμορφούμεθα ἀπὸ δόξης εἰς δόξαν). *Cf.* 2 Cor. iii, 8, 9, 11, etc.

avoid doing violence to his language, since the glorification, assured on God's part, is already begun actually and in principle; we satisfy the present object of the Apostle which is to confirm our hope by the blessings received by God; and, finally, we conform to his well-known custom of presenting salvation as a boon, which we already enjoy, and which we are nevertheless to hope for. Paul is not accustomed to establish between grace and glory and between initial election and final salvation the rigid line of demarcation which usually exists in our minds. For him there is no break of continuity; grace spontaneously changes into glory, as the plant becomes a tree by virtue of its vital force.

There remains the testimony of the Son, which corroborates and explains the testimony of the Father:

> It is God that justifieth: who shall condemn [us]? Christ Jesus that died, yea, that is risen also again, who is at the right hand of God, who also maketh intercession for us. Who can separate us from the love of Christ? . . . I am sure that neither death, nor life, nor angels, nor powers, nor things present, nor things to come, nor height, nor depth, nor any other creature, shall be able to separate us from the love of God, which is in Christ Jesus our Lord.[1]

Here is indeed the triumph of hope; it is not the endowment of a few privileged souls, but reaches out to all the just, for the charity of Christ embraces all who love him. We have four notable proofs of the love which Jesus Christ has for us. He has died to justify us; he has risen from the dead in order to associate us with his glory; he is seated at the right hand of the Father in order that we may reign with him; and he continues to intercede for us. The first two pledges lie in their effects, the last two guarantee us the efficaciousness of this love. Our assurance is not a mere persuasion; it is a certainty of faith; nothing can separate us from Christ except ourselves. From this point of view the certainty is conditional; for, if it is impossible to doubt the love of Christ for us, we cannot say without presumption that our love for Christ will never fail.

In concluding, Paul blends into one single proof the promise of the Son and the Father, and presents to us, as a supreme motive for hope, "the love of God which is in Christ Jesus," the love which the Father has for us in consideration of Jesus Christ who has so loved us.

Rom. viii, 33-35, 38-39. The Vulgate is without any note of interrogation: *Christus Jesus, qui mortuus est, immo qui et resurrexit, qui est ad dexteram Dei, qui etiam interpellat pro nobis.* But a very awkward phrase is thus obtained; it is necessary to supply a verb in this way: "*It is* Jesus who," and furthermore to understand the reply to the preceding question: " Who shall condemn us?" *No one; for it is Jesus,* etc. —On the other hand, the wondering note of interrogation suggested by us implies a very forcible negative reply.

3. This interpretation of Paul's thought, the most faithful possible, agrees with the general opinion of the Greek and Latin Fathers. All, with the exception of St Augustine in his second thoughts, are agreed on the three following points : Prescience, which is essentially an intellectual act, precedes predestination and directs it, the just not being foreknown because they are predestinated, but rather predestinated because they have been foreknown. Predestination is an act of the consequent will of God ; and in the text of St Paul it has reference to the gift of efficacious grace, and not directly to the bestowal of celestial glory. In this same text the words *foreknown, predestinated, called,* and *justified,* and very likely *glorified* also, designate the same persons, the friends of God, Christians whose faith is enlivened by charity.

Is it true that St Augustine, at the end of his career, abandoned the beaten path, to open up for himself new ways wholly unknown to his predecessors? In 428 A.D., two years before his death, his disciple Prosper of Aquitaine put to him this question, which he found very embarrassing : " How comes it that almost all our predecessors unanimously make the purpose and the predestination of God depend upon his prescience, so that God constitutes some vessels of honour and others vessels of dishonour, because he foresees the end of each and foreknows what their will and action will be with the help of divine grace?"[1] St Augustine does not dispute the fact, but limits himself to saying that before the advent of Pelagianism his predecessors were not obliged to insist on the necessity of grace, that they are not fundamentally opposed to his doctrine, and that he could even avail himself of them in order to defend it. All this is perfectly true, yet there must have been between them and him, either in the manner of speaking, or in the way of looking at the subject, or in the general point of view, very considerable differences for St Prosper to have been so struck by them. The history of his changes of opinion, instructive in many respects, helps us to understand it.

Up to 394 A.D. the Bishop of Hippo connected the " call according to the purpose " with the divine prescience, and he wrote unhesitatingly : " God predestines only him who as he foresees is to believe and to follow the divine call "; or again : " Him whom God foresees destined to believe hath God chosen, in order to give him the Holy Spirit." He keeps thus the problem on its true ground—namely, the efficacious call to faith. Unfortunately, as is seen by his writings and as he himself subsequently frankly acknowledges, he then erroneously extended the power which we have of responding

---

[1] Migne, XLIV, 953 (or among the letters of St Augustine, ccxxv, 8). St Augustine replies in *De praedest. sanctorum,* 27 (XLIV, 980). For the quotations from St Augustine and the opinions of the other Fathers, see Note H.

to the divine call. He thought not only that we are free to believe or not to believe—which he always admitted—but that faith is from us, while works are from God, which is quite inadmissible. This false distinction, which he subsequently and with reason condemns in heretics, is the more astonishing in him because it formally contradicts a text of St Paul, and because it has no foundation in the exegesis of the other Fathers. He does not fail to retract it at a later date and substitutes for it the orthodox doctrine that every saving act is from God, faith as well as works.

However, his exegesis did not follow the progress of his theology. In the last years of his life he devoted his attention especially to final perseverance, and applied to it the passage in which St Paul treats of the efficacious call to faith. The problem of the Apostle was thus displaced and carried over from that of predestination to grace to that of predestination to glory. For theology the harm was not serious, since the two questions are connected, and can be solved by the same principles; but it was a different thing for exegesis. The assertions of St Paul took a direction and an amplitude which he had not intended to give them, and his evident purpose of giving all the just a reason for hope was misunderstood.

This first deviation led to another. Directly Augustine understood by predestination a predestination to celestial glory, he had to imagine a twofold divine appeal, no longer as before an efficacious call and an ineffectual call, according to the affirmative or a negative reply of the will, but two efficacious calls, one of which is according to the purpose of God, because it is to be crowned by final perseverance, while the other would not be according to that purpose, because, in the designs of God, it would not be destined to last for ever. Here the language of St Augustine became quite unusual; none of his predecessors, except, perhaps, Ambrosiaster, had conceived of an efficacious call to faith which was not according to the purpose. This diversity of language proves that Augustine's thought and that of his predecessors do not move in the same spheres. Neither St Paul nor his interpreters form a complete theory of predestination. They start from one fact—the state of the just man—and show that this state includes in itself a sure reason for hope, because it is a sure guarantee of the benevolence and continuous protection of the heavenly Father. But the Bishop of Hippo wishes to sound the depths of the divine counsels, and sees clearly that he must go back even beyond prescience, otherwise the initiative of salvation would belong to man. What indeed is prescience if it be not the prevision of the human act under the influence of divine grace? The general decree of an order of grace and the individual offer of grace logically precede, therefore, prescience itself, and this again cannot be the first of the divine acts in the matter of our salvation. This the other Fathers do not deny, and St Paul teaches it often when he speaks of the plan of redemption, but he excludes it from the texts which concern us here.

It follows that St Augustine and the other Fathers are much more in agreement than a superficial view would make us think. All know well that the co-operation of man in the divine call presupposes grace, without which this co-operation is not even conceivable. They differ as exegetes, not as theologians. The usual exegesis, holding to the texts of St Paul, considers man *after* the use of his liberty, and it safeguards sufficiently the initiative of God, since nothing in the order of salvation is possible without the calling, which depends on God alone. Nevertheless, at the first glance, the difference between two men called in the same way, one of whom responds to the call, while the other resists it, would seem to lie only in their free act. Augustine carries the question further and higher, *before* the moment when man makes use of his liberty. He proves that the act of faith itself is a gift of God. He who responds actually to the divine call cannot have received more help; he has certainly received more benefit, and consequently more grace; and even, in a sense, has obtained more help since he has received it at the opportune moment. A call made efficacious by the effective consent of the man is a greater favour than the same call not followed by an effect through the resistance of his free will. Now the last reason for this divine predilection, calling such and such a man at the moment when God foresees that he will obey the call, cannot consist in the act itself of the man, nor in the foreknowledge of that act. It is the mystery of the distribution of the graces which God, by virtue of his prescience, knows are to be efficacious for one and ineffectual for another; a mystery which forces from St Paul the exclamation : *O altitudo!*

THIRD SECTION

THE SCANDAL OF THE REPROBATION OF THE JEWS

I—GOD FAITHFUL AND JUST IN THEIR REJECTION

1. God Free in his Choice. 2. God Master of his Mercies.
3. Exegesis of the Fathers.

1. At the moment when the development of dogma seems exhausted and we expect nothing more save the moral conclusion, a distressing and inexorable objection rises before

the Apostle, which he cannot but meet boldly. It is asserted that the great mass of the Jews, resisting the invitations of Christ, and baffling the efforts of the Twelve and of Paul himself, will remain outside the Church, into which, however, the Gentiles are streaming from all sides. A melancholy contrast this and an inexplicable enigma! Is it not the reversal of all the prophecies and a denial given by facts to the divine promises? Jehovah had proclaimed himself a hundred times the liberator and saviour of his people: the Messiah was to be first of all the redeemer of the Jews; Sion was designated in advance as the centre of the Messianic theocracy and a bond of union with the unbelieving nations. But now, not only are the Gentiles entering the Church without first passing through the Synagogue, but they are almost the only ones who are entering, while the Jews, whose rights seemed preponderant, if not exclusive, find themselves shut out from it.

Such is the problem, the examination of which fills three chapters (ix-xi), whose obscurity is proverbial. The difficulty is chiefly due to two causes: one, St Paul's well-known habit of isolating the different aspects of a question, of entrenching himself in them for a time, and of exploring their darkest corners, without troubling himself about possible misunderstanding and probable false interpretations; the other cause is the unparalleled number of biblical quotations which at every moment break the thread of the argument, cast into the mind of the reader ideas partially foreign to the thesis, and form a heterogeneous conglomeration of texts whose literal meaning it is indispensable to analyze, before deciding on their particular application. There is not perhaps in the whole of Scripture a page where it would be more dangerous to lose sight of the main thought, by exaggerating the significance of the details. Let us first see what the precise point of the question is. It is not " Why is this man predestined to glory and that one doomed to condemnation?" or " Why, in fact, is this man saved and that one rejected?" or even " Why is this man called to faith in preference to that man?" Paul's object is concrete and his aim perfectly practical. He wishes to remove the scandal caused by the unbelief of the Jews and to reply to the question " Why has the people of God, the natural heir to the Messianic blessings and promises, repudiated the Gospel, the only means of salvation?" We will give a general idea of his reply by saying that, of the three chapters devoted to the question, the first vindicates the justice and faithfulness of God, without entering into the heart of the problem; the second explains the why and wherefore of this on the part of man; while the third shows the providential reason for it.

Paul does not challenge a single one of the prerogatives of the Jews.[1] As *Israelites*, they bear the name of one of the greatest favourites of Jehovah; they enjoy the blessing of divine *adoption* and are, collectively and as a nation, children of God; to them was manifested the *glory* (*the Shekinah*), that supernatural splendour with which the ark and the temple were sometimes enveloped; to them belong the *covenants*, contracted under solemn circumstances between God and the people; to them belongs the *Torah*, established by the angels and promulgated by Moses amid the thunders of Sinai; theirs is also the only lawful *worship*, the only one worthy of God and approved by him; to them belong the Messianic *promises*, descending uninterruptedly from Abraham to the latest of the prophets; theirs are the *patriarchs*, the shield and pride of Israel; and, finally, above all, to them belongs the *Christ*, born of the lineage of Abraham and the blood of David according to the flesh, who is at the same time the sovereign God of all ages. These nine privileges, so glorious by the memories they evoke, so overwhelming by the contrasts they suggest, fall one after the other, like an ever sharper cry of pain, from the wounded soul of the Apostle, who could desire to be accursed for his brethren's sake and to pay for their salvation with his life and happiness.[2] And this long enumeration, characterized by so skilful a gradation and so poignant an effect, renders the interest of the problem more intense, and the paradox of the rejection of the Jews more perplexing. The Gentiles, who are nothing to God and to whom God is nothing, are called to faith, while the holy nation, the sacerdotal race, the house of Jehovah, is excluded from it! The natural heirs are disinherited, the legitimate children are supplanted by intruders, the promises seem to be forgotten, the contrasts violated. How can all this be reconciled with divine faithfulness and justice?

Let us first speak of faithfulness. The claims of the Jews

---

[1] Rom. ix, 4-5 : οἵτινές εἰσιν ᾿Ισραηλῖται·

> ὧν ἡ υἱοθεσία (adoptive sonship),
> καὶ ἡ δόξα (the supernatural radiance),
> καὶ αἱ διαθῆκαι (repeated covenants),
> καὶ ἡ νομοθεσία (Mosaic legislation),
> καὶ ἡ λατρεία (the whole system of revealed worship),
> καὶ αἱ ἐπαγγελίαι (Messianic promises).
> ὧν οἱ πατέρες (the patriarchs),
> καὶ ἐξ ὧν Χριστός, κτλ.

This last text, a magnificent testimony to the divinity of Jesus Christ, will be studied in the second part of this work. In the Latin version, some of the nine titles—particularly *obsequium*, which renders λατρεία somewhat incorrectly—are rather indiscriminate.

[2] Rom. ix, 3 : Ηὐχόμην γὰρ ἀνάθεμα εἶναι αὐτὸς ἐγὼ ἀπὸ τοῦ Χριστοῦ ὑπὲρ τῶν ἀδελφῶν μου.

rest upon a misunderstanding.   If they invoke the name of
Abraham, as a palladium which is to shelter them from all
evil, if they look upon the blood of Israel as a kind of sacrament which is to save them *ex opere operato,* without regard
to personal dispositions, their error is complete and inexcusable.   It is to misunderstand the sense and the import
of the divine promises.   There is an Israel according to
the flesh and an Israel of God : to the former nothing is due,
to the latter belongs the promise.   In the same way there is
the carnal posterity of Abraham, and there is his spiritual
posterity; the latter alone inherits the blessings : " All who
bear the name of Israel are not of Israel; neither are all they
that are the seed of Abraham, the children of Abraham."[1]
Sacred history furnishes the clear proof of these two facts.
Among all the children of Abraham, Isaac only, the son by
a miracle, the son of promise, inherits the blessings promised
to the line of Abraham; Ishmail and the sons of Ketura have
no part in it.   The title of " child of Abraham " is therefore
nothing in itself, and it is wrong to take advantage of it in
opposition to God, who remains the master of his gifts and
benefits.   It is exactly the same in the case of Isaac.   A new
selection is made among his children, and here God's liberty
of choice is still more evident.   The same external circumstances accompany the conception and birth of the twin-
brothers.   The only difference would be in favour of Esau,
who was the first to see the light.   Nevertheless, God's
choice, independent of all acquired right and all human consideration, falls on Jacob.

> For when the children were not yet born, nor had done any good or
> evil, that the purpose of God according to election might stand, not of
> works but of him that calleth, it was said to her : The elder shall serve
> the younger, as it is written : Jacob I have loved, but Esau I have hated.[2]

---

[1] Rom. ix, 6-7.

[2] ix, 11-13: Μήπω γὰρ γεννηθέντων μηδὲ πραξάντων τι ἀγαθὸν ἢ φαῦλον,
ἵνα ἡ κατ' ἐκλογὴν πρόθεσις τοῦ Θεοῦ μένῃ, οὐκ ἐξ ἔργων ἀλλ' ἐκ τοῦ
καλοῦντος, ἐρρέθη αὐτῇ ὅτι ὁ μ ε ί ζ ω ν δ ο υ λ ε ύ σ ε ι τ ῷ ἐ λ ά σ σ ο ν ι ·
καθὼς γέγραπται· τὸν 'Ιακὼβ ἠγάπησα, τὸν δὲ 'Ησαῦ ἐμίσησα.   There are
several remarks to be made concerning this difficult passage :—(*a*) The Latin
words *secundum electionem propositum Dei* ought to be understood *per modum
unius* as " the purpose which is according to election " (ἡ κατ' ἐκλογὴν πρόθεσις)
which depends only on the free choice.—(*b*) Similarly, the words *non ex
operibus sed ex vocante* refer not to what follows but to what precedes, and
ought to be included in the parenthesis of the Vulgate.—(*c*) The words
sicut scriptum est (καθὼς γέγραπται) are awkwardly placed near *dictum est ei*
and completed by *quum nondum nati essent aut aliquid boni egissent aut mali :*
which gives a false sense, contrary to the affirmation of the Apostle.   The
words of Malachias, to which St Paul refers, were not written *before*, but *after*
the merits and demerits of the two brothers.   The *sicut* does not indicate
an identity of situation but a similitude in the conclusions which Paul draws
from the two texts.—(*d*) Finally, it is useless to modify the *Jacob dilexi,
Esau autem odio habui*, as certain theologians think themselves obliged to do,

Since the Apostle bases his argument on scriptural texts, we must believe that he does not misinterpret their true meaning. Let us, therefore, go back to the two places cited. It was said to Rebecca :

> Two nations are in thy womb.
> And two peoples shall be divided out of thy womb
> And one people shall overcome the other,
> And the elder shall serve the younger.[1]

Neither in the text of Genesis nor in that of Malachias, mingled here in a composite citation, is there question of Esau and Jacob as individuals. They appear as racial chiefs, and are identified, according to biblical usage, with their posterity, which forms with them one and the same person morally. Esau himself was never the servant of Jacob; he was so only as the father of the Idumeans and in the person of his children. In the text of Malachias it is still more clearly a question of peoples, not individuals :

> I have loved you, saith the Lord; and you have said : Wherein hast thou loved us? Was not Esau brother to Jacob? saith the Lord, and I have loved Jacob, but I have hated Esau, and I have made his mountains a wilderness, and given his inheritance to the dragons of the desert. But if Edom shall say : We are destroyed, but we will return and build up what hath been destroyed; thus saith the Lord of hosts : They shall build up and I will throw down; and they shall be called the borders of wickedness and the people with whom the Lord is angry for ever.[2]

These two texts have this in common, that they refer to nations, not persons, but otherwise the two cases are entirely different. Before the existence of the two peoples and before the birth of their chiefs, independently of all merit acquired or foreseen, God destines for the Israelites, in preference to the Idumeans, the honour and the favour of being the depositaries of the Messianic hopes and the heirs of the promises. From this privilege flowed temporal and spiritual prerogatives with a special providence which guaranteed Israel from ruin. The Israelites were not, for all that, assured of salvation or preserved from infidelity; but they had, as members of the chosen people, one advantage over the others, and this they owed not to their own merits or to those of their fathers, but to the free choice of God. Malachias transports us to another point in the history of the two fraternal peoples. Irritated at their crimes, God raised up Nebuchadnezzar to chastise them both; but while Edom, as a nation, disappears from the face of the earth, Israel, as a nation, survives. Is this a purely temporal

---

as if the *hatred* were to be interpreted as a *lesser love*. These theologians do not reflect that love for guilty Jacob on the part of God is a love of pity, and the hate for Esau the sinner is the just hatred with which God pursues sin

[1] Gen. xxv, 23.   [2] Mal. i, 2-4.

favour? In itself, yes; in its cause and its effects, no. Israel is spared, guilty though it be, because it bears the hope of the world. In short, before all questions of merit, God chooses Israel in preference to Edom, and, after their common demerit, he pardons Israel in preference to Edom. The conclusion is that, in the absence of all merit, God is master of his preferences; in an equality of demerits, God is master of his mercies. These texts, as is evident, prove plainly the independence of God in the distribution of his graces, but have no direct relation to the eternal salvation of Jacob or the condemnation of Esau, and still less to the predestination or reprobation of man in general. If certain theologians had reflected on this, they would have spared themselves many idle theories.

Thus the faithfulness of God finds itself vindicated. God has kept all his agreements in the measure in which he made them; for he had never bound himself to any one of the individuals in question. He has detested Edom, because Edom was worthy of hatred; he has cherished Israel and still continues to love it, although Israel is unworthy of love; but that has not prevented many Israelites from having no part in these special favours. Has God been unjust in regard to them? We see that the Apostle's thought takes another direction: it was a question of nations; it is going to be a question of persons.

2. In this case, as in that, God preserves his independence. He confers his graces when and as he will. The example of Moses and Pharao shows this from two different points of view. Moses demands a favour to which no man is entitled, to look upon the face of God. God refuses it to him, although granting him another which he had not asked. To the poor man who stretches out his hand the rich man gives the alms he wishes to, or even none at all; justice does not oblige him to do anything. In the case of an absolutely gratuitous favour into which no antecedent merit can enter— as in the example admirably chosen by St Paul—the following conclusion is self-evident: *Non est volentis neque currentis sed miserentis est Dei.* This should not be translated, as a certain number of the Fathers, too anxious to preserve man's freedom of will, render it: "*It is not sufficient* to will and to run, it is necessary that God should show mercy"; or "it avails nothing to will or to run, *if* God does not show mercy." The only legitimate translation according to the text is that which St Augustine suggests: "It avails nothing to will and to run; *all* depends upon the God of mercies." A grace purely gratuitous, such as that to which Moses aspired, cannot be subordinated to the action of man nor conditioned by it.

The hardness of Pharao's heart proves essentially the same thing, for the *efficacious* grace of conversion is a purely gratuitous grace. The hard-heartedness of man can be considered as a chastisement from God, who gradually withdraws his aid, in punishment for former sins; it is thus that the Apostle explained the blindness of the heathen at the beginning of his epistle. But as far as Pharao is concerned, Scripture represents his obduracy as a result of the patience and long-suffering of God. God hardened him by multiplying miracles which should have touched him and blinded him by the power of light, as in the case of the Jewish contemporaries of Christ. Origen has very justly observed that Pharao begins to grow less obdurate under the hand of God, when he punishes him, and that his heart becomes harder again when God seems to temporize with him. In any case, as several Fathers, following Origen, remark, God never hardens a man unless he is already hard through his own fault, and he hardens him only for a purpose worthy of his justice and wisdom. Also the hardening is attributed sometimes to the man who is the real author of it by reason of his voluntary resistance, and at other times is attributed to God, who is the occasional cause of it through too much kindness, or who permits it through a just vengeance, while subordinating it to a higher end. It was said to Pharao : " To this purpose have I raised thee, in order that I may show my power in thee, and in order that my name may be declared throughout all the earth." The Greek word signifying " to excite " and " to raise up," it must be here taken in the second meaning, the only one conformable to the sense of the original, but it is proper to leave to the particle " in order that " (ὅπως) its natural value. There is on God's part more than a simple permission; there is intention and finality. The act of a general who abandons a rebellious army to the enemy, or that of a physician who gives up a refractory patient, is not a mere permission; it is a punishment or an act of vengeance. Let us remember, however, that God cannot directly will evil; he allows it only in order to correct it, or to direct it to something good. His designs are impenetrable : " He hath mercy on whom he will," for there is no will which he could not prevail upon to change by his grace; and " whom he will he hardeneth," by allowing him to persevere and to entrench himself in his obduracy, for reasons which he need not explain to anyone.

> Thou wilt say therefore to me : Why doth he then find fault ? for who resisteth his will ?
> O man, who art thou indeed that repliest against God ? Shall the thing formed say to him that formed it : Why hast thou made me thus ? Or hath not the potter power over the clay, of the same lump to make one vessel unto honour and another unto dishonour ? What if God, willing to show his wrath and to make his power known, endured with

much patience vessels of wrath, fitted for perdition, that he might show the riches of his glory on the vessels of mercy, which he hath prepared unto glory ? Even us, whom also he hath called, not only of the Jews, but also of the Gentiles.[1]

This objection no doubt aims at the aphorism of the preceding verse : " Therefore God hath mercy on whom he will; and whom he will he hardeneth." It is less against the reasoning of the Apostle than against the conduct of God, who, on the one hand, reproaches sinners, and, on the other, holds in his hands the hearts of men, as Scripture often declares. It is absurd, since it lets us suppose either that God is the author of sin, or that he complains of the sinner without reason; caprice, arbitrariness, or inconsequence. It relies on the material expression of a thought which found its limitation and its commentary in the context. The maxim *God hath mercy on whom he will, and whom he will he hardeneth,* drew its moral from the history of Moses and Pharao. God, in the bestowal of his purely gratuitous

Rom. ix, 19-24.—(A) Verse 19 contains the objection : *Dicis itaque mihi : Quid adhuc* (ἔτι, " things being thus ") *queritur ? Voluntati enim ejus quis resistit ?* (τίς ἀνθέστηκεν; in the perfect : " Who has ever resisted him ? No one.")

(B) Verses 20-21 contain, not the reply, but a plea in bar. The objection cannot stand. Paul contents himself with opposing it with three questions, which bear their reply in themselves :

(*a*) The first question (*O homo tu quis es qui respondeas Deo ?*) with the particle μενοῦνγε, not translated in the Vulgate, has in it a flavour of irony which could be well rendered by " indeed ! " The words *man* and *God* at the extremities of the sentence emphasize the contrast and accentuate the irony. Nonentity in presence of the infinite has only to be silent.

(*b*) The second question (*Numquid dicit figmentum ei qui se finxit : Quid me fecisti sic ?*) shows it still better, for it is absurd that the work should revolt against the workman ; a free quotation from Isaias xlv, 9-10 ; xxix, 16.

(*c*) The third question (*An non habet potestatem figulus luti ex eadem massa facere aliud quidem vas in honorem, aliud vero in contumeliam ?*) is brought in by the accidental mention of the potter, to whom God is often compared in Scripture, Isa. xxix, 16; xlv, 8-9; Jer xviii, 6; Ecclus. xxxvi, (xxxiii), 12-13. But Paul seems to have recalled especially Wisdom xv, 7, where it is not a question of God, but of a potter making various objects with the same clay: καὶ γὰρ κεραμεύς . . . ἐκ τοῦ αὐτοῦ πηλοῦ ἀνεπλάσατο τά τε τῶν καθαρῶν ἔργων δοῦλα σκεύη τά τε ἐναντία, πανθ' ὁμοίως· τούτων δὲ ἑτέρου τίς ἑκάστου ἐστὶν ἡ χρῆσις, κριτὴς ὁ πηλουργός. Observe that all the objects made by the potter are useful and good, although of unequal excellence and utility ; and it is thus that Paul considers them in another text, in which he seems to allude again to this same passage from Wisdom, 2 Tim. ii, 20-21 : *In magna autem domo non solum sunt vasa aurea et argentea, sed et lignea et fictilia ; et quaedam quidem in honorem, quaedam autem in contumeliam.* The vessels of wood and clay are less precious than those of gold and silver, but they have their value ; the vessels destined for common usage (*vasa ad contumeliam*) are less noble than the others (*vasa ad. honorem*), but they have their own kind of utility. After all, it is not this unequal utility which Paul in Rom. ix, 21 and the author of Wisdom also refer to, but the full liberty which the workman has to choose the purpose of his production, and consequently the obligation which the latter is under to accept without protest the condition which is assigned to it. The heart of the question is, however, not yet touched.

favours, has mercy on whom he will, as in the case of Moses; in the punishment of the guilty, from whom he withdraws his efficacious aid, or whom he overwhelms with new benefits, of which the sinner makes a bad use by his sin; he hardens whom he will, as he did in the case of Pharao. The objection, therefore, is groundless. Moreover, Paul does not reply to it directly; he contents himself with reproducing the usual answer of the inspired authors in similar cases.

It is enough to silence the objectors. Man never has the right to enter a plea against God, or to call him to account for his acts and designs. The creature has nothing for which to blame the Creator, any more than the work can blame the workman. It is probable that the Apostle has nothing else in mind : the majority of the Fathers have thus understood him, and the texts brought forward in proof say nothing more. The precise point of comparison then will be the attitude which the work should maintain towards its workman, the creature towards its Creator. Paul does not say " God *behaves* in regard to free creatures as the artisan behaves in regard to lifeless matter ;" he would, in doing so, destroy his own argument and would take away from God every right to complain, since no sensible workman has ever been known to blame the instrument fashioned by him for not

---

(C) Verses 22-24 contain an indirect reply under the form of a conditional question, the terms of which are to be weighed attentively : *Quod si Deus volens ostendere iram, et notam facere potentiam suam, sustinuit in multa patientia vasa irae apta ad interitum, ut ostenderet divitias gloriae suae in vasa misericordiae, quae praeparavit in gloriam? Quos et vocavit,* etc. It is evident that the sentence is interrupted. the quotation from Osee having carried the thought of the Apostle elsewhere ; but it is clear that it requires this complement : " What have you to object ?" or something similar : and the reply to the complete question is : " Nothing."

The vessels of wrath *have fitted themselves* for destruction (κατηρτισμένα εἰς ἀπώλειαν). There is no doubt that the past participle has in Greek the sense of the middle, for : (a) It is the meaning of this participle in the only place where it is again read (1 Cor. i, 10; compare the perfect participles of 2 Tim. ii, 21).—(b) If Paul had wished to express the passive, he would have done so frankly, using, for example, καταρτισθέντα.—(c) The change of construction and the employment of the active for the vessels of mercy (σκεύη ἐλέους ἃ προητοίμασεν εἰς δόξαν) shows that his intention is different, and that he does not wish to represent God as the author of the vessels of wrath. St John Chrysostom, followed by the best exegetes, paraphrases our text, therefore, very well by explaining it thus: κατηρτισμένον εἰς ἀπώλειαν, τουτέστιν ἀπηρτισμένον, οἴκοθεν μέντοι καὶ παρ' ἑαυτοῦ.

God endures patiently the vessels of wrath. The reason for this which St Paul gives (θέλων ὁ Θεὸς ἐνδείξασθαι τὴν ὀργήν) can be understood in two contrary senses: (1) "*Because* he wishes to manifest his anger," that is to say, with the purpose of showing subsequently how terrible his vengeance is (Origen, Ambrosiaster, St Jerome, St Thomas, Toletus, Estius, and the majority of the commentators). (2) "*Although* he wishes to manifest his anger"; from now on he is patient, in order to leave the sinner time to repent (Reithmayr, Cornely, Sanday, Godet, Weiss, etc.). This second interpretation alone appears to take account of ἐν πολλῇ μακροθυμίᾳ. *Cf.* Rom. ii, 4.

being better. Nor does Paul say "God *could* behave in regard to man as the workman in regard to his work," for he would strengthen the objection of the enemy, instead of removing it; and it is, moreover, evident that the conduct of the workman cannot be a standard for that of God. Paul does say "If God should treat his creature as the potter moulds his clay, the creature would not have the right to protest against him," for the work, as work, has no rights as against the workman. If we wish to push the comparison still further and see in the potter fashioning vessels for various uses the image of God fashioning at his pleasure the hearts and destinies of men, we shall do so only at our own risk and peril, without the warrant of the Apostle.

In any case, unless we distort the thought of Paul, we must never forget the differences which exist both on the part of the workman and on that of the work.

Differences on the Part of the Workman.—Man is capable of caprice, self-will, madness, injustice : God is not; and if he can do everything, he can do nothing contrary to his own wisdom. Man, unless he has lost his senses, does not get angry with the work of his hands, for he forms it as he likes, without either co-operation or resistance on the part of the work; on the contrary, the wrath of God bursts forth with justice and reason against the sinner, who frustrates his wishes and does not correspond with his graces.

Difference on the Part of the Work.—A free will cannot be compared with inanimate matter; and God does not manipulate liberty as the potter moulds the clay. If we wish at all hazards to stretch the comparison as far as that, we must at least observe that the common mass from which the artisan produces his works is good or indifferent and cannot serve as a symbol of the mass of humanity corrupted by original sin : an idea, moreover, completely foreign to the context.

The worst exegesis would be to identify the *vessels of honour* and *dishonour* with the *vessels of wrath* and *mercy*. Nothing authorizes this hypothesis, for the expression is different and the situation is not the same. The vessels designed by the potter for common use are not at all the object of his wrath; they are good and useful, like the vessels of honour, although of less excellence and less utility. On the other hand, the vessels of wrath and mercy are not vessels *destined and reserved* for wrath and mercy. It is a question of the past and present, not of the future. The vessels of mercy are the men on whom God has had mercy by calling them to faith. The vessels of wrath are those who by their unbelief deserve the just anger of God. They have " fitted themselves for destruction "; the attitude of God in regard to them is that of " enduring them with limitless patience," in order to give them a chance to repent, although justice would seem to counsel him to take speedy vengeance upon them.

3. The contrast of Esau and Jacob, the history of Moses and Pharao, the allegory of the potter, and the reflections which these recitals suggested to the Apostle, have from earliest times exercised the intelligence of Catholic exegetes.[1] Origen, as far as one can judge by the loose translation of Rufinus,[2] got out of the difficulty by making an imaginary adversary the mouthpiece of the most embarrassing texts of chapter ix, and by supposing that St Paul replies to every objection "God forbid!" Nevertheless, dissatisfied with an exegesis which, after him, was to have so much success, he takes up the texts again, one by one, and shows how they harmonize with the fact of man's free will. It is in the book of *Principles,* in which the question is treated openly, that we should seek his real thought.[3] The ardent champion of human freedom does not in the least fail to recognize the rôle of grace and God's initiative; but he remarks very justly that the duty of an interpreter is to harmonize apparently contradictory statements. A series of ingenious similitudes serve to explain Pharao's hardness of heart; the sun dries the earth and melts wax, the rain causes thistles to grow in one place and wheat in another; so the patience of God and the manifestation of his power, which would have certainly touched the heart of Pharao if he had been better disposed, only harden it. It was Origen who made famous the formula, so beloved by the Greek Fathers, that the work of salvation does not depend alone on the efforts of man, but also, and indeed chiefly, on the divine mercy. Under his pen, the comparison of the potter lost its terrifying mystery : it was the vessels of wrath which made themselves fit for destruction. Orthodoxy might have been able to follow him to the end, if he had not introduced the merits and demerits acquired in a previous existence to explain the unequal destinies of Esau and Jacob. The Cappadocian editors of the *Philocalia* omit this passage. St Jerome, who everywhere else follows his steps with a perhaps excessive docility, abandons him here unceremoniously.[4]

The influence exerted by Origen on St John Chrysostom is undeniable; but if he often gathers inspiration from the great Alexandrian, Chrysostom does not copy him.[5] The difficult

[1] See V. Weber (Catholic) *Kritische Geschichte der Exegese des IX. Kap., resp. der Verse 14-23 des Römerbriefs bis auf Chrysostomus und Augustinus einschliesslich,* Wurzburg, 1889.

[2] *Comment. in Epist. ad Roman.,* vii, 14-18 (XIV, 1141-1152).

[3] *Periarchon,* iii, 1 (Greek text in the *Philocalia,* chap. xxi).

[4] *Epist.* 120 *ad Hedibiam* (XXII, 997-1001).

[5] *Homilies* xvi-xix on the Epistle to the Romans.

texts are in his eyes objections presented by St Paul himself, in order to silence the unbelieving Jews. They do not yet contain the Apostle's reply, but they prepare the way for it by showing from Scripture that there are mysteries which man cannot explain. But if we wish to take them for his real thought, there is no objection to doing so. For example, the text *Non volentis neque currentis sed miserentis est Dei* will be understood in the sense that it is not sufficient to will and to run, but that grace is indispensable. " One must will and run and put one's trust in the divine goodness, not in one's own strength, according to those words : ' Not I alone, the grace of God in me.' " The comparison of the potter has for its aim to impose silence on bold questioners. To push the analogy between the workman and God any further would lead finally to absurdity. God has in his conduct in regard to man neither arbitrariness nor caprice, for he is wise. He cannot impute to his creature that of which he himself is the author, for he is just. The history of Pharao is brought up in objection; but Pharao has done everything to ruin himself, while God has neglected nothing to reform him, and has finally decided to punish him only when he sees that he is incorrigible. " In a word, whence comes it that some are vessels of wrath and others vessels of mercy? The reason for it lies in their own will. God, who is infinitely good, shows to all the same goodness." The difference between men depends on the different use which they make of God's graces : " All have not been willing to answer the divine call; but, so far as God is concerned, all have been saved, for all have been called."

Such is, with some differences of detail, the exegesis of the Greek Church. All the commentators, Theodoret, St John Damascene, Œcumenius, Euthymius, and Theophylact follow Chrysostom closely. St Basil, St Isidore of Pelusium, St Cyril of Alexandria, and others hardly differ from them, if it is permissible to judge of them by the brief quotations from the biblical *Catenae.* It is only just to say that the Greek writers never had anything to do with Pelagianism. Photius is almost the only one to mention the Pelagian controversies, and he does not even distinguish between Pelagians and semi-Pelagians.

The mysterious anonymous writer, called by agreement Ambrosiaster, holds a position midway between the Greeks and Augustine, who knows him and quotes him under the name of *Saint* Hilary. Ambrosiaster differs from the Greeks in that he regards the difficult texts in chapter ix, with perhaps one exception, as the real thought of Paul, and not as an objection made by some imaginary opponent; he differs from Augustine in that he explains all the acts of God—calling, election, predestination, justification, glorification—by his eternal prescience. This is, it may be said, the dominant idea of his commentary. If he speaks, like Augustine, of the predestined and elected to eternal salvation, if he understands by their glorification eternal glory, if he admits two kinds of calls to grace, one which is according to the purpose, because it has in reality glory for its final aim, another which is not according to the purpose, through the fault of man who neutralizes its effect, these partial agreements with Augustine only accentuate their radical divergencies. For, in the opinion of Ambrosiaster, the divine prescience has no respect of persons. God wishes the salvation of all men, but all men do not wish to be saved; he has mercy upon him who, as he foresees, is to respond to grace; his will is neither blind, nor arbitrary, nor destructive of free will; Pharao resists it, and God makes of him a terrible example of justice. Where the anonymous Ambrosiaster goes beyond the bounds of orthodoxy is when he utters this aphorism : *Praeparare unumquemque est praescire quid futurum est.* Moreover, it is plain that he does not touch the heart of the problem; he never speaks of anything but the *consequent* will of God; it is best to postpone the question, and in regard to this difficult matter the last word has not been said; it will be the rôle of Augustine to utter it.

Whatever admiration we may feel for the theological genius of the Bishop of Hippo, we cannot close our eyes to the faults of his exegesis. In the second of the *Various Questions to Simplicianus,* in which he considers the election of Jacob and the obduracy of Pharao, he proves perfectly that the calling of Jacob is wholly gratuitous and depends on no merit, actual or foreseen, either as a cause or even as a condition of the divine choice. But he forgets that, in the texts brought forward by St Paul, Esau and Jacob are nations, not individuals; that the calling of Jacob is a destination to the theocratic dignity and not a call to faith; that the love for Jacob and the hatred against Esau have relation to a period in their history when both had incurred guilt. He perceives this last point, it is true, but he does not draw from it the legitimate conclusions, so absorbed is he in the problem which engrosses him.[1] From the beginning of the Pelagian controversies, the theology of Augustine more and more intrudes upon his exegesis, and the latter sometimes suffers therefrom. If he had the merit of maintaining that, in the call according to the purpose, it is a question of God's purpose, that prescience is not the ultimate reason for the divine decrees relative to our salvation, and that the difficult passages in chapter ix of the

---

[1] *De divers. quaestion. ad Simplicianum,* book i, q. 2 (XL, 110-127). See Note H for the different opinions of St Augustine.

Epistle to the Romans express indeed the real thought of Paul, it is regrettable that he too often neglects the context and consultation of the original and the literal meaning of the biblical quotations, that he regards election and the purpose of God as a predestination to glory, and, finally, that he places himself on many points in opposition to all his predecessors.   But, even if he is not the prince of exegetes, he none the less remains the incomparable Doctor of grace.

II—Providential Reasons for the Abandonment of the Jews

1. Responsibility of the Unbelieving Jews.   2. Their Conversion, always Possible, One Day Certain.

1. Paul has the habit of making prominent apparently contradictory points of view, without always taking the trouble to reconcile them.   During his lifetime this method was more than once a pretext for accusations and a cause of misunderstandings.   Close the Epistle to the Romans at the end of chapter ix, and you will be tempted to sum up its doctrine in those maxims of profound meaning which are easy to be misrepresented as soon as they are separated from their context : " It is of no use to exercise our will, everything depends on God's good pleasure."   " God has mercy on whom he will, and whom he will he hardens."   " The destinies of man are in his hands like clay in those of the potter."   A false but specious conclusion would be that man has no part in securing his salvation and that his activity is completely absorbed by the divine initiative.   But, on reading a little further, we find the corrective.   We shall see that man responds voluntarily to the divine call, that he is the master of his eternal fate, that his unbelief is inexcusable, and that his obduracy fills up the measure of his iniquities.   In proportion as we isolate one of these contrasts by exaggerating it, we are Jansenists or Pelagians, disciples of Calvin or Arminius ; we predestinate man to salvation or condemnation without taking account of his actions, or we exalt the power of man to the point of suppressing the initiative and the independence of God.

The new aspect of Paul's doctrine can be formulated in the two following propositions with their proofs :[1]

The Jews' unbelief is their own fault.

In fact, they have sought salvation by a way which cannot lead them to it.   They cannot allege either ignorance or good faith ; their fault consists in having followed in the footsteps of their fathers, who were free and unbelieving like

[1] Rom. ix, 30–xi, 36.   Responsibility of the Jews (ix, 30–x, 21) ; hope of salvation for them, as for the Gentiles (xi, 1-36)

themselves. But if they wish, they can even now remedy the
evil by embracing the Gospel.

Moreover, the rejection of Israel is neither total nor final.
It has not been total, since the Church numbers already
thousands of Jewish Christians. It will not be final, for
there will come a day when the Jewish nation, as a whole,
will be converted.

It cannot be denied that they have a " zeal for God," but
theirs is a zeal which is unenlightened and " not according
to knowledge."[1] They have persisted obstinately in their
attitude to the stumbling-block, Jesus Christ, who offered
them salvation by faith.[2] They are counting only on the
observance of the Law, without reflecting that they are going
against the Law of which Christ is the aim and end.[3] They
wish to gain for themselves a justice of their own, which
dispenses them from humility and gratitude, and they misunderstand thus the true justice, the essential character of
which is to destroy pride.[4] Finally, they seek their salvation
in Jewish individualism, whereas " there is no difference
between Jews and Greeks,"[5] as the Scripture itself clearly
suggests. Blind and unhappy are those who stubbornly
remain in the steep and rugged path of the Law, when the
road opened by Christ is so straight, so wide, and so easy.
It is not a question of ascending to heaven to find a Saviour
there, since Jesus Christ has been made man ; it is not a
matter of descending into the deep, for God has brought
Christ up from it ; it is sufficient to believe in their heart that
Jesus is the Lord, and to confess with the mouth that God
hath raised him from the dead.[6]

The objection which this explanation calls forth is that the
unbelief of the Jews seems thus to be reduced to an invincible
and therefore excusable error. If they have taken the wrong
path, through " not knowing the justice of God "[7] it is a misfortune but not a fault. Paul does not give them the benefit
of this ignorance. The Gospel has been preached to them ;
it is impossible that they should not have heard it, for it
has resounded to the uttermost parts of the world.[8] But they
have not " obeyed the Gospel " ;[9] that is the true cause of
their unbelief. This spectacle, distressing as it is, has in it
nothing new for one who knows the history of Israel. Hardness of heart is traditional among the Jews. Isaias complained of it already in his day : " Lord," he said, " who
hath believed our report? . . . All the day long have I
spread my hands to a people that believeth not and con-
tradicteth me."[10] Long before Isaias, also, they had deserved

---

[1] x, 2.   [2] ix, 32.   [3] x, 4.
[4] x, 3 ; ix, 31-32.   [5] xi, 32.   [6] x, 5-10.
[7] x, 3.   [8] x, 18.   [9] x, 16.
[10] x, 21, quoting Isa. lxv, 2.

the same reproaches.[1] Their present unbelief, the object of
so much astonishment and scandal, is only one fact the more
to add to the annals of their apostasies.

2. But the door of the Church is not closed to them. Paul
continues to pray for them;[2] he would not pray for them if
he knew that they were rejected without a chance of returning. He tries, at the cost of many painful efforts, to win
some of them to Christ, and his endeavours are often
crowned with success.[3] It is unbelief which has broken them
off from the wild olive; but faith can graft them on again.[4]
We have here the exact opposite of chapter ix, and any
theory that neglects one of these aspects of the question
mutilates the Apostle's thought.

Nevertheless, the postponed question is not fully answered.
The Jews bear the penalty of their obduracy, and the responsibility for their rejection falls on them; the justice and
faithfulness of God are thus vindicated; but since he holds
the hearts of men in his hands, had not his wisdom and
goodness to make the chosen race the nucleus of the
Church and to enlarge rather than remove the ancient theocracy?

Such is the problem which Paul raises in his conclusion.
At the very outset he remarks that it is badly stated.
" Hath God cast away his people?" This question calls for
an energetic negation. In fact, it contradicts an affirmation
of Scripture thrice repeated; and the simple juxtaposition of
" God " and " his people " shows sufficiently the impossibility
of a rejection which would be on God's part an act of inconstancy, if not of unfaithfulness. " Certainly not; God
hath not cast away his people whom he foreknew."[5] Man
modifies his choices, because he does not foresee all the

---

[1] x, 19, quoting Deut. xxxii, 21.   [2] x, 1
[3] Rom. xi, 14 : *et salvos faciam aliquos ex illis.*
[4] xi, 23 : *Sed et illi, si non permanserint in incredulitate, inserentur.*
[5] Rom. xi, 1-2: Μὴ ἀπώσατο ὁ Θεὸς τὸν λαὸν αὐτοῦ; μὴ γένοιτο. . . . Οὐκ
ἀπώσατο ὁ Θεὸς τὸν λαὸν αὐτοῦ ὃν προέγνω. The reply, with the exception of the words ὃν προέγνω, is taken from Ps. xciii, 14, which the
question contradicts. See Ps. xciv, 4 and 1 Sam. xii, 22. The words
ὃν προέγνω, *quem praescivit,* are understood by St Augustine (*De dono persev.,*
xviii, No. 45) and his school as meaning " whom he predestined "; by Origen,
Chrysostom and their usual adherents as meaning "who he foresaw would
be faithful." For both of these schools the phrase is limitary and restrictive. But this cannot hold. In fact : (*a*) Paul would then take the
word " people " in an entirely different sense in the question and in the
reply, and the entire difficulty would remain.—(*b*) His answer would be a
truism and would amount to this : "God has not rejected those whom he
has predestinated," or more simply, "God has not rejected those whom
he has not rejected."—(*c*) To προέγνω is thus given the meaning of " predestine " which it has not, or else it is completed with an idea which nothing
suggests. It is better to leave to it its natural meaning (to know beforehand)
which suits the case perfectly.

inconveniences which may arise. But it is not so with God, who has chosen Israel for his people, in spite of their infidelities, which are foreseen The reason that Paul gives for this is that the gifts of God are without repentance. Israel, despite its present unworthiness, remains dear to God on account of the patriarchs; and their election in some way secures the divine faithfulness.[1]

But it is one thing to reject the people as a people, and another thing to permit the wandering away of individuals. In reality, individuals have never been protected against apostasy simply because they belonged to the chosen people. We see in sacred history that Providence has only seen to it that the defection should never be complete. That which distinguishes Israel from other nations is that it can be chastised, dispersed, and almost exterminated, but never without hope of return. God always leaves a *remnant*, an *offshoot*, a *seed*, in which is concentrated all the national life for a time, and wherein salvation shall again flourish. Among the examples of this providential action, which the prophets record on every page, Paul chooses one which adapts itself admirably to the conditions of that time. When Elias complained to God of the general apostasy which he saw, God replied to him that he had reserved seven thousand men, who had not bent the knee to Baal. This was the heart of the sacred nation, the hope of Israel and the living proof of God's fidelity. "Even so, then," concludes the Apostle, "at this present time also there is a *remnant* saved according to the election of grace."[2] The application is evident. It cannot be said that God has rejected his people now, any more than it could be said in the time of Elias.

Thus vanishes the theological objection; but there exists a difficulty which may be called one of feeling, or a popular objection. If, *de jure*, the nation, as nation, is not rejected, *de facto* the mass of its individuals is unbelieving. How can this fact be reconciled with the special providence with which God encompasses Israel?

Paul's reply is given in two words: the apostasy of the Israelites is neither absolute nor final. In other terms, those who are unbelieving to-day can be believers to-morrow; in

[1] xi, 29: Ἀμεταμέλητα γὰρ τὰ χαρίσματα καὶ ἡ κλῆσις τοῦ Θεοῦ. The Apostle is speaking of purely gratuitous gifts, such as the theocratic election. Having no other reason for their existence than the goodness of God, they give no occasion for repentance. Israel, as a nation, remains therefore dear to God (xi, 28: κατὰ τὴν ἐκλογὴν ἀγαπητοὶ διὰ τοὺς πατέρας), both because it is the chosen people and because it is descended from the patriarchs.

[2] xi, 5. This was the *remnant* that Isaias (vi, 13) compares to a tree ravaged by the axe and by fire, which he symbolizes by the name given to one of his children (vii, 3): *Shear Jashub, reliquiae convertentur* (Vulgate: *Qui derelictus est Jasub*). See Isa. x, 21, 22; Jer. xxiii, 3; Ezech. xiv, 22; Mic. ii, 12; v, iii; Soph. iii, 13, etc.

any case, at the end of the world Israel will repent and will come back to the Church as a whole. Here there is a theological teaching and a prophecy; but the Apostle mingles with these some profound considerations concerning the supernatural providence and the inscrutable ways of God.

Experience shows that the apostasy is not complete. Is not Paul himself, a Jewish offspring of purest blood, a Christian?[1] The Church at Jerusalem is flourishing; it has spread out into the whole of Palestine; a great number of Jews of the *diaspora* have embraced the Gospel. Some months after the sending of this Epistle, St James was able to tell St Paul of many thousands of converted Hebrews.[2] It is only a minority, but an important minority. It can increase; the Apostle hopes that it will do so, and, with this hope at heart, lavishes his efforts and prayers in abundance.

But as far as the ultimate conversion of Israel is concerned, hope is a certainty. Paul boldly proclaims "this mystery," either because he derives it from his own revelations, or because he presents it as an infallible consequence of the prophetic oracles : " Blindness in part has happened in Israel until the fulness of the Gentiles should come in, and so all Israel should be saved."[3] Wonderful tactics of God ! The Gentiles, at first incredulous, are called to faith, thanks to the unbelief of the Jews; the Jews refuse to believe in the mercy shown to the Gentiles, in order to be in their turn the object of mercy. " God hath concluded all in unbelief, that he may have mercy on all."[4] Is it not appropriate to exclaim here : " O the

---

[1] Rom. xi, 1. Another explanation is, however, possible.

[2] Acts xxi, 20 (πόσαι μυριάδες). *Cf.* Acts iv, 32 ; v, 14, etc.

[3] Rom. xi, 25-26, with a reference to the prophets.

[4] If the leaders of the Reformation refused to believe in the ultimate conversion of the Jews, it was only on account of dogmatic prejudices. Luther said that the Jews, being as hard as stone, steel, and the *devil* (for he brought the devil into everything), were not susceptible to conversion, Modern Protestants have, on the whole, returned to a better exegesis of St Paul, whose teaching is wholly unambiguous. The Apostle has already in the course of chap. xi given us a hint of the final conversion of the Jews (verses 11-12, 16, 23-24) ; now he announces it unhesitatingly (verses 25-26). The Greek text is still more explicit than the Vulgate : πᾶς Ἰσραὴλ σωθήσεται (*omnis Israel salvus fiet*, and not *fieret;* for it is a question of a fact, not of an intention). St Paul calls this *a mystery:* that is to say, conformably to his language, a plan of redemption which was the *secret* of God, because it proceeds from his free will ; but which has ceased to be a *secret* since God has revealed it to his confidants to be everywhere proclaimed. This mystery, this providential design, consists in this : God has permitted the blindness (*caecitas*) or rather obduracy (πώρωσις) of the majority of the Jews, in order to hasten the evangelization of the Gentiles, and to stimulate the Jews themselves to emulation ; but when the heathen nations in their entirety (τὸ πλήρωμα τῶν ἐθνῶν) shall have entered into the Church, the turn of Israel will come, and then *all* Israel will be *saved*. It is clearly a question here of

depth of the riches of the wisdom and of the knowledge of God?" And can we not here adore the incomprehensible judgements of God and his unsearchable ways? This is the closing word of the Apostle.

---

the Messianic *salvation*, and the *totality* is to be understood as meaning the mass of Israel as a nation, some individuals excepted. *The fulness of the nations* is to be interpreted in the same way. For details, see Cornely or Lagrange.

BOOK IV
THE CAPTIVITY

CHAPTER I

THE EPISTLES OF THE CAPTIVITY

I—Historic Outline and General Traits

1. Paul a Prisoner of Christ. 2. Characteristics common to these Epistles.

1. **T**HE three Epistles to the Colossians, the Ephesians, and the Philippians, together with the note to Philemon, which serves as a preamble or postscript to the first, form a group by themselves, still more closely related than the four great Epistles. To their common doctrinal traits and to their unity of time and place is added here an identity of scene and external setting. An ambassador of Christ in chains, Paul is a prisoner;[1] but he foresees his liberty as near at hand, and makes plans for the day of his deliverance.[2] His captivity is not strict; he enjoys a partial degree of liberty; he sees his friends, converses with his disciples, and even continues his active apostolate.[3] All these details make us think of Rome rather than of Cæsarea, and we locate the composition of these letters there, with entire certainty as regards the Epistle to the Philippians and with a very strong probability in regard to the other three. The latter were sent together by the same courier.[4] We think that a very short interval of time separates them from the Epistle to the Philippians, which, according to all appearances, is the last of the series. This brings us to the year A.D. 61 or 62.

The historical situation is not difficult to reconstruct. Onesimus, a slave of Philemon, had left his master, after having stolen from him.[5] Rome, that meeting-place of all misfortunes and sewer of all vices, promised in its immense and mixed cosmopolitan population a sure refuge for fugitive slaves, returned convicts, and adventurers of every kind. Onesimus fled thither. Perhaps he hoped to find help and protection with his master's friend. Actually he found something better still, faith and baptism. In sending him back to Colosse, Paul entrusted to him the little note, written with

---

[1] Eph. iii, 1 ; iv, 1; vi, 20 ; Philem. verses 1 and 9; allusion to chains, Phil. i, 7, 13, 14, 17 ; Col. iv, 4, 18 ; Philem. verses 10 and 13.

[2] Phil. i, 25-26 ; ii, 24 ; Philem. verse 22.

[3] Phil. i, 20 ; Eph. iii, 12 ; vi, 19 ; Philem. verse 8. See Acts xxviii, 34.

[4] Eph. vi, 21 ; Col. iv, 7 (Tychicus).

[5] This seems to be proved by Philem. verses 18-19: Εἰ δέ τι ἠδίκησέν σε ἢ ὀφείλει ἐμοὶ ἐλλόγα. . . . . ἐγὼ ἀποτίσω. Paul would not allude to this injustice, to this debt, and would not assume it, if he had not known of it by the avowal of the guilty man.

his own hand, which is our Epistle to Philemon. With him journeyed Tychicus, charged with a special message for the Church of Colosse. In this there was something unusual. Paul was not wont to build upon the foundations of others, and this Church was not his work. Epaphras was its missionary. It is true it was most intimately attached to Paul. The faithful met in the house of his friend Philemon, under the direction of Archippus, probably Philemon's son. There is even reason to suppose that Epaphras, alarmed by the dangers incurred by his converts, and too weak alone to resist the torrent of the new ideas, had begged for the assistance of someone stronger than himself. The humble missionary effaced himself behind the Apostle, whose intervention alone seemed able to avert the evil.[1] The theosophical doctrines, accompanied by strange practices, which were secretly making their way into Colosse, could not fail sooner or later to invade the neighbouring cities, Hierapolis and Laodicea, and thus in time to reach also the capital of the province, Ephesus, which was in close relations with the cities of the valley of the Lycus.[2] Paul, therefore, thought it appropriate to resume in a more general form the subject developed in the Epistle to the Colossians, leaving out all that it contained of a personal and local nature. This thought originated the circular letter, addressed to several Churches of Asia, and now known under the name of the Epistle to the Ephesians. The Epistle to the Philippians owed its origin to a quite casual circumstance. An inhabitant of Philippi, Epaphroditus, had brought to Paul, while still a prisoner, a generous contribution on the part of the former's fellow-citizens.[3] It seems that his intention was to devote himself to the Apostle's service; but he fell seriously ill, and had scarcely recovered before a feeling of homesickness seized him. Paul acquiesced in his wishes and gave him an affectionate letter for his compatriots, in which thanks and praises are most nobly and delicately expressed.

[1] It was Epaphras who pointed out to Paul the dangers which were threatening this young Christian community (Col. i, 8). The state of his converts caused him great uneasiness (ἀγωνιζόμενος) and lively apprehensions (πολὺν πόνον), Col. iv, 12, 13. How can his staying away from them be understood, unless he counted upon Paul's help? The tone of the letter shows that the most complete understanding and perfect harmony of opinions reigned between these two men.

[2] These three cities formed an isosceles triangle, at the base of which, about six miles long, were Hierapolis and Laodicea, opposite each other on the two sides of the Lycus, and at the apex of which was Colosse, up the river and on the Lycus itself, ten or twelve miles from each of them. The valley of the Lycus was the commercial route uniting Ephesus with Galatia and Cilicia.

[3] Phil. iv, 18. This Epaphroditus has nothing in common with the Epaphras of the preceding Epistles. Although Epaphras is the abridged form of Epaphroditus, the two names are always distinct in these Epistles.

2. In the Epistles of the captivity, several previously vital questions now pass to the second rank; some, up to this time scarcely hinted at, now assume a preponderating importance; but the new theories are always grafted on to the old doctrines, which thus still find an echo in the new writings. There is a development of thought, explained and justified by the circumstances, but nowhere is there a break in its continuity.

The judaizing crisis is over, the war formerly waged against the champions of Judaism is gradually dying down, and everywhere the conflict shows every sign of ending in the triumph of Paul's ideas. There remain, it is true, a few clouds on the horizon, and the sudden and violent outbreak against "dogs, evil workers, and the partisans of circumcision"[1] is a proof of it; but if the dogs still bark at a distance, they no longer dare to expose themselves to the terrible blows of the Apostle. The false teachers of Colosse are, it is true, tainted with Judaism, but it is a conciliatory Judaism, which no longer wishes to impose itself at any price, but is only too happy to be tolerated, a Judaism rather like that of the over-scrupulous Christians at Rome, who distinguished between certain days and certain meats. Although pitiless for errors of principle in the exponents of an uncompromising dogmatism, Paul knows how to condescend to the anxieties of timorous consciences; and this is why the tone of his polemics, in the face of enemies who are disarming, is so much milder. To make up for this, however, new tendencies are coming to light. The early preaching on the subject of Jesus had been simple. Men saw in him the Son of God, the Messiah, the Redeemer, the only Saviour, the supreme Judge. His birth from the lineage of David was recounted, as were his miracles, his teachings, his death, his resurrection, and the promise of his return in glory. Here were all the elements of a Christology, if they could be united and moulded into one system. But at first this was not thought of. It was enough to know that it was necessary to believe and to hope in him, to love him and obey him. Yet the innate need of knowing and comprehending was not to be long in asserting its rights, and it was only just to satisfy it. Whence came Jesus? What had he been in his previous existence? What was his rôle in the creation of the world and in the life of the Church? For want of an answer to these questions, converts sought to find a solution of the enigma in the ideas inherited from their fathers, which they had not entirely discarded at

---

[1] Phil. iii, 2-3: *Videte canes, videte malos operarios, videte* concisionem (κατατομήν). *Nos enim* sumus circumcisio (ἡ περιτομή). Note the sarcasm and the play on words. What makes the irony more biting is that κατατομή and κατατέμνω are used of mutilations forbidden by the Law (Lev. xxi, 5; 1 Kings xviii, 28; Isa. xv, 2).

the threshold of the baptistery, and they fashioned for themselves a theology of their own. It was, therefore, expedient to instruct them, to initiate them into the true wisdom, to unveil the mystery, and finally to elevate them to that higher knowledge of which they were so jealous and so proud. The first characteristic of this group of Epistles is, therefore, a highly developed Christology.

The second is a more precise teaching about the nature and constitution of the Church. The Church was on the way towards organization. Thanks to the efforts of Paul, the union between the two sections of Christianity was visibly progressing. It was now retarded only by the last pretensions of the Jewish Christians, who, no longer insisting on the entire observance of the Law, asked at least for some of it to be retained; it was also retarded by the very universality of the Church, composed as it was of peoples differing so greatly in mind, blood, customs, and language that they were jealous of one another and detested and despised one another. It was necessary to blend all this into one in Christ; for the Church is neither the sum of isolated believers, nor the aggregation of national Christian communities, but the mystical body of Christ, animated by one and the same Spirit, participating in the same life, aspiring to the same end, and under the authority of the same Head. Such is the most prominent truth in the Epistles of the captivity.

In running through them, we are struck by the importance given to the intellect. The words relating to intellectual knowledge, such as truth, science, doctrine, revelation, wisdom, comprehension, and light, together with their derivatives and the words of contrary meanings, are repeated lavishly. In the same category of ideas a certain number of terms make their appearance here for the first time. Formerly Paul seemed to make wisdom the endowment of the perfect; now he wishes it for all, as well as that superior knowledge which he himself designates as *superscience* (ἐπίγνωσις).[1] Finally, one of his keenest preoccupations is that of explaining the secret—hidden from past generations, but to-day revealed to the apostles and prophets—to which he applies the word *Mystery*. Let us not, however, exaggerate the contrast between these and the great Epistles. It is interesting to compare, in the two groups, the notions of justice, faith, grace, law, and sin. The theories, developed at length in the Romans or Galatians, are here recalled as axioms, as results acquired and accepted. But they often receive more concise and also more exact expression. "I desire," says the Apostle, "to have not my justice, which is of the Law, but that

---

[1] The Pauline word ἐπίγνωσις forms a bond of union between the different Epistles of Paul. It is found in each of the letters of the captivity, and of the pastorals. In the former it is especially frequent.

which is through the faith of Christ Jesus, the justice which is of God, founded upon faith."[1] We know well this justice engendered by faith, which the Law cannot attain, justice which is at the same time of God and of man—of God, because it emanates from him; and of man, because it is inherent in him; and we remark also that the grammatical ambiguity of "justice of God" has been removed. No less admirable in its conciseness is that other formula : " By grace you are saved through faith, and that not of yourselves, for it is the gift of God; not of works, that no man may glory."[2] If salvation—that is to say, habitual grace—is substituted for justification, it is because the controversy no longer turns on the *passage* from the state of sin to the state of justice. As the works of the Law are no more in question, it is works, indiscriminately considered, which take their place. The thesis is enlarged and generalized. But the rôle of faith, as a principle and means of salvation, the absolute necessity of grace, and its definition as a gift of God without regard to merit, are wholly characteristic of Paul and the final expression (*ut ne quis glorietur*) has also a thoroughly Pauline flavour.

II—THE NOTE TO PHILEMON

1. The Question of Slavery. 2. The Case of Onesimus.

1. This little masterpiece of tact, urbanity, nobility, and exquisite grace was the first Christian declaration of the rights of man. The question of slavery had already occupied the attention of the Apostle. He could not think of proclaiming it abolished. Social reasons, the security of the State, the peaceful penetration of Christianity, and the well-understood interests of the slaves themselves did not permit the.

---

[1] Phil. iii, 9 (see Rom. i, 17; iii, 21-22): μὴ ἔχων ἐμὴν δικαιοσύνην τὴν ἐκ νόμου, ἀλλὰ τὴν διὰ πίστεως Χριστοῦ, τὴν ἐκ Θεοῦ δικαιοσύνην ἐπὶ τῇ πίστει. The Pauline colouring of this passage is obvious and is now practically denied by no one. It is unnecessary to point this out in detail.

[2] Eph. ii, 8-10: Τῇ γὰρ χάριτί ἐστε σεσωσμένοι διὰ πίστεως· καὶ τοῦτο οὐκ ἐξ ὑμῶν, Θεοῦ τὸ δῶρον· οὐκ ἐξ ἔργων, ἵνα μή τις καυχήσηται. Αὐτοῦ γάρ ἐσμεν ποίημα, κτισθέντες ἐν Χριστῷ Ἰησοῦ, κτλ. We must remark : (a) Salvation already accomplished in principle (σεσωσμένοι). Cf. Rom. viii, 24; Titus iii, 5; 1 Cor. i, 18; xv, 2; 2 Cor. ii, 15.—(b) Salvation by (διά) faith, essentially Pauline. Cf. Rom. iv, 23-25; Gal. ii, 16; iii, 14-26; Phil. iii, 9, etc.—(c) The instrumentality of grace (τῇ χάριτι) or of faith, opposed to that of works (οὐκ ἐξ ἔργων). Cf. Rom. iii, 24 (δικαιούμενοι δωρεὰν τῇ αὐτοῦ χάριτι); xi, 6 (εἰ χάριτι οὐκέτι ἐξ ἔργων), etc.—(d) The choice of a means of salvation which takes away every pretext for boasting (ἵνα μή τις καυχήσηται. Cf. 1 Cor. i, 29 (ὅπως μὴ καυχήσηται πᾶσα σάρξ); iv, 7; 2 Cor. x, 17 and Rom. iv, 2.—(e) The transformation effected by grace, presented as a *creation* (ποίημα, κτισθέντες). Cf. 2 Cor. v, 17 (εἰ τις ἐν Χριστῷ καινὴ κτίσις); Gal. vi, 15 (καινὴ κτίσις), etc. —(f) The οὐκ ἐξ ὑμῶν corresponds to *Quid habes quod non accepisti?* (1 Cor. iv, 7), to Titus iii, 5, and is notoriously in the style of Paul.

The Roman Empire counted then ten times more slaves than citizens; a fortune of several thousands of *servi* was nothing exceptional, and some proprietors possessed more than twenty thousand. Suddenly to preach emancipation to these crowds would be to let loose civil war and provoke a cataclysm, in which the Empire might perish, and meantime would draw upon the infant Church terrible reprisals. Moreover, the experience of all the centuries shows how Utopian and fatal, even for its beneficiaries, is the too precipitate passage from servitude to liberty. To inculcate in a slave his dignity as a man, to teach the master to see in him a brother, to fill, little by little, the gulf between the castes by reminding Christians of their union in Christ and of their equality before God, was all that Christianity in its beginnings could do. The rest was an affair of time : the leaven of liberty, equality, and fraternity, deposited in the heart of the Church, would infallibly ferment in the course of centuries, bringing without shock or revolution on the one hand the progressive liberation of the slaves, and on the other the extension of the principles of justice and humanity which would thereafter render a return to slavery impossible.

Paul had bestowed upon the Galatians the charter of Christian liberty, when he wrote to them : "You are all the children of God by faith in Christ Jesus. For as many of you as have been baptized in Christ, have put on Christ. There is neither Jew nor Greek; there is neither bond nor free; there is neither male nor female. For you are all one in Christ Jesus."[1] For Christians, identified individually with Christ in the unity of his mystical body, the natural inequalities of race, condition, sex, no longer count for anything. A slave is as good as a free man. "Let every man," says St Paul again, "abide in the same calling in which he was called. Wast thou called being a bondman? Care not for it." There follows a phrase, ambiguous by reason of its conciseness, which has been interpreted in diametrically opposite senses : *Sed et si potes fieri liber magis utere.*[2]

---

[1] Gal. iii, 27-28 : πάντες γὰρ ὑμεῖς εἷς ἐστε. He says : "You are one and the same person," not "one and the same thing," because Christians form together only one mystical Christ.

[2] 1 Cor. vii, 20-21. The double meaning exists also in Greek : Ἀλλ᾽ εἰ καὶ δύνασαι ἐλεύθερος γενέσθαι, μᾶλλον χρῆσαι. It must, however, be confessed that the καὶ favours the first interpretation, which is that of the old Greek and Latin commentators and seems to harmonize better with the context and with Paul's thought. The pamphlets of Steinmann (Catholic) will be read with benefit : *Die Sklavenfrage in der alten Kirche,* Berlin, 1910, and *Paulus und die Sklaven zu Korinth,* Braunsberg, 1911. After having traced the history of the exegesis of 1 Cor. vii, 21 from Origen down, the author maintains that the meaning of the verse can very well be : "If nevertheless it is possible for you to become free, so much the better ; use your freedom as a good servant of Christ." But for this it is necessary to read too much between the lines.

In the opinion of some the Apostle counsels remaining in servitude : " Even if you can become free, remain rather a slave." According to others, he recommends seizing the chance of freedom, if it is offered. " If you can become free, take advantage of it." Whatever may be the reading adopted, the general thesis is the same : the slave called to faith being the freedman of Jesus Christ, and the freeman called to Christ being the bondman of Jesus Christ, the differences are external, accidental, without religious importance, and negligible from the Christian point of view. Christianity annuls neither marriages nor contracts, nor does it break the ties of relationship or subordination, but it transforms souls and renders them superior to human contingencies.

Paul marks out for masters as well as slaves their respective duties. Upon the latter he enjoins entire, sincere, heart-felt, and God-fearing obedience, without any pretence or base flattery, an obedience inspired by the thought of doing the will of God and sustained by the fear of his judgement and the hope of his everlasting recompense. To masters he prescribes justice and equity towards their slaves, forbids threats and bad treatment, and reminds them of the strict and infallible Judge who is no respecter of persons. The rights and duties of the slave ! What a strange Utopia in the eyes of the cultivated world of that age ! It was a question seriously debated by philosophers whether the slave had a soul. In any case, it could be only a servile soul, from which one must expect neither nobility nor morality. The slave had no more duties than an animal ; like the beast, he had only a task to fulfil.

As to his rights, the axiom universally accepted by jurists was that he could have none. The slave was a body, a beast of burden, a living machine, a piece of furniture. He was bought for the price of a horse, the same taxes were paid on him, he was trained and exploited in the same way, and the master was free to sell him off cheaply when he was old or used up. Moreover, his owner could with impunity fatten eels with him, let him be used for experiments in vivisection, condemn him to perpetual celibacy, abuse his sense of decency or even traffic in it, and separate him arbitrarily from his wife and children. If certain proprietors, through interest, apathy, fear, or humanity treated their slaves better, the latter remained none the less at the mercy of all sorts of passions and caprices. Societies for the protection of animals did not exist in Rome ; the laws of Hadrian, Antoninus Pius, and Marcus Aurelius, designed to free the *mancipia* a little from the power of despotic masters, were not yet enacted and were never efficacious. It was necessary to wait until the Christian idea, under Constantine, Theodosius, and Justinian, penetrated the customs of the nation as well as its code.

2. The case of Onesimus was serious. As a fugitive, the letter F would have been indelibly branded on his forehead with a red-hot iron, and his neck would have been encircled with an iron collar. As a thief, he would be left to the discretion of his owner, to die under the lash or to turn a millstone for the rest of his life. Paul knows all this, yet he does not fear to expose the guilty man to the vengeance and resentment of his master. He recognizes the rights of Philemon, and he was not willing to retain Onesimus without his master's consent; he does not ask him in so many words for the enfranchisement of the slave, but it is very evident that he counts on it and is sure of it. He clearly suggests to him this act of generosity, which will be the more meritorious the more spontaneous it is; he hints also that he *could* impose it on him by virtue of his paternal and apostolic authority; but, as a matter of fact, he does not impose it.[1] What he does ask of him unequivocally for Onesimus is his exemption from punishment. He, Paul, answers for the slave; he assumes his debt; and in a tone half in jest, half in earnest, he contracts formally to pay it, yet not without giving Philemon to understand that, if they were to settle their accounts, it would be Philemon who would remain the debtor.[2] Conformably to the principles of Christianity, Philemon is hereafter to regard his slave as a brother and a future companion in the glory of heaven.[3] With supreme delicacy, after having sketched this sublime ideal of Christian charity and generosity, Paul expresses the hope that his friend, not content with fulfilling all his wishes, will exceed them.

Our Epistle has often been compared with a letter written by Pliny the Younger on a similar subject and in an analogous situation. Although the letter of Pliny is very fine for a

---

[1] Commands, counsels and prayers are blended here to such a point that it is difficult to say where one ends and the others begin.

(A) Paul *begs* (παρακαλῶ): (*a*) as a friend (διὰ τὴν ἀγάπην), (*b*) as an old man (πρεσβύτης), (*c*) as an Apostle (Παῦλος), (*d*) as a prisoner of Christ Jesus (δέσμιος Χ. 'Ι.), in favour of his son whom he has begotten while in chains, that is, of his own bowels (τοῦτ' ἔστιν τὰ ἐμὰ σπλάγχνα).—(B) He only *counsels*, awaiting the consent of the interested party (χωρὶς τῆς σῆς γνώμης οὐδὲν ἠθέλησα ποιῆσαι), and his willing acceptance of his wishes)κατὰ ἑκούσιον).—(C) However, he could *command*, as the representative of Christ towards a Christian (πολλὴν ἐν Χριστῷ παρρησίαν ἔχων ἐπιτάσσειν); he counts on the *obedience* of Philemon (πεποιθὼς τῇ ὑπακοῇ); he even uses the imperative on occasion (προσλαβοῦ αὐτὸν ὡς ἐμέ, ἀνάπαυσόν μου τὰ σπλάγχνα).

[2] Paul promises to indemnify Philemon (18-20). Nothing is wanting to this contract, not even the signature of the debtor (ἐγὼ Παῦλος ἔγραψα τῇ ἐμῇ χειρί, ἐγὼ ἀποτίσω). But neither Paul nor Philemon has thought for a moment that the payment would have to be made in cash, as some modern exegetes think.

[3] Οὐκέτι ὡς δοῦλον ἀλλὰ ὑπὲρ δοῦλον, ἀδελφὸν ἀγαπητόν (verse 16). Philemon is to receive Onesimus, as he would receive Paul himself (15: ὡς ἐμέ).

pagan, the comparison is all in favour of the Apostle. Pliny begs his friend Sabinianus not to subject a runaway slave to torture. In future, should the slave commit the same offence again, his master may be pitiless in his anger, but for the moment the guilty man is sufficiently punished by the bitter reproaches and threats of Pliny himself. Very differently does Paul recommend to the mercy of Philemon the beloved spiritual son whom he has begotten while in chains.

Although the Apostle appreciates very highly man's moral independence, we may perhaps question whether his mind ever considered how much injustice and inhumanity there was in the slavery of ancient times. Among the Hebrews, slavery was usually voluntary and differed little from simple domestic service. For compatriots it ended after at most six years, without the formal consent of the interested party; and the legislator had foreseen the possibility that this consent would be freely given as quite an ordinary occurrence. In heathen circles it was entirely different, for there the slave was no longer a man. But there also acquired rights and interests existed which had to be guarded. The sudden stoppage of a machine so necessary for the working of the empire was too dangerous; and to abandon, without due preparatory steps, this institution, which had existed for so many centuries, would have been scarcely less unjust and immoral than its absolute maintenance. It was enough that the spirit of Christianity should gradually undermine its foundations and correct its abuses, while waiting for its final downfall.

CHAPTER II

THE PRE-EMINENCE OF CHRIST

I—THE FALSE TEACHERS OF COLOSSE

1. Ephesians and Colossians. 2. The Heresy of Colosse.

1. THE two Epistles to the Colossians and the Ephesians are in their relations to each other like the Epistles to the Galatians and the Romans. The shorter and the first written in each group serves respectively as a rough draft for its successor. The Epistle to the Colossians, more stirring, more lively, and more personal in character, aims at a precise and immediate result and attacks a determined adversary; the Epistle to the Ephesians, fuller, maturer, and more elaborate, avoids controversies and observes the regular trend of a dogmatic treatise. The subject is the same, as is the sequence of ideas; many expressions and turns of phrase are identical. However, the second is neither the duplicate nor the copy of the first. We recognize in them a mind which draws freely from its own resources under the influence of the same designs or the same needs; there is nothing visible here of the servile imitator, whose hand is betrayed by the excessive care it takes to conceal itself.

The Epistle to the Colossians has nothing special in it, save the polemic against the sectarians,[1] an occasional reference,[2] and some details of a personal nature.[3] On the other hand, the Epistle to the Ephesians has in it nothing particular except the introduction to the subject,[4] the definition and description of the mystical body,[5] and, finally, the description of the armour of God.[6] There are also in the portions peculiar to each several ideas and expressions common to both. Their relations become even closer in the section treating of morals. With the exception of two or three verses, all of the first chapter of the letter to the Colossians could be restored, if lost, by the aid of fragments taken here and there from the letter to the Ephesians, but placed in a different context. This minute similitude is a very strong proof of the authenticity of both Epistles.

An attempt to study them separately would lead to a thousand repetitions. It is better to seize upon the dominant

Col. ii, 1-9, 16-23.
[3] iv, 9-18.
[5] iii, 15-iv, 21 : v, 23-32.
[2] iii, 1-4.
[4] Eph. i, 3-14.
[6] vi, 10-17.

idea of each and to connect with it the parallel passages of the other. The principal idea of the Epistle to the Colossians is, beyond contradiction, the pre-eminence of Christ, considered whether in his divine life in the bosom of the Father or in his relations with the world; the important idea of the Epistle to the Ephesians is no less clearly the union of the faithful with Christ and in Christ, as members of the mystical body. The first might be headed : " Christ must be pre-eminent in all things;"[1] the second : " Christ is all in all."[2]

2. The hypotheses which have been brought forward in regard to the innovators of Colosse are as varied as the colours of the rainbow. One after another these sectarians have been called followers of Pythagoras, Epicureans, Stoics, Neo-platonists, Essenes, Pharisees, Ebionites, Cabalists, Chaldeans or Magi, Gnostics, partisans of Cerinthus or of Valentinus, and even—who would believe it?—pupils of Apollos or disciples of John. This strange medley, which does little credit to the critical discernment of the exegetes, and shows that their imagination is sometimes developed at the expense of their good sense, ought to teach us circumspection in the solution of a problem, of which the unknown factors exceed the known.

It is certain that a very large majority of the Christians at Colosse came from the ranks of the Gentiles. If there were some converted Jews among them, they must have been in a very small proportion, for Paul makes no allusion to their existence. The words " The Law which was against us, which was contrary to us "[3] do not at all prove the Jewish origin of the Colossians; for the Law was harmful to the Gentiles as well as to the Jews, although for different reasons. Moreover, before their conversion, the Colossians were " strangers "[4] to the theocracy of Israel; and they never received any other circumcision than the spiritual circumcision, Christ.[5] Nor is the fact of their having had a converted heathen, Epaphras, as their missionary without significance; for it is very difficult to imagine that he would have been able to constitute and organize a Church if the majority or a very considerable portion of its members had been of the Jewish race.

Nevertheless, the tendencies of the false teachers are clearly judaizing; not of that uncompromising Judaism which wanted to impose itself in Galatia or even in Corinth, but of a modified Judaism administered in small doses, a

---

[1] Col. i, 18.   [2] Col. iii, 11.   [3] Col. ii, 14.
[4] Col. i, 12: ἀπηλλοτριωμένοι. Cf. Eph. ii, 12: ἀπηλλοτριωμένοι τῆς πολιτείας τοῦ Ἰσραήλ.
[5] Col. ii, 11-13.

benign Judaism capable of concessions and compromises. The judaizing tendencies appear clearly from the following passage : " Let no man therefore judge you in meat or in drink, or in respect of a festival day, or of the new moon, or of the Sabbaths, which are a shadow of things to come, but the body " (that is, the reality and substance) " is of Christ."[1] He who possesses the body does not set his heart upon the shadow, and he who has the reality has nothing to do with the figure. New moons, Sabbaths, laws relating to foods and other Jewish prescriptions have no more importance or even signification; they had meaning only in so far as they prefigured the future. Now, those old precepts are dead for us, because Jesus Christ has nailed them to the cross in order to prevent them from tyrannizing any longer over men; and we are dead to them, since we participate mystically in the real death of Christ.

> If then you be dead with Christ from the elements of this world, why do you yet decree as though living in the world ? (They say to you) Touch not, taste not, handle not : which all are unto destruction by the very use, according to the precepts and doctrines of men.[2]

This Judaism is far from a pure and simple observation of the Law; mingled with it are arbitrary precepts which have never had the sanction of God, and which Paul, following the example of the Master, calls the traditions of men—such as restrictions concerning drinks, about which Moses had not said a word. On the other hand, the innovators do not seem to have insisted on circumcision; otherwise the Apostle would

---

[1] Col. ii, 16, 17 : *In cibo aut in potu.* The Mosaic prohibitions in regard to drinks concerned only certain persons (an officiating priest, Lev. x, 9 ; a Nazarite, Num. vi, 3) ; or certain particular cases (liquids contained in vessels which are defiled, Lev. xi, 34-36). But probably the strict Jewish sects, like the Essenes, Therapeutæ, and certainly the Rechabites, had extended the prohibitions of Moses and forbidden wine and fermented liquors.—*In parte* (ἐν μέρει, in point of) *diei festi, aut neomeniae aut sabbatorum.* These three words placed thus together include all the Jewish festivals, annual (ἑορτή), monthly (νεομηνία), weekly (σάββατα). Gal. iv, 10 (ἡμέρας παρατηρεῖσθε καὶ μῆνας καὶ καιροὺς καὶ ἐνιαυτούς) has the same enumeration in inverse order, the last word designating no doubt the sacred years (jubilee years).—*Quae sunt umbra futurorum ; corpus autem Christi.* These festivals were the shadow (σκιά), the figure, the type of the future— that is to say, of the Christian system. But the body (τὸ δὲ σῶμα), the reality, the antitype, *is* (understood here, because it is found in the preceding phrase) of Christ—that is, it belongs to him, concerns him.

[2] Col. ii, 20, 22 : *Si mortui estis* (εἰ ἀπεθάνετε, aorist), if you *died* with Christ in baptism, as you cannot doubt (Rom. vi, 2-6).—For *ab elementis hujus mundi,* see vol. ii, note Q.—*Quid adhuc tanquam viventes in mundo decernitis?* The meaning is doubtful and not very accurate. It should be : Why do you allow laws to be imposed upon you ? (δογματίζεσθε, passive or rather middle voice).—*Ne tetigeritis,* etc.: these are the arbitrary and purely human laws which it is desired to impose upon them (*secundum praecepta et doctrinas hominum*). These precepts are of *human* origin, in so far as they exceed the Mosaic rules.

not be satisfied with a disdainful allusion to the circumcision made by the hand of man,[1] which has not, like baptism, the power to strip us of " the body of the flesh "—that is to say, of the unwholesome influences which are opposed to the action of the Spirit.

From this it is evident that the Judaism of Colosse had scarcely any resemblance to that of the Pharisees of Jerusalem, Antioch, and Galatia. It was based upon a strange syncretism with speculations and practices of a very different origin. " Beware lest anyone cheat you by philosophy and vain deceit, according to the traditions of men, according to the elements of the world, and not according to Christ."[2] Here philosophy is not the study or the love of wisdom, but a mass of fanciful concepts, to which the chalatans of Colosse gave the decorative name of philosophy in order to hypnotize the masses, who are always impressed by great, high-sounding words. The Apostle gives them their real name of vain deceits. They were based upon " the traditions of men," and by that may be understood equally either the doctrines of a philosophical school, as, for example, that of Pythagoras, or the teachings which the Jewish sects of that time pretended to have received from Moses by oral transmission, or one of those hybrid systems resulting from a Judæo-pagan syncretism, so common in that period. The last hypothesis is certainly the most probable and the one that best takes account of this puzzling mixture of observances and contradictory speculations. The Jews contributed chiefly the practices to be observed; the pagan philosophers the ideas. Now all this—ideas and practices—is reckoned by St Paul among the elements of the world ($\sigma\tau\sigma\iota\chi\epsilon\hat\iota\alpha$ $\tau\sigma\hat\upsilon$ $\kappa\acute\sigma\sigma\mu\sigma\upsilon$). The elements of the world represent

---

[1] Col. ii, 11 : *In quo circumcisi estis circumcisione non manu facta* ($\dot\alpha\chi\epsilon\iota$-$\rho\sigma\pi\sigma\iota\dot\eta\tau\omega$) *in expoliatione corporis carnis, sed in circumcisione Christi.* The *sed* is superfluous and disturbs the meaning: "You were circumcised [at baptism] by a circumcision not made by the hand of man [that is by a *spiritual* one] which completely removes ($\dot\epsilon\nu$ $\tau\hat\eta$ $\dot\alpha\pi\epsilon\kappa\delta\acute\upsilon\sigma\epsilon\iota$) the body of the flesh, [I mean] the circumcision of Christ." Here the allusion to the circumcision *made by the hand of man* is indirect and contained in its opposite, circumcision $\dot\alpha\chi\epsilon\iota\rho\sigma\pi\sigma\acute\iota\eta\tau\sigma$. The allusion is direct in Eph. ii, 11 : *Vos gentes in carne, qui dicimini praeputium, ab ea quae dicitur circumcisio in carne, manu facta* ($\chi\epsilon\iota\rho\sigma\pi\sigma\iota\dot\eta\tau\sigma\upsilon$) : " You, Gentiles, who are called uncircumcised by what is called circumcision made by the hand of man in the flesh."

[2] Col. ii, 8: $\delta\iota\dot\alpha$ $\tau\hat\eta\varsigma$ $\phi\iota\lambda\sigma\sigma\sigma\phi\acute\iota\alpha\varsigma$ $\kappa\alpha\grave\iota$ $\kappa\epsilon\nu\hat\eta\varsigma$ $\dot\alpha\pi\acute\alpha\tau\eta\varsigma$, $\kappa\alpha\tau\grave\alpha$ $\tau\grave\eta\nu$ $\pi\alpha\rho\acute\alpha\delta\sigma\sigma\iota\nu$ $\tau\hat\omega\nu$ $\dot\alpha\nu\theta\rho\acute\omega\pi\omega\nu$, $\kappa\alpha\tau\grave\alpha$ $\tau\grave\alpha$ $\sigma\tau\sigma\iota\chi\epsilon\hat\iota\alpha$ $\tau\sigma\hat\upsilon$ $\kappa\acute\sigma\sigma\mu\sigma\upsilon$, $\kappa\alpha\grave\iota$ $\sigma\grave\upsilon$ $\kappa\alpha\tau\grave\alpha$ $X\rho\iota\sigma\tau\acute\sigma\nu$.—The name of *philosophy* was then highly honoured. Philo uses it continually to designate the Jewish religion, the Mosaic revelation; Josephus calls the Pharisees, the Sadducees and the Essenes schools of philosophy ($\phi\iota\lambda\sigma\sigma\sigma\phi\acute\iota\alpha\iota$ $\tau\rho\epsilon\hat\iota\varsigma$, *Antiq.*, xviii, 1, 2, etc.). It is not surprising if the deceivers at Colosse assumed the title of philosophers.—Like the Pharisees in Christ's time, and later like the Cabalists, the Gnostics were fond of appealing to *tradition. Cf.* St Hippolytus, *Philosophumena*, v, 7 ; vii, 20 ; Clement of Alexandria, *Strom.*, vii, 17.

the rudimentary notions which are suited to the childhood of humanity, and which wise men—or God himself, accommodating himself to its weakness—teach, like an alphabet, in order to prepare it for a higher, maturer, and diviner teaching. The Law of Moses also is included in this elementary institution. When he shall appear, in whom dwells the fulness of the Godhead bodily and in whom are hid all the treasures of knowledge and wisdom, those twilight glimmerings will disappear like shadows and all teaching that is not "according to Christ" will be disowned.

Two practices, the direct fruit of philosophic speculations, have not a very pronounced judaizing character : exaggerated asceticism and the little understood worship of angels. "These observances," says the Apostle, alluding to the various prohibitions to which the Colossians submitted, "have indeed a name for wisdom through an outward show of fervent piety and humility, and contempt for the body : [but] are not in any honour [since they only end in] filling out the flesh."[1] Here is a very unexpected effect of privations and austerities. Macerations of the body, voluntarily undertaken, can *"fill out the flesh,"* even while enfeebling the body. In this we recognize clearly the language and the teaching of Paul. What these abstinences were, on what principles they were authorized, and from what theoretical speculations they were deduced, the too abbreviated form of the discourse does not permit us to say. This feeling of excessive humility, allied to this claim to wisdom, honoured the worship of higher powers to the neglect of the only true Mediator. He therefore warns the faithful to be on their guard against the intrigues of this false devotee, who would deceive them after having deceived himself, "taking his stand upon visions, in

[1] Col. ii, 23 : ἅτινά ἐστι λόγον μὲν ἔχοντα σοφίας ἐν ἐθελοθρησκείᾳ καί ταπεινοφροσύνῃ καὶ ἀφειδίᾳ σώματος, οὐκ ἐν τιμῇ τινι πρὸς πλησμονὴν τῆς σαρκός. The Vulgate is here almost unintelligible, because : (*a*) no account is taken of the fact that *in superstitione et humilitate et non ad parcendum corpori* are the three things which give to these doctrines a " name of wisdom."—(*b*) *Superstitio* has a meaning that is too frankly unfavourable.—(*c*) *Non ad parcendum* ought to be translated by one word such as *vexatio* (Ambrosiaster) in order to retain the same construction.— The last phrase (*non in honore aliquo ad saturitatem carnis*) ranks in every way among the most difficult. Estius explains it thus : " These practices do not give to the body the honour which is its due, by subjecting it to excessive severities." But this sense is not satisfactory. Here *flesh* and *body* are not synonyms, and πλησμονή ought to retain the derogatory meaning which it usually has. The other explanations proposed are no more satisfactory. The only reasonable meaning seems to be that of seeing in οὐκ ἐν τιμῇ τινι πρὸς πλησμονὴν τῆς σαρκός an adversative clause suggested by the μέν of the preceding clause and of making them depend on ἔστι expressed at the beginning of the sentence : " These practices, *it is true* (μέν) are reputed to be pious, humble and austere; [*but*, in reality, they *are*] not very honourable (οὐκ ἐν τιμῇ τινι) : [they are only] for filling out the flesh (*i.e.*, develop bad instincts within us)."

vain puffed up in his carnal mind, and not holding the head,"[1] from which comes the whole vital nourishment to animate the mystical body. The *carnal* mind is one that is closed to the action of the Holy Spirit, but open to the suggestions of human nature, always subject to illusion and error. This leads us to suppose that the devotions of the Colossians were allied with their philosophical views and were the product of their visionary instincts.

What name should be given to these illuminati? It matters little and perhaps there is no name in use which would suit them. They have been called *Gnostic Essenes*.[2] These two words, at first sight, seem to be contradictory, historical Gnosticism being essentially anti-judaizing. But it was not so in the beginning; and the example of Cerinthus shows that Ebionite Judaism could accommodate itself to rudimentary Gnosticism. The title proposed is, therefore, acceptable, provided it is understood that it is not a question here of either Essenes or Gnostics in the strict sense of those terms. The Essenes were domiciled in the neighbourhood of the Dead Sea, and their presence is not discoverable, even sporadically, outside of the limits of Palestine and Syria. On the other hand, the orators of Colosse cannot be identified with any Gnostic sect known to history. The essential characteristics of this fickle and changeable heresy, Dualism, emanations of æons, in a word Docetism, are hardly noticeable in the errors of Colosse. If it be Essenism, it is not the Essenism of Palestine; and if it is Gnosticism, it is not the Gnosticism of the second century. Here is precisely where the difficulty lies; how can we explain the presence of judaizing tendencies in a Church in which the Jewish element was so small, and the Essene character of doctrines in a country so remote from Palestine, and the prevalence of Gnostic ideas before the appearance of Gnosticism itself?

Jews were very numerous in the valley of the Lycus. They had increased incredibly there since the time

---

[1] Col. ii, 18-19. The reading of the received text (ἃ μὴ ἑώρακεν), difficult from a grammatical point of view, has a very easy exegesis : " occupying himself with what he has *not* seen." On the contrary, the reading adopted by the critics, who omit the negation, gives quite a surprising interpretation. Is the text a corrupted one, as many suppose ? On the various conjectures about the true reading, see Abbott, *Internat. Critic. Comment.*, pp. 268-270.

[2] Lightfoot, *Colossians and Philemon*, 11, has two learned dissertations entitled : *The Colossian Heresy*, pp. 71-111, and *The Essenes*, pp. 347-417. The author clearly shows: (*a*) that Gnosticism is anterior to Christianity and independent of it ; (*b*) that it first allied itself with Judaism and broke definitely with it only towards the middle of the second century ; (*c*) that the tendencies of the Essenes had close relations with those of the Gnostics ; (*d*) that the heresy of Cerinthus represents a judaizing Gnosticism more developed than that whose traces are to be found in the Epistle to the Colossians. See A. L. Williams, *The Cult of the Angels at Colossae* (*Journal of Theol. Studies*, vol. x, April, 1909, pp. 413-438).

when Antiochus the Great had transplanted two thousand families of captive Israelites into Lydia and Phrygia. One hundred and twenty years before our era, the contribution sent by the district of Laodicea alone to the Temple at Jerusalem amounted to more than twenty pounds weight of gold, which presupposes an adult population of more than ten thousand free men. The religious influence of these Jews, abhorred and despised wherever they established themselves, is as certain as it is inexplicable. Their morality and the seriousness of their convictions were admired, and people went to their meetings and listened gladly to the reading of their sacred books, and though they rarely adopted circumcision, they did submit to other Jewish rites. This was so much the more the case because, without renouncing their strict monotheism, which gave them such a superiority over the poor pagan mythologies, the Jews knew how to adapt it to the theosophical speculations which were then so fashionable. The Essenes, the Therapeutæ, Philo, the Book of Enoch, the Sibylline Oracles, and the Fourth Book of Maccabees abundantly testify to this state of mind. Never had the Jews made such an effort to extend their proselytism under the cover of philosophy. To them the speciality of occult sciences was attributed. At Rome they were identified with the Chaldeans ; almost everywhere they passed for astrologers, and this reputation, far from proving injurious to them, enlarged the sphere of their activity.

This new Judaism was sure to find favour among the Phrygians, who had always been celebrated for their visionary tendencies. It might have been said that their very soil led them to such a mental state. Nature there, forbidding, racked, periodically convulsed by frightful earthquakes, and rent with crevices which still emit sulphurous vapours, appeared to be the scene of ancient conflicts between superhuman powers. Not far from Colosse there was visible at Hierapolis an entrance to the infernal regions, called Plutonium. An ancient philosopher of those regions, Thales, said : " The world is a living being and is filled with demons." The rites practised in honour of Cybele, Diana, and Sabazius show to what lengths the mystical exaltation of those populations could go. Phrygia was always a hot-bed of the most extravagant Gnostic sects, where men passed from the most unbridled licence to the strictest Puritanism. It was the fatherland of all fanaticisms and excesses.

II—The Primacy of Christ

1. Titles and Functions of Christ. 2. Head of the Angels. 3. In him
resides the Fulness, or Pleroma.

1. The errors of the Colossians obliged the Apostle to restore to Jesus Christ, together with his true place at the side of the Father, his part in the creation of the world and the life of the Church :

> God hath translated us into the kingdom of the Son of his love, in whom we have redemption through his blood, the remission of sins.
>
> Who is the image of the invisible God, the first-born of every creature ; for in him were all things created in heaven and on earth, visible and invisible, whether thrones, or dominations, or principalities, or powers.
>
> All things were created by him and in him, and he is before all, and by him all things consist.
>
> And he is the head of the body, the Church ; who is the beginning, the first-born from the dead, that in all things he may hold the primacy.[1]

St Paul, according to his custom, heaps upon the head of Christ, without caring for what we might call their chronological order, all the titles which belong to him by reason of his two natures. He is not inclined, any more than is St John, to divide Christ. In his anterior life, Christ is the image of God, the first-born, the creator, the preserver, the end of all things ; in his human life he is the first-born of the dead, the head of the mystical body, the redeemer of men, and the universal peacemaker ; in both he is the beloved Son and the end of creation ; he dominates all the celestial powers—in a word, he possesses the fulness. The greater part of these titles, found in several of Paul's letters, will be studied elsewhere. We mention here only the three points peculiar to this Epistle :

i. Christ is the image of the Father, the first-born of all creatures, the author, preserver, and end of all things.

ii. Christ is exalted above all heavenly spirits, whether as their creator or their chief.

iii. Christ possesses all fulness, both of divinity and of graces.

---

[1] Col. i, 14-20. (*a*) The whole passage, Col. i, 15-23, is dependent on the relative pronoun ὅς. (*b*) i, 15-17 has reference to the divine life of Christ, either in himself—as image of the Father—or in his relations with creation, before which he existed (πρὸ πάντων, πρωτότοκος), and of which he is the efficient cause (δι' αὐτοῦ), the preserver (ἐν αὐτῷ) and the end (εἰς αὐτόν). (*c*) i, 18-23 has reference to his human life, or rather to his theandric life, as head of the Church and first-born among the dead. (*d*) The grammatical construction of the two sections is the same : at first, proclamation of the fact (verses 15 and 18), then justification of the fact, beginning with an identical formula ὅτι ἐν αὐτῷ (verses 16-17 and 19-23).

The image of the invisible God—or, perhaps, more exactly, of God the unseen[1]—is an expression borrowed from the Book of Wisdom, and is, in reality, only a synonym of the Son. He who speaks of an image, speaks of resemblance and derivation. The son is the image of the father, of whom he is the living portrait, but the father is not the image of the son, although he bears a resemblance to him, because he is not derived from him. According to the powerful and strict expression of St Gregory Nazianzen : " The Word is image in so far as he proceeds from the Father, for it is of the nature of an image to be a reproduction, a copy of its archetype."[2] The invisible God of our text is evidently the Father. Invisibility belongs especially to him, considered either as God (and then it is common to him and to the Son, his perfect image), or considered as the Father, as St Paul seems to hint and as a great number of the ancient ecclesiastical writers have thought ; in this case, it would designate the personal and incommunicable attribute, by virtue of which the Father, source and principle of the Godhead, sends the other Persons, but is not sent by them.[3] As the image of the the Father, the Son is adapted to reveal him to men ; but it is not precisely this aptitude which exalts him to the position of the divine image ; he would be the image of the Father even if there existed no rational creature to receive his revelation, just as he would remain the Son, even though there should be no one to receive filial adoption from him.

The more perfect image, the better it expresses its model ; and it is possible to conceive of an image so perfect that it is the equal of its prototype. " Such is the Son of God, having within him the Father in his entirety, identical with the Father in every particular and differing from him only by the fact of being begotten."[4] However, the notion

---

[1] Col. i, 15 : ὅς ἐστιν εἰκὼν τοῦ Θεοῦ τοῦ ἀοράτου. The same phrase without the epithet τοῦ ἀοράτου is found in 2 Cor. iv, 4. Grammar, the usage of Paul, and theology require that Θεός (with the definite article) should designate the Father, and then the qualifying words τοῦ ἀοράτου must apply to him, as Father, in a special manner—that is, manifesting himself, as archetype in and by his image. The author of the Book of Wisdom (vii, 26) says of wisdom personified or personal : Ἀπαύγασμα γάρ ἐστι φωτὸς ἀϊδίου . . . καὶ εἰκὼν τῆς ἀγαθότητος αὐτοῦ. For the idea, see John i, 18. Philo also gives his Logos the title of image of God (De Mundi opif., 8 ; De confus. ling., 20, 28 ; De Profugis, 19 ; De Monarch., ii, 5 ; De Somn., i, 41) He derived his theory of the Logos-image from Gen. i, 26-27.

[2] Orat., xxx, 20 (XXXVI, 129).

[3] Petavius, De Trinitate, viii, 2, gives a long list of ecclesiastical writers, who attribute invisibility to the Father, as Father, either on account of our text, or on account of John i, 18.

[4] St John Damasc., De fide orthodox., i, 8 (XCIV, 816). Cf. De Imag., i, 9 (XCIV, 1240). St Chrysostom concluded that the Son is invisible because he is the perfect image of the invisible God (ἡ τοῦ ἀοράτου εἰκὼν καὶ αὐτὴ

of an image does not imply this, and equality, if it exists, must be deduced from other principles. The Son of God is the image of the Father, both because he is his *Word*—the Word, of its nature, expressing the intelligence which produces it—and because he is his Son; for generation, by virtue of its own concept, tends to reproduce the generative principle. But it is not certain that this relation between the Son and the image is in Paul's mind.

If the quality of image is at the same time absolute and relative, that of *first-born* is only relative, and consequently would be wanting in the case of nothing being created. The Fathers rightly observe that the expression "first-born of every creature"[1] can signify only " born before every creature."

ἀόρατος καὶ ὁμοίως ἀόρατος). Origen, before him, said the same thing (εἰ ἔστιν εἰκὼν τοῦ Θεοῦ τοῦ ἀοράτου, ἀόρατος εἰκών), text quoted by St Athanasius, *De decret. Nic.*, 27. Cf. *Periarchon*, II, vi, 3 (XI, 211).

[1] Col. i, 15 : πρωτότοκος πάσης κτίσεως ὅτι ἐν αὐτῷ ἐκτίσθη τὰ πάντα.

A. Three valuable points are furnished by the context: (*a*) Christ is the "first-born of every creature," *because* all things were created in him and because he is therefore not only superior, but anterior, to all things.— (*b*) Christ " is before all things, and all things consist in him " ; his priority in the duration of time is the reason of his pre-eminence.—(*c*) The words πάσης κτίσεως must be understood not in the collective sense (of the whole creation), but in the distributive sense (of every creature). Indeed: (*a*) we do not find any instance of πᾶσα κτίσις (every creature) being used for πᾶσα ἡ κτίσις (all creation).—(β) The assertion that κτίσις (the whole of creation), like κόσμος and other words of the same sort, can dispense with the definite article, is erroneous. That happens only when these words are preceded by an indefinite noun governed by a preposition, which is usually employed without a definite article : ἀπ' ἀρχῆς κτίσεως (Mark xiii, 19 ; 2 Peter iii, 4); πρὸ καταβολῆς κόσμου (Eph. i, 4 ; 1 Peter i, 20; John xvii, 24). This is not our case; moreover, the reason would be valueless with πᾶς, which in the sense of *totus* imperiously demands the article, on account of the confusion which its omission would create.

B. In its proper meaning the word πρωτότοκος signifies "first-born"— that is, *the one born first*, whether or not the first of a series. The first-born was thus called among the Jews and consecrated to God, before it was known whether he would have brothers. It is in this sense that Jesus is called the " first-born " of Mary (Luke ii, 7).—In the metaphorical sense, it means " beloved like a first-born, favoured like a first-born." Thus Israel was the *first-born* of God (Exod. iv, 22 : υἱὸς πρωτότοκος μοῦ Ἰσραήλ), and the theocratic king, the figure of the Messiah, is named *first-born* (Ps. lxxxviii, 28 : πρωτότοκον θήσομαι αὐτόν). It is possible that Heb. i, 6 and xii, 23 draw their inspiration from these two texts (Heb. xii, 23 referring to Exod. iv, 22, and Heb. i, 6 to Ps. lxxxviii, 28 ; but this last text is referred to rather in Heb. ii, 11, 12, 17).—It has been claimed that πρ. πάσης κτίσεως could be translated *sovereign of the whole world*. But πρωτότοκος does not mean " sovereign "; it is, metaphorically, "favoured like a first-born " and consequently " heir "; the ideas are akin yet different. Moreover, πᾶσα κτίσις does not signify " the whole world, all creation " (as πᾶσα ἡ κτίσις does); the sense is distributive, not collective.

C. Almost all the Fathers before and after Nicæa (Justin, Clement of Alexandria, Tertullian, Origen, Basil, Isidore of Pelusium, Chrysostom,

In fact, for the Son to be placed in the category of creatures, it would be necessary either for himself to have been created, or for the creature to have been produced by generation. Now, outside of him, nothing is begotten, since he is the only-begotten Son, and, on the other hand, he is not created himself, since all that has been created in heaven and on the earth has been created by him, in him, and for him. Finally, the three titles of Son, Image, and First-born refer to the divine life of the Word and are three aspects of his eternal generation; but there is between them this distinction, that the notion of Son is absolute in relation to created beings; that of Image is both absolute and relative; that of First-born is relative in its expression, since it includes the idea of a term exterior to the Son, yet rests upon an absolute perfection, independent of the existence of creatures.

"First-born of every creature" has nothing in common with "first-born among the dead."[1] His glorious resurrection being a kind of birth to a new life, Jesus Christ, who enters into this life of glory before all others, is justly called "the first-born of the dead," or, again, the "firstfruits of those who sleep." Although more highly esteemed than the rest of the harvest, the firstfruits are not different in kind. Thus Christ, although exalted incomparably above those whom he associates with him in his triumph, does not the less belong to the category of the resurrected. The appella-

---

Severianus, Theodoret, etc.) correctly understand this title of the pre-existent Christ. Some (Athanasius, Gregory of Nyssa, Cyril of Alexandria, Theodore of Mopsuestia) explain it as Christ incarnate, through an exaggerated fear of Arianism. But Paul has not yet come to the incarnation, and the πρωτότοκος ἐκ τῶν νεκρῶν, which occurs subsequently (i, 18) after the title "Head of the Church," is wholly different. Understood as referring to Christ incarnate, πρωτότοκος would indicate pre-eminence, as in Ps. lxxxviii, 28, and not priority; but how then can we explain the genitive πάσης κτίσεως, since the Son, according to what immediately follows, does not enter into the category of creatures?—On the other hand, πρωτότοκος is passive (begotten before) and not active (begetting before), as perhaps St Basil interprets it (Contra Eunom., iv) and St Isidore of Pelusium certainly does (Epis., iii, 31), who puts the accent on the penultimate, πρωτοτόκος.—In the compound πρωτότοκος the first element is, therefore, comparative (as in John i, 15 : πρῶτός μου ἦν) and refers to duration of time. Chrysostom (οὐχὶ ἀξίας καὶ τιμῆς ἀλλὰ χρόνου μόνον ἐστὶ σημαντικόν) and Theodoret (οὐχ ὡς ἀδελφὴν ἔχων τὴν κτίσιν, ἀλλ' ὡς πρὸ πάσης κτίσεως γεννηθείς) express this very well. The paraphrase of Justin (Dialog., 100, VI, 709) is also excellent: πρωτότοκον τοῦ Θεοῦ καὶ πρὸ πάντων τῶν κτισμάτων. Moreover, Paul himself paraphrases it, when he says, four lines further down (Col. i, 17) : καὶ αὐτός ἐστι πρὸ πάντων.—It is at least curious to hear a Rabbi of the Middle Ages (R. Bechaï) attribute to God himself the title of first-born of the world, because of his eternal pre-existence.

[1] Col. i, 18 : πρωτότοκος ἐκ τῶν νεκρῶν may be compared with Apoc. i, 5 (ὁ πρωτότοκος τῶν νεκρῶν) and 1 Cor. xv, 20 (ἀπαρχὴ τῶν κεκοιμημένων). Cf. 1 Cor. xv, 23.

tion of " first-born among many brethren "[1] is justified in the same way. Sanctifying grace really confers upon us the divine adoption as sons. Thenceforth the beloved Son deigns to receive us as brothers, and we truly share with him, although only by analogy, this title of sons of God. But who does not see how different is the relation of the Word to the creatures which are his handiwork? These are not his sisters, nor are they the daughters of God. He is, therefore, their " first-born " only because he precedes them in existence.

The different relations of the Son to the world are summed up in a monumental text : " All things are *by* him, *in* him, and *for* him."[2] The Son is the *efficient* cause, the *exemplary* cause, and the *final* cause of all beings.

St Paul's insistence on including all things " visible and invisible, in heaven and on the earth " in the creative activity of the Son is no less than that of St John himself. There is, however, a difference : it consists in the fact that St John, employing the aorist, indicates the first production of created beings, while St Paul, using the perfect, also designates the present relation of creatures to the Son, as to their Creator. They have been created by him and " they consist in him."[3] Without him, without the uncreated Wisdom, all creatures, incapable of enduring by themselves, would be scattered about, crumble to pieces, and again be lost in nonentity through mutual conflicts. He it is who preserves their existence, cohesion, and harmony. Philo's Logos, the uniting force of the universe, had the same rôle.

Not only have " all things been created by him " but " all

---

[1] Rom. viii, 29 : εἰς τὸ εἶναι αὐτὸν πρωτότοκον ἐν πολλοῖς ἀδελφοῖς. This is realized when we assume the *image*, the *form* of the Son of God (συμμόρφους τῆς εἰκόνος τοῦ υἱοῦ αὐτοῦ).

[2] Col. i, 16: ὅτι ἐν αὐτῷ ἐκτίσθη τὰ πάντα ... τὰ πάντα δι' αὐτοῦ καὶ εἰς αὐτὸν ἔκτισται. *Cf.* John i, 3. It is worthy of note that these three expressions appear respectively twice in the context (Col. i, 15-20) ; and refer the first time to the pre-existent Christ (i, 15-18), the other time to Christ incarnate (i, 19-20). Remark also that the three expressions refer to God without distinction of persons, Rom. xi, 36 : Ἐξ αὐτοῦ καὶ δι' αὐτοῦ καὶ εἰς αὐτόν. The Vulgate has *ex ipso et per ipsum et in ipso*, but we know that after *in* the accusative and ablative are very often put for one another.

[3] Col. i, 17 : πάντα ἐν αὐτῷ συνέστηκεν. Aristotle says (*De Mundo*, vi) : Ἐκ τοῦ Θεοῦ πάντα, καὶ διὰ Θεοῦ ἡμῖν συνέστηκεν. The parallelism of ideas is only apparent on account of the dative ἡμῖν. It is real; on the contrary, in the following phrase of Aristotle (*Ethic. Eud.*, vii, 9) : τὸ κοινὸν πᾶν διὰ τοῦ δικαίου συνέστηκεν, where the verb συνέστηκεν is used absolutely. Plato attributes the same function to the demiurge; Συνεστάναι τῷ τοῦ οὐρανοῦ δημιουργῷ αὐτόν τε καὶ τὰ ἐν αὐτῷ. Philo (*Quis rer. divin. heres*) assigns it to Providence: Συνέστηκε προνοίᾳ Θεοῦ. The word used by Aristotle, Plato, Philo and St Paul signifies, according to the context, " to preserve equilibrium, coherence." Reiske defines it quite well: *Corpus unum integrum, perfectum, secum consentiens esse et permanere.*

things have been created *in* him." The Apostle leaves us to divine how. Many of the Fathers, following St Hippolytus and Origen, suppose that it is in his quality as a divine exemplar, as the home of ideas and universal archetype. The hypothesis is attractive and, although it is necessary carefully to avoid ascribing to the apostles Platonian and Philonian speculations on the *intelligible world* (κόσμος νοητός), it is not easy to see how God created the world "in the Son," if the world were not in some way in the Son; but it was in him and could be in him only in an intelligible way, as in its model and exemplar. This explanation will find solid support in the prologue of St John, if the following punctuation be adopted : "What came into being was life *in* him."

An efficient cause (δι' αὐτοῦ) and an exemplary or formal cause (ἐν αὐτῷ), he is also the *final* cause (εἰς αὐτόν). The expression nevertheless surprises us. Not that the Son, as well as the Father, is not the final cause of his creatures; but finality would seem to belong to the Father by exclusive appropriation. We are therefore tempted to refer this title to the Word made man, to whom the whole universe is subordinated, as to the ambassador and representative of God; but, in the phrase of St Paul, the passage from the divine nature to the human nature not having been yet accomplished, it is better to keep to the simpler sense. Thus we once more establish the fact that the appropriation of the particles is not at all exclusive.

2. The dogmatizers of Colosse, through counting on the mediation of angels, ran the risk of overlooking the great Mediator. Perhaps some of them put between them and him only a difference of degree.[1] When needed Paul recommends respect for angels, but he would not have this shown at Christ's expense.[2] He knows that angels brought the Law to Moses;[3] that they dwell in heaven,[4] and in light;[5] that they are present at the solemn ceremonies of the Church,[6] and in the conflicts and triumphs of the Gospel;[7] that they will accompany the Supreme Judge at the last day;[8] and that one of them, an archangel, will give the signal for the resurrection.[9] He only forbids the arbitrary worship of angels, a worship which would be derogatory to the honour of Jesus Christ. Between them and him no comparison is possible; they are in the relation of the creature to the Creator, of the finite to the infinite. We shall not look for an explanation of Paul's mind in the speculations common at the beginning of our era, nor among

---

[1] This appears to result from Col. ii, 19: *non tenens caput.*
[2] 1 Cor. xi, 10 ; see Gal. iv, 14.
[3] Gal. iii, 19 ; see Heb. ii, 2.
[4] Gal. i, 8.
[5] 2 Cor. xi, 14.
[6] 1 Cor. xi, 10.
[7] 1 Cor. iv, 9.
[8] 2 Thess. i, 7
[9] 1 Thess. iv, 16.

the authors of the Jewish apocalyptical writings. These speculations had no uniformity in them. The Archangels, who then engaged much attention, were sometimes seven in number, arranged in the *Book of Enoch* in the following order: Uriel, Raphael, Raguel, Michael, Sariel, Gabriel, and Remiel; sometimes six, for example, in the *Targum of Jonathan;* sometimes five, with different names; and sometimes only four, enumerated without any fixed order. St Paul himself speaks only once of the Archangel, naming the Archangel St Michael, expressly mentioned by St Jude; he does not make the least allusion to the well-known triad of Seraphim, Cherubim, and *Ophanim,* "which guard the throne of the divine majesty and never sleep." Moreover, while in the lower period of Jewish demonology bad spirits possess an incredible variety of names, the good angels, whose rôle is very efficacious, are usually anonymous.

Four Pauline texts suggest the idea of an angelic hierarchy: Christ is victorious "above all principality and power and virtue and dominion, and every name that is named, not only in this world, but also in that which is to come."[1] All things have been created by the Son and for him: "Things visible and invisible, whether thrones, or dominations, or principalities, or powers."[2] Christ, at his glorious advent, "will bring to naught all principality and power and virtue."[3] Nothing can separate us from the love of Christ, "neither death, nor life, nor angels, nor principalities, nor things present, nor things to come, nor powers."[4]

But we soon perceive that the last two passages have only a purely verbal analogy with our question. The principalities, powers, and virtues which Jesus will destroy or overturn on the day of his triumph are not the angels, whom he would deprive of their thenceforth useless functions, as certain scholastics have claimed; they are the forces hostile to Christ, of whatsoever nature and by whatsoever name they are called; unless indeed we prefer to see in them the demons only, according to the opinion of some Fathers. If, in the text of the Epistle to the Romans, the angels, the principalities, and the powers were placed together, we could understand them to be one and the same class of spiritual beings; but being separated, according to the best reading, it is necessary to seek in them only moral forces or superhuman influences belonging to any order.

[1] Eph. i, 21: ὑπεράνω πάσης ἀρχῆς καὶ ἐξουσίας καὶ κυριότητος καὶ πάντος ὀνόματος, κτλ.

[2] Col. i, 16: ἐν αὐτῷ ἐκτίσθη τὰ πάντα . . . εἴτε θρόνοι εἴτε κυριότητες, εἴτε ἀρχαὶ, εἴτε ἐξουσίαι.

[3] 1 Cor. xv, 24: ὅταν καταργήσῃ πᾶσαν ἀρχὴν καὶ πᾶσαν ἐξουσίαν καὶ δύναμιν.

[4] Rom. viii, 38: οὔτε θάνατος, οὔτε ζωὴ, οὔτε ἄγγελοι, οὔτε ἀρχαὶ, οὔτε ἐνεστῶτα, οὔτε μέλλοντα, οὔτε δυνάμεις.

There remain the parallel passages of the Epistles of the captivity, which afford two lists of angelic spirits :

Principalities.	Thrones.
Powers.	Dominations.
Virtues.	Principalities.
Dominations.	Powers.

The different names must mark differences of rank or nature. Why should distinct words be used to signify one identical thing? If there are in heaven, as on earth, tribes and families, this presupposes a diversity of ranks, relations, and functions.[1] In what consists this celestial hierarchy and how many degrees it contains St Paul does not inform us any more than do the other writers, and we can say positively that he does not aim at teaching us anything about it. His enumerations follow one another without any fixed order, and it is certain that they are incomplete. Paul, who does not pretend to exhaust them, seems to attach very little importance to them. His evident purpose is to establish the truth that Jesus Christ is, as God, the Creator of all the angels; and, as man, he is the Head of all the heavenly powers, however highly placed we may imagine them to be.

But does he wish to affirm that the grace of the angels is derived from Christ? We do not think so. Nothing authorizes us to claim that the universal pacification, produced by the death of the Son, and in which the angels themselves have taken part, is a reconciliation of the angels with God, rather than a reconciliation of the angels with men, hitherto in rebellion against God.[2] From this it results that headship of the angels does not involve any community of supernatural life, but simply pre-eminence in dignity and honours. God has placed his Son *above* all the heavenly powers, and has given him to be the *Head* of the Church, which is his body.[3] Also Christ is not in the same way Head of men and Head of the angels. As the latter form part of his kingdom, he can well be called their Head, but he does not communicate to them vital nourishment, because they do not belong to his mystical body.

3. The Christology of the Epistle to the Colossians is comprised in this text: " The fulness of divinity dwells in Christ." The fulness or *pleroma* seems to have been one of the passwords of the innovators of Colosse; for, the first time that the Apostle uses the word *pleroma*, he speaks of it

---

[1] Eph. iii, 15. Πατριά signifies strictly " family, tribe, nation."
[2] Col. i, 20. *Cf.* Eph. i, 10.
[3] Eph. i, 21-23. The difference of relation between the angels, made subject by God to Christ, and the Church, which is the body of Christ and of which Christ is the Head, is quite clearly indicated in this phrase.

as of something known by all, and needing no explanation. This is a proof that the word formed part of his adversaries' terminology. St Paul seizes upon it in order to correct the abuse of it, as, in the opinion of many, St John wrests from the heretics of his time the term Logos and gives it an orthodox meaning.

What does the word *pleroma*[1] mean, and what in particular does the *pleroma of divinity* signify?

[1] The word πλήρωμα (found seventeen times in the New Testament and twelve times in St Paul) is always translated by *plenitudo*, except in Mark ii, 21 (*supplementum*), Mark vi, 43 ; viii, 20 ; Rom. xv, 29 (*abundantia*).—The verb πληροῦν having three meanings, (1) to fill, (2) to complete, (3) to accomplish, the word πλήρωμα, which is derived from it, will signify : (*a*) plenitude, (*b*) complement or supplement, (*c*) accomplishment. It designates, like other nouns ending in μα, either the result of the action, or the action itself considered as finished, and not properly speaking the action of filling, completing or accomplishing. The examples cited in contradiction to this statement, besides being very rare, are borrowed from the poets and cannot determine the ordinary usage of prose.

A. To the first meaning of *plenitude* (*that which is full* or *that which fills*) is joined the idea of a *whole*, of *totality*, frequent in profane as well as in biblical usage : πλήρωμα τῆς πόλεως means " the population of the city," and πλήρωμα alone signifies " the cargo, the tackle " of a ship, or, by extension, " the ship " itself, when it is loaded or fitted out. On the other hand, we have the biblical expression *the earth and the fulness thereof* (the earth and all that it contains), 1 Cor. x, 26, quoting Ps. xxiii, 1; *the fulness of the baskets* (basketfuls, Mark vi, 43 ; viii, 20) ; *the fulness of nations* (the whole of the pagan peoples, Rom. xi, 25) ; *the fulness of the Jews* (the entirety of the Jewish people, Rom. xi, 12), and perhaps *the fulness of the blessings of Christ* (all blessings, Rom. xv, 29).

B. The two other meanings are much less perfectly represented. Nevertheless, the meaning of *accomplishment* appears in the expression *fulness of the times* (Gal. iv, 4 ; Eph. i, 10) and in *plenitudo legis est dilectio* (Rom. xiii, 10, explained by xiii, 8 : *qui diligit proximum legem implevit*).—The notion of *complement* is shown in Matt. ix, 16 ; Mark ii, 21 (τὸ πλήρωμα τὸ καινόν, *supplementum novum*).

C. Here are the five texts in which the *pleroma* figures in the technical sense :

He is the principle, the first-born of the dead, obtaining the primacy in all things, for it hath pleased [God] that in him all *fulness* should dwell (Col. i, 19).

In him dwells bodily all the *fulness* of the Godhead, and you are filled in him (Col. ii, 9).

God has given him as Head to the Church, which is his body, the *fulness* of him who is fulfilled entirely in all (Eph. i, 23).

That you may know the charity of Christ, which surpasseth all knowledge, that you may be filled with all the *fulness* of God (Eph. iii, 19).

[Let us strive] to form a perfect man, having as our measure the *fulness* of Christ (Eph. iv, 13).

1. It is true that the *pleroma* is associated with the system of Valentinus, of which it forms an integral part ; but other sects also adopted it, formally invoking for its use the authority of St Paul. According to St Hippolytus (*Philosoph.*, v, 12 and x, 10 [XVII, 3162 and 3422]) the Peratae, a sect related to the Ophitae (snake-worshippers) and to the Naassenae, based upon Col. i, 19 and ii, 9 a conception of the *pleroma* which has nothing in common with the Apostle's theory. The Arab Monoimos (*Ibid.*, viii, 13 [XVII, 3359]) and the Naassenae (*Ibid.*, v, 8) also adopted the *pleroma* among their fantastic ideas. St Irenæus tells us of a Gnostic system, according to which

Later the Gnostics called *pleroma* the whole combination of divine emanations, the sum-total of the divine Being diffused throughout the universe. There are reasons for believing that this usage goes back to Cerinthus. If we could suppose that this terminology was current among the Colossians, we should obtain the following very acceptable meaning : the divine essence is not dispersed in a multitude of æons, forming a chain of links between matter and the absolute, as your false teachers tell you; it is entirely comprised and concentrated in Christ; " it dwells in him bodily."[1] But is not this exegesis an anachronism? Moreover, we arrive at the same result by leaving *pleroma* its usual meaning of totality. The plenitude of divinity will then be the combined sum of the perfections which constitute the divine essence : in other words, divinity itself.

God dwells in the souls and in the bodies of the just, as in his temple, but he dwells there by finite graces, always susceptible of growth, not in the fulness of his power and attributes; above all, he does not dwell there *bodily*. In order to dwell there thus, it is necessary that he be substantially united to humanity, so as to form with it a theandric compound, as the soul by dwelling in the body constitutes with it one single nature. The two theological texts, *In ipso inhabitat plenitudo divinitatis corporaliter,* and *Verbum caro factum est et habitavit in nobis,* are therefore equivalent. Only the mode of habitation is not the same. In St John it is a question of the *passing sojourn* of the Word made flesh, who condescends to plant his tent (ἐσκήνωσεν) for a moment in our midst; in St Paul it is a question of the immovable, permanent, and definitive residence (κατοικεῖ) of divinity in the humanity of Christ.

As for the other text, *In ipso complacuit omnem plenitudinem inhabitare,*[2] we must resist the temptation to seek here

---

Christ descended and entered into Jesus at his baptism in the form of a dove and then *re-entered into the pleroma,* after having taught men the truth of the invisible Father (*Contra haeres.*, i, 26; iii, 11; vii, 16; vii, 685, 880 and 920). In the first passage, where, however, the *pleroma* is not named (*revolasse iterum Christum de Jesu*), this doctrine is expressly ascribed to Cerinthus ; in the second text Cerinthus is mentioned in company with the Nicolaitans and other heretics.—The *pleroma* of Valentinus is very different from that which our Epistles allow us to suppose was preached by Paul's adversaries ; it is less the totality of the divine forces than the *home* of the æons, and it is thus opposed to the κένωμα, the *home* of phenomena and perishable beings. On the contrary, the fundamental meaning of *pleroma,* in *Palestinian* Gnosticism, is rather the biblical meaning of plenitude, the whole, totality.
  Cf. Lightfoot, *Colossians,* 11, 1892, pp. 255-271 : *On the meaning of* πλήρωμα.
  [1] Col. ii, 9: Ἐν αὐτῷ κατοικεῖ πᾶν τὸ πλήρωμα τῆς θεότητος σωματικῶς. This text is explained in the second volume.
  [2] Col. i, 19 : ἐν αὐτῷ εὐδόκησεν πᾶν τὸ πλήρωμα κατοικῆσαι.

again for the *pleroma* of divinity. The context is opposed to it, and the text scarcely resembles the preceding one. It lacks two essential words : *divinitatis* and *corporaliter*. Here it is a question of the plenitude of which St John speaks : *Vidimus . . . plenum gratiae et veritatis. . . . Et de plenitudine ejus nos omnes accepimus.* The fulness of divinity, dwelling bodily in the Saviour, brings to it a plenitude of graces. There are in him, therefore, two plenitudes, one of which is derived from the other. The plenitude of graces granted to the Saviour depends on the good pleasure of the Father—the subject of the verb *complacuit*—and it is subordinate to his functions as Head of the Church and as the universal Peacemaker. But it is not in Christ as grace is in the other saints ; it is there for good and all, it is permanent (κατοικεῖν) ; it proceeds naturally from the other plenitude, the *pleroma* of divinity ; it is the source, the superfluity of which overflows and fills the members of Christ. The more we compare the Epistle to the Colossians with the Prologue of St John, the more we discover its close relations therewith.

In the Epistle to the Ephesians, Paul wishes that the faithful may be filled " to the measure of (εἰς) all the *fulness* of God."[1] We do not believe, with St John Chrysostom, that he means here the absolute perfection of God ; for even if it is not unusual for the sacred writers to propose God to us as a perfect ideal, after whom we are to model our actions, it is certainly much more natural to see here the plenitude of graces and spiritual gifts of which God is the author. On the other hand, to understand by the " *pleroma* of God " Christ or the Church, when nothing in the sentence suggests either Christ or the Church, is to do violence to language.

Moreover, the Apostle represents Jesus Christ as giving lavishly his favours to the Church, " until we all meet into the unity of faith and of the knowledge of the Son of God, unto a perfect man, unto the measure of the age of the

---

[1] Eph. iii, 19 : *Ἵνα πληρωθῆτε εἰς πᾶν τὸ πλήρωμα τοῦ Θεοῦ.* Without the *πᾶν* we might understand this as meaning : " Be filled with the fulness of God," that is to say, as God is full. Compare : " Be ye perfect *as* your Father in heaven is perfect " (Matt. v, 48). But may it be said : Be perfect with *all* the perfection of God ?—Theodoret suggests : Be filled in such a manner that God may dwell perfectly in you ; more exactly : So as to be yourselves the fulness of God, or entirely full of God. Compare *Σπυρίδων πληρώματα* = baskets full. But this idea is new in the New Testament and we see no reason why *πᾶν* should be there.—There remains, therefore, the alternative : "All the riches of which God is the source, all his perfections which are communicable to the saints ": *Ut per haec efficiamini divinae consortes naturae* (2 Peter i, 4).—The difference will be noted that exists between *πᾶν τὸ πλήρωμα τοῦ Θεοῦ* (the fulness which belongs to God or which comes from God, possessive or causal genitive) and *πᾶν τὸ πλήρωμα τῆς θεότητος* (the fulness of the divinity, genitive of apposition—that is, the divinity in all its fulness).

fulness of Christ."[1] The perfect man is the mystical Christ, composed of the Head and the members, and destined for a perfection which it is possible to approach indefinitely, but the limit of which can never be attained. If the body corresponded fully to the Head, the mystical Christ would be a perfect man, in the sense that nothing of the perfection which he can and should possess would be lacking in him. The imperfections do not come from the Head, which has the plenitude; they proceed from the body which aspires and tends to perfection (ἄνδρα τέλειον), without ever being able to reach the highest summit. St Paul proposes as a model and standard for it (εἰς μέτρον), "the age of the fulness of Christ"—that is to say, the person of the glorified Christ, in that plenitude of perfection which the Apostle compares to the age of maturity, and which excludes all further progress and all new growth.

Finally, when the Church, the mystical body of Christ, is designated under the mysterious appellation : τὸ πλήρωμα τοῦ τὰ πάντα ἐν πᾶσιν πληρουμένου,[2] without dealing further in subtle

---

[1] Eph. iv, 13 : μέχρι καταντήσωμεν οἱ πάντες . . . εἰς ἄνδρα τέλειον, εἰς μέτρον ἡλικίας τοῦ πληρώματος τοῦ Χριστοῦ.   Observe that the Apostle writes οἱ πάντες (all together, collectively), and not πάντες (all individually, each one in particular).   In the same way he says εἰς ἄνδρα τέλειον and not εἰς ἄνδρας τελείους.   That the relation indicated by us is really in his mind, the continuation of the text shows : αὐξήσωμεν εἰς αὐτὸν τὰ πάντα, ὅς ἐστιν ἡ κεφαλή, Χριστός, κτλ.

[2] Eph. i, 23 : ἥτις ἐστὶν τὸ σῶμα αὐτοῦ, τὸ πλήρωμα τοῦ τὰ πάντα ἐν πᾶσιν πληρουμένου.   What is the exact meaning of πλήρωμα, and what is the voice (passive or middle) of the participle πληρουμένου?   These are two questions which require an answer.—(a) Everyone agrees (as opposed to Wetstein) that τὸ πλήρωμα is in apposition to τὸ σῶμα αὐτοῦ, and (as opposed to Oltramare) that it cannot signify " perfection, a perfect work."   Of the three meanings of πλήρωμα (accomplishment, fulness, complement), since the first is not suitable here, it is necessary to choose between the other two.   Haupt (Meyer's *Kommentar*, 8) defends energetically the meaning of *fulness ;* A. Ewald (Zahn Collection) prefers that of *complement ;* Barry (Ellicott Collection) and Abbott (*Intern. Commentary*), also prefer it, and rightly.   The sense of *completing* for πληροῦν (*cf.* Passow) and of *complement* for πλήρωμα (*cf.* Thayer) being incontestable, there is no objection to this explanation, as simple as it is natural.—(b) Some authors (Abbott, Ewald), who explain πλήρωμα as we do, taking the participle πληρουμένου in the transitive voice, obtain this antithesis : " The Church is the *complement* of him who *completes* all things."   But it is preferable to take πληρουμένου in the passive voice (who is completed), or still better in the reflexive (who completes himself). There is no objection to the accusative τὰ πάντα, for this is an adverbial expression signifying " in every way, entirely " (Herodotus, i, 122 ; v, 97 ; Xenophon, *Anab.* II, i, 1 : οἰόμενοι τὰ πάντα νικᾶν).   *Cf.* Scott's *Lexicon.*
    It is well to consult the erudite article of J. Armitage Robinson, " The Church as the Fulfilment of the Christ " (in *The Expositor*, fifth series, vol. viii, 1898, pp. 241-259).   The author compares our text with Col. i, 24 : ἀνταναπληρῶ τὰ ὑστερήματα τῶν θλίψεων τοῦ Χριστοῦ.   He regards the expression τὰ πάντα ἐν πᾶσιν as a sort of adverbial expression, similar to the English " all in all," or to the classical Greek παντάπασιν, but with more emphasis, and he invites us to compare 1 Cor. xii, 6 ; xv, 28 ; Col. iii, 1. Finally, he quotes in favour of his exegesis the ancient Latin version :

distinctions, and taking the *pleroma* in its most ordinary meaning, we understand that Christ is completed by the Church as the head is completed by the members. It is in vain that Christ fills everything with his plenitude; he none the less needs to be completed, in order to exercise his redemptive work; and the Church does complete him, as a passive power which he endows with his virtue, or as a receptacle which he fills with his graces. It is, therefore, justly called " the complement of him who fills all in every way," or, no doubt better, " the complement of him who is wholly completed in all " his members.

To sum it all up, the *plenitude of divinity* is divinity itself, or, in a technical sense, perhaps in use in the first century, it is " the sum-total of divine Being," in contrast to the separate portions and pretended emanations of that Being.

The *plenitude of God* is the union of supernatural blessings which he loves to bestow upon his friends, when he renders them participants in the divine nature, and of which he has made of Jesus Christ the universal depositary.

The *plenitude of Christ* is the superabundant measure of graces which the Saviour receives from his Father, that he may pour them out upon the Church, which is his body, and upon the faithful who are his members.

In an entirely different sense, the Church is the *plenitude of Christ,* because it completes and perfects him in the plan of redemption, the nourishment of grace being able to go from the Head to the members only through the medium of the body.

This last expression, the most remarkable of all, brings us face to face with the theory of the mystical Christ, which we must now briefly study.

---

supplementum ejus qui omnia et in omnibus impletur, also the first Syriac version, the Coptic versions, St John Chrysostom, and above all the very acute commentary of Origen, which the biblical catenæ have preserved to us.

CHAPTER III

THE CHURCH, THE MYSTICAL BODY OF CHRIST

I—THE MYSTICAL CHRIST

1. Analogy of the Human Body.   2. The Soul of the Mystical Body.
3. The Head of the Mystical Body

1.   THE principal subject of the Epistle to the
Colossians was the Person of Christ; that of
the Epistle to the Ephesians is the Church—
an extension of Christ in time and space, the
complement or *pleroma* of Christ.

The Apostle considers Christ in two very different ways.
When he identifies with Christ the true lineage of Abraham,
the sum-total of believers,[1] when he asserts that in baptism
we are immersed, buried in Christ,[2] when he says that Christ
has many members and that we are these members,[3] he is
not speaking of the natural Christ, but of the mystical Christ.
The natural Christ, the Word made flesh, the priest and
victim of Calvary, is a part, and indeed the principal part, of
the mystical Christ; but he is not the whole mystical Christ.
The mystical Christ is the true vine with its branches, it is
the wild olive with its boughs, it is Jesus the bridegroom
with the Church his bride, it is the Head together with all
its members. The natural Christ redeems us, the mystical
Christ sanctifies us; the natural Christ died for us, the
mystical Christ lives in us; the natural Christ reconciles us
to his Father, the mystical Christ unifies us in him. In a
word, the mystical Christ is the Church completing its
Head and completed by him.

The theory of the mystical body is not the product of the
growth of years. It is impossible to trace its gradual
development; it has no history. Apart from its application
and consequences, it is wholly contained in the remark of
the Saviour to Paul: "I am Jesus, whom thou persecutest."
It would be incomprehensible if we saw in it merely an
abstraction, a purely mental creation. It is a reality, of the
moral order indeed, but a genuine reality, since it is the
subject of prerogatives, of essential qualities, and of rights.
Mystical is not the opposite of real, and there are realities
outside of what can be touched and weighed. Let us remark,

Gal. iii, 16.   [2] Rom. vi, 3.
[3] 1 Cor. xii, 12 ; Gal. iii, 27, etc.

however, that this reality is expressed by a metaphor, like all immaterial and transcendental objects, and to appreciate fully the value of a metaphorical term it is necessary to go back to the comparison concealed under the metaphor. The best illustration of the mystical body will therefore be the analogy of the human body.

Two things are essential to a perfect organism : the variety of its organs, with the diversity of position, structure, and functions which this implies; then, their unity in a common principle of life and movement. Without diversity of parts, we have an inert mass, not an organism; and without a unity of motive force and vital principle, we should have an aggregate of living beings, but not an animated body. To these two original conditions is added the relation of dependency, included implicitly in the idea of an organism, by which the members are subject to reciprocal influence and become fitted for collective action. Very far from injuring unity, diversity beautifies and completes it. " The body is not a single member, but many. . . . If all were only one member, where would be the body?" Diversity of organs, identity of life : such is the formula of the human body, and such is also the formula of the mystical body.

2. For every living body a soul and a head are necessary : the soul of the mystical body is the Holy Spirit; the Head is the adorable person of Jesus Christ.

Not only does the Holy Spirit dwell in the Church and in every just Christian, as in his temple,[1] but he is there as a principle of cohesion, movement, and life.[2] And he does not act in us as if he were outside of us; he unites himself so closely with our inward activity that our action is his and his is ours. Thus we live by him and are moved by him.[3] It is he, in fact, who, causing the name of " Father " to rise from our hearts to our lips, testifies that we are the children of God. As the form specifies the being, so the presence of the life-giving Spirit within us confers upon us our supernatural distinction, our adoptive sonship.[4] The Holy Spirit being the Spirit of the Lord, it is by him that we become *conformable* to the image of the Son of God. For " he who is joined to the Lord is one Spirit "[5] with him, in so far as he is enveloped in the same atmosphere of the divine life. Thus St Paul, every time that he speaks of our supernatural *transformation,* is careful to make the Spirit of God intervene.[6]

Since this is the rôle of the Holy Spirit, it is necessary that

---

[1] Rom. viii, 9-11 ; 1 Cor. iii, 16 ; vi, 19.
[2] 1 Cor. xii, 4-11 ; Eph. iv, 4.
[3] Rom. xii, 11 ; ix, 14 ; Gal. v, 16, 18, 25.   [4] Rom. viii, 14-17.
[5] 1 Cor. vi, 17.   [6] 2 Cor. iii, 18.

he should take part in the birth of the mystical Christ, or, rather, in his growth and development, for the mystical Christ is born no more. The elements of the human organism live or die according as the soul lays hold upon it or lets it go; it is the same with the elements which constitute the mystical body : " For as the body is one and hath many members; and all the members of the body, whereas they are many, yet are one body, so also is Christ. For in one Spirit were we all baptized into one body . . . and in one Spirit we have all been made to drink."[1]   If the reference here were to drinking of the Eucharist, this would be a very bold and singular mode of speech. The Greek aorist shows that it is a question of a single fact; hence we can think only of the reception of the Holy Spirit through the laying on of hands—in other words, confirmation. It is, therefore, baptism and confirmation which incorporate us into the mystical Christ ; and this by an infusion of the Holy Spirit which puts us into vital communication with the Head and into organic relation with one another—a double relation which Paul happily designates by the phrase : *the communion of the Spirit*.[2]

3. Whoever speaks of a head implies thereby pre-eminence and superiority, a vital influx and community of nature, a principle of unity and measure of perfection. These are, indeed, the various relations which the Apostle reveals to us in the six passages in which Jesus Christ is represented as the Head of the Church in the Epistle to the Colossians still discreetly and without insistence, but in the Epistle to the Ephesians with more precision and a complete firmness of touch.

> Christ is the *Head* of all principality and power (Col. ii, 10).
> He is the *Head* of the body, the Church (Col. i, 18).
> As the husband is the *head* of the wife, so Christ is the *Head* of the Church, being the Saviour of his own body (Eph. v, 23).
> God hath made him *Head* over all the Church, which is his body, and the complement of him who is fulfilled entirely in all (Eph. i, 23).
> Not holding the *Head*, from which the whole body . . . groweth (Col. ii, 19).
> Let us grow up to the measure of him who is the *Head*, Christ (Eph. iv, 15).

The first of these texts expresses merely pre-eminence. When Jesus Christ is called the Chief (or Head) of all principality and power, it is probable that this title has no relation with the allegory of the human body ; for even if the

[1] 1 Cor. xii, 12, 13.
[2] 2 Cor. xiii, 13; Phil. ii, 1 (κοινωνία πνεύματος). It is directly the *community* of ideas and sentiments, which is the work of the Holy Spirit in the soul of the faithful, but this very community presupposes a *common* participation in the gifts of the Holy Spirit.

grace of the angels were obtained from the mediation of Christ, there would still be wanting, to complete the allegory of the body, the community of nature. Also Christ is called Head of the angels, without the angels having ever been called the body of Christ, which proves that he is their Head ($\kappa\epsilon\phi\alpha\lambda\dot{\eta}$) only by his supereminent dignity.

Perhaps it will be necessary to understand the next text in the same way : " He is the Head of the body, the Church, as he is the beginning, the first-born of the dead, that in all things he may hold the primacy." The dominant idea of the passage is the primacy. It is, therefore, possible that the Apostle, in awarding to Christ the title of Head of the Church, has not here anything else in view, although the reference to the allegory of the body is explicit.

But in the four remaining passages the idea of pre-eminence is neither the only nor even the most prominent idea. By virtue of a very common biblical metaphor, husband and wife are one flesh, one body, of which the husband is the head, " as Christ is the Head of the Church and the Saviour of his own body." Here the comparison to the human body is complicated by an allusion to the mutual relations of husband and wife. Christ and the Church are mutually related, like husband and wife ; on one side love and protection, on the other respect and obedience ; but the husband and wife are in their turn mutually like the head and the body in the human compound. Their union is perfect ; they are one and the same principle of activity, one soul and one life, without detriment to the primacy which belongs to the head.

Still more remarkable is the text which was discussed above in reference to the *pleroma:* " God hath made him *Head* over all the Church, which is his body, and the complement of him who is fulfilled entirely in all " his members. Jesus Christ, perfect God and perfect man, needs a complement in order to form the mystical body. We may even say that from this point of view he is not sufficient unto himself ; for the head, which centralises all the sensations and determines all the body's movements cannot exercise the vital functions without an organism which completes it and which is substantially united with it. Strictly speaking, the head is the complement of the body for the same reason that the body is the complement of the head ; but it is natural that the part that is less noble should be presented as the complement of the other.

The rôle which St Paul assigns to the head in order to make it the symbol of Christ is truly extraordinary when he warns the faithful against the Colossian visionaries, the forerunners of the promoters of schisms and heresies :

> Let no man baulk you [of the palm], under the guise of humility and the worship of angels, relying upon visions, in vain puffed up by his carnal mind, and not holding the head, from which the whole body, being supplied with nourishment and compacted by joints and bands, groweth unto the increase [willed] of God.[1]

Neglecting the fine shades of expression, which are difficult to render, the sense of the phrase is clear. Since the Christian stands to Christ in the relation of member to head, to isolate oneself from Christ is to consign oneself to helplessness and death; and this is what the visionaries of Colosse were practically doing, who, giving themselves up to their dreams and puffed up with carnal thoughts, were seeking patrons and mediators outside of him. The head, in truth, is for the whole body and for each of its parts a prin-

[1] Col. ii, 18 : Μηδεὶς ὑμᾶς καταβραβευέτω θέλων ἐν ταπεινοφροσύνῃ καὶ θρησκείᾳ τῶν ἀγγέλων, ἃ ἑόρακεν ἐμβατεύων, εἰκῇ φυσιούμενος ὑπὸ τοῦ νοὸς τῆς σαρκὸς αὐτοῦ,

19: καὶ οὐ κρατῶν τὴν κεφαλήν, ἐξ οὗ πᾶν τὸ σῶμα διὰ ἀφῶν καὶ συνδέσμων ἐπιχορηγούμενον καὶ συμβιβαζόμενον αὔξει τὴν αὔξησιν τοῦ Θεοῦ.

(A) 18: *Nemo vos seducat, volens in humilitate et religione angelorum, quae non vidit ambulans, frustra inflatus sensu carnis suae,*

(B) 19: *Et non tenens caput, ex quo totum corpus per nexus et conjunctiones subministratum et constructum crescit in augmentum Dei.*

A. Verse 18 presents three principal difficulties :

(*a*) The *meaning* of καταβραβευέτω. Only two examples of this word are known in the profane writings of antiquity, and it is questionable whether it means here to *baulk of the palm* (βραβεῖον) by a fraudulent trick, or by an unjust sentence given by a βραβεύς (umpire of a combat). The second meaning is preferable, for it is adopted by the Greek commentators; it corresponds well to verse 16 (μή τις ὑμᾶς κρινέτω) and it gives a very satisfactory interpretation, without having against it the two known examples.

(*b*) *Meaning* of θέλων. Most of the exegetes join θέλων to ἐν ταπεινοφροσύνῃ (*delighting in* a [false] humility and in a [mistaken] worship of angels). Others take θέλων absolutely (let no one *voluntarily, with deliberate purpose*). Others again understand the infinitive καταβραβεύειν (let no one *wishing* [to baulk you of the palm] really baulk you by an injudicious kind of worship). The first interpretation is evidently the more simple; it is a Hebrewism that St Paul may well have borrowed from the usage of the Septuagint.

(*c*) *Meaning* of ἃ ἑόρακεν ἐμβατεύων, supposing that it is the true reading, instead of ἃ μὴ ἑώρακεν of the received text and of the Vulgate. See p. 285, note 1. The verb ἐμβατεύειν signifies properly " to penetrate into, to take possession of, to invade," and figuratively " to scrutinize, to apply oneself to," perhaps " to rely upon." *Prying curiously into his* (*pretended*) *visions, relying upon them*, well describes the state of mind of the Colossian visionaries and gives an interpretation which dispenses us from having recourse to conjectural and always dangerous corrections of the text.

B. Verse 19 is much more clear in its entirety.—(*a*) With the accusative, κρατεῖν means " to attach oneself strongly to, to adhere to;" for example, 2 Thess. ii, 15 : κρατεῖτε τὰς παραδόσεις (adhere firmly to the traditions), etc.—(*b*) The *constructio ad sensum* of τὴν κεφαλήν ἐξ οὗ offers no difficulty, since the *Head* is in fact a *person*, and there is no need of taking ἐξ οὗ as neuter (whence), which is not very natural. — (*c*) Ἐπιχορηγεῖν means " to furnish, to provide with," and the passive participle is well rendered by the Vulgate *subministratum*. — (*d*) Συμβιβαζόμενον is less accurately translated by *constructum ;* it is rather " bound together, so united as to

ciple of unity, cohesion, and growth; separated from the
head, the body is incapable even of remaining in the condition of a corpse; it soon disintegrates and is resolved into
its ultimate elements. The union of the body with the head,
and the vital influence of the head over the body take place
by means of joints and ligaments, such as nerves, muscles,
tendons, and cartilages. St Paul does not explain here the
symbolism of it; but in the parallel passage of the Epistle to
the Ephesians, where the allegory is pushed farther, he
likens to these channels of communication the apostles, the
prophets, the evangelists, pastors, and teachers; it is, therefore, probable that the metaphor of the ligaments and
articulations indicates here also the *charismata*.

Let us now examine the parallel text, relieved of a parenthesis foreign to our subject. Paul is explaining why God
has set in the Church persons endowed with *charismata:*

> He has set them for the perfecting of the saints, for the work of the
> ministry, for the edifying of the body of Christ : until we all come to the
> unity of faith and of the full knowledge of the Son of God, unto a perfect
> man, unto the measure of the age of the fulness of Christ ; that . . .
> cleaving to the truth in charity we may in all things grow up in him
> who is the Head, even Christ : from whom the whole body, being
> compacted and fitly joined together, through the co-operation of every
> part in its own measure, maketh increase of the body, unto the edifying
> of itself in charity.[1]

---

form a whole," referring to the component parts.—(*e*) The ordinary sense
of ἀφή is " contact " or " touch " (the sense of touch). The second meaning
is not suitable here and, moreover, would require the noun in the singular.
It is necessary, therefore, to abide by the first. It is possible to translate " joints, articulations," provided we understand by that, not the joined
or articulated parts, but the *points of contact* of these parts. See Lightfoot
on this text.—(*f*) Σύνδεσμος (in the plural σύνδεσμοι or σύνδεσμα) possesses
in anatomy the special meaning of *ligament* (a bundle of fibrous tissues
serving as a means of binding the bones or cartilages) ; but this technical
sense should not be pressed here, and it may be used for the muscles,
tendons and nerves.—(*g*) The accusative τὴν αὔξησιν (in αὔξει τὴν αὔξησιν τοῦ
Θεοῦ) is not in order to strengthen αὔξει, but to bring in the complement
τοῦ Θεοῦ and to mark the nature and the origin of this growth. It is a
growth willed by God and produced by him.

The construction of the phrase is simple. The skeleton of it is : ἐξ οὗ πᾶν
τὸ σῶμα αὔξει. Two qualificatives are attached to τὸ σῶμα, to indicate
the conditions of the growth : the body must be "nourished, maintained "
(ἐπιχορηγούμενον), and moreover " solidly united into a whole " (συμβιβαζόμενον),
and it is so united by means of the many contacts (ἀφαί) which enable
the various parts to communicate with one another and by means of the
ligaments (σύνδεσμα) which keep them united. Note that ἀφαί refers
especially to ἐπιχορηγούμενον, and σύνδεσμα to συμβιβαζόμενον.

[1] Eph. iv, 12 : πρὸς τὸν καταρτισμὸν
τῶν ἁγίων εἰς ἔργον διακονίας, εἰς οἰκοδομὴν τοῦ σώματος τοῦ Χριστοῦ,
   13 : μέχρι καταντήσωμεν οἱ πάντες
εἰς τὴν ἑνότητα τῆς πίστεως καὶ τῆς
ἐπιγνώσεως τοῦ υἱοῦ τοῦ Θεοῦ, εἰς
ἄνδρα τέλειον, εἰς μέτρον ἡλικίας τοῦ
πληρώματος τοῦ Χριστοῦ. . . .

(A) 12 : *ad consummationem sanctorum in opus ministerii, in aedificationem corporis Christi:*

(B) 13 : *donec occurramus omnes in
unitatem fidei, et agnitionis filii Dei,
in virum perfectum, in mensuram
aetatis plenitudinis Christi. . . .*

It is evident that St Paul mingles and superimposes the incongruous images of a body and an edifice; moreover, he regards the body not only as the trunk, distinct from the head, but also as the entire organism; all of which are causes of obscurity and embarrassment. His thought, the richness of which no commentary exhausts, may be analyzed thus : The mystical Christ, composed of the Church and its Head, aims to become a *perfect man;* which is to be understood as a collective personality. The growth which the Apostle here has in view is intensive rather than extensive; it consists in the increase of faith and supernatural knowledge, since the *charismata* to be employed refer chiefly, if not

---

15 : ἀληθεύοντες δὲ ἐν ἀγάπῃ αὐξή-σωμεν εἰς αὐτὸν τὰ πάντα, ὅς ἐστιν ἡ κεφαλή, Χριστός,

16 : ἐξ οὗ πᾶν τὸ σῶμα συναρμολο-γούμενον καὶ συμβιβαζόμενον διὰ πάσης ἁφῆς τῆς ἐπιχορηγίας κατ᾽ ἐνέργειαν ἐν μέτρῳ ἑνὸς ἑκάστου μέρους τὴν αὔξησιν τοῦ σώματος ποιεῖται εἰς οἰκοδομὴν ἑαυτοῦ ἐν ἀγάπῃ.

(C) 15 : *veritatem autem facientes in charitate, crescamus in illo per omnia, qui est caput, Christus,*

(D) 16 : *ex quo totum corpus compactum et connexum per omnem juncturam subministrationis, secundum operationem in mensuram uniuscujusque membri, augmentum corporis facit in aedificationem sui in charitate.*

A. Verse 12 depends on ἔδωκεν (God hath given to the Church Apostles, prophets, etc., *for . . . for . . . for*): (a) Chrysostom considers these three "*fors*" as co-ordinate and *directly* dependent on ἔδωκεν. The change of preposition (πρός ͜ and εἰς) is not absolutely opposed to this, but the place of the second member is then peculiar and contrary to all logical order. —(b) Many make the first clause dependent on ἔδωκεν and the other two (beginning with εἰς) similarly dependent on the first (De Wette, Olshausen, etc.), or similarly on ἔδωκεν, but in a different relation than on πρός (Abbott : God hath given the Apostles and prophets *in view of . . . for . . . for*).—(c) The simplest exegesis is, perhaps, to subordinate the three clauses to one another. God has established Apostles and prophets *in order to* "perfect" the Christians (to render them *qualified* for their mission); καταρτίζειν comes from ἄρτιος, "apt, complete, perfect," *in order that* these Christians may perform well the duties of their ministry and *that so* the body of Christ be edified. The only difficulty is to grant a "ministry" to every Christian : but the word "ministry" has the widest meaning, and from the moment that St Paul concedes to every Christian the possession of a *charisma* (verse 7) he also necessarily takes it for granted that each has a ministry to fulfil.

B. Verse 13 expresses the final aim towards which tend the *charismata* of teaching, of which mention has just been made : to produce the unity of faith and supernatural knowledge in order to prevent the fluctuations of doctrine and the crafty intrigues of the false teachers (verse 14). Although the Apostle has especially in view this particular point, he enlarges his thesis and speaks of the growth of the Church in general. The Church in its entirety is to *tend to become a perfect man* (εἰς ἄνδρα τέλειον)—that is to say, to form in its perfection the mystical Christ. Consequently it should take as its standard and ideal the *physical Christ,* who is its Head, and he, having attained all the fulness desired (πλήρωμα), all its normal development—twofold meaning of ἡλικία—can, therefore, henceforth grow only in his members, of which he still remains the ideal *measure* (μέτρον).

C. In verse 15 is expressed the condition of that growth which the Apostle has chiefly in view : to be united to Christ by a sincere faith, animated and sustained by charity. The words ἀληθεύοντες ἐν ἀγάπῃ go together, and

exclusively, to preaching; but the growth is effected only in charity, without which faith is nothing. The growth in faith and charity must be proportioned to the *power of the charismata* received by the faithful, for these are conferred less for the personal sanctification of their possessors than for the common benefit of the Church. This growth, having for its object the formation of a perfect man, has for a standard the perfection of the Head. The Head of the Church has all *the fulness of graces* which his title and his rôle require; he has attained his *fulness of age,* or, what amounts to the same thing, his *full stature* (according to the double meaning of the Greek ἡλικία); he cannot grow any more so far as he himself is concerned, but only in his members. Finally, as the essential condition of growth in each of the organs is that they should adhere to one another and should be closely united to the head, whence all the vital current proceeds, it is necessary that all the parts of the body should be bound together by a manifold system of tissues and ligaments, which put them into communication with the centre of life and cause the divine nourishment to circulate even to the extremities of the body.

To sum up, then, we see that the head is, in St Paul's opinion, the centre of the personality, the knot which binds

---

ἀληθεύειν does not mean simply "to tell the truth," but to "practise, cultivate and love it"; for the verbs in -εύω signify the doing of the action expressed by the corresponding substantive in -εια. Now ἀλήθεια means not only "veracity," but "truth" in the widest sense. This condition was developed in verse 14 on its negative side: not to be fickle like children (νήπιοι), nor to be lifted up and tossed about like waves (κλυδωνιζόμενοι) by the winds of changeful doctrines (παντὶ ἀνέμῳ τῆς διδασκαλίας) through the action of deceitful men (ἐν τῇ κυβείᾳ = by *deceit, trickery*), by crafty men (ἐν πανουργίᾳ = by *craftiness*), who only seek to lead men astray by their perfidious stratagems (πρὸς μεθοδείαν πλάνης).

D. Verse 16 bears a great resemblance to Col. ii, 19. The essential words are ἐξ οὗ πᾶν τὸ σῶμα τὴν αὔξησιν τοῦ σώματος ποιεῖται = [the Head], thanks to whom the whole body *achieves by itself and for itself* (ποιεῖται in the middle voice) its growth. The expression τοῦ σώματος is repeated, instead of αὐτοῦ, because this demonstrative pronoun might refer to μέρος which precedes. As in Col. ii, 19, the conditions of growth are expressed by two participles; but συναρμολογούμενον is substituted for ἐπιχορηγούμενον because the dominant idea here is the *unity* of the Church, while in the other case it was *union* with its Head. The two participles συναρμ. and συμβιβ., are nearly synonymous, but the former signifies rather *apte connexum*, and the latter *solide colligatum*. The words διὰ πάσης ἀφῆς τῆς ἐπιχορηγίας are variously interpreted. First, they can refer to what precedes and can designate a *means of union* of the mystical body (Abbott); or they can refer to that which follows and can indicate a *condition of growth* of this same body (Haupt). The word ἀφή, signifying properly "contact," and ἐπιχορηγία, signifying "supplying, provisioning," the translation "supplying through every contact" (with the source of graces and gifts) gives us quite a satisfactory meaning, which we may adopt. The idea may be equally applied to the union and growth of the mystical body.

the organism together, the focus of all the vital current. It remains only to know whether he applies his scientific conception of the human head to Christ, the Head of the Church, or if, on the contrary, seeing what Jesus Christ is in relation to the Church, he has had an intuition of the part played by the head in the human compound. It would not then be his psychology that has coloured his religious utterances; it would be his religious ideas that have left their mark upon his psychological language.

II—THE GREAT MYSTERY

It is in the Epistles of the captivity, and chiefly in the Epistle to the Ephesians, that the mention of the great Mystery and the expression *In Christo Jesu* recur with exceptional frequency. As these two points occupy an important place in the general doctrine of the Apostle, and as they will be elsewhere explained and enlarged upon, it will now be sufficient merely to bring them to the reader's notice.

The Mystery *par excellence* is the design conceived by God from all eternity, but revealed only in the Gospel, to save all men without distinction of race, identifying them with his well-beloved Son in the unity of the mystical body. This idea is now so familiar to us that we can hardly conceive how it could have been the most characteristic feature of St Paul's teaching, even to the point of being called his Gospel; but this idea, so simple in itself, swept away all privileges and put an end to the claims which Israel had made for centuries. Think of the passions which it unchained at first in the bosom of the Church itself, of the conflagrations which it would have kindled but for the intervention of the apostles, of the persecutions which it stirred up against the Doctor of the Gentiles, and of the posthumous calumnies which it brought upon him from the judaizing writers of the second century. It was the suspicion of having violated the laws of Israel by introducing a stranger into the Temple that caused his arrest and an imprisonment of nearly five years;[1] also he loves to call himself the prisoner of Jesus Christ for the sake of the Gentiles and a martyr for their just claims.

To the doctrine of the mystical body the formula *In Christo Jesu* is also very closely linked. The Christ here named is less the glorified Head of the Church than the mystical Christ, including the Head and the members, the trunk and the branches; in a word, the living temple of the Holy Ghost. It is the Christ upon whom we are grafted by faith, in whom we are buried by baptism, with whom the Apostle invites us to clothe ourselves through charity and good works.

[1] Acts xxi, 28. The grievance of Paul's enemies is that he has preached against the Jewish people and the Law. *Cf.* Eph. iii, 1; vi, 19-20; Col. iv, 3.

The question whence Paul derived this phrase is of secondary importance. There is certainly something unusual about it. Nothing of the kind is found among the profane writers, and the Fathers of the Church stand astonished before this extraordinary expression. However, there are in the Septuagint, and especially in the deuterocanonical books, some fairly similar expressions. The phrase in the Book of Wisdom that " the just live for ever and that their recompense is *in* the Lord " makes us think irresistibly of the expression *In Christo Jesu*. This form of speech was able to become general only because Christ was considered as an element in which the life and activity of the Christian is exercised. St John, in the allegory of the vine, and St Paul, in the theory of the mystical body, adopted this formula independently of each other, but Paul is peculiar in that he uses it without any explanation, as a set formula, of the meaning of which none of his readers can be ignorant.

CHAPTER IV

THE EPISTLE TO THE PHILIPPIANS

I—THE GREAT CHRISTOLOGICAL TEXT

1. Historic Framework. 2. The Form of God and the Form of a Slave.

1. PHILIPPI, Paul's first conquest on European soil,[1] was always his favourite church. In this uncultured, simple population of Roman colonists he had found docile minds and loving hearts. For their sake he modified the absolute rule which he had imposed upon himself of accepting neither presents nor subsidies from his converts.[2] He knew the depth and sincerity of their affection too much to fear being indebted to them. The Philippians showed themselves worthy of this confidence; they revealed no trace of heresy, schism, or faction; there were only a few personal rivalries, and the principal business was the settlement of a quarrel between two women.[3] Paul's angry outburst against the Judaizers is sufficiently accounted for by the notoriety of their attacks and the anxieties which these continually caused the Apostle; it is unnecessary to suspect their actual presence and propaganda in Philippi itself.[4]

In this heart to heart talk as a father with his dearly loved children, perfect order and strict sequence are not to be looked for. No Epistle less resembles a treatise on morals or theology. Paul exhorts, encourages, consoles, and, above all, opens his heart freely. His dominant feeling is spiritual joy. He repeats constantly : " I rejoice in my tribulations; rejoice with me," until he finally feels obliged · to excuse himself for insisting so much on this point.[5]

One of the first reasons why he rejoices is the favourable turn which his trial is taking at Cæsar's tribunal. Paul will send Timothy to Philippi as soón as the affair becomes a little clearer; but, he adds, " I trust in the Lord that I myself also shall come to you shortly." Not that he is greatly elated by the prospect of a speedy deliverance; his only desire is that Christ may triumph either by his own life or by his death, a noble indifference which keeps him in suspense between the natural wish on the one hand to live in order to work again, to make the Gospel bring forth fruit,

---

[1] Acts xvi, 12.
[2] Phil. iv, 15-16 ; I Cor. ix, 12-15 ; 2 Cor. xi, 9.
[3] Phil. iv, 2, 3.
[4] Phil. iii, 2, 3.
[5] Phil. ii, 18 ; iii, I ; iv, 4, etc.

to serve his neighbour, and to glorify his Master, and on the other hand the happiness of dying, in order to be with Christ, his love and his life. But heaven decides in favour of the first alternative : " I know that I shall abide and continue with you all for your furtherance and joy of faith." The attitude of the Jews in regard to him, the kindly disposition of the tribunal, and even the slowness of a trial which has been dragging on for more than four years, all make him anticipate a favourable result.

Moreover, and this is a second motive for rejoicing, his captivity does not hinder the continuance of his preaching. The guards who take turns in watching him hear him speak of Jesus Christ. His situation makes him conspicuous and excites curiosity; it is one of the first steps towards the spread of the Gospel. The success of his defence and his henceforth certain liberation inflame the zeal and courage of the Christians. What matters it, after all, that some are preaching the word of God stimulated by a feeling of envy and desire of preferment, and that they redouble their activity in order to strengthen their party and to render the detention of the Apostle more bitter ; what matters it, if only Christ is preached and the Gospel continues its conquests? " I rejoice at it," says Paul, forgetful of himself, " and I shall always rejoice."

But his greatest cause of joy—or, at least, the one nearest his heart—is the unalterable affection of the Philippians, which was only waiting for a chance to " break into flower " again. The attentions, devotion, and unselfishness of Epaphroditus, whom he calls his brother, his fellow-worker, his companion in arms, and his visible providence, have touched him deeply. After the tribulation of a long illness, from which he has scarcely recovered, this generous man has manifested the desire to see his native land once more. Paul, therefore, sends him in his place to his beloved converts, happy to be able to give him this consolation and all of them this joy.

2. It is in the midst of this effusion of paternal tenderness in a letter filled with cordiality, delicacy, and kindly allusions, that there suddenly and most unexpectedly appears the most precise and finished statement of Pauline christology. It is amazing to come upon this sublime doctrine, thrown off merely by the way in an exhortation, without any latent notion of controversy, as if it were a question of an ordinary dogma which had been known and believed by all of them for a long time, and which it is sufficient to recall to make it the foundation for a moral admonition. This is truly surprising and, indeed, wholly inexplicable, unless we suppose that the pre-existence of Christ and the union in his

person of divinity and humanity formed part of the apostolic catechetical teaching and belonged to those elementary articles of which no Christian should be ignorant.

Paul urges the faithful to brotherly unity, to humility, and to that generous self-denial which makes us prefer the interests of others to our own, in imitation of him who is our perfect model :

> For let this mind be in you which was also in Christ Jesus.
> Who, being in the form of God, thought it not robbery to be equal with God ; but emptied himself, taking the form of a slave, being made in the likeness of men.
> And in habit found as a man, he humbled himself, becoming obedient unto death, even to the death of the cross.
> For which cause God also hath exalted him and hath given him a name which is above all names, that in the name of Jesus every knee should bow of those that are in heaven, on earth and under the earth, and that every tongue should confess that the Lord Jesus Christ is in the glory of God the Father.[1]

An inquiry whether Paul is treating here of the pre-existent or of the historical Christ would be very misleading. Paul is speaking of the Person of Jesus Christ, and, as usual, refers to this single subject statements which may belong either to pre-existence, to the state of humiliation, or to the glorified life. It is the task of exegesis to distinguish and classify them according to the meaning and the context.

Since we know by experience what the simplest text often

---

[1] Phil. ii, 5-11 : τοῦτο φρονεῖτε (var. φρονείσθω) ἐν ὑμῖν ὃ καὶ ἐν Χριστῷ Ἰησοῦ·

A. ὃς ἐν μορφῇ Θεοῦ ὑπάρχων οὐχ ἁρπαγμὸν ἡγήσατο τὸ εἶναι ἴσα Θεῷ, ἀλλὰ ἑαυτὸν ἐκένωσεν μορφὴν δούλου λαβών, ἐν ὁμοιώματι ἀνθρώπων γενόμενος·

B. καὶ σχήματι εὑρεθεὶς ὡς ἄνθρωπος ἐταπείνωσεν ἑαυτὸν γενόμενος ὑπήκοος μέχρι θανάτου, θανάτου δὲ σταυροῦ·

C. διὸ καὶ ὁ Θεὸς αὐτὸν ὑπερύψωσεν, κτλ.

It is plain that the whole phrase depends on the relative pronoun ὅς (qui) and refers consequently to the same subject, the person of Christ, but in three different conditions :

(a). To the pre-existent Christ, verses 6 and 7a (ὃς ἐν μορφῇ . . . γενόμενος).—The Latin cum in forma Dei esset weakens a little the Greek ἐν μορφῇ Θεοῦ ὑπάρχων, because it allows us to suppose that this condition is temporary and may one day cease. On the contrary, ὑπάρχων better indicates permanence : " Existing then and still existing in the form of God."

(b). To the historical Christ, verses 7b and 8 (καὶ σχήματι . . . σταυροῦ).—The Vulgate punctuation is here defective ; the phrase ought to begin and not end by et habitu inventus ut homo. In fact, Christ took the form of a slave and became like men at the moment of the incarnation, but he was recognized (εὑρεθείς) as man by his whole visible exterior (σχήματι, habitu) only after the incarnation.

(c). To the glorified Christ, verses 9-11 (διὸ καὶ . . . πατρός).—In διὸ καί (propter quod et), καί marks reciprocity and might be translated by " in return." The διό seems to refer to the last phrase only—that is to say, the voluntary humiliation of Jesus ; it indicates, therefore, the recompense due to the merits of Christ. If it were wished to refer it to all that precedes, it would indicate the logical consequence, and would offer a virtually double meaning ; the Father exalts his Son both because this exaltation is seemly to the Son as God, and also because it is due as a recompense to him as man.

becomes in the hands of commentators who distort it into contrary meanings, it is a pleasant surprise to be able to note here the almost unanimous agreement of the patristic tradition. Truth to tell, the Greek and Latin Fathers do not seem to suspect that there are any real difficulties here. After a short exegesis, and sometimes without any explanation, they hasten to make war upon the heresies of their time. It is wonderful to hear St John Chrysostom, in a finely poetic burst of eloquence, invite his hearers to behold the great heretical leaders, Arius, Sabellius, Marcion, Valentinus, Manes, Paul of Samosata, Apollinarius of Laodicea, Marcellus of Ancyra, together with his supernumeraries Sophronius and Photinus, all smitten down under the impetuous blows of Paul. "In the contests of the amphitheatre, if nothing equals the pleasure of seeing one of the competitors violently collide with the chariots of his rivals, overturn both the four-horse cars and their drivers, and then, while on all sides the air is rent with applause and acclamations, fly on alone from one end of the arena to the other towards the goal and finish of the race, as if borne on through space by the intoxication of triumph and the frenzy of the spectators : how do we not rejoice to see the Apostle of Christ beat down to earth, all together and by a single blow, all the erections of error and all the arsenals of the devil together with their architects?"

The other Fathers also employ similar language, almost to the point of enthusiasm. Are not, therefore, the difficulties raised by many modern exegetes due rather to a defective method and to that far too common mania for neglecting the plain meaning of a text which should cast light upon the rest, in order to cling obstinately to obscure or ambiguous expressions without even perceiving that the doubtful points are at the extreme periphery of the question and do not in the least affect the general signification of the whole?

The main point is to know to which will of Christ (human or divine) the self-renunciation, proposed to the Philippians as an example of self-abnegation, refers. Traditional exegesis does not hesitate. It finds this self-humiliation in the very act of the incarnation, and regards it consequently as an effect of the divine will. Some exegetes, however, who though few in number are very resolute, are of a different opinion.[1] For them the self-renunciation, perhaps simul-

---

[1] Velasquez, *Ep. ad Philip.*, vol. i, p. 351, is the first Catholic theologian who has maintained this theory. He ingenuously claims to be the inventor of it. *Dicerem confidentius expositionem meam, si aliquem indubitatum, praeter me, auctorem ejus reperissem.* If he had sought carefully, he would have found two predecessors : Ambrosiaster and the Pseudo-Jerome (Pelagius). The first is very plain, the second less so. Both of them give warning that their exegesis is disputed.

taneous with the incarnation, logically occurs after it in point of time, and consequently depends upon the human will. Their reasons are specious but not convincing. They say, an act which would logically precede the incarnation would be common to the three divine Persons and would not belong distinctively to the pre-existent Christ. It would not, therefore, be for us an example of humility and abnegation, which are virtues incompatible with the perfection of divinity. Finally, it would not be meritorious, and Christ would not owe his exaltation to it. We say again that these reasons are not decisive. The act of the Word, in accepting incarnation, is an act *voluntatis notionalis* (purely personal) and consequently belonging to the Son only; it can be said also that the incarnation is looked upon as a distinctively personal (hypostatic) function and not as an act of will or power. Observe that St Paul does not say " Have the mind which Christ Jesus *had,*" but " Have a mind like that which *was* in Christ Jesus." Now, Christian opinion has always regarded the act of the incarnation as an incentive to self-abnegation and renunciation; it is authorized so to regard it by the Apostle himself, who does not fear to propose for our imitation him who " being rich " with all the riches of heaven, " became poor for our sake, that he might by his poverty make us rich." If it be objected that the incarnation, either as a divine act or as a hypostatic function, is not meritorious, the reply is easy. In the words of St Paul there are several actions, one of which at least, and the last mentioned—the obedience of the cross—designates the human will of Christ and calls his glorious exaltation a recompense : " He humbled himself, becoming obedient unto death, even to the death of the cross; for which cause God also hath exalted him." If anyone should absolutely insist on making the words " for which cause " refer to all that precedes, it would be necessary to say that the words indicate fitness as well as merit. Nothing, therefore, obliges us to abandon the traditional opinion; on the contrary, even apart from reasons of authority, everything invites us to maintain it. It is just to remark, however, that the modern view of Velasquez and his followers, while safeguarding the divinity of Jesus Christ, is rejected by exegesis rather than by orthodoxy.

What is the meaning of the form of God? The word *form* designates, in the New Testament, something deep and intimate, very distinct from externals and appearances, touching the essence of being and inseparable from it. We find this same meaning also in the contemporaries of the Apostle, Josephus and Philo. The latter says that the form of God cannot receive, like a medallion, a super-impression or a false stamp; while the former affirms that God, invisible in his form and majesty, manifests himself to us by his works and benefits. We can thus understand why the Greek Fathers, with their keen comprehension of the terms of their language, unhesitatingly make the form of God identical with divinity itself. Sometimes they give, as a synonym for form, either *nature,* or *substance,* or *essence,* although undoubtedly they are not ignorant of the metaphysical difference of these concepts; sometimes they understand by form the specific character, although calling attention to the fact that in the Absolute, in which a mingling of act and power cannot exist, its specific character is its very being. Moreover, since the form of God is the very opposite of the form of a slave, and since the latter can finally signify nothing but human nature, " to be in the form of God " and " to be God " are necessarily equivalent expressions. The Word could not take the form of a slave without becoming truly man, and no more can he be in the form of God without being truly God. This latter expression appeared to the Fathers still more clear and indisputable than the former, and several of them made use of it to prove the reality of the human nature of Christ against the heresy of the Docetæ. It is not necessary, therefore, for the strict maintenance of our own conclusion, to interpret form in the sense of the ἐντελέχεια of Aristotle, although this philosophical meaning, known by the contemporaries of the Apostle, may very likely have passed into common usage.[1]

A point too often forgotten, and nevertheless of capital importance, is that the Word existed in the form of God *before* the acts of human will and before the effects of the divine will. The present participle (ὑπάρχων), taken in connection with the aorists, acquires an imperfect sense and signifies existence without any limit of time. It coincides with the precise time of duration expressed by the aorist, but it also goes beyond it in both directions, for it logically precedes that indivisible instant and yet does not necessarily end with it. Moreover, it is here, as usual, *causative*—the adversative sense being only exceptional in such constructions—and is to be translated : *" Because* he was in the form

---

[1] The μορφή of Aristotle is opposed to matter (ὕλη) as act (ἐντελέχεια) is opposed to power (δύναμις). But apart from this special philosophical sense, the form is always closely related to the essence of the being. Plato says that it is impossible for a god to wish to change his form (*Repub.*, ii, p. 381c) : μένει ἀεὶ ἁπλῶς ἐν τῇ αὐτοῦ μορφῇ. Philo also, in speaking of the true God (*Leg. ad Caium*, 14, vol. ii, p. 561) : οὐ γὰρ ὥσπερ τὸ νόμισμα παράκομμα, καὶ Θεοῦ μορφὴ γίνεται. And Josephus (*Contra Apion.*, ii, 22) : ὁ Θεὸς ἔργοις μὲν καὶ χάρισιν ἐναργής . . . μορφὴν δὲ καὶ μέγεθος ἡμῖν ἀφανέστατος. It follows that the form is something intrinsic to the nature, something inseparable from divinity.—For the New Testament, see, Lightfoot, *Philippians* 14, London, 1900 : *The Synonyms* μορφή and σχῆμα, pp. 127·133. For the exegesis of the Fathers, see note 1.

of God." The paraphrase of Estius is, therefore, excellent: *Cum esset ac sit in natura Dei, id est cum esset ac sit verus Deus.*[1]

II—CHRIST'S SELF-STRIPPING

1. *Exinanivit semetipsum.* 2. The *Kenosis.*

1. Hitherto we have purposely refrained from discussing the much-disputed clause *non rapinam arbitratus est esse se aequalem Deo sed exinanivit semetipsum.* In reality it adds nothing essential to the Apostle's teaching, although it specifies and circumscribes it. It is not surprising, therefore, that the Fathers lay little stress upon it and that they let us infer their thought rather than express it formally. They are right; for the different shades of exegesis in the explanation of this detail do not seriously affect the signification of the whole.

And first, what is the precise meaning of equality with God? Is it equality of substance, or equality of rank and honours? No doubt equality of condition presupposes equality of nature; and no one has a right to divine honours if he is not really God. From this word the Fathers therefore legitimately inferred the consubstantiality of the divine Persons; but the question is to know whether they did this by reasoning as theologians or by analysis as exegetes. It is certain that the Greek expression (εἶναι ἴσα Θεῷ) has not the direct meaning of "to be *equal to* God," but "to be *on an equality with* God, in the same rank as he."[2] And thus several Fathers indeed understand equality with God,

---

[1] The causative participle ὑπάρχων has nothing to do with time. Chrysostom observes very justly that ὑπάρχων is not γενόμενος. The latter awakens the idea of becoming (as in ἐν ὁμοιώματι ἀνθρώπων γενόμενος, or γενόμενος ὑπήκοος), the former marks stable and permanent existence. Nor is it a simple synonym of ὤν. Joined to an adjective or to an adjectival expression, ὑπάρχων gives the reason of the quality announced (Luke xxiii, 50; Acts ii, 30; vii, 55; xvii, 24, 29; Rom. iv, 19; 1 Cor. xi, 7; 2 Cor. viii, 17; xii, 16). It follows that the state indicated by ὑπάρχων not only co-exists at the time indicated by the verb (ἡγήσατο), but is logically anterior to it. It could be translated by "finding himself," or, as is given in the margin of the English Revised Version, "being originally." In the Vulgate, *cum sit* would serve better than *cum esset.*

[2] The expression is very common since Homer. It signifies always " to be on a footing of equality with someone " and not " to be equal to someone." Compare the *Odys.,* xi, 304 (τιμὴν δὲ λελόγχασ᾽ ἴσα θεοῖσιν); xv, 520; *Iliad,* v, 71; xv, 439; Euripides, *Hel.* 8, etc. The adverbial plural ἴσα is equivalent to the neuter singular ἴσον and to the expressions ἐξ ἴσου, ἐν ἴσῳ, εἰς τὸ ἴσον. Tertullian's translation *pariari Deo* is very exact, although of doubtful Latinity. The English Revised Version renders very well the shade of distinction by " on an equality with God," replacing the words of the old Authorized Version "equal to God." If Paul had wished to express equality of substance, he would have employed the adjective which gave the idea with no ambiguity.

since they say that the Word, in becoming flesh, renounced that equality for his human nature.

Another doubt. The Greek ἐκένωσεν ἑαυτόν, like the Latin *exinanivit semetipsum,* may have an absolute or a relative sense. If taken absolutely, it ought to be translated by "he annihilated himself, ceased to be"; taken relatively, it would mean "he stripped himself."[1] The second meaning is indisputably the more natural; but the commentators ask of what could the Word strip himself. It cannot be the form of God, since on every hypothesis the form is inherent in the nature and is virtually identical with it. Would it not be, then, the equality of homage and honours? No one can renounce his nature, but he can renounce the rights which that nature confers. On giving to these two expressions their exact value, we obtain a meaning characterized by an easy exegesis and an irreproachable theology.

On the whole, the only serious difficulty consists in defining the relation of the parts of the sentence : *Non* rapinam *arbitratus est esse se aequalem Deo: sed exinanivit seme-tipsum* (οὐχ ἁρπαγμὸν ἡγήσατο τὸ εἶναι ἴσα Θεῷ, ἀλλὰ ἑαυτὸν ἐκένωσεν).[2] The Greek word ἁρπαγμός, like the Latin

---

[1] The adjective κενός, which properly signifies "empty of something" which the context indicates, takes also frequently an absolute meaning: "without effect, fruit, force, object" (1 Cor. xv, 14; xv, 58; see Eph. v, 6; Col. ii, 8; 1 Thess. ii, 1). The verb κενοῦν may follow this meaning and signify "to render vain, void, without effect" (Rom. iv, 14; 1 Cor. i, 17; see 1 Cor. ix, 15; 2 Cor. ix, 3). It is for exegesis to decide.

[2] Joined to ἡγεῖσθαι, ποιεῖσθαι, and similar words, ἅρπαγμα is synonymous with ἕρμαιον, εὕρημα, and means "to regard as a prey, to consider as a precious acquisition, as an unhoped-for treasure"; Heliodorus, *Aethiop.,* vii, 11 and 20 (οὐχ ἁρπαγμα οὐδὲ ἕρμαιον ἡγεῖται τὸ πρᾶγμα) ; Plut., *De Alex. fortit.,* i, 8 (οὐδὲ ὥσπερ ἅρπαγμα καὶ λάφυρον διανοηθείς), etc. Cicero translates this Greek expression literally in the orations against Verres (*ut omnium bona praedam tuam duceres*).

The question is to know whether it is necessary to give to ἁρπαγμὸν ἡγεῖσθαι the same sense as to ἅρπαγμα ἡγεῖσθαι. By its form the former is active (theft, larceny) and the second is passive (prey, booty). But we must note two things : (*a*) Many nouns in μός often have the passive signification ; we find in Herodotus φραγμός (vii, 36) and φράγμα (viii, 52) taken in the same sense of a barrier; similarly σταλαγμός and στάλαγμα are treated as synonyms by Æschylus (*Eumen.,* 246 and 808).—(*b*) All the Greek Fathers consider ἁρπαγμός as the equivalent of ἅρπαγμα. No doubt the Latin translations of Origen and Theodore of Mopsuestia have *rapina,* but this word was passive as well as active (*a thing stolen* or *the action of stealing*). Outside of the commentators on our text, we find ἁρπαγμός employed absolutely like ἅρπαγμα in Eusebius, *In Luc.,* vi (Mai, *Nova Patr. bibl.,* iv, 165 : ὁ Πέτρος ἁρπαγμὸν τὸν διὰ τοῦ σταυροῦ θάνατον ἐποιεῖτο) and in St Cyril of Alex. (*De adorat.,* i, 25 : οὐχ ἁρπαγμὸν τὴν παραίτησιν ἐποιεῖτο).

On the other hand, ἁρπαγμός is so rare that it is necessary to give up determining its meaning by profane usage. It is found in only two pagan authors, subsequent to Paul : the grammarian Phrynichus (Bekker, *Anecd. gr.,* i, 36, where ἁρπαγμός is connected with ἅρπασις and consequently transitive) and Plutarch (*De educ. pueror.,* 15 : τοὺς μὲν Θήβῃσι καὶ τοὺς Ἤλιδι φευκτέον ἔρωτας καὶ τὸν ἐν Κρήτῃ καλούμενον ἁρπαγμόν, the reading of the manu-

rapina, can be active or passive; in other terms, it can signify larceny or booty. In general, the Latin commentators keep to the meaning suggested by the Vulgate : " Because he was in the form of God he did not regard equality with God as a theft; *however,* he stripped himself by taking the form of a servant." The Word could not regard the being equal to the Father as a usurpation, since, being in the form of God, he is consubstantial with the Father; nevertheless, the just appreciation of his greatness did not prevent him from stripping himself. The majority of the Greeks, at least, those who have expressed their thought clearly to us, explain the relation of the terms differently : " Because he was in the form of God, the Word did not consider divine equality as a prey or booty on which one seizes with avidity, through fear of being deprived of it if it is abandoned for a moment, *but on the contrary,* he stripped himself of it by assuming the form of a servant." As is evident, the difference in punctuation expresses perceptibly the divergence of the two interpretations : in the one, there is only one subordinate phrase whose meaning is complete only after the last part; in the other, the phrases are co-ordinated and we might stop after the first. But both affirm equally clearly that divine equality belongs to the Word

---

scripts instead of τόν ἐκ Κρήτης of the old editions). This last example shows that ἁρπαγμός had in Crete the very special meaning of *raptus amasii,* a meaning the origin of which is no mystery. The shameful morals of the Cretans to which Plutarch alludes (see Aristotle, *Politics,* ii, 8) are well known. Plato formally accuses them of having invented the fable of Ganymede in order to have authority for their evil conduct (*Leges,* i, p. 636 D). To express the rape of Ganymede, or other similar rapes effected by the gods, the verb ἁρπάζειν was established by use :

> Ἤτοι μὲν ξανθὸν Γανυμήδεα μετιέτα Ζεὺς
> Ἥρπασεν ὃν διὰ κάλλος.

Thus sings the author of the *Homeric Hymn to Aphrodite,* 202-203. See also Pindar (*Olymp.,* i, 64) and Athenæus (*Sophist. conviv.,* xiii, 2, p. 566 D). Only it is very improbable that St Paul knew this technical meaning and still more unlikely that he supposed it known to the Philippians. Moreover, I do not see what could be extracted from it for the comprehension of our text.

The other pleas in favour of the active sense of ἁρπαγμός do not seem to have given any more satisfactory results. According to J. Ross (*Journal of Theol. Studies,* x, 1909, pp. 573-574) Jesus did not consider his equality with God as a *means of stealing* or as an *encouragement to theft* (" Christ Jesus did not think that to be on an equality with God spelt rapacity, plundering, self-aggrandizement "). J. Agar Beet (*Expositor,* 3rd ser., vol. v, 1887, pp. 115-125) had already proposed to translate : " He deemed not his being equal to God *a means of grasping.*"

To maintain at all hazards the transitive sense of ἁρπαγμός, Cremer (*Wörterbuch,* 9, p. 184) regards it as expressing the action not *in fieri* but *in facto esse ;* and he proposes this rather far-fetched translation : *Er hielt das Gottgleichsein* nicht für identisch mit dem Auftreten, dem Hendeln eines ἅπαξ.

As for those who, like Arius, take ἁρπαγμός for *res rapienda,* it is better not to mention them, since ἁρπαγμός surely cannot have that signification.

by right of birth and that he can claim it without injustice. When Arius insinuated that, if Christ had not arrogated to himself divine equality, it was because he recognized that he had no right to it, all Catholics rose in indignation against this perverse exegesis, revived in our day by some heterodox writers.

Thus, from the simple point of view of the theologian, the two interpretations are almost equivalent. But four principal reasons make us prefer that of St John Chrysostom and his school : *the authority of the Greek Fathers,* much more capable of appreciating the demands of their language; *the context,* which makes us expect a lesson of humility rather than the direct assertion of the dignity of Christ; *the etymology,* which seems to impose on the expression ἁρπαγμὸν ἡγεῖσθαι this definite meaning; lastly, *grammar,* the usage of which is better respected in translating ἀλλὰ by " but " than by " however."

On this hypothesis, we will try to analyze the successive stages of St Paul's mind.

Christ, pre-existing in the form of God and being, therefore, God, when he thought of becoming man, did not consider the divine honours to which he was entitled as a possession which he had to guard jealously.

On the contrary, he stripped himself of them voluntarily in becoming man, concealing the form of God under the form of a slave.

The example of humility and abnegation is less in the will of the Word decreeing the lowliness of the mortal life (for this will is common to the three divine Persons) than in the fact of the hypostatic union itself.

After the incarnation, the human will completes the self-stripping; it accepts the death of the cross, together with the life of obedience and renunciation that prepares for it and is its crown.

It is for this—for this act of obedience and voluntary humiliation—that God, fitting the recompense to the merit, exalts him beyond measure and makes him sit at his right hand.

2. From this imperfectly understood text has arisen the extravagant theory of the *kenosis,*[1] or self-stripping of the

---

[1] The word *kenosis* (κένωσις) is derived from the expression ἐκένωσεν ἑαυτόν (Phil. ii, 6). The first one to make use of it is, perhaps, the Pseudo-Hippolytus (*Contra Beron. et Helic.*, x, 832). In this text again κένωσιν is not certain : ἕνωσιν would do just as well, if not better. St Gregory Nazianzen, (*Orat.*, xxxvii, 3 [XXXVI, 285]) gives an excellent definition of it : κένωσιν λέγω τὴν τῆς δόξης οἷον ὕφεσίν τε καὶ ἐλάττωσιν. Moreover, the texts of the Fathers have nothing in common with the modern systems of the *kenosis.* They are discussed in the article *Kenosis* by Loofs, *Realencykl. für prot. Theol.*², vol. x, 1901, pp. 248-256.

Word made flesh. Fundamentally, the *kenosis* owes its first origin to the difficulty of conceiving two complete natures united in one single person; either one of the two natures was absorbed by the other, or they were blended in such a way as to produce a new nature, or one of the two was diminished in order that, completed by the second, it could thus form with it one unique whole. Truth to tell, Arius was the inventor of it, although the word did not originate with him. He admitted three parts in Christ :- a body, an irrational soul (ψυχὴ ἄλογος), and the Word, or Logos, supplying for the reasonable soul of other men. The human nature of Christ was, therefore, incomplete; and the Logos, which was neither eternal nor infinite, nor God in the proper sense of the term, could not become an integral part of a finite nature without itself undergoing some change. So the Arians granted that the Logos was not *physically* unchangeable, although *morally* he was so, as he was incapable of sin. In opposition to Arius, Apollinarius of Loadicea strongly maintained the full divinity of the Logos; but he, like Arius, makes it the third element of the unique nature of Christ, which is, therefore, composed of a body, a sensible soul or vital principle, and the Logos, performing the function of a reasonable soul. In vain he protests that in this fusion the Word remains unchangeable; all his teaching and the comparisons which he uses refute his assertion : Christ, in fact, is, according to him, neither wholly God nor wholly man, but a mixture of man and God, as the mule stands midway between the horse and the ass, and as the colour grey is a blending of white and black. All the Monophysites, by admitting the fusion of the two natures, had fatally to end in the same error, unless they turned to Docetism.

Two of Luther's ideas contributed much to implant the *kenosis* in the heart of Protestantism. Luther maintained, contrary to the common opinion, that the self-stripping of which St Paul speaks could not have been effected by the divine will of the Word, because the Word, in becoming flesh, had not himself been able to empty himself. Moreover, he understood the *communicatio idiomatum* in the strange sense that the human nature of Christ really possesses the attributes of the divine nature and, reciprocally, that the divine nature possesses the attributes of the human nature. Jesus Christ, as man, would therefore be omniscient, omnipotent, infinite. The Lutherans subsequently returned to the ordinary exegesis, understanding St Paul's text as referring to the Word himself; but many accepted the conclusion which Luther feared—although quite wrongly—namely, that the Word, in emptying himself, had thereby lost something of his divinity. Nor did it require long to see that the *communicatio idiomatum,* in Luther's sense, was ruled out, since the humanity of Christ could not be everywhere. Some tried to safeguard the master's doctrine by saying that the humanity of Christ possessed the attributes of divinity *by right,* but that it concealed them and only made a secret use of them, or even that it voluntarily stripped itself of them by refusing to make any use of them. The majority further added that the attributes of the divine nature can perfectly well be communicated to human nature, but not *vice versa;* yet they made reservations as to the *ubiquity* of the humanity of Christ, which is, indeed, something unintelligible.

Modern defenders of the *kenosis* prefer to take a philosophical stand. A certain school of philosophy identifies the person with consciousness; the loss of consciousness (or the feeling of the ego) would be equivalent to the annihilation of the person. Two consciousnesses in the same subject would be two persons. There are not, therefore, in Christ a divine consciousness *and* a human consciousness; there is only a divine consciousness *or* a human consciousness. With this principle it is impossible to escape the *kenosis,* unless by saying that the humanity of Christ is absorbed in his divinity. Thomasius, the theorist of the system, would have the consciousness of the Word become a human consciousness capable of evolution and progress. Others think that the incarnation consists in taking the predicate *man* in place of the predicate *God,* by ceasing to be God (Hofmann). Or else Christ changed the divine ego for a human ego, and there is a momentary cessation of the intimate life of the Word; the Father ceases to beget the Son, and the Holy Spirit proceeds from the Father only (Gess). Several, taking their stand on the heresy of Arius and Apollinarius, make the Word play the rôle of the mind or intellectual principle in the human organism (Gaupp). At all events, the incarnation means for the Word the loss or lessening of the divine form.[1] If the immutability of God is brought forward as an

---

[1] Whoever is curious to know more of these foolish speculations has only to read Dorner, *Ueber die richtige Fassung des dogmatischen Begriffs der Unveränderlichkeit Gottes* (*mit besonderer Beziehung auf das gegenseitige Verhältniss zwischen Gottes übergeschichtlichem und geschichtlichem Leben*) in *Jahrbücher für deutsche Theol.,* vol. i, 1856, pp. 361-416 (*Die neueren Läugnungen der Unveränderlichkeit des persönlichen Gottes*) and vol. ii, 1857, pp. 440-500; (*Die Geschichte der Lehre von der Unveränderlichkeit Gottes bis auf Schleiermacher nach ihren Hauptzügen historisch-kritisch dargestellt*), with two replies to Dorner by Liebner, *Christologisches, Ibid.,* vol. iii, pp. 349-366; and by Hasse, *Ueber die Unveränderlichkeit Gottes und die Lehre von der Kenosis des göttlichen Logos mit Rücksicht auf die neuesten christol. Verhandlungen, Ibid.,* vol. iii, pp. 366-417.
It would be neither possible nor useful to enumerate all the modern forms of the *Kenosis.* Bruce, in his work entitled *The Humiliation of Christ,* arranges them in four general types, which he calls : (1) *Absolute dualistic;* (2) *absolute metamorphic;* (3) *absolute semimetamorphic;* (4) *real but rleative.*

objection to the holders of this singular theory, they reply
either that we do not know in what the divine immutability
consists, or that God can do everything that is not incompatible with his moral character—in other words, with his
holiness.

We have said in what the stripping of the incarnation consists for the Son of God. He willed freely to unite with
a nature subject to limitations of every sort. There are, first,
the *metaphysical* limitations. The humanity of Christ is
created and consequently finite; infinite in dignity, as being
hypostatically united with a divine person, but finite in its
essence and endowed with a perfection which does not
exhaust all the power of God; apart from the fact that it
does not even occupy the highest rank in the scale of actual
beings. There are also the *economic* limitations, concerning
the rôle and the office of Redeemer in the present plan of
providence; Christ had to suffer and to die before entering
into glory, and to conquer by his merit an exaltation which
belonged to him by right of birth. There are also—we know
not in what measure—the *voluntary* limitations. Let us not
forget that the hypostatic union, since it does not directly
influence the human nature of Christ, could bring no physical
change to the body, or to the soul, or to the intellectual
faculties of his holy humanity. Here a vast field is left open
for voluntary renunciation. Christ wished to be born poor;
he took upon himself spontaneously our pains and our
infirmities; he knew the temptations and the anguish of the
agony; he made himself the slave of his adopted brethren;
above all, he renounced, for his earthly existence, the divine
honours which were his by right. By this voluntary self-
stripping, effected in his holy humanity, the Word was
stripped of himself, since he forms only one Person with that
humanity.

The *Kenosis* is relative or absolute according as the Logos lays aside the divine
attributes partially or wholly; it is dualistic or metamorphic according as
the Logos remains distinct from the human soul of Christ or is identified with it.

BOOK V
THE PASTORAL EPISTLES

CHAPTER I

THE HAND AND THE MIND OF PAUL

I—AUTHENTICITY

1. Tradition and Resemblances.   2. Style and Ideas.

1. THE name of *Pastorals,* which serves to designate St Paul's three letters to his disciples Timothy and Titus, goes back only to the middle of the eighteenth century, and is not a very happy one; but as it is now customary and makes for brevity of speech, we see nothing inappropriate in keeping it for this group of Epistles, closely related by date, style and subject.

Without discussing here in detail the texts of St Barnabas, St Clement of Rome, St Ignatius, St Polycarp, St Justin, and of Hegesippus, which take for granted already the knowledge and use of the Pastorals, it may be asserted that the testimony of tradition in their favour is as explicit and unanimous as it is for the most indubitable Epistles; for in the present case the questions of authenticity and canonicity are blended : if these letters are not authentic, they are the work of a forger, and the Fathers would not knowingly have admitted a fraud into the canon of the inspired books.   The two or three discordant voices of Marcion, Basilides, and Tatian, who naturally rejected writings that condemned their errors in advance, counted for nothing, and Eusebius did not hesitate to number the Pastorals among the books whose authenticity was indisputable.

Since the time of Schleiermacher, who, in 1807, declared the First Epistle to Timothy apocryphal, many critics have extended this negative verdict to all three Epistles, and the reaction of good sense, which has little by little restored to the Apostle most of the works the paternity of which was denied by the school of Tübingen, has not yet ended in dissipating all doubts on this subject.   However, a number of contemporary scholars have again gone halfway towards tradition, perceiving in the Pastorals large authentic fragments, which were later amplified by some unknown person desirous of sheltering his own ideas or arguments under the ægis of Paul.   Several have taxed their ingenuity in trying to pick these out; but their very divergent systems, the arbitrariness of which is self-evident, satisfy hardly anyone save the authors themselves.   The partisans of the theory of fraud pure and simple, if they were not more rational, were at least more logical.

Strangely enough, the two reasons usually advanced against attributing the Pastorals to the Apostle—apart from the question of style, of which we shall have occasion to speak subsequently—turn out to be positive proofs of their authenticity. These are the nature of the errors refuted and the hierarchical position of the churches.

Sometimes the argument runs as follows : " The Pastorals, dating from the second century, ought to attack Gnosticism, the great heresy of that period;" or, *vice versa:* "The Pastorals, being directed against Gnosticism, are not anterior to the second century." Both arguments are equally valueless; both contain a clear begging of the question, and together they form a fine example of the vicious circle.

Gnosticism is Protean in its variations. Which Gnostics do they mean? Baur named Marcion, Hilgenfeld spoke of Saturninus, others of Valentinus or of a forerunner of Valentinianism. Holtzmann more prudently avoids being definite, thinking doubtless that, among the innumerable systems comprised under the general name of Gnosticism, there will surely be found one to answer the description of the Pastorals. But there is nothing of the kind. The different Gnostic sects in the second century are all hostile to Judaism, and, if they retain some fragments of the New Testament, it is the better to combat the Old. Now, the persons aimed at in the Pastorals have unmistakable tendencies towards Judaism.

To-day we call *Gnostics* all those dreamers, smitten with Greek or oriental philosophy, who sought a solution for the problem of evil in dualism. It was not so in the second century. The title of Gnostic still had a favourable meaning, so that Clement of Alexandria used it to designate the perfect Christian. It had been claimed only by a group of obscure sects : Ophites or Naassenes, Sethians, Peratæ, and Cainites, all worshippers of the infernal Serpent, or admirers of the first murderer, but having absolutely nothing in common with the Judaizers mentioned in the Pastorals. Neither Marcion, nor Valentinus, nor Basilides, nor yet the crowd of contemporary heretics—Encratites, Ebionites, Docetæ, and others—were then looked upon as *Gnostics.*

Moreover, the name matters little. What is of capital importance is the following fact : the persons aimed at by the Pastorals are not heretics in the proper sense of the term. Twice some individuals are denounced as apostates;[1] elsewhere it is a question of unbelieving Jews;[2] but in regard to these people Titus and Timothy received no mission; they

---

[1] 1 Tim. i, 20 ; 2 Tim. ii, 17-18.　　　　[2] Titus i, 15-16.

were neither to command them nor to count on their obedience; they are only to avoid them and to make the disciples avoid them. Their true mandate concerns other persons and other doctrines.

What are these doctrines? Curious questions, the only effect of which is to inflame men's minds and to stir up disputes,[1] wars of words,[2] senseless propositions,[3] old wives' tales,[4] idle gossip.[5] The circulators of this trash are not, strictly speaking, heretics. They have not broken with legitimate authority, they attend the meetings of Christians, they come in contact every day with the other believers. Timothy remains at Ephesus just to tell them to stop chattering.[6] Titus, too, is told to shut their mouths.[7] He is to warn them once or twice kindly;[8] he is to proceed against them with all severity only if they throw off the mask and refuse to obey.

What a difference between this benignant attitude and the usual uncompromising stand taken against the Gnostics of every sect and every denomination! What a contrast also between St Paul's present mildness and the thunderbolts with which he threatens the Galatian Judaizers, or the severity displayed against the false teachers of Colosse! This is because the situation is wholly different; the preachers of Crete and Ephesus are not undermining the foundations of the Gospel or compromising its solidity; they are only dimming its lustre. For want of reflection the critics go hunting in all directions through Gnostic systems for comparisons of admitted inconsistency. They need not have hunted so far; the *Book of Jubilees,* a work rather earlier than the Christian era, offers an excellent specimen of the nonsense which charmed the innovators of Ephesus and Crete. Nothing is wanting there; neither endless genealogies nor Jewish fables, nor old wives' tales, nor senile disputes about the Torah. Some converts who had formerly been in touch with the doctors of the Synagogue still found amusement in these things.

The second design of the supposed forger, who is said to betray himself in spite of all the precautions taken to throw his readers off the scent, is his care to favour the monarchical transformation of the episcopacy.

In the second century, we are assured, a revolution took place in the government of the Church. From amidst the colleges of priests, who presided conjointly over the Christian assemblies, rose one individual more influential, more

---

[1] 2 Tim. ii, 2-3.
[2] 1 Tim. vi, 4.
[3] 1 Tim. vi, 20 ; 2 Tim. ii, 16.
[4] 1 Tim. iv, 7.
[5] Titus iii, 9.
[6] 1 Tim. i, 3.
[7] Titus i, 11.
[8] Titus iii, 10.

ambitious or more able than the rest, who claimed for himself
primacy over the others. This was not done at first, as can
be easily imagined, without some opposition on the part of
his evicted colleagues; but the centralization of power in the
hands of one man offered such advantages for the common
weal that no notice was taken of individual protests, and
the new system soon became general. The principle of
monarchical episcopacy having been once found, it was
necessary to promote it, to cause it to be accepted everywhere, and to break down all resistance. Such, it is said,
is the aim of the author of the Pastorals, and it is for this
reason that he assumes the mask of the Apostle and puts on
his authority.

How many are the errors and sophisms in these few lines !
Among other baseless hypotheses, it is supposed that Titus
and Timothy are bishops, without the name, and that they
are ordered to appoint other bishops. Nothing is more
contrary to sound exegesis and historical reality. Monarchical
episcopacy is essentially stationary, autonomous, and permanent; the bishop is settled in a diocese which he governs
by his own authority, without any other temporal limit than
the end of his life. Now, Titus and Timothy exercise only a
kind of superintendence over a group of churches; and they
exercise it in the name of Paul, as his representatives and
delegates, with a purely temporary title, ready to leave their
posts and functions at the first sign from the Apostle. They
may have received, they certainly have received, episcopal
consecration; but they are not bishops in the monarchical
sense of the word, because they have no dioceses to govern.
The primitive dioceses coincided practically with the Greek
city; they comprised the town with its suburbs and a territory
of moderate extent. There were bishops of Ephesus, Smyrna,
Pergamos, Gortyna, Gnossus, and much smaller localities;
and there were never, at least in the East, bishops appointed
over entire provinces. Nevertheless it is precisely the island
of Crete, without any more special localization, which is
assigned to Titus. He is to establish priests there in every
city; which proves that the episcopacy is not yet constituted
there. The jurisdiction of Timothy appears, indeed, to overlap the city of Ephesus with its immediate environs; for
Paul, in leaving him there for a time, which he supposes is
to be brief, instructs him to ordain priests and deacons, a
mission not especially urgent and necessary if it were a
question of the small Christian minority of a single city.

Titus and Timothy are also distinguished from the
stationary and autonomous bishops by two other circumstances; first, that they have no authority of their own; and
secondly, that they do not even possess a permanent title to
their delegated authority. They take the place of Paul

during his absence with a very clearly defined mandate—namely, to assign worthy ministers, to provide for good order, and to silence imprudent teachers.[1] This mandate is for a relatively short time only; Titus is not to retain it even till the return of the Apostle; he is definitely ordered to rejoin his master, when Tychicus or Artemas come to relieve him;[2] and, as a matter of fact, in the following year we see him setting out for Dalmatia.[3]

Are these bishops as they were conceived to hold office at the beginning of the second century when·St Ignatius wrote his letters? At that time each city had one pastor only, appointed for life, in whose hands all powers were concentrated to the extent in which he himself judged it proper to exercise them : the government of the church, the bestowal of all the sacraments, and the administration of ecclesiastical property and of charitable institutions. A contemporary of St Ignatius, especially in Asia Minor, where the radical critics prefer to locate the composition of the Pastorals, would have been wholly incapable of imagining such a situation as that which our Epistles present to us. But, supposing he were able to execute this archæological feat, far from contributing to the evolution of the hierarchy, he would have brought it back violently to a state of things existing half a century before. His work would not indicate progress, but retrogression. That the Pastorals and the letters of St Ignatius are products of the same social conditions is beyond belief. Hesse, among others, has quite understood this. "The letters of St Ignatius," he says, "are without any doubt of a later date than the Pastorals."[4] An interval of some fifty years is necessary to explain the changes which have taken place in the organization of the Christian communities. And as Hesse persists, in spite of everything, in placing the date of the Pastorals at the beginning of the second century, he sees himself obliged to assign the letters of Ignatius to the reign of Marcus Aurelius (161-180). The absurdity of this consequence ought to have shown him the error of his point of departure.

On the contrary, everything becomes simple and natural as soon as we see in the Pastorals the work of Paul himself. The situation of the churches of Ephesus and Crete is exactly that which we discover in all the Christian communities founded during the lifetime of the Apostle, with the one difference that the church of Ephesus, already a dozen years old, has now reached a rather more advanced phase of its development.

[1] 1 Tim. i, 3 ; Titus, i, 5.   [2] Titus iii, 12.
[3] 2 Tim. iv, 10.
[4] H. Hesse, *Die Entstehung der Hirtenbriefe*, Halle, 1889, p. 338.

2. The difficulty of style is specious in a different way. By style we mean here especially the use of words; for the style itself, although less concise, less eloquent, and less vigorous than that of the polemical passages of the great Epistles, does not differ noticeably from that of the moral passages. The syntax—that is to say, whatever in the style is more personal and less capable of imitation—is the same. Hence the philologists, the best judges in such matters, express no doubt as to the Pastorals' authenticity : an evident proof that the difficulties originate less in the style itself than in a prejudice, to the support of which the choice of language is later dragged in. It is true, the proportion of new words is considerable, and a certain number of expressions familiar to Paul, and of particles which he usually seems unable to dispense with, are entirely wanting; but, on the other hand, on all the pages are found expressions which are not his and turns of speech unused by him. As arguments of this sort are convincing only by an accumulation of details, there has been drawn up a list of Pauline words which are looked for in vain in the Pastorals, and also, as a sort of counter-proof, a whole series of expressions frequent in the Pastorals, but absent from the other Pauline writings. But a careful examination of these lists does not give a decisive result. The touchstone of style must be handled with great circumspection. The attempt has been made with Plato, Dante, Shakespeare, and Bossuet, but the most unlooked-for conclusions have always been reached. This is because the vocabulary of writers is modified and transformed with age, it becomes richer or poorer in a curious way, favourite words are subsequently completely discarded, and others replace them for a time, until terms which seemed to have been forgotten return to favour. There is here an interesting psychological problem, which it would be well to study thoroughly before formulating aphorisms.

The problem becomes further complicated in the case of an author whose diction shows no traces of the purist. Paul's mother tongue was Hebrew as much as Greek, and, without even considering the part which his different secretaries might have taken in the editing of his letters, his vocabulary was no doubt influenced by the many dialects and idioms which he heard in his travels. The new subjects treated in the Pastorals also necessitated a more extended use of words. More than half of those peculiar to this group of Epistles designate either the false teachers and their false doctrines, or the system of morals which it was proper to oppose to them, or the qualities requisite for priests and deacons. The presence of most of the others is purely accidental, and whoever is astonished at finding nowhere except in the Pastorals the words "cloak," "parchment," "stomach," "blacksmith," "modesty," "fear," "ancestors," and "grandmother," should be asked why things as rare as wind and water are mentioned only in the Epistle to the Ephesians. These minute researches are games of patience which may yield useful philological observations, but too often degenerate into puerilities.

More significant than the language of the Pastorals is their doctrine. The critics most hostile to their authenticity are compelled to concede that the Pastorals bear the stamp of one and the same author, and that this author, whoever he may be, is very familiar with the teaching of St Paul. By studying them closely, it will be perceived that most of the views peculiar to these Epistles are connected with the Epistles of the captivity. The latter evidently hold an intermediate position, and are like a bridge uniting the great Epistles and the Pastorals. Let us confine ourselves to two or three examples :

> But when the goodness and kindness of God our Saviour appeared, not by the works of justice which we have done, but according to his mercy, he saved us by the laver of regeneration and renovation of the Holy Ghost ; whom he hath poured forth upon us abundantly through Jesus Christ our Saviour ; that, being justified by his grace, we may be heirs according to hope of life everlasting.[1]

Almost all these expressions betray the hand of Paul. The "laver of regeneration and renovation," which is evidently baptism, already receives the name of *laver* or *bath* in the Epistle to the Ephesians, and this name reappears nowhere

---

[1] Titus iii, 4-6: Ὅτε δὲ ἡ χρηστότης καὶ ἡ φιλανθρωπία ἐπεφάνη τοῦ σωτῆρος ἡμῶν Θεοῦ, οὐκ ἐξ ἔργων τῶν ἐν δικαιοσύνῃ ἃ ἐποιήσαμεν ἡμεῖς ἀλλὰ κατὰ τὸ αὐτοῦ ἔλεος ἔσωσεν ἡμᾶς διὰ λουτροῦ παλινγενεσίας καὶ ἀνακαινώσεως Πνεύματος ἁγίου, οὗ ἐξέχεεν ἐφ' ἡμᾶς πλουσίως διὰ Ἰησοῦ Χριστοῦ τοῦ σωτῆρος ἡμῶν, ἵνα δικαιωθέντες τῇ ἐκείνου χάριτι κληρονόμοι γενηθῶμεν κατ' ἐλπίδα ζωῆς αἰωνίου.—This text is admirably adapted for a study of the relations and differences between the Pastorals and the rest of Paul's Epistles. We point out several of them in the text, but it will not be without benefit to add others here. (a) χρηστότης is a *Pauline* word, as well as χρηστεύομαι and χρηστολογία.—(b) φιλανθρωπία is not used by St Paul, but the predilection for compounds of φιλός which is observable in the Pastorals, is also found in the other Epistles.—(c) God is not elsewhere called σωτήρ, which is a title reserved for the Son. But we know that Paul is accustomed to apply to the Son all that belongs to the Father and *vice versa*.—(d) Λουτρόν is Pauline (Eph. v, 26) and used precisely to designate baptism.—(e) Ἀνακαίνωσις is Pauline (Rom. xii, 2) precisely in the same sense; as well as ἀνακαινόω (2 Cor. iv, 16 ; Col. iii, 10).—(f) Δικαιόω, δικαιοσύνη, ἔλεος and χάρις, without being exclusively Pauline, are words of which Paul makes a preponderant use, and which he employs exactly as they are here employed.—(g) As much could be said of κληρονόμος and of ἐλπίς in the context where they are found.—(h) Πλουσίως is wholly in the style of Paul, who loves to use it for the *richness* of the divine mercy and wisdom.—(i) But what is perhaps most characteristic is *salvation* presented as an accomplished fact (ἔσωσεν ἡμᾶς) and yet an object of our hope (κατ' ἐλπίδα). It is difficult to admit that a forger could furnish so many and such delicate coincidences with the true Paul.

else in the New Testament. The idea, if not the term of
"regeneration," recurs frequently in the canonical writings,
especially in those of St Paul. Strictly speaking, baptism is
not regeneration, but the instrument of regeneration; it is
the maternal body which gives us birth and clothes us with
Christ, not as with a strange attire, but as it were with a
vital form which changes our most intimate relations and
makes of us a new creature. The word, as well as the idea of
"renovation," belongs rightly to St Paul, and also the way
in which this renovation is effected, thanks to the intervention
of the Holy Spirit, shed in our hearts by the Father or by the
Son without distinction. Very Pauline also is the part played
by grace. The theory of a justice of our own is rejected,
the influence of works is denied, everything is left to mercy.
The state of justice makes us *heirs* of everlasting life and, as
in St Paul, we are saved here below in reality and in hope.
It is true, the old antithesis of "works and faith" is here
replaced by that of "works and grace," but the tendency to
this substitution is shown already in the Epistles of the
captivity, as if Paul wished to cut short the unhappy
ambiguity of which his doctrine had been the pretext, that
works are useless and that faith takes the place of everything. It may be also that, in proportion as the distance
from the Christian origins increased, the act of faith appeared
less indissolubly connected with baptism and justification.
The children of Christian families were born candidates
for baptism, and little by little faith came to be regarded as
a supernatural habit, rather than a sudden act, revolutionizing
the whole moral being.

Elsewhere Paul exhorts Timothy to dare and to suffer
everything for the Gospel of God, "who hath delivered us
and called us by his holy calling, not according to our works,
but according to his own purpose and grace, which was
given us in Christ Jesus before the times of the world; but is
now made manifest by the apparition of our Saviour Jesus
Christ, who hath destroyed death and hath brought to light
life and incorruption by the Gospel."[1] There is scarcely a

---

[1] 2 Tim. i, 9, 10 : (Θεοῦ) τοῦ σώσαντος ἡμᾶς καὶ καλέσαντος κλήσει ἁγίᾳ, οὐ κατὰ
τὰ ἔργα ἡμῶν ἀλλὰ κατὰ ἰδίαν πρόθεσιν καὶ χάριν, τὴν δοθεῖσαν ἡμῖν ἐν Χριστῷ
Ἰησοῦ πρὸ χρόνων αἰωνίων, φανερωθεῖσαν δὲ νῦν διὰ τῆς ἐπιφανείας τοῦ
σωτῆρος ἡμῶν Χριστοῦ Ἰησοῦ, καταργήσαντος μὲν τὸν θάνατον φωτίσαντος
δὲ ζωὴν καὶ ἀφθαρσίαν διὰ τοῦ εὐαγγελίου. Here again it is appropriate to point out some relations between the Pastorals and the other
Epistles : (*a*) πρόθεσις in this sense is exclusively Pauline (Rom. viii, 28 ;
ix, 11 ; Eph. i, 11 ; iii, 11 ; 2 Tim. i, 9 ; iii, 10).—(*b*) Ἀφθαρσία also (Rom. ii, 7 ;
1 Cor. xv, 42, 50, 53, 54 ; Eph. vi, 24 ; 2 Tim. i, 10).—(*c*) καταργεῖν, used
twenty-five times by Paul, is found elsewhere only in Heb. ii, 14 and Luke
xiii, 7 ; but the expression καταργεῖν τὸν θάνατον (1 Cor. xv, 26 ; 2 Tim. i, 10)
is doubly remarkable.—(*d*) The χρόνοι αἰώνιοι (Rom. vi, 25 ; 2 Tim. i, 9;
Titus i, 2) are not less so.—(*e*) The φανερωθεῖσαν νῦν (2 Tim. i, 10) is also
to be compared with the φανερωθέντος νῦν of Rom. xvi, 26 ; and these two

phrase here which does not bear the stamp of Paul: the *purpose* or good pleasure of God, *incorruption*, the *destruction* of death, the strange expression *times of the world* as opposed to the " to-day " of the Gospels, in which is *manifested* the grace decreed before all ages. Paul does not commonly regard heavenly glory as the direct and sole end of God's purpose or decree. The good pleasure of God, absolutely free and independent, guided by his mercy and not by the sight of pre-existent works and merits, leads finally to the individual's calling and initial salvation, which is blended with it. Nevertheless, this gracious determination is subordinated to the redemption of Christ Jesus, outside of whom there is neither grace nor salvation.

We like rediscovering these absolutely pure Pauline doctrines, with their precise terminology and fixed formulas, in a group of Epistles where certain heterodox theologians complain of searching in vain for the theories of Paul on grace and justification. But these theories no longer have the polemical form necessitated by the controversies of the great Epistles. It is not with these that the Pastorals should be compared, but rather with the letters addressed to the Thessalonians, or, better still, with the Epistles of the captivity.

II—HISTORICAL SETTING

1. Late Date of these Epistles.   2. Proof of Authenticity.

1. It is expedient to reduce as much as possible the interval which separates the two Epistles to Timothy, between which comes the letter to Titus. In both of them we see the Apostle a prey to the same cares and apprehensions, combating the same errors, and warding off the same dangers. The uniformity of his language betrays the same mental state and proves that similar circumstances imprint upon his mind an analogous train of thought. If our conjectures are well founded, the Pastorals were written within the space of a year—the last of Paul's life.

In the spring of the year 66 the Apostle made a general tour of the East. He went from south to north along the Asiatic coast, left Timothy at Ephesus to check the false teachers, and pushed on to Macedonia. From there he apparently wrote the First Epistle to Timothy, fearing that

---

passages should be carefully compared for the idea as well as for the expression.—(*f*) Here again, as in the Epistle to Titus and in the other Epistles of St Paul, salvation is presented as an accomplished fact (τοῦ σώσαντος ἡμᾶς) and identified with the efficacious call.—(*g*) Finally, everyone knows that the characteristic formula ἐν Χριστῷ ’Ιησοῦ is exclusively Pauline. The relations of thought are at once evident, and they are so frequent and so subtle that no unprejudiced person will believe them the work of a forger.

some unforeseen obstacle might prevent his return to Asia,[1]
perhaps also in order to reply to the doubts of a disciple afraid
of his own youth and responsibility.   When did he go to Crete
to found the church whose organization he charges Titus to
complete?   We cannot say.   After this hasty visit, we find
him on the way to Nicopolis, where he resolved to spend the
winter.[2]   There he ordered Titus to rejoin him as soon as
Tychicus or Artemas landed in Crete to replace him.[3]   Subsequently he descended the shore of the Mediterranean; at
Troas he was the guest of Carpus, at whose house he left
a cloak and books; at Miletus he lands Trophimus, who is
sick; he puts into Corinth and leaves there Erastus, another
of his companions.[4]   But we have no means of clearing up
the doubtful incident of his arrest.

In the Second Epistle to Timothy we find him a prisoner in
Rome.   A citizen of Ephesus has had time to learn of his
captivity and to discover him after a long search.[5]   The
Apostle feels the burden of solitude keenly.   Demas has just
deserted him in a cowardly manner.   He himself has had
to send Titus to Dalmatia, Crescentius to Galatia or to Gaul,
and Tychicus to Ephesus.   Luke alone is with him.[6]   He
has no hope left on earth : " For I am even now ready to be
sacrificed, and the time of my dissolution is at hand.   I have
fought a good fight, I have finished my course, I have kept
the faith.   As to the rest, there is laid up for me a crown of
justice, which the Lord, the just Judge, will render to me in
that day; and not only to me but to them also that love his
coming."[7]   This letter is a last appeal to his beloved disciple ;
Paul wishes to see him once more before he dies, and fears
already that it is too late, so imminent does the end appear.

2. The fact that the composition of the Pastorals falls
outside the historical setting of the Acts, far from weakening their authenticity, gives it additional support.   It is not
possible to escape from this dilemma : " Either Paul's career
did not end at the point where the book of the Acts concludes,
or the Pastoral Epistles are unauthentic."   All attempts which
have been made to distribute them along the known life of
the Apostle have failed, in spite of prodigies of ingenuity.
In order to explain both their resemblance to one another

[1] The final notes of the manuscripts which make the Epistle originate from
Laodicea in Phrygia or from Nicopolis or Athens or Rome, are only more or
less conjectural.
[2] Titus iii, 12 undoubtedly refers to Actia Nicopolis in Epirus.   Probably
the Apostle wished to revisit Illyria, evangelized by him on his travels
(Rom. xv, 19).
[3] It was probably Artemas and not Tychicus who took the place of Titus,
for, a little later, we see Tychicus despatched to Ephesus (2 Tim. iv, 12).
[4] 2 Tim. iv, 13, 20.   [5] 2 Tim. i, 16-17.
[6] 2 Tim. iv, 10-12.   [7] 2 Tim. iv, 6-8.

and their lack of resemblance to the rest, it is necessary to make them a separate group, confined to a very short period of time, and to place them at the end of Paul's life.

This period leaves us as much in the dark as would all the apostolic story without the record of the Acts; but the difficulty of reconciling the allusions in the Pastorals with some established facts is precisely one more proof in favour of their authenticity. A forger, familiar with the style and writings of Paul, would not designedly scatter contradictions throughout a skilful imitation which he wished to pass off as the genuine work of the master. He would link up his pretended correspondence with historical circumstances; and he would bring forward the same persons and carefully preserve their rôle and character. The author of the Pastorals, if he be other than Paul, proceeds in a way contrary to common sense. He introduces for the first time a crowd of strangers : Hymenæus, Philetus, Phigellus, Hermogenes, Lois and Eunice, Crescens, Carpus, Eubulus, Pudens, Linus, Claudia, Onesiphorus, Alexander, Artemas, and Zenas. The details concerning them are brief, precise, and well suited to the epistolary form in which it is not necessary to instruct the gallery. Most of these personages are charged with a rôle which they did not seem prepared to play. How was it possible to foresee the defection of Demas, and why send him to Thessalonica? What had Tychicus and Titus himself to do in Crete? Apollos, Erastus, and Trophimus are not where they were expected to be. A forger, who esteems Timothy enough to have two apocryphal letters addressed to him, would have idealized his portrait; at least, he would not have detracted anything from the praises which Paul in his public letters bestows upon his favourite disciple; certainly he would not have represented him as timid, irresolute, and distrustful of his youth and strength. There are things that are not invented. The recommendation to Timothy to drink a little wine for his stomach's sake and to bring to the Apostle the books and parchments left behind at the house of Carpus, charming as an expression of actual life realistically drawn, would be cold and puerile if penned by an imitator.

CHAPTER II

DOCTRINE OF THE PASTORALS

I—THE ERRORS ATTACKED

1. Errors pointed out to Titus. 2. Errors pointed out to Timothy.
3. Common Characteristics.

1.   **A**NXIETY to keep intact the deposit of faith, with arrangements for the choice of sacred ministers, form the principal subject of this group of Epistles. The Apostle feels the need of safeguarding the word of God against the morbid attacks of an unbridled imagination and the unwholesome assaults of unsystematic knowledge. Sound, vigorous truth will serve as an antidote to the pernicious doctrines which, like gangrene, threaten to invade the body of the Church.[1] The danger of contamination made such a lively impression upon him that he repeats these medical metaphors on almost every page, as he usually reiterates all ideas which have forcibly taken possession of his mind.

Before making any conclusions, let us allow him to speak for himself. To Titus he writes in these terms :

> There are many disobedient, vain talkers and seducers, especially they of the circumcision ; who must be reproved ; who subvert whole houses, teaching things which they ought not, for filthy lucre's sake. . . . Rebuke them sharply, that they may be sound in the faith ; not giving heed to Jewish fables and commandments of men, who turn themselves away from the truth. All things are clean to the clean ; but for them that are defiled and to unbelievers nothing is clean ; but both their mind and their conscience are defiled. They profess that they know God, but in their works they deny him, being abominable, incredulous, and to every good work reprobate.[2]

---

[1] 2 Tim. ii, 17 : Ὁ λόγος αὐτῶν ὡς γάγγραινα νομὴν ἕξει. The expression νομὴν ἔχειν, " to extend, to spread," is used of fire, ulcers and cancerous affections. In the same order of ideas he speaks of "sound doctrine" (ἡ ὑγιαίνουσα διδασκαλία, 1 Tim. i, 10 ; 2 Tim. iv, 3 ; Titus i, 9 ; ii, 1) ; "wholesome words" (ὑγιαίνοντες λόγοι, 1 Tim. vi, 3 ; λόγος ὑγιής, 2 Tim. i, 13) ; "persons sound" in the faith (Titus i, 13 ; ii, 2). These figures of speech were then common ; λόγοι ὑγιαίνοντες is from Philo, *De Abraham*, 38. Plutarch, *De aud. poet.*, 4, has the expression ὑγιαίνουσαι περὶ θεῶν δόξαι. The metaphor of health naturally suggests those of sickness, 1 Tim. vi, 4 (νοσῶν), of pollution and infection, Titus i, 15 (μεμιαμμένοι, μεμίανται). Another remarkable medical metaphor is κεκαυτηριασμένοι (or κεκαυστηριασμένοι) τὴν ἰδίαν συνείδησιν, 1 Tim. iv, 2.

[2] Titus i, 10, 11, 13, 16. It is important to note that from verse 15 on the subject changes and that thereafter it is a question of other persons and other errors. Titus is to forbid those under his authority to listen to *Jewish fables*

> Avoid foolish questions and genealogies and contentions and strivings about the law ; for they are unprofitable and vain. A man that is a heretic, after the first and second admonition, avoid ; knowing that he that is such an one is subverted and sinneth, being condemned by his own judgement.[1]

The errors pointed out offer us the following characteristics :

It is a question of doctrines spread extensively among the faithful, for Paul commands Titus to silence those who propagate them, to rebuke them sharply, and, in case of obstinate persistence, to avoid them ; but he does not mean to exclude all foreign influences ; and those who " profess that they know God, but in their works deny him," are no doubt unbelieving Jews, and not Judaizers.

These doctrines are preferably addressed to the recruits from Judaism ; they are disputes about the Law, which must have been due to Jews or Judaizers ; they dispose their hearers to listen to the disseminators of Jewish fables and arbitrary rules, referring to ritual purifications, and to the difference between clean and unclean articles of food.

What especially strikes the Apostle is less the falsity of these doctrines than their *vanity* and *uselessness*. Their propagators are actuated by a low desire for gain. They are *vain talkers,* who deceive the simple by the charlatanism of their *foolish questions* and *curious genealogies.* Instead of discussing with them, it is necessary to command them to hold their tongues and, if they persist in talking, to exclude them from the Church.

2. Let us now observe the errors mentioned in the two letters to Timothy :

> I desired thee to remain at Ephesus when I went into Macedonia, that thou mightest charge some not to teach otherwise, nor to give heed to fables and genealogies without end ; which minister questions rather than the edification of God, which is in faith. Now the end of the commandment is charity from a pure heart and a good conscience and an unfeigned faith. From which things some, going astray, are turned aside unto vain babbling ; desiring to be teachers of the Law, understanding neither the things they say, nor whereof they affirm.[2]
> Now the Spirit manifestly saith that in the last times some shall

---

and the *commandments of men who reject the truth.* He clearly alludes here to the unbelieving Jews, whose fatal influence was still able to make itself felt by their compatriots converted to the faith, and he continues to characterize them in the two following verses : nothing is clean to these men who are defiled ; they profess in vain that they know God ; for in their works they deny him, refusing to embrace the truth.

[1] Titus iii, 9-11. There are here two very different injunctions : (*a*) Avoid foolish questions and contentions which may arise among the faithful.— (*b*) Set aside the *heretic* (αἱρετικὸν ἄνθρωπον) after one or two admonitions ; do not have anything more to do with him and regard him as excluded from the Church (see 1 Tim. i, 20 ; 2 Tim. iv, 14 ; 1 Cor. v, 5).

[2] 1 Tim. i, 3-7.

depart from the faith, giving heed to spirits of error and doctrines of devils, speaking lies in hypocrisy and having their conscience seared, forbidding to marry, to abstain from meats, which God hath created to be received with thanksgiving by the faithful and by them that have known the truth. For every creature of God is good, and nothing to be rejected that is received with thanksgiving; for it is sanctified by the word of God and prayer.[1]

If any man teach otherwise and consent not to the sound words of our Lord Jesus Christ, and to that doctrine which is according to godliness, he is proud, knowing nothing, but sick about idle questions and strifes of words; from which arise envies, contentions, calumnies, evil suspicions, endless disputes of men perverted in mind, and who are destitute of the truth, supposing that godliness is a means of making money.[2]

Charge them before the Lord not to strive about words to no profit, but to the subverting of the hearers. Endeavour to show thyself approved unto God, a workman that needeth not to be ashamed, rightly administering the word of truth. But shun profane and vain babblings, for they grow much towards ungodliness, and their speech spreadeth like a canker, of whom are Hymeneus and Philetus; who have erred from the truth, saying that the resurrection is past already, and have subverted the faith of some.[3]

Know also this that in the last days shall come on dangerous times; Men shall be lovers of themselves, covetous, haughty, . . . having an appearance of godliness, but denying the power thereof. Now these avoid. For of these sort are they who creep into houses and lead captive silly women loaded with sins, who are led away with divers desires; ever learning, and never attaining to the knowledge of the truth. Now as Jannes and Jambres resisted Moses, so these also resist the truth, men corrupted in mind, reprobate concerning the faith. But they shall proceed no farther; for their folly shall be manifest to all men, as theirs also was.[4]

For there shall come a time, when they will not endure sound doctrine; but, according to their own desires, they will heap to themselves teachers, having itching ears; and will indeed turn away their hearing from the truth, but will be turned unto fables.[5]

Three of these texts relate to the present; the other three—the second and the last two—to the future.[6] The errors actually propagated have exactly the characteristics which we have cited in the Epistle to Titus. They are doctrines spread among the faithful, since Timothy receives a mandate to silence those who propagate them. The latter are evidently Jews by nationality, for they boast of being doctors of the Law. The doctrines themselves are not so much heresies as idle questions, adapted to excite contentions, disputes over words which lead to nothing, vain chatter and gossip. The expressions met with in the Epistle to Titus recur here also continually. The situations, therefore, are identical.

But error can live only provided that it grows. It spreads like a cancer. The Apostle foresees in the future a flood of false doctrines advancing simultaneously with a corruption

[1] 1 Tim. iv, 1-4.   [2] 1 Tim. vi, 3-5.   [3] 2 Tim. ii, 14-18.
[4] 2 Tim. iii, 1-9.   [5] 2 Tim. iv, 3-4.
[6] *In novissimis temporibus* (1 Tim. iv, 1); *in novissimis diebus* (2 Tim. iii, 1); *erit tempus* (2 Tim. iv, 3).

of morals. And these will be only the present aberrations carried to their highest power. They are already active in obscurity. As they grow worse, the spirit of contention will proceed to actual schism. The truth will no longer be endured; there will be apostasies from the faith; crowds will gather about false teachers and false prophets, who will openly preach diabolical doctrines. It will no longer be a question merely of fables and genealogies, wordy disputes, quarrels relating to the Law, and arbitrary, fruitless practices; marriage will be forbidden, and certain animals will be condemned as bad, either under the influence of dualism or of a misapprehended asceticism. Finally, the love of money will engender a thousand detestable abuses, and the mask of hypocrisy will be a cover for the worst excesses.

3. Combining all these features into a complete picture and without distinguishing too much the future from the present, a very exact idea can be formed of these preachers, their motives, and their doctrines.

The preachers are Jews or Judaizers. They belong especially to the circumcision;[1] they call themselves doctors of the Law;[2] they have a liking for Jewish fables;[3] they are particularly given to disputes about the Law;[4] they resist the truth, as the two celebrated impostors resisted Moses.[5]

They are seducers,[6] hypocrites,[7] insubordinate,[8] vain babblers,[9] perverted in mind,[10] having itching ears,[11] incapable of apprehending the truth,[12] eager for money[13] and for popularity, men who cause division in the Church and in families,[14] who make coteries and foster schisms.

The doctrines which they propagate are not so much heresies as innovations, dangerous from their very uselessness, for they keep up an unhealthy curiosity, feeding the mind with idle fancies and accustoming it to what is false and unreal. A word, difficult to translate,[15] sums up very well

---

[1] Titus i, 10 : μάλιστα οἱ ἐκ τῆς περιτομῆς.
[2] I Tim. i, 17 : νομοδιδάσκαλοι.
[3] Titus i, 14 : Ἰουδαϊκοῖς μύθοις.
[4] Titus iii, 9 : μαχὰς νομικάς.　　　　　　　　[5] 2 Tim. iii, 8.
[6] Titus i, 10: φρεναπάται. Cf. I Tim. iv, I : προσέχοντες πνεύμασι πλάνοις.
[7] 2 Tim. iii, 5 : ἔχοντες μόρφωσιν εὐσεβείας.
[8] Titus i, 10 : ἀνυπότακτοι.
[9] I Tim. i, 6 : ματαιολογία. Cf. Titus i, 10 : ματαιολόγοι. Their vain discourses are only old women's fables (I Tim. iv, 7, μῦθοι γραώδεις).
[10] 2 Tim. iii, 8.　　　[11] 2 Tim. iv, 3.　　　[12] 2 Tim. iii, 7.
[13] I Tim. vi, 5, 10; Titus i, 11.　　　[14] I Tim. iii, 6.
[15] I Tim. i, 3; vi, 3 : ἑτεροδιδασκαλεῖν. This verb 'cannot mean " to have other masters," as Otto, Kölling and Hesse have asserted with mis-directed erudition. It does not come directly from διδασκαλεῖν, which does not exist, but is formed like other Pauline words : ἑτεροζυγεῖν (2 Cor. vi, 14), ἀγαθουργεῖν (Acts xiv, 17), τεκνογονεῖν (I Tim. v, 14), τεκνοτροφεῖν (I Tim. v, 10), οἰκοδεσποτεῖν (I Tim. v, 14), from a noun ἑτεροδιδάσκαλος

the teaching of these doctors who teach without authority.
In general they do not teach things *contrary* to the doctrine
of the Apostle, but they inculcate things which he has
judged to be superfluous or perilous to preach, and they
teach the articles of his Gospel *differently* from him. Paul
explains the nature of these innovations by forbidding the
faithful to " seek after fables and genealogies without end."[1]
We are tempted to think here of the Greek writers of
mythologies, or of those historians of origins who collected
fables about the gods and *genealogical lists,* which formed
the principal basis of primitive history. But the words of
St Paul do not allow us to think either of the legends of
pagan mythologies or of the genealogies of the gods and
heroes. For these fables are distinctly described as being
Jewish, and the parallel passage shows that they were propagated by people *who call themselves doctors of the Law.*
After this statement it is impossible to see in them anything
but *foolish babbling* and *gossip,* like that with which the
Talmudical books are crammed. As to the *genealogies
without end* and especially without profit, the apocryphal
books of the Old Testament, composed about the beginning
of the Christian era, offer us more than one example of them.
The mind that is in love with novelties allows itself to be
dazzled by the mirage of all these sophisms. " O Timothy,
keep that which is committed to thy trust, avoiding the profane novelties of words and oppositions of knowledge falsely
so called, which some professing have erred concerning the
faith."[2] First idle questions, then foolish objections and

(Eusebius, *Hist.*, iii, 12), in use or not. The meaning of ἑτεροδιδάσκαλος,
compared with καλοδιδάσκαλος (Titus ii, 3), νομοδιδάσκαλος (I Tim. i, 7),
ψευδοδιδάσκαλος (2 Peter ii, 1), is not doubtful. It is " he who teaches
something *else*" than Paul's teaching. It is true that, in departing from the
apostolic rule, there is great danger of falling into error and that one usually
ends there. This is why ἑτεροδιδασκαλεῖν, like ἑτερόδοξος and ἑτεροδοξεῖν
(Josephus, *Bell.*, viii, 5 ; S. Ignatius, *Magn.*, viii, 1 ; *Smyrn.*, li, 2), easily
assumes a derogatory meaning, and why the Fathers also generally take
the expression in the sense of " to teach error "; while in itself it signifies
merely " to teach novelties." The Apostle explains his thought and indicates
to us the nature of these novelties by adding : μηδὲ προσέχειν μύθοις καὶ
γενεαλογίαις ἀπεράντοις.

[1] Polybius, *Hist.*, IX, ii, 1 : τὰ περὶ γενεαλογίας καὶ μύθους. These
legendary stories were called μυθογραφία (Strabo, I, ii, 35), μυθογραφεῖν
(*Ibid.*, III, iv, 4), from the word μυθογράφος, an "historian of origins."
Primitive or genealogical history was designated by ὁ γενεαλογικὸς τρόπος
(Polybius, IX, i, 4) ; Philo (*Vita Mosis*, ii, 8) calls the historical part of the
Pentateuch τὸ γενεαλογικόν.

[2] I Tim. vi, 20 : ἐκτρεπόμενος τὰς βεβήλους κενοφωνίας (the Vulgate
reads : καινοφωνίας, *vocum novitates*) καὶ ἀντιθέσεις τῆς ψευδωνύμου γνώσεως.
It is in the last words that Baur saw an allusion to the famous work
of Marcion, entitled *Antitheses:* an utterly untenable opinion. St Irenæus
certainly took the title of his work from our text: ἔλεγχος καὶ ἀνατροπὴ
τῆς ψευδωνύμου γνώσεως, but when he applies it to the Gnostics (II, xiv, 7)

sterile cavillings, and finally the loss of faith : such is the course of error.

II—ECCLESIASTICAL DIGNITARIES

1. Priests and Deacons.   2. Qualities required of Candidates.
3. Widows and Deaconesses.

1. In the authentic letters of St Ignatius, at the beginning of the second century, the terminology and the prerogatives of the ecclesiastical hierarchy are already completely settled. There are three distinct orders : the bishop, always one alone;[1] the priests, closely associated with the bishop and so intimately united with one another that they are usually designated by the collective name of πρεσβυτέριον, or sacerdotal college;[2] finally, lowest of all, the deacons, who owe obedience to the priests and to the bishop, as the simple laity owes obedience to them.   The bishop, the presbyterate, and the deacons constitute the clergy; the clergy and the laity constitute the Church.[3]   The episcopate is stationary and monarchical; Ignatius is bishop of Antioch, Polycarp of Smyrna, Onesimus of Ephesus, Polybius of Tralles, Damasus of Magnesia.   The bishop performs or presides over the ceremony of baptism and of the agape, the solemnization of marriage, and, above all, ·the consecration of the Eucharist; but it is permissible for him to delegate his authority.   The priests and deacons are to exercise no function without the knowledge of the bishop.[4] the laity have absolutely no share in the government of the Church; their duty is to obey the

---

he just leaves aside ἀντιθέσεις, which suggests nothing to him.   It is noteworthy that in Eusebius (*Hist.*, III. xxxii, 8) the words τῷ τῆς ἀληθείας κηρύγματι τὴν ψευδώνυμον γνῶσιν ἀντικηρύττειν ἐπεχείρουν are those of Eusebius himself and not of Hegesippus, as the interpolation by Migne between parentheses (xx, 284-285) might lead one to believe.   In the time of Hegesippus γνῶσις, with or without the epithet ψευδώνυμος, did not yet designate the *Gnostics*, a name which is attributed by Irenæus to some obscure sects only.—Tertullian informs us what the *antitheses* or *oppositions* of Marcion were.   As to those which St Paul commands the faithful to banish, Chrysostom sees in them futile objections unworthy of a reply. They are called ἀντιθέσεις " oppositions," either merely because they are *opposed* to the true doctrine or perhaps because they are *opposed* among themselves.   Are we to think of the rabbinical method of citing authorities *for and against* on every question?   As it is a matter of Jews or Judaizers, the hypothesis is not improbable.

[1] *Ignatii epist.*, *Eph.*, i, 3 (Onesimus of Ephesus): *Ad Polyc.* (Polycarp of Smyrna); *Trall.*, i, 1 (Polybius of Tralles); *Magnes.*, ii (Damasus of Magnesia).   As all the bishops named have their see fixed and occupy it alone, there is no reason to believe that it is not the same with the Bishop of Syria mentioned in *Roman.*, ii, 2.

[2] *Ephes.*, ii, 2 ; iv, 1 ; xx, 2, etc. (fifteen times).

[3] *Magnes.*, xiii, 1 ; *Smyrn.*, xii, 2 ; *Philad.*

[4] *Smyrn.*, viii, 1-2 ; for marriage, *Polyc.*, v, 2 ; *Smyrn.*, ix, 1 (*qui clam episcopo aliquid agit, diabolo servit*).

bishop, or the bishop and the presbyterate, or the bishop, the presbyterate, and the deacons;[1] for the two inferior orders are united to the bishop as the strings to the lyre;[2] there is only one Eucharist, only one body of Christ, only one chalice of his blood, only one altar, only one bishop, with the presbyterate and the deacons.[3]

The Pastoral Epistles, however, reveal an organization much more primitive than this, a fact which refutes the paradox of the critics who claim that they were written long after the beginning of the second century by a forger desirous of promoting the hierarchy, which was then in process of formation. But the subsequent evolution, which was effected very rapidly and everywhere in the same direction, with all the characteristics of a legitimate development, proves that the essential lines of it had been traced out beforehand by the apostles, according to instructions given by the Master and under the ever-vigilant impulse of the Holy Ghost. It can, therefore, be of use to us in interpreting the doubtful data of the apostolic age; but it would be a fallacy to transport to those distant times the functions and appellations of a later epoch. Every author should be studied separately, and no one has a right to suppose à priori that all are speaking of the same things in the same terms.

In St Paul the ecclesiastical terminology is undecided. If ἐπίσκοπος always designates a sacred minister, πρεσβύτερος has frequently the meaning of "an old man," and διάκονος rarely signifies anything but "servant or helper." On the other hand, the heads of the Church sometimes receive other titles: those of Thessalonica, for example, are called *presidents*. The language used is still unfixed, and it is surprising that an end was so soon put to its first indecision.

By common accord the name *deacon,* rather than any synonym, was decided on for the inferior ministers of worship.[4] Perhaps δοῦλος was discarded because of its servile

---

[1] The bishop must be revered like the Lord, *Eph.*, vi, 1; *Trall.*, ii, 1; vii, 1. Obedience and respect are due to the bishop and the priests, *Eph.*, ii, 2; xx, 2; *Magn.*, 2; *Trall.*, xiii, 2; similarly to the bishop, priest and deacons, *Philad.*, vii, 1; *Trall.*, iii, 1; *Polyc.*, vi, 1.

[2] Eph. iv, 1.   [3] *Philad.*, 4.

[4] The word διάκονος is found eight times in the Gospel in its ordinary meaning of *servant* (Matt. xx, 26; xxii, 13; xxiii, 11; Mark ix, 35; x, 43; John ii, 5-9; xii, 26) and twenty-two times in St Paul. The other writers of the New Testament do not use the word, and St Luke himself does not employ it in relating the institution of the seven Gentile deacons, although he designates their ministry under the name of διακονία (Acts vi, 1-4). It receives in St Paul the most varied applications. The prince is the διάκονος of God (Rom. xiii, 4); Jesus Christ is διάκονος of the circumcision (Rom. xv, 8); the apostolic workmen are διάκονοι of Christ (1 Cor. iii, 5; 2 Cor. iii, 6; vi, 4; xi, 23). Paul claims this title for himself (Eph. iii, 7; Col. i, 23-25; *cf.* 2 Cor. xi, 23); he gives it to Timothy (1 Thess. iii, 2; 1 Tim. iv, 6), to Tychicus (Eph. vi, 21; Col. iv, 7), to Epaphras (Col. i, 7), to a woman, Phœbe (Rom. xvi, 1). Διάκονος has only three times the

associations, ὑπηρέτης because it made one think of the sacristan of the Jewish synagogue, θεράπων because it recalled the custodian of certain idolatrous chapels. However this may be, διάκονος was soon chosen to the exclusion of every other title, and it is curious that St Luke in describing the election of the first seven Gentile deacons does not make use of it. In Paul's writings the word deacon has already received its hierarchical stamp; the Apostle sends special greetings to the διάκονοι of Philippi, and he enumerates the qualities to be required of the διάκονος in order to be able to confer upon him the laying on of hands. No doubt is here possible; the reference is certainly to the diaconate and deacons.

For the higher functions the most general terms, freed by their very vagueness from any association with compromising ideas, were also the most suitable. One of these is the word πρεσβύτερος.[1] Almost all ancient societies—those, at least, where pure aristocracy did not reign—were governed by a council or senate of *elders*. At first, this was the privilege of age; later, it was a hereditary title. In all the epochs of sacred history, under Moses, under the Judges, under the monarchy, and at the return from the captivity, we perceive everywhere the presence of these elders. During the period of Judaism, properly so called, they were at the head of the synagogues; they exercised an authority in the cities and villages analogous to that of our municipal officers, and a notable number of them were members of the great Sanhedrim of Jerusalem. Hence they are constantly mentioned in the New Testament in company with the scribes and high priests. To designate the spiritual directors of the Christian churches the word ἱερεύς was discarded, since it recalled the levitical priest and the pagan *sacerdos* or *sacrificulus*. The word πρεσβύτερος was fixed upon because it had the advantage of being understood by the Jews, who were everywhere governed in civil and in religious matters by a council

---

hierarchical meaning which concerns us here. The Apostle salutes the ἐπίσκοποι and the διάκονοι of Philippi at the same time as the whole church (Phil. i, 1); and he enumerates the qualities requisite for deacons (1 Tim. iii, 8-14). "To minister the office of deacon" is called twice διακονεῖν (1 Tim. iii, 10-13), but this verb retains its usual meanings elsewhere. With St Paul διακονία signifies "ministry, service," in the most different senses, or designates a special *charisma* (Rom. xii, 7; 1 Cor. xii, 5), but is not used for the function of a deacon.

[1] The word πρεσβύτερος is used in the sense of ecclesiastical dignitary in all cases where the Vulgate translates it by *presbyter* (1 Tim. v, 17-19; Titus i, 5; James v, 14). It has the same meaning in Acts xx, 17 (where the *seniores Ecclesiae* are those whom Paul subsequently calls ἐπίσκοποι, xx, 28) as well as in Acts xv, 4, 6, 22, 23; xvi, 4 (where the *seniores* are the same persons as the *presbyteri* of Acts xv, 2. The whole number of the *elders* of the people is called collectively πρεσβυτέριον (Luke xxii, 66; Acts xxii, 5), and Paul gives this name once to the college of the *elders* of the Church (1 Tim. iv, 14).

of *elders;* while it was familiar to the Greeks, to whom it recalled, outside of political and municipal titles, the members of certain committees instituted for the celebration of festivals, the service of the temples, or the burial of the associates. But while the community at Jerusalem employed it to the exclusion of every other name, the Gentile churches adopted it only gradually and concurrently with ἐπίσκοπος.

This third title is still more indeterminate than the two preceding ones.[1] It signifies in Scripture " guardian, overseer, inspector, commissioner." At Athens it was applied to special delegates, like the *Harmosts* of Sparta, whom the city sent out to organize new colonies or conquered countries. In Batanea and the Decapolis it was the title of officials charged with administering the property of a temple. Elsewhere the functions were different, but the brevity of the texts referring to them seldom allows us to define them exactly. Hence we cannot say with certainty why, in the ecclesiastical hierarchy, the ἐπίσκοπος held the highest rank, above the πρεσβύτερος. Can it be because the latter word naturally awakened the idea of a large number of persons, united in a priestly college to exercise the same duty, whereas the function of an ἐπίσκοπος was often conferred on one person only, without any division of authority? Let us hasten to add that for St Paul the two words are synonymous.

In the salutation which he addresses to the clergy of Philippi he distinguishes only two classes—the ἐπίσκοποι and

---

[1] The word ἐπίσκοπος (always translated by *episcopus*) occurs five times in the New Testament, four times in the sense of an ecclesiastical dignitary (Acts, xx, 28 ; Phil. i, 1 ; 1 Tim. iii, 2 ; Titus i, 7) and once figuratively (1 Peter ii, 25). Jesus Christ is the shepherd and the ἐπίσκοπος of our souls. This word is quite frequent in the Septuagint, where it is translated פָּקִיד, and is used by Homer (*Il.*, xxii, 255 ; *Od.*, viii, 163) in the most general sense. Homer, Æschylus, Pindar, Sophocles, Plato and Plutarch apply it to the gods. A character in Aristophanes (*Birds*, 1022) arrogates to himself this title in the special sense which it had at Athens : " I come here," he says, " as ἐπίσκοπος, having obtained (this office) thanks to the bean," used by the citizens for voting.

Ἐπίσκοπος ἥκω δεῦρο τῷ κυάμῳ λαχών.

A commentator on Aristophanes (edit. Didot, p. 490) and Harpocration (edit. Dindorf, p. 129), quoting Theophrastus, liken these commissioners of Athens to the *Harmosts* of Lacedaemon. Arrian (*Ind.*, xii, 5) and Appian (*Mithr.*, 48) designate by this word inspectors or commissioners from other countries. 1 Macc. i, 51 applies it to the delegates of Antiochus Epiphanes. The inscriptions, especially those of Rhodes, offer several examples of it. See Deissmann (*Neue Bibelstudien*, p. 57). The functions performed by these ἐπίσκοποι do not seem particularly important. Once an ἐπίσκοπος is pointed out in the personnel of a temple of Apollo (*Inscr. Gr. Maris Aegæi*, Berlin, 1891, No. 731).

Ἐπισκοπή is once the office of an ἐπίσκοπος (1 Tim. iii, 1) ; once (Acts i, 20, quoting Ps. cviii, 8) it is an *office*, a *post*, in general ; the other two times (Luke xix, 44 ; 1 Peter ii, 12) it is the scriptural name for the " day of *visitation*."

the deacons.[1] The former, precisely because of their numbers, can only be the *elders* of the Church, for it is unheard of that one single city should have had several bishops. If it be supposed that the ἐπίσκοποι were bishops, the omission of the second rank could not be well explained.

The matter is still clearer in the passage where Paul orders Titus to establish πρεσβύτεροι in *each* city; he requires that they should be distinguished by their virtue and stainless reputation, *for*, he adds, the ἐπίσκοπος must be irreproachable.[2] His mode of reasoning would be a sophism if the two terms were not synonyms. On the other hand, if it were a question of the highest rank of the hierarchy, he would not use the plural, since each city had only one bishop.

Another proof. After having sent to Miletus the πρεσβύτεροι of Ephesus—that is to say, the heads of that particular church, who certainly were not bishops, since he subsequently has to leave Timothy in Ephesus to exercise episcopal duties there—Paul addresses them in these terms : " Take heed to yourselves and to the whole flock wherein the Holy Ghost hath set you as ἐπίσκοποι."[3] Thus, beyond a doubt, these two terms are used indifferently to denote the same persons, and are applied to the members of the second rank of the hierarchy—in other words, to priests.

In the only text which gives rise to discussion this will be remembered : " If a man desire the office of an ἐπίσκοπος, he desireth a good work. It behoveth, therefore, an ἐπίσκοπος to be blameless."[4] The parallelism and the list of the qualities to be required of this dignitary show plainly enough that the ἐπίσκοπος of the Epistle to Timothy is the same as that of the Epistle to Titus; now the latter, as we have seen, is not a bishop, but a priest.[5]

2. We do not know what virtues Paul would have required from the future bishop if the monarchical episcopate had already existed in his churches. But we can form some idea

---

[1] Phil. i, 1 : τοῖς οὖσιν ἐν Φιλίπποις σὺν ἐπισκόποις καὶ διακόνοις.

[2] Titus i, 5-7 : ἵνα καταστήσῃς κατὰ πόλιν π ρ ε σ β υ τ έ ρ ο υ ς . . . εἴ τίς ἐστιν ἀ ν έ γ κ λ η τ ο ς . . . δεῖ γὰρ τὸν ἐπίσκοπον ἀ ν έ γ κ λ η τ ο ν εἶναι.

[3] Compare Acts xx, 17 with Acts xx, 28. St Irenæus supposes that Paul convoked the *bishops* of Ephesus and the *neighbouring cities* to Miletus. But in the text of the Acts only the church of Ephesus is in question.

[4] 1 Tim. iii, 1-2. Compare Titus i, 5-7.

[5] The synonymous character of the two terms πρεσβύτερος and ἐπίσκοπος in the New Testament was recognized by most of the ancient commentators : St John Chrysostom, Theodore of Mopsuestia, Theodoret, Ambrosiaster, St Jerome, Pelagius, Ammonius (in Cramer's *Catena in Act.* p. 337). But while Chrysostom adheres to *the simple synonymy of the names* (*In Philip. hom.*, i, 1 [LXXII, 183] we have οἱ πρεσβύτεροι τὸ παλαιὸν ἐ κ α λ ο ῦ ν τ ο ἐπίσκοποι . . . και οἱ ἐπίσκοποι πρεσβύτεροι; cf. *In Epist.* 1 *Tim. hom.*, xi, 1 ; *In Epist. ad Tit. hom.*, ii, 1), Jerome seems to admit the *primitive identity of the two orders* (*Epist.* cxlvi *ad Exuperant.*, XXII, 1193. Cf. *Epist.*, lxix *ad Oceanum*).

of them from those which he praises in Titus and Timothy, missionary bishops who served him as assistants. These are, above all, zeal, piety, fidelity, courage when put to the test, firmness in the performance of duty, the spirit of faith, and a life of self-abnegation and self-sacrifice. But the list of the qualities required of the *elders* exists in duplicate in the Pastoral Epistles, with certain differences not devoid of interest :

> It behoveth, therefore, a bishop to be blameless, married once only, sober, prudent, of good behaviour, chaste, given to hospitality, a teacher, not given to wine, no striker, but gentle, pacific, disinterested, but one that ruleth well his own house, having his children in subjection with all chastity—for if a man know not how to rule his own house, how shall he govern the Church of God ?—not a neophyte, lest, being puffed up with pride, he fall into the judgement of the devil. Moreover, he must have a good testimony of them who are without, lest he fall into reproach and the snare of the devil.
> I left thee in Crete . . . that thou shouldest ordain elders in every city, as I also appointed thee; if any be blameless, married once only, having faithful children, not accused of riot or unruly—for an *ἐπίσκοπος* must be without crime, as the steward of God ; not arrogant, not subject to anger, not given to wine, no striker, not greedy of filthy lucre ; but given to hospitality, a lover of goodness, prudent, just, pious, continent, embracing the true doctrine as it has been taught, that he may be able to exhort in sound doctrine and to convince the gainsayers.[1]

St Paul wishes a candidate who is worthy of the priesthood to fulfil three fundamental conditions : *he must be apt to teach, he must have a well-regulated house, and he must have been married only once.* The Protestants formerly made superhuman efforts to take from the words μιᾶς γυναικὸς ἀνηρ[2] their natural meaning. Some, despairing

---

[1] 1 Tim. iii, 3-7; Titus i, 6-9. There are some differences in these two lists : (*a*) *Three* qualities of the candidates for holy orders are peculiar to the first list : he must be *worthy* in his exterior (κόσμιος), *not a neophyte* and *esteemed by the pagans.*—(*b*) *Three* also are peculiar to the second: a *friend of good* (or perhaps of *good people*, φιλάγαθος), *just* (δίκαιος), pious (ὅσιος).—(*c*) The *twelve* others are common to the two lists, but *seven* are expressed by synonyms : *married once only*, *prudent* or *circumspect* (σώφρων), *hospitable* (φιλόξενος), *not a drinker* (μὴ πάροινος), *nor violent* (μὴ πλέκτης), *nor arrogant* (μὴ αὐθάδης, Titus i, 7 ; ἐπιεικής, 1 Tim. iii, 2), *neither disputatious* nor choleric (μὴ ὀργίλος, Titus i, 7 ; ἄμαχος, 1 Tim. iii, 2), *nor avaricious* (ἀφιλάργυρος, 1 Tim. iii, 2 ; μὴ αἰσχροκερδής, Titus i, 7), but *sober* (νηφάλιος, 1 Tim. iii, 2 ; ἐγκρατής, Titus i, 8), *irreproachable* (ἀνεπίληπτος, 1 Tim. iii, 2 ; ἀνέγκλητος, Titus i, 6-7), *able to teach* (διδακτικός, 1 Tim. iii, 2 ; in Titus i, 9 a periphrasis), *managing his house well* (a different expression in the two Epistles).
As is apparent, the terms are not quite synonymous. Ἀφιλάργυρος (" who loves not money, disinterested ") says much more than μὴ αἰσχροκερδής (" not grasping at gain ") ; Ἐγκρατής (" temperate, continent ") is stronger and more general than νηφάλιος (" sober ") ; Ἐπιεικής (" affable, approachable ") seems to express the virtue, of which αὐθάδης (" arrogant ") is the defect. The same remark applies to ἄμαχος (" pacific "), compared with μὴ ὀργίλος (" not irascible "). We shall notice, later on, the shade of difference between ἀνεπίληπτος and ἀνέγκλητος.
[2] Compare μιᾶς γυναικὸς ἀνὴρ (Titus i, 6 ; 1 Tim. iii, 2) with ἑνὸς ἀνδρὸς γυνή (1 Tim. v, 9), the meaning of which is not doubtful.

of winning their case, adopted the explanation proposed by Vigilantius and so vigorously denounced by St Jerome : " he must be married, he must have a wife." But it is evident that a candidate is not unsuited for ecclesiastical functions because he follows the example and counsel of St Paul himself. Most of them, therefore, maintain that the Apostle means merely to exclude anyone who is a bigamist or a polygamist, one who has still, or who has ever had, more than one wife *at the same time.* Their great reason is that he asks nothing more of the clergy than of the laity, and that he formally permits laymen to marry again. Now, the first assertion is a pure begging of the question; the second is just, but then the man who remarries retires from the clergy. It is not a fault for which he is blamed; but he fails to fulfil a required condition, just as does the neophyte, or one who is ignorant or incapable. Rationalistic exegesis has this good feature, that it is not afraid to attack Protestant orthodoxy boldly. It returns, therefore, without hesitation to the meaning maintained by Catholics, and many Protestants are accepting that meaning to-day. Indeed, it is impossible otherwise to explain the expression ἑνὸς ἀνδρὸς γυνή " married once only," which designates the widow who is admitted to the service of the Church. Only the desire to make lawful a personal situation, and afterwards the sectarian spirit, could cause the adoption of such a manifest distortion of Paul's thought.

In making fidelity to the first conjugal tie an absolute condition for elevation to the priesthood, the Apostle was no doubt guided by symbolical reasons; but it is certain that this was, especially at that epoch, a token of respectability. For the same motive, St Paul insists that the candidate for the priesthood, if he be married, should be at the head of an exemplary family and a well-regulated household.[1] The questionable conduct of his wife or children would lessen his influence and hamper his action, just as inability to maintain good order in his family and his affairs would show that he is unfitted for the government of the Church. The recommendations in regard to the good reputation of the candidate, either in the midst of the Christian community or among the pagans, are of the same character. How could the new priest win for himself the respect and sympathy of unbelievers if his conduct, after baptism, had been scandalous, or not wholly conformable to the severe moral code of the Gospel? His apostolate among them would be destined to failure in advance, for people do not readily listen to a preacher whom they do not respect. In the Christian communities which had been recently founded, it happened to be

[1] I Tim. iii, 4. This presupposes that the family is Christian ; but Titus i, 6 says so expressly (τέκνα ἔχων πιστά).

sometimes necessary to take consecrated ministers from among the new converts. But experience had shown the disadvantages of this course. Hence Paul forbids Timothy to lay his hands too soon upon anyone, and in particular adjures him not to ordain a neophyte,[1] for fear that, puffed up with pride by such a rapid elevation, he may have the fate of Lucifer. The injunction was a timely one for the Church of Ephesus, already ten or twelve years old, but it had less application to that of Crete, which, according to all appearances, had just been established. That is why the message to Titus omits this last clause.

As to the inward characteristics of one who is to be honoured by admission to the priesthood, one forcible word expresses them admirably : he must be *irreproachable,*[2] by reason of his high dignity and because he is the representative of God on earth. This word says everything : it comprises exemption from gross vices which would ruin his authority—such as avarice, anger, arrogance, brutality, drunkenness—and also the possession of virtues which will increase his prestige, such as sobriety, prudence, modesty, hospitality, justice, and purity of morals.

The qualities demanded of deacons are the same in due measure :

> Let deacons in like manner be chaste, not double-tongued, not given to much wine, not greedy of filthy lucre ; holding the mystery of faith in a pure conscience.
> And let these also first be proved ; and so let them minister without reproach as deacons.
> The women in like manner chaste, not slanderers, but sober, faithful in all things.
> Let deacons be the husbands of one wife ; who rule well their children and their own houses. For they that have ministered well shall purchase to themselves a good degree and much confidence in the faith which is in Christ Jesus.[3]

The deacons are to be exempt from three vices which would completely disqualify them in the eyes of the public—duplicity, intemperance, and avarice.

On account of their many and delicate relations with the laity, they had to guard themselves especially against the danger of *duplicity.*[4] They will avoid, therefore, saying now that a thing is white and now that it is black, and speaking

---

[1] I Tim. v, 22 : χεῖρας ταχέως μηδενὶ ἐπιτίθει.

[2] The word ἀνεπίληπτος (employed in I Tim. iii, 2) is perhaps a little stronger than ἀνέγκλητος (Titus i, 5). This would mean, according to a commentator on Thucydides (v, 17), one who is not only *actually* irreproachable, but one who offers no ground for criticism (μὴ παρέχων κατηγορίας ἀφορμήν. Theodoret gives almost the same definition.

[3] I Tim. iii, 8-13. The verse concerning women is explained later.

[4] We understand δίλογος like δίστομος, δίψυχος, δίγλωσσος.

sometimes in one way, at other times in another, in order to please their hearers or, at least, not to displease them.

The frequent visits which were part of their functions imposed upon them, more than others, the duty of sobriety.[1] Excesses of this sort, or even a general lack of decorum, would have been both injurious to their ministry and contrary to edification.

Lastly, *cupidity*[2] would have brought them into absolute disrepute. Doubtless the Apostle is not here alluding to possible embezzlements in the administration of worldly properties, of which the deacons had charge, but rather to the temptation of turning their ministry to their own personal advantage—for example, by accepting presents voluntarily offered. This indirect exploitation of the Gospel would be clearly the pursuit of sordid gain.

Paul also wishes the deacon to enjoy the prestige arising from *gravity* of manners and *dignity* of conduct, and, finally, to hold " the mystery of the faith in a pure conscience."[3] What has this incongruous injunction to do here? What does the mystery of the faith mean, and what relation has it with a pure conscience? We think that it is not a question of the subjective faith of the deacons, but of the mysteries of the Gospel, of which they are, in a certain measure, the dispensers. Whatever may be the precise meaning of this enigmatical expression, from the deacon is demanded an exemplary life and not merely the absence of the gross faults which would render him unqualified for his duties. This is why he must undergo a period of trial and is to be definitely promoted only if the test results to his honour and to the satisfaction of all.

3. On the border-line, and in a grade lower than the ecclesiastical hierarchy, were there then regularly appointed virgins and deaconesses?

In the passage of the Epistle to the Corinthians, in which the Apostle advises both sexes to observe continence and virginity, he bases his counsel on the greater liberty which they have for God's service, without any allusion to a special aptitude for serving the Church. The vow of virginity is presented as an act of individual perfection.[4] There are already virgins, but the *order* of virgins does not yet exist; above all, it has not yet taken a place beside the hierarchy. The pious Phœbe was a " servant " ($\delta\iota\acute{\alpha}\kappa o\nu o s$) of the

---

[1] *Non vino multo deditos.* But he does not demand that they should be abstainers. *Cf.* 1 Tim. v, 23.

[2] *Mὴ αἰσχροκερδεῖς.* *Ne sint turpilucricupidi* (a word of Plautus in *Trinummus*, I, ii, 63.

[3] *Ἔχοντας τὸ μυστήριον τῆς πίστεως ἐν καθαρᾷ συνειδήσει.*

[4] 1 Cor. vii, 8-9, 39, 40.

Church of Cenchræa, and a "patroness" (προστάτις) of the Christians who were employed at Corinth and of Paul himself.[1] This means that she had voluntarily consecrated herself to the *service* of the Church, and that she used her influence for the benefit of her co-religionists. In the terminology of St Paul, she had received from the Holy Spirit the *charismata* of the *deaconry* (διακονία) and of *help* (ἀντίληψις). Phœbe is called διάκονος, just as are Epaphras, Tychicus, the preachers of the Gospel, and all who serve the cause of the faith; she is not a deaconess in the ecclesiastical sense of the word. The wives of the deacons, mentioned in the First Epistle to Timothy, who are bound to more modesty, regularity of life, and piety, in order not to compromise the ministry of their husbands, are not deaconesses either.[2] The deaconesses whom the customs of the East made it necessary to establish in certain Asiatic provinces came only later.[3] There is no trace of them in the writings of St Paul.

The institution of widows, on the contrary, goes back to the apostolic age. They had their prototype in the pious women who accompanied our Lord from city to city, and

---

[1] Rom. xvi, 1-2 : οὖσαν διάκονον τῆς ἐκκλησίας τῆς ἐν Κενχρεαῖς (*quae est in ministerio ecclesiae*). The word διάκονος in St Paul is too indeterminate to be regarded by itself as a hierarchical term. We think that the services which justify Phœbe's epithet of διάκονος are indicated subsequently, xvi, 2 : καὶ γὰρ αὐτὴ προστάτις πολλῶν ἐγενήθη καὶ ἐμοῦ αὐτοῦ. She possessed the *charisma* of the διακονία (Rom. xii, 7; 1 Cor. xii, 5), which has nothing to do with the diaconate.

[2] 1 Tim. iii, 8-10 : Διακόνους ὡσαύτως σεμνούς . . . ἔχοντας τὸ μυστήριον τῆς πίστεως ἐν καθαρᾷ συνειδήσει· (καὶ οὗτοι δὲ δοκιμαζέσθωσαν πρῶτον, εἶτα διακονείτωσαν ἀνέγκλητοι ὄντες)· γυναῖκας ὡσαύτως σεμνάς, μὴ διαβόλους, νηφαλίους, πιστὰς ἐν πᾶσιν. Διάκονοι ἔστωσαν μιᾶς γυναικὸς ἄνδρες, κτλ. The first accusative διακόνους depends on δεῖ εἶναι expressed previously (iii, 2), before the qualities required of the ἐπίσκοπος. It is a question whether the accusative γυναῖκας also depends on δεῖ εἶναι or on the participle ἔχοντας which qualifies the deacons. In the latter case, these women would be simply the wives of the deacons, to whom a more exemplary conduct is prescribed, which is also required from the children of ecclesiastical dignitaries (iii, 4-12). In the former case, they might have the rank of deaconesses, since they are enumerated after the two orders of the local clergy. But this hypothesis seems wholly improbable. Indeed, why should Paul call these deaconesses "women," instead of giving them the name of διάκονοι, which is both feminine and masculine? And how can we suppose that he is speaking of deaconesses before he has finished speaking of deacons, cutting thus in two the enumeration of their qualities and aptitudes? It is necessary, therefore, to make the accusative γυναῖκας depend on the participle ἔχοντας, and to regard verse 10 as a parenthesis. There is doubtless a slight carelessness in style in attaching to the same verb two objects so incongruous (τὸ μυστήριον τῆς πίστεως and γυναῖκας); but no one will say that such carelessness is contrary to Pauline usage. On the other hypothesis the carelessness and confusion would be serious in another way.

[3] They are mentioned in the *Apostolic Constitutions*, ii, 26; iii, 15 (διάκονοι); viii, 19, 20, 28 (διακόνισσαι). Pliny the Younger (*Epist.*, x, 97) put two Christian servants (*ancillae*) to the torture: *quae ministrae dicebantur. Ministrae* is the Latin translation of διάκονοι or διακόνισσαι.

perhaps in those whom certain apostles, such as Peter and the brethren of the Lord, caused to attend them.[1] Paul recognizes that a widow has complete liberty to contract a second marriage, although he advises her in general to remain in the state of widowhood.[2] This somewhat vague advice might open the door to certain inconveniences, and the Apostle, instructed by experience, saw himself obliged to make it precise. He makes it a duty for persons in easy circumstances to receive the widows of their families who desired to remain unmarried, so that they may not be a burden to the Church. Paul gives us to understand that generous women willingly accepted the duty of supporting widows at their expense, in order not to burden the common fund. As for the widows who were still young and without resources, he advises them to marry again.[3] No doubt there had been some abuses in the community. Some widows were attracted by the prospect of idleness and independence, and caused their names to be inscribed on the books of the Church, making profession of widowhood. But soon, disappointed as to Christ and impelled by sensual desires, they offered the melancholy spectacle of levity, idleness, devotion to trifles, running from house to house and scandalizing everybody by their impertinent chatter. They are guilty of having violated their sworn faith and of having furnished to the evil-minded a pretext for calumniating the Gospel. Paul wishes that henceforth there should be inscribed on the books of the Church (καταλεγέσθω) only widows who are at least sixty years old, whose conduct has been tested, whose life is exemplary, and who do not cause fear of either scandal or inconstancy. To true widows (ταῖς ὄντως χήραις) who make profession of widowhood under the sanction of the Church, are to be paid the honours which their state, their virtues, and the services which they render deserve. It was they, no doubt, who by their lessons and example trained young Christian maidens to piety and good conduct; they also perhaps taught the faith to the neophytes of their sex. Working indirectly for the altar they had the right to live of the altar. The Apostle does not grant them any other prerogatives. He, who forbade women to speak in the church, was not disposed to assign them a share in the exercise of its sacred functions.

---

[1] 1 Cor. ix, 5. *Cf.* viii, 2; Luke xxiii, 49; Mark xv, 40-41.
[2] 1 Cor. vii, 39-40.   [3] 1 Tim. v, 3-16.

BOOK VI
THE EPISTLE TO THE HEBREWS

CHAPTER I

INTRODUCTION

I—The Question of Authorship

1. Character and Style of the Epistle. 2. Eastern and Western Tradition. 3. Pretended Relations with Philo. 4. Various Conjectures.

1. ALONE among the Epistles of the New Testament the Epistle to the Hebrews is anonymous. The introduction, in which the author usually discloses his name and titles, is suppressed. The allusion to chains—which might be those of Paul—rests upon a false reading.[1] Some rather vague characteristics, which present certain difficulties, have suggested St Paul, but may very well suit other writers : " Know ye that our brother Timothy is set at liberty; with whom (if he come shortly) I will see you. . . . The brethren from Italy salute you."[2] This is the most definite detail; and in these few words there are three ambiguities. Elsewhere the author seems to distinguish himself very clearly from the first generation of Christians and to number himself among those who have received the Gospel at second hand.[3] At least, nothing thus far betrays a distinct personality.

The style completes our bewilderment. Nothing differs more from the language and manner of Paul. I do not speak merely of the choice of words, to which too much importance is often given in questions of authenticity, although the absence of certain expressions and particles which Paul does not seem able to dispense with, and the presence of phrases

---

[1] Heb. x, 34 : τοῖς δεσμοῖς μου. In spite of the antiquity of this reading, attested by the *Sinaiticus* and five other uncial manuscripts (E H K L P), it is certainly necessary to read with the Vulgate : τοῖς δεσμίοις, *vinctis.*

[2] Heb. xiii, 23-24 : Γινώσκετε τὸν ἀδελφὸν ἡμῶν Τιμόθεον ἀπολελυμένον. . . . Ἀσπάζονται ὑμᾶς οἱ ἀπὸ τῆς Ἰταλίας.—(a) Γινώσκετε is probably in the imperative, as in Gal. iii, 7, but it might be in the indicative.— (b) ἀπολελυμένον signifies probably " delivered from prison," but it might signify " declared absolved of an accusation brought against him."— (c) οἱ ἀπὸ τῆς Ἰταλίας may be translated " the brethren *who are in Italy,*" or " the brethren who are *natives of Italy,*" whatever may be their place of sojourn at the time. As the preposition ἀπό is the principal argument of those who maintain that the Epistle was not written in Italy, but was addressed to a community of Italy, Deissmann's note (*Theol. Rundschau*, vol. v, p. 64) will be read with interest, which proves, referring to Bröse (*Theol. Stud. und Krit.*, 1898, pp. 351-360) that at that epoch οἱ ἀπὸ Ἰταλίας currently signified " those who are in Italy."

[3] Heb. ii, 3 : ὑπὸ τῶν ἀκουσάντων εἰς ἡμᾶς ἐβεβαιώθη (σωτηρία).

foreign to his terminology, give us food for thought; I refer to the diction in its broadest sense, images, comparisons, and the way of conceiving and presenting things. We can only subscribe to the verdict of Origen : " The style of the Epistle called that to the Hebrews is of a totally different character from that of the Apostle. . . . The Epistle is written in better Greek, as everyone who is capable of forming a judgement in this matter must admit." It is sufficient to read the first paragraph, so musical, so well balanced and harmonious, to be convinced that it is not of Paul's writing. And the sequel does not belie the promises of the beginning. No biblical author, not even excepting St Luke, writes so purely. There are few Hebraisms, and very few of those irregularities and inaccuracies—anacolutha, hyperbata, sense constructions—which fairly swarm in the Pauline Epistles. The perfect connection of the ideas in the discourse, the art of natural transitions, the oratorical tone maintained without effort, the mastery of a language which is always copious and rhythmical, distinguish him clearly from Paul. The eloquence of the latter, made up of passion and logic, resembles an impetuous torrent which bursts its dykes, while the Epistle which we are now considering is like a majestic river, the windings of which only afford relief from its monotony.

The Epistle is full of reminiscences and biblical allusions; but its way of quoting and using the Old Testament is very far from Pauline. The Apostle almost always quotes from memory, often combining fragments of texts, while the author of this Epistle copies his manuscript of the Greek Bible word for word and never allows himself to make composite citations. Although he usually follows the Septuagint version, Paul does not fail to have recourse to the original when it is too divergent; the author of this Epistle, on the contrary, nowhere shows any knowledge of the Hebrew, even in case of remarkable divergence between the two texts. Paul only attributes directly to God the words put by Scripture into the mouth of God; the other calls *words of God* even scriptural passages, in which God is spoken of in the third person. Finally, the formulas of quotation are entirely different, as a simple comparison is sufficient to show : the Epistle to the Hebrews does not once employ the expression *as it is written* ($\gamma \acute{\epsilon} \gamma \rho a \pi \tau a \iota$), which is the usual form of the Apostle.

2. And yet it is the best judges of style, the Fathers of Alexandria, who unanimously, as far back as one can go, see in it the work of Paul. Clement, following his master Pantænus, Origen, St Dionysius, St Peter, St Alexander, St Athanasius, Didymus, St Cyril, Euthalius—Arius himself apparently—all, without one exception, agree in this. Not

that they shut their eyes to the differences in style. In order
to explain it, Clement supposed that the letter, written
originally in Hebrew, had been translated into Greek by St
Luke—an untenable hypothesis undefended now by anyone.
If there is one thing positive, it is that the Epistle was composed in Greek. Never has a translation had such supple-
ness and freedom of movement. The author of it makes use
of the Septuagint exclusively, even when its writers depart
from the original text. He pours forth a perfect stream of
plays upon words, assonances, and alliterations to a degree
impossible in a translator. The art with which he rounds
his periods would be an unheard-of literary feat if he had to
deal with the little juxtaposed and co-ordinated clauses of
some Hebrew original.

Finally, to say nothing of the rest, the reasoning based
upon the double meaning of the word διαθήκη—covenant and
testament—would be absolutely impossible in Hebrew.
According to Origen, the ideas are Paul's and the diction
that of one of his disciples known to God alone. "The
historical documents which have come down to us," adds
Origen, "name either Clement, Bishop of Rome, or Luke,
the author of the Gospel and the Acts," as the writer of this
Epistle. Thus, though fully conscious that there are difficulties, Origen holds to what he calls the ancient tradition
and practically, forgetting his doubts as critic and linguist,
he quotes the Epistle without hesitation under Paul's name.
Eusebius does the same, although he places it once among
the number of disputed writings, out of deference to the
opinion of others. All the Greek Church, with the Council
of Antioch (264) and that of Laodicea (390), with St Gregory
Thaumaturgus, St Cyril of Jerusalem, St Isidore of Pelusium,
St Epiphanius, St Basil and the two Gregories, St John
Chrysostom and Theodore of Mopsuestia, Severianus of
Gabala, the Syrian Church with the Peshitto, with St
Ephraem and St James of Nisibis, give the same testimony
as the Alexandrians. In a word, the East is unanimous.

Very different was the situation in the West. Known at
Rome, from the time of the first century, by St Clement,
who makes use of it as his own property, the Epistle to the
Hebrews was not generally regarded either as authentic or
canonical. The Muratorian fragment and the priest Caius
recognize only thirteen Epistles of St Paul. Neither St
Irenæus nor St Hippolytus, according to Gobar, admit its
authenticity; it is a fact that the former does not once quote
from it in his great work against heresies, and it is doubtful
whether he ever makes an allusion to it. St Cyprian refrains
also from citing it; and when he affirms, with several other
Latin writers, that Paul wrote to seven churches, he seems,
indeed, equivalently to deny that it is the work of the Apostle.

Tertullian, on what ground is unknown, attributes it to Barnabas, and the way in which he quotes it shows quite well that he does not believe it to be canonical. Among the heretics, Marcion rejected it; but, on the contrary, the banker Theodotus, the leader of the obscure sect of the followers of Melchisedech, accepted it. We do not know what the attitude of Novatus and Novatian was in regard to it, but we have no reason to claim, as has sometimes been done, that they took advantage of it to deny the Church's right to remit sins. In the fourth century doubts on this point still persisted, and were not yet dissipated in the fifth. Nevertheless, St Jerome exaggerates when he maintains that the Latins were not accustomed to receive the Epistle as canonical; there were disputes and disagreements, and there was no unanimity either in one direction or the other. If Ambrosiaster and Pelagius do not comment on it, if Phebadius, Optatus of Milevis, Zeno, Vincent of Lerins and Orosius make no use of it, if the codex Claromontanus and the codex Mommseianus exclude it from their canon, Victorinus, Hilary of Poitiers, Ambrose of Milan, Lucifer of Cagliari, Pacian, Faustinus and Rufinus are favourable to it; Pelagius and Ambrosiaster quote it sometimes unreservedly; and Philaster, contradicting himself, treats somewhere as heretics those who attribute it to anyone but Paul. It must be said that Philaster, according to the fine observation of St Augustine, attaches to the word " heretic " a meaning peculiar to him. But when the Council of Hippo in 393 and that of Carthage in 397 had inscribed in the list of canonical books thirteen Epistles of Paul and the Epistle to the Hebrews of the same Apostle, when Innocent I in his letter to Exuperius of Toulouse in 405 and the Council of Carthage in 419 had simply catalogued fourteen Epistles of St Paul, the old doubts about its canonicity disappeared, and, although no new argument was brought forth in favour of its authenticity, little by little people accepted the general opinion or at least the usual way of speaking about it. Only the scholars, such as Isidore of Seville, retained the memory of the past discussions, the trace of which still exists in the place assigned to the Epistle, either in the tenth rank, or at the end of the Pauline Epistles, or even outside of the series.

It was precisely when the question appeared to have been decided irrevocably by three councils of which he had been the soul, that Augustine began to doubt its authenticity. His scruples increased steadily and, while formerly he had been accustomed to quote the Epistle as Paul's, he abstained from doing so in his last years, or did so only with express reservations. The idea did not occur to him that the decision of a council would settle the question, any more than it occurred to St Jerome, who, after having been present at the Roman Council where the Epistle to the Hebrews had been

for the first time attributed to Paul, did not fear to write :
*Nihil interesse cujus sit, cum ecclesiastici viri sit et quotidie
Ecclesiarum lectione celebretur.* The public reading of the
Epistle was an argument in favour of the canonicity, but did
not at all prejudice the authenticity of an anonymous writing.
To bind canonicity to authenticity and to maintain, as Cajetan
did, that, if the Epistle were not from Paul, it would not be
canonical, is one of the greatest of theological errors. It is,
indeed, only by an abuse of language that authenticity is here
spoken of, for *authentic* is the opposite of *apocryphal,* and
nothing in the Epistle leads us to suspect that the author
wished to pass himself off as Paul.

Since Origen's time the question has not advanced.
Although originated by Clement of Alexandria, accepted by
Eusebius and St Jerome, and adopted subsequently by several
theologians of the Middle Ages, the hypothesis of a translator
who clothed the Hebrew original of Paul in Greek, even
taking the word translator in the broadest sense, is wholly
abandoned to-day and does not now merit a refutation.

On the other hand, the authors suggested instead of Paul
are not very satisfactory. Harnack proposes Aquila and
Priscilla, especially the latter, because of some doubtfully
feminine touch discoverable in the Epistle. Godet, without
much more foundation, thought of Silas. Some ancient
writers name Luke and Clement of Rome, either as trans.
lators or editors. It is certain that Clement knew and made
use of our Epistle, but his style is so different that it can be
affirmed with certainty that it does not belong to him. He
co-ordinates his sentences instead of subordinating them, he
abounds in doxologies, he quotes Scripture in a way peculiar
to himself, and, finally, all his ideas and his manner of expressing them show another cast of mind. Against St Luke we
should be less positive, principally because of the authorities
who favour him. He has this in common with the author
of the Epistle, that he writes Greek with purity and moves
in the sphere of Pauline ideas. His relations with Timothy
and his sojourn in Rome furnish two other favourable data.
As Clement of Alexandria remarked, there exists between
the Epistle and the Acts a certain affinity in the use of words
and in diction. But in addition to the fact that the points
of contact have nothing decisive or even striking in them,
how can we persuade ourselves that St Luke, a converted
pagan, could know the Mosaic ritual so thoroughly and take
so much interest in observances of no value in his eyes?
And St Luke nowhere betrays the peculiar rhetoric and
Alexandrine culture with which the writer of the Epistle
seems imbued. It is this last characteristic which has caused
some to think of Apollos as the author, who was put forward
by Luther and supported by numerous critics. Apollos was
one of the confidants of Paul and was acquainted with

Timothy; he was from Alexandria and might have frequented the school of Philo; he was very eloquent and "very well versed in the Scriptures." But that proves at most that Apollos *might* have composed the Epistle to the Hebrews, if there were no decisive objection. Now it is not easy to see either when or how Apollos could have acquired the right to speak as a master to the Jewish-Christian Church, and it must not be forgotten that the theory which attributes our Epistle to him is wholly devoid of historical foundation and traditional support.

As far as hypotheses go, Barnabas is to be preferred. He has in his favour the positive testimony of Tertullian and of a considerable part of the West. He was a Jew by race, a Hellenist by education; as a Levite, he was familiar with the Mosaic ritual, and as a citizen of Cyprus Alexandrian literature must have been familiar to him; moreover, he possessed great authority in Jerusalem and in the churches of Palestine. It is true, if the Epistle published under his name more than a century ago was his work, we could not think of him for a moment, but the scholars of our day are more and more agreed that the so-called Epistle of Barnabas is not by Barnabas at all. Hence there is no longer any valid objection to him, and he could be considered as the editor of the Epistle under the direction or the inspiration of Paul himself.

3. Certain modern critics, giving up all hope of finding the name of the great unknown, are satisfied with pointing out as the author an Alexandrine, or "a disciple of Paul, tinged with Philonism."[1] This formula is deceptive. If we limit ourselves to a general and superficial comparison, we easily find quite numerous points of contact between our author and Philo; but if we press the parallel with texts in support, most of the similarities vanish or take a contrary meaning. Philo, indeed, calls his Logos high priest, messenger, mediator, and intercessor; but what honourable titles does he not give to the Logos?[2] Moreover, the Logos of Philo

---

[1] Jülicher, *Einleitung in das N.T.*[4], 1901, p. 135. The author considers the dependence upon Philo very likely. Davidson, more reserved (*Introduction*,[2] London, 1882, vol. i, p. 219), says merely *probable*. On the other hand, Riehm, Reuss, Weiss, Beyschlag and Schmiedel see hardly any connection; while other critics (Siegfried, Holtzmann, Ménégoz, etc.) regard it as almost certain. Bruce (in Hastings' *Dict. of the Bible*, vol. ii, p. 335) thus comes nearest the mark: "An infallible means of misunderstanding the Epistle would be to be too sure that the author belongs to the school of Philo."

[2] *Quis rer. divin. heres.* (Mangey, vol. i, p. 501). The Logos is the *luminous cloud* (Exod. xiv, 19) which protects friends and removes enemies. It is called on this occasion ἀρχάγγελος, μεθόριος, ἱκέτης, πρεσβευτής, and further on (p. 504) μέσος τῶν ἄκρων ἀμφοτέροις ὁμηρεύων. It is difficult to imagine a title of honour which Philo does not apply to the Logos.

is high priest of the universe, the immense temple of divinity, as reason is the high priest of that other temple of God, man;[1] what connection is there here with the high priest of the new covenant? We are assured that the Logos of Philo, like the Son in the Epistle to the Hebrews, is called the ἀπαύγασμα and the χαρακτήρ of the divine substance; but the Epistle certainly borrows the former appellation from the Book of Wisdom; and in Philo it is the human soul, not the Logos, that is the χαρακτήρ of God.[2] Some have wished to see a striking analogy in the way in which the two authors treat the history of Melchisedech; but Philo emphasizes chiefly the offering of bread and wine, of which the Epistle says not a word, and the resemblance is reduced finally to a very ordinary etymology, for no one is ignorant of the fact that in Hebrew *melek* signifies king and that *zedeq* means justice.[3]

As for the rest, the use of allegory by the two writers has nothing in common : the allegories of Philo are only moral symbols tending towards an accommodative sense; those of the Epistle to the Hebrews, if we insist on calling them by that name, are prophetic types. The same difficulty—still more pronounced—exists at another point where similarities are sought for in vain. The two writers often oppose heaven to earth, the visible to the invisible, the temporal to the eternal, the image to reality; but while the Alexandrian philosopher turns towards the past and, beyond the world of phenomena, contemplates the world of ideas, the intelligible world (κόσμος νοητός) which has served him as an archetype, the gaze of the saintly writer is constantly turned towards the future, and the events of Jewish history are the book in which he reads the destiny of the heavenly Jerusalem, unchangeable and eternal. We will not dwell upon similarities of less value, many of which are purely imaginary.[4] Have not some critics claimed that " the word of God more piercing than any two-edged sword "[5] ought to be derived from the

---

[1] *De Somniis*, i (Mangey, vol. i, p. 653).

[2] *Quod deter. pot. insid.* (vol. i, p. 207). After having said that the spirit is the essence of the soul (πνεῦμά ἐστιν ἡ ψυχῆς οὐσία) Philo defines the spirit thus : οὐκ ἀέρα κινούμενον ἀλλὰ τύπον τινὰ καὶ χαρακτῆρα θείας δυνάμεως.

[3] *Leg. alleg.*, iii (vol. i, pp. 102-103).

[4] Holtzmann (*Lehrbuch der neutest. Theolog.* 1889, vol. ii, p. 294) says that the Logos of Philo is, like the Son of the Epistle, *Erhalter und Träger der Welt* (I[3] φέρων τὰ πάντα = *Quis divin. rerum her.* 7 τὰ ὄντα φέρων καὶ τὰ πάντα γεννῶν). There is here a twofold and serious mistake. Philo does not write τὰ ὄντα φέρων, but τὰ μὴ ὄντα φέρων (this is the text of the manuscripts and editions, including that of Wendland) ; moreover, he does not say this of the Logos, but of God.

[5] Heb. iv, 12 : ὁ λόγος τοῦ Θεοῦ ἐνεργὴς τομώτερος ὑπὲρ πᾶσαν μάχαιραν δίστομον. The *word* is here the word of the prophets and definitely, the word (προφορικός) of the Word (ἐνδιάθετος). The idea that the word is more piercing than a sword is very common among the sacred (Eph. vi, 17 ;

λόγος τομεύς of Philo? As if the *dividing* Logos of Philo were anything but a demiurge, occupied in separating the elements of chaotic matter, a conception entirely foreign to the Epistle. The word more piercing than a sword (λόγος τομώτερος) is the prophetic word, infallibly attaining its aim. As to the verb μετριοπαθεῖν (to moderate one's feelings or passions), which belonged to the philosophical language of that age, one must be truly short of arguments to maintain that the author of the Epistle must have borrowed it from Philo.[1]

4. If the dependence of the Epistle upon Philo is more and more problematical in proportion as it is closely studied, its dependence on Paul—a dependence of ideas, not of words —becomes from day to day more evident. It is admitted at present by the majority of critics. The impression received from a repeated reading of it is well expressed by one of the best biblical linguistic scholars : " The resemblance of its thoughts with those of Paul becomes at once apparent with constantly increasing evidence, and at the same time we are more and more surprised that anyone should have been found to attribute its style and diction to Paul."[2] We are, therefore, brought back to the opinion of Origen, shared again in our day by the majority of critics and exegetes, both Catholic and heterodox. Origen distinguished between the author and the editor, making the share taken by the latter a very large one. Paul would then have furnished the ideas and inspiration, and a disciple of Paul, known only to God, would have collected them into a whole from memory, adding the necessary explanations to them.[3] It is to him that the diction,

---

Apoc. i, 16 ; ii, 12, etc.) and profane writers. The verse of Phocylides (116) presents a striking analogy with our text :

Ὅπλον τοι λόγος ἀνδρὶ τομώτερόν ἐστι σιδήρου.

As to the λόγος τομεύς of Philo (*Quis rerum divin. heres.*, Mangey, vol. i, pp. 491, 503, 506) apropos of Gen. xv, 10, it is the divine Intelligence, which divides all creatures and leaves without division only itself and human reason (νοῦς, λογισμός, which becomes τομεύς in its turn).

[1] See Cremer, *Wörterbuch*,[9] 1902, pp. 799-800.

[2] Moulton, *Commentary for English Readers*, vol. iii, (1884), p. 279.

[3] Eusebius, *Hist. eccl.*, vi, 25 (XX, 584-585) has preserved for us the actual words of Origen : Ἐγὼ δὲ ἀποφαινόμενος εἴποιμ' ἄν ὅτι τὰ μὲν νοήματα τοῦ Ἀποστόλου ἐστὶν ἡ δὲ φράσις καὶ ἡ σύνθεσις ἀπομνημονεύσαντός τινος τὰ ἀποστολικὰ καὶ ὡσπερεὶ σχολιογραφήσαντος τὰ εἰρημένα ὑπὸ τοῦ διδασκάλου. He adds that if any church regards the Epistle as being Paul's, it is to be praised, for the ancients have handed down this opinion to us not without cause. But God only knows who really *wrote* it (τίς δὲ ὁ γράψας τὴν ἐπιστολὴν τὸ μὲν ἀληθὲς Θεὸς οἶδεν). Some propose Clement of Rome (ἔγραψε τὴν ἐπιστολήν); others Luke. Thus, according to Origen, the editor of the Epistle is not a simple copyist writing under dictation, but a writer (γράψας, ἔγραψεν), whose is the diction and the composition (ἡ φράσις καὶ ἡ σύνθεσις), but who records the thoughts and words (τὰ νοήματα, τὰ

the arrangement of the parts, in a word the composition, is due. He was the writer of a work of which Paul
remains the author. It was said formerly in the same sense
that the second Gospel was the Gospel of Peter, and the third
Gospel that of Paul, because St Mark and St Luke were
thought to have reproduced respectively the preaching of the
two great apostles. The hypothesis of Origen is sufficiently
elastic to yield to all the requirements of criticism. It takes
account of the similitudes and the differences, and satisfies the
data of tradition. We think it is necessary to adhere to this,
and to-day the majority of Catholics, with infinite shades of
opinion that it is neither possible nor useful to discuss, think
the same. Directly or indirectly, the basis of the Epistle is
Paul's; the form is that of an unknown person, whose name
is known to God alone.

II—HISTORICAL SETTING AND CENTRAL IDEA

1. The Epistle is addressed to Jewish Christians in Palestine.
2. Dominant Idea and Division.

1. The question of date and destination has only a secondary
interest for the theologian. Let the critics, if they will, look
for the recipients of this Epistle at Rome or Alexandria, at
Antioch, Corinth, Thessalonica, nay, even at Ravenna or the
town of Jamnia. Most of these fantasies are not worth
referring to; at most the partisans of Rome and Alexandria
deserve a word of mention. Alexandria would have some
chance if the recipients of an Epistle were necessarily of the
same country as the author, and if the author could not have
acquired Alexandrian culture outside of Alexandria; but it is
a bad sign for a theory if it must be built upon a pure hypothesis; and how can it be explained that the Alexandrian
Fathers, always from the very first unanimous in their reception of our Epistle as canonical, never had the least suspicion that this Epistle was written to their Church? The
only motive for thinking of Rome is the salutation of the
brethren of Italy, if we understand by οἱ ἀπὸ τῆς Ἰταλίας
not the Christians residing in Italy, but those who are natives
of Italy. An ambiguous phrase is very little upon which to
establish an hypothesis, which is, moreover, devoid of any
traditional foundation, and so much the more as this text,
even in the most favourable sense, brings us indeed to Italy,
but not to Rome. Is it conceivable that in the Roman
Church, composed in a very large majority of converted

εἰρημένα)¹ of the Apostle, which he has preserved in his memory (ἀπομνη-
μονεύσαντος), and which he explains or comments on, when there is need of
it, as formerly grammarians and annotators did in the case of obscure
passages of the classic authors (σχολιογραφήσαντος).

pagans, there was so great an infatuation for the Mosaic ritual that it was in danger of apostatizing rather than give it up? To say that the author only addresses a little group of Jewish Christians (Zahn), or that he is writing only to the particular assembly gathered in the house of Aquila and Priscilla (Harnack), is to complicate an arbitrary inference with an improbability.

The old theory which placed the receivers of this Epistle in Palestine is still the most probable. It possesses a respectable amount of tradition in its favour which no opposing tradition outweighs, and the title (πρὸς Ἑβραίους), although not forming part of the primitive text, goes back at least to the second century, since it is found in all the manuscripts and in all the translations; finally, it has in its favour the incredible variety and inconsistency of the hypotheses which men have tried to substitute for it. Above all, it possesses, together with the concordant facts of date and place, intrinsic characteristics; " a pronounced ' smack of Jewish soil ' and such a complete absence of any allusion to pagan civilization, that we have difficulty in understanding how the slightest indication can be found in it of readers who have left paganism."[1]

In our opinion, it is impossible to place the composition of this Epistle later than the catastrophe of A.D. 70. The Temple is still standing, and the Mosaic ritual still in full vigour. The author, it is true, refers to the biblical description of the tabernacle and to the written legislation of the Pentateuch without taking into account the modifications introduced into it in the course of time, either because he takes it for granted that practice is conformable to the rule, or, rather, in order to give his typology a scriptural foundation; but the reader constantly feels that he is not fighting with shadows, but that his polemic is aimed at actual realities. After the fall of the Temple, which marked the end of sacrifices, and after the ruin of Jerusalem without any human hope of its restoration, the state of mind of those to whom the Epistle was addressed would be an insoluble enigma. But, previous to that fateful date, their temptation is explicable. They regretted the loss of the worship of their ancestors, with the pomp and splendour of its solemnities, poorly compensated for, in their eyes, by the spiritual character of Christianity. Detested, calumniated, and persecuted as turncoats by their compatriots, thoughts of discourage-

---

[1] Ménégoz, *Théol. de l'Ép. aux Hébreux*, p. 28. The arguments of Weizsäcker, Schürer, Pfleiderer and von Soden, who think that the recipients were pagan converts, reduce themselves first to the mention of the *living* God (iii, 12; ix, 14; x, 31), a biblical expression liked by the author, but which obviously does not indicate the quality of his readers ; secondly to the enumeration of elementary doctrines (vi, 12) better suited, it is said, to Gentile neophytes than to Jewish converts.

ment and apostasy invaded their souls. Some were looking backward and perhaps were already beginning to experience a spirit of defection. They were on the eve of a great national crisis; Judaism was struggling in the convulsions of a death-agony which might have to many the appearance of a resurrection. The hour was a critical one for the Jewish Christians. It was necessary for them to make common cause with the fanatical patriots of the nation or else to break with them, defying their anger and maledictions; it was necessary for them to deny Christ or to go with him out of the camp, bearing his reproach. The Jewish Christians chose the latter course when, in A.D. 66 or 67, at the approach of Titus, they took refuge in Pella, not without leaving behind them, doubtless, more than one misguided or undecided brother. It is to strengthen them in the faith that the Apostle sent them his Epistle.

2. The Epistle to the Hebrews is a real letter and not a thesis or a homily. It has the well-arranged plan, the regular advance, and the fine concatenation of proofs and developments characteristic of the dogmatic treatise; it recalls also the homily by its oratorical tone, loftier than that required in ordinary correspondence, and by the continual introduction of speculative views and ethical conclusions. Nevertheless, it must certainly be placed in the epistolary category. It is addressed to a limited circle, whose strong and weak points are perfectly well known to the author, who exalts their virtues, reproves their faults, and tries to ward off their dangers. The Epistle is not, therefore, a treatise; it is a letter which has in it something of the homily, if you will, and which its author defines most accurately when he calls it "a word of exhortation." As such, its aim is immediate and practical; the dogma in it is not the occasion of its moral teaching; it is the moral teaching which is the reason for the existence of the dogma. The author—who makes no secret of it—wishes to restrain the Jewish Christians who are on the very brink of the abyss. He shows them how fatal would be their fall, and how senseless also, since it would be a return from the perfect to the imperfect, from the light of the Gospel to the twilight of the old order of things. In order to prove that the law of grace is a better religion, he establishes the fact that it is a religion which is definite, immutable, ideal, and eternal.

Since every religion is meant to facilitate man's approach to God and to unite us with him, it follows that the value of a religion must be measured by the more or less efficacious way in which it attains this aim. Now, the duty of bringing about this close relation between heaven and earth falls especially upon the priest, the appointed intermediary between man and God. Here, therefore, are the three postulates which the author of the Epistle constantly presupposes and which the reader must never lose sight of. The value of a religious institution is measured by the union which it produces between man and God. This union is the more intimate in proportion as the mediating priest approaches the ideal. The value and efficacy of the sacrifice assign his position to the priest. But while the parallel between Judaism and Christianity, which forms the real subject of the Epistle, remains hidden, or hardly appears upon the surface, the contrast between the mediators of the two religions and their sacerdotal functions form its apparent and external framework. The long passages concerning morals are so closely connected with the proofs and are introduced so naturally that they do not interrupt the course of the demonstration.

At first glance we distinguish the following three parts, in which dogma and morals blend in a harmonious whole : the *Person of Christ* in contrast to that of other mediators, prophets, angels, Moses, and Joshua. Exhortation to obedience and fidelity (chaps. i-iv).—*The Priesthood of Christ*, a priest according to the order of Melchisedech in contrast to the Levitical priesthood. Exhortation to the ideal and most perfect (chaps. v-vii).—*The Sacrifice of Christ* in contrast to the sacrifice of the day of expiation. The dangers of unbelief, the worth of faith, exhortation to perseverance (chaps. viii-xiii).

We shall follow this division, adding a supplementary chapter on the contrast between the two covenants and the two systems, a contrast which is the underlying basis of the Epistle.

CHAPTER II

CHRIST THE MEDIATOR

I—THE PERSON OF CHRIST

1. The Son of God, the Image and Imprint of the Father. 2. Creator of the World. 3. Phase of Humiliation and Life of Glory.

1. JUDAISM, independently of its priesthood, had three kinds of mediators : the prophets, the angels, and Moses. The prophets were extraordinary messengers, commissioned at moments of great religious crisis to warn the people against apostasies and to keep alive the Messianic hope.[1] The whole Old Testament shows us the active rôle of the angels as messengers of God, but it is especially in the covenant of Sinai that their action is exercised.[2] As to Moses, whose name alone evokes the idea of the mediator *par excellence*,[3] he arrives at the end of the series, after the prophets and the angels, as the final stage of an ascending gradation. How small these mediators become when compared with Jesus ! Comparison in this case serves only to make more prominent his incomparable grandeur. The *prophets* spoke in the name of God, or, rather, God spoke in them and by them ; but this was *aforetime,* in distant ages, and to the *patriarchs,* long since dead, and in the childhood of the race ; and their revelation was *fragmentary,* distributed by instalments, in time and space. *Now,* on the contrary, at the end of the ages and after all the providential preparations for the event, God has spoken to *us,* heirs of the patriarchs, by the *Son* and in him. It is evident that a revelation made little by little, in scraps and fragments (πολυμερῶς) and in divers manners, by figures, symbols, and allegories (πολυτρόπως) is neither perfect nor final, and cannot be put on the same level with the revelation of him who possesses in himself all the treasures of wisdom and knowledge.[4]

[1] On the rôle of the prophets *cf.* Isa. xlii, 6 ; xlix, 8 ; liv, 10 ; lxi, 8 ; Jer. xxxi, 31 ; l, 5 ; Ezech. xxxvii, 26 ; Ps. ii, 18, etc.

[2] Heb. ii, 1 ; the Law is ὁ δι' ἀγγέλων λαληθεὶς λόγος. Gal. iii, 19 and Acts vii, 53 express the same thought, which is also found in Josephus, *Antiq.*, XV, v. 3. Deut. xxxiv, 2 and Ps. lxvii, 17 point out the presence of the angels at Sinai, but without mentioning their active ministry.

[3] Gal. iii, 19, 20 : μεσίτης, with or without the article, is certainly Moses.

[4] Heb. i, 1 :

PROPHETS.   JESUS CHRIST.

Πολυμερῶς καὶ πολυτρόπως
πάλαι ὁ Θεὸς   ἐπ᾽ἐσχάτου τῶν ἡμερῶν τούτων
λαλήσας   ἐλάλησεν
τοῖς πατράσιν   ἡμῖν
ἐν τοῖς προφήταις   ἐν Υἱῷ.

367

The angels are the executors of the divine wishes; they are, after all, only ministers of God assigned to the service of the elect, and they may be compared to the atmospheric agents. Not only is the function of the angels to serve (λειτουργικὰ πνεύματα), but their service is subordinated to the welfare of the elect; the lightning and the tempest also bear the same names and fulfil, proportionately, the same offices; God makes the winds his messengers (ἀγγέλους) and flaming fires his ministers (λειτουργούς). Christ is the Son, begotten in the eternal Now; his throne abides for ever; the heavens are the work of his hands; he changes them at will, though he himself is incapable of change or of decline. His supremacy over the angels is already apparent in his name; he is the Son of God in an incommunicable way; he is God, and what the Old Testament says of Jehovah is applicable to him, or rather is said of him. Consequently, he is the Creator, he is eternal, he is the universal King; and the angels also owe him homage.

As for Moses, he was the faithful steward of the house of God; but he was there only as a servant, and the house did not belong to him. Christ, however, as the Son, governs his own house—that is to say, his Church; for he it is who has founded it.

The supreme dignity of Christ is derived entirely from his divine sonship. He is incomparably above the prophets because he is the Son; he eclipses the angels because he is the Son; he is superior to Moses because he is the Son; he is the only mediator of creation as well as of redemption because he is the Son; he is heir of all things because he is the Son; and he is eternally a priest because he is the Son. Although he is said to have brethren who sometimes take the title of sons, yet, when it is a question of the Son only, of the Son *par excellence,* of the Son of God, no ambiguity is possible, and everyone thinks of the Son by nature, of the only-begotten Son, born of the Father before all the ages.[1]

The personality of the Son remains unchangeable alike in his divine pre-existence in the bosom of the Father, in his historical manifestation as Mediator, Saviour, and Priest,

---

Formerly is opposed to *to-day*, the *patriarchs* to *us*, the *prophets* to the *Son*, and the difference of the two Testaments appears from this very contrast. Only, the first clause remains without a counter-clause.

[1] He is *the* Son of God, iv, 14 ; vi, 6 ; vii, 3 ; x, 29. God says to him *my* Son, i, 5 ; v, 5 ; he is *the* Son, i, 8 ; he is Son (without article), i, 2 (ἐν υἱῷ, contrasted with the prophets) ; i, 5 (εἰς υἱόν, contrasted with the angels) ; iii, 6 (ὡς υἱός, contrasted with Moses) ; v, 8 and vii, 28 (καίπερ ὢν υἱός and υἱὸν εἰς τὸν αἰῶνα τετελειωμένον, as high-priest, antitype of Melchisedech, with a tacit contrast to the high-priest Aaron). The absence of the article is explained by the fact that the title of Son has become a kind of proper name. —Moreover, Christians also are *sons*, xii, 5-8 and ii, 10-14, because *the* Son adopts them as brothers, ii, 11, 13.

and in his glorified life beyond the range of history. The different attributes which apply to him under this triple mode of existence are often united in the same sentence and enumerated without change of subject. This phenomenon, which can be verified in the prologue to St John's Gospel and in the christological passages of the Epistles to the Colossians and to the Philippians, is especially striking in the Epistle to the Hebrews. The following are two examples taken from the beginning :

> God hath spoken to us by the Son (historical existence),
> Whom he hath made heir of all things (glorified existence),
> By whom also he made the ages (divine pre-existence).

Or, observing the chronological order :

> The brightness of his glory,
> The imprint of his substance,
> Upholding all things by the word of his power,
> After having made expiation for sins,
> He sat down at the right hand of the majesty on high.

Eternal pre-existence, historical existence, glorified survival ; such is the natural framework in which we can classify the principal christological ideas of this epistle.

Moreover, the ideas referring to eternal pre-existence are arranged under three heads : the titles of Christ pre-existent, his part in creation, his divine nature.

Jesus Christ, from all eternity, is the Son of God ; he is the brightness of the Father's glory and the imprint of his substance. We have already spoken of the first name.

The expression *brightness of the Father's glory* (ἀπαύγασμα τῆς δόξης αὐτοῦ) is borrowed from the Book of Wisdom, where the parallelism defines the meaning both of the brightness and of the glory. Eternal wisdom " is a breath of the power of God and an effluence of the pure glory of the Almighty . . . for it is a radiancy of the eternal light, a faithful mirror of the activity of God, and an image of his goodness."[1] The brightness is explained by the effluence, and the glory is explained by the light. Glory, indeed, in the Bible does not mean public esteem, or reputation, or honour ; it means effulgence, splendour, and, by extension, beauty and majesty. The glory of the Father is the splendour and majesty of him who dwells in inaccessible light, in whom is light, and who is himself the light which is incapable of suffering eclipse or obscurity, and of whom the glory which

---

[1] Wisdom vii, 26 : ἀπαύγασμά ἐστι φωτὸς ἀϊδίου. By its passive termination ἀπαύγασμα designates, not the act of shining, but the image or light emitted by the radiation. This was well understood by the Greek commentators. This meaning is made certain by the text of Wisdom, where ἀπαύγασμα corresponds in the other parts of the sentence to ἀτμίς (breath), ἀπόρροια (effluence), ἔσοπτρον (mirror), εἰκών (image).

sometimes enveloped the sanctuary—the *Shekinah* of Jewish theology—was the symbol. The Son is not his reflection—for in what could the Father be reflected?—but his resplendence, and, to come still nearer to the Greek word ἀπαύγασμα, he is the result of this refulgence. The Father is, therefore, conceived as a glowing sun which pours forth its rays; but while in the shining bodies known to us there is always a dark nucleus, a fuel or a residuum of light; in God, in whom all is light, the brightness is absolute, and is reflected in an image equal to itself. Chrysostom was, therefore, right to see in the refulgence of the glory of the Father the equivalent of the article of the Creed. *Lumen de Lumine;* and the other Greek commentators, following Origen,[1] are right in inferring that this refulgence, inseparable from the luminous centre from which it emanates, is eternal like itself. Nevertheless, the divinity of the Son does not result from the refulgence itself, but from the fact that an emanation from God cannot be other than of his substance and infinite.

The Son is, moreover, the imprint of the substance of the Father: χαρακτὴρ τῆς ὑποστάσεως αὐτοῦ. It is of little use to remark that ὑπόστασις designates the substance and not the person. This term in this sense is not found in the Bible, and would not be suitable here; for how could the Father reproduce in the Son precisely that which distinguishes them? Nor must χαρακτήρ be translated by seal or stamp. The Greek word has not that signification, and the metaphor would not correspond to the idea. It is rather the Father who would be the stamp, making an adequate imprint of himself, with all the energy of his substance. The χαρακτήρ is the characteristic trait of a person or thing, its exact reproduction; it is used, in particular, in speaking of the portrait on a medallion, or of the imprint graven on a coin; Philo gives as its synonyms "image" (εἰκών), "copy" (μίμημα), "representation" (ἀπεικόνισμα).[2] "Rational nature is the image of the divine and the invisible, being marked by the seal of God, of whom the Logos is the imprint."[3] Thus the word, according to Philo, is not the seal (σφραγίς) of God; it is the imprint (χαρακτήρ) graven on this seal. But we should exceed the scope of our text if we applied to it Philo's conception of the Word, a representation of God, which marks us in his image and renders us participants in the divine nature. The imprint is not a mere copy; it is the exact reproduction of the model, with an idea of causality,

---

[1] Orig. *In Jerem. homil.* ix, 4. St Gregory of Nyssa, *Cont. Eunom.*, viii, (XLV, 773), says very poetically the same thing. Origen insists elsewhere (*In Joan.*, xxxii, 18) on this idea that the Son is the brightness of *all* the glory of the Father, from which the consubstantiality of the persons can be deduced.

[2] *Quod. deter. pot. insid.*, 23 (Mangey, vol. i, p. 207).

[3] *De. plant. Noe*, 5 (Mangey, vol. i, p. 332).

which the word " copy " does not awaken in our minds. There is, therefore, a perfect reciprocal relation between the refulgence and the imprint; both offer us the image of the Father, and both are derived from the Father.

Son, refulgence, imprint are almost synonymous terms, by which the attempt is made to express in human language the innermost activity of God. The Word is always designated by names which express his eternal procession and consequently his fitness to reveal to us the Father, whom no one has ever seen and whom no one can see, except in his Image, the Son. But it would be a grave error to think that, outside of his function of Mediator and Revealer, the Word is nothing else. The Son would be the Son, even though he had not to lead us to the Father; the glory of God would emit its rays, even though there were no mortal eye to contemplate that splendour; and as much must also be said of the imprint which the Father makes of his substance. These titles are relative, but have an intrinsic and necessary relation, independent of the existence of God's creatures. On the contrary, those of Creator and Preserver, which we have still to examine, are conditioned by the existence of finite beings.

2. The Son is the Creator of the world : " By whom also God made the ages,"[1] and it cannot be doubted that the *ages* mean the sum-total of all things limited by time and space. Nothing shows that the Gnostic notion of divine emanations, or *eons,* was already current at this time. Moreover, the author, to avoid all ambiguity, is careful to define the *ages: Fide intelligimus aptata esse saecula verbo Dei ut ex invisibilibus visibilia fierent.*[2] The ages correspond to the worlds of Jewish theology. In the Talmud God is called the Creator of the ages (*boreh 'olamîm*); in Scripture God is called king of the ages or God of the ages.[3] In both places "ages" are used for "worlds." The Son is also the Preserver of the universe : " He upholdeth all things by the word of his power."[4] If the function of Creator appears subordinate ($\delta\iota$' $o\tilde{v}$) because it is performed according to the order of divine processions, that of Preserver is presented as independent and absolute : an apparent singularity, for the preserva-

---

[1] Heb. i, 2 : $\delta\iota$' $o\tilde{v}$ $\kappa\alpha\grave{\iota}$ $\dot{\epsilon}\pi o\acute{\iota}\eta\sigma\epsilon\nu$ $\tauo\grave{\upsilon}s$ $\alpha\grave{\iota}\tilde{\omega}\nu\alpha s$. That $\delta\iota\acute{\alpha}$ does not in itself indicate an instrument appears from ii, 10 ($\delta\iota$' $o\tilde{v}$ $\tau\grave{\alpha}$ $\pi\acute{\alpha}\nu\tau\alpha$), where it designates the creative causality of the Father.

[2] xi, 3. This meaning is usual in Wisdom (xiii, 9 ; xiv, 6 ; xviii, 4) and in Philo, Josephus, Clemens Romanus, etc.

[3] 1 Tim. i, 17 ; Tob. xiii, 6-10 ; Ecclus. xxxvi, 22.

[4] i, 3 : $\phi\acute{\epsilon}\rho\omega\nu$ $\tau\epsilon$ $\tau\grave{\alpha}$ $\pi\acute{\alpha}\nu\tau\alpha$ $\tau\tilde{\omega}$ $\dot{\rho}\acute{\eta}\mu\alpha\tau\iota$ $\tau\tilde{\eta}s$ $\delta\upsilon\nu\acute{\alpha}\mu\epsilon\omega s$ $\alpha\grave{\upsilon}\tauo\tilde{\upsilon}$. Paul (Col. i, 17 : $\tau\grave{\alpha}$ $\pi\acute{\alpha}\nu\tau\alpha$ $\dot{\epsilon}\nu$ $\alpha\grave{\upsilon}\tau\tilde{\omega}$ $\sigma\upsilon\nu\acute{\epsilon}\sigma\tau\eta\kappa\epsilon\nu$) expresses almost the same idea still more concisely.

tion of things is only the virtual continuation of the creative act. Perhaps the sacred writer wishes to make us understand that the mediation of the Son does not imply dependence, and that his creative activity is not that of a minister or instrument.

Some Fathers have seen the divinity and creative activity of the Son in a text which can be translated in two ways: " He who hath ordered all things is God," or, " It is God who hath ordered all things." The second translation seems to us preferable. The author has just affirmed that Christ, " apostle and high priest of our confession," was faithful to him that made him [apostle and high priest], " as was also Moses in all his house "—that is to say, in the house of God. But there are two differences: one is that Moses was faithful in the capacity of a servant, while Christ was faithful in the capacity of a Son; the other is that Moses is a part of the house of God, of which Christ is the director and the founder. Now it is evident that the director of a house is of greater value than the house itself or any part of it; hence the superiority of Christ over Moses. Here comes the passage in dispute: *Omnis namque domus fabricatur ab aliquo; qui autem omnia creavit, Deus est.*" This, we think, should be translated thus: " For every house is ordered by someone; but it is God who has ordered all things."[1] These words cannot explain the preceding verse, which is perfectly plain, and, therefore, refer to the one before the last, in which it is said that Christ was faithful to him who made him his representative, as Moses was in the house of God. Although Christ, as high priest, is the founder and orderer of this edifice—for his sacrifice reverberates into the past—it is God, after all, who orders all things and places in his house Moses as a servant and Christ as his Son.

Leaving this passage aside, the Son receives elsewhere the name of God, even with the definite article: ".Thy throne, O God, is for ever and ever."[2] The author unhesitatingly applies to him Old Testament passages referring to Jehovah and expressing attributes specifically divine: " Thou in the beginning, O Lord, didst found the earth, and the heavens are the works of thy hands. They shall perish, but thou abidest for ever."[3] That the angels are commanded to adore him[4] is the foreseen and necessary consequence of his transcendent dignity. It is hard to see what the prologue of St John's Gospel and the Epistles to the Philippians and Colossians add to this express affirmation of the divinity of Christ.

---

[1] iii, 4: Πᾶς γὰρ οἶκος κατασκευάζεται ὑπό τινος, ὁ δὲ πάντα κατασκευάσας Θεός. The word Θεός is not the predicate but the subject of the proposition.

[2] Heb. i, 8-9.   [3] i, 10-12.   [4] i, 6.

3. Although he is God, Jesus Christ is none the less man. While still in the bosom of the Father, the Son requests that a body be prepared for him.[1] He wishes to be a partaker in the flesh and blood of humanity, like the adoptive sons,[2] and to become like unto them in all things except sin.[3] This his rôle of priest demands.[4] He will submit, therefore, to the test and will come off victorious.[5] He will possess all the virtues to the highest degree : confidence in God,[6] fidelity,[7] compassion,[8] and, above all, obedience, which he will learn in the school of suffering.[9] Outside of the Gospels, no inspired writing is more abundant in allusions to the mortal life of Jesus : his descent from the tribe of Judah,[10] progress in grace and wisdom,[11] signs and wonders attesting his divine mission,[12] tribulations and persecutions, the agony and prayers in the Garden of Olives,[13] his voluntary death[14] and crucifixion outside the city gates.[15] Perhaps the name of Jesus is chosen in preference to that of Christ,[16] in order better to inculcate the truth of his human nature. But nowhere also is the *communicatio idiomatum* more perfect; and has not *Participavit carni et sanguini,* compared with *Corpus aptasti mihi,*[17] the same value, as a theological formula of the incarnation, as the *Verbum caro factum est* of St John or the *In ipso inhabitat omnis plenitudo divinitatis corporaliter* of St Paul?

The glorified life of Christ is represented as the fruit of his self-abnegation and death. The ignominy of the cross is the prelude to his triumphal reign. Heir of the world by right of birth, the Son becomes so by a new title by right of conquest, and he acquires at the same time the right to hold fellowship with his co-heirs. Here we recognize ideas familiar to Paul; but—a fact worthy of notice—the Epistle mentions the resurrection only once, and that casually,[18] while it delights to describe Jesus, the high priest of humanity, entering into the heavenly sanctuary for ever open, and seating himself at the right hand of the Father, as advocate and intercessor :[19] " Having completely cleansed away sins, he sat down on the right hand of the majesty on high." " We have a high priest, who hath sat down on the right hand of the throne of majesty in the heavens, a minister of the holy place and of the true tabernacle." " But this man, having

---

[1] x, 5, 9. [2] ii, 14. [3] iv, 15 ; v, 7-8 ; vii, 26.
[4] ii, 17. [5] ii, 18 ; iv, 15. [6] ii, 13.
[7] ii, 17 ; iii, 2. [8] iv, 15. [9] vii, 7-8.
[10] vii, 14. [11] ii, 10 ; v, 9 ; vii, 28. [12] ii, 4.
[13] v, 7. [14] xii, 2. [15] xiii, 12.
[16] The word Jesus occurs ten times *alone*, Christ nine times, Jesus Christ three times ; Christ Jesus never. On the contrary, in St Paul, Jesus rarely occurs *alone*, and Christ Jesus is very frequent.
[17] ii, 14 and x. 5. [18] xiii, 20.
[19] iv, 16; vi, 20; vii, 26; ix, 11, 12, 24.

offered one sacrifice for sins, hath sat down for ever on the right hand of God." "Instead of the joy set before him, he endured the cross, counting the shame as nothing, and hath now sat down on the right hand of the throne of God."[1] In the other writings of the New Testament Jesus takes his place at the right hand of the Father as one who triumphs, as a king and judge; in the Epistle to the Hebrews it is pre-eminently in the capacity of priest that he does so, and he there continues his office of mediator.

II—THE PRIESTHOOD OF CHRIST

1. Jesus Christ as High-Priest. 2. After the Order of Melchisedech.

1. The comparison with the other mediators—prophets, angels, and Moses—prepared the mind for the supreme Mediator, for " the great high priest who hath entered into the heavens." The high priest having once been named, everything converges towards him. Does not the author of the Epistle propose to demonstrate that Christianity is the perfect, ideal, and final religion, and is not the level of a religion marked by its priesthood?

Jesus Christ is priest and high priest: priest after the order of Melchisedech in the capacity of sacred mediator; high priest, as the antitype of Aaron, whom he replaces.[2] But there is no other distinction between these two titles, and the name of high priest does not here imply a hierarchy of which Christ is the Head: "For every high priest taken from among men is ordained for men in the things that appertain to God, that he may offer up gifts and sacrifices for sins; who can be indulgent towards them that are ignorant and that err; because he himself also is compassed with infirmity. And therefore he ought, as for the people, so also for himself, to offer for sins. Neither doth any man take the honour to himself, but he that is called by God, as Aaron was."[3]

---

[1] i, 3 ; viii, 1 ; x, 12 ; xii, 2.

[2] Jesus Christ is called priest (ἱερεύς) according to the order of Melchisedech in the quotations from Ps. cix, 4 and the allusions to this text (v, 6; vii, 15, 17, 21); he is ἱερεὺς μέγας ἐπὶ τὸν οἶκον τοῦ Θεοῦ (x, 21). Everywhere else he is ἀρχιερεύς with different qualifications: ii, 27 (ἐλεήμων καὶ πιστός), iii, 1 (τῆς ὁμολογίας ἡμῶν), iv, 14 (μέγας), iv, 15 (δυνάμενος συμπαθῆσαι), v, 10, vi, 20 (κατὰ τὴν τάξιν Μελχισεδέκ), vii, 26 (ὅσιος, ἄκακος, ἀμίαντος, κτλ.), ix, 11 (τῶν γενομένων ἀγαθῶν).

[3] v, 1-4. The words " taken from among men " are not restrictive ; they apply to all high-priests. It is necessary, therefore, to understand it as: Every high-priest, *being* taken from among men, etc. The verb μετριοπαθεῖν which we translate " to act with indulgence," on account of the dative which follows, signifies absolutely "to be moderate in passions or sentiments." Aristotle said, according to Diogenes Laërtius, that the philosopher ought not to be *insensible*, but *sensible in moderation* (ἔφη τὸν σοφὸν μὴ εἶναι μὲν ἀπαθῆ, μετριοπαθῆ δέ). The word is common in Philo ; it is found also in Josephus.

We have not here—a point too frequently forgotten—a definition of the priest, or even of the high priest, but merely of the Hebrew high priest. All the traits mentioned are not applicable to Jesus Christ or are so only by analogy, as the type represents on a large scale the antitype with some imperfections which the latter rejects. Yet, on the whole, the description may serve as an outline for a study of the priesthood of Christ, for it well expresses the essential characteristics of the priest—namely, his rôle as mediator, the common life which it assumes, the divine vocation which is its condition, and the sacrifice which is its primordial function.

The priest is, above all, a mediator. " He is appointed for men in the things which concern the worship of God." If man owed to God only an individual worship, he would load the altar with his own offerings and would pour out upon it his own libations and the blood of victims, with no need of an intermediary. But everywhere and always, in every society which has not made a public profession of atheism, men have felt that they owed God a social worship. Naturally, the most worthy man in the community was intrusted with it : in the family, the father ; in the tribe, the patriarch ; in the nation, the king. However, when society had outgrown the patriarchal clan, impelled by an instinct which does honour to human nature, the solemn functions of the priesthood were usually confided to a special caste, freed from secular cares and interests, a severe guardian of traditions and rites, deemed more acceptable to the divinity and from that very fact better fitted for its rôle.

But, as we have said, the author of this Epistle does not speak of the priest in general. He does not ask himself what the priest would be in a state of nature, nor what he would be if humanity had not fallen. His gaze does not leave the world of actual realities nor go beyond the biblical horizon. He takes the human race as it is, burdened with the consciousness of sin, and powerless to hew out a path to heaven for itself. If we ignored the barrier which sin raises between God and ourselves, we could only imperfectly understand the rôle which he assigns to the high priest, a rôle which consists chiefly " in offering oblations and sacrifices for sins." The priest remains, indeed, the representative of men with God, but, in fact, he now represents a sinful humanity ; he is always intrusted with what pertains to the worship of God, but, as the normal relations between God and man are disturbed, his first aim is to re-establish them. Jesus Christ comes on earth, therefore, to wipe out sin ; he becomes incarnate because God no longer accepts Aaronic sacrifices, and his purpose is realized when he has fulfilled the purification of sins.

In order to be the mandatory, the ambassador and the
religious head of humanity, the high priest must belong to
the human family. It is by virtue of the solidarity which
unites us to our common father that the sin of Adam is our
sin, and it is by the same bond of solidarity that the justice
of Christ will be our justice. St Paul has already made us
familiar with this idea. "For both he that sanctifieth and
they who are sanctified are all [sons] of one and the same
[father]. . . . Therefore, because the children are partakers
of flesh and blood, he also himself in like manner hath been
partaker of the same. . . . For nowhere doth he [come to
the aid] of the angels, but to the seed of Abraham. Wherefore it behoved him in all things to be made like unto his
brethren."[1] The complexity of this passage is due chiefly
to two causes : first, the author wishes to explain at the same
time the necessity and the expediency of the incarnation
and of the other humiliations of Christ; then, instead of
approaching the question directly as a dogma to be established, he attacks it indirectly as an objection to be removed. In exalting Jesus Christ to an incomparable height
above all creatures, he has not been able to conceal the
transitory phase of humiliation which places him below the
angels. He replies that Christ *had* to partake of our nature
in order to be priest, and of our temptations in order to be a
perfect priest.[2] Not that there can be in the Most High a
real necessity; there are only reasons of expediency and
hypothetical necessities; but from the moment that, in the
designs of God, the Son is deputed to save men by a
sacerdotal act, it is necessary that he should be able to call
them his brethren. Otherwise he would be their Head, as he
is the Head of the angels, but he would not be their high
priest. From this point of view " the sanctifier and the
sanctified " must have the same origin. In order, as a priest,
to save the race of Abraham, he must belong to it. That is
what makes the incarnation necessary; but it is a conditional
necessity, subordinated to the plan of redemption.

The Epistle does not separate the idea of the priest from
that of the perfect priest. The ideal pontiff of a guilty
humanity, after having assumed human nature, must participate in the sufferings and death which are now the common
lot of men. " For it became him, for whom are all things,
and by whom are all things, and who bringeth many children
unto glory, to perfect the author of their salvation by sufferings."[3] In voluntarily undergoing death, Jesus Christ intends not only to take all power away from the present
master of death, Satan, but he wishes also to deliver us from
that servile fear of death which has held us in bondage. In

---

[1] Heb. ii, 11-17.   [2] ii. 17, 18. *Cf.* v, 1-3.   [3] ii, 10

taking upon himself our miseries and our infirmities, he makes himself more capable of understanding our needs and our weaknesses, our temptations and our failures, and, finally, of sympathizing with us in that perfect temperament which knows how to avoid at once excessive indulgence and excessive severity ($\mu\epsilon\tau\rho\iota o\pi a\theta\hat{\epsilon}\iota\nu$). Yet the resemblance has a limit. "We have a high priest who can have compassion on our infirmities, but one tempted in all things, like as we are, yet without sin."[1] The reason for this is clear. The more the priest has to draw near to God in order to draw his brethren to him also, the more he needs to be holy; the more it is his mission to expiate sins, the more it becomes him to be himself exempt from them. If he were compelled to sacrifice for his own sins, before thinking of the sins of the people, he would need another priest to supply his own insufficiency. "It was, therefore, fitting that we should have such a high priest, holy, innocent, undefiled, separated from sinners, and made higher than the heavens."[2]

2. In natural religion the priest is indicated either by his worthiness or by the choice of those whom he represents : God approves of him, but does not nominate him. In supernatural religion it is otherwise. God, when he reveals the worship with which he wishes to be honoured, entrusts the care of it to whomsoever he pleases. Whoever dares, without a divine call, to meddle with the sacred functions of the priesthood would be an intruder and a usurper. Aaron having been regularly invested with the high priesthood, together with his descendants, an express call from the Most High is needed to replace them. This is the case with Jesus Christ : "He did not glorify himself, that he might be made a high priest : but he that said unto him : 'Thou art my Son : this day have I begotten thee,' "[3] called him to the summit of the high priesthood. Although the Son is Son from all eternity, these words are, according to the Psalmist, addressed to him only at the moment when he assumes human nature. In becoming man, he is *ipso facto* consecrated priest—that is to say, an accredited mediator of the human race with God. His Father confirms to him this dignity with an oath : "The Lord hath sworn, and he will not repent : thou art a priest for ever according to the order of Melchisedech."[4] The exclusive prerogative of Aaron is thus revoked. But this transfer of the priesthood is not limited to a mere substitution of persons; it is equivalent to the change of the priesthood itself which, from the order of Aaron, passes to the order of Melchisedech.

This mysterious person, who appears and disappears in

[1] iv, 15. *Cf.* ii, 17.
[3] Heb. v, 5, quoting Ps. ii, 7.
[2] vii, 26. *Cf.* iv, 14.
[4] v, 6 ; Ps. cix, 4.

the Bible like a meteor, interests the author of this Epistle only as a type of Christ. Three circumstances impress him : the etymology of the names, the conduct of Abraham in regard to the priest-king of Salem, and the silence of Scripture concerning his origin.

The name Melchisedech signifies "king of justice," and king of Salem means "king of peace." Now the reign of the Messiah is to be the reign of peace and justice. Melchisedech is priest and king; Christ is also priest and king, and our Epistle, with one exception, always associates his royalty with his priesthood. The ideal priesthood, at the end of its evolution, is thus brought back to its primitive conception. The meeting of the patriarch with the king of Salem furnishes two other typical details, the signification of which is almost the same : "Melchisedech blesses Abraham, and Abraham pays him tithe."[1] It is an accepted principle that a blessing descends from the father to the child, from the king to the subject, from the priest to the layman ; in a word, from the superior to the inferior. It is equally evident that the payment of tithe is an act of subjection to a higher authority, royal, sacerdotal, or divine. Now Melchisedech blesses him in whom all the nations of the earth are to be blessed, and receives from him in the form of tithe the best of the booty. By this twofold act all the posterity of Abraham, yet unborn, without excepting the priestly sons of Levi, virtually recognize the superiority of Melchisedech and, with greater reason, him of whom Melchisedech is only the figure. The silence of Scripture is even more fertile in typical applications. According to the sacred narrative, Melchisedech was "without father, without mother, without genealogy"; his days have "neither beginning nor end," since sacred history mentions none of his ancestors, nor the date of his birth or death. The genealogy essential to levitical priests is to him a matter of indifference. Possessing the priesthood by personal right and not by inheritance, neither the quality of his ancestors nor his mother's country could be a hindrance. The high priest according to the order of Melchisedech will have the same privilege, and his blood-descent from Judah will set no obstacle in the way of his priesthood. But it is first necessary that the prerogative of Aaron should be abolished. This is the object of God's oath.

Petavius and Bellarmine made a collection of the texts of the Fathers who see in the bread and wine offered by Melchisedech a symbol of the Eucharist. The author of our Epistle could hardly dwell upon this typical signification without compromising his thesis and weakening his course of reasoning. It is probable that he makes allusion to the

[1] vii, 2.

Eucharist when he says: "We have an altar from which those have not the right to eat who remain in the service of the tabernacle." But here, concerned as he is to demonstrate that Christ perfects for ever the elect by one sacrifice only, that the offering for sin becomes useless when once sin is abundantly expiated, and that the insufficiency of the ancient sacrifices results precisely from their repetition, he could not make prominent either the oblation (the Eucharist) which is repeated, or the victim who is sacrificed at stated periods on the altar. Otherwise he would have had to explain why the Eucharistic sacrifice reproduces and commemorates—though without multiplying it—the bloody sacrifice of Calvary.

The silence in regard to the sacrifice of Melchisedech has, nevertheless, given rise to serious misunderstandings. It has been claimed that Christ was, at the same time or successively, a priest according to the order of Aaron and also according to the order of Melchisedech: according to the order of the former by his sacrifice, according to the order of the latter by his dignity; or according to the order of Aaron on earth, and according to the order of Melchisedech in heaven. But it has not been considered by the supporters of these claims that, according to the explicit teaching of the Gospel, these two orders are incompatible. Jesus Christ cannot be a priest of the order of Aaron if he takes the place of that order and if he is a priest only in virtue of the abolition of the Aaronic priesthood. "If he were on earth— that is, if his priesthood belonged to the typical and figurative sphere in which Aaron's order operated—he would not even be a priest, since others were charged with the offering of gifts in accordance with the Law."[1] Jesus Christ is, therefore, a priest according to the order of Melchisedech only, and he remains so for ever. We must not confound the sacerdotal dignity with the function of the priesthood. The priest does not become a priest at the moment when he offers the sacrifice, for he has the right to offer it only because he is already a priest. The sacerdotal consecration of Jesus Christ coincides with the incarnation. It is as he comes into the world that he says to the Father by the mouth of the Psalmist: "Sacrifice and oblation thou wouldest not; but a body thou hast prepared for me. Holocausts and sacrifices for sin did not please thee. Then said I: Behold I come . . . that I should do thy will, O God."[2] The will of God is that he should die, and he will die at the appointed hour; this will be his sacrifice. But he is a priest from the first moment of his mortal life, and it is his divinity, as the Fathers say, that consecrates his humanity.

The eternity of his priesthood is explained by the same

---

[1] Heb. viii, 4. [2] x, 5-7, quoting Ps. xl, 7-9.

principle. If the priest were a priest only in so far as he offers sacrifice or as he has the possibility of offering it, the priesthood of Christ would have only a relative eternity and would necessarily end at the latest on the day when the blood-less sacrifice which he offers through the ministry of his representatives until the consummation of the world shall terminate. But it is not so. His priesthood is eternal be-cause he holds it " not according to the law of a carnal com-mandment, but according to the power of an indissoluble life."[1] The ritual institution, which makes the priests of the lineage of Aaron, is valid only till their death, and the com-mission which it confers expires with life; but the hypostatic union, which consecrates Christ a priest, is indissoluble, and consequently his priesthood has no end. The others cannot remain priests always, "hindered from it as they are by death; but he retains a priesthood which nothing can take from him, because he himself continueth for ever . . . always living to make intercession for us."[2] In whatever way this intercession may be interpreted, it is evident that it does not cease with the mortal life of Christ, and that, consequently, death is not for him, as for the others, the extreme limit of his priesthood. In him the priesthood is not an accident separable from the person. Mediator of humanity because he is God Incarnate, it is impossible that he should ever cease to be such. Jesus, the high priest, will always be the appointed representative of the people whom he has saved, and he will always exercise the functions of high priest, were it only in offering to the Father the fruit of redemption by means of an oblation which is virtually eternal. But even should he not make use of this power, he preserves it for ever, and this it is which constitutes him high priest for eternity.[3]

III—THE SACRIFICE OF CHRIST

The specific function of the priest is sacrifice : " Every high priest is appointed to offer gifts and sacrifices; there-fore it was necessary that he also should have something to offer." In the present state of fallen humanity, the principal aim of sacrifice is expiation for sin; and it is as an expia-tion for sin that the Epistle to the Hebrews considers the sacrifice of Christ, although it mentions different kinds of sacrifices—gifts ($\delta\hat{\omega}\rho a$), oblations ($\pi\rho o\sigma\phi o\rho a\iota$), immolations ($\theta v\sigma\iota a\iota$), holocausts ($\dot{o}\lambda o\kappa a v\tau\dot{\omega}\mu a\tau a$)[4]—which the unique sacri-fice of the cross abolishes and replaces.

---

[1] vii, 16.   [2] Heb. vii, 23-25. Allusion to Ps. cix, 4.

[3] Although we avoid taking sides with one or another of the scholastics, Vasquez seems to us to be right as against Lugo, when he maintains that the eternity of Christ's priesthood is absolute and not merely relative.

[4] The word $\delta\hat{\omega}\rho o v$ is associated three times out of five with $\theta v\sigma\iota a$ (v, 1 ; viii, 3 ; ix, 9, always with the verb $\pi\rho o\sigma\phi\epsilon\rho\epsilon\iota v$), which would lead us to

To be convinced that the immolation of Calvary is a sacrifice in which Jesus Christ is at the same time priest and victim, it is sufficient to read the four following texts, of which the first announces the fact; the second, the mode; the third, the efficaciousness; and the fourth, the infinite value :

> Who needeth not daily, as the high-priests [of the Jews], to offer sacrifices, first for his own sins, and then for the people's; for this he did once, in offering himself.[1]
>
> How much more shall the blood of Christ, who by the Holy Ghost offered himself [a victim] unspotted unto God, cleanse our conscience from dead works to serve the living God ?[2]
>
> So also Christ was offered once to take away the sins of many ; the second time he shall appear, without sin, unto the salvation of them that expect him.[3]
>
> But this man, offering one sacrifice for sins, hath sat down for ever on the right hand of God. . . . For by one oblation he hath perfected for ever them that are sanctified.[4]

The immolation of Calvary is compared, in passing, by way of contrast, with the holocausts of the Mosaic ritual, with the sacrifice of the red cow and with the sacrifice by which the covenant of Sinai was sealed.[5] But the author does not dwell on these analogies; he hastens to come to the most perfect or the least imperfect of the rites of the ancient Law, that of the day of Atonement. Celebrated only once a year, in the presence of the whole assembly and amid the most solemn surroundings, the sacrifice of Atonement was also the only one in which the high priest was obliged to officiate in person, and it was, above all, the sacrifice for sin.[6] None, consequently, better typified the sacrifice of Christ.

The whole spectacle is described with a richness of details,

---

suppose that it indicates unbloody sacrifices, while θυσία would indicate bloody sacrifices ; but elsewhere (viii, 3, ὄντων τῶν προσφερόντων κατὰ νόμον τὰ δῶρα) it seems to include all sorts of sacrifices, and in xi, 4 it is synonymous with θυσία.—Besides the three cases where it is associated with δῶρον (v, 1 ; viii, 3; ix, 9), the word θυσία is associated with προσφορά (x, 5, 8) in a citation (Ps. xl, 7) ; it is employed to designate the sacrifice of Abel (xi, 4) and the sacrifice for sin either in the Old Testament or in the New (vii, 27; ix, 23, 26; x, 1, 11, 12, 26) ; twice it is taken in a metaphorical sense (xiii, 15, 16, " sacrifices of praise ").—It might be thought that προσφορά, united with θυσία and to ὁλοκαύτωμα in the quotation from Ps. xl, 7 (Heb. x, 8), is a sacrifice without blood, but it is used precisely for the sacrifice of Christ (x, 10, 14) and of the sacrifice for sin (x, 18, προσφορὰ περὶ ἁμαρτίας). We see that the author does not endeavour to distinguish between the different kinds of sacrifices; he retains only the generic notion of them, which he finds verified in the sacrifice of the Cross.

[1] Heb. vii, 27.   [2] Heb. ix, 14.
[3] Heb. ix, 28.   [4] Heb. x, 12-14.
[5] Holocausts (x, 6-8), red cow (vi, 13), sacrifice of the Covenant (ix, 15, 23).
[6] Lev. xvi, 1-34 ; xxiii, 26-32 ; Num. xxix, 7-11. Cf. Exod. xxx, 10; Lev. xxv, 9. For the Jewish tradition see the treatise of the Mishna entitled Yômâ. The name is significant, יוֹם הַכִּפֻּרִים, ἡμέρα ἱλασμοῦ (or ἐξιλασμοῦ), dies expiationum or propitiationis.

the significance of which is not always clear.[1] Several features of it seem to have no connection with its typical meaning. Perhaps the author points them out in order to show that he appreciates the splendour of the national worship, that he takes an interest in these souvenirs, and that he does not think himself obliged to depreciate the past in order to magnify the present. The division of the tabernacle into two parts, separated by a veil, which was raised only once a year before the high priest alone, is essential to the type. It signified, as the author goes on to explain, that the access to the sanctuary was not yet open. The rôle of the high priest, on the day of Atonement, was to reconcile the people with God; by offering the blood of the victims in the Holy of Holies.[2] It is not necessary to divide the mystery of this single action into two; for the high priest entered only that day into the Holy of Holies to offer up the blood there, and he could offer it up only in the Holy of Holies. In general, the Hebrew high priest did not perform in person the act of immolation. The sacred text seems to indicate that he himself did strike the victim on the day of Atonement, but he could have done it by an intermediary without changing the value or the signification of the rite. What was important for this sacrifice was that he should himself offer up the blood, and that he should offer it up in the Holy of Holies. These two acts, which are, in reality, only one, form an integral part of the same symbolism. The great error of the Socinians was to divide what, by its nature, ought to remain indissolubly united. Jesus Christ, being a priest by their consent only through the sacrifice, and the sacrifice of Christ being only the oblation of his blood made in the eternal sanctuary, there resulted therefrom this paradox, contradicted on every page of the Epistle to the Hebrews, that the death of Christ is not a sacrifice, that Jesus Christ was not a priest on earth, and that he became one only on entering heaven on the day of the Ascension.

The author does not propose to give a complete account of the typology of the rites of the Atonement. He says nothing of the scapegoat, which would seem to lend itself readily to comparisons. He mentions, in, passing, but in another setting, the burning of the victim[3] outside the camp, a figure or symbol of the execution of Jesus outside of the city gate. In general, he confines himself to the rôle of the high priest. He makes an application of it to Christ by way of comparison and contrast. But the contrasts preponderate. In the type compared with the antitype there is a difference in four essential points:

The Preparations for the Sacrifice.—Aaron sacrifices for

---

[1] Heb. ix, 1-10.   [2] Heb. ix, 7. *Cf.* Exod. xxx, 10; Lev. xvi, 16.
[3] Heb. xiii, 11-12.

himself before attending to the wants of the people; Jesus Christ, a high priest, " holy, innocent, separated from sinners, and made higher than the heavens," has not to sacrifice for himself, since, being without sin, he is always ready to exercise his ministry.[1]

The Place of the Sacrifice.—On the one hand, a perishable tabernacle, earthly, made by the hand of man, and figurative; on the other, an eternal sanctuary, celestial, built by God, ideal and perfect.[2]

The Matter of the Sacrifice.—There, the blood of bulls and goats, irrational animals; here, the blood of a pure victim, of the high priest himself, of the beloved Son.[3]

The Fruits of the Sacrifice.—The Jewish high priest enters for a moment into the Holy of Holies, only to emerge from it again immediately, and he has not the right to conduct any-one thither. Jesus Christ enters heaven never to leave it again, and he brings thither after him all those who are partakers in his sacrifice. The sacrifice of Aaron must be periodically repeated, because it does not obtain the desired result; the sacrifice of Christ is necessarily one only, because it is not compatible with its perfection that it should be re-newed, and because the death of the single victim can take place only once.[4]

The positive relation of the type to the antitype consists entirely in the fact that both high priests open for themselves the Holy of Holies by means of the blood of Atonement. Yet this unique feature should not be unduly emphasized. On the day of Atonement a certain time elapsed between the death of the victim and the offering up of its blood upon the mercy-seat. In the sacrifice of the cross this interval does not exist; the oblation coincides with the death, and the entrance into the Holy of Holies coincides with the oblation. From that moment heaven is virtually open and the moment of actual entrance into it has no more importance.

In fact, to make this entry coincide with the day of the Ascension would materialize the relations of type and anti-type too much. In order to continue in this line, it would be necessary to ascertain what the heavenly mercy-seat is which Jesus Christ sprinkles with his blood. At the instant when Jesus expires, everything is consummated: immola-tion, offering, the sprinkling of blood, and the right to enter heaven. The partisans of the heavenly sacrifice forget this. Separating the death of the victim from the oblation of blood, they either regard the former as a simple preparation which is not an essential part of the sacrifice, and are then obliged

---

[1] Heb. ix, 7 ; *cf.* v, 3 (for Aaron) ; vii, 26-27 (for Christ).
[2] Heb. ix, 11 ; *cf.* vi, 19, 20 ; viii, 2 (λειτουργὸς τῆς σκηνῆς τῆς ἀληθινῆς).
[3] Heb. ix, 12-14. *Cf.* x, 4-9 ; ix, 23, etc.
[4] Heb. ix, 15, 28. *Cf.* x, 1-3 ; vii, 27, etc.

to conclude with the Socinians that Jesus Christ was not a priest on earth, and that he inaugurates his priesthood only on entering into the life of glory—which is manifestly contrary to the apostolic doctrine; or else they see in the two actions two distinct sacrifices, and, without denying the value of the sacrifice of the cross, dream of a heavenly sacrifice differing from the other in the manner of oblation, somewhat as the Eucharist differs from the bloody sacrifice of Calvary; but this new opinion, suspicious by its very novelty, has not the slightest foundation in our Epistle.

CHAPTER III

THE TWO COVENANTS

I—THE CONTRAST BETWEEN THE TWO COVENANTS

TO show the superiority of the New Testament over the Old, and to establish at the same time the absolute and definitive character of the Gospel, is, as we have said, the real, though disguised, purpose of the Epistle. Three fundamental points are connected with this thesis : the contrast between the two covenants, the obligations of the new dispensation, and the fulfilment of the promises.

The idea of a new covenant, with Jesus as Mediator, is not peculiar to the Epistle to the Hebrews. Paul has already cited the text of Isaias which announced it;[1] he and St Luke expressly connect the institution of the Eucharist with a new covenant concluded in the blood of Jesus,[2] and the other two synoptists express the same thought in almost identical words.[3] What is original in our Epistle is the fact that it grafts the new covenant on the old, and makes the Church come out from the Synagogue without any lapse of continuity, as the fruit grows from the flower or the stem from the seed.[4] Under a paradoxical form, which contains a grain of truth, it has been possible to declare that " the author of the Epistle is an evolutionist and St Paul a revolutionist. . . . One abolishes the law, the other transfigures it."[5] At bottom, the difference of the point of view is much less : Paul depicts admirably the harmony and affinity of the two Testaments, and the author of the Epistle is no less radical than Paul in regard to the imperfection and the rejection of the

[1] Rom. xi, 27-28, quotation from Isa. lix, 20 combined with xxvii, 9. Paul also speaks of the *two* Testaments (Gal. iv, 24), of the Old (2 Cor. iii, 14), and of the New (1 Cor. xi, 25 ; 2 Cor. iii, 6).

[2] 1 Cor. xi, 25 and Luke xxii, 20 (ἡ καινὴ διαθήκη ἐν τῷ αἵματί μου).

[3] Matt. xxvi, 28 and Mark xiv, 24 (τὸ αἷμά μου τῆς διαθήκης, variant reading : καινῆς). The Epistle to the Hebrews also calls the blood of Jesus Christ " the blood of the covenant " (x, 29) ; and " the blood of the everlasting covenant " (xiii, 20).

[4] From another point of view there is, however, a distinction between the two Covenants. Jeremias had announced a " new covenant " (viii, 8) ; by this he indicated clearly that the " first " (ix, 15 : πρώτη) was drawing near its end (viii, 13). Jesus Christ is the *Mediator* of this new and better Covenant, ix, 15 (διαθήκης καινῆς μεσίτης ἐστίν) ; xii, 24 (νέας) ; viii, 3 (κρείττονος) ; he is the *surety* of a better Covenant (vii, 22 : ἔγγυος). Between the words καινή and νέα there is this difference, that the latter designates *newness*, the former denotes *youth* and *vigour*.

[5] Ménégoz. *La théol. de l'ép. aux Hébreux*, Paris, 1894, pp. 197 and 190.

Mosaic Law. It might almost be said that he is more so, for he denies to the Law the praise with which St Paul is so liberal, and he readily insists upon its revocable blemishes. It was a "carnal," intrinsically "invalid and useless" Law, which from that very fact must one day be repudiated. Incapable of "bringing anything to perfection,"[1] it consequently could have only a relative and transitory character; for the author always presupposes the existence of a supernatural system which really opens to man a way of approach to God.

The Old Testament, in comparison with the New, had three great disadvantages : It was a strictly bilateral contract, liable to be annulled from its very nature. The means established to bind it closer were insufficient. Moreover, it bore the characteristics of a simple sketch, a preparation.

The Ancient Law was a διαθήκη in the sense of a covenant (berîth), but not in the sense of a testament; the new Law is both at the same time. Now, from the moment that the testator is dead, the testament is irrevocable. We recognize here an idea common to Paul and to the editor of the Epistle. A second point of contact is that the promise made to the lineage of Abraham partakes of the nature of a testament— Paul calls it also διαθήκη—in that it is a unilateral contract, whereby God binds himself, without making his bond dependent on any external circumstance.[2] The pact of Sinai, on the contrary, was a contract of the kind known as : do ut des, facio ut facias. If the people violated its engagements, God was released from his; hence sacred history is nothing but a series of infidelities on the part of the Jews and of partial abandonments on the part of God, soon followed by short-lived reconciliations. Jeremias predicted the end of this state of things, the instability of which indicated sufficiently clearly its transitory character : " I will perfect with the house of Israel and the house of Juda a new covenant : not according to the covenant which I made with their fathers on the day when I took them by the hand to lead them out of the land of Egypt. Since they continued not in my covenant, I, too, have left them, saith the Lord."[3]

The great defect of the ancient contract was its tendency to

---

[1] Heb. vii, 16 (κατὰ νόμον ἐντολῆς σαρκίνης); vii, 18 (διὰ τὸ αὐτῆς ἀσθενὲς καὶ ἀνωφελές); vii, 19 (οὐδὲν γὰρ ἐτελείωσεν ὁ νόμος).

[2] Heb. ix, 16-27. Gal. iii, 17 contrasts the gracious testament made in favour of Abraham and confirmed by God under an oath with the Mosaic Covenant concluded long after (διαθήκην προκεκυρωμένην ὑπὸ τοῦ Θεοῦ . . . νόμος οὐκ ἀκυροῖ).

[3] Heb. viii, 8-12 (cf. x, 16-17), quoting Jer. xxxi, 31-34. In the text of Jeremias the principal difference between the two Testaments consists in the fact that the Old having been violated (οὐκ ἐνέμειναν ἐν τῇ διαθήκῃ μου), God uses reprisals and withdraws from his people (κἀγὼ ἠμέλησα αὐτῶν), while in the New, God pledges himself unconditionally to be the God of his people (ἔσομαι αὐτοῖς εἰς Θεόν, κτλ.), to be propitious to them and to forget their iniquities (ἵλεως ἔσομαι . . . τῶν ἁμαρτιῶν αὐτῶν οὐ μὴ μνησθῶ ἔτι).

become old and to die at last of senility,[1] a tendency which did not find a sufficient corrective in the Mosaic institutions. The perpetual sacrifice had, indeed, for its object to symbolize the covenant and to revive feeling in its behalf; on the other hand, the sacrifices for sins, which reached their culmination on the day of Atonement, aimed at reconciling the contracting parties by effacing the memory of the acts of unfaithfulness. But all this produced a "carnal justification" only, in virtue of a sort of legal fiction; for it is evident that the blood of animals could neither wash away sin nor purify the conscience.[2]

The Old Testament, therefore, could be only a sketch. Hence the Psalmist predicts a new priesthood, destined to supersede that of Aaron; he announces a new sacrifice which shall render the levitical ritual obsolete; Jeremias prophesies a new covenant which will inevitably take the place of the former.[3] However, this new covenant is not so much the violent destruction of the old one as its consummation. The relations of the two Testaments are expressed by these four words: shadow (σκιά), figure (ὑπόδειγμα), antitype (ἀντίτυπος), similitude (παραβολή).[4] The shadow is opposed to the substance, the antitype to the truth, the figure and similitude to reality. It may be remarked here that the language of the Epistle differs from that of the other sacred writers: it calls *antitype* what Paul would call *type;* and its *type* is the model presented to Moses on Sinai with an injunction to reproduce it; the *image* (εἰκών), which it opposes to the shadow, is the *body* (σῶμα) of Pauline terminology. But the editor of the Epistle insists more than anyone on the figurative character of the Mosaic system, and expresses it usually by the antitheses of earth and heaven, present and future, material and immaterial, copy and archetype.

---

[1] Heb. viii, 13 (τὸ παλαιούμενον καὶ γηράσκον ἐγγὺς ἀφανισμοῦ).

[2] Heb. ix, 9-10 ; x, 4, 11.

[3] Ps. cix, 4 ; Jer. xxxi, 31-34. *Cf.* Heb. vii, 11-22 ; viii, 6-13.

[4] Heb. x, 1 (σκιὰν ἔχων ὁ νόμος τῶν μελλόντων ἀγαθῶν οὐκ αὐτὴν τὴν εἰκόνα); viii, 5 (οἵτινες ὑποδείγματι καὶ σκιᾷ λατρεύουσιν τῶν ἐπουρανίων); ix, 24 (οὐ γὰρ εἰς χειροποίητα εἰσῆλθεν ἅγια ἀντίτυπα τῶν ἀληθινῶν). These three characteristic texts show well how the *shadow*, the *figure* and the *antitype* are in contrast to the image (reality), to future things, to true things, to heavenly and divine things. We again find ὑπόδειγμα (iv, 11 ; ix, 23) and παραβολή (ix, 9), with the same contrast. On the contrary τύπος (viii, 5), which is found elsewhere only in a quotation from the Septuagint, signifies the pattern given to Moses, when he received the command to build the tabernacle.

II—The Obligations of the New Covenant

1. Necessity of Faith.   2. Dangers of Unbelief.

Two words sum up the moral teaching of our Epistle : faith and perseverance. " Let us draw near [to God] with a true heart in fulness of faith. . . . Let us hold fast the confession of our hope without wavering."[1] Such is the refrain which occurs repeatedly under different forms. This moral anxiety explains at once the different rôles which faith is called upon to play respectively in the Epistle to the Hebrews and in the four great Epistles of Paul. In the latter it was a question of the effects of a faith which is in its beginning; in the other it is a question of the fruits of a faith that perseveres.

The author defines this faith in a way which, no doubt, is not in the manner of Aristotle, by genus and difference, but which suits it perfectly and distinguishes it from everything that it is not. " Faith is the substance of things hoped for, the evidence of things unseen."[2] The Greek word ὑπόστασις has three well-established meanings : foundation, firm con-

---

[1] Heb. x, 22-23 (κατέχωμεν τὴν ὁμολογίαν). Cf. iv, 14 (κρατῶμεν τῆς ὁμολογίας).

[2] Heb. xi, 1 : Ἔστι δὲ πίστις ἐλπιζομένων ὑπόστασις πραγμάτων, ἔλεγχος οὐ βλεπομένων. Whether the comma is put after πραγμάτων, as we have put it, or before it, as certain editors do, the meaning is not changed.—The word ὑπόστασις is found five times in the New Testament (2 Cor. ix, 4 ; xi, 17 ; Heb. i, 3 ; iii, 14 ; xi, 1). The Vulgate always translates it by substantia. It seems possible to establish the following derivation : (a) foundation (etymological meaning of ὑπό and ἵστημι, like sub-stantia) ; (b) reality (common, popular meaning) ; (c) substance (philosophical meaning, that which forms the basis of being, beneath accidents and phenomena) ; (d) subject, theme of a discourse and, in general, object, matter ; (e) firm confidence (in Ps. xxxviii, 8, ὑπόστασις corresponds to the Hebrew tôheleth and in Ruth i, 12 and Ezech. xix, 5 to tiqvāh).

In the New Testament, outside of our text (Heb. xi, 1), ὑπόστασις signifies twice " matter " (2 Cor. ix, 4 ; xi, 17) ; once " substance "·(Heb. i, 3) ; and once, apparently, " firm persuasion " (Heb. iii, 14).—(a) 2 Cor. ix, 4 : Ne cum venerint Macedones mecum et invenerint vos imparatos erubescamus nos (ut non dicamus vos) in hac substantia (the addition τῆς καυχήσεως of the received text comes from xi, 17). Paul sends the collectors of funds ahead of him so that, when he arrives at Corinth with his Macedonians, he and the Corinthians may not have to blush in this matter (ἐν τῇ ὑποστάσει ταύτῃ) as he said previously in hac parte (ἐν τῷ μέρει τούτῳ). The sense of " persuasion " or of " confidence " which might suit erubescamus nos would not suit ut non dicamus vos.—(b) 2 Cor. xi, 17 : Quod loquor non loquor secundum Deum sed quasi in insipientia, in hac substantia gloriae (ἐν ταύτῃ τῇ ὑποστάσει τῆς καυχήσεως). The meaning seems to be: in this subject of glorying, or rather: in this matter (this motive) of glorying myself. Nevertheless the translation " in the confidence which I show in glorifying " is not absolutely excluded by the context.—(c) Heb. i, 3 : figura substantiae ejus (τῆς ὑποστάσεως αὐτοῦ). The Son is the imprint of the substance of the Father, of the divine nature such as it is in the Father. The word ὑπόστασις has here its philosophical meaning of substance ; the meaning of person is much more recent.—(d) Heb. iii, 14: Participes enim

viction, reality. Taken apart from the context, each of these three meanings may well enter into the definition of faith. Faith is, indeed, the foundation of hope and, in general, of all our supernatural life; it is also a persuasion, so firm and assured that it leaves no room for doubt; finally, it is the reality of the things for which we hope, in so far as it is a taking possession by anticipation of blessings to come, and prevents our hopes from being vain or fantastic. St Thomas prefers the first of these meanings, to which he attaches the Latin word *substantia* itself : " The object of hope," he says, " is contained in embryo in faith, as the object of knowledge is contained in embryo in its rudiments; therefore faith is the foundation of hope, as the rudiments are the foundation of knowledge." Nevertheless, the last meaning—that of reality—appears preferable to us, for the first either resolves itself into this (the foundation of a thing being only its *substratum,* its reality), or else it takes the object of hope for hope itself; which is inadmissible, since the text has ἐλπιζομένων and not ἐλπίδος. On the other hand, the second meaning would destroy the parallelism between the two parts of the definition, for if ὑπόστασις can signify persuasion, ἔλεγχος, which makes a pendant to it, does not mean subjective conviction. Faith is, therefore, not only a pledge, but also an instalment of the blessings hoped for. According to the expression of St Thomas, it is a commencement within us of the life eternal; because, following the explanation of St Augustine, to believe what one does not see is to deserve to see what one believes.

Again, faith is the evidence of things unseen : ἔλεγχος οὐ βλεπομένων. If it were permissible to translate ἔλεγχος by conviction, there would be given to ὑπόστασις the meaning of persuasion, and the whole verse could be translated thus : Faith is a persuasion of things hoped for, a conviction of things unseen. Unfortunately, usage does not authorize this meaning : ἔλεγχος signifies, indeed, an argument to be refuted, refutation, evidence, and the action of convincing, but never subjective conviction. The Vulgate translation is, therefore, quite exact : *argumentum non apparentium.* Those things which are not seen are not only things invisible by their nature, but those which escape the perception of our

---

Christi effecti sumus, si tamen initium substantiae *ejus usque ad finem firmum retineamus* (τὴν ἀρχὴν τῆς ὑποστάσεως—the pronoun *ejus* corresponds to nothing in the Greek). Here we think that ὑπόστασις signifies "firm persuasion" or "confidence." This appears, in our opinion, from the parallelism of idea and expression with Heb. iii, 6 (*Si fiduciam et gloriam spei usque ad finem firmam retineamus*), where τὴν παρρησίαν καὶ τὸ καύχημα τῆς ἐλπίδος corresponds to our τὴν ἀρχὴν τῆς ὑποστάσεως. This is evident also from the contrast with the *cor malum incredulitatis* which precedes.—From these very different interpretations it is plain that the meaning of ὑπόστασις can be determined only by the context.

minds. Without having seen them, we yet know by faith
that they exist : faith takes for us the place of proof. It is
evident that this part of the definition is much more extended
than the former; it includes the objects of faith in their
entirety, past, present, and to come, all that we believe on
the testimony of God; while the other part of the definition,
confounding itself with the object of hope, is by that very
fact limited merely to the realities of the future.

The numerous examples of faith which fill the entire
eleventh chapter will make clear and definite whatever is
vague in this summary description. In all these instances,
without exception, faith denotes the acceptance by the intelligence of the divine testimony; but, as the truth to be believed
on the statement of God is not impressed upon the intellect by
its own evidence, there is always an intervention of the will
which renders the act of faith free and meritorious. Apart
from these two points, common to them all, the different acts
of faith present a certain variety. Three kinds can be distinguished :
    " By faith we understand that the world was framed by the
word of God, so that what is seen was not made of things
visible." Here the act of faith resolves itself into an act of
the intellect, and includes only its essential parts : acceptance by the mind of the testimony of Scripture and intervention of the will, inclining the intellect to admit, on the attesta-
tion of God, a fact remote from us, which is incapable of any
verification.
    When the divine testimony has a promise as its object,
faith naturally is allied to hope, and the two virtues, without
absolutely blending, go hand in hand. Such was the faith
of Sara, of Isaac, of Jacob, of Joseph, and of the patriarchs
in general, whose faith was trustful, and whose hope was
faithful. Sometimes that which is promised requires a miracle
dependent on the faith of man : then it is necessary to have
that lively faith which moves mountains. It was by faith
that the waves of the Red Sea parted and the walls of
Jericho fell.
    Most frequently the divine testimony consists of a com-
mand, or at least involves an obligation other than faith
itself. Faith, if it be sincere, must be active. By faith Noe
built the ark; by faith Abraham left his country, lived in exile
and resolved to sacrifice his son; by faith Moses defied the
wrath of Pharao, despised the pleasures of Egypt and
obeyed the divine commands; it was by faith also that Rahab
the harlot welcomed the Hebrew spies, and that the judges,
the prophets and the saints of the Old Testament braved so
many perils, endured so many persecutions, and underwent
the most cruel forms of death.

It is " by faith " that these holy persons " received the testimony." It is true, Scripture, which praises their justice and recounts their great deeds, does not always specially mention their faith. But that is not necessary, for, according to Habacuc, " the just man lives by faith." Faith is the measure of justice, and justice is the proof of faith. In this way the faith of Abel and Henoch is explained. Scripture does not make express mention of it, but it says of Abel that he offered a more excellent sacrifice than his brother, and that his blood cried for vengeance; and of Henoch that he pleased God and deserved thus to be caught up to heaven. The author concludes thence that this was on account of their faith, either by virtue of the text of Habacuc, which makes justice depend on faith, or in the case of Henoch in particular, by the reflex principle that without faith it is impossible to please God. How is it possible to please God without going to him? And how can one go to him without believing in his existence and his providence? Without doubt God, when known only by the light of reason, can attract the soul; but this philosophical notion does not correspond with the plan of our salvation in its present state of sublimity. It is less easy to see why faith in the existence of God is not sufficient. Is it not because the soul is unable to rise towards God *sicut oportet,* if it does not look upon him as its ultimate end and, in its present state, as its supernatural end?

2. The more necessary faith is, the more fatal is unbelief. Twice the author seems to describe apostasy as an irreparable evil. To appreciate the meaning of these passages, they must be placed in their context : " If we sin wilfully after having full knowledge of the truth, there is now left no sacrifice for sins; but a certain dreadful expectation of judgement and the rage of a fire which shall consume the adversaries. Whoever broke the law of Moses died without mercy under [the testimony of] two or three witnesses; how much more do you think he deserveth worse punishments, who hath trodden under foot the Son of God, and hath esteemed as a common thing the blood of the covenant, by which he was sanctified, and hath offered an affront to the Spirit of grace?"[1] The sin referred to by the Apostle is certainly not any ordinary kind of sin, even a serious one, but the sin which surpasses all others, apostasy. The general tendency of the Epistle, which makes everything converge on faith, and the circle of ideas in which the author moves, already allow us to suspect this. The exhortation which precedes and that which immediately follows, where only sincere faith, immovable hope and faithfulness in attendance at religious assemblies are in

[1] Heb. x, 26-29 : *cf.* vi, 1-8.

question, confirm this impression, which the allusion to Moses, punishing idolatry with death on the testimony of two or three witnesses, corroborates still more strongly.   The sin itself is described as an act which tramples under foot the Son of God, which regards the blood of the covenant as common or unclean, which is an insult to the Holy Spirit, and which takes place after a full knowledge of the truth of which it can only be the negation.   All these characteristics agree in showing deliberate apostasy, blasphemy against the Holy Ghost.   This sin will never be forgiven either in this world or in the world to come, because it dries up the source of grace and closes the path to repentance.   Without faith, indeed, it is impossible to please God or to be reconciled with him.   To the Christian who relapses into Judaism in the full knowledge of what he is doing, there remains no more sacrifice for sin, either in the Mosaic dispensation, which provided no sacrifice for crimes of this kind, or in Christianity, which possesses only one sacrifice, that of the new covenant with which the apostate has broken.   Doubtless God, who raiseth the dead, can always restore to life the withered seed of grace and light again the extinguished torch of faith, but the author had no need to refer to such a hypothetical miracle at the very moment when he was depicting the consequences of apostasy in such sombre colours.

His intention appears still more evident in the second passage.   He wishes to give the Hebrews food for men, not milk for babes, although their instruction does not seem to correspond to their age in the faith.   He leaves aside, therefore, the elementary dogmas which are taught to catechumens, for, he adds : " It is impossible for those who were once illuminated, have tasted also the heavenly gift, and were made partakers of the Holy Ghost . . . and are fallen away, to be renewed again to penance, crucifying again to themselves the Son of God and making him a mockery."   It is for exegetes to determine the precise sense of each of these phrases. They will, however, no doubt agree that it is not a question here of any ordinary fault, but of a serious falling away (παραπεσόντας), which puts those guilty of it on the level of unbelieving Jews.   In order to bring them back to the point whence they fell, it would be necessary to lead them again through all the stages of Christian initiation and to move them anew to repentance.   But this road is not travelled twice.   The author does not say that their conversion is impossible for God to accomplish, and that there is no more hope for them ; but he says that it is " impossible " for the preachers of the Gospel to " renew them to penance " and to prepare them for it again.   And in order to make us understand in what this renewal and preparation consist, he gives us a warning that he will abstain from repeating the instructions which are given to catechumens to prepare them for baptism. The power of the Church to remit sins was not in question.

III—THE CONSUMMATION

1. Rest in God.   2. Gradual Initiations.

1. Union with God is the supreme end and aim of our existence, the final goal of man's aspirations, the instinctive, if not the fully realized, purpose of all worship. This happy consummation is expressed in our Epistle by a most felicitous phrase : " God's rest "—that is to say, the rest which God enjoyed after the work of creation and redemption, the rest which he wishes us to enjoy with him and in him, the rest of which he is both the author and the end, and the rest which he proposes for our hope, either as a gratuitous gift, a heritage, or a recompense. Faithful to his typological method, the sacred writer sees the symbol of it in the promised land for which the Hebrews longed, less as the end of their wanderings than as the centre of the theocracy, where they would be nearer God, in his domain and under his ægis.[1] For a long time unbelief had kept them remote from it ; and when they entered into it, after having strewn the sands of the desert with their dead bodies, they perceived that they had received only an instalment of the divine promises. The prospect receded, and they caught glimpses of another " rest of God," from which the Psalmist adjures them not to exclude themselves by their hardness of heart : " There remaineth, therefore, a final Sabbath for the people of God. For he who hath entered into this divine rest, the same also hath rested from his works, as God did from his. Let us hasten, therefore, to enter into that rest, and beware of disobedience,"[2] which barred the entrance to it to the unbelieving Jews. This rest of God is Jesus, the antitype of Josue, who promises and assures it to us.

2. But to find access to it, it is necessary to undergo a series of initiations which are the *raison d'être* of Christ's

---

[1] The thought is developed at length (Heb. iii, 7–iv, 11) under the form of a moral commentary on Psalm xciv, 7-11, with continual allusions to Num. xiv, 21, 23. The central idea is the oath which God makes in his wrath : εἰ εἰσελεύσονται εἰς τὴν κατάπαυσίν μου.

[2] Heb. iv, 9-11 : ἄρα ἀπολείπεται σαββατισμὸς τῷ λαῷ τοῦ Θεοῦ. The *therefore* (ἄρα) is justified by the σήμερον of the Psalmist (xciv, 7). It is evident how the *rest* (κατάπαυσις and once σαββατισμός) is put into connection with the rest of the Creator : ὥσπερ ἀπὸ τῶν ἰδίων ὁ Θεός.—Finally it is faith which assures the entrance to it (iv, 3 : εἰσερχόμεθα γὰρ εἰς τὴν κατάπαυσιν οἱ πιστεύσαντες), and it is unbelief (iii, 19 : οὐκ ἠδυνήθησαν εἰσελθεῖν δι' ἀπιστίαν) or disobedience (iv, 1) which excludes us from it (iv, 6 : οὐκ εἰσῆλθον δι' ἀπείθειαν).

priesthood, and are expressed by the four words "expiate, purify, sanctify, perfect." These are almost synonymous terms, yet have interesting shades of meaning. The word "expiate" (ἰλάσκεσθαι)—corresponding to the Hebrew *kipper*—is essentially sacerdotal. It designates the action of the priest who cleanses from sin or washes away moral stains in the blood of the victims. The rôle of the high priest Jesus is to "expiate the sins of the people"[1] by his own blood, and thus to render God propitious to them. This is why St John calls him "a propitiation for our sins," and St Paul a "propitiator" or "means of propitiation";[2] for the two effects are correlative, and God is appeased in proportion as our sins receive an adequate expiation. "Purify" (καθαρίζειν) means almost the same thing. Blood is the great means of expiation, and it is also the usual means of purification. The Son "accomplishes the purification of sins"[3] (maketh purgation of sins) by his blood;[4] for "almost all things, according to the Law, are cleansed with blood; and without shedding of blood there is no remission of sins."[5] What the purification, which is accomplished by Jesus as priest, has peculiar to itself is that, in contrast to the Mosaic rites, it is spiritual and internal, reaches the conscience, and is absolute and final.[6]

Expiation and purification are, as it were, the other side of sanctification and perfection; the former annihilate sin, the latter substitute a positive perfection for it. To "sanctify" is to consecrate a being to God by separating it from profane use, to allot it to divine worship, to make a person fit for that worship. But, while the holiness produced by the ancient rites was merely legal, the holiness peculiar to the New Testament transforms souls: an identical terminology thus covers entirely different conceptions. It is no longer the blood of the victims that "sanctifies by making purification according to the flesh";[7] it is "the blood of the [new] covenant;"[8] it is the voluntary act of the true high priest,[9] offering himself as a sacrifice that *consummates* and consecrates for ever, once for all, those whom it sanctifies.[10]

The word "consummation" is perhaps the most characteristic word of the Epistle. To perfect (τελειοῦν) is to make perfect (τέλειος)—that is to say, to bring to an ideal terminus

---

[1] Heb. ii, 17 : εἰς τὸ ἰλάσκεσθαι τὰς ἁμαρτίας τοῦ λαοῦ.

[2] 1 John ii, 4: Αὐτὸς ἱλασμός ἐστιν περὶ τῶν ἁμαρτιῶν ἡμῶν. It is God who sends him in this character (1 John iv, 10). It is also God who establishes him (ἱλαστήριον, Rom. iii, 25).

[3] Heb. i, 3 : καθαρισμὸν τῶν ἁμαρτιῶν ποιησάμενος.

[4] Heb. ix, 14.   [5] Heb. ix, 22.   [6] Heb. x, 2.

[7] Heb. ix, 13.   [8] Heb. x, 29.   [9] Heb. x. 10.

[10] Heb. x, 14.

(τέλος), which marks a being's attainment of perfection.[1] The Mosaic Law was rejected because it was unable to *perfect* anything.[2] The saints of the Old Testament caught glimpses of this ideal goal, yet never reached it, for it was not fitting that they should be *perfected* before us.[3] Jesus Christ was the first perfected; for " it became him [God], for whom are all things and by whom are all things, who had brought many children unto glory, to *perfect* the author (or chief) of their salvation, by suffering."[4] The chief (ἀρχηγός) precedes his soldiers to the assault, and conducts them into the place, after being himself the first to enter in. Therefore, " although he was the Son, he learned obedience in that he had to suffer, and being *perfected,* he became to all that obey him the cause of eternal salvation."[5] Everywhere he marches in front and clears the way. " He is *perfected* for eternity,"[6] and we are *perfected* with him.[7]

Here we note some differences and still more similitudes between Paul and the editor of the Epistle. The latter saves us by following Christ and through the mediation of Jesus as high priest; the former saves us in Christ Jesus and in union with the mystical Christ; the one accentuates the distinction between the author of salvation and those who benefit by it;

---

[1] The word τέλος signifies " end," but with the secondary idea of a result obtained, of the extreme limit of efforts or aspirations. (Cremer, *Wörterbuch*[9], Gotha, 1902.) Thence comes the special meaning of its derivatives.

The adjective τέλειος itself has nothing special about it in this Epistle; it qualifies *mature* age (v, 14) in contrast to childhood, and it indicates the *perfect* tabernacle (ix, ii), as contrasted with the figurative tabernacle. But the use of the verb τελειοῦν and its derivatives τελείωσις and τελειότης is very remarkable in the following associations of ideas : (*a*) Christ is *consummated,* or made perfect through suffering (ii, 10), and that for ever (vii, 28).—(*b*) Christ is in this way the ideal High Priest, capable of sympathizing with us in our sorrows and our miseries (ii, 17-18 ; iv, 14-16).—(*c*) He becomes thus fitted to *consummate* or to make perfect "for ever and by one single oblation " (x, 14) those who are united to him. *Cf.* v, 9 and xii, 23. He is the *finisher* (τελειώτης, xii, 2) of our faith, which he renders efficacious and perfect. We might be tempted to compare the τελείωσις of our Epistle with the τελεταί or initiations into the pagan mysteries. The comparison was early made by certain Fathers, like St Justin and Clement of Alexandria. But it is much more probable that the Epistle remains on Jewish ground, for τελειοῦν and τελείωσις express in the Septuagint the *consecration* of high priests (Exod. xxix, 9; Lev. xvi, 32; Num. iii, 3, etc.), and the ram sacrificed on that occasion was called κριὸς τελειώσεως, *aries consecrationis* (Exod. xxix, 22, etc.). We see from this the close relation which exists between the terms to *consummate,* to *consecrate,* to *sanctify* (in the biblical sense), to *inaugurate* and to *initiate,* and we can understand the play on words made by Philo (*Vita Mosis,* ii, 17, vol. II, p. 157) on the *consecration* (τελείωσις) of Hebrew high priests and the *initiations* (τελεταί) of the profane mysteries.

[2] Heb. vii, 19 (οὐδὲν ἐτελείωσεν ὁ νόμος); ix, 9 (μὴ δυνάμεναι κατὰ συνείδησιν τελειῶσαι τὸν λατρεύοντα); x, 1 (οὐδέποτε δύνανται τοὺς προσερχομένους τελειῶσαι).

[3] Heb. xi, 40.   [4] Heb. ii, 16.   [5] Heb. v, 9.
[4] Heb. vii, 28.   [7] Heb. x, 14.

the other makes prominent the identity between the Head and the members. Neither is ignorant of the fact that the individual application of redemption has still to be made; and that the blood of Jesus purifies the soul only by virtue of the sacramental rite; but both love to consider the rôle of Christ as completed in a single act, his voluntary sacrifice; and the restoration of humanity as being complete in principle through the loving obedience of the Son. Both agree that we are saved only in hope, but our hope is certain, and the closest bond exists between the commencement of salvation and its consummation. "You are come to Mount Zion and to the city of the living God, the heavenly Jerusalem, and to the company of myriads of angels, and to the Church of the firstborn whose names are written in the heavens."[1] Thus we move already in the sphere of heavenly realities; faith is an acquisition by anticipation of the blessings hoped for, charity is an instalment of glory, and the Church the entrance of heaven.

[1] Heb. xii, 22-23.

DETACHED NOTES

NOTE A—THE CHRONOLOGY OF ST PAUL'S APOSTOLATE

I—The Four Fixed Dates in His Apostolate

THESE are obtained by establishing a certain synchronism between a fact in Paul's life and a dated event of secular history. Let us observe, however, that a problem of chronology hardly lends itself to strict and mathematical demonstration. It is usually solved by the examination of convergent probabilities which check and verify one another and must harmonize with the whole of the various data. As, in the period we are considering, the list of the Roman emperors serves as a scale for our chronological calculations, we must bear that list always in mind. The years of their reigns are reckoned from the day on which they were invested with the power of the tribunate :

> Caligula from March 18, 37 A.D.
> Claudius from January 25, 41 A.D.
> Nero from October 13, 54 A.D.

In the official documents the title of reigning emperor, besides his years of power as tribune, denoted in addition the actual number of his consulships and the number of times he had been acclaimed as *Imperator* by his triumphant legions; but the last two data are of themselves insufficient, because the mention of the third consulate, for example, remained unchanged until the fourth was obtained, which might occur several years later ; and it is the same as regards the succession of imperial acclamations which followed one another at very irregular intervals.

1. *The Conversion of Paul.*—Some scholars of our time (Blass, Harnack, and O. Holtzmann) think that Paul's conversion closely followed the death of Jesus. We cannot share this opinion. The story of the Acts gives us the inevitable impression that a considerable time elapsed after that event. The Church passed through several stages exactly recorded by St Luke : the gradual increase in the number of the faithful (Acts ii, 17; iv, 4; v, 14; vi, 7), its social and religious organization by the holding of property in common (iv, 32-v, 11) and by the institution of the first seven

Hellenist deacons (vi, 1-6), the open break with the Synagogue (vi, 8-15), the spread of Christianity beyond Judæa and Galilee to Samaria and Damascus (viii, 1; viii, 27; ix, 19), and a complete change in the respective attitude of the Pharisees and Sadducees in regard to the disciples of Christ.

The conversion of Paul is closely connected with the martyrdom of Stephen. But under the strict, dictatorial, and distrustful government of Pilate, how is it possible to imagine such proceedings as were carried out against the holy deacon, his condemnation to death by the Sanhedrim, his summary execution, and the official mandate given to Saul by the high priest to go and ferret out the partisans of the new religion in Damascus and to bring them in chains to Jerusalem? Would Pilate, so anxious to preserve order in the streets, and so prompt to repress the encroachments of the Jews, have tolerated these attempts to secure greater freedom? The unexpected death of Festus in the year 62 and the anarchy which preceded the arrival of his successor, Albinus, were needed in order to make it possible for the Sanhedrim to get rid of suspected persons and to put James, the brother of the Lord, to death, so as to throw all the blame upon a popular insurrection in which no one would have seen anything, and the responsible authors of which it would be impossible to discover. A similar situation, in fact, presented itself in the spring of the year 36, when Vitellius sent Pilate to Rome, giving the administration of his office in the meantime to Marcellus. In the history of that epoch there is certainly no more favourable moment in which to place the martyrdom of Stephen than that in which the authority of Marcellus was still insecure and when it might have been supposed that the governor of Syria, Vitellius, whose policy was always to treat the Jews with caution, would close his eyes to their illegal actions. No time is therefore better adapted than this for the discretionary mission given to St Paul, provided the other chronological data do not raise any obstacle to it.

On the contrary, they fit in admirably with this date. We know that, *three years* after his conversion, shortly before returning to Jerusalem (Gal. i, 18), Paul had to fly by night from Damascus in order to escape (2 Cor. xi, 32-33) the ethnarch of Aretas IV, King of the Nabatæans. According to some recent authors (O. Holtzmann, Zahn, and Clemen), this ethnarch of Aretas was not the governor of the city, but the national chief of the Arabs who resided there, what one would call to-day a consul-general. This idea may claim to be original, but it is not a happy one. Can anyone imagine the diplomatic agent of a king who was so unpopular in Rome as Aretas putting a Roman city in a state of siege, in order to seize Roman citizens who were not the least dependent on

him, and whom the Roman authority would have been powerless to protect? These are proceedings which the *consuls-
general* of European powers have never allowed themselves
to carry out, even in Turkey. Aretas IV was therefore at
that time master of Damascus.

Now in 33-34 the Syrian capital still belonged to the
Romans, since its coins bear up to that date the stamp of
Tiberius. Moreover, it seems absolutely impossible that,
during the lifetime of that emperor, Aretas ever took possession of Damascus by force or received it by royal favour.
As a matter of fact Tiberius, towards the end of his life,
regarded with great displeasure the intrigues of the Arab,
who was waging war without his consent against Herod
Antipas, tetrarch of Galilee. The governor of Syria had
even received orders to march on Petra and had arrived at
Jerusalem, when the news of the death of Tiberius, which
took place on March 18, 37, caused him to suspend the
proposed expedition. But if Aretas had rendered himself
guilty of an act of direct aggression against the Romans,
he would not have got out of the affair so easily. Moreover,
it would have been inexplicable, on this hypothesis, why
Vitellius did not at once march directly on Damascus, in
order to recover the property of Rome instead of under-
taking a distant and difficult campaign. It has been supposed, not without some probability, that Caligula, whose
policy was often the reverse of that of his predecessor, may
have given Damascus to the King of the Nabatæans, as
he gave to Herod Agrippa the tetrarchy of Philip. That
would explain why there are no Damascus coins with the
heads of Caligula and Claudius, the series of imperial coins
beginning again only in 62 or 63. The taking possession of
Damascus by King Aretas could not, therefore, have been
anterior to the accession of Caligula (March 18, 37), nor
could the conversion of Paul have preceded the year 34, even
reckoning as complete the *three* years which elapsed before
the escape from Damascus. For these reasons the spring of
the year 36, coinciding with the recall of Pilate and the
martyrdom of Stephen, in all probability marked the conversion of the Apostle, which decisive reasons, to be presented later, prevent us from delaying longer.

2. *Meeting of St Paul and the Proconsul Gallio at Corinth.*
—This has been generally placed in the year 52. An inscription, coming from the excavations of Delphi, and published
in 1905 by M. Bourguet, confirms this date. The inscription,
which is very fragmentary, consists of twelve lines of uncertain length. But whatever difficulty the restitution of the
details may offer, two results are certain. First, when
Claudius wrote his letter to the city of Delphi, Gallio was

proconsul of Achaia, for the reading of the sixth line leaves no doubt of it: ('Ιού)νιος Γαλλίων ὁ φ(ίλος) μου κα(ὶ ανθύ-) πατος (τῆς 'Αχαιας); and the mention of ἀνθύπατος could not be retrospective. In the second place, the letter was written *after* the epoch at which Claudius had been saluted as *Imperator* for the twenty-sixth time and *before* the twenty-seventh imperial salutation; the figure XXVI (κϚ), which is read in the second line, cannot refer to anything else. Everyone is agreed on these two points.

We have now to settle the time. The twenty-seventh salutation of Claudius is twice mentioned without any date and four times with an interesting date. These latter documents inform us that Claudius had been saluted emperor for the twenty-seventh time in the year 52, or, more exactly, before August 1, 52. What is exactly the date of the twenty-sixth salutation? We have just seen that it was certainly before August 1, 52, and we know, moreover, that on January 25, 51, Claudius received his twenty-second imperial salutation; finally, we deduce from other epigraphic documents that the twenty-sixth salutation, the one which interests us especially, coincides with the twelfth year of the tribunate of Claudius (from January 25, 52, to January 24, 53). It is evident, therefore, that five imperial salutations (from the twenty-third to the twenty-seventh) were decreed to Claudius between January 25, 51, and August 1, 52. Now in looking over the *Annals* of Tacitus, we observe that the year 51 was not particularly fruitful in military successes, while the year 52 has to its credit some notable advantages won from the Clitae of Cilicia and from the Silures of South Britain. It is, therefore, almost certain that the twenty-sixth imperial salutation dates from the first half of the year 52, and even more probably from the spring of that year, at the moment of the resumption of military operations. Consequently, the letter of Claudius must have been written between the month of April and August 1, 52. See *Recherches de science religieuse,* vol. iii, 1912, pp. 374-378, on the inscription of Delphi and its chronological consequences.

Gallio was then proconsul of Achaia. The term of a proconsul's office lasted for a year, and cases of their continuance in office were very exceptional and must not be taken for granted without proof. An exception is much less probable for Gallio, since the climate of Greece did not agree with him (Seneca, *Epist.* 104). The proconsuls entered on their duties in the month of April or May. In reality, their authority began from the day when they set foot in their provinces. The letters of Cicero assure us of this positively; but as the majority of these magistrates were in no hurry to depart, Claudius allowed them an extreme limit of delay, after which they must all have left Rome. According to Dio

Cassius (LX, 11 and 17) this was at first (in 42) the new moon of April, and a little later (in 43) the 15th of the same month. For those who used public vehicles the journey from Rome to Corinth could hardly have taken more than a month, so that May 15 at the latest found them at their post. Gallio would, therefore, have been in Achaia from May, 52 to May, 53.

In spite of everything, even regarding it as settled that the letter of Claudius to Delphi was written in the first seven months of 52 and that the proconsulship of Gallio had only the normal duration of one year, there remain two causes of uncertainty : first, we do not know in what month Claudius wrote his letter to Gallio; second, the meeting of this magistrate with Paul might have occurred at any moment during his government. St Luke tells us merely that it took place *during* the proconsulship of Gallio (Acts xviii 12 : Γαλλίωνος ἀνθυπάτου ὄντος). However, it is more natural to think of the beginning than of the end of it in this connection. The enemies of the Apostle might have taken advantage of the arrival of a new magistrate to try to destroy Paul, and the *considerable* time which the latter passed at Corinth after his sentence (Acts xviii 18 : Παῦλος ἔτι προσμείνας ἡμέρας ἱκανάς) is better explained if Gallio was still there to protect him. But this is only a conjecture, and the door must be left open for the contrary hypothesis.

In conclusion : by the strictest interpretation of facts, Paul and Gallio might have met at Corinth at any time from May, 51 A.D., to May, 53; but for the reasons given above the probability in favour of the year 52 is much the greatest.

3. *Recall of Felix and Arrival of Festus.*—St Paul had been a captive for two years at Cæsarea (Acts xxiv, 27) when Nero recalled the procurator Felix and appointed Festus as his successor. While most historians and exegetes place this event in the year 60, allowing of the deviation of a year more or less, a resolute minority holds to one of the years 54, 55, or 56. Two reasons are alleged in favour of an early date.—1. According to Josephus (*Antiqu.* XX, viii, 9) the procurator Felix, who had been accused by the Jews to the emperor, owed his escape from punishment only to the influence of his brother Pallas, then all-powerful at Nero's court. Now, if Tacitus is to be believed, Pallas fell into disgrace, or at least lost his influence at court, under the consuls of the year 55 (*Annals* XIII, 14; *cf.* 11), or, more exactly, a little before the murder of Britannicus in February, 55 (*Annals* XIII, 15). —2. Eusebius in his Armenian *Chronicle* assigns the recall of Felix to the last year of Claudius (54) and, in the Latin *Chronicle* translated by St Jerome, to the second year of Nero (October, 55—October, 56) In any case, according to both

Eusebius and Josephus, the departure of Felix must have been before the year 57.

These two proofs are very precarious. First, in the case of Josephus. It is utterly impossible that between October 13, 54, the date of the accession of Nero, and the beginning of February, 55, the date of the death of Britannicus—that is to say, in less than four months and in the dead of winter—the emperor's order recalling Felix should have arrived in Palestine, that the latter should have gone to Rome, that his case should have been prepared in refutation of the charges made against him, and finally that it should have been non-suited at the imperial tribunal. One of two things, therefore, is true : either Josephus, in order to explain the scandalous acquittal of Felix, has purely and simply deceived himself in attributing it to the influence of Pallas ; or else Pallas, though having fallen from his position of omnipotence at court, still retained sufficient power to be useful to his friends. The second alternative is hinted at by Tacitus (*Annals* XIII, 14) when he says that Pallas, although in disgrace, had stipulated that he should not be questioned and disturbed about anything in the past. But on both hypotheses the argument drawn from Josephus is without force or value.

The text of Eusebius is not convincing. For the chronology of the procurators of Judæa Eusebius depends upon Josephus (*Cf.* Schürer in *Zeitschrift für wissenschaft. Theologie,* 1898, pp. 21-42). Now Josephus, who accords ten years (from 52 to 62) to the two governments of Felix and of Festus, says nothing of their respective duration ; and Eusebius in his *History* imitates his reserve. But as he is obliged in his *Chronicle* to give precise dates, he thinks it well to divide the whole term of the two governments into two equal parts. The arrival of Festus is, therefore, placed in the second year of Nero's reign, that is in 57, for it must not be forgotten that Eusebius makes the reign of Nero begin at the commencement of the Syrian year (September, 55) which followed the death of Claudius, and that consequently his dates are a year too late. Dependence, therefore, is not to be placed upon the data of his *Chronicle,* even admitting that the Latin version has preserved the real figures.

On the other hand, we have four plausible reasons for retarding the departure of Felix and the arrival of Festus to 59 or 60.—1. The first time that Felix, *two years before his recall* (Acts xxiv, 27), found himself confronted by Paul, the latter said to him : " Knowing that *for many years* thou hast been judge over this nation, I will willingly answer for myself before thee " (Acts xxiv, 10). Now, even taking into consideration the usual brevity of the imperial delegations (less, however, under Tiberius, Claudius, and Nero), it is difficult to admit that "*many years*" (ἐκ πολλῶν ἐτῶν) represents a period of less than five or six years; and we know by Josephus, compared with Tacitus, that Felix had entered on his office in 52. He was not, therefore, recalled before 59 or 60.—2. At the time of Paul's arrest, the abortive insurrection of an Egyptian adventurer is already ancient history. But this attempt, which is in any case later than the accession of Nero (October 13, 54), does not date from the first year of Felix. That carries us back to almost the same epoch for the change of procurators.—3. All the probabilities indicate that the government of Festus was much shorter than that of Felix; for Josephus, who dwells at some length on the deeds and exploits of Felix, has almost nothing to say about Festus. The latter died in the first half of the year 62, since his successor, Albinus, came in that year to Jerusalem for the Feast of Tabernacles. By allowing him a government of two years, three years at most, historical surmises are best satisfied. He would then have replaced Felix in 59 or 60.—4. Finally, from the meeting with Gallio to the commencement of the captivity of Paul, there ensued not less than five years. As the meeting took place in 52 or 53 at the latest, that brings us to 57 or 58 for the beginning of the captivity and to 59 or 60 for the recall of Felix.

We have purposely neglected to mention two data which appear to us too indefinite : the marriage of Felix with Drusilla, sister of Herod Agrippa I (Acts xxiv, 24), and the journey to Rome of Josephus in 64 (*Vita,* 3) to obtain the release of some priests whom Felix had sent captive thither. See on the former point Turner, *Dictionary of the Bible,* vol. i, p. 417, and on the second Zahn, *Einleitung*[3], vol. i, p. 650.

Ramsay (*A Fixed Date in the Life of St Paul,* in the *Expositor,* May, 1896, pp. 336-345), basing his conclusions on a text of the Acts (xx, 6-7), has tried to show that St Paul's captivity necessarily took place in 57, and that, consequently, the replacing of Felix by Festus occurred in 59. But he supposes without valid proof that Paul left Philippi *immediately* after the Azymes—that is to say, 22 Nisan. Now, although the Apostle desired to reach Jerusalem before Pentecost, forty-two days were quite sufficient for the journey; the proof that he was not in so much haste is that he landed at Troas for a week's stay. The trip from Philippi to Troas took *five* days; the stay in that city *seven* days; Ramsay concludes that Paul left Troas the *eleventh* day after his departure from Philippi; but this might have been on the twelfth or even the thirteenth day, by counting as full days both the passage by sea and the stay at Troas. Finally, the author, reasoning as if the two preceding hypotheses were surely true, and observing that Paul departed from Troas on a Monday (Acts xx, 7-11), deduces from this the fact that he left Philippi on a Friday (22 Nisan), and that the 15 Nisan or the Passover was, therefore, that year on a Friday. Now, he adds, the only year—between 56 and 59—when the Passover occurred on a Friday was precisely the year 57. Such accuracy, however, must not deceive us. It is almost impossible to say on what day of the week the paschal solemnity fell in any year whatever, since we do not know how the Jews at that time determined the first day of their lunar months.

Let us be content to assert, with that high degree of probability which in history very closely resembles certainty, that the replacing of Felix by Festus, in the midst of the captivity of Paul, occurred in 59 or 60, but more probably in 59.

4. *Date of Paul's Martyrdom.*—We are quite sure that St Peter and St Paul suffered martyrdom at Rome in the reign of Nero, but we do not know whether this was in the same year and on the same day, and it seems that June 29, the day on which the Church celebrates their feast, is the anniversary of the removal of the relics of both apostles in the year 258, during the persecution of Valerian. Several learned contemporaries declare with axiomatic certainty that the great apostles must have perished during the summer of the year 64, with the other Christians put to death by Nero after the conflagration of Rome (July, 64). It is gratuitously taken for granted that Nero's persecution lasted only a few weeks, at most several months. But Suetonius, who mentions the persecution of the Christians without connecting it with the fire, notes well the permanent cause of it : *Afflicti suppliciis Christiani, genus hominum superstitionis novae ac malificae (Nero, 16)*. The reason alleged is *superstition*—that is to say, a new cult, not a recognized one, illicit and, therefore, dangerous from the Roman point of view. There was no need of a decree or a special law; the Christians were now pursued by the higher law of public safety in the name of a primordial principle of government, which is considered essential to the preservation of the empire. If it had not been so, the correspondence between Pliny and Trajan would have no sense. The well-understood text of Tacitus presents no obstacle to this interpretation : *Primum correpti qui fatebantur, deinde indicio eorum multitudo ingens, haud perinde in crimine incendii, quam odio humani generis convicti sunt (Annals* XV, 44). The immediate occasion, the first pretext, is indeed the fire; but soon the motive for the persecution changes, the accusation becomes general and may assail any Christians in whatever place they are found, without the least connection with the Roman disaster; their

crime is *hatred for the human race*—that is to say, their
religious isolation, which kept them away from the temples
and public offices, and their intolerance of other religions.
Hereafter no other complaints are invoked against them; if
they confess, their crime is proved; if they are silent, their
denunciators will be believed. It is to this state of things
that the First Epistle of St Peter alludes. At the moment of
the conflagration St Paul was far from Rome, in Spain or in
the East; he was arrested in Asia Minor and conveyed to
the capital to be tried there. Neither his capture nor his condemnation can have any connection with the burning of
Rome.

II—Intermediate Dates

With our four dates thus determined, it will be easy to
trace Paul's apostolic career. For the sake of greater clearness, let us divide it into two unequal parts, Paul's meeting
with the proconsul Gallio forming the point of intersection.

1. *From Paul's Conversion to his Meeting with Gallio.*—
There are three principal stages : the return to Jerusalem
after his conversion, the persecution of Agrippa soon followed
by his death, the meeting of the apostles to settle the question
of the Mosaic observances.

There is nothing special to be said about the visit to
Jerusalem *three years after* Paul's conversion (Gal. i, 18).
The only doubt is whether this means three complete years
or two years and a fraction. The story of the Acts does not
help us to solve this question. St Luke does not speak of
the journey to Arabia, although he seems to indicate quite
clearly two separate sojourns in Damascus; the first one of
a few days only (Acts ix, 19 : ἡμέρας τινάς), the other much
longer (Acts ix, 23 : ἡμέραι ἱκαναί). It is between the two that
the journey to Arabia is to be inserted, but there is nothing
conclusive as to the whole duration of this period. However,
as St Paul makes it evident that he was not in special haste
to go to the other apostles (Gal. i, 16 : εὐθέως οὐ προσανεθέμην),
perhaps he magnifies the delay as much as the import of the
discourse allows him to. If his conversion falls within the
first months of the year 36, the return to Jerusalem may then
have taken place in the second part of the year 38.

Paul then resided for several years in his own country
(Gal. i, 21 ; Acts ix, 30). He was brought out from his retirement by Barnabas, when the extraordinary increase of
the Christian community at Antioch made the need of new
missioners felt (Acts xi, 24, 25). They worked there together
one entire year, and were together sent as delegates to
Jerusalem to carry to the brethren there the aid which was

intended for them in view of the predicted famine (Acts xi, 26-30). It is very remarkable that St Luke inserts the recital of the persecution and the death of Herod (Acts xii, 1-23) between the arrival at Jerusalem and the return of the two delegates to Antioch (Acts xi, 30 and xii, 25). Is this not to make us understand that these events are synchronous? And this he expresses quite clearly elsewhere by saying that they took place about the same time (Acts xii, 1 : κατ' ἐκεῖνον τὸν καιρόν). The date of the death of Herod Agrippa I can be determined with sufficient exactitude. Very soon after the death of Tiberius (March 16, 37) this crowned adventurer received from Caligula the tetrarchies of Philippi and Lysanias with the title of king, and a little later also obtained the plundered wealth of Herod Antipas. On his accession (January 25, 41) Claudius added to this Judæa and Samaria. Now, Josephus expressly states that Agrippa reigned over all Judæa only three years, and we know from the Acts (xii, 3) that he died soon after the Passover. This was, therefore, in the first months of the year 44, at the moment when he was about to celebrate at Cæsarea the solemn games in honour of Claudius who had returned from Britain in triumph in the spring of this same year. When it is objected that the famine of which St Luke speaks raged chiefly in 45 or 46, it is forgotten that bad harvests were frequent during the reign of Claudius, that a general famine is almost always preceded by several years of scarcity, and that, moreover, the help sent by the Christians of Antioch to their brethren in Jerusalem was despatched thither in advance, through belief in a prediction. The date proposed has, moreover, the advantage of explaining why St Luke puts the delegates from Antioch in touch, not with the apostles, scattered by the persecution, but with the elders of Jerusalem (Acts xi, 30); and also why St Paul in the Epistle to the Galatians (i, 11–ii, 1) does not mention a journey in which manifestly he had not been able to come into contact with his colleagues in the apostolate. The only reason for referring the persecution to the year 42 seems to have been to place the dispersion of the apostles twelve years, more or less, after the Passion, and the departure of Peter for Rome, twenty-five years before his martyrdom.

The interval between the persecution of Herod and the apostolic gathering at Jerusalem cannot be directly determined; for we do not know how much time Paul and Barnabas spent at Antioch after their return from Palestine (Acts xii, 25) and we have no data by which to measure the duration of the first mission. All that can be stated positively, in view of the length of the journey made, the number of churches founded and certain more or less definite chronological data, is that it must have taken several years; without counting that, on their return, before the troubles which made the meeting in Jerusalem necessary, the two missionaries resided quite a long time in Antioch (Acts xiv, 28 : χρόνον οὐκ ὀλίγον). By assigning to this period a total duration of four or five years, the probabilities are best accounted for.

This brings us to the year 49 or 50. Let us see if this date coincides with the testimony of St Paul. He mentions two visits to Jerusalem : one, three years after his conversion, to see Peter (Gal. i, 18 : ἔπειτα μετὰ τρία ἔτη ἀνῆλθον εἰς Ἱεροσόλυμα); the other after an interval of fourteen years to settle the question about the observances of the Law (Gal. ii, 1 : ἔπειτα διὰ δεκατεσσάρων ἐτῶν πάλιν ἀνέβην εἰς Ἱεροσόλυμα). Do these *fourteen years* include the *three* years mentioned above, or not? Certainly the preposition employed in the second case (διά instead of μετά) and the iterative particle (πάλιν) lead us to see in διὰ δεκατεσσάρων ἐτῶν the interval included between the two visits. The three years, if added to the fourteen, would make a total of seventeen, or at least of sixteen, counting fractions of years as full years. As the meeting of the apostles cannot be later than the year 50, nor the conversion of Paul previous to the year 34, it would be necessary to fix these two events at their extreme dates. But the text of the Epistle to the Galatians does not force us to this course. In fact, the second chapter is not the logical sequel to the first chapter. Here Paul proves that he has not learned his Gospel from men, but from Jesus Christ himself; there he shows that his Gospel was sanctioned by the leaders of the Twelve, and it is for this purpose that he is led to speak of the meeting at Jerusalem; but his aim is not to enumerate all his journeys to the Holy City, and he establishes no connection between those which he mentions. The *three years* of Gal. i, 18 and the *fourteen years* of Gal. ii, 1, instead of joining together, may therefore overlap each other; so much the more as St Paul by the very tendency of his argument is led to enlarge as much as possible the time passed apart from the other apostles, as well as the period of his unchallenged apostolate. Consequently, if his conversion took place in the spring of the year 36, as there are good reasons to suppose, the meeting at Jerusalem would have occurred towards the end of the year 49 or at the beginning of the following year.

The sojourn of Paul at Antioch, after the meeting at Jerusalem, appears to have been of short duration (Acts xv, 36 : μετὰ δέ τινας ἡμέρας). But it is difficult to estimate at less than a year the length of the visit to the churches of Cilicia and Galatia, with the missionary journey across Macedonia and Greece to Corinth (Acts xv, 41–xviii, 1). Paul found in the latter city Aquila and Priscilla, who *had just arrived* there (Acts xviii, 2 : προσφάτως), by reason of the decree of Claudius expelling the Jews from Rome. Tacitus does not speak of this decree, and contents himself with mentioning, in reference to the year 52, a severe and inefficacious measure against the astrologers (*Annals* XII, 52). Suetonius mentions it without dating it (*Claud.*, 25). Orosius (*Hist.* VII, 6) places it in 49, and refers to Josephus who, in the works which have come down to us, has written nothing of the sort. The authority for it is not great, but the date given by Orosius fits in very well with our other data. Paul would thus have rejoined Aquila towards the end of the year 50, and would have appeared before Gallio in the first half of 52 after a sojourn of eighteen months in Corinth (Acts xviii, 11).

2. *From the Meeting with Gallio to the Martyrdom.*—
Paul remained still for some time in Corinth (Acts xviii, 18 : ἔτι προσμείνας ἡμέρας ἱκανάς. Note the meaning of ἱκανός in St Luke). This *considerable time* must not be included in the eighteen months mentioned above (xviii, 11); that would be contrary to the literary usage of the author. Every time that St Luke gives a date, the utmost limit of that date is the event which he is about to relate. For example, the missionaries " spend an entire year at Antioch " (xi, 20) until the incident mentioned immediately after. The same is true of the sojourn in Ephesus (Acts xix, 8-10) presently to be considered.

Paul then betook himself to Antioch by way of Jerusalem. The third mission seems to have followed quite closely upon the second (Acts xviii, 23 : ποιήσας χρόνον τινὰ ἐξῆλθεν). However vague these hints may be, it does not seem possible to make the third mission begin sooner than six months after Paul's meeting with Gallio. The Apostle longed to keep the promise given to the Ephesians; yet he reached Ephesus by a long détour, halting to console and strengthen the different churches found along his route. Such a journey can scarcely have lasted less than six more months.

Paul's stay at Ephesus is divided into three periods : the *three months* during which he preaches in the synagogue (Acts xix, 8); the *two years* which he devotes to teaching in the school of Tyrannus (xix, 10); and the uncertain length of time which he still passed at Ephesus after sending Timothy and Erastus to Macedonia (xix, 22 : αὐτὸς ἐπέσχεν χρόνον εἰς τὴν 'Ασίαν). Following the principle above mentioned, this last sojourn is not to be included in the two years and three months. Indeed, in his address to the elders of Ephesus, Paul asserts that he has remained among them for the space of three years (xx, 31 : τριετίαν, *per triennium*).

It is possible that the insurrection of the silversmiths, which occurred about this time (xix, 23 : κατὰ τὸν καιρὸν ἐκεῖνον), hastened his departure from Ephesus. This obliged him to await in Macedonia the return of Timothy, who had not rejoined him at Troas (2 Cor. ii, 13); for he did not wish to appear in Corinth before the settlement of all the disputes. At Corinth he remained three months (Acts xx, 3) and left it again towards the time of Easter, since he wished to arrive at Jerusalem for Pentecost, which he actually did (xx, 16). About a year had elapsed since his departure from Ephesus.

From this day on the story of the Acts becomes very circumstantial. The Apostle, who was made a prisoner at the time of the feast of Pentecost, consequently in May or June, is kept a captive at Cæsarea two entire years (Acts xxiv, 27 : διετίας πληρωθείσης) until the arrival of the procurator Festus. But the new examination of his case and the formalities attending his appeal to Cæsar delay his shipment to Rome, and it is only in the autumn that the vessel which is to convey him sets sail for Italy (xxvii, 9). As the navigation was slow and difficult, interrupted by several halts, one of which lasted three months at Malta after the shipwreck (xxviii, 14), they reached Rome only in the spring, about the month of March. Paul was a prisoner there two years more (xxviii, 30), so that the whole duration of his captivity was five years, perhaps less two or three months. Beginning at Pentecost of the year 57, it ended about Easter of the year 62. Adding up the different numbers thus detailed, we obtain almost ten years as the interval between the meeting with Gallio and the end of his first captivity.

3. *Synoptic View.*—The preceding considerations can be expressed in a view of the whole subject, in which the chances of error are very limited :

	Year
Martyrdom of St Stephen ; conversion of Saul	Spring, 36
First visit of St Paul to Jerusalem	Autumn, 38
Sojourn of St Paul in Cilicia	39–43
Paul brought by Barnabas to Antioch	Spring, 43
Martyrdom of St James the Greater ⎫ Miraculous deliverance of St Peter ⎪ Sudden death of Herod Agrippa I ⎬	March-April, 44
Barnabas and Paul sent to Jerusalem ⎭	
Departure for the first great mission	44–45
Meeting of the Apostles ; conflict at Antioch	Autumn, 49
Departure for the second mission	Spring, 50
Arrival of Paul at Corinth	Winter, 50–51
Meeting with the proconsul Gallio	Summer, 52
Departure for the third mission	Spring, 53
Arrival at Ephesus	Autumn, 53
Departure from Ephesus	Summer, 56
Beginning of the first captivity	Pentecost, 57
Festus succeeds Felix	Summer, 59
Voyage to Rome ; sojourn at Malta	Winter, 59–60

	Year
End of St Paul's first captivity - -⎫ Martyrdom of James, brother of the Lord ⎭ · ·	Spring, 62
Last missionary journey, Spain, Asia - - - -	62–66
Second arrest of St Paul - - - - -	66
Martyrdom of the Apostles Peter and Paul - - -	66–67

Let us not forget that neither the extreme points of this list (the conversion of Paul and the martyrdom of the great apostles) nor the two principal intermediate points (the meeting of Paul and Gallio at Corinth and the replacing of Felix by Festus) are dated with absolute strictness. The conversion of Paul is fixed in the year 34 or in the year 36, according as one adds together or blends the figures furnished by the Epistle to the Galatians (i, 18, and ii, 1); but it cannot be placed either before 34, because of 2 Cor. xi, 32, or after 36, on account of the apostolic council, which cannot have been subsequent to the year 50. The precise time of the death of Saints Peter and Paul is likewise unknown. All that can be affirmed with certainty is that they suffered martyrdom *towards the end* of the reign of Nero. The meeting of Paul with Gallio must have taken place between May, 51 and May, 53, the proconsulship of Gallio, according to the inscription of Delphi, being confined to these limits; but the reasons for fixing it in the summer of the year 52, although very strong, are not absolutely decisive. Finally, we know that Festus succeeded Felix between 58 and 60; but, to be more exact, it is necessary to have recourse to extrinsic considerations.

These uncertainties being conceded, we might modify the schedule given above by advancing by two years the beginning of the period and retarding by a year most of the other dates, with the exception of the events of 43 and 44, maintained in their place by the synchronism of the death of Herod Agrippa :

	Year
Conversion of Paul - - - - - -	34
Meeting of the Apostles at Jerusalem - - - -	50
Meeting of Paul with Gallio - - - -	Spring, 53
Beginning of Paul's captivity - - -	Summer, 58
Arrival of Festus - - - - -	Summer, 60
End of the first captivity - - - -	Spring, 63

These results must suffice. It is very improbable that new discoveries in the fields of epigraphy or history will ever bring any important corrections. Moreover, they would have very little interest for the exegete and the theologian.

The Epistles of Paul abound with quotations, allusions, and reminiscences the examination of which becomes a necessity for the exegete and theologian desirous of not imputing alien ideas to the Apostle. The citations in the Epistle to the Hebrews are studied separately in Note K.

I—COLLECTION OF QUOTATIONS CONTAINED IN PAUL'S EPISTLES

1—*Actual Quotations with Formulas of Quotation.*

Epistle.	Passage quoted.	Formula.	Remarks.
Rom.:			
i, 17	Hab. ii, 4	καθὼς γέγρ.	From the Septuagint.
ii, 24	Is. lii, 5	*Id.*	*Id.* (omission).
iii, 4	Ps. l, 6+cxv, 11	καθάπερ γέγρ.	*Id.* (composite).
iii, 10-12	Ps. xiii, 1-3	καθ. γέγρ. ὅτι	
iii, 13a	Ps. v, 10	. . . . .	⎫
iii, 13b	Ps. cxxxix, 4	. . . . .	⎬ Series; from the Septuagint with different readings.
iii, 14	Ps. ix, 28 (x, 7)	. . . . .	⎪
iii, 15-17	Is. lix, 7-8	. . . . .	⎪
iii, 18	Ps. xxxv, 2		⎭
iv, 3, 9, 22	Gen. xv, 6	ἡ Γραφὴ λέγ.	From the Septuagint.
iv, 7-8	Ps. xxxi, 1-2	Δα. λέγει	*Id.*
iv, 17	Gen. xvii, 5	καθ. γέγρ. ὅτι	*Id.*
iv, 18	Gen. xv, 5	κατὰ τὸ εἰρημ.	*Id.*
vii, 7	Ex. xx, 17 (Deut. v, 21)	ὁ νόμ. ἔλεγεν	*Id.*
viii, 36	Ps. xliii, 23	καθ. γέγρ. ὅτι	*Id.*
ix, 7	Gen. xxi, 12	Special form	*Id.*
ix, 9	Gen. xviii, 10, 14	*Id.*	Variation (compos.).
ix, 12	Gen. xxv, 23	*Id.*	From the Septuagint.
ix, 13	Mal. i, 2-3	καθάπερ γέγ.	*Id.*
ix, 15	Ex. xxxiii, 19	τῷ Μω. γέγ.	*Id.*
ix, 17	Ex. ix, 16	λέγ. ἡ Γραφή	After the Hebrew.
ix, 25·26	Hos. ii, 25+ii, 1	ἐν τῷ Ὡσ. λέγ.	Free, composite.
ix, 27-28	Is. x, 22-23	Ἡσ. κράζει	Septuagint (with variations).
ix, 29	Is. i, 9	Special form	From the Septuagint.
ix, 33	Is. viii, 14 + xxviii, 16	καθὼς γέγρ.	Composite.
x, 5	Lev. xviii, 5	Μω. γράφει	Very free.
x, 6-9	Deut. xxx, 12-14	Special form	Commentary.
x, 11	Is. xxviii, 16	λέγει ἡ Γρ.	Very free.
x, 15	Is. lii, 7	καθάπ. γέγρ.	*Id.*
x, 16	Is. liii, 1	Ἡσ. λέγει.	Septuagint.
x, 19	Deut. xxxii, 21	Μω. λέγει.	*Id.* (variation)
x, 20	Is. lxv, 1	Ἡσ. λέγει.	*Id.* (inversion)
x, 21	Is. lxv, 2	*Id.*	*Id.*
xi, 3	1 Kings xix, 10	λέγει ἡ Γρ.	Very free.
xi, 4	1 Kings xix, 18	λέγει ὁ χρημ.	After the Hebrew.
xi, 8	Is. xxix, 10+ Deut. xxix, 3	καθάπ. γέγρ.	Composite.

Epistle.	Passage quoted.	Formula.	Remarks.
Rom. :			
xi, 9-10	Ps. lxviii, 23-24	Δα. λέγει.	Septuagint (variations).
xi, 26-27	Is. lix, 20 + xxvii, 9	καθὼς γέγρ.	Composite.
xii, 19	Deut. xxxii, 35	γέγραπται	After the Hebrew.
xii, 20	Prov. xxv, 21-22	Id.	After the Septuagint.
xiii, 9	Ex. xx, 13-15 + Deut. v, 17-19	Special form	Composite.
xiv, 11	Is. xlv, 23 + xlix, 18	γέγραπται	Id.
xv, 3	Ps. lxviii, 10	καθὼς γέγρ.	After the Septuagint.
xv, 9	Ps. xvii, 50	Id.	
xv, 10	Deut. xxxii, 43	πάλιν λέγει	⎫ Series ; after the Septua-
xv, 11	Ps. cxvi, 1	καὶ πάλιν	⎬ gint (with inversions).
xv, 12	Is. xi, 10	πάλ. Ἡσ. λέγ.	⎭
xv, 21	Is. lii, 15	καθὼς γέγρ.	After the Septuagint.
1 Cor. :			
i, 19	Is. xxix, 14	γέγραπται	Septuagint (with varia- tions).
i, 31	Jer. ix, 22-23, etc.	καθὼς γέγρ.	Very free.
ii, 9	Is. lxiv, 3+lxv, 17	Id.	Id.
iii, 19	Job v, 12-13	γέγραπται	After the Hebrew.
iii, 20	Ps. xciii, 11	καὶ πάλιν	Septuagint (with varia- tions).
vi, 16	Gen. ii, 24	φησίν	After the Septuagint.
ix, 9	Deut. xxv, 4	ἐν τῷ Μω. γέγρ.	Id.
x, 7	Ex. xxxii, 6	ὥσπερ γέγρ.	Id.
xiv, 21	Is. xxviii, 11-12	ἐν τῷ νόμῳ γ.	Very free (Hebrew ?)
xv, 45	Gen. ii, 7	οὕτως γέγρ.	Free.
xv, 54-55	Is. xxv, 8+Os. xiii, 14	ὁ λόγος ὁ γ.	Composite.
2 Cor. :			
iv, 13	Ps. cxv, 10	κατὰ τὸ γεγρ.	After the Septuagint.
vi, 2	Is. xlix, 8	λέγει	Id.
vi, 16	Ez. xxxvii, 27	καθ. εἶπεν ὁ θ.	⎫ Series ; after Septuagint,
vi, 17	Is. lii, 11-12	. . . . .	⎬ very free.
vi, 18	2 Sam. vii, 14	. . . . .	⎭
viii, 15	Ex. xvi, 18	καθὼς γέγρ.	Septuagint (with inver- sions.)
x, 9	Ps. cxi, 9	Id.	After the Septuagint.
Gal. :			
iii, 8	Gen. xii, 3	Special form	Septuagint (with varia- tions).
iii, 10	Deut. xxvii, 26	γέγρ. ὅτι	Septuagint, free.
iii, 13	Deut. xxi, 23	ὅτι γέγρ.	Septuagint (with varia- tions.)
iv, 22	Gen. xvi, 15, etc.	γέγραπτ. ὅτι	Without textual quota- tion.
iv, 27	Is. liv, 1	γέγραπται	After the Septuagint.
iv, 30	Gen. xxi, 10	λέγει ἡ Γρ.	Septuagint (with varia- tions.)
v. 14	Lev. xix, 18	Special form	After the Septuagint.

Epistle.	Passage quoted.	Formula.	Remarks.
Eph. :			
iv, 8	Ps. lxvii, 19	διὸ λέγει	Neither Hebrew nor Septuagint.
v, 14	?	διὸ λέγει	*Id.*
vi, 2-3	Ex. xx, 12 (Deut. v, 16)	Special form	Septuagint (with variations.)
1 *Tim.:*			
v, 18	Deut. xxv, 4	λέγει ἡ Γρ.	Septuagint (with inversions).
2 *Tim. :*			
ii, 19	Num. xvi, 5 ; Is. xxvi, 13	Special form	Septuagint (with variations.)

2—*Tacit Quotations, Allusions, Reminiscences.*

Epistle.	Passage referred to	Epistle.	Passage referred to.
Rom. :		1 *Cor. :*	
i, 20-32	Wisdom xiii, 1 and *passim.*	x, 5	Num. xiv, 16.
		x, 6	Num. xi, 4, 34.
i, 23	Ps. cv, 20.	x, 20	Deut. xxxii, 17.
ii, 6	Ps. lxi, 13.	x, 21	Mal. i, 7, 12.
ii, 11	Ecclus. xxxii, 15-16.	x, 22	Deut. xxxii, 21.
*iii, 20	Ps. cxlii, 2.	x, 26	Ps. xxiii, 1
iv, 11.	Gen. xvii, 10-11.	xi, 7	Gen. i, 27.
iv, 25	Is. liii, 4-5.	xi, 25	Ex. xxiv, 8 ; Zach. ix, 11.
v, 5	Ps. xxi, 6.	xiii, 5	Zach. viii, 17.
*v, 12	Gen. ii, 17 ; iii, 19.	xiv, 25	Is. xlv, 14, etc.
*vii, 2-3	Deut. ii, 1-4.	*xiv, 34	Gen. iii, 16.
vii, 11	Gen. iii, 13	xv, 25	Ps. cix, 1.
viii, 33	Is. l, 8-9.	xv, 27	Ps. viii, 7.
viii, 34	Ps. cix, 1.	xv, 32	Is. xxii, 13.
*ix, 7	Gen. xxi, 12.		
ix, 18	Ex. iv, 21 ; vii, 3, etc.	2 *Cor. :*	
ix, 20	Is. xxix, 16 ; xlv, 9, etc.	iii, 3.	Ex. xxxi, 18 ; Ez. xi, 19, etc.
ix, 21	Wisdom xv, 17.		
*x, 13	Joel iii, 5.	*iii, 7-18	Ex. xxxiv, 29-35, etc.
*x, 18	Ps. xviii, 5.	v, 4	Wisdom ix, 15.
xi, 1-2	Ps. xciii, 14, etc.	v, 10	Ecclus. xii, 14.
xi, 32	Wisdom xi, 23.	v, 17	Is. xliii, 18-19.
*xi, 34-35	Is. xl, 13 ; Job xli, 3.	vi, 9	Ps. cxvii, 17-18.
xii, 16-17	Prov. iii, 7+iii, 4.	vi, 11	Ps. cxviii, 32.
		vii, 6	Is. xlix, 13.
1 *Cor.:*		viii, 21	Prov. iii, 4 (LXX).
i, 20	Is. xix, 11, 12+ xxxiii, 18.	ix, 7	Prov. xxii, 8 (LXX).
		ix, 10	Is. lv, 10+Os. x, 12.
*ii, 16	Is. xl, 13.	x, 17	Jer. ix, 23.
v, 7	Ex. xii, 21.	xi, 3	Gen. iii, 4, 13.
v, 13	Deut. xxii, 24, etc.	xiii, 1	Deut. xix, 15.
vi, 2	Wisdom iii, 8.	*Gal. :*	
vi, 12-13	Eccl. xxxvii, 28+xxxvi, 23.	i, 15-16	Is. xlix, 1+Jer. i, 5.
		*ii, 16	Ps. cxlii, 2.
vi, 17	Deut. x, 20 ; xi, 22.	*iii, 6	Gen. xv, 6

Epistle.	Passage referred to.	Epistle.	Passage referred to.
Gal.:		1 *Thess.:*	
*iii, 11.	Hab. ii, 4.	ii, 16	Gen. xv, 16; 2 Macc. vi, 14.
*iii, 12	Lev. xviii, 5.	iv, 5	Jer. x, 25.
*iii, 16	Gen. xii, 7, etc.	iv, 8	Ez. xxxvii, 14.
vi, 16	Ps. cxxiv, 5.	iv, 13	Wisdom iii, 18.
Eph.:		v, 8	Is. lix, 17.
i, 18	Wisdom v, 5.	v, 22	Job i, 1, 8; ii, 3.
i, 20	Ps. cix, 1.	2 *Thess.:*	
i, 22	Ps. viii, 7.	i, 8	Is. lxvi, 15.
ii,13-17	Is. lvii, 19; lii, 7.	i, 9-10	Is. ii, 10, 11, 19, 21.
ii, 20	Is. xxviii, 16.	i, 10	Zach. xiv, 5+Ps. lxvii, 36.
*iv, 25	Zach. viii, 16.	i, 12	Is. lxvi, 5.
*iv, 26	Ps. iv, 5.	ii, 4	Dan. xi, 36; Ez. xxviii, 2.
v, 2	Ps. xxxix, 7; Ez. xx, 41.	ii, 8	Is. xi, 4.
v, 18	Prov. xxiii, 31 (LXX).	ii, 13	Deut. xxxiii, 12.
*v, 31	Gen. ii, 24.	1 *Tim.:*	
*vi, 14a	Is. xi, 5.	ii, 6	Is. liii, 11-12.
*vi, 14b	Is. lix, 17.	ii, 12	Gen. iii, 16.
*vi, 17	Is. xlix, 2.	ii, 13	Gen. ii, 7.
Phil.:		ii, 14	Gen. iii, 6.
i, 19	Job xiii, 16.	*v, 19	Deut. xix, 15.
ii, 10-11	Is. xlv, 23.	vi, 1	Is. lii, 5.
*ii, 15	Deut. xxxii, 5.	vi, 15	Deut. x, 17; Dan. ii, 47.
ii, 16	Is. xlix, 4; lxv, 23.	2 *Tim.:*	
iv, 3	Ps. lxviii, 29.	iv, 14.	Ps. lxi, 13: Prov. xxiv 12.
iv, 18	Ez. xx, 41.	*Titus:*	
Col.:		ii, 5	Is. lii, 5.
ii, 3	Is. xlv, 3.	*ii, 14	Is. liii, 12.
ii, 22	Is. xxix, 13.		
iii, 1	Ps. cix, 1.		
iii, 10	Gen. i, 27.		
1 *Thess.:*			
ii, 4	Jer. xi, 20.		

In the passages marked with a star the quotation or allusion is manifestly intentional. St Paul makes many more allusions to the Old Testament than we have been able to indicate. It has been impossible for us to take into account the passages which refer to a fact or a thought of the Old Testament, but without any expression common to both; for example, Rom. v, 12 (*cf.* Gen. ii, 17; iii, 19; vi, 23); 1 Cor. xi, 8-9 (*cf.* Gen. ii, 18-23), etc.

II—Manner of Quoting the Bible

1. *Formulas of Quotation.*—If reminiscences are numerous in all the Epistles, express quotations are hardly found outside of the four great Epistles. The exceptions are 1 Tim. v, 18 (λέγει ἡ Γραφή); 2 Tim. ii, 19; probably Eph. vi, 2-3; and perhaps Eph. iv, 8 and v, 14 (διὸ λέγει). The most usual formula of quotation is γέγραπται, employed thirty times (without counting 1 Cor. iv, 6: τὸ μὴ ὑπὲρ ἃ

γέγραπται) it is true, with the variations of readings : Rom. xii, 19; xiv, 11; 1 Cor. i, 19; iii, 19; ix, 9; Gal. iii, 10; iv, 22, 27 (γέγραπται γάρ); Rom. i, 17; ii, 24; iii, 10; iv, 17; viii, 36; ix, 33; xi, 26; xv, 3, 9, 21; 1 Cor. i, 31; ii, 9; 2 Cor. viii, 15; ix, 9 (καθὼς γ.); Rom. iii, 4; ix, 13; x, 15; xi, 8 (καθάπερ γ.); 1 Cor. x, 7; xiv, 21; xv, 45; Gal. iii, 13 (various readings).

This manner of quoting is met with in the Synoptics, the Acts, the I^a. Petri, but not in John. Sometimes, but more rarely, the authors are quoted by their names: David, Rom. iv, 6; xi, 9 (λέγει); Moses, Rom. x, 5 (γράφει), x, 19 (λέγει); Isaias, Rom. ix, 27 (κράζει); ix, 29 (προείρηκεν); x, 16, 20; xv, 12 (λέγει). These formulas of quotation are also in use among the other sacred writers. A quite common formula with Paul is λέγει ἡ Γραφή, Rom. iv, 3; ix, 17 (τῷ Φαραώ); x, 11; xi, 2 (ἐν Ἡλείᾳ—that is to say, in the portion of the Books of the Kings where there is mention of Elias); Gal. iv, 30; 1 Tim. v, 18. Then Scripture can be personified, Gal. iii, 8 (προϊδοῦσα); iii, 22 (συνέκλεισε). This way of quoting is employed occasionally by John vii, 38, 42; xix, 37; James ii, 23; iv, 5; and 1 Peter ii, 6. God is substituted five times for the Scripture, 2 Cor. vi, 16 (καθὼς εἶπεν ὁ Θεός); Rom. ix, 15 (τῷ Μωϋσεῖ λέγει); Rom. ix, 25 (ἐν τῷ Ὡσηὲ λέγει); 2 Cor. vi, 2; Gal. iii, 16. In the last four cases "God" is not named, but it is certainly necessary to understand the word. It is to be remarked that in all these examples the words quoted were put into the mouth of God, and it is equally so with ὁ λόγος τοῦ Θεοῦ (Rom. ix, 6).

It may be asked, therefore, whether in the unusual form of the Epistle to the Ephesians (iv, 8; v, 14: διὸ λέγει) it is necessary to understand "God" or "the Scripture," or, indeed, to take λέγει impersonally, "some one says, it is said," and not see in it a Scriptural quotation. What would favour the latter alternative is the fact that Eph. v, 18 is nowhere found in the Old Testament, and that Eph. iv, 8 strangely modifies the text quoted. Some other exceptional formulas show the little fixity found in the language of St Paul: Rom. iv, 18 (κατὰ τὸ εἰρημένον); 2 Cor. iv, 13 (κατὰ τὸ γεγραμμένον); 1 Cor. xv, 54 (ὁ λόγος ὁ γεγραμμένος); Rom. vii, 7 (εἰ μὴ ὁ νόμος ἔλεγεν); Rom. ix, 9 (ἐπαγγελίας ὁ λόγος); and Rom. xi, 4 (τί λέγει αὐτῷ ὁ χρηματισμός;) are explained by special reasons. By comparing the formulas employed in the Epistle to the Hebrews, it will be perceived that they are entirely different; γέγραπται is never used; and, on the contrary, we find a very frequent use of the impersonal εἶπεν, λέγει, εἴρηκεν, φησίν.

2. *Free and Composite Quotations.*—Quotations according to the Hebrew are quite rare: Rom. xi, 35 (Job xli, 3); 1 Cor. iii, 19 (Job v, 13), and perhaps Rom. ix, 17; xi, 14; xii, 19. As examples of intentional modification, cited from

the translation of the Septuagint, can be mentioned: Rom. ix, 17: εἰς αὐτὸ τοῦτο ἐξήγειρά σε, instead of Ex. ix, 16: ἕνεκεν τούτου διετηρήθης, because Paul wishes to prepare the conclusion: Ἄρα οὖν ὃν θέλει ἐλεεῖ, ὃν δὲ θέλει σκληρύνει, Rom. xi, 4: κατέλιπον ἐμαυτῷ ἑπτακισχιλίους ἄνδρας, οἵτινες οὐκ ἔκαμψαν γόνυ τῇ Βάαλ, instead of 1 Kings xix, 18: καὶ καταλείψεις ἐν Ἰσραὴλ ἑπτὰ χιλιάδας ἀνδρῶν, πάντα γόνατα ἃ οὐκ ὤκλασαν γόνυ τῷ Βάαλ, Rom. xii, 19: Ἐμοὶ ἐκδίκησις, ἐγὼ ἀνταποδώσω, instead of Deut. xxxii, 35: Ἐν ἡμέρᾳ ἐκδικήσεως ἀνταποδώσω. As Heb. x, 30, is absolutely like Rom. xii, 19, perhaps the quotation is made from a Greek version differing from the Septuagint. Perhaps also the same thing could be said of 1 Cor. xiv, 21, quoting Is. xxviii, 11-12, very freely. But it is more probable, as St Jerome supposes, that Paul has in mind here the Hebrew form. The version of Aquila (ὅτι ἐν ἑτερογλώσσοις καί ἐν χείλεσιν ἑτέροις λαλήσω τῷ λαῷ τούτῳ) is almost identical with the text of Paul.

The *free quotations* are explained either by the fact that Paul almost always quotes from memory, or because the slightly modified text is better adapted to his subject. Thus 1 Cor. iii, 20: Κύριος γινώσκει τοὺς διαλογισμοὺς τῶν σοφῶν (instead of τῶν ἀνθρώπων, Ps. xciii, 11), ὅτι εἰσὶν μάταιοι. 1 Cor. xv, 45: Ἐγένετο ὁ πρῶτος ἄνθρωπος Ἀδὰμ εἰς ψυχὴν ζῶσαν (instead of Ἐγένετο ὁ ἄνθρωπος εἰς ψυχὴν ζῶσαν, Gen. ii, 7). 2 Cor. vi, 18: καὶ ἔσομαι ὑμῖν εἰς πατέρα, καὶ ὑμεῖς ἔσεσθέ μοι εἰς υἱοὺς καὶ θυγατέρας (instead of: Ἐγὼ ἔσομαι αὐτῷ εἰς πατέρα καὶ αὐτὸς ἔσται μοι εἰς υἱόν, 2 Sam. vii, 14). Gal. iv, 30: μετὰ τοῦ υἱοῦ τῆς ἐλευθέρας (instead of υἱοῦ μοῦ Ἰσαάκ, Gen. xxi, 10). Rom. x, 20 (Is. lxv, 1, *transposed*). Rom. xiii, 9 (where the order of the commandments does not agree either with Ex. xx, 13-14, or with Deut. v, 17-19).

The habit of quoting from memory can also account generally for the *composite citations*.

The following are some examples:

1 Cor. xv, 54-55: κατεπόθη ὁ θάνατος εἰς νῖκος.	Is. xxv, 8: κατέπιεν ὁ θάνατος ἰσχύσας.
ποῦ σου, θάνατε, τὸ νῖκος; ποῦ σου, θάνατε, τὸ κέντρον;	Hos. xiii, 14: ποῦ ἡ δίκη σου, θάνατε; ποῦ τὸ κέντρον σου, ᾅδη;
Rom. xi, 8: Ἔδωκεν αὐτοῖς ὁ Θεὸς πνεῦμα κατανύξεως, ὀφθαλμοὺς τοῦ μὴ βλέπειν καὶ ὦτα τοῦ μὴ ἀκούειν, ἕως τῆς σήμερον ἡμέρας.	Is. xxix, 10: πεπότικεν ὑμᾶς Κύριος πνεύματι κατανύξεως. Deut. xxix, 3: καὶ οὐκ ἔδωκεν Κύριος ὁ Θεὸς ὑμῖν καρδίαν εἰδέναι καὶ ὀφθαλμοὺς βλέπειν καὶ ὦτα ἀκούειν, ἕως τῆς ἡμέρας ταύτης.

It will be seen similarly that in Rom. ix, 33, the quotation from Is. xxviii, 16, is modified by the remembrance of Is. viii,

14; that in 1 Cor. ii, 9, quoting Is. lxiv, 3, the addition of καὶ ἐπὶ καρδίαν ἀνθρώπου οὐκ ἀνέβη is probably occasioned by recalling Is. lxv, 17: οὐδ' οὐ μὴ ἐπέλθῃ αὐτῶν ἐπὶ τὴν καρδίαν. An unusually free quotation is Eph. iv, 8-11. Here the Septuagint, obscure as regards the meaning, translates the Hebrew literally, Ps. lxvii, 19: ἔλαβες δόματα ἐν ἀνθρώπῳ (or ἀνθρώποις). Not only does St Paul change the person, but he transforms the text thus: ἔδωκεν δόματα τοῖς ἀνθρώποις. Instead of receiving the tribute of men, God gives to men his favours. Can this be, as has been sometimes supposed, in virtue of a targum, according to which God *receives* only in order to *return* with interest?

Finally, the following quotation, made with the regular formula διὸ λέγει, is not found in Scripture. Eph. v, 14: Ἔγειρε, ὁ καθεύδων, καὶ ἀνάστα ἐκ τῶν νεκρῶν, καὶ ἐπιφαύσει σοι ὁ Χριστός. The Biblical text most like it is Is. lx, 1: Φωτίζου, φωτίζου (Vulgate, following the Hebrew; *Surge, illuminare*), Ἰερουσαλήμ, ἥκει γάρ σου τὸ φῶς, καὶ ἡ δόξα Κυρίου ἐπὶ σὲ ἀνατέταλκεν. But is it possible to admit such a free quotation, even supposing that the Apostle was influenced by the recollection of Is. ix, 2, xxvi, 19, and lii, 19? St Jerome, after having searched in vain for this text in Scripture, offers the hypothesis that it is taken from some apocryphal writing. But the word ὁ Χριστός is opposed to this, and, besides, St Paul would not quote an apocryphal text with the formula διὸ λέγει. On the other hand, the rhythmical tone of the passage has led to the conjecture that the Apostle is reproducing a liturgical fragment, inspired by the passages of Isaias mentioned above. There will be found a similar case in 1 Tim. iii, 16, but without the formula of quotation, although the context suggests the idea of a quotation.

NOTE C—THE DECREE OF JERUSALEM

I—The Meaning of the Decree

Apart from the restriction in regard to the persons comprised in the decree, the differences between James's proposal and the resolution finally adopted are very small.

ADVICE OF JAMES (ACTS XV, 19-21).	DECREE OF THE APOSTLES (ACTS XV, 28, 29).
Μὴ παρενοχλεῖν	Μηδὲν πλέον ἐπιτίθεσθαι ὑμῖν βάρος
τοῖς ἀπὸ τῶν ἐθνῶν ἐπιστρέφουσιν ἐπὶ τὸν Θεόν,	(τοῖς κατὰ τὴν Ἀντιόχειαν καὶ Συρίαν καὶ Κιλικίαν ἀδελφοῖς)
ἀλλὰ ἐπιστεῖλαι αὐτοῖς	πλὴν τούτων τῶν ἐπάναγκες,
τοῦ ἀπέχεσθαι τῶν ἀλισγημάτων τῶν εἰδώλων	ἀπέχεσθαι εἰδωλοθύτων
καὶ τῆς πορνείας καὶ πνικτοῦ καὶ τοῦ ἅιματος.	καὶ αἵματος καὶ πνικτῶν καὶ πορνείας.

Instead of the technical term εἰδωλοθύτα, St James employs the biblical word "pollutions of idols." The order of the three other points differs : "fornication, things strangled, blood" in the speech of James; "blood, things strangled, fornication" in the decree. The assembly contents itself with affirming that the measure taken is necessary (ἐπάναγκες), but James gives a reason for it (γὰρ) which for us is very obscure on account of its conciseness : "For Moses is read every Sabbath in all the synagogues." As this tends to prove that it is well to limit the boundless liberty of the Gentiles in the mixed communities, James means, it seems, that all the Jews and all the proselytes know, through the public reading of the Pentateuch, the restrictions laid upon strangers who desire to live among Israelites, and they must therefore expect to see the same restrictions imposed upon converts from the Gentiles. In fact, these four points prescribed for strangers (προσήλυτοι in the Septuagint) under penalty of death are found in Leviticus (chaps. xvii and xviii) : Lev. xvii, 7, for things sacrificed to idols (the text here directly indicates only the prohibition of sacrificing victims to false gods, but with a clear allusion to the sacred feast, considered as the same thing, Ex. xxxiv, 15; Num. xxv, 2); Lev. xvii, 10-12, for blood; Lev. xvii, 13-14, for strangled animals. The object of the fourth prohibition is disputed. We think that it has to do chiefly—but perhaps not exclusively—with marriages between relatives in the degrees of consanguinity and affinity forbidden by Leviticus (xviii, 7-18) both for strangers residing in Israel and for the Israelites themselves. These marriages between blood-relatives are indicated in Leviticus by the expression: צְדָרָה גְּלוֹת (ἀποκαλύψαι ἀσχημοσύνην, *reve-lare turpitudinem*). It is to be observed that the same Hebrew expression גלוי צדיות denotes in the Talmud the fourth Noachic law. See Schürer, *Geschichte des jüd. Volkes,* Leipzig, vol. iii, 1909, p. 179. For this particular meaning of πορνεία, see Cornely, *Comment. in 1 Cor.,* pp. 119-121. We do not mean, of course, that the apostles borrowed the four restrictions from Leviticus, or even that they thought directly of the Mosaic legislation; but the rules of Leviticus concerning strangers had to be obeyed with more or less strictness by all those who, to any extent whatever, desired to associate themselves with Israel. Now, as in the mixed churches of Syria and Cilicia the majority of the neophytes had had relations with the Synagogue before their conversion, the four rules must have been carried out in practice there, and it was proper, in order to preserve uniformity and to avoid offending the Jews, to sanction this measure and to apply it universally. The motive for it, alleged by St James, is thus readily explained.

II—OCCIDENTAL FORM OF THE DECREE

In the texts which represent what is called by common consent the occidental tradition, the proposal of James and the decree of the apostles are formulated in a very different manner, as follows:

Acts xv, 20: ἀλλὰ ἐπιστεῖλαι αὐτοῖς τοῦ ἀπέχεσθαι τῶν ἀλισγη-μάτων τῶν εἰδώλων καὶ τῆς πορνείας καὶ τοῦ αἵματος καὶ ὅσα μὴ θέλουσιν ἑαυτοῖς γένεσθαι ἑτέροις μὴ ποιεῖν.

Acts xv, 28, 29: ἀπέχεσθαι εἰδωλοθύτων καὶ αἵματος καὶ πορνείας καὶ ὅσα μὴ θέλετε ἑαυτοῖς γένεσθαι ἑτέρῳ μὴ ποιεῖν.

Instead of four restrictions of positive law we should thus have three prohibitions of natural law—idolatry, murder, and fornication—to which would be joined the *golden rule* of not doing to others what we do not wish that others should do to us. On one side or on the other there is an intentional modification, and it certainly seems that the Oriental text keeps the original reading. If the decree had been originally drawn up in its occidental form, it is difficult to see any motive for changing it. On the contrary, it is perfectly comprehensible that the canonical form of the decree may have shocked and astonished the weak ones of the flock, especially during the judaizing disputes of the first two centuries. Moreover, the fact of the interpolation of the *golden rule* appears evident in the discourse of James, as well as in the decree itself. In fact, if it were a question of an elementary moral law, which of course was applicable to all Christians, the reason alleged by St James would no longer have any sense, and the restriction of the precept to the proselytes of Syria and Cilicia would be incomprehensible.

We have left out of consideration the hypothesis of Blass, according to which St Luke himself is said to have produced two editions of the Acts : one a Roman one, represented now by the *occidental* text, the other a revised edition, which is our *oriental* text. Even if this hypothesis had some foundation, it would still not be possible to depend on it in regard to the passages referring to the apostolic decree, which constitute an absolutely special case in which intentional manipulation seems beyond doubt. For the purport of the occidental text, see G. Resch, *Das Aposteldekret nach seiner ausserkanonischen Textgestalt,* 1905 (*Texte und Untersuch.*).

III—The Understanding of the Decree in the First Centuries

As regards the blood and meats not drained of blood, the variations are very curious. The apostolic Fathers do not seem to be acquainted with this law. St Ignatius (*Ad Philad.,* vi, 1 ; *Ad Magnes.,* viii, 1 ; x, 3 ; Funk, *Patres apost.,*[2] 1901, pp. 268, 236, and 238) and the author of the so-called *Epistle of Barnabas* (iii, 6 ; x, 9 ; *ibid.,* pp. 44 and 70) denounce the judaizing practices in general, but do not specially mention our decree. The author of the *Epistle to Diognetus* (iv, 1-6 ; *ibid.,* pp. 394-396) points out in proper terms the Jewish customs in regard to meats and finds them ridiculous, without admitting, it would seem, any restriction for Christians. The *Didache* (vi, 3 ; *ibid.,* p. 16 : περὶ δὲ τῆς βρώσεως, ὃ δύνασαι βάστασον· ἀπὸ δὲ τοῦ εἰδωλοθύτου λίαν πρόσεχε· λατρεία γάρ ἐστι θεῶν νεκρῶν), while energetically proscribing meats sacrificed to idols, seems to allow the rest. The Fathers of the second century take a positive stand against partaking of blood. If Justin (*Contra Tryph.,* 35), Aristides (*Apol.,* 15), and Athenagoras (*Legatio,* 26-27) content themselves with expressing horror for meats sacrificed to idols, we know from Lucian (*De morte Peregr.*) that among the Christians there were meats which were forbidden, and we have evidence that towards the end of the second century there was abstinence from blood among the Christians of Lyons, Carthage, Rome, and Alexandria. See, for the Gauls, the reply of Byblis to the judge (in Eusebius, *Hist. Eccl.,* V, i, 26 : πῶς ἂν παιδία φάγοιεν οἱ τοιοῦτοι, οἷς μηδὲ ἀλόγων ζῴων αἷμα φαγεῖν ἐξόν) ; for Northern Africa, Tertullian (*De monog.,* 5 ; *Apol.,* 9) ; for Italy, Minucius Felix (*Octav.* 30 ; *tantum ab humano sanguine cavemus, ut nec edulium pecorum in cibis sanguinem noverimus*) ; for Egypt, Clement (*Paedag.,* ii, 7 ; *Strom.,* iv, 15, etc. ; above all, *Paedag.,* iii, 3, end; Ὄλοιντο οἱ θῆρες οἱ φυλακτικοί, οἷς τὸ αἷμα ἡ τροφή· οὐδὲ γὰρ θιγεῖν αἷμα τοῖς ἀνθρώποις θέμις). Clement is the first to refer expressly to the apostolic decree with which he seeks to harmonize the injunctions of Paul (*Strom.*, iv, 15).—The apocryphal Clementine literature is especially explicit about these interdictions, *Homil.* vii, 8; viii, 19, to which the golden rule is sometimes joined (*Homil.* vii, 3). See Nestle, *Zum Erstickten im Aposteldekret* in *Zeitschrift für neutest. Theol.* vol. vii, 1906, pp. 254-256; Funk, *Didascalia et Constit. apost.*, Paderborn, 1906, vol. I, p. 583.

The Fathers are unanimous in forbidding meats sacrificed to idols, without entering into the distinctions which we find in the First Epistle to the Corinthians. They can be divided into three schools :

1. The first maintain intact the teaching of Paul : the meat offered to idols is not defiled by the fact of the offering itself, and its prohibition is due to other circumstances—scandal, danger to one's neighbour, participation in idolatrous worship. Minucius Felix says (*Octav.* 38) : *Quod vero sacrificiorum reliquias et pocula delibata contemnimus, non confessio timoris est, sed verae libertatis assertio. Nam etsi omne quod nascitur, ut inviolabile Dei munus, nullo opere corrumpitur; abstinemus tamen, ne quis existimet aut daemoniis, quibus libatum est, cedere, aut nostrae religionis pudere.* The commentary of Ambrosiaster is excellent on this point. Later, St Cyril of Alexandria defended this opinion very well (*In Julian.*, vii).

2. But several regard meat sacrificed to idols as being defiled through the consecration of it to false gods, from which it follows that the eating of it is intrinsically bad and cannot be allowed in any case. St Cyril of Jerusalem is particularly explicit on this subject. (*Catech.* iii, 3, XXXIII, 430): Ὥσπερ γὰρ τὰ τοῖς βωμοῖς προσφερόμενα τῇ φύσει ὄντα λιτὰ μεμολυσμένα γίγνεται τῇ ἐπικλήσει τῶν εἰδώλων, thus the water of baptism is sanctified by the invocation of the three divine Persons. Cf. *Catech.* xix, 7, and xxii, 7, where meat offered to idols is compared to the Eucharist. Origen (*Contra Cels.*, viii, 28) appears, indeed, to have shared this opinion, which is certainly that of St Jerome (*Comment. in Matth.* xv, 11; see *Comment. in Tit.* i, 15) and of St Augustine (*De bono conjug.*, 16; *Epist. ad Public.*, xlvii, 6).

3. The other Fathers seem also to incline towards this second opinion; but they content themselves in general with condemning absolutely meats sacrificed to idols, without giving their reasons, and do not even distinguish between public, ritual eating, which constitutes a scandal or an act of idolatry, and private, secret eating, which can be illicit only in so far as the meat sacrificed to idols has contracted some defilement. See the *Teaching of the Apostles*, Aristides, Athena-

goras, St Justin, at the places indicated above. Moreover, Tertullian (*De spectac.*, 13; *De praescript.*, 33; *De corona,* 10) and St John Chrysostom (*in* 1 *Cor., Hom.* xxv, and *in* 1 *Tim., Hom.* xii) protest vigorously against the use of meats offered to idols.

On this question, *cf.* K. Böckenhoff (Cath.) *Das apost. Speisegesetz in den ersten fünf Jahrhunderten,* Paderborn, 1903; and, above all, K. Six, S.J., *Das Aposteldekret, seine Entstehung und Geltung in den ersten vier Jahrhunderten,* Innsbruck, 1912.

On the decree in general, *cf.* J. Thomas, *L'Église et les Judaïsants à l'âge apostolique* (in *Rev. des quest. hist.,* 1889, vol. ii., pp. 400-460); M. Coppieters, *Le décret des apôtres* (in *Rev. Bibl.,* 1907, pp. 31-58, 218-239); H. Wilbers (in *Studiën,* 1907, pp. 193-214). The subject is a question of the day, and has been treated in recent times by Harnack (1899), Hilgenfeld (1899), A. Seeberg (1906), Sanday (1908), Kirsopp Lake (1911), and several others. See Six, pp. x-xii.

NOTE D—THE *CHARISMATA*

I—The Four Lists

These are as follows, in order of date :

(A) 1 Cor. xii, 8-10.
1. Word of wisdom.
2. Word of knowledge.
3. Faith (miraculous).
4. Graces of healing.
5. Working of miracles.
6. Prophecy.
7. Discernment of spirits.
8. Gift of tongues.
9. Interpretation of tongues.

(B) 1 Cor. xii, 28-30.
1. Apostles.
2. Prophets.
3. Doctors.
4. Miracles.
5. Graces of healing.
6. Help (or assistance).
7. Gifts of government.
8. Glossolalia.

(C) Rom. xii, 6-8.
1. Prophecy.
2. Ministry.
3. Doctor.
4. Exhorter.
5. Almsgiver.
6. President.
7. Shewing mercy.

(D) Eph. iv, 11.
1. Apostles.
2. Prophets.
3. Evangelists.
4. Pastors.
5. Doctors.

This would make in all (9 + 8 + 7 + 5) twenty-nine *charismata*. But it is obvious : First, that the names in list D—except evangelists and pastors—are already found in the others; second, that in lists A and B, forming, properly speaking, two fragments of one and the same list, the following *charismata* : prophecy, healing, and the working of miracles, are repeated, and that the *kinds* of tongues (γένη γλωσσῶν) have their equivalent in the *glossolalia* (γλώσσαις λαλοῦσιν) ; third, that the *charismata* of prophet and doctor in list C are already mentioned in list B.

This list of *twenty* charismata could be extended by taking into account certain other manifestations of the Holy Spirit (1 Cor. xiv, 26), or, on the contrary, shortened by pushing the synonymity of the terms still further ; the λόγος σοφίας, for example, was the attribute of the apostles and prophets, the λόγος γνώσεως was that of the doctors ; but neither constituted the *complete* charisma of prophet or doctor.

A different division is suggested by Paul (1 Cor. xii, 4-6) : There are diversities of *charismata,* but the same Spirit ; and there are diversities of *ministries,* but the same Lord ; and there are diversities of *operations,* but the same God that worketh all in all.

We might be tempted to refer the *operations* (miracles, healings, etc.) to the *Father,* the *ministries* (pastors, doctors, etc.) to the *Son,* and the other charismata (gift of tongues, discernment of spirits, etc.) to the Holy Ghost. But it is evident that these are three different aspects of the same graces. In fact, although God is he who "*worketh* all in all," the Holy Spirit is designated a little later as the author of all the *charismata,* of whatever nature they may be, especially of the *operations.* He it is who *worketh* (ἐνεργεῖ) *all these things* and who distributes them (διαιροῦν) to each one as he pleases. A division of charismata could not, therefore, be founded on this text.

II—DISTINCTION OF "CHARISMATA"

Four of them form a sort of hierarchy among themselves :— apostles, prophets, evangelists, doctors (1 Cor. xii, 28 : καὶ οὓς μὲν ἔθετο ὁ Θεὸς ἐν τῇ ἐκκλησίᾳ π ρ ῶ τ ο ν ἀποστόλους, δ ε ύ τ ε ρ ο ν προφήτας, τ ρ ί τ ο ν διδασκάλους, ἔπειτα δυνάμεις κτλ). Elsewhere the evangelists are inserted between the prophets and the doctors, but the descending gradation, without being enumerated as in the preceding case, appears very clear (Eph. iv, 11) : Ἔδωκεν τοὺς μὲν ἀποστόλους, τοὺς δὲ προφήτας, τοὺς δὲ εὐαγγελιστάς, τοὺς δὲ ποιμένας καὶ διδασκάλους. There seem to be only *four* classes here, although there are *five* names, for the last two are governed by the same definite article. St Jerome, no doubt following Origen, has noted this (*Comment. in Ephes.,* iv, 11) : *Non enim ait: alios autem pastores et alios magistros, sed alios pastores et magistros, ut qui pastor est esse debeat et magister.* In any case, pastors and doctors are clearly distinguished from apostles, prophets, and evangelists.

The *apostles* named here are not the Twelve. St Paul doubtless means those missionaries who, impelled by the Spirit of God, left all to go and found new communities of Christians in a heathen land. The *Didache* gives us some very curious details about them (*Doctr. duod. apost.,* xi, 3, in Funk, *Patres apost.,*[2] 1901, vol. I, p. 26). The *apostle* is to be received like the Lord himself ; but if he stops *more than two days* in a community already established, or if in departing he asks for money, he is to be regarded as a false prophet —that is, as not really having the *charisma* of the apostolate. This honoured title was eagerly sought for. Paul attacks with his shafts of sarcasm the deceitful workmen who falsely arrogate to themselves the name of apostles (2 Cor. xi, 13 : μετασχηματιζόμενοι εἰς ἀποστόλους Χριστοῦ) and John congratulates the Bishop of Ephesus on having unmasked these hypocrites (Apoc. ii, 2 : τοὺς λέγοντας ἑαυτοὺς ἀποστόλους καὶ οὐκ εἰσίν).

"To edify, to exhort, to console :" such was the triple rôle of the *prophets* (1 Cor. xiv, 3). The gift of *exhortation* (Rom. xii, 8) is, therefore, to prophecy what the part is to the whole. The *Didache* (xi, 7-12) also takes up the subject of the *prophets,* and indicates by what signs they are to be recognized; it guarantees to them board and lodging, it commands the faithful to pay them the tithe, and it adds this characteristic trait (*Doct. duod. apost.*, xv, 1, in Funk, *Patres apost.*,[2] 1901, vol. I, pp. 32-34) : " Choose for yourselves, therefore, bishops and deacons worthy of the Lord . . . for they also exercise among you the ministry of prophets and doctors." This text proves that bishops of the second rank, or priests, and the deacons had a certain analogy with the prophets and doctors respectively, and that, in case *charismata* are wanting, the graces pertaining to the ordinary ministry take their place.

The *doctor,* like the prophet, was commissioned to teach. But while the prophet appealed especially to the heart, the doctor spoke chiefly to the mind. He was an inspired catechist, or at least one raised up providentially and endowed with the word of knowledge, just as the word of wisdom was the usual attribute of the prophet (1 Cor. xii, 8).

There remains the *evangelist.* Everything leads us to believe that he was meant to strengthen the new churches, but not, perhaps, to found them. He was thus distinguished from the *apostle.* The episcopal character, with which the apostles were regularly invested, was less necessary to him. Philip, one of the first seven Hellenist deacons, is termed an evangelist (Acts xxi, 8), and Paul exhorts Timothy to do the work of an evangelist (2 Tim. iv, 5). Theodoret calls them itinerant preachers. It is needless to add that these evangelists have nothing in common with the authors of the four Gospels.

Of most of the other *charismata* we have only the name with some vague traits. Of six of them, divided into two groups, bodily acts of mercy are the main object.

The *almsgiver,* moved by a supernatural impulse, distributes his gifts to the poor. He must exercise the simplicity which frees him from egotism, from regard for the approval of men, and from ostentation (Rom. xii, 8 : ὁ μεταδιδοὺς ἐν ἁπλότητι). The *dispenser of mercy* assists the unfortunate, the prisoners, or the sick. His special virtue consists in an agreeable, cheerful manner which doubles the value of the benefit conferred and serves as an antidote to the monotony of his life of devotion (Rom. xii, 8 : ὁ ἐλεῶν ἐν ἱλαρότητι).— The possessor of the *charisma* called ἀντιλήψεις (aid or help), according to St John Chrysostom, also took care of the poor and the sick. We should rather think that he put at the service of his brethren his skill, his influence, and his resources (1 Cor. xii, 28). Indeed ἀντιλήπτωρ means "defender," and ἀντιλαμβάνεσθαι signifies "to come to help, to give a hand to the stumbling."

The gifts of faith, healing, and miracles are closely related. Considered as a *charisma, faith* is not the theological virtue, although it is allied to it; it is the faith that is able to remove mountains and to work miracles (1 Cor. xii, 9). It can be defined as "an invincible confidence, founded on theological faith and assured by a supernatural instinct, that God, in a given case, will manifest his power, his justice, or his mercy." St Cyril of Alexandria describes it (*In Joan.*, xi, 40): ὸν δογματικὴ μόνον ἐστὶν ἀλλὰ καὶ τῶν ὑπὲρ ἀνθρώπου ἐνεργητική. It is of this that the Saviour speaks in Mark xi, 22 (*Habete fidem Dei*); it is for this that his disciples beg in Luke xvii, 5 (*Adauge nobis fidem*). Paul (1 Cor. xiii, 2) alludes to the words of Christ (Matt. xvii, 20), who promises to faith the power to remove mountains. The opposite to this *charisma* has a special name—ὀλιγοπιστία (Matt. xvii, 20), ὀλιγόπιστος (Matt. vi, 30; viii, 26; xiv, 31; xvi, 8; Luke xii, 28).—*The gift of healing,* permanent or transient, is not to be confounded with this lively faith. The shadow of Peter, the garment of Paul, like the mere contact with Jesus, restored health (Acts v, 15; xix, 12; Luke vi, 19).—*The gift of miracles* is of the same nature as the preceding, and is distinguished from it only by its more extended object. Paul enumerates them together, and unites them with faith, so as to show by the structure of the sentence that they form a group (1 Cor. xii, 9): ἐτέρῳ πίστις . . . ἄλλῳ δὲ χαρίσματα ἰαμάτων . . . ἄλλῳ δὲ ἐνεργήματα δυνάμεων. Further on (1 Cor. xii, 28) faith is omitted.

The other *charismata*—pastors, rulers, ministries, gifts of government—show no decided difference of meaning. They must have designated a supernatural aptitude for governing the Christian community before the regular hierarchy was established. The most generally used word—(κυβερνήσεις, 1 Cor. xii, 28)—is rightly understood by exegetes as referring to the government of the Church, whose head is the pilot or steersman. The vague word *ministry*—(διακονία, Rom. xii, 7; 1 Cor. xii, 5)—designates services of an inferior order. The *ruler* (προϊστάμενος) whose characteristic is zeal (Rom. xii, 8) no doubt directed the still imperfectly organized religious assemblies. This is the title which Paul gives to the heads of the Church of Thessalonica a few months after its foundation (1 Thess. v, 12). As to the *charisma* of *pastor*—(ποιμήν, Eph. iv, 11)—which appears to be one of the clearest, yet in reality is one of the most obscure, the Apostle seems almost to identify it with the *charisma* of doctor, or at least to attribute it to the same persons. It is impossible to say whether it had for its special object teaching or government.

III—Glossolalia

For this extraordinary *charisma* Paul uses very different expressions: γλῶσσαι (1 Cor. xii, 10; xiii, 8; xiv, 22) γένη γλωσσῶν (xii, 10, 28), λαλεῖν γλώσσῃ (xiv, 2, 4, 13, 27) or γλώσσαις (xii, 30 ; xiii, 1 ; xiv, 5, 6, 18, 23, 39), γλῶσσαν ἔχειν (xiv, 26), λαλεῖν λόγους ἐν γλώσσῃ (xiv, 19), προσεύχεσθαι γλώσσῃ (xiv, 14). Compare 1 Cor. xiv, 2, 15, 16, where γλώσσῃ is replaced by τῷ πνεύματι, and notice the corresponding gift of *interpretation* : ἑρμηνεία (xii, 10), διερμηνεύειν (xii, 30 ; xiv, 5, 13, 27), διερμηνευτής (xiv, 28). The passage 1 Cor. xiv, 9 is also to be considered.

The explanation which we have followed is that of all the Fathers, of Catholic commentators in general, and of a great number of Protestant theologians. It alone avoids doing violence to the texts. It is, in fact, necessary to suppose that *glossolalia* was an articulate, intelligible language, since it was a prayer, a psalm, a benediction, a thanksgiving (1 Cor. xiv, 14-16); that it had a connected meaning, since it expressed concepts (1 Cor. xiv, 19, λόγους ἐν γλώσσῃ λαλῆσαι ; *cf.* xiv, 9); and that it was susceptible of interpretation (1 Cor. xiv, 27, etc.); finally, that it was a language resembling foreign tongues (1 Cor. xiv, 21, etc.) and comparable to the means which men and angels use to communicate their thoughts (1 Cor. xiii, 1).

Many modern Protestants—and all the Rationalists, of course—declare this explanation unacceptable because it presupposes a miracle and because it is psychologically impossible to speak a language that one has not learned. They have recourse, therefore, to one or the other of the two following hypotheses :

1. Γλῶσσα *signifies the Organ of Speech.*—Hence the gift of tongues consists in inarticulate sounds produced by the vibrations of the tongue, similar to the babbling of young children (Meyer, Eichhorn, Holsten, Baur, Neander, Steudel, de Wette, Zeller, Ewald, Hilgenfeld, etc.). However, in order to have something in which the *charisma* of interpretation can work, the majority of these authors admit, in the gift of tongues, sighs and even a few words without connection : " Some strange sounds which the possessors of this gift pronounced, and in which were mingled Greek, Syriac, the words *anathema, maran atha* . . . embarrassed these simple people greatly " (Renan : *Saint Paul,* p. 409; *cf.* p. 412 : *bégaiements inarticulés*).

2. Γλῶσσα *signifies Obscure Speech.*—The word γλῶσσα was, in fact, sometimes taken in the sense of an *archaic, strange,* unusual expression, and consequently one which was obscure and unintelligible for the common people. The possessor of this gift spoke a kind of dialect or an enigmatical language like that of the priestess of Delphi, and the *Alexandra* of Lycophron. Such is the opinion maintained by Bleek, Heinrici, and Schürer.

For these different systems, see Heinrici, Meyer's *Komm.*[8], pp. 371-382, and J. Weiss, Meyer[9], 1910, pp. 335-9; the

Protestant bibliography of *charismata,* and especially about the gift of tongues, in Th. Simon, *Die Psychologie des Ap. Paulus,* Göttingen, 1897, pp. 114-115; or, still better, in Mosiman, *Das Zungenreden geschichtlich und psychologisch untersucht,* Tübingen, 1911.   E. Lombard (*De la glossolalie chez les premiers chrétiens et les phénomènes similaires,* Lausanne, 1910) presents with much skill the rationalistic point of view and furnishes some curious comparisons.   At the present time the reality of the gift of tongues is beginning to be recognized, almost as we have presented it, and to be explained by the mysterious phenomena of the subconscious mind.

There is a good monograph on this subject by Englmann (Catholic)—*Von den Charismen,* etc., Ratisbon, 1848.   That of Hilgenfeld (*Die Glossolalie in der alten Kirche,* Leipzig, 1850), conceived in an entirely different spirit, adds nothing very important.

NOTE E—PROPITIATION, EXPIATION, REDEMPTION

The ideas of *propitiation* and *expiation* correspond to the Greek ἱλαστήριον; *redemption* is the translation of the word ἀπολύτρωσις.

I—THE WORD Ἱλαστήριον.

1. *Meaning outside of the Septuagint.*—If we leave aside the Greek translators of the Pentateuch and Philo, who evidently is dependent on the Septuagint, we find among the secular writers of antiquity only six examples of the adjective ἱλαστήριος or of the substantive ἱλαστήριον.

(*a*) In an inscription of Cos, before the time of St Paul :—" The people [offers this ex-voto] as a ἱλαστήριον to the gods for the health of Cæsar Augustus, son of God." (Paton and Hicks, *The Inscriptions of Cos*, Oxford, 1891, no. 81, p. 126: Ὁ δᾶμος ὑπὲρ τᾶς αὐτοκράτορος Καίσαρος θεοῦ υἱοῦ Σεβαστοῦ σωτηρίας θεοῖς ἱλαστήριον).

(*b*) In another inscription of Cos of uncertain date (*Ibid.* no. 347, p. 225) ἱλαστήριον designates, as in the former case, a votive object or a monument erected in honour of Jupiter to make him propitious.

(*c*) In the apocryphal Fourth Book of Machabees is a text which is very interesting both in idea and expression : " By the blood of these pious men, and by their expiatory death, God saved oppressed Israel" (xvii, 22 : διὰ τοῦ αἵματος τῶν εὐσεβῶν ἐκείνων καὶ τοῦ ἱλαστηρίου θανάτου αὐτῶν, ἡ θεία πρόνοια τὸν Ἰσραὴλ προκακωθέντα διέσωσεν). Here ἱλαστήριος is an adjective and awakens the idea of expiation rather than that of propitiation, for the author has just said that the country has been purified, thanks to these martyrs, ὥσπερ ἀντίψυχον γεγονότας τῆς τοῦ ἔθνους ἁμαρτίας.

(*d*) In Josephus (*Antiq.* xvi, 7, 1 : περίφοβος δ' αὐτὸς ἐξῄει καὶ τοῦ δέους ἱλαστήριον μνῆμα λευκῆς πέτρας ἐπὶ τῷ στομίῳ κατεσκευάσατο) Herod comes trembling out of the tomb of David, which he has violated, and causes to be placed at the entrance, as if to perpetuate the remembrance of his fear, an expiatory monument of white stone. The word ἱλαστήριον is more naturally an adjective referring to μνῆμα than a substantive in apposition with μνῆμα. The motive which suggests the erection of this monument evokes rather the idea of expiation than that of propitiation.

(*e*) In Dion Chrysostom (*Orat.* xi, p. 355, ed. Reiske : ἱλαστήριον Ἀχαιοὶ τῇ Ἰλιάδι) it is certainly a substantive. This is the inscription cut upon a splendid ex-voto offered to the goddess Athene.

(*f*) In a papyrus of the second century A.D., published by Grenfell and Hunt (*Fayum Towns and their Papyri*, London, 1900, p. 313, No. 337:—τοῖς θεοῖς εἰλαστη(ρί)ους θυσίας ἀξιω(θέ)ντες ἐπιτελεῖσθαι), the word is adjectival.

In the above examples the word is a substantive three times (*a, b,* and *e*); it is an adjective twice (*c* and *f*); *d* remains doubtful. As an adjective it means "one who makes expiation or propitiation"; as a substantive it signifies "a means or object of expiation or propitiation," according as it is a question of making reparation for a past fault or of ensuring the future favour of a divinity; but these two motives can very well be expressed by the same word. We see that, if the idea of sacrifice is not contained in the word itself, it is not on that account excluded from it, since *expiatory* or propitiatory *sacrifices* are spoken of (Example *f*).

Cf. Deissmann, *Bibelstudien,* Marpurg, 1895, pp. 121-132, or *Bible Studies,* Edinburgh, 1903, pp. 124-135; the article *Mercy Seat* in the *Encyclop. Biblica,* and *Zeitschrift für neutest, Wissenschaft,* vol. iv, 1903, pp. 193-212.

2. *Meaning in the Septuagint.*—It is known that ἱλαστήριον corresponds to the Hebrew *kappōreth,* which meant the golden covering of the ark. The first time that the writers of the Septuagint meet with it (Ex. xxv, 16) they translate: Καὶ ποιήσεις ἱλαστήριον ἐπίθεμα χρυσίου καθαροῦ. Deissmann formerly supposed (*Bibelstudien,* p. 122-132) that *kappōreth* was translated by ἐπίθεμα and that the adjective ἱλαστήριον was added, either by allusion to the etymology (*kipper,* "to expiate, to make propitious"), or in order to recall the fact that here it is not an ordinary covering. He is now of the opinion (*Zeitschrift für neutest. Wissenschaft,* vol. iv, 1903, p. 201) that ἱλαστήριον translates *kappōreth* and that ἐπίθεμα is there only to indicate the form of this "instrument of propitiation."

Heretofore it was customary to derive *kappōreth* from an obsolete verb—*kāfar*—to which was attributed the basic signification of "to cover"; this word would, therefore, have signified only a "cover" and, by antonomasia, "the cover of the ark of the covenant." But contemporary philologists give to *kāfar* the basic meaning of "to wash, to efface," a meaning which the Syriac, Arabic, and Assyrian render very probable (*cf.* Delitsch, *Assyr. Handwörterbuch,* 1896, p. 347; Genenius-Buhl, *Hebr. Handwörterbuch*[14], 1905, p. 324; E. König, *Lehrgebäude der hebr. Sprache,* ii, 1, Leipzig, 1895, p. 201). The form *kipper* has the same meaning, but is taken always in a figurative sense, as "to efface, to expiate" sins. From this come *kōfēr,* λύτρον, *propitiatio,* and *kappōreth,* ἱλαστήριον, *propitiatorium.* The old Lutheran theory of sins *covered,* not *effaced,* is destroyed at one stroke.

An interesting question, but one which does not concern us here, is that of knowing whether the word *kappōreth* itself, with the idea which it awakens, belongs particularly to the Hebrew, or whether it was common to other Semitic religions. It is certain that in the Koran *kaffārah*—which corresponds exactly with the Hebrew *kappōreth*—is an "expiation" or a "means of expiation" (*cf.* Hughes, *Diction. of Islam²*, London, 1896, p. 259), and that *kuppuru,* corresponding to the Hebrew *kipper,* plays a certain rôle in the Babylonian religion (see Zimmern in *Die Keilinschr. und das A.T.³,* Berlin, 1903, p. 601).

3. *Meaning of the Word in St Paul.*—The meaning appears from what has been said. The word ἱλαστήριον is more probably a substantive than an adjective. It signifies a "means of expiation" or "of propitiation," or perhaps both : it is to be decided by the general doctrine of St Paul and by the context. Although the idea of sacrifice is not directly contained in the word, it is included in the phrase ἐν τῷ αὐτοῦ αἵματι. Deissmann concedes it as well as Bruston (*Les conséquences du vrai sens de ἱλαστήριον,* in *Zeitschrift für neutest. Wissenschaft,* vol. vii, 1906, pp. 77-81). Jesus Christ is, therefore, rightly represented as a *victim of expiation,* or *of propitiation.* It must not be forgotten through the ἀπολύτρωσις which precedes.

The ideas of *expiation* and *propitiation* are very closely related, for God is appeased or made propitious only in so far as sin is expiated, and the same redeeming act produces at the same time this double result. Consequently the derivatives—which are however rare in the New Testament—of ἵλεως (Matt. xvi, 22 ; Heb. viii, 12) can be taken generally in either sense. This is the case with ἱλαστήριον of which we have just spoken. When St John says (1 John ii, 2 ; iv, 10) that Jesus Christ is ἱλασμὸς περὶ τῶν ἁμαρτιῶν ἡμῶν, and that his Father sent him as such, we may understand it as "propitiation" or "expiation"; although the second meaning is more natural. In Heb. ii, 17 the latter meaning is imposed by the context: εἰς τὸ ἱλάσκεσθαι τὰς ἁμαρτίας τοῦ λαοῦ.

But perhaps there is nothing to choose between these two meanings; for the sacrifices of the Old Law had the double effect of expiating sin and of appeasing God, and this double effect could be expressed by the same word. Now in St Paul, as well as in the rest of the New Testament, the death of Christ is often represented as a sacrifice.

We take no account of the opinion of Origen, revived by Ritschl after several others, who understands ἱλαστήριον in the sense of *mercy-seat.* The mercy-seat was the covering of the ark, which was sprinkled with the blood of the victims on the great day of the Expiation, and where Jehovah was believed to be seated between the cherubims of gold. But what relation is there between Jesus Christ shedding his blood for the salvation of the world and the mercy-seat sprinkled with blood, which would rather represent the altar of the Cross? And how can it be supposed that this typical signification, unknown to all Scripture, could have ever occurred to the minds of Paul and his readers? This explanation is now rightly almost entirely abandoned.

II—The Word " Redemption "

The word "redemption" (λύτρωσις and ἀπολύτρωσις, nouns denoting action, from the verbs λυτροῦν and ἀπολυτροῦν) in the Old Testament means the theocratic *deliverance* (*ge'ullāh*) promised to the faithful people by Jehovah, the Redeemer of Israel (*gō'ēl*). In the New Testament it is the Messianic deliverance obtained by the blood of Christ offered as a ransom (λύτρον, Matt. xx, 28; Mark x, 45; or ἀντίλυτρον, 1 Tim. ii, 6). The comparison of the Synoptics with St Paul is interesting:

MATT. XX, 28; MARK X, 25.		PAUL (1 TIM. II, 6).
Δοῦναι τὴν ψύχην αὐτοῦ	==	Ὁ δοὺς ἑαυτὸν
λύτρον ἀντὶ	=	ἀντίλυτρον
πολλῶν	=	ὑπὲρ πάντων.

1. The identity of the two formulas is evident: for δοῦναι τὴν ψύχην αὐτοῦ is a Hebrew form for "to give oneself, to deliver oneself up"; the composite ἀντίλυτρον is equivalent to the two words λύτρον ἀντί, and the equivalence of πολλῶν and πάντων is established by numerous examples. Paul adds only the shade of meaning in ὑπέρ, "in favour of" contained implicitly in the formula of the Synoptics.

2. Although, strictly speaking, "redemption" may signify simply deliverance, without any allusion to the price paid or received, its etymological value must be preserved to it for the following reasons : (*a*) The word λύτρον, which in the Septuagint is used to translate the Hebrew *kōfēr, ge'ullāh,* and *pidiōn,* signifies the *price of the ransom* of slaves (Lev. xix, 20), of captives (Isa. xlv, 13), the *ransom* of life (Exod. xxi, 30; Num. xxxv, 31).—(*b*) The word λύτρουν means also, strictly, "to deliver someone by paying his ransom" (Num. xviii, 15-17).—(*c*) The synonyms ἀγοράζειν (1 Cor. vi, 20; vii, 23; 2 Pet. ii, 1; Apoc. v, 9; xiv, 3-4) and ἐξαγοράζειν (Gal. iii, 13; iv, 5) show that the idea of a ransom has not entirely disappeared from the metaphor.

3. The redemption of the New Testament is, therefore, the deliverance of men obtained by paying either the ransom (λύτρον) or the price due (τιμή—1 Cor. vi, 20; vii, 23). This price, as the Synoptics, in full accord with Paul, teach us, is the blood of Christ. The word "redemption" is used generally to denote the real, though imperfect, deliverance of grace; sometimes also the complete deliverance of glory (Rom. viii, 23; Eph. iv, 30; Heb. ix, 12; perhaps also Eph. i, 14).

NOTE F—TERMS REFERRING TO PREDESTINATION

I—To Predestinate, Predestination

The verb *to predestinate* occurs only six times in four distinct texts (Acts iv, 28; Rom. viii, 29, 30; 1 Cor. ii, 7; Eph. i, 5, 11), for in Rom. i, 4 (praedestinatus *est Filius Dei*) the Greek word is ὁρίζειν and not προορίζειν.

(*a*) In Acts iv, 28 (*facere quae manus tua et consilium* decreverunt *fieri*, προώρισεν) to predestine signifies simply *to decide in advance,* and has no relation to theological predestination.

(*b*) In 1 Cor. ii, 7 (*loquimur Dei sapientiam . . . quam* praedestinavit Deus ante *saecula in gloriam nostram*) the object of the predestination is not a person, but a thing, the revelation of the divine counsels.

(*c*) In Rom. viii, 29 (*quos praescivit et* [καὶ, etiam] praedestinavit) we see that prescience precedes predestination, and that they have here the same range of meaning; that is, they are applicable to the same subjects.

(*d*) From Rom. viii, 30 (*quos et* praedestinavit *hos et vocavit*) it appears that predestination, having the same scope as calling, cannot have as its end, at least directly, eternal life.

(*e*) In Eph. i, 5 (Praedestinavit *nos in adoptionem filiorum*) the end of the predestination is filial adoption, completed in this life.

(*f*) In Eph. i, 11 (*in quo et nos sorte vocati sumus,* praedestinati *secundum propositum ejus qui operatur omnia secundum consilium voluntatis suae*) it is equally common to all believers, and has as its end the efficacious call to faith.

To sum up, *to predestinate* is an act *peculiar to God*—that is to say, an act which in the New Testament always has God as its subject—by which God *decrees a thing which has relation to the scheme of salvation* (although the soteriological meaning is less clear in Acts iv, 28), but *which is never directly eternal glory.*

If the word *predestination* were employed by St Paul, the meaning corresponding to the verb would be: *A divine, eternal, and absolute decree, logically subsequent to prescience, by which God destines man to a supernatural benefit* (Examples *c, d, e, f*) *or a benefit to man* (Example *b*).

But we should be greatly mistaken if we imagined that this notion is applicable to the language of all the Fathers. Here are three definitions which differ diametrically from one

433

another and which are no less foreign to the terminology of St Paul. The definition of St Augustine is well known : *Praeparatio beneficiorum quibus certissime liberantur quicumque liberantur.* That of St John Damascene could not be more contrary. According to him, " God foresees everything, but does not predestine everything : Ὥστε τῆς θείας προγνωστικῆς κελεύσεως ἔργον ἐστὶν ὁ προορισμός. God predestines according to his foreknowledge, which is something that is not dependent upon us " (*De fide orthod.* ii, 30; XCIV, 972).

At the very opposite extreme is the definition of St Isidore of Seville (*Sentent.* ii, 6; LXXXII, 606) : *Gemina est praedestinatio sive electorum ad requiem, sive reproborum ad mortem. Utraque divino agitur judicio ut semper electos superna et interiora sequi faciat, semperque reprobos ut infimis et exterioribus delectentur deserendo permittat.*

The theologian may employ terms in a new sense, provided he defines them; but he renders himself guilty of paralogism by supposing at once that the new interpretation is precisely that of the sacred writers or of tradition. Cajetan, for example, thinks that the preposition *prae* in the verb *praedestinare* denotes a priority over prescience : *Etiam prius quam praesciret praedestinavit.* He calls this a profound mystery. An unintelligible mystery, well and good; but St Paul does not teach it.

II—PURPOSE, GOOD PLEASURE, WILL OF GOD

If we except the Biblical expression " shew bread " (οἱ ἄρτοι τῆς προθέσεως, Matt. xii, 4; Mark ii, 26; Luke vi, 4: ἡ πρόθεσις τῶν ἄρτων) and two passages in the Acts (xi, 23, xxvii, 13) where πρόθεσις evidently designates, according to the context, the will of man, πρόθεσις is exclusively Pauline and usually signifies the will of God. The thing is indubitable in 2 Tim. i, 9 (God has delivered and called us οὐ κατὰ τὰ ἔργα ἡμῶν, ἀλλὰ κατὰ ἰδίαν πρόθεσιν καὶ χάριν) and also in Eph. i, 11 (προορισθέντες κατὰ πρόθεσιν τοῦ τὰ πάντα ἐνεργοῦντος κτλ.) and also in Eph. iii, 11 (κατὰ πρόθεσιν τῶν αἰώνων ἣν ἐποίησεν ἐν τῷ Χ᾽Ι.) This meaning appears still clearer in Rom. ix, 11 (ἵνα ἡ κατ᾽ ἐκλογὴν πρόθεσις τοῦ Θεοῦ μένῃ), since it is here expressly a question of the " purpose of God." These examples (outside of which πρόθεσις is used only in 2 Tim. iii, 10) are sufficient to determine with certainty the sense of Rom. viii, 28 (τοῖς κατὰ πρόθεσιν κλητοῖς οὖσιν), where we cannot understand thə " purpose " as the purpose of man, without an extreme violence of interpretation. To sum up, in St Paul (apart from 2 Tim. iii, 10: *assecutus es meam doctrinam,* propositum, *fidem*), πρόθεσις, *propositum,* signifies always God's plan of redemption. The corresponding verb προτίθεσθαι is taken once in the theological sense indicated above (Eph. i, 9: κατὰ τὴν εὐδοκίαν αὐτοῦ, ἣν προέθετο ἐν αὐτῷ), once for the resolution of man (Rom. i, 13 : *proposui venire ad vos*), and once in a special sense imposed by the context and parallel passages (Rom. iii, 25).

A synonym of πρόθεσις is the *will* of God (θέλημα), not the will that commands, but the will that disposes (Rom. i, 10; xv, 32; 1 Cor. i, 1; 2 Cor. i, 1; viii, 5; Gal. i, 4; Eph. i, 1, 5, 9, 11; Col. i, 1; 2 Tim. i, 1); another synonym which is still closer is the *good pleasure* (εὐδοκία, Eph. i, 5, 9, and εὐδοκεῖν, 1 Cor. i, 26; Gal. i, 15; Col. i, 19); these words, applicable alike to God and man, are determined by the context.

It is necessary to observe that in πρόθεσις the preposition πρό suggests no idea of *priority*, but has rather a local sense (the action of *proposing* to oneself to do something, or of having it *in* mind). Priority, when it exists, must be expressed by another term, for example in Eph. i, 11, προορισθέντες κατὰ πρόθεσιν and Eph. iii, 11, κατὰ πρόθεσιν τῶν αἰώνων (equivalent to κατὰ πρόθεσιν αἰώνιον).

From all that precedes it results that πρόθεσις designates in St Paul *an eternal act of the consequent and absolute divine will referring to a particular benefit;* for example, to an efficacious call.

III—Foreknowledge, Prescience

The word "prescience" (πρόγνωσις) is not Pauline. It is found only four times in the Bible (Acts ii, 23; 1 Pet. i, 2; Judith ix, 6; xi, 16) and is used each time to denote the prescience of God, except in Judith xi, 16. Among secular writers it is met with only after the commencement of the Christian era, with the meaning of foresight, and especially of medical prognosis.—Προγινώσκω is much more common and is a purely Greek word. It signifies "to know beforehand, first of all," without any accessory idea. See examples in Passow or in Cremer. The aphorism of Aristotle (*Eth. Nic.* vi, 3) is famous: ἐκ προγιγνωσκομένων πᾶσα διδασκαλία. It is a purely intellectual act. It is the same in Wisdom vi, 13; viii, 8; xviii, 6. It is not found elsewhere in the Old Testament. In the New it appears five times, and is twice applied to the knowledge of men (2 Pet. iii, 7; Acts xxvi, 5: προγινώσκοντές με ἄνωθεν), once to the prescience of God in relation to his providence (1 Pet. i, 19: Christ, the lamb without spot, is προεγνωσμένος πρὸ καταβολῆς κόσμου). For Rom. xi, 2, see p. 264, note 5; and for Rom. viii, 29, see p. 243, note 2 and p. 244, note 1.

All this shows that προγινώσκω cannot mean directly and principally an act of will; but the sense of "approving prescience" can be admitted, when used of God foreseeing the moral good of his creatures.

IV—To Call, Called, A Call or Vocation

1. *To call* (*vocare*, καλεῖν) is used of God and of men: in both cases it means either "to give a name" or "to call to a function."

2. *Called* (*vocatus*, κλητός) in the New Testament always has the theological sense of *called by God*. Paul is called to the apostolate (Rom. i, 1; 1 Cor. i, 1); all the faithful are called saints or are called to sanctity (*vocati sancti*, κλητοὶ ἅγιοι, Rom. i, 7; 1 Cor. i, 2), called of Jesus Christ (Rom. i, 6), or simply called (1 Cor. i, 24; Jud. 1; Apoc. xvii, 14; *vocati et electi et fideles*). Those who love God are *secundum propositum vocati* (Rom. viii, 28; the word *sancti* added by the Vulgate, although it is not the text, does not alter the meaning). In St Matthew (xx, 26; xxii, 14) only, the word "called" comprises the invited guests who do not respond to the call: *Multi vocati pauci vero electi*.

3. *Vocation* (*vocatio*, κλῆσις) is also a word reserved to God. It is the efficacious call to faith (1 Cor. i, 26; vii, 20; Eph. i, 18; iv, 1, 4; Phil. iii, 14; 2 Thess. i, 11; Heb. iii, 1; 2 Pet. i, 10), and exceptionally to the dignity of the elect (Rom. xi, 20).

To sum up, when *to call* has God for its subject, and does not mean merely to give a name, Paul always has in mind an efficacious vocation. *Called* (except in Matt. xx, 26; xxii, 14) always indicates one who has accepted the divine call: the end of the call is, twice, the apostolate, but everywhere else grace and justification. *Called* practically means *Christian*, alluding to the favour of God and the gratuitous nature of the benefit. Similarly, *vocation* is always efficacious vocation: its end is generally sanctifying grace; once it refers to the Mosaic theocracy.

V—To Elect, Elected, Election

These words, which are rare in St Paul, do not always mean a divine action.

1. *To elect* (*eligere*, ἐκλέγεσθαι) is used of men (Luke x, 42; xiv, 7; John xv, 16; Acts vi, 5; xv, 22, 25); of Jesus Christ choosing his apostles (Luke vi, 13; John vi, 70; xiii, 18; xv, 16, 19; Acts i, 2); of God (Acts i, 24; xiii, 17; xv, 7; 1 Cor. i, 27, 28; Eph. i, 4; Jas. ii, 5). In the latter case it always refers to things to be done (except Eph. i, 4).

2. *Elected* (*electus*, ἐκλεκτός) is usually synonymous with *called*, to which it adds a notion of selection or preference. Once it may mean *the elect of heaven* (1 Tim. v, 21: *Testor coram Deo et J.C. et electis angelis*); but various interpretations of this expression are given, either as referring to

angels *eminent in dignity* (Birping), or to angels in possession of *eternal blessedness* (Estius), or to angels *chosen* for the protection of men.

3. *Election* (*electio, ἐκλογή*) is a synonym of vocation with the notion of preference and choice (Rom. ix, 11; xi, 5, 7, 28; 1 Thess. i, 4; 2 Pet. i, 10: *Certam / vestram vocationem et electionem faciatis*). In *vas electionis* (Acts ix, 15) there is an idea of excellence rather than of choice.

To sum up : *To elect* is not applied only to God, while God is the sole source of the *elect* and *election* in the New Testament. Except in 1 Tim. v, 21, where *elect* signifies, perhaps, elect unto glory, *elect* usually (fifteen times) means *one who has accepted the divine call*, but with a notion of favour and of choice on the part of God; exceptionally it also means *excellent, precious* in Rom. xvi, 13; Luke xxiii, 35; 1 Pet. ii, 4, 6. In Col. iii, 12 and 2 John 1 and 13 the sense is doubtful. *Election* always signifies *vocation* with the shade of meaning indicated above. It implies either the dignity of the apostle (Acts ix, 25) or the dignity of a chosen people (Rom. ix, 11), or, elsewhere, the dignity of a Christian.

NOTE G—ADAM'S SIN AND ITS CONSEQUENCES

I—Passage from St Paul (Rom. v, 12-21)

It is indispensable first of all fully to appreciate the parallel, most frequently revealed in contrast, between Adam and Christ. The use of special type below clearly shows the current of thought : *the argument of parity,* which forms the principal idea, is in heavy face; the *argument à fortiori,* which is grafted on to it, is in roman, and the *digressions* are in italics.

Verse 12. Propterea sicut per unum hominem peccatum in hunc mundum intravit, et per peccatum mors, et ita in omnes homines mors pertransiit in quo omnes peccaverunt :
Verse 13. (*Usque ad legem enim peccatum erat in mundo: peccatum autem non imputabatur, cum lex non esset.—* Verse 14. *Sed regnavit mors ab Adam usque ad Moysen etiam in eos qui non peccaverunt in similitudinem praevaricationis Adae,* [**qui est forma futuri**]).

Verse 15. Sed non sicut delictum, ita et donum : si enim unius delicto multi mortui sunt; multo magis gratia Dei et donum in gratia unius hominis Jesu Christi in plures abundavit.

Verse 16. Et non sicut per unum peccatum, ita et donum : nam judicium quidem ex uno in condemnationem : gratia autem ex multis delictis in justificationem.—Verse 17. Si enim unius delicto mors regnavit per unum : multo magis abundantiam gratiae et donationis et justitiae accipientes, in vita regnabunt per unum Jesum Christum.

Verse 18. Igitur sicut per unius delictum in omnes homines in condemnationem : sic et per unius justitiam in omnes homines in justificationem vitae.— Verse 19. Sicut enim per inobedientiam unius hominis, peccatores constituti sunt multi : ita et per unius obeditionem justi constituentur multi.

Verse 20. Lex autem subintravit ut abundaret delictum. Ubi autem abundavit delictum superabundavit gratia ;

Verse 21. Ut sicut regnavit peccatum in mortem, ita et gratia regnet per justitiam in vitam aeternam, per Jesum Christum Dominum nostrum.

1. *The Parallel between Adam and Christ.*—The first phrase begins with a comparison which is not finished. The long parenthesis which fills verses 13 and 14 naturally explains this lack of sequence, without importance as regards the meaning, for the unexpressed term of comparison is sufficiently indicated by the short clause which terminates the

phrase—*qui est forma* (τύπος) *futuri.* The *type,* in fact, is correlative with the *antitype.* It is, therefore, unnecessary to supply the lacking term of comparison, as Origen proposes to do : *Ita et per unum hominem justitia introivit in mundum et per justitiam vita, et sic in homines omnes vita pertransiit, in qua omnes vivificati sunt* (translation of Rufinus, Book V, No. 1), or else as follows : *Things occur in the work of reparation wrought by Christ,* just as by one man sin entered into the world, etc. Patrizi, in a dissertation excellent from other points of view (*Commentat. tres,* Rome, 1851, pp. 26-39 : *De peccati originalis propagatione a Paulo descripta*), tries to prove that the phrase is complete and that the words *et sic* (καὶ οὕτως) begin the apodosis. This hypothesis, which is contrary to the unanimous opinion of the interpreters, is absolutely forbidden by the rules of grammar, for καὶ οὕτως (*et sic*) is not equivalent to οὕτως καί (*sic et*). A question of less importance is that of knowing to what διὰ τοῦτο (*propterea*) refers. The best exegetes of all schools—Cornely, Sanday, Meyer-Weiss, etc.—rightly think that St Paul refers to the whole beginning of the chapter (Rom. v, 2-11), in which the fruits of Christ's redemption are summarized.

The parallel, once introduced, is resumed later on in verses 18, 19, and 21. Everywhere else it gives way to the contrast.

2. *Basis of the Parallel and Contrast between Adam and Christ.*—This is to be sought, on the one hand, in the *representative character common to both,* and, on the other, in the fact that Christ represents humanity *better and more efficaciously* than Adam. The reasoning of Paul assumes, therefore, one of these two forms :

(*a*) *As* Adam was able to destroy us, *so* Christ will be able to save us.

(*b*) *If* Adam, by his sin, made us sinners, *how much more* will Christ, by his justice, be able to make us just.

From one end of the passage to the other the *single* cause is contrasted with the *multiple* effects. For example :

Verse 18. *One* man only transgresses. . . . *All* men are condemned.

One author of justice. . . . *All* men justified.

Verse 19. *One* man only disobeys. . . . *The many* are made sinners.

One man only obeys. . . . *The many* are made just.

What we translate by *the many* (*un grand nombre*) corresponds to the Greek οἱ πολλοί.

This expression is very difficult to render in French, and

still more difficult, perhaps, in Latin. If the word *plusieurs* (Osterwald) is used, it gives the erroneous idea that it does not mean all; if the word *tous* is employed (Crampon), it is not a translation, but a commentary; if *la plupart* is chosen (Oltramare), universality seems to be improperly excluded; if *les plusieurs* (Godet) is used, exactitude is gained at the expense of correctness; perhaps *beaucoup* (Segond) renders the true shade of meaning best, provided it is not *exclusive*. It is evident that by οἱ πολλοί (here, as in Rom. xii, 15; 1 Cor. x, 17) Paul means *all*, but *totality* is not the salient idea; it is *multiplicity* as contrasted with unity. The amplification *all, whatever their number,* brings out this last idea, but with too much emphasis on the total number. The most exact meaning of οἱ πολλοί is *whatever their number.*

II—ADAM'S FALL AND JEWISH THEOLOGY

Did the Jews contemporary with St Paul admit the existence of original sin? The question thus worded is very badly stated. If a Jew had been asked if man was guilty of any other sin than personal sins, he would no doubt have answered in the negative, for by the word " sin " he meant only those in which the individual will has a part. It is a matter of words and definitions. Original sin is not a sin like other sins. It is admitted to-day that it does not consist of concupiscence only, nor in a morbid germ inoculated into the body, but in the deprivation of the supernatural justice which Adam had received in trust, in order that he might transmit it to his race. But few problems have needed more intense and continuous theological labour for their solution. It is a long road from St Augustine to the fifth session of the Council of Trent, as we can easily convince ourselves by reading, for example, J. N. Espenberger, *Die Elemente der Erbsünde nach Augustin und der Frühscholastik,* Mainz, 1905 (*in Forsch. zur christl. Lit. u. .Dogmengesch.,* vol. x, Part I).

This, therefore, is admittedly the way in which the question should be stated. Was the sin of Adam for humanity a fall, a decadence, from the point of view of supernatural or preternatural gifts? To the question thus put all Jews—at least those who were not imbued with the dualistic principles of Greek philosophy—would have replied affirmatively, for they admitted generally—(1) That the sin of Adam has caused men to lose the privilege of immortality, or, rather, of exemption from death. (2) That it has produced, or at least developed, the יצר הרע, the *cor malignum,* concupiscence. (3) That it has taken from them the good-will and familiar companionship of God. (4) That Adam represented the human race contained in his loins. (5) Finally, many thought that the Messiah would restore the blessings lost in Adam. This was sufficient to cause the Jewish or judaizing readers of St Paul to have no objections against these two propositions which sum up chapter five : " By one man sin entered into the world, and through sin death.—As all die through the deed of Adam, all shall be made alive through Christ (the Messiah)."

The principal Jewish texts relating to this question are very accessible, and it would be superfluous to reproduce them. The reader may consult Tennant, *The Sources of the Doctrine of the Fall and Original Sin,* 1905; Isr. Lévi, *Le péché originel dans les anciennes sources juives,* Paris, 1907; J. B. Frey, *L'état originel et la chute de l'homme d'après les conceptions juives au temps de Jésus-Christ* (in the *Revue des sciences philos. et théol.,* vol. v, 1911, pp. 507-545); Lagrange, *Epître aux Romains,* Paris, 1916, pp. 113-118; Porter's monograph, *The Yeçer hara': A Study of the Jewish Doctrine of Sin,* New York, 1901 ; and the more general works of Bousset, *Die Religion des Judentums*[2], Berlin, 1906, pp. 462-470; Weber, *Jüdische Theologie*[2], Leipzig, 1897, pp. 218-225. The last-named writer is perfectly right in saying that the Talmudic theology admits an *original debt,* but not an *original sin* in the sense of a necessity to sin (p. 224 : *Es gibt eine* Erbschuld, *aber keine* Erbsünde; *der Fall Adams hat dem ganzen Geschlechte den Tod, nicht aber die Sündigkeit im Sinne einer Notwendigkeit zu sündigen verursacht*).

What is most interesting and too little noted in the texts is the representative character of Adam at the time of his disobedience. *Cf.* Eisenmenger, *Das entdeckte Judentum,* Königsberg, 1711, vol. ii, pp. 81-82. The following are some of the briefest texts. R. Bechai writes : *Primus homo causavit mortem omnibus generationibus suis* (אדם הראשון גרם מיתה לכל תולדותיו). R. Isaac Caro says, referring to Ecclesiasticus xxv, 24 : *Non obstantibus istis non morimur nisi per peccatum primi hominis.* R. Menachem is still more positive : *Cum peccavit ille totus mundus peccavit,* כאשר חטא הוא כל העולם חטא, et iniquitates ejus portavimus. The reason given by R. Menachem is that Adam contained within himself all his posterity : Notum est mortem decretam fuisse in primum hominem *qui erat princeps mundi et radix omnium generationum* (שהיה שר העולם ועקר כל הדורות). Happily, all that Adam caused us to lose will be restored to us by the Messiah. On this point see Weber, *Jüd. Theologie*[2], pp. 380-382. This idea is very old, for it is found already in the *Testaments of the Patriarchs* (*Levi,* xviii, 10-12).

The Dominican, Raymond Martini, in his celebrated *Pugio fidei,* Paris, 1651, Part III, chapters vi-ix, pp. 463-497, reproduces in Hebrew a very large number of texts borrowed from the rabbis of all epochs; but he gives a definition of original sin which we cannot accept (p. 463): *Originale peccatum dicitur apud nos fomes peccati*, scilicet *concupiscentia*, vel *concupiscibilitas*, quae quandoque dicitur *lex membrorum*, quandoque *languor naturae*, quandoque *lex carnis*.

The ideas of modern Jews on this subject are vague and incoherent; they seem, moreover, to attach only a small importance to the question. See in *The Jewish Encyclopedia* the articles on *Adam, Fall, Original Sin*.

NOTE H—PREDESTINATION AND REPROBATION

In the Epistle to the Romans, St Paul says that God " has predestined the just to be made conformable to the image of his Son " (Rom. viii, 28-30), and he speaks several times of the rejection of Israel. As contradictory theories have arisen from these expressions, let us see what foundation they have in the exegesis of the Fathers.

I—PRESCIENCE AND PREDESTINATION
ROM. VIII.

28. Οἴδαμεν δὲ ὅτι τοῖς ἀγαπῶσι τὸν Θεὸν πάντα συνεργεῖ εἰς ἀγαθὸν, τοῖς κατὰ πρόθεσιν κλητοῖς οὖσιν·

Scimus autem quoniam diligentibus Deum omnia cooperantur in bonum, iis qui secundum propositum vocati sunt [sancti].

29. ὅτι οὓς προέγνω, καὶ προώρισεν συμμόρφους τῆς εἰκόνος τοῦ υἱοῦ αὐτοῦ, εἰς τὸ εἶναι αὐτὸν πρωτότοκον ἐν πολλοῖς ἀδελφοῖς·

Nam quos praescivit, et praedestinavit conformes fieri imaginis Filii sui, ut sit ipse primogenitus in multis fratribus.

30. οὓς δὲ προώρισεν, τούτους καὶ ἐκάλεσεν· καὶ οὓς ἐκάλεσεν, τούτους καὶ ἐδικαίωσεν· οὓς δὲ ἐδικαίωσεν, τούτους καὶ ἐδόξασεν.

Quos autem praedestinavit, hos et vocavit: et quos vocavit, hos et justificavit; quos autem justificavit, illos et glorificavit.

Exegesis of the Greek Fathers.

(A) As far as it is possible to judge, all the Greek writers who have treated of this text are agreed on all the essential points and differ only in details of interpretation, whose accessory character in regard to the present question it is easy to prove.

(*a*) All of them make predestination depend upon prescience, in the sense that God predestines to grace and to faith all those, and only those, whose response to the divine call or to the grace of vocation he foresees.

(*b*) All of them understand by the predestination, of which Paul speaks in this place, predestination to the efficacious grace of the vocation; that is to say, to the call not only offered by God, but accepted by man; and all of them apparently understand by the glorification mentioned later, that glorification which takes place in this life through the sanctifying grace which renders us " conformable to the image of the Son of God."

(*c*) But the greatest merit of the Greek exegetes is to have noted clearly the aim of the Apostle, which is to give to *all* the just, "to all those who love God," a reason for hope, by showing them by past benefits that God is with them, that he continues to protect them, and that he will abandon them only if they abandon themselves.

(*d*) Consequently they admit that in this phrase : τοῖς ἀγαπῶσι τὸν Θεὸν πάντα συνεργεῖ εἰς ἀγαθόν, τοῖς κατὰ πρόθεσιν κλητοῖς οὖσιν, the two clauses have the same *extent* of meaning; the second does not *limit* the first, but explains it; in other words, all those who love God are called according to the purpose and the blessings enumerated—prescience, predestination, vocation, justification and glorification—are common to them all, a fact which permits them all and commands them all to indulge in hope.

After this it is easy to see that the three divergences noted in the exegesis of the Greek Fathers have no great importance.

(*e*) In the phrase τοῖς ἀγαπῶσι τὸν Θεὸν πάντα συνεργεῖ εἰς ἀγαθόν, most of them, with Chrysostom, take "God" as the subject; others (among whom perhaps Origen is to be counted) take as subject of συνεργεῖ the neuter πάντα. In reality, whether God "makes everything work together for the good of his friends," or "all things work together to the good of the friends of God," makes no noteworthy difference in the thought; since the benefit is common to all the friends of God, and since, after all, it is God who, by a special providence, is the author of it.

(*f*) Urged by an ill-founded fear of favouring fatalism, the Greek Fathers (with the exception of Origen and St Cyril of Alexandria) understand by κατὰ πρόθεσιν the "purpose" of man. But neither the general sense of the passage nor its theological import is thereby changed; since, according to them, *all those who are called* are called according to the purpose, and *all the friends of God* are called thus. It is, therefore, only a fault of exegesis, πρόθεσις in St Paul meaning a divine act.

(*g*) Finally, the same Fathers, referring to the two categories of those invited in the Gospel (Matt. xx, 16; xxii, 14), sometimes oppose to those who have accepted the divine call, and who are said to be *called according to the purpose,* those who have not accepted it. Thus St Chrysostom, St Isidore of Pelusium, Diodorus of Tarsus, Theodore of Mopsuestia, Photius, and the regular disciples of Chrysostom. This is another fault of exegesis, for in the terminology of Paul there is only one category of the *called,* the κλητοί ; but this fault has no serious influence on the understanding of the text, since, as a matter of fact, all the *called according to the purpose* are Christians, and *vice versa.*

(B) Of the Greek commentaries before A.D. 400, those of Origen and Chrysostom, which have exerted the most in-

fluence on Oriental exegesis, are precisely those which have
come down to us, one in the original, the other in a Latin
translation. They deserve special examination.

(a) *Origen and his School.*—The translation of Rufinus is
only an abridged adaptation, in which we do not always
recognize Origen's thought. The reader is left free to understand by *secundum propositum* the will of man or the will
of God; the *glorification,* of which the Apostle speaks, takes
place, at least in part, in this life; the *prescience* is an
approving knowledge which precedes and directs the predestination; two vocations can be distinguished—that which,
being followed by the effect desired, is according to the
purpose, and that which is not so followed through the fault
of man. All this is fairly in accord with the mind of Origen,
but we may always suspect in it the hand of Rufinus. Fortunately, SS Basil and Gregory, in their collection of selected
passages from Origen, have inserted a long one taken from
the *Commentary on the Epistle to the Romans,* in which our
text is explained (Robinson : *The Philocalia of Origen,* Cambridge, 1893, chap. xxv, pp. 226-231). The characteristic
feature of this commentary is its clear distinction of the
divine acts—before justification, vocation; before vocation,
predestination; before predestination, prescience. " If predestination came first, the fatalists would be right; but
prescience precedes it " (ἀνωτέρω δέ ἐστι τοῦ προορισμοῦ ἡ
πρόγνωσις). God sees the present and foresees the future; but
neither vision nor prevision have any influence on their object;
far from creating it, they presuppose it. *Conformity* to the
Son of God is the resemblance which grace or adoptive
sonship gives; the *purpose* is indeed the purpose of God, but
it follows the prescience upon which it is founded; finally,
the verb συνεργεῖ is intransitive (all things work together)
and not transitive (God makes all things work together).
But this last point is of secondary importance.

(b) *St John Chrysostom and his School.*—Chrysostom's
commentary is admirable in its clearness and logic—*In
Roman. hom.* xv, 1-2 (LX, 540-542). God is the subject of
συνεργεῖ, and it is God who works all things together for the
good of those who love him; the translator, therefore, ought
not to have kept the *cooperantur* of the Vulgate.—There are
two categories of those who are called—those who have come
because their will (πρόθεσις) is good (and who are therefore
κλητοὶ κατὰ πρόθεσιν) and those who have not wished to come
(πρόθεσιν ἐνταῦθά φησιν, ἵνα μὴ τὸ πᾶν τῇ κλήσει δῷ . . . ὅτι
οὐχ ἡ κλῆσις μόνον, ἀλλὰ καὶ ἡ πρόθεσις τῶν καλουμένων τὴν
σωτηρίαν εἰργάσατο). In fact, the divine call forces no one; all
have been called, but all have not obeyed the call. *Conformity*
to the Son of God is that which sanctifying grace gives (Ὅπερ
γὰρ ὁ Μονογενὴς ἦν φύσει, τοῦτο καὶ αὐτοὶ γεγόνασι κατὰ χάριν).—

The glorification has already taken place; it is that which adoptive sonship confers (Ἐδόξασε διὰ τῆς χάριτος, διὰ τῆς υἱοθεσίας).—Finally, the aim of the Apostle is to confirm the hope of Christians, and to show them, from the benefits already received from God in the past, those which they have a right to expect in the future (Εἰ τοῖς μέλλουσί τινες διαπιστοῦσιν, ἀλλὰ πρὸς τὰ ἤδη γεγενημένα ἀγαθὰ οὐδὲν ἄν ἔχοιεν εἰπεῖν· οἷον, τὴν ἄνωθεν τοῦ Θεοῦ πρὸς σὲ φιλίαν, τὴν δικαίωσιν, τὴν δόξαν). Note the ἤδη and the δόξαν which give the true note of this whole commentary.

The commentators who come after Chrysostom often merely copy him. Nor shall we say anything of compilers like Œcumenius, Euthymius, and Theophylact. Theodoret seems as mindful of Origen as of Chrysostom (LXXXII, 141-143): Ὧν προέγνω τὴν πρόθεσιν, τούτους προώρισεν ἄνωθεν· προορίσας δὲ καὶ ἐκάλεσεν· εἶτα καλέσας διὰ τοῦ βαπτίσματος ἐδικαίωσεν· δικαιώσας δὲ ἐδόξασεν υἱοὺς ὀνομάσας, καὶ Πνεύματος ἁγίου δωρησάμενος χάριν. Thus prescience at the base, glorification at the summit, but a glorification which is realized here on earth through the gift of the Holy Spirit. Prescience has for its object the purpose of man.—The same note is apparent in the brief annotations of *Photius*, who well apprehended the import of the passage as a motive for hope (CI, 1244). All the benefits which the Apostle enumerates (prescience, predestination, vocation, justification, glorification) have been already conferred on all the just, and they are to all of them a sure guarantee of divine favour in the future. The πρόθεσις is the γνώμη of man.

(C) *Other Greek Commentators.* — The biblical *Catenae* make us acquainted with a certain number of patristic texts taken from commentaries now lost (Cramer : *Catena in epist. ad Roman.*, Oxford, 1844, pp. 147-150 and 262-276; above all, the *Greek* Vatican manuscript 762, which is more complete and more correct).

(a) The master of St John Chrysostom, *Diodorus of Tarsus*, is careful to remark that prescience precedes predestination : πρῶτον ἐφῆ προγινώσκειν τὸν Θεὸν εἶτα προορίζειν (*Greek* Vatic. 762, fol. 118, wanting in Cramer). He is of opinion that the meaning would be clearer if the order were reversed : "‹Those whom he glorified, those he also justified," etc. Moreover, all these benefits take place here on earth. The whole commentary recalls Origen, except that Diodorus understands by πρόθεσις the *purpose* of man and makes it a preliminary condition of predestination : Τίνας δὲ προώρισεν; οὓς προέγνω· τοὺς κατὰ πρόθεσιν κλητοὺς ὄντας, τοῦτ' ἔστιν τοὺς διὰ τὴν ἰδίαν πρόθεσιν ἀξίους ὄντας κληθῆναι καὶ συμμορφω θῆναι Χριστῷ.

(b) There are only very short fragments of the writings of Theodore of Mopsuestia (LXVI, 832): God makes all things work together for the good of those who love him (τοῖς ἀγαπῶσιν αὐτὸν ἀγαθῶν πρόξενος γίνεται Θεός), although he tolerates the wicked and does not deprive them of his benefits. The call "according to purpose" is that which is freely accepted by the will (πρόθεσις) of man : Τούτων γὰρ ᾔδει καὶ πάλαι ὁ Θεὸς τὴν περὶ αὐτὸν [this is the reading of the Greek Vatic. 762 ; Cramer, followed by Migne, reads περὶ αὐτῶν, which appears meaningless] πρόθεσιν οἷα τίς ἔσται, ὅθεν αὐτοὺς καὶ ἐκάλεσεν ἐπὶ τῷ τῆς οἰκείας ἀξίως τιμῆσαι προαιρέσεως. Man can, however, do nothing without grace (*In Rom.* viii, 38) : οὐκ ἔτι τῇ οἰκείᾳ δυνάμει, τῇ δὲ τοῦ Χριστοῦ συνεργίᾳ τὸ πᾶν ἐπιτρέψας.

(c) The passionate opponent of St Chrysostom, *Severianus of Gabala,* does not seem to have had any antipathy for his exegesis. The *Catenae* give us only two of his short notes, one of which shows that he had clearly apprehended Paul's general idea (the love of the Father and the Son for us is a certain sign [τεκμήριον] that they will finish their work), while the other lets us see that he understood by the *conformity* to the Son of God, to which we are predestined, the conformity produced by sanctifying grace (τῆς εἰκόνος τοῦ Υἱοῦ ἀντὶ τοῦ ἁγίου Πνεύματος).

(d) The exegesis of *St Cyril of Alexandria* (LXXIV, 828-829) differs from that of Chrysostom in only one point : πρόθεσις, which is the same thing as βούλησις, designates at the same time the will of God and the will of man (κλητοὶ γεγόνασί τινες κατὰ πρόθεσιν, τήν τε τοῦ κεκληκότος καὶ τὴν ἑαυτῶν). The idea and the rôle of prescience are the same as in Chrysostom. All are called, but all do not accept : Οὓς εἰδὼς πόρρωθεν ὁποῖοί τινες ἔσονται, ἀφώρισεν εἰς τὸ τῶν μελλόντων μετασχεῖν ἀγαθῶν, τούτους καὶ ἐκάλεσεν, ὥστε διὰ τῆς ἐπ' αὐτὸν πίστεως ἀπολαῦσαι δικαιώσεως. The good Cardinal Mai, who first edited the scholia of St Cyril, thinks himself obliged to remark here : *Observent scholastici praedestinationem post praevisa merita a Cyrillo perspicue traditam,* rather a needless observation, for the doctrine of St Cyril has in this respect nothing which interferes with the teaching of his predecessors : Εἰδὼς ἄνωθεν τοιούτους ἐσομένους αὐτούς, ἀνάλογα τῇ περὶ αὐτῶν διαθέσει πόρρωθεν αὐτοῖς ηὐτρέπιζεν ἀγαθά. The whole of this commentary should be read.

(e) *Gennadius* (following Cramer's *Catena,* p. 148, and the most correct text of the *Greek* Vatic. 762) agrees with his predecessors. God makes all things work together for the good of those who love him : πάντα αὐτοῖς τὰ περὶ αὐτοὺς συμβαίνοντα γίνεσθαι παρασκευάζει πρὸς ἀγαθόν, ἅτε καὶ κατὰ τὴν ἀγαθὴν αὐτῶν πρόθεσιν προσκεκλημένους αὐτούς. . . . The conformity to the image of the Son is adoptive sonship.

An unknown writer, supposed to have lived in the sixth century and whom the *Catenae* call *Theodore the Monk,* accentuates still more than the others the vocation according to the *purpose* of man (ὁ μὲν γὰρ Θεὸς καλεῖ πάντας οὐ πᾶσι δὲ συνεργεῖ ἀλλὰ τοῖς εὐσεβῆ πρόθεσιν ἔχουσιν) and moreover follows Chrysostom and Origen. It is the Holy Spirit that makes everything work for the good of the friends of God (τὸ Πνεῦμα συνεργεῖ, ὅ ἐστι συμπράττει) ; 'the glorification and conformity to the image of the Son, the end and aim of the predestination, take place here on earth through grace. See, for information about this person, Hastings, *Dictionary of the Bible*, extra vol., 1904, p. 519.

(*f*) To the Greek commentators can be added St Ephrem (*Comment. in Epist. Pauli,* Venice, 1893, after the Armenian version) : "*Justificavit* per fidem et baptismum ; *glorificavit* per dona Spiritus.'' Other Greek Fathers, although not professedly explaining our text, show us how they understand it. Thus *St Cyril* of Jerusalem, *Procatech.*, i (XXXIII, 333) ; περιμένει [ὁ Θεὸς] τὴν γνησίαν προαίρεσιν. Διὰ τοῦτο ἐπήγαγεν ὁ Ἀπόστολος λέγων· Τοῖς κατὰ πρόθεσιν κλητοῖς οὖσιν· Ἡ πρόθεσις γνησία οὖσα κλητόν σε ποιεῖ (on the orthodoxy of these words see the note of Touttée in Migne).—For *St Basil* and *St Athanasius* the conformity to the image of the Son of God, to which the just have been predestined, is received here on earth through the gift of the Holy Spirit. *Basil. Adv. Eunom.* v (XXIX, 724 : Εἰκὼν δὲ Υἱοῦ τὸ Πνεῦμα, καὶ οἱ τούτου μεταλαμβάνοντες υἱοὶ σύμμορφοι) ; *Athan. Epist. ad Serap.*, i, 24 and iv, 3 (XXVI, 588 and 641). Both refer to Rom. viii, 29. *St Isidore of Pelusium* comments twice on our text. The first time, *Epist.*, iv, 13 (LXVIII, 1061), he limits himself to saying that God never abandons men of goodwill. In the second passage, *Epist.*, iv, 51 (LXVIII, 1101), he follows St John Chrysostom so closely that he must have had his writings before him : Οὐ γὰρ ἡ κλῆσις μόνον (πάντες γὰρ ἐκλήθησαν μὲν οὐχ ὑπήκουσαν δέ)· ἀλλὰ καὶ πρόθεσις τῶν κεκλημένων τὴν σωτηρίαν εἰργάσατο. Οὐ γὰρ ἠναγκασμένη γέγονεν ἡ κλῆσις οὐδὲ βεβιασμένη, ἀλλ' ἑκούσιος.

If St John Damascene does not differ from the others in regard to doctrine, he differs from them much in respect of terminology. According to him, prescience extends to everything, even to free acts, while predestination includes only necessary acts, *De fide orthod.*, ii, 30 (XCIV, 972) : Πάντα μὲν προγινώσκει ὁ Θεὸς, οὐ πάντα δὲ προορίζει. Προγινώσκει γὰρ τὰ ἐφ' ἡμῖν, οὐ προορίζει δὲ αὐτά. And even for necessary acts predestination follows prescience : Προορίζει δὲ τὰ οὐκ ἐφ' ἡμῖν κατὰ τὴν πρόγνωσιν αὐτοῦ. It is a style of language that is quite unusual and which it is sufficient to note in passing.

2. *Exegesis of the Latin Fathers before St Augustine.*

We possess only the commentary of Ambrosiaster and that of Pelagius, more or less recast in an orthodox sense ; but the thought of St Hilary, of St Ambrose, and of St Jerome is known to us by their works.

At once we perceive that the point of view of the Latins differs much from that of the Greeks. This is perhaps due to the evolution which took place at an early date in the signification of the words *predestined* and *predestination*. In Latin the words *praedestinatio* and *praedestinatus* had a meaning of their own and tended to assume the *theological* sense to which we are now accustomed—namely, that of predestination to glory or to grace and glory, while they had preserved in Greek the meaning which may be called *exegetical* —that which they have in St Paul—of predestination to faith and grace. Such titles as *De praedestinatione sanctorum* or *Praedestinatus,* translated literally into Greek, would not have been understood, for they brought in a new notion with which the Greek language was not yet acquainted.

This explains why the Latin Fathers, in speaking of predestination, lay much more stress on the *merit* of man, and do not fear to assign to predestination causes outside of God. This is because they are speaking of predestination to glory, as Latin usage allows them to do. For example :

(a) St Hilary, In Psalm. lxiv, No. 5, on the text *Multi vocati sed pauci electi,* says (IX, 415) : *Itaque non res indiscreti judicii est electio, sed ex meriti delectu facta discretio est. Beatus ergo quem elegit Deus, beatus ob id, quia electione sit dignus.*

(b) St Ambrose, De fide, v, 83, on Rom. viii, 29 (XVI, 665) : *Apostolus ait:* Quos praescivit et praedestinavit, *non enim ante praedestinavit quam praesciret, sed quorum merita praescivit, eorum praemia praedestinavit.*

(c) St Jerome, Epist. 120 ad Hedibiam x (XXII, 1000) : *Non salvat [Deus] irrationabiliter, et absque judicii veritate, sed causis praecedentibus; quia alii non susceperunt Filium Dei, alii autem recipere sua sponte voluerunt.*

(d) The exegesis of *Ambrosiaster* (XVII, 127-128) is very curious : *Hi secundum propositum vocantur, quos credentes praescivit Deus futuros sibi idoneos; ut antequam crederent scirentur. . . . . Istos quos praescivit sibi devotos, ipsos elegit ad promissa praemia capessenda. . . . Conformes* fieri imaginis Filii sui. *Hoc dicit quia ideo praedestinantur in futurum saeculum ut similes fiant Filio Dei. . . . Quos autem justificavit, hos et magnificavit. Hoc dicit quod supra, quia quos praescivit Deus aptos sibi, hi credentes permanent. . . . De ceteris quos non praescivit Deus, non est illi cura in hac gratia, quia non praescivit illos futuros idoneos. At si credant aut eligantur ad tempus . . . non permanent ut magnificentur.* The basis of the system is that there are two categories of the called—those who, being certain to persevere to the end, are called according to the purpose and are the object of prescience and of predestination (to glory), and those who do not persevere and who are not either known in advance (like the faithful) or predestined.

(e) *Pelagius* (XXX, 684-5), whose commentary must have been retouched, establishes a suspicious identity between prescience and predestination : *Praedestinare idem est quod praescire.* He adds : *Ergo quos praevidit conformes futuros in vita, voluit ut fierent conformes in gloria.. . . .* Quos autem praedestinavit, hos et vocavit. . . . *Quos praescivit credituros, hos vocavit. Vocatio autem volentes colligit, non invitos. Aut certe discretio non in personis, sed in tempore est.* This is the clearest statement that is found in him. Is this the theory of Ambrosiaster on the double vocation, which the final perseverance differentiates? On the other hand, does not the identity established between predestination and prescience tend to suppress predestination, so as to keep foresight only, to which the divine decree is bound? It would then be pure Pelagianism. If, on the contrary, prescience was lost in predestination and was only one aspect of it, we should have the error of the predestinarians.

In any case, the very special terminology of Pelagius and Ambrosiaster prepares us for the variations of Augustine.

3. *Successive Opinions of St Augustine.*

The exegesis of St Augustine on chapters eight and nine of the Epistle to the Romans underwent in the course of time a radical transformation. *Cf.* K. Kolb, *Menschliche Freiheit und göttliches Vorherwissen nach Augustinus,* Freiburg i. Br., 1908, and V. Weber, *Kritische Geschichte der Exegese des IX Kapitels, resp. der Verse 14-23 des Römerbriefs bis auf Chrysostomus und Augustinus einschliesslich,* Würzburg, 1889.

First Phase.—In 388, Augustine interpreted St Paul as the other Fathers did; but his language in favour of the goodwill of man which precedes conversion is more difficult than that of his *predecessors.* He wrote, for example, *De diversis quaestion. octoginta tribus,* lviii, No. 4 : *Praecedit aliquid in peccatoribus, quo quamvis nondum sint justificati, digni efficiantur justificatione; et item praecedit in aliis peccatoribus quo digni sint obtusione* (another reading, *obtunsione*). No. 5 : *Parum est velle nisi Deus misereatur; sed Deus non miseretur, qui vocat ad pacem, nisi voluntas praecesserit; quia in terra pax hominibus bonae voluntatis* (XL, 72-73). In the *Retractations,* i, 26 (XXXII, 628), he explains the last phrase by saying that he spoke *post paenitentiam,* for the call to repentance, which precedes the will, is itself an act of mercy.

In 394, in his *Expositio quarumdam propos. ex epist. ad Roman.,* lv (XXXV, 2076), he thus explains Rom. viii, 28-30 :

Propositum Dei accipiendum est, non ipsorum. . . . *Non enim omnes qui vocati sunt, secundum propositum vocati sunt: hoc enim propositum ad praescientiam et ad praedestinationem Dei pertinet; nec praedestinavit aliquem, nisi quem praescivit crediturum et secuturum vocationem suam, quos et electos dicit. Multi enim non veniunt, cum vocati fuerint: nemo autem venit qui vocatus non fuerit.* In this passage St Augustine does not depart from the usual exegesis. If he distinguishes between two categories of the called, conformably to the Gospel parable of the invited guests, several Fathers had done so before him. Origen, St Cyril of Alexandria, Pelagius himself, it seems, understand as he does the *propositum* (πρόθεσις) as the purpose of God. Now, he adds, this purpose of God which is exercised in the act of vocation, that is, in the order of execution, is related to prescience and predestination; that is to say, to the order of intention. All this is quite correct, and Augustine, in his *Retractations* (i, 23), finds nothing in it to take back. But a little further on he wrote, *Propos.* lx (XXXV, 2079) : *Non elegit Deus opera cujusquam in praescientia, quae ipse daturus est; sed fidem elegit in praescientia; ut quem sibi crediturum esse praescivit, ipsum elegerit cui Spiritum sanctum daret, ut bona operando etiam vitam aeternam consequeretur.* . . . *Quod ergo credimus, nostrum est; quod autem bonum operamur, illius qui credentibus in se dat Spiritum sanctum.* Likewise, *Propos.* lxi *(ibid.)* : *Nostrum enim est credere et velle, illius autem dare credentibus et volentibus facultatem bene operandi.* This was to put himself in open opposition to St Paul (Eph. ii, 8) and all the Fathers. Also, St Augustine did not fail to retract this and to substitute for his previous assertions the Catholic formula, *Retract.* i, 23 (XXXII, 621-622) : *Utrumque nostrum est propter arbitrium voluntatis et utrumque tamen datum est.* . . . *Utrumque ipsius est, quia ipse praeparat voluntatem; et utrumque nostrum quia non fit nisi volentibus nobis.*

Second Phase.—After 397, in his letter to Simplicianus, he condemned the unfortunate expressions, which had escaped him up to that time, and formulated a new theory which can be regarded as his definitive, final thought, since he finds in it nothing to eliminate in his *Retractations* and returns to it unreservedly in the *De praedest. sanctorum,* 4, and in the *De bono preserverantiae,* 20. Commenting on Rom. ix, 10-29, he thus sums up the aim of Paul : to show that no one ought to boast of his merits, since merit is not possible without grace, which depends upon God alone. In fact, faith, even when initial and imperfect, presupposes the saving thought; that is to say, the divine call. Now, the call of God is an absolutely gratuitous grace : *Nemo enim credit qui non*

*vocatur. Misericors autem Deus vocat, nullis hoc vel fidei
meritis largiens; quia merita fidei sequuntur vocationem
potius quam praecedunt. . . . Nisi ergo vocando praecedat
misericordia Dei, nec credere quisquam potest, ut ex hoc
incipiat justificari et accipere facultatem bene operandi. Ergo
ante omne meritum est gratia (De divers. quaest. ad Simplician.,* ii, 7; XL, 115). Augustine proves that the election
of Jacob in preference to Esau does not depend on his *foreseen*
works any more than on his actual works; but he reasons
always as if it were a question of a *personal* call to Jacob and
of an *efficacious* call to faith, while it is really a question of
the *theocratic election* of Israel and of the relations of two
peoples compared with each other. Moreover, he supposes
that the words of the prophet (*Jacob dilexi, Esau autem odio
habui*), although, in fact, subsequent to the appearance of the
two brothers, refers to the moment which precedes their
birth (*ibid.,* No. 4): *Quod quidem scriptum est in propheta
qui longe posterior prophetavit quam illi nati et mortui sunt;
sed tamen illa sententia videtur commemorata qua dictum est,
Et major serviet minori, et antequam nati et aliquid operati
essent.* The exegetical foundation for this is wanting, and
the reasoning employed suffers from it.

The great doctor recovers all his advantages when he
starts to prove that man's goodwill is a gift of God (*ibid.,*
No. 12): *Quia non praecedit voluntas bona vocationem, sed
vocatio bonam voluntatem, propterea vocanti Deo recte tri-
buitur quod bene volumus, nobis vero tribui non potest quod
vocamur.* Here we are brought to the crux of the problem—
the distribution of the graces, especially of the first one,
the *initium fidei,* and of the last, final perseverance. God
calls this one and he comes; God calls that one and he does
not come; it is because God has shown mercy to the former
by calling him at the moment when he will obey the call: *Illi
electi qui congruenter vocati; illi autem qui non congruebant
neque contemperabantur vocationi,* non electi, quia non secuti,
quamvis vocati . . . *quia etiamsi multos vocet, eorum tamen
misereatur, quos ita vocat quomodo eis vocari aptum est ut
sequantur* (*ibid.,* No. 14, XL, 119).

Third Phase.—In the *De praedest. sanctorum,* iii-v, Nos. 7-
10 (XLIV, 964-968), Augustine briefly relates the history of
his change of opinion, which he attributes to a better comprehension of this text: *Quid habes quod non accepisti? Si
autem accepisti quid gloriaris quasi non acceperis?* He
adds: *Mihi Deus . . . revelavit.* From that time on he
often uses the passages of St Paul without regard to context,
and he views them only under the aspect which is most
favourable to his thesis.

Thus he seeks in the Apostle a support for his suggested
doctrine of a *double call, De corrept. et gratia,* 23 (XLIV,

929) : *Illi enim* [qui secundum propositum *vocati sunt*] *permanent usque in finem; et qui ad tempus inde deviant, revertuntur, ut usque in finem perducant quod in bono esse coeperunt. De praedest. sanctor.,* 32 (XLIV, 983) : *Ait* Ipsis autem vocatis, *ut illos* (the others) *ostenderet non vocatos: sciens esse quamdam certam vocationem eorum qui secundum propositum vocati sunt, quos ante praescivit et praedestinavit conformes imaginis Filii sui.*

At the same time he withdrew more and more from the consideration of prescience and seems at times even to confound it with predestination. *De dono persever.,* 47 (XLV, 1022) : *Haec dona Dei, quae dantur electis secundum Dei propositum vocatis, in quibus donis est et incipere credere, et in fide usque ad vitae hujus terminum perseverare . . . si nulla est praedestinatio quam defendimus, non praesciuntur a Deo: praesciuntur autem; haec est igitur praedestinatio quam defendimus. Unde aliquando eadem praedestinatio significatur etiam nomine praescientiae.* Cf. *De praedest. Sanctor.,* 34 (XLIV, 985-986).

K. Kolb, in the work previously quoted, claims that predestination, as St Augustine understands it, in the last stage of his thought, is irreconcilable with freewill. P. Morard, O.P., reviewing this book in the *Revue Thomiste* (1909, p. 340), recognizes that the doctrine of St Augustine is " neither Thomistic nor Molinistic," but he denies that " it rather approaches Molinism." It is thought to maintain a middle course difficult to define. In reality its course varies from one work to another, and these variations ended only with the death of the great doctor.

Towards the year 428, St Prosper wrote to the Bishop of Hippo, who had almost reached the end of his career (among the letters of Augustine, ccxxv, 8, or *P.L.* XLIV, 953) : *Illud qualiter diluatur, quaesumus patienter insipientiam nostram ferendo demonstres, quod retractatis priorum de hac re opinionibus, pene omnium par invenitur et una sententia, qua propositum et praedestinationem Dei secundum praescientiam receperunt; ut ob hoc Deus alios vasa honoris, alios contumeliae fecerit, quia finem uniuscujusque praeviderit, et sub ipso gratiae adjutorio in qua futurus esset voluntate et actione praescierit.* Apart from the ambiguity of the word *quia,* St Prosper states the question admirably. St Augustine replies, *De praedest. Sanctor.,* 27 (XLIV, 980) : *Certe si de divinarum Scripturarum tractatoribus qui fuerunt ante nos, proferrem defensionem hujusce sententiae, quam nunc solito diligentius contra novum Pelagianorum defendere urgemur errorem; hoc est, gratiam Dei non secundum merita nostra dari, et gratis dari cui datur, quia neque volentis neque currentis, sed miserentis est Dei; justo autem judicio non dari cui non datur, quia non est iniquitas apud Deum: si hujus ergo sententiae defensionem ex divinorum eloquiorum nos praecedentibus catholicis tractatoribus promerem; profecto hi fratres, pro quibus nunc agimus, acquiescerent: hoc enim significastis litteris vestris.* We must content ourselves with this general reply, which can be perfectly well accepted; but it is to be regretted that the illustrious doctor did not examine in detail the texts of his predecessors.

Père Allo, O.P., presents an able defence of Augustine's third view in the *Revue des sciences phil. et théol.* (vol. vii, 1913, pp. 263-273). He does not say, like Cajetan : *Etiam antequam praesciret Deus praedestinavit.* He grants that προγινώσκειν precedes—not actually in God, but in the logical order—the act called προορίζειν, the intelligence preceding the will. But he adds : " In Pauline usage the word πρόγνωσις expresses something much more limited than the prescience of the metaphysicians . . . it implies already, in some manner, predestination, and never has for its object the reprobate (pp. 272-3)." Are there not here two ambiguities? What does the word *implies* mean? And is it a question here of (Pauline) predestination to grace, or of (scholastic) predestination to glory? P. Allo relies upon scriptural phrases like the following : *Novit Dominus viam justorum,* without thinking that it is said of sinners : *Novit Dominus opera eorum.* God *knows the way of the just* in order to approve and crown it, he *knows the way of the wicked* in order to reprove and punish it; and in this sense the foreknowledge of moral good and evil does *imply in some manner* predestination and reprobation; but it does not follow from this that to know signifies to approve or to reprove, nor that prescience is to be practically identified with predestination.

For myself I hold to the distinction made by St Thomas : In God predestination *differt a praescientia secundum rationem, quia praescientia importat* solam *notitiam futurorum, sed praedestinatio importat causalitatem quamdam respectu eorum* (Rom. viii, 29).

II—Reprobate and Reprobation

It is by a veritable abuse of language that a doctrine of reprobation is imputed to St Paul, in the sense that this word has acquired in modern theology. The word *reprobation* does not exist in his writings, any more than the verb *to reprobate* does. As for the adjective which the Vulgate translates by *reprobus,* it is used of a person or an object " who or which does not bear an examination or test " (ἀδόκιμος), and consequently " useless and worthless," as, for example, a coin of bad alloy. It is the opposite of *probatus* (δόκιμος). It is perfectly evident that such a judgement, rejecting or approving a subject submitted to examination, even if it were pronounced by God, would belong essentially to a *consequent* act of the will, and would therefore have nothing to do with *antecedent* reprobation, which is here in question. 1 Cor. ix, 27 : *Ne cum aliis praedicavero ipse reprobus* (ἀδόκιμος) *efficiar.* *Cf.* Rom. i, 28; 2 Cor, xiii, 5, 6, 7; 2 Tim. iii, 16; Titus i, 16. Moreover, it is not from these passages, but from certain phrases in the Epistle to the Romans, detached from their context and thus commented on by St Augustine, that the partisans of antecedent reprobation, positive or negative, claim to draw their arguments. Calvin, Luther, and Jansen make them the foundation of their sombre theories; but while the last two adopt the hypothesis of original sin, which, according to them, has destroyed freewill, the Genevan reformer deduces reprobation as well as predestination from the supreme power of God over his creatures and from his sovereign independence, by virtue of which " he ordains some to eternal life and others to eternal damnation " (*Instit.,* III, xxi, 5).

It is for Catholic partisans of negative reprobation to see that they keep clear of these teachers of heresy, so that they may not fall under the anathema which strikes them. It is for them also to prove, if they can, that there exists any real difference between being condemned to damnation in advance with infallible certainty, and being *excluded from heaven, not admitted there, being neglected or abandoned, not reckoned in the number of the elect;* and this by virtue of an *antecedent volition* of God, under any hypothesis whatever. It has been remarked, and not without justice, that the verdict of the Roman Censor had exactly the same result, whether he erased the names of certain unworthy patricians or whether he neglected to inscribe them in the list of Senators.

We think that we have shown that St Paul lends no support to these systems. As to the thought of St Augustine, about which so little is understood, we cannot examine it here. But if his faithful disciple, St Prosper of Aquitaine, has comprehended him correctly, we have no difficulty in subscribing to it. (*Pro Augustino responsiones,* xii, LI, 184) : *Voluntate exierunt, voluntate ceciderunt. Et quia praesciti sunt casuri, non sunt praedestinati. Essent autem praedestinati, si essent reversuri et in sanctitate ac veritate mansuri.* If non-predestination (or negative reprobation) results from the fact that God foresees that they will not persevere (*quia praesciti sunt casuri*), all difficulty disappears; only we must no longer speak of *antecedent* reprobation, either positive or negative.

NOTE I—THE FORM OF GOD AND THE FORM OF A SERVANT

(Phil. ii, 5-11.)

ii, 5 : τοῦτο φρονεῖτε ἐν ὑμῖν ὃ καὶ ἐν Χριστῷ Ἰησοῦ,
6. ὃς ἐν μορφῇ Θεοῦ ὑπάρχων
οὐχ ἁρπαγμὸν ἡγήσατο τὸ εἶναι ἴσα Θεῷ,
7. ἀλλὰ ἑαυτὸν ἐκένωσεν μορφὴν δούλου λαβών, ἐν ὁμοιώματι ἀνθρώπων γενόμενος· καὶ σχήματι εὑρεθεὶς ὡς ἄνθρωπος 8. ἐταπείνωσεν ἑαυτόν κτλ.

It is important to distinguish well the principal questions, which affect the doctrinal signification of the text, from the secondary questions, which concern only the details. On the essential points tradition is in complete agreement, although the precise meaning of some terms gives room for discussion.

The reader may consult the important monograph of H. Schumacher, *Christus in seiner Präexistenz und Kenose nach Phil.* ii, 5-8, Part I; *Historische Untersuchung,* Rome, 1914 (*Biblioth. de l'Institut biblique*). He will find there the complete bibliography of the subject (pp. xiii-xxx), an ample harvest of patristic passages, and a summary account of the protestant and rationalistic systems (pp. 193-229). This book would deserve unreserved commendation if the author did not direct the whole force of his argument to a secondary point (the meaning of the word ἁρπαγμός) and if he did not start from a preconceived position which exposes him to the temptation of straining his texts.

I—DOCTRINAL POINTS ON WHICH THERE IS AGREEMENT

These are four in number.

1. All the Fathers and ecclesiastical writers—except Ambrosiaster and Pelagius, who nevertheless are conscious of being out of the current of common tradition—regard Phil. ii, 6-7a *as applying to the pre-existent Christ,* and consequently consider the stripping (ἐκένωσεν) as something accomplished by the *divine will* of the incarnate God. The thought of the Fathers originates in the fact that they make the stripping consist in the incarnation itself, and cannot therefore attribute it to the human will of Christ.

On this point there is no possible doubt. The declaration of Velasquez is significant (see p. 313, note). The only exceptions are Pelagius and Ambrosiaster. The former comments thus (XXX, 845) : In forma Dei, *in qua erat, sive quia absque peccato erat: ad imaginem Dei scilicet.* Formam servi

456

accipiens, *ita ut etiam pedes lavaret apostolorum.* All this
can refer only to Jesus Christ as man. But Pelagius adds a
remark which does not seem in place and which is, perhaps,
the marginal note of some scandalized reader : *Multi prae-*
terea hunc locum ita intelligunt quod secundum divinitatem
se humiliaverit Christus, secundum formam scilicet, secundum
quam aequam aequalitatem Dei non rapinam usurpaverit,
quam naturaliter possidebat. Et exinanivit se, *non substan-*
tiam evacuans, sed honorem declinans: formam servi, *hoc est*
naturam hominis inducendo. Ambrosiaster, on the contrary,
is very explicit (XVII, 408-9) : *Christus semper in forma Dei*
erat, quia imago est invisibilis Dei. Sed apostolus de Dei
Filio, cum incarnatus homo factus est, tractat dicens: Hoc
sentite in vobis quod et in Christo Jesu, *id est Deo et homine.*
Qui cum in forma Dei esset, *inter homines utique conversatus,*
verbis et operibus apparebat ut Deus. Forma enim Dei nihil
differt a Deo. . . . Sed semetipsum exinanivit, *hoc est*
potestatem suam ab opere retraxit. . . . Formam servi
accipiens, *dum tenetur et ligatur et verberibus agitur. . . .*
Non enim mihi, sicut quibusdam, videtur sic formam servi
accepisse dum homo natus est. Thus, then, for Ambrosiaster,
to take the form of a servant is to accept humiliations and
sufferings ; *to strip himself* is to conceal his power ; *to be in*
the form of God is to show himself as God in his acts and
words after his incarnation. However, the contrary opinion
is mentioned. I do not take into account the so-called letter
of St Dionysius of Alexandria to Paul of Samosata. This
work, which is much more recent, is by a questionable author.
Cf. Bardenhewer, *Geschichte der altchristl. Lit.,* 1903, vol. ii,
p. 188.

2. *The Form of God is his Divinity.*—Another point
common to all—without excepting even the two dissenters
mentioned above—is the way of understanding the form of
God as being identical with his divinity. The synonymy is
variously explained : the form of God is sometimes thought
to signify his nature, sometimes his substance, at other times
his essence, or, again, his specific character or his substantial
image, or the sum total of the divine perfections and attributes ; but these variations are manifestly accidental, since
under any and every hypothesis *the form of God is God.*

(a) Some identify the form of God purely and simply with
the *substance of God* (οὐσία, *substantia*) : St Basil, *Contra Eunom.,*
i, 18 (XXIX, 552 : Ἐγὼ γὰρ τὸ ἐν μορφῇ Θεοῦ ὑπάρχειν
ἴσον δύνασθαι τῷ ἐν οὐσίᾳ Θεοῦ ὑπάρχειν φημί) ; St
Gregory of Nyssa, *Contra Eunom.,* iv (XLV, 672 : Ἡ δὲ μορφὴ
τοῦ Θεοῦ ταὐτὸν τῇ οὐσίᾳ πάντως ἐστίν) ; St Cyril of Alexandria,
De incarnat. Domini, x (LXXV, 1432 : Ἡ μορφὴ τοῦ Θεοῦ οὐσία τοῦ
Θεοῦ) ; Theodoret, *Dialog.,* ii (LXXXIII, 189 : τῆς θείας οὐσίας
ἡ ἰδιότης). On this point Apollinarius of Laodicea, *Antirrh.*

contra Eunom. (*Texte und Unters.*, vii, 3, p. 206) speaks like St Basil : τὸ ἐν μορφῇ Θεοῦ ἐν οὐσίᾳ ἐστὶ Θεοῦ· οὐ γὰρ ἄλλο μορφὴ καὶ ἀλλὰ οὐσία Θεοῦ, ἵνα μὴ σύνθετος.

(*b*) Others identify the form of God with the *nature of God* (φύσις, *natura*). Thus St John Chrysostom, *Homil.*, vi, 1 and 2 (if the form of a servant means, as cannot be doubted, the human nature, the form of God must mean the divine nature : ἡ μορφὴ τοῦ Θεοῦ, Θεοῦ φύσις) ; Anastasius the Sinaite, *Hodegos*, x (LXXXIX, 172 : Ἡ δὲ μορφὴ φύσις ἐστίν, ὥς φησιν τῶν ἁγίων διδασκάλων χορός), who moreover also explains form by substance (*ibid.*, 180) ; St John Damascene, *Advers. Nestor.*, x (XCV, 1193), who invokes all tradition in this sense ; among the Latins, St Hilary, *De Trinit.* xii, 6 (X, 437 : *Esse in forma Dei non alia intelligentia est quam in Dei manere natura*). Victorinus, if we understand him correctly (*Adv. Arium*, 4, VIII, 1119 : *Filius Dei forma Dei est, id est vita quae est forma viventis*), is thinking of the principle of operations rather than of the specific character. See in his *Comment.* (VIII, 1207 : *Quid forma ? Non figura, non vultus, sed imago et potentia*) a rather obscure theory.

(*c*) Others, without further explanation, say that the form of God is his *divinity* : St Athanasius, *Contra Arian. Orat.* iii, 5 (XXVI, 332 : ἡ θεότης καὶ ἡ ἰδιότης τοῦ πατρός) ; St Ambrose, *De fide*, v, 8 (XVI, 698) : *Quid est in Dei forma, nisi in divinitatis plenitudine ?*) ; Ambrosiaster (XVII, 408 : *Forma Dei nihil differt a Deo*).—Many reach this identification by means of the following reasoning : "As he who possesses the *form of a man* is evidently man, he who possesses the *form of God* is certainly God." Thus St Hilary, *De Trinit.*, x, 22 (X, 360), St Basil, *Contra Eunom.*, i, 18 (XXIX, 552).

(*d*) Tertullian must be studied separately. He read in his Latin version or translated thus : *In effigie Dei constitutus non rapinam existimavit pariari Deo, sed exhausit semetipsum accepta effigie servi* (*Adv. Marcion.*, v, 20, edit. Kroymann, Vienna, 1906, pp. 647-8). *Effigies* is not a good translation of μορφή. Tertullian maintains that it ought to be understood as *imago* in Col. i, 15—a substantial image which establishes no inequality between God the Father and God the Word (*Sermo Deus*). The equation—the *form* or *image of God = God*—was, even in his eyes, so certain that he made use of it to prove that *effigies servi* designated a *veritable* humanity, not an appearance, a phantom without reality : *Quod si in effigie et imagine* [*Dei*], *qua filius Patris, vere Deus, praejudicatum est etiam in effigie et imagine hominis, vere hominem inventum.*—Can this synonomy of μορφή and εἰκών also be found in St Gregory Nazianzen, *Orat. theol.*, iv, 3 (XXXVI, 105 : τῷ τὴν θείαν εἰκόνα δουλικῇ μορφῇ συγκεράσαντι)?

3. *The Stripping* (κένωσις) *took place at the moment of the Incarnation ;* it is nothing but the act of the incarnation ; for

all the Fathers interpret the words "taking the form of a servant " in the sense of " assuming human nature." Consequently the example of self-abnegation which St Paul proposes to the Philippians is already realized in the incarnation itself, although it is continued in the life of humiliation and obedience of the incarnate Word.

Origen, *In Jerem.* xiv, 9 (ed. Klostermann, 1901, p. 114 : Αμα γὰρ ἀνέλαβε τὴν τοῦ δούλου μορφὴν καὶ ἑαυτὸν ἐκένωσεν) ; cf. *In Joann.*, xx, 16, ed. Preuschen, 1903, p. 350 ; Chrysostom, *In Phil. hom.*, vii (LXII, 229 : πῶς ἐκένωσεν; μορφὴν δούλου λαβών) ; Eusebius, *De eccles. theol.*, i, 20 (ed. Klostermann, 1906, pp. 90-91).—It would be easy to multiply quotations ; but the fact is not disputed. It is because he cannot fail to recognize it and does not wish to depart too far from the common opinion of the Fathers, that Velasquez also makes the self-stripping coincide with the incarnation. He asks for only just one moment of respite in order to allow time enough for the human will of Christ to accept a poor, miserable existence in place of the glorious condition of which he had the choice. For it is in this *act of the human will* that Velasquez places the self-stripping and it is in this that he departs from the patristic tradition : *Tam exinanitionem quam formam servi de vera carne et substantiali hominis forma, quam Christus suscepit, potius accipienda putamus, frequentissimae Patrum interpretationi assentientes :* si tamen ipsi nobis vel unicum saltem temporis instans velint liberaliter retribuere. But this *one little instant* that he demands changes the exegesis of the text completely.

4. *The Form of God and the Form of a Servant unite without Confusion or Mixture.*—The self-stripping, therefore, does not signify any diminution whatever of the form of God. Christ is perfect God and perfect man. From the fourth century on this was expressed by an almost stereotyped formula : *Manens quod erat, assumpsit quod non erat.*

The stereotyped formula is found in St Gregory Nazianzen, *Orat. theol.*, ii, 19 (XXVI, 100 : Ὁ μὲν ἦν διέμεινεν, ὁ δὲ οὐκ ἦν προσέλαβεν), St Cyril of Alexandria, *De incarn. Dom.*, 8 (LXXV, 1428 : Μένων γὰρ ὃ ἦν, ἔλαβεν ὃ οὐκ ἦν), Basil of Seleucia, *Orat.* 9 (LXXXV, 137 : Μεμένηκε γὰρ ὃ ἦν, λαβὼν ὃ οὐκ ἦν), St Ambrose, *De fide*, v, 8 (XVI, 1196 : *Non remittens utique quod erat, sed assumens quod non erat*), Theophilus of Alexandria, translated by St Jerome, *Epist.*, 98 (XXII, 795 : *Mirum in modum coepit esse quod nos sumus et non desivit esse quod fuerat*), and many others, sometimes under a less incisive, but still more precise form ; for example, St Leo the Great, *Sermon.* xxiv, 3 (LIV, 205 : *Qui verus est Deus, idem verus est homo*) and xxiii, 2 (LIV, 201 : *Sicut formam servi forma Dei non adimit, ita formam Dei servi forma non minuit*); so also St Augustine, *Contra serm. Arian.*, 8 (XLII, 689 : *Cum in forma Dei, antequam ab illo forma servi esset accepta, nondum erat filius hominis sed filius Dei; cui Patris aequalitas rapina non erat sed natura. . . . Nondum ergo erat Christus, quod esse coepit cum semetipsum exinanivit, non formam Dei amittens sed formam servi accipiens).*

II—Points on which Agreement is only Partial

1. *Meaning of* οὐχ ἁρπαγμὸν ἡγήσατο τὸ εἶναι ἴσα Θεῷ.

All the ecclesiastical writers—with the exception of Novatian —see in these words the affirmation of a right belonging to the Word before the incarnation. Indeed, whatever may be the precise meaning of ἁρπαγμός and in whatever connection this phrase may be taken, whether with what precedes or with what follows, the fact that for the Word to think that his equality with God was not an ἁρπαγμός, proves beyond question that he was in the legitimate and undisputed possession of that right.

Novatian starts from the postulate that Christ, as man and also as God, *obeys* his Father in all things, *De Trinit.*, 22 (III, 930): *Denique et ante carnis assumptionem, sed et post assumptionem corporis, post ipsam praeterea resurrectionem, omnem Patri in omnibus rebus oboedientiam praestitit pariter ac praestat.* He never dared to compare himself with his Father. *Quamvis se ex Deo Patre Deum esse meminisset nunquam se Deo Patri aut comparavit aut contulit.* The text of St Paul proves this: *Ex quo probatur nunquam arbitratum illum esse rapinam quamdam divinitatem, ut aequaret se Patri Deo.* Thus Christ did not regard his divinity (of an inferior order) as an *occasion, motive,* or *means of unlawfully arrogating to himself* equality with his Father; and this is what Novatian understands by *rapina.* This frankly heretical and no less arbitrary doctrine has found in our time very numerous followers among the rationalists of all schools. Most of them conceive the thing as Novatian does—Christ has not abused his high dignity (his divine form) to try to make himself equal to God. Thus Sabatier writes (*L'Apôtre Paul*[3], p. 274): " He did not seek by egoism and pride to pose as an equal of God, and to usurp at once divine equality. He resisted that first temptation to magnify his being." So also, but with variations, Baur, Hilgenfeld, Beyschlag, B. Weiss, Holtzmann, Deissmann, etc. Christ did not pretend to have an equality which did not belong to him, perhaps alluding to Adam (Brückner) or to Lucifer (J. Weiss), who wished to make themselves equal with God. Others, starting from a *certain* equality with God, which they think belonged to Christ, affirm that the latter did not take advantage of it to exalt his claims (Pfleiderer, Von Soden, Cremer, J. Agar Beet, J. Ross, etc.). *Cf.* pp. 317-8, note.

But while many Fathers insist upon *the assertion of this*

right and treat the proposition as a complete phrase to which nothing is lacking, others think that St Paul wishes, above all, to give *a lesson of self-abnegation,* and consequently subordinate· the phrase to the proposition which follows it. The first take ἁρπαγμός in the active sense (theft, larceny, unjust acquisition); the others take it in the passive sense (booty, a windfall, unlawful possession) as a synonym of ἅρπαγμα. The latter conceive the line of thought as follows : " Subsisting in the form of God, he did not fear to lose divine equality (*or* he did not seek to take advantage of it), *but on the contrary* he stripped himself of it." The former present the association of ideas as follows : " Subsisting in the form of God, he had a full right to regard himself as equal to God. *Nevertheless* he stripped himself." It may be said that the Latin Fathers favour in general this last exegesis, while the Greek Fathers favour the other; but the absence of all commentary or the conciseness of the texts does not always allow us to state with assurance what their opinion was.

(A) For the *passive sense* of ἁρπαγμός it will suffice to question the masters.—(*a*) Origen (*In Joan.* i, 32, ed. Preuschen, 1903, p. 41) says that Christ, in humiliating him-self even unto death, " manifested more goodness for us than if, regarding it as a ἁρπαγμός to be equal to God, he had refused to make himself a slave for the salvation of the world " : Πλείονα . . . τὴν ἀγαθότητα φαίνεσθαι τοῦ Χριστοῦ, ὅτε ἑαυτὸν ἐταπείνωσε γενόμενος ὑπήκοος μέχρι θανάτου, θανάτου δὲ σταυροῦ, ἢ εἰ ἁρπαγμὸν ἡγήσατο τὸ εἶναι ἴσα Θεῷ, καὶ μὴ βουληθεὶς ἐπὶ τῇ τοῦ κόσμου σωτηρίᾳ γένεσθαι δοῦλος. Cf. *In Joann.,* vi, 57 ; *ibid.,* p. 166.—(*b*) Theodore of Mopsuestia (*Comment.,* ed. Swete, Cambridge, 1880, vol. i, p. 216) : *Non magnam [Christus] reputavit illam quae ad Deum est aequalitatem, et elatus in sua permansit dignitate, sed magis pro aliorum utilitate praeelegit humiliora sustinere.* (*c*) St John Chrysostom presents his thought at great length and with perfect clearness (*Comment. Hom.,* vii, 1 ; LXII, 227-9) : " Whatever has been stolen, whatever is retained unjustly, is clung to desperately, and we dare not relinquish it for an instant, for fear of losing it ; it is otherwise with that which is received by nature and is sure to be found again whenever desired." Thus the usurper does not dare to lay aside his sceptre nor the tyrant his purple ; while the legitimate king is not afraid to go without the insignia of royalty. And yet the comparison is not a perfect one, for there is no dignity that man holds by reason of his nature. But what has the Son of God to fear by humiliating himself ? Ὁ τοῦ Θεοῦ υἱὸς οὐκ ἐφοβήθη καταβῆναι ἀπὸ τοῦ ἀξιώματος · οὐ γὰρ ἁρπαγμὸν ἡγήσατο τὴν θεότητα, οὐκ ἐδεδοίκει μή τις αὐτὸν ἀφέληται τὴν φύσιν, ἢ τὸ ἀξίωμα. Golden words !— (*d*) Isidore of Pelusium follows St Chrysostom step by step

(*Epist.*, iv, 22 ; LXXVIII, 1072): Εἰ ἕρμαιον ἡγήσατο τὸ εἶναι ἴσον, οὐκ ἂν ἑαυτὸν ἐταπείνωσεν. . . . Δοῦλος μὲν γὰρ καὶ ἐλευθερωθεὶς καὶ υἱοθεσίᾳ τιμηθεὶς ἅτε ἅρπαγμα ἢ εὕρημα τὴν ἀξίαν ἡγησάμενος, οὐκ ἂν ὑποσταίη οἰκετικὸν ἔργον ἀνύσαι, ὁ δὲ γνήσιος υἱός κτλ. Thus a freedman, an adopted son, does not wish to stoop to perform servile work, because he considers his condition and his newly acquired rank as a ἕρμαιον, a εὕρημα, or a ἅρπαγμα. The legitimate son, on the contrary, does not fear to forfeit his rank, because he receives from nature his quality of sonship. The great interest of this commentary consists in the fact that St Isidore replaces ἁρπαγμός by ἅρπαγμα, and that he exactly defines the meaning of it by means of the synonyms εὕρημα (a find, an unhoped for discovery) and ἕρμαιον (a good windfall, a profit due to Hermes, the god of merchants and thieves), whose signification with ἡγεῖσθαι, ποιεῖσθαι, and similar words is not doubtful.

(B) Among the defenders of the *active sense* of ἁρπαγμός are usually reckoned all those who conclude from our text that Christ has not *stolen* his equality with God, because he derived it from his nature. Such are Didymus the Blind (*De Trinit.*, i, 26 ; XXXIX, 389), St Cyril of Jerusalem (*Catech.*, x, 9 ; XXXIII, 672 : Οὔτε γὰρ υἱὸς ἥρπασεν, οὔτε πατὴρ ἐφθόνησε τῆς μεταδόσεως), Apollinarius of Ladoicea or the author of the *Dialog. de Trinit.*, ii (in *Texte und Untersuch.*, vii, 3, p. 280 : Οὐχ ἥρπασεν ἀλλ᾽ ἔχει τῇ φύσει), St Isidore of Pelusium (*Epist.*, i, 139 ; LXXXVIII, 273: Οὐχ ἥρπασε θεότητα καὶ βασιλείαν, ἀλλ᾽ ἔμφυτον ἔσχε πρὸ τῶν αἰώνων), St Cyril of Alexandria (*De Incarn. Domini*, 10; LXXV, 1429), etc. From the fact that Christ is in legitimate possession of divine equality, it can be very well concluded that this possession has not an unjust or illegitimate origin ; but from a strictly exegetical point of view one must say with Chrysostom (*Homil.*, vii, 1 ; LXII, 299): Οὐκ εἶπε· οὐχ ἥρπασεν, ἀλλά· οὐχ ἁρπαγμὸν ἡγήσατο.

Nor should it be supposed without examination that the Latin Fathers took *rapina* in the active sense in their reading *non rapinam arbitratus est;* for the word *rapina* has both meanings. It is, therefore, almost always the context which decides (*cf.* A. d'Alès, *Recherches de science relig.*, 1910, pp. 260-9).

Moreover, it is all the less useful to go deeply into these controversies because for the theologian the two meanings amount to the same thing—*a thing which one possesses without having usurped it* (the passive meaning of ἁρπαγμός) being a legitimate possession, and a legitimate possession not being the fruit of *usurpation* (active meaning).

Finally, all ecclesiastical writers find in the τὸ εἶναι ἴσα Θεῷ the assertion that the Son is equal to the Father, a fact so well known that it needs no proof. Whether they arrive at this conclusion by way of reasoning and as theologians, or by way of analysis and as exegetes, whether they admit the grammatical equivalence between ἴσα Θεῷ (adverb) and ἴσος Θεῷ (adjective), or whether they deduce it from the text and from the context, what does it matter? For all, in the last analysis, the Word indisputably possesses divine equality, and this equality expresses or presupposes equality of nature; in other words, consubstantiality.

2. *Exact Meaning of* ἐκένωσεν ἑαυτόν, *exinanivit semetipsum.*

In general, the Fathers limit themselves to saying that Christ stripped himself in becoming man, but without explaining how. Nevertheless, their brief remarks seem to favour one or the other of the two following notions :

(A) *The Self-Emptying is taken in an Absolute Sense, as an Act of Abasement or Condescension on the part of a Divine Person assuming a Created Nature.*—For a God to unite himself hypostatically to a finite being, whoever he may be, is a kind of moral forfeiture. From this point of view the quality and condition of the creature who is elevated to the divine personality are of no importance, for, since nothing can fill the abyss which separates the finite from the infinite, the distance between God and the most perfect or most. glorious of his creatures remains the same—immeasurable. In every hypostatic union, through the *communicatio idiomatum,* the Infinite becomes finite, the Creator becomes a creature, he who is equal to God becomes inferior to God; and it is in this that the abasement of the incarnate Word consists.

Perhaps this theory will not be found expressly developed in the writings of the Fathers, but it can be deduced from their utterances : when, for example, they say that the Word descends (κατέρχεται, καταβαίνει) into an inferior nature (Augustine, *In Psalm.* ciii, *serm.* iv, 8, XXXVII, 1384: *Ut autem sit mediator* descendat *a superiore ad inferiorem, ab aequalitate Patris; faciat quod ait apostolus:* Semetipsum exinanivit); or when they express the abasement of Christ by the well-known formula : *Manens quod erat, assumpsit quod non erat; μένων ὃ ἦν, ἔλαβεν ὃ οὐκ ἦν.* The scholastics, on the contrary, take pleasure in discussing it. They were drawn to it by the usual commentary : *Exinanire est ab invisibilitatis suae magnitudine se visibilem demonstrare.* The interpretation of the commentary is borrowed literally from St Gregory the Great (*Moral.* ii, 23, LXXV, 576). St Thomas gives a somewhat different turn to it : Inane *opponitur pleno; natura autem divina satis est plena . . . natura autem humana non est plena . . . sed inanis.* Cornelius a Lapide, expatiating in this sense, endeavours to prove that if God is Being, the creature is non-being or nonentity. Before the incarnation, says Cajetan, Christ was *absolutely and in every respect* equal to the Father; after the incarnation he is so only in a certain way and as God; which seems to constitute a loss, a fall. The prince of commentators on St Paul, Estius, is of the same opinion : Semetipsum exinanivit, *quasi dicat: non alienum deposuit, sed semetipsum, qui verus erat Deus, ad imum usque dejecit, ac divinitatem quodammodo exuit.* This is not from having taken a human nature subject to suffering and death, but from having united himself to a creature *quae respectu Dei totius creaturae Domini, servilis est.* Finally, according to this explanation, which will perhaps seem a little too finely drawn, to abase oneself is to make oneself small resembling nonentity, limited in time and space and in one's manner of being and appearing (χωρητός). We know the fine definition of St Gregory Nazianzen (*Orat.* xxxvii, 3 ; XXXVI, 285) ; 'Αλλ' ἐπειδὴ κενοῦται δι' ἡμᾶς, ἐπειδὴ κατέρχεται (κ έ ν ω σ ι ν δὲ λέγω τὴν τῆς δόξης οἷον ὕφεσίν τε καὶ ἐλάττωσιν) διὰ τοῦτο χωρητὸς γίνεται. But does not this *abasement* (ὕφεσις), this *lessening* (ἐλάττωσις) of the divine *glory,* in which the *emptying* (κένωσις) consists, correspond rather to the following notion, which we are now to set forth ?

(B) *The Emptying is taken in a relative sense, as the act by which the Word renounces something which he could and should have.*—This something evidently cannot mean the divine nature, which does not permit of any increase or decrease; it is therefore something which proceeds from that nature, which is inherent in it, although separable from it, such as external glory would be, or the honours due to divinity—adoration, gratitude; in a word, the treatment it deserves from rational creatures. Now, of all these external advantages the Word voluntarily stripped himself by taking the form of a slave and by uniting himself to a nature destined in the plans of God to ignominy, suffering, and death.

This conception of the divestment of the Word is not only orthodox, but so natural that it is surprising that the Fathers did not think of it. Also it is not new, although it is rather hinted at than explicitly formulated.—In a letter from the Church of the Gauls, written in 178 and cited by Eusebius (*Hist.,* v, 2, ed. Schwartz, 1903, p. 428), it is said that those who openly professed Christ, covered with glorious wounds which had been received for the faith, refused the title of martyrs to which they had a right, in this respect imitating Christ : ὃς ἐν μορφῇ Θεοῦ ὑπάρχων οὐχ ἁρπαγμὸν ἡγήσατο τὸ εἶναι ἴσα Θεῷ. Is not this clearly to insinuate that the Word renounced for his human nature the honours which were due him as God ?—The decrees of the Council of Antioch against Paul of Samosata are very probably apocryphal, but they offer us an interesting example of ancient exegesis, confirmed moreover by other authorities (Mansi, vol. I, p. 1037): Jesus Christ πεπίστευται Θεὸς κενώσας ἑαυτὸν ἀπὸ τοῦ εἶναι ἴσα Θεῷ. St Hilary expresses himself in exactly the same way. Although he often affirms that the form of God is unchangeable and imperishable (Cf. *De trinit.*, viii, 47; X, 271; and x, 22; X, 360), he does not hesitate to say on occasion that Christ abandoned his equality with God or even his divine form (*De trinit.*, viii, 45; X, 270): *Exinanivit se ex Dei forma, id est ex eo quod aequalis Deo erat;* and again (*ibid.*, xii, 6; X, 437): *quia ex Dei aequalitate, id est ex forma ejus in servi formam, decederet.* This proves that the Bishop of Poitiers interpreted equality with God sometimes in the absolute sense, at other times in the relative sense, in regard to the rights inherent in the divine nature, of which Jesus Christ divested himself in his human nature.

In the same way we must explain all the Fathers who take ἐκένωσεν ἑαυτόν in the relative sense of *self-stripping* and not in the absolute sense of *total emptying*. To strip oneself is to abandon something, which can here be only the external glory or honours due to God. We know already the texts of St John Chrysostom, according to which Christ " did not fear to descend from his rank or dignity " (LXX, 229: οὐκ ἐφοβήθη καταβῆναι ἀπὸ τοῦ ἀξιώματος), because he knew that he would find them again whenever he should wish to. Is not this what St Isidore of Pelusium also affirms when he says that " if the Son of God had considered equality with God as an acquisition that could be wrested from him he would not have abased himself " (*Epist.*, iv, 22; LXXVIII, 1072)? And what other sense can be given to the words of Theodore of Mopsuestia, previously quoted (p. 461)?

It is hardly necessary to caution the reader that this conception has nothing in common with the hypothesis of Velasquez. In his opinion it is the *human will* of Christ which renounced the divine prerogatives, immediately after the incarnation; for the Fathers it is the *Word* who renounced them in exchange for human nature, *before* the incarnation. The man Christ, according to Velasquez, wished to acquire the divine honours by conquest instead of receiving them as a gift; the Son, according to the Fathers whose opinions we have presented, did not wish, in becoming man, to take advantage of the rights which his eternal generation conferred upon him.

Some readers will ask if the meaning of Paul is not virtually a twofold one, whether the *self-stripping* effected in the person of Christ—without any distinction between divine and human will—could not include at the same time the fact of the incarnation itself and the consequences of the life of humiliation accepted by Christ. This interesting question, which would be of value also for 2 Cor. viii, 8 (*propter vos egenus factus est, cum esset dives*), would lead us too far.

NOTE J—AUTHENTICITY OF THE PASTORAL EPISTLES

To one who wishes to form an independent judgement on the origin of the Pastoral Epistles three things seem worthy of attention—the unanimity of tradition, the insuperable contradictions found in negative criticism, and the resemblances and points of difference in the Pastoral compared with the unchallenged Epistles.

I—THE UNANIMITY OF TRADITION

The unanimous testimony of the early Church acquires still more force if it is borne in mind that here authenticity and canonicity are not two distinct questions, since these Epistles, if they were not authentic, would be intentional forgeries.

The Muratorian Canon (l. 60-64), Tertullian (*Praescr.*, 6; *Contra Marcion.*, v, 21; *De resurr. carnis*, 22; *De pudic.*, 14; *Scorp.*, 13), St Irenæus (*Contra haeres.*, i, 1; ii, 14; iii, 3, etc.), Clement of Alexandria (*Cohort.* 1 and 9, etc.), all of whom unhesitatingly attribute the three Pastoral Epistles to Paul, show us the Catholic tradition established in the whole Church before the end of the second century. These Epistles formed part of the old Latin version as well as of the Syriac version, and this fact proves clearly that they were regarded as letters written by Paul. Eusebius (*Hist. eccl.*, iii, 3), who, with the curiosity of an archæologist, brings up all the doubts which had been raised on the subject of the authenticity and canonicity of the sacred books, has nothing to say concerning the attribution of the Pastorals to Paul, which seems to him certain. It is the same with Origen (*In Matth.*, ser. 117, XIII, 1769), who records, merely as worth remembering, the abortive attempt of those who had dared to reject the Second Epistle to Timothy.

We know that Marcion received, in his Canon of the New Testament, only the Gospel of Luke and ten Epistles of Paul, not without making certain suppressions and excisions in them which he thought necessary or useful. He therefore excluded the Pastoral Epistles (Tertullian, *Adv. Marcion.*, v, 21; St Jerome, *Preface to the Commentary on the Epist. to Titus*). Basilides did the same, according to St Jerome, while Tatian rejected only the two Epistles to Timothy (St Jerome, *loc. cit.*). This fact is of no consequence, and Clement of Alexandria has given the real reason for it (*Stromat.*, ii, 11; VIII, 989): Ὑπὸ ταύτης ἐλεγχόμενοι τῆς φωνῆς (1 Tim. vi, 20-21) οἱ ἀπὸ τῶν αἱρέσεων τὰς πρὸς Τιμόθεον ἀθετοῦσιν ἐπιστολάς. Marcion undoubtedly might have expurgated them, as he did the others

(St Irenæus, *Contra haeres.*, i, 29; *cf.* iii, 12); but there would have been eight passages in them to cut out, and so it seemed to him simpler to eliminate them entirely.

The Pastoral Epistles were known long before the outbreak of Gnosticism. There is perhaps no Pauline Epistle which has been made more use of by the apostolic Fathers. Compare Barnabas xiv, 6, with Titus ii, 14. If καταργεῖν τὸν θάνατον (Barn. v, 6) depends upon 1 Cor. xv, 20 and not on 2 Tim. i, 10, it is difficult to suppose that the characteristic expressions ἐπισωρεύοντες ταῖς ἁμαρτίαις (Barn. iv, 6) and φανερωθῆναι ἐν σαρκί (Barn. v, 6; vi, 7, 9) are not derived from 2 Tim. iii, 6 (σεσωρευμένα ἁμαρτίαις) and from 1 Tim. iii, 16 (ἐφανερώθη ἐν σαρκί).—In Clement of Rome are found again a certain number of words peculiar to the Pastoral Epistles: ἀγωγή, ἀναζωπυρεῖν, βδελυκτός, πρόσκλισις, etc., the adjectives εὐσεβής, σεμνός, σώφρων, and entire phrases, like " lifting up pure hands to heaven" (1 Tim. ii, 8; Clem. *ad. Cor.* xxix, 1) and "ready to every good work" (Tit. iii, 1; Clem. *ad Cor.*, ii, 7), where the union of meaning and expression seems impossible to be accidental. Ignatius and the Pastoral Epistles have in common a certain number of rare words which seem to indicate a literary connection: ἀναζωπυρεῖν, ἀναψυχεῖν, ἑτεροδιδασκαλεῖν, κατάστημα, etc.—The relations of *Polycarp*, iv-vi, with the Pastoral Epistles, especially the textual extracts, *Polyc.*, iv, 1 (1 Tim. vi, 7-10) and *Polyc.*, ix, 2 (2 Tim. iv, 10) testify in the same sense.—One cannot help feeling that the Epistle to Diognetus, xi, 3, alludes to 1 Tim. iii, 16, and that Justin, *Dial.*, 47, is inspired by Tit. iii, 4. Finally, the passage from Hegesippus quoted by Eusebius (*Hist. Eccl.*, iii, 32) is understood clearly only when compared with 1 Tim. i, 3 and vi, 4, 20.

II—INSUPERABLE CONTRADICTIONS OF THE NEGATIVE CRITICISM

1. *Radical Negation.*—After the attacks of Schleiermacher and some others against the First Epistle to Timothy, Baur (*Die sogen. Pastoralbriefe,* etc., 1835) sought by internal criticism of the three letters to prove that they had been composed towards the middle of the second century to combat Gnosticism and to promote the ecclesiastical hierarchy already in process of formation. He was followed—but with modifications sometimes equivalent to the transformation of the system—by Hilgenfeld, Schwegler, Volkmar, Schenkel, and also by Pfleiderer, Beyschlag, Weizsäcker, H. Holtzmann, and S. Davidson. It can, however, be stated that at present this system is quite out of fashion. The direct refutations of Baur, or the works in favour of the authenticity of the Pastorals, have certainly contributed less to this result than the constantly increasing recognition of the three

following facts : (*a*) The principal argument of Baur rests on a false interpretation of Eusebius (*Hist.*, iii, 32). See p. 340, note 2.—(*b*) The errors combated in the Pastoral Epistles do not agree with any of the forms of historical Gnosticism, whether the composition of these Epistles be placed towards 170, as Volkmar has done, or towards 150, as Schenkel and Hilgenfeld suppose, or towards 140, as Baur himself holds, or under Hadrian, as Hausrath believes, or between Hadrian and Trajan, as Pfleiderer argues, or, finally, under Trajan, as Beyschlag and Jülicher affirm.—(*c*) Nor does the hierarchy supposed by the Pastoral Epistles any better correspond to the situation acquired by the Church after the beginning of the second century. These letters, which are alleged to have been composed to promote the growing hierarchy, far from marking a state of progress, would have indicated a retrogression.

2. *Partial Authenticity.*—The hypothesis of an intentional forgery appears so unlikely in certain parts of the Pastoral Epistles that the critics most disposed to admit it have always asked themselves if there were not authentic portions in them. Renan, who supports Baur's theory, which was in vogue in his day, does not hesitate to write with his usual indecision (*St Paul, Introduction,* pp. xlviii-xlix) : " Are the three Epistles in question apochryphal from beginning to end, or has someone in composing them made use of authentic letters addressed to Titus and Timothy, which have thus been manipulated in a sense conformable to the ideas of the time and with the intention of lending the authority of the Apostle to the developments which the ecclesiastical hierarchy was taking? This is difficult to decide. Perhaps in certain parts —at the end of the Second Epistle to Timothy, for example— notes of different dates have been combined; but even then we must admit that the forger has taken great liberties."

Harnack maintains more decisively the same view (*Chronol. der altchristl. Liter.,* Leipzig, 1897, p. 480). He believes that the Pastoral Epistles " were fashioned after some genuine Pauline letters." But how much is authentic? " One can unhesitatingly include in the genuine portion very considerable fragments of the Second Epistle to Timothy, and perhaps a good third of the Epistle to Titus. As to the First Epistle to Timothy, if it is impossible to prove that a single verse is distinctly traceable to Paul, it is nevertheless not improbable that there is in that Epistle also a Pauline foundation, but one that has been retouched." Certain critics, however, are less severe on the First Epistle to Timothy. Knoke, for example (*Commentar zu den Pastoralbriefen,* Göttingen, 1889), after having cut it up into twenty-two tiny fragments, which he then sews together again with the patience of a mosaic-worker, forms out of them three distinct letters. The first, comprising seven fragments and thirty verses, he thinks was written at Corinth by St Paul; the second, containing nine fragments and fifty-five verses, was sent from Cæsarea also by St Paul; the third, having only six fragments and twenty verses, was composed after the Apostle's death, but in a Pauline spirit. The final editor, in combining them, naturally retouched them. According to Knoke, the Second Epistle to Timothy is authentic, but the order has been greatly disturbed; in the Epistle to Titus there is nothing apocryphal except ch. i, vv. 7, 9, 12, 13. The curious thing about this is that we arrive finally, by a long détour, almost at the conservative theory of authenticity. Clemen is much less liberal than Knoke, but he is still more precise (*Paulus, sein Leben und Wirken,* Giessen, 1904, p. 146). According to him, the authentic parts are : (a) 2 Tim. iv, 19-22a and Titus iii, 12-14, written in 57 ; (b) 2 Tim. iv, 9-18 in 61 ; (c) 2 Tim. i, 15-18 in 62. Nothing more is wanted than the month and the day.

In the last half-century a great number of critics—Ewald, Hausrath, Hitzig, Hesse, Pfleiderer, MacGiffert, Bacon, Moffatt, and many others, without speaking of Harnack, Knoke, and Clemen, already mentioned—have tried to discover with their lynx eyes the authentic portions of the Pastoral Epistles. But the results do not agree. What one declares certainly apocryphal is proclaimed by another to be certainly authentic. See some specimens of these dissections in Moffatt's *The Historical New Testament*[2], Edinburgh, 1901, pp. 700-8. If we had to award the palm for arbitrariness, we should be tempted to give it to Krenkel (*Beiträge zur Aufhellung der Geschichte und der Briefe des Apostels Paulus,* Brunswick, 1890). The authentic fragments of the Pastorals are, in his opinion, (a) a letter written to Titus by St Paul at the time of his second visit to Corinth (Tit. iii, 12 + 2 Tim. iv, 20 + Titus iii, 13); (b) a letter written to Timothy or to Aristarchus by St Paul when a captive at Cæsarea (2 Tim. iv, 9-18); (c) a letter written by St Paul during his captivity at Rome to a disciple who had remained at Ephesus (2 Tim. iv, 19 + i, 16-18[b] + iv, 21). Mathematicians do not proceed with greater minuteness.

3. *Present State of Independent Criticism.*—The systematic failure of the innumerable attempts to explain the origin of the Epistles, by supposing them to be apocryphal, sanctions more and more their authenticity pure and simple. We can account for them by the avowal of Moffatt, who favours, in the *Encycl. biblica,* col. 5096, the opinion of Baur and Holtzmann. "Although the opinion we adopt," he says, "is indisputable, it is unfortunately not undisputed. The traditional opinion survives." It survives, in fact, so well that Moffatt himself, although excluding Catholics and Protestants

suspected of orthodox prejudice, cites in favour of authenticity more authorities than for the opposite opinion; and he is obliged, in order to produce a goodly number, to put into the second list names which ought not to be included in it. Sabatier, for example, has always declared that he remained neutral. " We could decide for or against the authenticity of these Epistles only by doing violence to our interior conviction and by going beyond the positive results of an impartial exegesis by following the logic of an *a priori* system" (*Encyclop. des sciences relig.*, vol. x, p. 251; cf. *L'Apôtre Paul*³). Harnack admits authentic parts. Most of the others, although agreed in rejecting authenticity, do so for diametrically contrary reasons. In a word, we can affirm, with an Anglican author, that we are on the way to recover the Pastoral Epistles and that we have been very foolish ever to suppose them lost (*Expository Times,* 1907, p. 245).

III—Resemblances to and Differences from the Unchallenged Epistles

1. *The Vocabulary.*—Von Soden has calculated that the Pastoral Epistles contain in all 897 words, of which 304 are not employed elsewhere by St Paul, while 171 of them are lacking in the rest of the New Testament. Thayer (*Lexicon of the N.T.*⁴, 1901, pp. 706-707) gives a still longer list of words peculiar to these Epistles, but he includes among them certain particular expressions (ἡ μακαρία ἐλπίς, πιστὸς ὁ λόγος, κτλ.) and several special received readings (διάβολος as an adjective; ἐνδύνω intransitive; ὑγιαίνω in the metaphorical sense; προφήτης said of a poet, etc.). Taking this list as a basis to proceed from, an anonymous writer has shown (*Church Quarterly Review*, 1907, I) that, of the 191 words attributed properly to the Pastorals, 13 ought not to be in the list, 83 are used in the Septuagint and could not be unknown to Paul, 52 are in the classics or in the works of his contemporaries, and finally that not one of the others, examined one by one, bears the mark of a date later than the death of the Apostle.

It is generally agreed to-day that the *hapax legomena* do not signify anything of importance, but the opponents of authenticity always lay great stress on the expressions which are frequent in the Pastorals, and absent from the other Epistles, or *vice versa.* The most conspicuous instances are these. The following expressions are completely lacking in the other Epistles: εὐσέβεια and kindred words (13 times in the Pastorals); ἀρνεῖσθαι (6 times); προσέχειν τινί (5 times); ὠφέλιμος (4 times); σωτήρ, applied to God (6 times), δεσπότης instead of κύριος (4 times); βέβηλος (4 times); ζήτησις and ἐκζήτησις (together 4 times); παραιτεῖσθαι (4 times); πιστὸς ὁ λόγος (5 times); the metaphor of health and sickness applied to doctrines (10 times). To this list might be added some expressions elsewhere very rare : σώφρων and derivatives (in all 10 times, as against Rom. xii, 3 ; 2 Cor. v, 13) ; διδασκαλία (15 times against 4 ; καθαρός (6 times against Rom. xiv, 20) ; καλός as an epithet—for example, in the remarkable expression καλὸν ἔργον.—On the other hand, one searches in vain in these Epistles for particles used so commonly in the others : διό, διότι, ἄρα. The word περισσός, elsewhere, with its derivatives, so frequent, does not appear here at all.

All these facts combined produce on the reader's mind an impression unfavourable to authenticity; but this first impression diminishes and disappears when it is borne in mind that the same result is obtained by taking, as a basis, any group of letters. Everywhere we may observe very great differences in the use of words and the temporary employment of some special favourites. What is the cause of this phenomenon? We have noted several reasons for it. In any case this difficulty, although perhaps more conspicuous in these Epistles, is not peculiar to them.

The objection based upon etymology is studied in detail by Jacquier (*Histoire des Livres du N.T.*[6], 1906, vol. i, pp. 357-368) and Wohlenberg (*Die Pastoralbriefe*[2], Leipzig, 1911, collection Zahn, pp. 50-58).

2. *The Ideas and Style.*—Everyone is agreed in recognizing the striking resemblances in style and thought which exist between the Pastorals and the other Pauline writings. Jülicher (*Einleitung*[4], p. 140) confesses that they are the work of a disciple very familiar with the ideas and language of the master, and that his skill consists precisely in not using too freely the words which call him to mind. The imitation is so successful that a great number of contemporaneous critics—and the least disposed to feel the influence of tradition—do not hesitate to see in many a passage the hand of Paul. The list of these resemblances will be found in the *Dictionary of the Bible,* by Hastings, and in the *Dictionary of the Apostolic Church* (1918, vol. ii, pp. 590-1), by the same editor. After having studied it, the reader will no doubt agree with the author's conclusion that there is nowhere any trace of conscious imitation. A forger would have here performed a veritable miracle and, moreover, a miracle which was not typical of the manners of that time.

3. *The Facts and Allusions.*—Since on any hypothesis the author was very familiar with the language, doctrine, and history of the Apostle, it would be supposed that he would adapt the setting of his writings to the well-known life of Paul, and that he would cause those persons to appear in them who play a part in the other Epistles. Now, what happens is just the reverse. The Apostle stays where he was not expected to be seen, and most of his customary associates

are different. These new actors are presented as a matter of course and without a word of explanation, as if their situation had nothing unusual about it.

Of the sixteen names which appear here for the first time, four are mentioned without any detail (2 Tim. iv, 21 : Eubulus, Pudens, Linus, Claudia). All the others are accompanied by a characteristic trait : Loïs and Eunice (2 Tim. i, 5), the grandmother and mother of Timothy, are praised for the sincerity of their faith, Onesiphorus (2 Tim. i, 16; iv, 19) for his devotion. Paul recommends to Titus (iii, 13) Zenas, the lawyer; he proposes to send Artemas to replace him (iii, 12); he has left some books and clothing with Carpus (2 Tim. iv, 12); he announces that Crescens has departed for Galatia or Gaul (2 Tim. iv, 10). The persons hostile to the Apostle are also admirably characterized : Phygellus and Hermogenes (2 Tim. i, 15) have turned their backs upon him; Hymenæus and Philetus (2 Tim. ii, 17) have apostatized; the first (1 Tim. i, 20) has been delivered over to Satan, as well as a certain Alexander who perhaps must be distinguished from Alexander the coppersmith (2 Tim. iv, 14 : ὁ χαλκεύς). In any case, this individual seems to have nothing in common with the Alexander of Acts xix, 33.

On the other hand, nothing suggested the cowardly desertion of Demas (2 Tim. iv, 10; cf. Col. iv, 14; Philem. 24), nor the sending of Tychicus to Crete (Tit. iii, 12; cf. Acts xx, 4; Col. iv, 7; Eph. vi, 21) or even to Ephesus (2 Tim. iv, 12), nor the illness of Trophimus at Miletus (2 Tim. iv, 20; cf. Acts xx, 4; xxi, 29), nor the voyage of Apollos to Crete (Tit. iii, 13), nor, finally, the landing of Erastus at Corinth (2 Tim. iv, 20).

On the subject of the Pastoral Epistles four decisions of the Biblical Commission were published on June 12, 1913. The first affirms that they are canonical and authentic. The second rejects as arbitrary and untenable the hypothesis of authentic fragments which are supposed to have furnished an unknown editor material for the Epistles we now possess. The third declares that the objections deduced from the style, the errors combated, and the developed hierarchy in no respect weaken their authenticity. Finally, the fourth places the date of the composition of the Pastorals between the first captivity of St Paul and his martyrdom.

NOTE K—ORIGIN OF THE EPISTLE TO THE HEBREWS

I—Patristic Tradition

The ecclesiastical writers of the first five centuries, whose opinion is known to us, can be divided into three classes : (1) those who reject both the canonicity and the authenticity of the Epistle, (2) those who admit both, (3) those who accept the canonicity without expressing an opinion on the question of authenticity or else making positive reservations on the subject. We mean here by *authenticity* the attribution of the Epistle to Paul ; for since it is anonymous, and nothing indicates that the author wished to pass himself off as Paul, there can be no question of authenticity in the strict sense of the term.

1. *Fathers Hostile to Canonicity and Authenticity.*—These are all Western. The Muratorian Canon does not mention the Epistle, and equivalently excludes it by saying that Paul wrote to seven churches. St Hippolytus, on the testimony of Photius, *Biblioth.*, cxxi and ccxxxii (CIII, 404 and 1104) and the priest Caius, as Eusebius tells us, *Hist. eccl.*, vi, 20 (XX, 273), and as St Jerome says, *De viris ill.*, 59 (XXIII, 706), also did not receive it. It was the same with St Irenæus, as Stephen Gobar informs us in Photius, *Biblioth.*, ccxxxii (CIII, 1104), and as we might conclude from the fact that the Bishop of Lyons does not quote the Epistle even once in his great work against heresies. Eusebius claims, it is true, *Hist.*, v, 26 (XX, 509), that Irenæus " mentions and quotes it " in another writing, but he does not say that he quotes it as canonical or as the work of Paul. Tertullian attributes it to Barnabas, and the way in which he speaks of it shows that he does not believe it to be canonical, *De pudic.*, 20 (II, 1021). The same is true of the author of the *Tractatus Origenis* (ed. Batiffol, Paris, 1900, p. 108). St Cyprian is not acquainted with it, for not only does he make no use of it, but he is one of those who assert that Paul wrote only to seven churches, *De exhort. mart.*, 11 and *Testim. contra Jud.*, i, 20 (IV, 668 and 689). Ambrosiaster and Pelagius exclude it from their commentary on the thirteen Pauline Epistles. Nothing indicates that Victorinus commented on it. Finally, the famous catalogue of the *Claromontanus* omits it, unless it be mentioned under the name of Barnabas. All these facts are the more astonishing because, in the first century, St Clement

of Rome transcribes long passages from the Epistle, although he does not quote it expressly. At the end of the fourth century, the doubts entertained by the Westerns still continued to exist (St Jerome, *De viris ill.*, 59 and *Comment in Is.*, vi, 2).

2. *Fathers Favourable to Canonicity and Authenticity.*— The Easterns, who never doubted the canonicity of the Epistle, in general accept its authenticity also without discussion, for they quote it under the name of Paul, comment on it among the other Epistles of Paul, or even reply to arguments brought against its Pauline origin.—*Alexandria:* St Denys, *Epist. ad Fabian.*, 2 (X, 1297); St Peter, *Epist. can.* 9 (XVIII, 485); St Alexander, *De Ariana haer. epist.* i, 2 (XVIII, 557, 565); St Athanasius, *Serm. contra Arian.*, ii, 1, 6, 7 (XXV, 148, 153); Didymus, *De Trinit.*, i, 15 (XXXIX, 317); St Cyril, *Thesaur. de Trin.*, 4, 7 (LXXV, 37, 40); Euthalius, *Argum.* in *Epist. Pauli* (LXXXV, 776), etc.— *Palestine:* St Cyril of Jerusalem, *Catech.*, x, 18; xv, 28; xvii, 20 (XXXIII, 684, 912, and 992); St Epiphanius, *Haeres.*, xlii, 12 (XLI, 812).—*Cappadocia:* St Basil, *Adv. Eunom.*, i, 14, 48 (XXIX, 345, 553); St Gregory Nazianzen, *Carm. de Script.*, 135 (XXXVII, 474); Amphilochius, *Ad Seleuc.*, 308 (XXXVII, 1597); St Gregory of Nyssa, *Adv. Eunom.*, 1 (XLV, 364, 369).—*Syria:* Council of Antioch, A.D. 264 (Mansi, *Concil.*, vol. i, p. 1038); St Chrysostom, Theodore of Mopsuestia, and Theodoret comment on the Epistle and affirm in their preface that it is by Paul. Theodoret (LXXXII, 673-676) is particularly keen on this subject. The Latin translation of the commentary of Theodore has been published by Swete; some fragments of it were possessed in Greek (LVI, 952). To this list must be added the Fathers who wrote in Syriac : St Ephrem (*Op. syr.*, vol. i, p. 159; vol. i, p. 30, etc.), who at the head of his commentary, preserved in Armenian and published in Latin by the Mechitarists of Venice, defends the authenticity *ex professo;* moreover, St James of Nisibis (Galland, *Biblioth. Pat.*, vol. v, pp. xiii and xvi), as well as the new school of Nisibis, on the testimony of Junilius, *Part. div. leg.*, i, 6 (LXVIII, 19).— *Latins:* St Hilary, *De Trinit.*, iv, 11 (X, 104), etc.; Lucifer of Cagliari (XIII, 782); Faustinus, *De Trinit.*, 2 (VIII, 61); St Ambrose, *De fuga saec.*, 16 (XIV, 577), etc.; Rufinus, *Symbol.*, 37 (XXI, 374).

3. *Fathers who accept Canonicity with Reservations as to Authenticity.*—The apostolic and sub-apostolic Fathers— except Clement—make little use of the Epistle. The ῥαντισμὸς αἵματος of Barnabas (v, 1) may have been borrowed from 1 Pet. i, 2 as well as from Heb. xii, 24. However, Polycarp (xii, 2) gives to Christ the title of *eternal High Priest* (cf. Heb. iv, 14), Justin (*Apol.*, 12) that of *Apostle* (cf.

Heb. iii, 1) and of *priest according to the order of Melchisedech (Contra Tryph., 113)*. On the other hand, the instances
of borrowing on the part of Clement are evident : *Ad Corinth,*
xxxvi, 1-5 (Heb. i, 3-13), ix-x, xviii (Heb. xi), etc. But the
tacit quotations of St Clement do not at all clear up the
question of the author. Clement of Alexandria, the first who
formally attributes the Epistle to Paul (Eusebius, *Hist.,*
vi, 14, vol. XX, 549 and 552), sees clearly the difficulty of his
thesis and gives an unacceptable solution of it. Origen (*ibid.,*
vi, 25, vol. XX, 584) so much extends the idea of authorship
that he can be ranked indiscriminately among the partisans
of authenticity. The doubts of which Eusebius speaks (*Hist.,*
iii, 3, vol. XX, 217) refer less to authenticity than to
canonicity. St Philastrius, *Haeres.,* lxxxviii (XII, 1199),
after having given a catalogue of the canonical books in
which figure *thirteen* Epistles of St Paul, without any
mention of the Epistle to the Hebrews, adds almost immediately, *Haeres.,* lxxxix (XII, 1200) : "Others, denying
that the Epistle to the Hebrews was written by Paul,
attribute it either to the Apostle Barnabas, or to Clement,
Bishop of Rome, or to Luke the Evangelist." He then
claims that, if it is not generally read in the churches, it is
because of interpolations made by heretics and on account
of certain difficult passages. The lengthy arguments of
Euthalius (LXXXV, 776) and those of St Ephrem in favour
of authenticity show that it was disputed. St Jerome repeats
to satiety that the Romans and the Latins in general do not
accept the Epistle and do not believe it to be Paul's, *De vir.
ill.,* 59 (XXIII, 669) ; *In Isa.* iii, 2 (XXIV, 94 : *quam Latina
consuetudo non recipit*) ; *In Isa.* viii, 18 (XXIV, 121), cf.
Epist. lxxiii *ad Evang.,* 3 (XXII, 678) ; *In Matt.* xxvi, 8-9
(XXVI, 192). He says that St Paul wrote to *seven* churches
only, *Epist.* liii *ad Paulin.,* 8 (XXII, 548 : *Paulus apostolus
ad septem ecclesias scribit; octava ad Hebraeos a plerisque
extra numerum ponitur*) ; *In Zachar.* viii, 23 (XXV, 1478).
Personally, although he quotes the Epistle as Paul's, he
seems to take little interest in the question, *In Jer.* vi, 31
(XXIV, 883 : *Hoc testimonio apostolus Paulus, sive quis
alius scripsit Epistolam, usus est ad Hebraeos*) ; *In Eph.* ii,
18 (XXVI, 475) : *Nescio quid tale et in alia Epistola, si quis
tamen eam recipit,* etc.) ; *In Titus* ii, 2 (XXVI, 578 : *Relege
ad Hebraeos Epistolam Pauli apostoli, sive cujuscumque
alterius eam esse putas, quia jam inter ecclesiasticas est
recepta*). The holy doctor firmly maintains the canonicity,
but attaches little importance to the authenticity, Epistle
cxxix *ad Dardan.,* 3 (XXII, 1103) : *Illud nostris dicendum
est, hanc epistolam quae inscribitur ad Hebraeos non solum
ab ecclesiis Orientis, sed ab omnibus retro ecclesiasticis
Graeci sermonis scriptoribus, quasi Pauli apostoli suscipi;*

*licet plerique eam vel Barnabae vel Clementis arbitrentur; et
nihil interesse cujus sit, cum ecclesiastici viri sit et quotidie
ecclesiarum lectione celebretur.   Quod si eam Latina consuetudo non recipit, etc.*   Cf. *De vir. ill.,* 5 (XXIII, 617);
In Is. iii, 9 (XXIV, 99).—St Augustine in the second period
of his life imitated the reserve of St Jerome.   He also
believes firmly in the canonicity of the Epistle, *De peccator.
meritis et remiss.,* i, 50 (XLIV, 137) : *Ad Hebraeos quoque
Epistola, quanquam nonnullis incerta sit, tamen quoniam . . .
magis me movet auctoritas ecclesiarum orientalium quae hanc
etiam in canonicis habent, quanta pro nobis testimonia con-
tineat, advertendum est.*   But he does not appear to attach
much importance to the question of authenticity, and in his
last writings he never declares his opinion categorically, *De
civit. Dei,* xvi, 22 (XLI, 500 : *In Epistola ad Hebraeos quam
plures apostoli Pauli esse dicunt, quidam autem negant. . . .).*
The curious feature of the affair is that he never appeals to
previous Councils in regard to it.

II—QUOTATIONS FROM THE OLD TESTAMENT

It is impossible to enumerate all the reminiscences and
allusions contained in the Epistle to the Hebrews; certain
chapters (xi, for example) are literally full of them.   We have
wished to notice only direct quotations with a *formula of
quotation,* but there are also a certain number of quotations
which, though they be unavowed, are none the less textual.
For example, iii, 2-5 (Num. xii, ·7); iii, 17-18 (Num. xiv,
22-29); vii, 1-10 (Gen. xiv, 17-20); ix, 28 (Is. liii, 12); x, 13
(Ps. cix, 1, Septuagint); x, 38 (Hab. ii, 3-4); xii, 15 (Deut.
xxix, 18); xii, 28 (Deut. ii, 4); xiii, 6 (Ps. cxvii, 6,
Septuagint).

In the list on p. 477 there will be remarked especially :

1. The great variety of quotation formulas.

2. The complete absence of the formula γέγραπται γάρ, of
which Paul is so fond.

3. The usual source (Pentateuch and Psalms, rather than
the Prophets).

4. Almost always it is God himself who speaks, instead of
the writer quoted.   The quotations usually follow the text of
the Septuagint, even when this differs from the Hebrew.
Three, however—vi, 13-14 (quoting Gen. xxii, 16-17); ix, 20
(quoting Exod. xxiv, 8); x, 30 (quoting Deut. xxxii, 35)—
differ at the same time from both the Hebrew and the
Septuagint.

Direct Quotations with Formula of Quotation.

Chapter	Passage Quoted	Formula of Quotation
i, 5ᵃ	Ps. ii, 7	τίνι εἶπεν :
i, 5ᵇ	2 Sam. vii, 14	καὶ πάλιν [εἶπεν]
i, 6	Deut. xxxii, 43	λέγει
i, 7	Ps. ciii (civ), 4	λέγει
i, 8-9	Ps. xliv (xlv), 7-8	πρὸς τὸν υἱὸν [λέγει]
i, 10-12	Ps. ci (cii), 26-28	καὶ [πρὸς τὸν υἱὸν λέγει]
i, 13	Ps. cix (cx), 1	πρὸς τίνα . . . εἴρηκεν
ii, 6-8	Ps. viii, 5-7	διεμαρτύρατο δὲ πού τις
ii, 12	Ps. xxi (xxii), 22	οὐκ ἐπαισχύνεται . . . καλεῖν λέγων
ii, 13ᵃ	2 Sam. xxii, 3	καὶ πάλιν [λέγων]
ii, 13ᵇ	Is. viii, 17-18	καὶ πάλιν [λέγων]
iii, 7-15	Ps. xciv (xcv), 7-11	λέγει τὸ πνεῦμα
iv	Ps. xciv (xcv), 11	καθὼς εἴρηκεν
iv, 4	Gen. ii, 2	εἴρηκεν γάρ που
iv, 5	Ps. xciv (xcv), 11	καὶ ἐν τούτῳ πάλιν
iv, 7	Ps. xciv (xcv), 7-8	καθὼς προείρηται
v, 5	Ps. ii, 7	ὁ λαλήσας πρὸς αὐτόν
v, 6	Ps. cix (cx), 4	καθὼς καὶ ἐν ἑτέρῳ λέγει
vi, 13-14	Gen. xxii, 16-17	ὁ Θεὸς . . . ὤμοσεν . . λέγων
vii, 11-13	Ps. cix (cx), 4	ἐφ' ὃν λέγεται ταῦτα
viii, 5	Ex. xxv, 40	φησίν
viii, 8-12	Jer. xxxi, 31-34	μεμφόμενος λέγει
ix, 20	Ex. xxiv, 6-8	λέγων
x, 5-7	Ps. xxxix (xl), 7-9	εἰσερχόμενος . . . λέγει
x, 15-16	Jer. xxxi, 33-34	μαρτυρεῖ τὸ πνεῦμα
x, 30ᵃ	Deut. xxxii, 35	οἴδαμεν τὸν εἰπόντα
x, 30ᵇ	Deut. xxxii, 36	καὶ πάλιν
xi, 18	Gen. xxi, 12	πρὸς ὃν ἐλαλήθη ὅτι
xii, 5	Prov. iii, 11-12	ὡς υἱοῖς διαλέγεται
xii, 20	Ex. xix, 13	τὸ διαστελλόμενον
xii, 21	Deut. ix, 19	Μωϋσῆς εἶπεν
xii, 26	Agg. ii, 6.	ἐπήγγελται λέγων
xiii, 5	Deut. xxxi, 6-8	αὐτὸς γὰρ εἴρηκεν

Three direct quotations and an implied one are common to both Paul and the Epistle : Gen. xxi, 12 (Heb. vi, 13-14 ; Rom. ix, 7) ; Deut. xxxii, 35 (Heb. x, 30 ; Rom. xii, 19) ; Ps. viii, 5-7 (Heb. ii, 6-8 ; Eph. i, 22) ; Hab. ii, 3 (Heb. x, 37 ; Gal. iii, 11 ; Rom. i, 17).

III—HYPOTHESES AS TO THE AUTHOR OR EDITOR

1. *St Barnabas, Author or Editor.*—To the positive testimony of Tertullian, *De pudic.*, xx (II, 1021 : *Volo ex redundantia alicujus etiam comitis apostolorum testimonium superducere.* Exstat enim et Barnabae titulus ad Hebraeos; *et utique receptior apud ecclesias* epistola Barnabae *illo apocrypho* Pastore *moechorum*), we can add the author (Gregory of Elvira?) of the *Tractatus Origenis* (ed. Batiffol, Paris, 1900, p. 108) : *Sed et sanctissimus Barnabas:* Per ipsum offerimus, *inquit,* Deo laudis hostiam labiorum confi-

tentium nomini ejus (Heb. xiii, 15). The testimony of the *Claromontanus* is disputed, but the stichometry assigned to the *Epistle of Barnabas* suits the Epistle to the Hebrews and is not suited to the Epistle published under the name of Barnabas. The texts of St Jerome and of St Philastrius have been already given. A certain number of Catholic and Protestant critics and historians (among others Fouard, Salmon, and Zahn) accept this hypothesis, which seems to correspond quite well with the different data.

2. *St Luke or St Clement, Authors or Translators.*—The hypothesis of a translator, conceived by Clement of Alexandria (Eusebius, *Hist.*, iii, 38), is given by Eusebius (*Hist.*, vi, 25) and by St Jerome (*De viris ill.*, 5), with no allusion to Clement. Origen thinks (Eusebius, *Hist.*, vi, 25) that Clement or Luke are not the translators, but the editors, of the Epistle, and this new theory is mentioned by St Philastrius (*Haeres.*, 89), who adds Barnabas to the two others, and by St Jerome (*Epist. ad Dardan.*, cxxix, 3), who names only Luke and Barnabas. Many exegetes and critics embrace the hypothesis of Origen, giving their preferences either to Luke (Hug, Zill, Döllinger, Huyghe, etc.) or to Clement (Theodoret, Euthalius, Bisping, Kaulen, Cornely, etc.), urging in the case of both certain affinities of style which appear to us very problematical.

3. *Apollos, Author or Editor.*—Whether Luther was the first to think of Apollos or not, his authority has certainly won over some adherents to this hypothesis, which, thanks to the defence of it by Bleek, was for some time the prevalent opinion among protestant critics. Some Catholics also adopted it, Belser (*Einleitung in das N.T.*, 1901, pp. 600-601) among others.

4. *Aristion, Author.*—This hypothesis was proposed by J. Chapman, O.S.B., *Aristion, author of the Epistle to the Hebrews,* in the *Revue Bénédictine,* vol. xxii (1905), pp. 49-62. It is thus stated on p. 51 : "I only ask that it be assumed here, for the sake of argument, that *the last twelve verses* (of Mark) *are a composition by a single author,* whose name is not of the slightest importance in this article. I then claim to be able to show that *this author is apparently also the writer of the Epistle to the Hebrews."* This is, therefore, an hypothesis grafted on another hypothesis. Dom Chapman undertakes to prove that Aristion is the real author of the last portion of the Gospel of Mark, but we have not yet seen this demonstration. Moreover, it does not appear to us clear from a study of his article that the author of the end of Mark and of the Epistle to the Hebrews is one and the same person. The basis for a comparison is, in fact, too narrow to result in a firm conclusion.

5. *Prisca or Priscilla, Author, perhaps in Collaboration with her Husband Aquila.*—This clever idea has created some noise in the world, thanks to the notoriety of Harnack, *Probabilia über die Adresse und den Verfasser des Hebräerbriefes* (in *Zeitschrift für neutest. Wiss.*, 1900, pp. 26-41). Belser sets it forth and refutes it (*Einleitung*, pp. 611-615) at a greater length than it deserves. These unfounded conjectures should be left to their ephemeral fate.

6. *Silas or Silvanus, Author.*—The candidature of Silas has won some partisans, at the expense of Apollos, since Riehm has shown that the former has as many rights—purely hypothetical ones, however—to be regarded as the author of the Epistle.

7. It should not be thought that the above-named authors are the only ones for whom the paternity of the Gospel is claimed. Ramsay has thought of the deacon *Philip* (*Expositor*, June, 1899), and there remain among the associates of St Paul enough persons to exercise the cleverness of the critics, without any need for recourse to St Peter. *Cf.* Velch (*The Authorship of the Epistle to the Hebrews*, London, 1899). But the greater part of our contemporaries have given up the attempt to discover the great and mysterious unknown; they are content to propose an *Alexandrian Jew;* that is to say, a Jewish writer imbued with the culture commonly called Alexandrian.

In closing it seems fitting to transcribe here the opinion of the learned P. Cornely, one of the stoutest champions of the authenticity of the Epistle, understood in the sense that the Apostle is the *auctor* but not the *scriptor* of it (*Introd.*[2], vol. iii, 1897, p. 529) : *Paulinam originem asserentes neque quaestionem hanc cum illa de canonicitate conjungimus, ut priore negata alteram negandam esse censeamus, neque sententiae illorum adversamur qui cum Paulo* auctore *alium ex viris apostolicis* scriptorem *epistolae agnoscunt. Namque* canonicitatem *epistolae non labefactari, etiamsi quis incertum esse ejus auctorem diceret, manifestum est consideranti non paucos esse libros canonicos, quorum auctores humani ignorantur. . . . Erravit ergo Cajetanus, qui* nisi *Pauli esset epistola, non perspicuam esse ejus canonicitatem* asseruit, ac profecto ad apostolicam ejus originem non attendentes ejus canonicitatem tueri possumus.

The Biblical Commission on June 24, 1914, promulgated the three following decisions : (1) In view of the tradition of the Eastern Church and of that of the Western Church from the fourth century, in regard to the documents of the Councils and ecclesiastical usage, the Epistle to the Hebrews is to be held as canonical—which is a tenet of faith—and should be numbered among the authentic Epistles of Paul.—(2) The arguments alleged against its authenticity (unusual exordium, language, quotations, divergences) are not sufficient to invalidate it, and certain facts of internal criticism, like the similarity of ideas and words, confirm it.—(3) It is not, however, necessary to think—*salvo ulteriori Ecclesiae judicio*—that the Apostle not only conceived and produced it in its entirety under the inspiration of the Holy Spirit, but also gave to it its present form (*ipsum eam totam non solum Spiritu Sancto inspirante concepisse et expressisse, verum etiam ex forma donasse qua prostat*).

We are therefore brought back to the distinction between substance and form, which most Catholics of our time maintain with Origen. This is the conclusion of a long study published by P. Méchineau in the *Civiltà Cattolica* (February, 1916, to August, 1917). P. Méchineau calls the writer who gave the Epistle its present form an *estensore,* but he contents himself with presenting the various opinions of Catholics without taking sides with any.

APPENDIX

ANALYSIS OF THE EPISTLES

THE genius of Paul is universally considered to be characterized by two traits: first, a dialectical energy which pursues to the utmost limit one idea, turning it about for inspection under all its aspects; and, second, the intensity of a soul entirely absorbed in the feeling or thought of the moment. A mind of this stamp cannot fail to imprint upon its works a seal of unity. This is, indeed, what strikes one most forcibly in the writings of the Apostle. His digressions are not mere side issues; they are due to a desire to solve an intervening difficulty or to illumine some detail necessary for the comprehension of his thesis. When the accessory question is completely settled, Paul enters again into his subject rather by means of a word that recalls it than by a direct transition, or returns to his point of departure by a sort of roundabout reasoning. Therefore, with all consideration for the freedom of manner characteristic of the epistolary style, and without wishing to reduce everything to a strict method of procedure, it is nevertheless imperatively necessary never to lose sight of the dominant idea.

Is it necessary to caution the reader that the central idea of the Epistles is not always a thesis? Sometimes it is a feeling to be inspired or an aim to be secured. The phrase which theologians so readily detach from its context, in order to occupy themselves with it almost exclusively, as if it were the very quintessence of the Epistle, is often only an incident, the omission of which would scarcely disturb the construction of the letter. This is true, for example, of the great christological text in the Epistle to the Philippians, of the passages of the Epistles to the Corinthians about the necessity of grace, and even, to a lesser degree, of the verses in the Epistle to the Romans on original sin and predestination. At least the dogmatic text is generally subordinated to the central idea, from which it appears that the duty of the attentive reader is to replace it in its natural framework.

We have tried here to free the thought of Paul from the accessory ideas which burden it, and to reduce it to its essential elements, in order better to show its sequence and logical connection. It has been difficult to escape entirely the charge of arbitrariness and of a wish to reduce everything to a system, since the same idea has not the same degree of importance in the eyes of all readers. But to avoid transcribing the whole text of the Epistles involved self-restraint and throwing some things overboard.

We had thought at first of preserving, as far as possible, the very words of St Paul, being well aware that these terms have not in most cases an exact equivalent. Only in proceeding thus we should have been obliged to accompany our résumé with a running commentary, in order to render it intelligible to those who had not previously studied the terminology of the great Apostle. This would have been to fail in our object and to deprive this analysis of the only merit to which it aspires—that of informing the reader quickly where he is to find what he is seeking and of guiding him through the obscure labyrinth of complex arguments.

For reasons of practical convenience, we shall follow the usual order of our Bibles. But the reader will please bear in mind at the same time the chronological order, and not forget the respective place of each group :

1. First and Second Epistles to the Thessalonians.

2. Great Epistles (First and Second to the Corinthians, Galatians, Romans).

3. Epistles of the Captivity (Philemon, Colossians, Ephesians, Philippians).

4. Pastorals (First to Timothy, Epistle to Titus, Second to Timothy).

5. Epistle to the Hebrews.

I—THE EPISTLE TO THE ROMANS

The *plan* of the *dogmatic* part (i-xi) is very regular. The *exhortation* (xii-xvi) forms something entirely apart, with no connection with the rest.

With a few notions about the apostolate, the *superscription* (i, 1-7) includes the elements of a concise Christology.

The *introduction* (8-17), in the form of a thanksgiving, contains a eulogy of the faith of the Romans, an expression of the lively interest which the Apostle takes in them, and finally the statement of his subject.

Proposition: " The Gospel is an agent of God for the salvation of every one that believeth, of the Jew first and also of the Greek; for the justice of God is revealed therein, from faith unto faith, as it is written : The just shall live by faith " (16-17).

The *division* of the doctrinal part is taken from the phrase : *The Gospel is an instrument of salvation for every one that believeth, beginning with the Jews.* The Apostle first establishes the fact that true justice is derived, not from nature or

the Law, but from the Gospel (i-iv); he then explains the
bond of causality that exists between justice, initial salvation,
and completed, definite salvation (v-viii); and finally he raises
the objection of the unbelief of the Jews which seems to
destroy his assertion " To the Jew first and also to the Greek "
(ix-xi).

PART I

THE GOSPEL AN INSTRUMENT OF SALVATION FOR ALL MEN

SECTION I

TRUE JUSTICE IS DERIVED ONLY FROM THE GOSPEL (i-iv)

I—*This Justice is not found Outside of the Gospel*
(i, 18–iii, 20).

1. *The Gentiles never had it* (i, 18-32).—They indeed
knew God, whose attributes are reflected in our world of
sense (18-20); but far from paying him the honour and
adoration which they owed him, they prostituted them to the
vilest creatures (21-24). Therefore God repays them with
insult for insult; they shall themselves be the executors of his
vengeance and shall cover each other with shame through
the impure fires with which they are inflamed (24-27). God
abandons them to the dominion of their reprobate sense and
allows them to fall into the most shameful debaucheries (28-
31). Not only do they violate the law of nature, but, by
an excess of malice, they applaud those who violate it (32,
Greek).

2. *The Jews never had it* (ii, 1–iii, 20)—(*a*) *Their greater
light does not hinder them from imitating the pagans,* whom
they despise (ii, 1-3). They thus heap up against themselves
an abundance of wrath with the incorruptible judge (4-12).
For it is not the knowledge but the observance of the Law
that justifieth (13), since the pagans also have an internal
light which for them takes the place of the Law (14-16). The
Jews are all the more inexcusable since they cannot so well
use the pretext of ignorance; and their Law, of which they
are so proud, turns to their accusation (17-24).—(*b*) *Circumcision is of no use without the observance of the Law* (25-29).
—This assertion detracts nothing from the honourable prerogative of the Jews and makes the fidelity of God in regard
to them only the more conspicuous (iii, 1-8). As for true
justice, Jews and Gentiles are equally deprived of it (9).
Scripture abundantly proves this, especially as to the Jews
(10-18). So that no one will be able to boast before God
(19-20).

II—*The Gospel promises it and gives it, in accordance with the Prophecies.*

1. In a fine general survey Paul shows us *in the Gospel all the causes of justification:* the *efficient* cause, God the Father; the *meritorious* cause, the blood of Jesus Christ; the *instrumental* cause, faith; the *formal* cause, the justice of God communicated to man; the *final* cause, the glorious manifestation of the immanent justice of God (21-26). Conclusion : man is justified by faith without the works of the Law; and this is true of the Gentiles as well as of the Jews, for God is the God of both (27-30).

2. Moreover, this is entirely *according to Scripture* (iii, 21 and 31). Abraham was justified by faith and not by works. If it had been otherwise there would have been room for boasting; but no, his justification is gratuitous, and God gives him justice in return for faith, which is not the equivalent of justice (iv, 1-5). Neither does David, aspiring to be just, count upon himself, but upon God alone (6-8). That which proves that justice does not depend on circumcision is that Abraham was declared just before he was circumcised (9-12). He was also made heir of the divine blessings and father of the faithful before the appearance of the Law; these blessings cannot, therefore, now depend upon the Law, for this would be to annul the promises made independently of it (13-22). Thus all blessings will pass to the spiritual posterity of Abraham by the means which made him the depositary of them; that is to say, by faith (23-25).

SECTION II

CERTAINTY OF OUR HOPE (v-viii)

This section (v-viii) begins and ends in the same way by affirming that our hope is certain : " Hope confoundeth not " (v, 5) and " We are saved by hope " (viii, 24). There are two great *divisions*—removal of hindrances (vi-vii), and positive reasons for hope (viii).

Presentation of the Subject (v, 1-11).—Being justified, we have peace, free access to God, therefore hope (v, 1-2), strengthened by tribulations (3-4), guaranteed by the gift of the Holy Spirit (5) and by the death of Christ (6-8). If Jesus died for us when we were sinners, how much more will he make us live by his life, now that we are just (9-11).

I—*Removal of Hindrances to Hope: Sin, Death, and the Flesh in Coalition with the Law* (v, 12–viii, 11).

1. *Sin conquered* (v, 12-22).—By Adam's sin, sin entered into the world, bringing death in its train (12); for death is not the punishment of actual sins, seeing that it strikes down even those who have not transgressed (13-14). But the new Adam restores with usury what the first Adam took from us (15-17). All men are made sinners by the disobedience of Adam; all men will be made just by the obedience of Christ (18-19). In vain does the Law multiply sin, grace abounds still more (20); the reign of sin is ended, that of justice begins (21).

2. *Death conquered* (vi).—Baptism, a mystical death and burial, communicates to us the life of Christ in all its fulness : life of the soul through grace, life of the body by the seed of a glorious resurrection (vi, 3-7). Whence the obligation to maintain this mystical death, pledge of life eternal (8-14), and to withdraw ourselves more and more from the empire of sin, by dedicating ourselves voluntarily to the service of justice, according to the engagements contracted at baptism and the requirements of our new nature (15-23).

3. *The Flesh conquered, and the Law, unconscious auxiliary of Sin and the Flesh, is abolished* (vii, 1–viii, 11).

(*a*) *Death of the Law to the Christian or of the Christian to the Law.*—Death is the end of obligation (vii, 1); thus, in marriage, the death of one of those thus united renders the other free (2-3). Now, bodily union with Christ is the mystical death of the Christian, which frees him from all subjection in respect of the Law (5-6).

(*b*) *Why is the Law abolished?*—It is not because the Law is sin, but because it makes us know sin (7); sin makes use of it to inspire us with bad desires (8). Sin, which was sleeping, regains its vigour thanks to the Law, and thereby robs man of the life of the soul (9-11). The Law is good in itself, but sin takes advantage of it to produce death (12-13). The last cause of it is our inborn corruption (14). I do not what I would, and I do what I would not : a proof that it is sin, a foreign element grafted on my nature, which works evil in me (15-20). There are in me two laws—that of reason, which approves the good, and that of the members or of sin, which inclines to evil; sad dualism which grace alone can heal (21-25).

(*c*) *The Flesh itself is now powerless.*—By his incorporation into Christ the Christian masters the law of sin and death (viii, 1-2). Christ, by dying for us, confers upon us the power to attain to the justice which the Mosaic Law had not been able to give (3-4). Of course, the conflict between the flesh and the spirit still continues, incessant, implacable (5-8), but the presence of the Spirit assures us the victory; it is a certain pledge of life for both soul and body (9-11).

II—*Immovable foundations of our Hope* (vii, 12-39).

1. *The whole creation predicts our future glory.*—It was formerly subjected, in spite of itself, to sinful man (18-19), but with the assurance of being one day delivered, together with man himself (20). Therefore it awaits impatiently its own glorification and ours (21-22).

2. *The Holy Spirit guarantees it to us.*—He puts upon our lips the name of Father (15); he attests thus our filial adoption (16) and consequently our right of being heirs, provided that we participate in Christ's suffering, in order that we may share in his glory (17-18). The firstfruits of the Spirit are the earnest of blessedness (23-25); the Spirit inspires us with desires for happiness which cannot be frustrated (26-27).

3. *God the Father promises it to us.*—He makes all things work together for the good of the just (28); all the effects of predestination, from the call to faith to the glory of heaven, are connected in his designs (29-30). If, then, God is for us, what have we to fear (31-33)?

4. *Jesus Christ wins it for us and holds it in reserve for us.*—Having died and risen again for us, he is now seated at the right hand of the Father to intercede for us (34). Nothing in heaven or on earth can separate us from the love which Jesus Christ has for us (35-39).

SECTION III

UNBELIEF OF THE JEWS (ix-xi)

Paul recognizes the fact with unspeakable sorrow (ix, 1-3); he enumerates, without weakening them, the nine prerogatives of the Jews (4-5); but (1) the objection in no way impugns the faithfulness or the justice of God—(2) the blame for the rejection of the Jews falls on the Jews themselves—(3) this rejection, partial and transient, is allowed for very wise ends.

I—*Neither the Faithfulness nor the Justice of God is involved in it* (ix, 6-29).

1. *The Faithfulness of God.*—God had made promises to Israel, to the *lineage* of Abraham; but all the descendants of Abraham or of Jacob have not the right to that title (6-7). Among the children of Abraham, Isaac alone is heir to the promises (8-9); a new selection is made between the children of Isaac, a purely gratuitous election (10-12), which to the

Idumeans and the guilty Hebrews means a very different
treatment (13).

2. *The Justice of God.*—To accuse God of injustice is
blasphemy (14). There is no injustice in refusing a purely
gratuitous favour like that which Moses asked for (15).
From this point of view everything depends upon the
liberality of God and nothing upon the efforts of man (16).
Nor is there any injustice in punishing criminals, such as
Pharao, and in not according them the *efficacious* grace of
conversion (17). From this new point of view God hath
mercy on whom he will have mercy, and whom he will he
hardeneth (18). If it be objected that then God has no longer
any right to complain of man (19), in the first place man
never has the right to lay the blame for this on God, for it is
absurd for the work to attack the workman (20), since the
latter is under no obligation to his work (21); secondly, God
can without injustice patiently endure sinners fit for perdition,
in order to make more glorious the wonders of his grace in
the just whom he has prepared for glory (22-23). Now, this
is what God, according to Osee, does in behalf of the Gentiles
(24-26) and also in favour of the *remnant* of Israel, as Isaias
predicted (27-29).

II—*The Jews are Responsible for Their Rejection* (ix, 30–x, 21).

Wishing to conquer justice by their own efforts (ix, 30-31),
they stumbled at the stone of offence (32-33). Their zeal is
sincere, but not according to knowledge (x, 1-2). They do
not know what true justice is, and they forget that Christ is
the end of the Law, the only author of salvation (3-4). Un-
wise and unhappy, they enter upon an impracticable path,
when the way of faith is so easy. It is not a question either
of ascending into the heavens, or of going down to the
depths; it is sufficient to believe in one's heart in the Lord
Jesus and to confess him with the mouth (5-11). There is no
more difference between Jew and Greek; whoever confesses
the name of the Lord shall be saved (12-13). Let not the
Jews pretend ignorance; the voice of the Apostles has resounded to the ends of the world (14-18). They have refused
to hear (16), and their unbelief, predicted by Moses (19), was
already deplored by Isaias in the Jews of his time (20-21).

III—*Their Rejection, Partial and Transient, is Providential* (xi).

1. *Partial.*—God has not rejected *his people,* for there are
Christians among the Jews (xi, 1-2): as in the time of Elias,
in spite of general unfaithfulness, there is a group of men
faithful to Jehovah (3-4); as in all the epochs of Jewish

history, there is a *remnant* saved by grace (5-6). The others were blind, according to the prophetic words of Moses and of David (7-10).

2. *Transient and providential.*—Their fall, which God has permitted in order to bring the Gentiles to the faith, is not final (11). Their return to God will be much more productive in fruits of salvation than their defection (12 and 15). In view of this, Paul spares no effort to gain some of them (13-14).—If the branches of the wild olive (the Gentiles) have been grafted on to the true olive (the people of God), while the natural branches (the Jews) were cut off, how much more easily will the latter be grafted on again if they are converted, and the former be rejected if they are unfaithful (16-24)?— Israel is blinded only for a time; the prophets predict their ultimate conversion (25-27); God, whose favours are never repented of, loves them always because of the patriarchs (28-29); he has his designs of mercy for the Jews as well as for the Gentiles (30-32). Oh, the depth of the divine counsels (33-36)!

PART II

CONCLUSION AND MORAL PRECEPTS

Nor does the exhortation, which does not seem especially appropriate to the thesis of the first eleven chapters, appear to be due to the particular situation of the church of Rome. Perhaps Paul wished to add to the most complete presentation of his doctrine of grace the fullest compendium of his code of social morality.

I—GENERAL PRECEPTS OF SOCIAL MORALITY (xii-xiii)

1. *Reciprocal duties of Christians as members of the Mystical Body.*—Having stated by the way the two principles of Christian morality : the new nature, source of new obligations, and the will of God manifested in the Gospel (xii, 1-2), the Apostle briefly recalls his theory of the mystical body, expounded at greater length to the Corinthians. As we are members of one body, so are we members one of another (3-5), with different functions in relation to the different *charismata* which are all for the common good (6-8). The duties which devolve from them can be summed up in one word—brotherly love (9-10). The immediate applications of this are : Self-forgetfulness (11-12), making oneself all things to all men (13-16), returning good for evil (17-21).

2. *Duties towards Authority.*—Authority comes from God (xiii, 1); to resist it is to resist God himself (2) and to expose oneself to the just punishment of the prince who beareth not

the sword in vain (3-4). Conscience and fear alike preach to us submission (5). Let us therefore pay tribute to the sovereign, as to the representative of God, and, in general, let us render to everyone what is his due (6-7).

3. *The precept of Charity, an epitome of our social duties.*—The only debt of the Christian is the debt of love (8). All the commandments are comprised in this law, and in this sense it can be said that love is the fulfilling of the Law (9-10). Time presses; the day is at hand; let us cast off the works of darkness; let us put on Jesus Christ (11-14).

II—APPLICATION OF THE PRECEPT OF CHARITY
(xiv, 1–xv, 13)

Let charity reign between the enlightened Christian and " him that is weak in faith," who abstains from certain foods and observes certain days (xiv, 1-2, 5). The latter ought not to despise the other as if he were less perfect, nor ought the former to *judge* one who is scrupulous in the matter (3-4). Both act with the intention of pleasing their Master (6-8); both are dependent on the judgement of Christ only, before whose tribunal we shall appear (9-13). In theory the enlightened Christian, for whom no food is impure, is right (14). But charity (15), the blessing of peace (16-18), edification (19) may require sacrifices of us (20). It is praiseworthy to abstain even from meat and wine, if we thereby avoid scandalizing the weak (21-23). After the example of Christ, the strong ought to bear the weak with patience (xv, 1-3). Let the Romans be thoroughly imbued with that self-abnegation so eloquently taught by Christ (4-7), who has embraced both Jews and Gentiles with the same love (8-13).

The *conclusion,* exceptionally elaborated, comprises some personal communications, a long series of salutations, and various recommendations.

1. *Personal Communications.*—The Apostle excuses himself for having written so freely to the Romans, of whose good instruction he is aware (xv, 14-15), but he is under obligations to all the Gentiles (16-19). No doubt he has made it a law unto himself not to build on another man's foundation (20-21), and it is this which has hitherto hindered him from going to Rome (22); but now that his work in the East is finished he will go to Spain by way of Rome (23-25), as soon as he has carried to Jerusalem the amount of his collections (26-29). He beseeches the faithful to pray heaven for the success of this mission (30-33).

2. *Salutations.*—Paul warmly commends Phœbe, who, according to all appearances, was to deliver the Epistle to them (xvi, 1-2). Then he sends salutations to a great number

of persons and Christian families, with a word of praise for each (3-16).

3. *Various Recommendations.*—(*a*) To avoid those who cause dissensions and seducers (17-18).—(*b*) The companions of Paul send their salutations to their brethren of Rome (21-24).—(*c*) A solemn *doxology* for the end (25-27).

II—FIRST EPISTLE TO THE CORINTHIANS

Each of the nine or ten points treated in this Epistle is without connection with the rest and might form an Epistle by itself. It is evident, however, that the first six chapters find fault with disorders of which Paul had learned from third parties, while in the ten concluding ones the Apostle settles cases of conscience propounded to him, for the most part, if not exclusively, by the Corinthians themselves. This is a principle on which to found a *division,* which is rather precarious and artificial, but sufficient for our purpose.

The *superscription* (i, 1-3), in which Sosthenes is associated with Paul, is unusually solemn. The Epistle is addressed, not only to the church of Corinth, but to ' all that invoke the name of our Lord Jesus Christ," wherever they may be.

The *introduction* (i, 4-9), in the form of a thanksgiving, contains a warm eulogy of the Corinthians. The Apostle desires that God may finish his work in them, and this wish leads him easily to his first admonition.

PART I

DISORDERS (i-vi)

I—FACTIONS AND INTRIGUES (i-iv)

The Corinthians take sides for this or that preacher (i, 10-12). Paul expresses his indignation at this (13); he rejoices that he has baptized almost no one at Corinth and that he has preached there only the doctrine of the Cross, so that they cannot make use of his name to stir up intrigues (14-17).—In reproving this disorder, he has in view two things : (1) to justify his manner of acting and to re-establish his legitimate authority, (2) to show in general how unreasonable these factions are.

1. *A personal question*—(*a*) *Excellence of the Doctrine of the Cross preached by Paul.*—The *verbum Crucis,* foolishness in the eyes of the world, is wisdom to the elect (18).

God is pleased to confound "the wisdom of the world" by saving, through "the foolishness of preaching" them that believe (19-21). The Cross, which is foolishness to the Greeks eager for wisdom, a stumbling-block to the Jews desirous of miracles, manifests to all who believe, whether they be Jews or Greeks, the power and the wisdom of God (22-24) : the wisdom, since it triumphs over that which appears wise; the power, since it casts down that which seemed powerful (25). A proof of this are the Corinthians, deprived of the qualities which the world esteems; it is, however, by them that God confounds the world (26-28). Thus no one will be able to glory save in the Lord (29-31).

(b) *Justification of Paul's conduct.*—He wished to know only Jesus Christ crucified (ii, 1-2). He despised the subtleties of human wisdom, in order that the faith of the Corinthians might rest on God alone (3-5). This is not because he is ignorant of the true wisdom, unknown to the princes of this world and invisible to every human eye (6-9), but which the Holy Spirit, who searcheth the deep things of God, has revealed to the Apostles (10-12). He knows how to preach it on occasion, without mixing it up with the dross of worldly wisdom, reserving it for men who are *spiritual,* alone capable of comprehending it (13-16). Now the Corinthians are still children in the faith and need the milk of children (iii, 1-2) ; they are still carnal; in a word, they are *men* (3), as they show by their conduct (4).

2. *A general question.* — *The abetters of factions misunderstand the role of the apostles*—(A) *The apostles are coadjutors of God.*—They work in subordination, each in his own sphere; but really God is the only worker, for it is he alone who builds the edifice, he alone who giveth increase to the harvest (5-8). The faithful are, therefore, the field of the heavenly husbandman, the temple of the divine architect (9). Considered as God's labourers, the missionary workers are one and the same (8); nevertheless, it does not follow that they have not individual duties and responsibilities : (a) Some add to the foundation (to the doctrine of Christ preached by Paul) precious materials, gold, silver, and marble; each of them shall receive a reward proportionate to his work (10-12; *cf.* 8 and 14).—(b) Others employ for the building wood, hay, straw, mean and perishable materials; the fire of God's judgement shall destroy their work, and they themselves shall be saved only by going through the fire (13-15). (c) Finally, others, instead of building, weaken and destroy the temple of God by their wicked doctrines; and them, too, shall God destroy (16-17).

(B) *The Apostles are for the Faithful, and the Faithful are for Christ* (21-23).—There is, therefore, folly and madness in giving allegiance to any one man (18-21).

(C) *The Apostles are the dispensers of the Mysteries of God* (iv, 1).—They are, therefore, to be faithful to their mandate and submissive to their employer (2). But it is not for men to judge them. Paul despises these premature judgements (3); he avoids judging himself although he is not conscious of having failed in doing his duty; he wishes to be dependent only on the judgement of God (4-5). Here Paul condemns without any circumlocution and no longer in veiled terms the conduct of the Corinthians (6-7); he contrasts the claims of the faithful with the tribulations of the Apostles, made into a spectacle for the whole world (8-13); he reminds them that he is their father in the faith (14-16) and that he will know how to use with them severity or mercy, as the case may need (17-21).

II—Tolerance in regard to the Man Guilty of Incest (v)

A Christian had contracted a marriage with his stepmother, which was illicit even in the eyes of the pagans (v, 1). Paul is astonished and indignant that he has not been expelled from the Church (2). He pictures himself as being in the midst of the faithful, delivering up to Satan the body of the guilty man in order to save his soul from damnation (4-5). He wishes all in the Church should be *azymoi,* and that they should purge out the old leaven; that is to say, the scandal (6-8). The Apostle takes advantage of the occasion to remove a misunderstanding. In a previous Epistle he had forbidden all relations with fornicators (9). He was not speaking of pagans, but of Christians whose mode of life is bad. With these he forbade them to maintain even ordinary social relations (10-11). As for unbelievers, God will judge them (12-13).

III—Lawsuits before Pagan Tribunals (vi)

To ask justice from the unjust—that was the usual name for pagans—is contrary to all reason (vi, 1). Let Christian judges be taken, for Christians shall one day judge the world and the angels themselves (2-3). These temporal interests are so trifling that they should be confided to the humblest members of the Church (4). Yet no; Corinth has men capable of acting as judges (5). Lawsuits between brethren are in themselves an abuse, but what is intolerable is to have them judged by unbelievers (9). Better to suffer injustice than do that. What shall be said of one who commits such a fault (7-8)? Know this, that sinners shall not enter into the kingdom of heaven (9-10). You are regenerate; let your life correspond to your new condition (11).

The question of lawsuits may be considered as a parenthesis. Paul returns without any transition to the case of the man guilty of incest, and combats the false principle that all things are lawful to the Christian (12). No, all things are not lawful, and fornication is intrinsically bad, and for three reasons : (a) *It is an injustice,* for the body belongs to the Lord, who destines it for a glorious resurrection (13-14)—(b) *it is a sacrilege,* for we are the members of Christ : whoever wrongs his own body prostitutes a member of Christ (15-18) —(c) *it is a profanation,* for we are the temple of the Holy Ghost (19-20).

PART II

CASES OF CONSCIENCE

FIRST QUESTION

Marriage and Celibacy (vii)

In principle it is better to abstain from sexual relations, but the danger of incontinence comes in to modify this principle (vii, 1).

1. *Conjugal Relations.*—They are advisable in order to obviate the peril of impurity (2); they are obligatory in order to fulfil the conjugal duty (3), for each party to the marriage belongs to his or her partner (4). But abstention is allowable if it takes place (a) by common agreement, (b) for a worthy purpose, (c) for a limited time (5). The Apostle, while permitting conjugal relations, does not impose them (6); on the contrary, he would like to confer on everyone the gift of continence (7).

2. *Indissolubility of Marriage.*—Less perfect than celibacy, marriage is, nevertheless, advisable in order to avoid incontinence (8-9). The Lord has instituted it absolutely indissoluble, and neither of those who are married can repudiate the other. If they separate, they are forbidden to make a new marriage (10-11).

3. *The Pauline Privilege.*—A marriage contracted in unbelief holds good when one of the parties embraces the faith (12-14); but if the unbelieving party separates from the other, the believer becomes free again and can use his liberty without scruple (15-16). This does not impair the general principle of remaining in the state in which the party was when the Gospel was received (17). Whether circumcised or uncircumcised, no matter (18-20). Whether bond or free is all the same from the Christian point of view (21-23). In brief, let every man abide in the state in which the faith has found him (24).

4. *Excellence of Virginity.*—The general principle is applicable to unmarried persons of both sexes (26-27). It is

not that marriage is not perfectly allowable, but it exposes the parties to tribulations of the flesh (28). The fashion of this world passeth away; it is necessary to make use of the world without becoming attached to it (29-31). Paul would have his converts be without solicitude (32); this is the advantage which the virgin and the celibate have, who think only of the things of God, while married people are distracted by a thousand earthly cares (33-34). Paul, in speaking thus, thinks only of removing the obstacles which impede the exercise of religion (35). If anyone fears dishonour for the virgin who is under his care, and if he thinks it suitable to give her in marriage, he can do so without sin (36-37). Moreover, other things being equal, the father who gives his daughter to a husband doeth well; and yet in keeping her a virgin he doeth better (38).

5. *The state of Widowhood.*—On the death of her husband the woman is free to remarry, provided she marry a Christian (39). Paul is of the opinion that she will do better to remain a widow, and he is sure that his opinion is in conformity with the spirit of God (40).

SECOND QUESTION

THINGS SACRIFICED TO IDOLS (viii-x)

1. *General Principles.*—In matters of conduct, theoretical knowledge is not enough; there is needed a knowledge that is inspired by charity (viii, 1-3). In itself, food sacrificed to idols is nothing (4), since there is only one God, from whose dominion nothing can be taken away (5-6). But there are some ill-balanced consciences to which meat offered to idols seems intrinsically impure (7), and we must avoid scandalizing these (8-10). For the scandal may cause a brother for whom Christ died to perish (11), and therefore the causer of the scandal sins against Christ himself (12). God forbid that I should scandalize my brother for a morsel of meat (13)!

2. *Paul's Example.*—He is as much an Apostle as the Twelve (ix, 1), and he is unquestionably the Apostle of the Corinthians (2); he could therefore live at the expense of the faithful (3-4) and have himself cared for by a Christian woman like the other Apostles (5-6). Every labourer lives at the expense of his employer (7), and the Mosaic Law forbids the muzzling of the ox that treadeth out the corn (8-11). Paul renounces his rights in order not to hinder his preaching (12). He knows that under the old Law, as under the Gospel, the ministrant at the altar lives from the altar (13-14). But his glory, which is more to him than life, is to preach the Gospel without charge (15-18). Therefore he makes himself

all things to all men, in order to win them to Christ (19-23). Like the competitors in the stadium, supported by the hope of winning the crown, he embraces all kinds of self-denial, that he may not be deprived of the prize (24-27).

3. *Warning against idolatrous acts.*—The Hebrews providentially rescued from Egypt (x, 1-2), provided miraculously with food and drink (3-4), offended God and perished in the desert (5). This teaches us to fear concupiscence (6), to flee the idolatry of which they were guilty (7-8), not to tempt Christ, and not to murmur as they did (9-10). All this happened to them figuratively and was recorded for our instruction (11). Let everyone take heed (12) and rely on the help of God (13).

4. *Practical solution of the cases mentioned.*—Every act of idolatry is forbidden (14). Judge ye yourselves (15). Is not the Eucharist the communion of the body and the blood of the Lord (16-17)? Are not the Jewish priests, in making sacrifices, partakers of the altar (18)? Thus, to participate at an idolatrous banquet is to sit at the table of devils and to hold communion with the idol (19-22). As for the rest, it is needful to consider the question of edification (23-24). All that is sold in the market may be bought without hesitation, and the invitations of unbelievers accepted without scruples (25-27). But if any food is pointed out as having been sacrificed to idols, it is proper to abstain from it in order not to scandalize those present (28-30). Seek in everything the glory of God and the spiritual welfare of your neighbour (31-33); such is the lesson which the example of Paul and of Christ teaches us (xi, 1).

THIRD QUESTION

The Veiling of Women (xi, 3-16)

1. *Mystical reason.*—The subordinate relation which exists between man and woman should be made a reality in religious assemblies; the man will show his authority by praying with uncovered head; the wife will show her submission by praying with her head covered (3-5). The woman was derived from the man and created for the man (7-9); in presence of the angels also she should wear the sign of this dependency (10), which is not, however, without compensation, since the man needs the woman and is born of woman (11-12).

2. *Natural propriety.*—Long hair, a kind of natural veil, is an indication of the desire of nature that a woman should remain veiled (13-15).

3. *Custom of the Churches.*—Such is, moreover, the custom everywhere. This argument cannot be answered (16).

FOURTH QUESTION

The Agape and the Eucharist (xi, 17-34)

1. *The Agape.*—The Apostle has been informed of various abuses (xi, 17). Separate groups and *schisms* are formed in the church (18-19); there are distinct individual repasts, with a lack of decorum and a shocking irregularity which make this ceremony resemble an unholy feast deserving severe reproof (20-22).

2. *The Eucharist.* — Remember the institution of the Eucharist, which I have delivered unto you, as I myself received it from the Lord (23). Jesus blesses and distributes the consecrated bread and chalice, and bids the repetition of this act as a memorial of his death (24-26). To eat this bread or to drink this chalice without the proper dispositions is to make oneself guilty of the body and blood of the Lord (27). Self-examination, therefore, is required in order not to eat and drink unto condemnation (28-29). The frequent deaths and illnesses among the Christians of Corinth are God's warnings, which they should take to heart if they would escape condemnation (30-32).

3. *Practical decision.*—Wait for one another, and go not to church to satisfy your hunger. The other points shall be set in order on my return (33-34).

FIFTH QUESTION

The Charismata (xii-xiv)

I—*General Notions* (xii).

1. *Criteria for Charismata.*—Whoever says, *Anathema to Jesus* is moved by an evil spirit; whoever says, *Jesus is the Lord* is moved by the Holy Ghost (xii, 1-2).

2. *Origin of the Charismata.*—However different they may be, the *charismata* come from God only (4-6).

3. *Purpose of the Charismata.*—The Holy Spirit distributes them as he will and to whom he will for the common good (7-11).

4. *Variety of the Charismata.*—This is necessary to the organization of the Church, the mystical body of Christ, just as the variety of the members is necessary to the human organism (12-20). All, even the humblest, have their functions and their utility, as all the members, even the least honourable, contribute to the functional activity of the body and to the welfare of the other members (21-27). This is why

God has placed in the mystical body first apostles, secondly prophets, thirdly doctors, then other graces of a lower order which complete and embellish it (27-30).

II—*Charity is Worth More than Charismata* (xiii).

1. The *great rule* is to desire the best—that is, the most profitable—of the *charismata;* but there is something more excellent than all this: this is charity (xii, 31), for without it the most wonderful gift of tongues is only a vain noise (xiii, 1), the sublimest prophecy and a faith capable of moving mountains are nothing (2), and the most heroic acts have no value (3).

2. Enumeration of *fifteen virtues* that accompany charity (4-7).

3. *Another privilege of charity* is that it endureth always, never faileth (8), while on the contrary the gift of prophecy shall be lost in the fulness of the beatific vision; the gift of tongues is incompatible with the perfection of heavenly happiness; and the gift of knowledge, dim and partial, will be eclipsed in the light of glory (9-12). Still more, of the three *permanent* virtues, contrasted with the transient *charismata,* charity is the greatest (13).

III—*Prophecy and Glossolalia* (xiv).

In comparison with the gift of tongues, prophecy is superior (xiv, 1).

1. The possessor of the gift of tongues (*glossolalos*) speaks only to God, for no one understands him; but the prophet speaks to men words of edification, consolation, and exhortation; he edifies the whole Church, while the possessor of the gift of tongues edifies only himself (2-6).

2. The words of the latter resemble the sounds of an instrument playing an unknown tune or a discourse in a foreign language (7-11). It is essential to strive unto the good of the Church (12-15); now, the gift of tongues without the gift of interpretation is of little use, for it is not understood (16-19).

3. God threatened to speak to his people, as a punishment, in an unknown tongue (20-22).

4. An unbeliever, entering the Church, would ridicule the *glossolalos,* while on the contrary the exhortation of the prophet would touch his heart (23-25). These are so many reasons for preferring the gift of prophecy.

IV—*Practical Instructions about the use of Charismata.*

1. In public meetings, avoid confusion and give heed to edification (26). Let two or three speakers in tongues at most speak one after the other, and let there be someone to interpret what is said. If there be no interpreter, let them keep silence and speak only to God (27-28).

2. Likewise with the prophets : only two or three are to speak in the same meeting, and the others will listen and judge (29-33).

3. Let the women keep silence in the churches (34-37).

4. Esteem spiritual gifts, but let all things be done according to order (38-40).

SIXTH QUESTION

THE RESURRECTION OF THE DEAD (xv)

I—*The Fact of Christ's Resurrection.*

The death of Christ for our sins, his burial, and his resurrection on the third day, all in conformity with the prophecies : such is the immovable foundation of our faith and one of the fundamental articles of Paul's Gospel (xv, 1-4). This fact is attested by numerous eyewitnesses : Peter, the Twelve, more than five hundred brethren, of whom the most are still living, Paul himself, the least and last of the Apostles (5-8). The remembrance of his miraculous conversion calls forth an outburst of humble gratitude (9-11).

II—*The Reason for the Resurrection.*

The resurrection of Christ is indissolubly linked with ours ; he would not have risen if we were not also to rise, or, rather, we are bound to rise if he has risen (12-13). Now, if Christ be not risen, the testimony of the Apostles is false, the faith of the converts is vain ; the just, dead in Christ, are lost ; the faithful who are living are of all men most miserable (14-19) ; absurd suppositions.—Death is the result of the act of one man, Adam ; the resurrection will be the act of one man, the new Adam ; therefore Christ is called the *firstfruits of the dead ;* he comes first, but the others necessarily follow him, as the harvest follows the firstfruits (20-24).—Christ must triumph over all his enemies, according to the prophets ; he will therefore also triumph over death—which will take place in the resurrection of the just—and then he will be able to inaugurate his eternal kingdom, under the orders of the

Father (24-28).—The hope of the resurrection is so firmly
implanted in the Christian consciousness that it manifests
itself by some believers having themselves baptized for the
dead (29), and especially by the courage with which the
Apostles confront all dangers (30-32).—A vehement attack
upon sceptics (33-34).

III—*The Manner of the Resurrection.*

The comparison of the seed : the grain dies to live again ;
it lives again only on condition that it dies ; and God gives it
a new body, according to its species (35-38).—Animate and
inanimate beings are more or less perfect, the stars are more
or less brilliant ; it will be the same at the resurrection of the
dead (39-42). The bodies of the elect will have the attributes
of incorruption, glory, power, and spirituality (43-44). I say
spirituality, for as we at birth receive the image of the
terrestrial man, so we shall receive at our resurrection the
image of the heavenly man (45-49). Nothing weak or corruptible can enter into the kingdom of heaven (50). — A
previous transformation is necessary for this. Therefore
listen to this mystery : at the sound of the last trump the
dead shall rise incorruptible, and we (the living) shall be
transformed (53). Then the sting of death shall be broken,
as the prophets declare (54-56).—Doxology and exhortation
(57-58).

The *conclusion* contains, together with instructions about
the collection (xvi, 1-4), items of personal news about Paul
(5-9), a pressing recommendation of Timothy (10-11), some
details concerning Apollos (12) and the three envoys from the
Corinthians (15-18), and finally the usual salutations and
good wishes (19-24).

III—SECOND EPISTLE TO THE CORINTHIANS

The unity of the Epistle is seen in the plan pursued by the
Apostle—to prepare for his arrival in Corinth by removing
the difficulties which prevent his immediate return. These
obstacles are of three kinds—*the doubtful feelings* of the
Corinthians towards him, *the affair of the collection,* still in
suspense, *the actions of his enemies.* Paul declares on
several occasions that he will not return to Corinth before all
these difficulties have been settled. If his spiritual children
had not full confidence in him, his return would be darkened
by sadness, and he wishes to avoid such sorrow (ii, 2-3) ; if

the collection were not completed, he would have to blush before his companions (ix, 4-5); finally, if the Corinthians did not themselves punish the guilty, he would be obliged to deal severely with them (xiii, 10).

It is evident that the first part is, above all, *apologetic,* the second *persuasive,* and the third *polemical.* Numerous words of reminder, scattered here and there, tighten the bond which rather loosely unites these three parts.

In the *superscription* Paul associates Timothy with himself and addresses all the faithful in Achaia at the same time as the Corinthians.

The introduction, in the form of a thanksgiving, is one of Paul's most beautiful passages. He blesses God for consoling him in his tribulations in order to teach him how to console others in their trials. Between him and the believers reigns a perfect communion of joys and sorrows. This motive permits him to remind them of the superhuman struggles which he had endured at Ephesus and delicately to attribute his victory to the prayers of the converts (i, 3-11).

PART I

APOLOGETIC

Paul Explains and Justifies his Conduct (i-vii)

He was accused of *inconstancy* in his conduct, of a *lack of sincerity* in his preaching, and of *despotism* in his government. These three grievances become somewhat involved in the apologia of the Apostle, as they were in the mouths of his enemies, and it is not always possible to separate them. Paul opposes to them first, in general, the testimony of his own conscience (i, 12-13) and the inward conviction of the Corinthians themselves (14).

1. *Inconstancy.*—He had at first determined to go directly from Ephesus to Corinth (15) and to return to this latter city after a rapid visit to Macedonia (16). He had to change his plan, but he did not do so thoughtlessly (7-18). His *yes* has always been *yes,* like the *yes* of the Son of God himself (19-21). If he postponed his voyage, it was in order to spare them (22-23). He did not wish his return to be for them and for himself an occasion of sadness (ii, 1-2); and the severe letter which he sent them had for its aim precisely to smooth difficulties away (3-4). He comes back, on this occasion, to the affair of the man guilty of incest, the cause of their disagreements. The guilty man has been reprimanded by the majority in the Church (5-6). That is enough; Paul forgives him and begs that he may be forgiven (7-8).

He intended, in writing to them, to put their obedience to the test (9), but he did not wish to show excessive severity which might be doing a service to Satan (10-11). His anxiety to know what the Corinthians would do deprived him of all rest (12-13). Finally Titus has reassured him, and he thanks God for it (14).

2. *Lack of sincerity.*—The passage ii, 15-17 serves as a transition to what follows : " We are not like many others who adulterate the word of God : we speak to you in perfect sincerity, as from God and before God, in Christ." After having apologized for appearing to commend himself, when he has no need of any letter of commendation other than the Church of Corinth itself (iii, 1-3), he explains the reasons for his confident uprightness, of which God alone is the author (4-6). The ministry of the Apostles, compared with that of Moses, is so glorious that it naturally inspires confidence and frankness (7-12). So the Apostles do not veil their faces when they speak to the people, as Moses did, whose veil will rest upon the eyes and hearts of those who read him until the day of their final conversion (13-16). The Spirit of God is a spirit of liberty (17), and all Christian believers, contemplating the glory of God face to face, are transformed into his divine image (18). The Apostles themselves, imbued with the dignity of their mission, repudiate all pretence and subterfuge (iv, 1-2). Only the unbelievers willingly find their preaching doubtful (3-6).

Far from making them cowardly, the realization of their weakness increases their confidence in God (7). Perils of death ; nay, death itself ; nothing, in fact, disheartens or discourages them (8-15). If their bodies perish, their inner man is renewed day by day (16), and the prospect of eternal blessings sustains and animates them. They know that, when they shall emerge from this perishable tabernacle, an imperishable habitation awaits them (v, 1). No doubt they would be glad to be clothed upon with glory without being deprived of their mortality, a thing which is possible only if the day of the Lord shall find them alive (2-5) ; but they are resigned, happy to depart from the body to be with Christ (6-8). They try in every state to please God, knowing that we must all appear before his judgement-seat (9-10). This is a new reason for sincerity (11).

3. *Arrogance and despotism.*—The Apostle approaches this delicate subject with new rhetorical precautions (v, 12). He justifies his apostolic liberty, which is travestied by his enemies, with two reasons. The charity of Christ constrains him, and he does not wish to know anyone according to the flesh (14-18). He has received the commission to reconcile men to God, and he must fulfil this duty (v, 19–vi, 2). He traces here the ideal of the apostolic workman

(vi, 3-10), and, in order to unite example with theory, he addresses to the Corinthians one of those impassioned exhortations which have brought disagreements between them and him (vi, 11–vii, 1). He then protests again that he has not been excessively severe (vii, 2-3), and concludes by relating what has happened between his departure from Ephesus and the arrival of Titus, who brought him such consoling news from Corinth (4-16).

PART II

HORTATORY

Aim : to organize the Collection (viii-ix)

First Motive: Emulation.—The Macedonians, in spite of their extreme poverty, had distinguished themselves by their generosity (viii, 1-2); they had given voluntarily as much as they could (3-4). This spectacle moves the Apostle to complete the collection already begun in Corinth (5-6); the Corinthians, who excel in everything, cannot remain behindhand on only this one point (7). The Apostle does not force them; he only wishes to stimulate their charity by comparing it with that of others (8). He reminds them that Jesus Christ made himself poor in order to make us rich (9). His advice is, moreover, justified by the well-known zeal of the Corinthians (10-12). It is not a question of making themselves destitute in order to enrich others (13), but of establishing among Christians that sort of equality which reigned between the Jews who collected the manna (14-15). Paul guarantees and recommends his three messengers (16-24).

Second and Third Motive: Self-Esteem and Interest.— These two motives, touched on casually in chapter eight, are developed in chapter nine. The last chapter would seem to have been added later, or written after an interruption.—Paul everywhere praises the zeal and generosity of the Corinthians (ix, 1-2). If they were not ready in time, what a shame it would be for him and for them (3-5) !—The interest to which he appeals is a *supernatural interest.* The heavenly harvest is proportioned to the seed sown, and especially to the quality of the seed (6-7). God is generous towards us in proportion as we are generous towards him (8-11). The giving of alms causes thanksgiving to rise to heaven, and this returns in blessings upon the donor (12-15).

PART III

POLEMICAL

Aim : to overthrow his Enemies (x-xiii)

1. *Threats to agitators.*—Paul conjures his enemies not
to compel him on his return to exert the energy of which
he gives proof when he is absent from them (x, 1-2). His
person is weak, but his weapons are those of God himself
(3-4), from whom he has received power to humble the proud
and to punish the rebellious (5-6). He yields to his adversaries in nothing and does not fear to boast of that power
which God has given him, not to destroy, but to edify (7-8).
His Epistles, it is said, are strong and terrible, but his person
does not correspond with them (9-10); now, when confronting
his opponents, he will be as he is in his letters (11). There
are some who, measuring themselves by themselves,
erroneously believe themselves to be something (12); he
measures himself by the authority which God has conferred
upon him (13), and which he has gained for himself by
evangelizing Corinth (14). He does not make a pedestal of
the labours of others (15) and does not usurp the merit of
others (16). Thus he puts into practice the adage : " He that
glorieth, let him glory in the Lord " (17-18).

2. *Reproaches for the Corinthians who listen to them.*—
Paul feels a holy jealousy for the Church of Corinth (xi, 1);
he would like to preserve it for Christ as a chaste virgin (2);
he fears for it the seduction of which Eve was a victim (3),
a seduction which is inexcusable, for the agitators do not
preach to them another Christ, nor confer upon them another
Spirit, nor preach to them another Gospel (4). Paul, in spite
of his rude speech, is not inferior to any of the great Apostles
in works and in knowledge (5-6). He is blamed for his
modesty and for his disinterestedness (7); in fact, he has
taken wages from other churches in order not to be a burden
to them (the Corinthians) (8-9); he glories in it, but he is
calumniated for it by those who see in it a want of affection
(10-11). He wished to deprive his enemies of the means of
resembling him in this respect (12); for these false apostles,
these deceitful workmen, wish to transform themselves into
apostles of Christ (13), as Satan transforms himself into
an angel of light (14); but they shall have an end worthy of
their conduct (15).

3. *Paul yields in nothing to any man.*—The Apostle
apologizes for speaking so much in favour of himself and
for appearing in this respect to imitate his detractors (xi, 16-
18). The Corinthians, who suffer them so patiently, will
know how to suffer him (19-20). Moreover, he fears no com-

parison (21). He is a Hebrew, an Israelite, a child of Abraham, a minister of Christ, as much as or more than they are (22-23).—(a) *What Paul suffered for Christ:* Five times flogged (24), three times beaten with rods, once stoned, thrice shipwrecked (25), innumerable labours, and perils of every kind (26-27), and solicitude for all the churches (28-29). But Paul wishes to glory only in his weakness (30). He calls God to witness (31), and then in conclusion he recalls his escape from Damascus (32-33).—(b) *What Jesus Christ has done for Paul:* Visions and revelations of the Lord (xii, 1), transportation to the third heaven (2-3), communication of unspeakable mysteries (4); this is still another subject for self-glorification, if he wished to glory in anything but his infirmities (5-6). As an antidote to these favours, God has given him a buffet from Satan (7), and refused to free him from it in spite of his prayers (8); Paul rejoices in the thought of making the power of God triumph through his weakness (9-10).

4. *Paul, on his return to Corinth, will act with energy.*— His title of Apostle gives him the right to speak thus (11-12). The Corinthians can reproach him with only one thing: his own disinterestedness and that of his messengers; but this reserve in regard to them has not been caused by lack of affection (13-19). He fears that, on his arrival, he will not find them such as he would desire to have them (20-21); for he is resolved this time to treat the guilty without indulgence (xiii, 1-4). Let them, therefore, try themselves and prove themselves seriously (5-9). If he writes this to them, it is to spare them severity (10).

A very brief *conclusion* contains the usual counsels, salutations, good wishes, and blessings (11-13).

IV—EPISTLE TO THE GALATIANS

The *central idea* of this Epistle is contained in this formula (v, 1): *Christ has given you liberty; stand firm, therefore, and do not fall back under the yoke of servitude.* The fact of Christian liberty is at first established by history (i-ii), then demonstrated by the nature of the Gospel system (iii-iv), and finally studied in its consequences (v-vi).

The *superscription,* longer than usual, includes two considerations in harmony with the object of the letter (i, 1-5).

The *introduction* in the form of a thanksgiving, and the eulogy of the recipients, being omitted, the Epistle begins *ex abrupto.*

PART I

CHRISTIAN LIBERTY ESTABLISHED BY HISTORY (i-ii)

1. *By Paul's constant and authorized preaching.*—The Apostle is astonished that the Galatians forget his Gospel so quickly (i, 6-7) and pronounces an anathema against whoever should teach any other Gospel (8-9). He gives them to understand that he is calumniated by anyone who pretends that he had formerly more condescension in his preaching (10-11). His Gospel does not accommodate itself to the desires of men, for it comes from God (11-12). In fact, Paul, a bitter persecutor (13) and a fanatical Pharisee (14), was one day suddenly enlightened by the Son of God and received the mandate to preach him to the Gentiles (15-16). Instead of going to Jerusalem to receive instruction from his predecessors, he retired into Arabia (17). After three years he came to see Peter, but abode with him only fifteen days (18-20). He lived then without any connection with the Christians of Judæa (21-22), who learned only by hearsay of his conversion and his apostolate (23-24).

2. *By the sanction which the chief Apostles gave to Paul's Gospel.*—Paul explained to them in private the Gospel which he preaches to the Gentiles, the first article of which is exemption from the Mosaic Law (ii, 1-2). They approved it and did not oblige him to circumcise Titus (3-5). Much more, the pillars of the Church, James, Peter, and John, expressly recognized his mission, gave him the right hand of fellowship, and shared with him the field of the apostolate, recommending to him only the care of the poor in Jerusalem (6-10).

3. *By the conflict at Antioch.*—As Peter, through fear of the Judaizers, withdrew from the Gentile converts who observed not the Law. Paul reproved him publicly (11-14) and explained to him before everyone the reasons which militate in favour of Christian liberty, and which were accepted by the chief of the Apostles (15-21).

PART II

CHRISTIAN LIBERTY DEMONSTRATED BY JUSTIFICATION
(iii-iv)

This part becomes rather obscure because it conceals a latent course of reasoning which can be presented thus : " The Christian is free as regards the Law, if the Law is neither the cause nor the essential condition nor the complement of justification." This conditional proposition is evident to the Apostle, who is satisfied with proving the truth of the condition, namely, that the Mosaic Law plays no part in the justification of the Christian.

1. *Proof from experience* (iii, 1-6).—If the image of the Crucified displayed to the Galatians is not sufficient to dispel their error (1), a simple question will open their eyes : Whence comes the Holy Spirit which they received at baptism? From faith or from the Law? From faith, no doubt, since they had never observed the Law (2). Now, having begun in the Spirit, they would like to finish in the flesh (3-4) ! And now also, whence come the miraculous manifestations of the Holy Spirit? Always from faith; the Law has nothing to do with them (5).

2. *Scriptural Proof.*—Abraham, according to Scripture, was justified by faith (6), and it is also by faith that we become the children of Abraham (7). In fact, all the nations are to be blessed in him (8); now they cannot obtain these blessings by means of the Law, because it is a source of curses (9-10). Christ, taking on himself the curse of the Law, has redeemed us from it (11-13), in order that by faith we may share in the blessings of which the faithful Abraham is the depositary (14).

3. *Theological Proof derived from the nature of the Promise and of the Law.*—(A) The blessings promised to Abraham and his posterity are a gratuitous and unconditional benefit, a testament with no restrictive clauses and confirmed by an oath (15-16); the Law is a bilateral contract, requiring the intervention of a mediator, burdensome for both parties; moreover, it does not confer justice, but on the contrary increases transgressions, as facts prove (19-22). It is therefore impossible that it should supervene, as something *perpetual,* 430 years after the gratuitous promise of God, and that the inheritance promised to the posterity of Abraham should be affected by it, for this would be plainly to annul the divine promise (17-18).

(B) The same conclusion is forced upon us if we consider what the Law is in the sight of God.—(*a*) The Law is the schoolmaster who leads us to Christ (23-24); it has finished its rôle and must disappear when the pupil attains maturity, when he receives the results of true sonship. This is what took place at baptism (25-29).—(*b*) The Law is the childhood of humanity. The child of tender age is treated as a servant and is subjected to subordinates, but when the time appointed by his father comes he is free and master of his acts (iv, 1-2). So, too, in the fulness of time, on the arrival of Christ, the Jews are emancipated and the Gentiles receive the adoption of sons (3-5). The proof of this is in the name of Father, which the Holy Spirit puts upon their lips (6-7). How, then, can the Galatians, who have been enlightened through the Gospel, think of retrograding to that inferior state, which in its imperfection resembles that from which the Gospel

has freed them (8-11)?—Here Paul opens his heart and recalls
the touching care the Galatians had for him in former times
(12-15). Can he have become odious to them because he has
told them the truth (16)? Let them beware of flatterers
(17-18). For his part, he bears them always in his heart and
would gladly speak to them words of tenderness, like a
mother to her nursling (19-20).

4. *Scriptural illustration from the history of the son of
Abraham.*—Ishmael, son of the bondwoman, was a son
according to the flesh; Isaac, the son of a freewoman, was a
son according to the promise (21-23). It is the allegory of
the two Testaments (24). One, represented by Hagar, gives
birth only to slaves (25); the other, typified by Sara, produces only freemen (26-28). The Synagogue persecutes the
Church, as Ishmael persecuted Isaac (29); but God orders the
bondwoman to be cast out, for she shall have no part in the
inheritance (30-31).

PART III

CONSEQUENCES OF CHRISTIAN LIBERTY (v-vi)

1. *Direct corollary.*—The first duty of the Christian is to
stand fast in this liberty which Christ has won for him (v, 1).
Whosoever has himself circumcised binds himself to observe
the Law in its entirety, and loses the advantages of faith; he
falls from grace (2-4). Justice depends only on faith
informed by charity; circumcision availeth nothing (5-6).
Paul warns the Galatians against seducers (7-10), defends
himself from a calumny brought against him (11), and ends
with an imprecation upon the Judaizers (12).—However,
Christian liberty is not licence; it presupposes charity, which
is the epitome of the Law (13-15). It requires a struggle of
the spirit against the flesh and the ultimate victory of the
spirit (16-18). Paul enumerates on this occasion the *works* of
the flesh (19-21) and the *fruits* of the Spirit (22-23). Whoever belongs to Christ crucifies his flesh (24); whoever lives
in the Spirit follows the impulses of the Spirit (25).

2. *Various Counsels.*—Mutual consideration and support
(vi, 1-2). Avoidance of vainglory (3-4). Deference on the
part of the catechumen towards the catechist (6). Sowing
seed for eternal life (7-9). Doing good to all men, especially
to those of the faith (10).

Conclusion, written by Paul with his own hand (11). New
warning against seducers, who preach circumcision not from
motives of zeal, but from those of self-love and self-interest
(12-13). The Apostle, for his part, will glory only in the cross
of Christ, with whom he is crucified and whose marks he
bears (14-17).—Final greeting (18).

V—EPISTLE TO THE EPHESIANS

The *aim* is to explain the supreme *Mystery,* or secret design conceived by God from all eternity and realized in the Gospel, to save all men without distinction by uniting them with Christ by a bond so intimate that they form in him and with him only one *mystical body.* In other words, the conjugal union of Christ with his Church, a union sung by the prophets and of which the Song of Songs is the magnificent epithalamium. One and the same flow of ideas permeates the whole Epistle. The watchwords are : *Mystery* (i, 9 ; iii, 3, 49 ; v, 32 ; vi, 19), *Church* (i, 22 ; iii, 10, 21 ; v, 23, 32), *Body* (i, 23 ; ii, 16 ; iv, 2, 12, 16 ; v, 23, 28, 30), *Head* (i, 22 ; iv, 15 ; v, 23), the verbs compounded with σύν marking the mystical identity of Christians among themselves and with Christ, and the formula *In Christo Jesu.*

The *superscription* can be taken as typical, if the words ἐν Ἐφέσῳ are authentic.—The *introduction,* in the form of a thanksgiving, forms part of the body of the Epistle.

PART I

The Mystery of Incorporation with Christ (i-iii)

1. *The Mystery conceived by God from all eternity* (i, 3-14).—The Father has blessed us in Christ (3), chosen in him before the foundation of the world (4), and predestined by adoptive Sonship (5), by reason of his goodwill and in view of his own glory (6), but not without the intervention of his Son (7). The mystery which God has revealed to us (8-9) is his intention to re-establish all things in Christ in the fulness of times (10). Consequently (11) the Jews believe first (12) ; then the Gentiles, called in their turn (13), receive the same gifts of the Holy Spirit (14).

2. *The Mystery realized in the Church* (i, 15—ii, 22).—The Apostle prays God incessantly (i, 15-16) to give to the faithful the spirit of wisdom and revelation (17-18), that they may comprehend what they owe to Christ, who is exalted infinitely above all creatures (19-21) and is the incomparable head of the Church which is his complement (22-23). The Gentiles, formerly dead in their sins (ii, 1-3) have been made alive in Christ by a marvellous effect of grace and divine mercy (4-9), and have been called to serve God by the exercise of virtue (10). They are no longer *uncircumcised* (11) ; they are no more without Christ, without God, and without hope (12-13). Jesus has broken down the barrier which separated Jews from Gentiles, and has united the two peoples in one body (14-16). No more hatred and rivalry between them, but, on the

contrary, perfect equality (17-18). The Gentiles, like the others, belong to the city, the house of God (19), built on the foundation of the Apostles (20), living stones of the temple of the Holy Spirit (21-22).

3. *Revelation of the Mystery* (iii).—Paul redoubles his supplications (iii, 1 and 14-15) that God may strengthen *the inner man* of the converts (16-17) and make them appreciate the grandeur and the profundity of this Mystery and the incomprehensible love of Christ (18-19).—Here is inserted a long digression (iii, 2-13), in which Paul claims a special knowledge of the Mystery (2-4) now revealed to the Apostles and prophets (5) : namely, that the Gentiles are fellow-heirs, members of the same body, sharing in the same promises (6). Paul, in spite of his unworthiness, has received a mandate to preach this Mystery (7-9), that the higher powers may learn through the Church the marvels of divine wisdom (10-13).—*Doxology* (20-21).

PART II

CHRISTIAN MORALS (iv-vi)

I—*General Principles.*

1. *Positive Principle:* To lead a life *worthy of their vocation* (iv, 1); in particular, to " keep the unity of the Spirit in the bond of peace " (2-3), conformably to the *seven* elements of union which the profession of Christianity includes (4-6). The *charismata,* due to the liberality of Christ (7), who has descended to earth and ascended to heaven that he might fill all things (8-11), far from injuring the union, are designed for the edification of the mystical body (12) and have for their aim to instil in all the faithful the vigour of Christ and to make them increase unto the measure of their Head (13-16).

2. *Negative Principle:* Not to imitate the pagans (iv, 17), who are given over to impure passions (18-19), but to put off the old man (20-22) in order to put on the new man (23-24). Therefore, no more lies (25), no more anger (26-27), no more stealing (28), no more evil speech (29) : all things which grieve the Spirit of holiness (30). Imitate the gentleness of God (iv, 31-v, 1); imitate Christ (2). Let Christians flee with horror the vices of the flesh (3-5); they are no longer children of darkness, but children of the light (6-12); let them be watchful, therefore, in temperance and the giving of thanks (13-20).

II—*Special Applications.*

1. *Duties of various social positions.* — (a) *Duties of women:* To be subject to their husbands, as the Church is subject to Christ (22-24).—(b) *Duties of husbands:* To love

their wives, as Christ loves the Church; for marriage is symbolical of the union of the Church and Christ (25-33).— (c) *Duties of children:* Obedience (vi, 1-3).—(d) *Duties of fathers:* Tenderness and devotion (4).—(e) *Duties of servants:* Supernatural submission (5-8).—(f) *Duties of masters:* Gentleness inspired by the fear of God (9).

2. *Panoply of Virtues.*—In order to struggle against the world and the powers of darkness (10-13), the Christian must put on the *girdle* of truth, the *breastplate* of justice (14), the *sandals* of promptitude (15), the *shield* of faith (16), the *helmet* of salvation (17), and the *sword* of the spirit (18), Let him add to these vigilance and prayer (19-20).

Conclusion: Personal news (21-22) and greetings (23-24).

VI—EPISTLE TO THE PHILIPPIANS

Deeply touched by the continued affection of the Philippians, who had sent him a generous contribution, and by the filial devotion of one of them, Epaphroditus, the Apostle writes them a letter of thanks. Joy is the feeling with which he is overflowing and which he wishes also to inspire. This fragile bond unites the different parts of the Epistle, in which it is not necessary to seek for any other plan.

The *superscription* is addressed to the clergy and the faithful.—The *introduction,* in the form of a thanksgiving, forms part of the body of the Epistle.

1. *Various reasons for joy.*—The first is *his recollection of the Philippians,* who have never failed to lend him assistance (i, 3-6). He cherishes them all in his heart, and everything is shared between them (7-8). He wishes fervently that God may complete his work of mercy in them (9-11).—A second reason for joy is the *favourable turn* that affairs are taking. The Gospel is gaining converts even in the Pretorium (12-14). If the feelings of the preachers of the faith are not always pure, what matters it, provided that Christ be preached (15-18)? Paul desires only to glorify Christ, whether by his life or by his death (19-21); death seems to him the more desirable because it would unite him with the object of his love; but he accepts life with courage and resignation, that he may continue to work (22-24). He knows that he will see his beloved converts again (24-26). May he be able to perceive that they are doing honour to the Gospel and that they bravely stand by him in his persecutions (27-30)!

2. *He begs them to fulfil his joy.*—This will be done by charity, abnegation, and mutual devotion (ii, 1-4), of which

Jesus Christ offers them such a perfect example, who, being God (5-6), stripped himself by becoming man (7-8), and, by his voluntary humiliation, deserved his incomparable exaltation (9-11). Let them, therefore, co-operate with grace (12-13) and, by the practice of all the virtues, put the seal upon their common joy (14-18).

3. *He wishes himself to contribute to this.*—It is for this that he has determined to send them Timothy, of whom he makes a magnificent eulogy (19-23). Even more, he hopes to come to them himself (24). Meanwhile he sends Epaphroditus back to them, whose recovery and devotion to his person he relates, commending him warmly to the faithful (25-30).

4. *Attack on the Judaizers.*—In vain do they make for themselves a merit out of circumcision (iii, 2-3). From the point of view of material advantages, Paul would have no cause to envy them (4-6), even if he did not despise all that for the sake of Jesus Christ (7-8); he esteems only the justice that comes from faith (9-10) and the happiness of being like his Master in everything (11-12). Not that he flatters himself that he has attained perfection, but, with his gaze fixed upon the mark, like the runners in the stadium, he presses towards it with all his might (13-16). He can, therefore, without pride offer himself as an example (17) and warn the converts against the enemies of the cross (18-19). The life of the Christian is in heaven, the end of his hope (20-21).

5. *Recommendations.*—The Apostle urges the faithful to concord (iv, 1-3), to spiritual joy (4-5), to confidence (6), to peace (7), and to the practice of the principles of morality which he has taught them (8-9). He recalls his former relations with the Philippians, who have just sent him renewed assistance (10-16); he thanks them delicately—less, however, for the gift itself than for its proof of their affection (17-18). —Doxology (19-20), salutations (21-22), and greetings (23).

VII—EPISTLE TO THE COLOSSIANS

While the Epistle to the Ephesians explained the *Mystery of Christ,* this one chiefly describes the *Pleroma of Christ*—his incomparable dignity.

The *superscription* and the *introduction* are the same.

PART I

SUPREME DIGNITY OF CHRIST (i-ii)

1. *The Pleroma of Christ* (i, 3-23).—After a thanksgiving, with which he mingles a delicate eulogy of the Colossians (i, 3-8), Paul wishes them an ever-clearer perception of the truth of the Gospel, together with a conduct corresponding to such knowledge (9-11), in order duly to honour the Son of God, who has called them to his kingdom (12-14).—This Son is, *in his divine life,* the image of the Invisible, the first-born of all creatures, the exemplary and efficient cause of *all* creatures (15-16).—*As man* he is head of the Church and the first-born from the dead (18); he possesses *fulness* (19). By his blood he reconciles all things (20); he reconciles the Gentiles to God (21) and destines them to holiness (22), provided they persevere in the faith (23).

2. *Paul is specially charged to proclaim this Mystery* (i, 24–ii, 3).—He fills up the sufferings of Christ (24) by having preached the mystery of the incorporation of the Gentiles into the mystical body (25-27). He will not fail to fulfil his mandate (28-29). May the Colossians enter more and more into the depth of this mystery (ii, 1-3) !

3. *Avoid errors which are against the dignity of Christ* (ii, 4-23).—Present in spirit with the converts (4-5), Paul admonishes them to be anchored in the faith (6-7) and to be on their guard against a pretended philosophy, a human invention disavowed by Christ (8). In him dwelleth the *fulness of the Godhead* bodily (9), and we partake of his *fulness* (10); in him we receive the circumcision of the heart (11); in him we die and live mystically (12-13), delivered from sin, from the Law, and from hostile powers (13-15).—Therefore, no more legal observances (16-17), no more imaginary mediators who make us neglect Christ (18-19). Dead in Christ (20), let us renounce arbitrary devotions belonging to a spirituality which is without knowledge (21-23).

PART II

CHRISTIAN MORALITY (iii-iv)

1. *General Principle: To die with Christ in order to rise with Him.*—(A) The Christian who is dead and risen with Christ should be in accord with his mystical death and resurrection (iii, 1-4).—(B) He must complete this state of death and develop this divine life (*a*) by mortifying the passions (5-8), (*b*) by putting off the old man and putting on the new (9-11). —(C) To be clothed with Christ means to practise all the

virtues, especially charity (12-14). The immediate fruits are : Peace (15), gratitude (16), purity of intention (17).

2. *Application to the various conditions of Life.*—(a) Wives and husbands (18-19);—(b) Children and parents (20);—(c) Servants and masters (iii, 21–iv, 1).

3. *Divers Recommendations.*—Prayer, above all for Paul's intentions (iv, 2-4) ; circumspection (5-6).—Personal news (7-9).—Mutual salutations (10-17).—Final greeting (18).

VIII—FIRST EPISTLE TO THE THESSALONIANS

As a fatherly outpouring of gratitude, tenderness, and entire devotion, this Epistle has for its *aim* to console and reassure the converts. The determining *motive* is relegated to the end of the Epistle (iv, 13-18).—The *superscription* is briefer than usual.

PART I

Thanksgiving for the Past and for the Present
(i-iii)

I—*For the Past* (i, 2–ii, 12).

1. *First Theme: How converts make the Gospel bear fruit.*—The activity of their faith is praised, the firmness of their hope, the ardour of their charity (i, 4-5). Embracing the Gospel with joy in spite of persecutions (6), they have served as an example to the faithful in Macedonia and Achaia (7). Everyone praises their ardent faith (8), their sincere, enlightened, and enduring conversion (9-10).

2. *Second Theme: How Paul has behaved towards converts.*—Braving tribulations and opprobrium, he preached Christ to them boldly (ii, 1-2), without any secret design (3-4) of flattery, interest, or vainglory (5-6), without even claiming his rights (7). Like a mother who cherishes her children in her bosom, he could have wished to give them his life as well as the Gospel (8). He worked day and night lest he should be a burden to them (9), because he loved them like a father (11-12).

II—*For the Present* (ii, 13–iii, 13).

1. *First Theme: Perseverance of converts.*—The word of God continues to bear fruit in them (ii, 13); they imitate the Christians of Palestine (14), exposed to persecution

33

from the Jews (15), who thus fill up the measure of their crimes (16).

2. *Second Theme: Good news brought by Timothy.*—Paul has desired greatly to see his Thessalonians again (17-20). Not being able to leave Athens, he sent them his faithful fellow-labourer Timothy to confirm them in the faith (iii, 1-5); this messenger has just returned, bringing the most consoling news (6-8). How can he thank God enough for so much joy (9-10)! May he complete his work of salvation in them (11-13)!

PART II

INSTRUCTIONS FOR THE FUTURE (iv-v)

1. *General exhortation.*—To put into practice Paul's teachings (iv, 1-2). Above all, to avoid impurity and injustice (3-8). A recommendation to charity is superfluous (9-10); the Apostle confines himself to inculcating the love of good order and work (11-12).

2. *Instruction as to the dead.*—The Christian ought not to mourn excessively the death of his relatives (iv, 13), for Jesus will raise them again from the dead (14). At the last day the living shall not precede the dead (15); the dead shall rise *first,* at the first sound of the last trump (16); *then* shall the living go to meet Christ, to remain, all together, with him (17). Let this be their consolation (18).—As regards the time, the converts know all that it is necessary to know, that Christ will come as a thief in the night (v, 1-3). But they will not be surprised, for they are not in darkness and are on the watch (4-7). Let them therefore put on the armour of faith, charity, and hope (8-9), and let them console themselves with the thought that, whether living or dying, they are destined to live with Jesus Christ (10-11).

3. *Various recommendations.*—To love and revere their superiors (12-13); to aid the brethren (14); to do good to all (15); to persevere in joy and thanksgiving (16-18); to esteem the *charismata* highly (19-20); to be circumspect (21-22).— Wishes for their perfection (23-24), request for prayers (25), salutations and benediction (26-28).

IX—SECOND EPISTLE TO THE THESSALONIANS

Its manifest *aim* is to reassure the faithful as to the pretended nearness of the *parousia.*—The *superscription* has nothing special in it, and the *introduction* belongs to the body of the Epistle.

PART I

ESCHATOLOGICAL PICTURE (i)

The Apostle begins by thanking God for his converts' progress in faith and charity, and especially for their perseverance in the midst of persecution (i, 3-4). This thought suggests to him the idea of the justice of God, who owes it to himself to repair disorder (5). A just punishment awaits the persecutors (6); a not less just recompense is reserved for the persecuted (7), when Jesus, preceded by an avenging fire, comes to punish unbelievers (8), who will be banished for all eternity from the face of the Lord (9), while the saints will reign with him (10). May God complete his work of grace and mercy in the converts (11-12)!

PART II

INSTRUCTION AS TO THE PAROUSIA (ii)

The faithful are not to let themselves be troubled under any pretext whatever by the nearness of the *parousia* (ii, 1-2), for two anticipatory signs will precede it : the apostasy foretold in the Gospel and the appearance of the great adversary (3), who will wish to be taken for God (4). The Apostle has explained all this orally (5), and the Thessalonians know, therefore, the obstacle that impedes the coming of the Antichrist (6). No doubt the mystery of iniquity already worketh, but it is hindered by the *obstacle* (7). When this obstacle shall disappear, the *man of sin* will be revealed, to be soon overthrown by the triumphal return of Christ (8), after having wrought many signs and wonders (9), to seduce many (10) whose blindness God will permit in punishment for their iniquities (11-12).

PART III

VARIOUS RECOMMENDATIONS (iii)

The Apostle implores the converts' prayers for the Gospel to bear fruit and escape the snares of the wicked (iii, 1-2). On his side, he promises them the help of God and hopes that the Thessalonians will profit by it (3-6). He urges them to keep at a distance the idle and disobedient (6), who forget his teachings and his example of an orderly and laborious life (7-10). He earnestly recommends these wayward souls that they should work in silence (11-12). He orders the others to put these unruly brothers away from them, to bring them back to a better life, and to admonish them with charity (13-16).—Salutations and benediction (17-18).

X—FIRST EPISTLE TO TIMOTHY

Paul sends his disciple some rules and counsels, which follow one another in the order in which they occur to him. The mutual relation of these groups of ideas is not very apparent.

The *superscription* (i, 1-2) is quite unlike the usual kind. The *introduction* is *ex abrupto*.

1. *Combat false doctrines.*—Timothy will silence the restless men who teach frivolous and dangerous innovations (i, 3-5). Several foolishly boast of being teachers of the Law (6-7), and are ignorant of the fact that even if the Law is good, provided it be used lawfully (8), nevertheless it has not been made for the just man, but for the sinner (9-10). This is the Gospel of Paul (11), converted by a prodigy of mercy and a miracle of grace (12-16), the honour of which he attributes to God (17). Timothy, faithful to his vocation, will fight the good fight against the enemies of the faith (18-20).

2. *Organize public prayer* (ii).—God, who desires the salvation of all men (for Jesus Christ, the universal mediator, has given himself for the redemption of all), desires also that our prayers should include all men without exception (ii, 1-7). The Apostle describes the dispositions and attitude of men (8) and women (9-10) during prayer. The latter are not to teach in public (11-12), for woman is inferior to man (13-14), although in the accomplishment of her duties she has a great means of sanctification (15).

3. *Make a good choice of Sacred Ministers* (iii).—The ἐπίσκοποι must be the possessors of the virtues which their office requires, and exempt from defects which would injure their ministry (iii, 1-7). The deacons also (8-13). Paul insists upon the exemplary conduct of their wives (11) and on the necessity of first testing those charged with any sacred ministry (13). He fears that he cannot rejoin his disciple soon (14-15), and ends with a lyrical passage on the *mystery of godliness* (16).

4. *Resist the beginning of Innovations* (iv).—The Spirit foretells a sort of hypocritical dualism in the last days (iv, 1-5). Timothy must avoid it, unmask it, and fight it (6-11). In spite of his youth, he must be a finished model of all the virtues, in particular of pastoral solicitude (12-16).

5. *Widows and Elders.*—Treat everyone according to his

condition (v, 1-2). Honour true widows (3), who are distinguished for the good government of their families and for a life without reproach (4-8). Inscribe on the books of the Church only widows of sixty years old and upwards, who are of exemplary conduct (9-10). Young widows will do better to marry again, because they run too much risk of losing the faith and of creating scandal (11-15). Pious women are invited to take care of widows who are without resources, in order to relieve the Church of burdens (16).—Honour the *elders* and provide for their needs (17-18); do not lightly receive accusations against them, but reprove them if they are guilty (19-20); only lay hands upon any man with full knowledge (22).

6. *Various recommendations*—[here the sequence of his ideas seems to be wanting, and we may ask if the text has not been disturbed].—Counsels to Timothy (23).—Neither good nor evil is unnoticed (24-25).—Duties of servants and masters (vi, 1-2).—Attack upon innovators (3-5).—Eulogy of piety and disinterestedness (6-10).—Paul exhorts his disciple to continue to practise all the Christian virtues (11-12); he adjures him to be without reproach in the name of God and of Jesus Christ, who suffered under Pontius Pilate and whom the Father (may he be praised !) shall bring again in glory at the appointed time (13-16).—Warn the rich against making a bad use of their riches (17-19).—Keep safe the deposit *of the faith* (20-21).

XI—SECOND EPISTLE TO TIMOTHY

Paul, foreseeing his approaching end, writes a letter of instruction and encouragement to his favourite disciple.—The *superscription* differs a little from the usual form.—The *introduction,* in the form of a thanksgiving, with the eulogy of Timothy and of his mother and grandmother, leads on naturally to the main body of the Epistle (i, 3-5).

PART I

EXHORTATION TO COURAGE AND CONSTANCY
(i, 6–ii, 13)

1. *Special subjects.*—(a) The Apostle recalls to Timothy, naturally timid and distrustful, and fearful of the difficulties and responsibilities of his office, the *fervour of his episcopal ordination* (i, 6), the spirit of strength and of charity which

he then received (7). He must not, therefore, be ashamed of the Gospel nor of Paul, the prisoner of Christ (8), for it is the Gospel of salvation, of grace and light (9), of which Paul is proud to be the preacher (11-12). Timothy also will faithfully guard the treasure of the faith (13-14).

(b) Paul here recalls the Asians' ingratitude to him and the admirable devotion of Onesiphorus (15-18) : a fault to avoid, an example to follow.

2. *General subjects.*—(a) The Apostle, inviting Timothy to transmit his teaching to faithful men (ii, 1-2), urges him again to *fight* as a soldier of Christ, anxious only to please his Master (3-4), to *strive* as the athlete who aspires to victory (5), and to *labour* as the husbandman who prepares for an abundant harvest (6-7).

(b) Let us associate ourselves with the sufferings of Christ, in order to be saviours, like him (8-10), and to partake in his immortal life and reign with him (11-13).

PART II

How to deal with Innovators (ii, 14–iv, 8)

1. *Instruct and enlighten them, but do not argue with them.*—Discussion is useless (14) ; it is enough to present the truth clearly (15). It is necessary, above all, to avoid profane questions which degenerate into ungodliness (16-19), but be not surprised to find in the Church this mixture of good and evil, which is inevitable in every great institution (20-21). Let the pastor teach sound doctrine, but not engage in futile inquiries or vain disputes (22-26).

2. *Rebuke them severely and without indulgence.*—In the last days there shall be an overflow of iniquity under the mask of godliness (iii, 1-5). The actions of intriguers and seducers are seen already (6-8), but they shall be finally unmasked (9). Timothy knows well the teachings of the Apostle with whose trials he himself has been associated (10-13) ; let him guard carefully this deposit (15) and be devoted to the Scriptures, which are inspired by God and profitable to teach, to reprove, to convince, and to instruct (16-17). Make no concessions to error (iv, 1-2). The day will come when men will be impatient of the truth (3-4) ; but Timothy must fulfil his ministry resolutely (5). As for Paul, his career is ended ; he has fought valiantly (7) ; he has now only to receive his crown (8).

Conclusion.—Come quickly with Mark, for all my companions except Luke are absent (iv, 9-12).—Bring me my cloak and books (13).—Beware of Alexander, my deadly enemy (14-15).—All have left me, but God has come to my aid (16-17).—Doxology, salutations, final greeting (18-22).

XII—EPISTLE TO TITUS

The Apostle's double *aim* is clearly indicated : *to correct abuses* and *to establish elders* everywhere (i, 5). These two points are treated in the reverse order.—The *superscription* assumes an abnormal development ; in this new Christian community Paul feels the need of energetically affirming his apostolate (i, 1-4).

PART I

QUALITIES OF THE ELDERS ($\pi\rho\epsilon\sigma\beta\acute{v}\tau\epsilon\rho\iota$)

1. *Four preliminary conditions:* (*a*) A spotless reputation ; (*b*) the husband of one wife; (*c*) Christian and obedient children; (*d*) aptitude for teaching.
2. *Exemption from five sins:* (*a*) Pride; (*b*) anger; (*c*) drunkenness; (*d*) brutality; (*e*) avarice.
3. *Practice of seven virtues:* (*a*) Hospitality; (*b*) love of goodness; (*c*) prudence; (*d*) justice; (*e*) holiness (*f*) continence; (*g*) zeal for the truth (i, 6-9).

Knowledge and 'ove of the truth are necessary for the priest, that he may refute the charlatans, who swarm (10-11), especially in Crete (12). Titus will take care to rebuke them and resist them (13-14). Some among them are wholly corrupt and deny God by their works (15-16).

PART II

REFORM OF MORALS AND REPRESSION OF FALSE DOCTRINES (ii-iii)

1. *Duties suitable to various conditions.*—(*a*) *Old men:* Sobriety, prudence, etc. (ii, 2).—(*b*) *Old women:* Modesty, reserve, good example, etc. (3).—(*c*) *Young women:* Conjugal and maternal love, good housekeeping (4-5).—(*d*) *Young men:* Temperance (6) ; let Titus set them an example (7).—(*e*) *Slaves:* Obedience and fidelity (9-10).—The object of these precepts is to silence calumny (8) and to honour the Gospel by showing that it is a good school of morals (10-15).
2. *The Christian's general duties.*—Practice of the Christian *virtues* as the antithesis of the *vices* in which unbelievers are plunged (iii, 1-3).—The grace of the Saviour and baptismal regeneration are to transform the whole man and prepare him for his heavenly heritage (4-7). The Christian must be an example to others (8).

In *closing*, the Apostle begs Titus to avoid foolish questions (9) and to shun the fomenter of contentions (10). He gives him again some items of news and some practical advice (11-14), and concludes, as usual, with good wishes and benedictions (15).

XIII—EPISTLE TO PHILEMON

In spite of its brevity, this has all the integral parts of the other Epistles : the usual *superscription* (1-3), *introduction* as a thanksgiving, with a eulogy of the person addressed (4-7), *presentation of the subject,* united with the touching request of an old man, a prisoner of Christ and a tender spiritual father (8-10), and crowned with a fervent appeal to the noblest motives of generosity, supernatural advantage, justice, faith, and Christian brotherhood (11-20).

In *conclusion* the Apostle expresses the assurance that his friend will go beyond his wishes (21), bespeaks his hospitality for himself in advance (22), and sends him his greetings and benedictions (23-25).

XIV—EPISTLE TO THE HEBREWS

The manifest *aim* of this Epistle is to check the downward course of the Jewish Christians, who were on the verge of apostasy. Consequently the author shows that the Christian religion is superior to the Mosaic religion because its mediator, Jesus Christ, is, beyond comparison, superior to all other mediators in respect of his *person,* his *priesthood,* and his *sacrifice.*

A word of exhortation (xiii, 22), in which morality is everywhere closely connected with dogma ; after the thesis (x, 18), the hortatory portion is pursued alone.

PART I

THE EXCELLENCE OF CHRISTIANITY IS PROVED BY
THAT OF ITS MEDIATOR (i–x, 17)

*First Contrast—The Person of Christ and Other
Mediators* (i-iv).

1. *Christ and the Angels.*—(a) The Son of God, the brightness and image of the Father (i, 1-3), is distinguished from the angels by the fact that he is the Son (4-6), whereas the

angels are servants (7); Christ is King, eternal, immutable, creator, God (8-13); the angels are at the service of the elect (14).

(b) *Moral Application.*—If the violators of the Law promulgated by the angels were so severely punished, what will be the fate of those who despise the message of the Son (ii, 1-4)? God has put all things under the feet of Christ (5-7), but has made him pass through a transitory phase of humiliation (8-9); for it was becoming that the Saviour should be in all respects like his brethren (10-13), that he should teach them to brave death (14-15), and that he should become a perfect high priest through trial (16-18).

2. *Christ and Moses.*—(a) They have this in common—that they were *faithful to their charge* (iii, 1-2); but Moses was faithful as a member of the house of God which belongs to Christ (3-5); and he was so as a servant, while Christ is faithful as a Son (6).

(b) *Moral Application.*—The Psalmist exhorts us not to harden our hearts (7-15), as the Hebrews did to the voice of Moses, and were therefore excluded from the land of promise (16-19). We also are called to enter into the rest of the Lord (iv, 1-10); let us not close the entrance to it by unbelief; our High Priest is able to conduct us thither (11-16).

Second Contrast—The Priesthood of Christ and that of the Levites (v-viii).

1. *Christ the High Priest.*—(a) *Definition of the High Priest as applied to Christ:* Representing men before God (v, 1) and willing to help the unfortunate through the feeling of his own weakness (2), the High Priest is to offer up expiatory victims (3) and cannot assume this office without a divine vocation (4).—Christ is called by God to the priesthood (5-6), has been subjected to trials, and has learned obedience through suffering (7-8). What distinguishes him from the others is that he is a priest for ever according to the order of Melchisedech (9-10).

(b) *Hortatory digression:* The author complains that the Hebrews still need the milk of children, when they ought to be able to bear food for grown men (11-14). Nevertheless, he will not return to the elementary articles of the faith (vi, 1-3), for it is impossible to renew again to penitence Christians who have knowingly and deliberately become unbelievers (4-6), like a sterile soil which drinks in the dew of heaven in vain (7-8). In spite of these severe words, he is full of confidence in them (9-12); for God has promised with an oath to Abraham to bless his spiritual posterity (13-20).

2. *High Priest according to the Order of Melchisedech.*—(a) Melchisedech is the type of Christ, as Scripture represents

him (vii, 1-3). He blesses Abraham, who pays tithes to him; he is therefore doubly superior to the great patriarch, and all the more to the sons of Levi (4-10). How much more must the priesthood of Christ, a priest after the order of Melchisedech, be superior to the levitical priesthood (11-19)! Unlike the former priesthood, Jesus Christ is made a priest by a solemn oath and is a priest eternal (20-28).

(b) *Theological conclusion:* We have a perfect High Priest who replaces the ancient priesthood (ix, 1-7). But the transference of the priesthood implies the transference of the covenant, according to the prophecy of Jeremias (8-13).

Third Contrast.—The Sacrifice of Christ and that of Aaron (ix–x, 17).

1. *Typology of the Tabernacle.*—Description of the tabernacle (ix, 1-6) with its two parts, one of which was reserved for the high priest when offering the blood of expiation, to signify that access to God was not yet free (7-10). Christ, as High Priest, opens it by his blood to all true worshippers of God (11-14). Therefore he is the mediator of the new covenant which he seals with his blood (15-17).

2. *The Sacrifice of the Covenant.*—The first was ratified by the blood of animals (18-22); the new covenant by the blood of the High Priest (23).

3. *The Sacrifice of Expiation.*—This was only the annual renewal of the sacrifice of the covenant, the effect of which was neutralized by time. It had to be repeated every year; that of Christ is of necessity unique (24-28).—The first had only a restricted value; that of Christ, possessing an infinite value (x, 1-10), is able to *perfect* for ever those for whom it is offered (11-18).

PART II

EXHORTATION TO PERSEVERE IN THE FAITH (x, 18–xiii)

First Theme: The Intercession of Jesus.—By his blood he has opened for us a way of access to heaven (x, 19-20); let us follow him without wavering (21-23), exhorting one another to constancy (24-25).

Second Theme: The Calamity of Unbelief.—Wilful unbelief is without a remedy (26-27), for it tramples underfoot the blood of the new and eternal covenant (28-31).

Third Theme: Remembrance of Past Fervour.—After their baptism the faithful had endured persecution with joy (32-34). Make one more effort; the reward is near (35-39).

Fourth Theme: The Example of the Patriarchs.—Eulogy

of the faith of the patriarchs (xi, 1-2) : faith of Abel (4), of Henoch (5-6), of Noe (7), of Abraham and Sara (8-19), of Isaac (20), of Jacob (21), of Joseph (22), of Moses (23-28), of Josue (29-31), of Rahab (30), of the judges, prophets, and saints of the Old Testament (32-40).

Fifth Theme: The Example of Jesus.—He preferred the ignominy of the cross to joy ; wherefore his Father has caused him to sit at his right hand (xii, 1-3). The Hebrews have not yet undergone the trial of blood (4) ; their afflictions are only paternal and salutary lessons sent by God who loves them (5-13).

Sixth Theme: Punishments reserved for Unbelievers.—Do not imitate Esau, who, having foolishly sold his heritage of blessings, repented of it later bitterly, but in vain (14-17). Nor imitate the Israelites, deaf to the voice of Jehovah amid the thunders of Sinai. The place where you stand is holier than Sinai ; it is Mount Sion, the city of the living God, the heavenly Jerusalem, the company of angels, the Church of the first-born (18-29).

Various Recommendations.—Charity and hospitality (xiii, 1-3), continence (4), detachment from the world (5).—Respect and obedience to superiors (7 and 17).—Renunciation of Jewish sacrifices and the following of Jesus crucified without the city gates : Christians have something better than victims offered up in the temple (8-16).—Request for prayers (18-19).—Desires for perfection (20-21).—Personal news and final greeting (22-25).